MANUAL OF
ENGLISH GRAMMAR AND COMPOSITION

MANUAL OF
ENGLISH GRAMMAR AND COMPOSITION

IN SIX PARTS

BY

J. C. NESFIELD

GYAN

Published by

GYAN

Gyan Publishing House
5, Ansari Road
Daryaganj, New Delhi-110002
Phone: 011-47034999, 9811692060
E-mail: books@gyanbooks.com

Distribution Network
gyanbooks.com
India, USA, Canada, UK, Australia

ISBN: 978-93-6208-831-4 (HB)
First Published, 1898

2nd Impression 2024

Printed at: Gyan Press, Delhi.

MANUAL OF ENGLISH GRAMMAR AND COMPOSITION
Author: J. C. NESFIELD

MANUAL OF
ENGLISH GRAMMAR
AND COMPOSITION

BY

J. C. NESFIELD, M.A.

AUTHOR OF 'ENGLISH GRAMMAR PAST AND PRESENT,' 'HISTORICAL ENGLISH AND DERIVATION,' ETC.

IN SIX PARTS

I.—PARSING AND ANALYSIS
II.—COMPOSITION: FORCE AND PROPRIETY OF DICTION
III.—ENLARGEMENT OF VOCABULARY: FIGURES OF SPEECH
IV.—PROSE AND POETRY
V.—HISTORY OF THE LANGUAGE
VI.—SOUNDS, SYMBOLS, AND SPELLINGS
APPENDIX ON DERIVATIONS

MACMILLAN AND CO., LIMITED
ST. MARTIN'S STREET, LONDON
1908

PUBLISHERS' NOTICE

OWING to the increasing importance attached to Phonetics, a sixth Part bearing the name of *Sounds, Symbols, and Spellings*, and consisting of three chapters, has been added to this book. The first chapter deals with "Letters, Accents, and Syllables," the next with "Vowel-Sounds and how they are spelt," the last with "Consonantal Sounds and how they are spelt." The system followed in this Part is that on which all the best authorities on Phonetics are agreed, viz. Dr. Sweet, Professor Skeat, Miss Laura Soames, and Dr. Murray (in the Introduction to the Oxford Dictionary).

Besides the new matter furnished in Part VI., an Appendix on Derivations (mainly based on Skeat's *Etymological Dictionary*) has been added at the close of the book. The Appendix gives five different lists of Derivatives—the first consisting of Words derived from Proper Names, the second of Words formed by Composition, the third of Derivatives from Teutonic (mainly A.S.) Roots, the fourth of Derivatives from Latin Roots, the fifth and last of Derivatives from Greek Roots.

Nothing has been added to the price of the book on account of the additional matter thus furnished, which consists altogether of seventy-six pages.

CONTENTS

PART I.—PARSING AND ANALYSIS.

PART II.—COMPOSITION: FORCE AND PROPRIETY OF DICTION.

PART I.—PARSING AND ANALYSIS.

CHAPTER I.

ANALYSIS IN OUTLINE.

This chapter assumes that the student has a rough knowledge of the Parts of Speech to start with.

1. **Sentence.**—When one person says something to another, or puts what he says into writing, he uses a combination of words which is called a sentence :—

Fire burns.

Here "fire" is the thing talked about. The word "fire," though it names the thing, does not make a sentence. It is a *name*, and nothing more. It is only by adding such a word as "burns" to the word "fire," that is, by *saying* what the thing (fire) does, that we can make a sentence.

Definition.—A sentence is a combination of words, in which something is *said* about something else.

Note.—That which is "*said*" may be an assertion, or a command, or a question, or a wish, or an exclamation,—whatever, in fact, can be expressed by a Finite verb (on the meaning of Finite verb see § 5). Thus there are five different kinds of sentences :—

(*a*) **Assertive**, affirming or denying. (*Indicative Mood.*)
A man's success *depends* chiefly on himself. (*Affirmative.*)
He *did* not *get* much help from others. (*Negative.*)

(*b*) **Imperative**, commanding or prohibiting. (*Imperative Mood.*)
Rely chiefly on your own efforts. (*Command, Advice.*)
Do not *rely* much on the help of others. (*Prohibition.*)

(*c*) **Interrogative**, asking a question. (*Indicative Mood.*)
Have you *finished* that task?

(*d*) **Optative**, expressing a wish. (*Subjunctive Mood.*)
Thy kingdom *come*, thy will *be done*.

(*e*) **Exclamatory**, expressing some emotion. (*Indicative Mood.*)
What a foolish fellow you have been!

2. **Subject and Predicate.**—Every sentence, when it is expressed in full, consists of two parts, a Subject and a Predicate.

In a very short sentence like "fire burns," the word "fire" (which is called a Noun) expresses the whole of the Subject, and the word "burns" (which is called a Finite Verb) expresses the whole of the Predicate.

However long a sentence may be, it can always be divided into the same two parts as the shortest sentence :—

Subject	*Predicate.*
(1) Fire	burns.
(2) A fierce fire	burnt down my house.
(3) A fierce fire, breaking out yesterday,	completely burnt down my house.
(4) A fierce fire, suddenly breaking out yesterday afternoon,	completely burnt down my house and many others in the same street.
(5) A fierce fire, suddenly breaking out yesterday afternoon at four o'clock,	completely burnt down my house and all the other houses in the same street except five.

Definitions.—The Subject of a sentence is a word or words denoting what we speak about.

The Predicate is a word or words by which we say something about the thing denoted by the Subject.

Note 1.—In *grammar* the Subject is not "what we speak about," but "the *word or words denoting* what we speak about." Grammar deals exclusively with words, and this fact has to be recognised in all the definitions.

Note 2.—Such a sentence as "Go!" is elliptical. Here the Subject "thou" or "you" is understood. Still more elliptical is a sentence in which the Subject and the Finite verb are both understood :—

Companion, hence !—SHAKSPEARE.

To express this sentence in full, we have to say—

Companion, *go thou* hence !

3. Nominative or its equivalent.—The predicate-verb has for its Subject some noun or noun-equivalent of the same number (Singular or Plural) and the same person (First, Second, or Third) as the verb itself. The noun that stands as Subject to a verb is invariably in the Nominative case, and so it is best to call it a Nominative at once.

Fire | burns.

Here "fire" is the Nominative to the predicate-verb "burns."

A pronoun is a very common form of noun-equivalent :—

He | is standing outside.

We cannot say "*Him* is standing outside." So the pronoun like the noun must be in the Nominative case.

Another form of Nominative is a Gerund or Verbal noun ending in *-ing* :—

Walking | is good for health.

Sometimes an Infinitive is used as an equivalent to the Nominative :—

To walk | is good for health.

Sometimes a **clause** (that is, a sentence which is part of a larger sentence) is used as an equivalent to the Nominative. This is called a Noun-clause, because it does the work of a noun :—

Whom the gods love | die young.—*Proverb.*

4. **Enlargement of Nominative.**—The Nominative is sometimes enlarged by a word or words that add something to its meaning.

The commonest form of enlargement is an adjective or a participle; and both forms of enlargement may occur together :—

A *fierce* fire }
A *fierce* fire, *breaking out* yesterday, } burnt down my house.

Another very common form of enlargement is a noun or pronoun in the Possessive case :—

My prospects | are not bad.
A *fox's* tail | is of a tawny colour.

Another form of enlargement is a noun in apposition (*i.e.* referring to the same thing as the other noun) :—

John, *the baker*, has taken a new shop.

Another form of enlargement is a preposition followed by a noun :—

My prospects *in life* | are not bad.
A bird *in the hand* | is worth two in the bush.

Sometimes a clause can be used to enlarge the Nominative. This is called an Adjective-clause, because it enlarges the noun as an adjective would do.

The house *in which we live* | has been sold.

5. **Finite Verb.**—Any part of a verb that can be used for saying something about something else (in any of the five senses shown in § 1) is called Finite.

The word "finite" means "limited." A Finite verb is so called, because it is limited to the same person (*First*, *Second*, or *Third*) and to the same number (*Singular* or *Plural*) as its Nominative :—

(*a*) I *see* him. (*b*) They *see* him.

In both sentences the *form* of the verb "see" is the same.

But in (*a*) the verb is in the *First* person, because its Nom. "I" is in the *First* person, and in the *Singular* number, because its Nom. "I" is *Singular*. Similarly in (*b*) the verb is in the *Third* person, because its Nom. "they" is in the *Third* person, and *Plural*, because its Nom. "they" is Plural.

Note.—Those parts of a verb which are not finite, that is, are not limited to number and person, are of three kinds :—(1) the **Infinitive** mood, as "I wish *to retire*"; (2) a **Participle**, as "a *retired* officer"; (3) a **Gerund** or Verbal noun, as "I think of *retiring*." These, though they are parts of a verb, have lost what is most essential in the verb-character; that is, they do not enable us to *say* anything about anything else, and therefore they can never be the verb of a Predicate.

6. Completion of Finite Verb.—Some verbs make a complete sense by themselves. If so, they are called Intransitive verbs of Complete Predication :—

Fish *swim*. Rivers *flow*. All animals *die*.

Other verbs do not make a complete sense by themselves, but require some word or words to be added for this purpose. Such additional word or words are called the **Completion**.

The Completion may be either (*a*) an Object, or (*b*) a Complement; and there is one class of verb (Factitive, see below) that requires both :—

(*a*) **Object** :—

A verb that requires an object is called Transitive. "Transitive" means "passing over" or "passing on." A verb is Transitive, when the action denoted by it does not stop with the doer, but passes on to something else :—

Ships traverse *the ocean*. He shot *a tiger*.

There is no sense, or at least a very imperfect sense, in saying "Ships traverse," "He shot."

A Transitive verb may even have *two* objects :—

He asked *me a difficult question*.

To say "he asked" gives a very incomplete sense. "He asked me" brings the sense a step nearer to completion. But the sense is not really completed till we say, "He asked me a difficult question."

(*b*) **Complement** :—

This word is used to denote any kind of completion except the object or objects to a Transitive verb. Transitive verbs which need a complement as well as an object are called **Factitive**; Intransitive verbs which need a complement are called **Copulative**.

That grief drove him (Object) *mad* (Complement) (*Factitive.*)
He seems *to be mad* (Complement) . . . (*Copulative.*)

If we omit the complement, and say "That grief drove him," or "He seems," the sentences are almost meaningless. It is the complement which furnishes what was wanted to complete the sense in either sentence.

7. Extension of Finite Verb.—The Finite verb is said to be "extended," when its meaning is increased by an adverb or by some word or words that have the force of an adverb:—

That grief *nearly* drove him mad.
That grief drove him mad *all of a sudden.*

Here the meaning of "drove" is extended in the first sentence by the adverb *nearly*, and in the second by the adverbial phrase *all of a sudden.*

Sometimes the Finite verb is extended by a clause. A clause so used is called an Adverb-clause, because it has the force of an adverb:—

The news drove him mad, *as soon as he heard it.*

The sentence italicised extends the meaning of "drove" by mentioning the time of the action.

8. Scheme of Analysis.—Sentences are analysed according to the following scheme, the details of which have been already explained in §§ 3-7:—

The new master soon put the class into good order.
A bird in the hand is worth two in the bush.
Evil communications corrupt good manners.
Without any necessity, he asked me a rude question.

I. SUBJECT.		II. PREDICATE.			
Nominative or Equivalent.	Enlargement of Nominative.	Finite Verb.	Completion of Finite Verb.		Extension of Finite Verb.
			Object.	Complement.	
master	(1) The (2) new	put	the class	into good order	soon.
bird	(1) A (2) in the hand	is	...	worth two in the bush.	
communications	Evil	corrupt	good manners.		
He	...	asked	(1) me (2) a rude question	...	without any necessity.

Analyse the following sentences according to the model:—

1. A certain fowler, having fixed his net, withdrew to a little distance, that the birds might not be afraid to come.
2. A flight of pigeons, led by their king, was by chance passing through the sky at this time.
3. They caught sight of the rice-grains scattered by the fowler near the net.
4. The pigeon who was king of the rest then asked his rice-loving followers this question—
5. Why are rice-grains lying here in this lonely place?
6. We will see into this thing.
7. We must be cautious in our movements.
8. One conceited pigeon among the rest gave them bad advice.
9. He told them to fly down to the rice-grains and satisfy their hunger.
10. Having listened to this bad advice and flown down, they began to peck up and swallow the grains.
11. On beginning to peck they were all caught in the net.
12. Then they blamed their rash and imprudent friend for having given them such bad advice.
13. They ought rather to have blamed themselves for having listened to him.
14. The king now told them what to do.
15. At one moment and with one united movement springing suddenly up fly off with the net.
16. Small things become strong by being united among themselves.
17. Even mad elephants can be held fast by a rope made of thin blades of grass.
18. The pigeons acted on this advice.
19. Making a sudden spring together, they flew up into the air, carrying the net with them.
20. At first the fowler hoped to see them come down again to the earth.
21. Flying along as fast as they could, they passed out of sight with the net about them.
22. In this way the fowler lost both his net and the pigeons.
23. The pigeons then said to their king:—"O king, what is the next thing to be done?"
24. The king directed them to a certain place.
25. There his friend, the king of the mice, received them kindly.
26. The king of the mice set them all free by nibbling through the net.
27. Thus the whole troop of pigeons escaped by means of union.
28. All men should profit by this lesson.
29. A chariot will not go on a single wheel.
30. A creeper, having nothing to support it, must fall to the earth.—*Digest of Eastern Fable.*

SUMMARY OF CHAPTER I.

Sentence: a combination of words in which something is said about something else (§ 1).

Subject: the word or words denoting what we speak about (§ 2).

Predicate: the word or words by which we say something about the thing denoted by the subject (§ 2).

Clause: a sentence that is part of a larger sentence (§ 3).

Nominative or its equivalent: the noun or noun-equivalent that fixes the number and person of the Finite verb (§ 3).

Noun-clause: a clause that does the work of a noun (§ 3).

Enlargement of Nominative: an adjective or adjective-equivalent that enlarges the meaning of the Nominative (§ 4).

Adjective-clause: a clause that does the work of an adjective (§ 4).

Finite verb: any part of a verb that is limited to number and person (§ 5).

Non-finite parts of a verb: those parts of a verb that are not limited to number or person, viz. the Infinitive, the Participle, and the Gerund (§ 5).

Transitive verb: one that requires an object (§ 6).

Intransitive verb: one that does not require an object (§ 6).

Factitive verb: a Transitive verb that requires both a complement and an object (§ 6).

Copulative verb: an Intransitive verb that requires a complement (§ 6).

Extension of Finite verb: an adverb or adverb-equivalent that extends the meaning of a Finite verb (§ 7).

Adverb-clause: a clause that does the work of an adverb (§ 7).

CHAPTER II.—THE PARTS OF SPEECH IN OUTLINE: PHRASES.

SECTION 1.—THE PARTS OF SPEECH.

The definitions given in this chapter will not be repeated in subsequent chapters.

9. **The Parts of Speech.**—The different kinds of words used for different purposes in a sentence are called Parts of Speech.

Until we see a word *in a sentence*, we are often unable to say to what part of speech it belongs:—

(*a*) *Water* the roses. (*b*) Take some *water*. (*c*) A *water* bird.

In (*a*) *water* is a verb. In (*b*) it is a noun. In (*c*) it is an adjective, or a noun used as an adjective.

10. **Noun.**—Take such a sentence as the following:—

The *howling* of the *wolf* filled the *flock* with *terror*.

Here *howling* is the name of an action; *wolf*, of an animal; *flock*, of a multitude; *terror*, of a feeling. So *howling*, *wolf*, *flock*, *terror* are all nouns.

Definition.—A noun is a word used for naming anything.

Note 1.—The word "thing" in this definition stands for person, place, quality, action, feeling, collection, etc., anything, in fact, that we can speak about. It is so used in all the definitions that follow.

Note 2.—*Noun* and *name* both mean the same thing at bottom. *Noun* is from Latin *nomen*, a name. *Name* is from Anglo-Saxon *nama*, a name.

11. Pronoun.—Take such a sentence as the following:—

I told James that the snake *which you* saw in the garden would do *him* no harm, if *he* let *it* go *its own* way.

Here *I* is used for the speaker; *you* for the person spoken to; *him* and *he* for "James"; *which*, *it*, and *its own* for "snake." So all these words are pronouns.

Definition.—A pronoun (Latin *pro*, for, instead of) is a word used instead of a noun. (It is, in fact, a substitute word or proxy. It denotes a thing without being a name for it.)

Note 1.—Pronouns in the First and Second persons save the *mentioning* of a noun, and in the Third the *repetition* of one. The speaker, however, can give his own name, if he chooses:—

We, *John Cade*, so termed of our supposed father, etc.
2 *Henry VI.* iv. 2, 33.

Usually, however, the speaker simply says "I" without giving his own name, and in addressing any one he simply says "you" without mentioning the name of the person spoken to.

Note 2.—Pronouns are also used as substitutes for a noun-equivalent:—

Climbing up rocks is an amusement to me; but *that* (=climbing up rocks) is a labour to you.

12. Adjective.—A noun standing by itself is sometimes of too general a meaning to indicate the thing to which the writer or speaker is referring

Supposing the noun to be "house," the speaker might wish to point out some particular house. He would then have to say "*this* house," or "*that* house," or "*the other* house."

Or he might wish to allude to the quantity, as "the *whole* house"; or to the number, as "*one* house," "*four* houses"; or to the serial order, as "the *first* house," "the *fourth* house."

Or he might wish to describe the kind of house, as "a *little* house," "a *comfortable* house," "an *untidy* house," etc.

Or he might wish to speak about several houses in a distributive sense, as "*each* house," "*every* house."

Any word thus added to a noun is called an Adjective (Lat. *adjectivus*, "used for adding on"). The noun and adjective thus combined make a kind of compound noun. Sometimes this compound noun can be written as a single word, as "greatcoat," "blackguard," "nobleman," "halfpenny," "quicksands," "sweetheart," etc., every one of which can easily be broken up into a simple noun and an adjective that precedes it.

Definition.—An adjective is a word that enlarges the meaning and narrows the application of a noun.

Enlargement of meaning is necessarily accompanied by a narrowing of application. This is a vital point. Thus the noun "house," so long as its meaning remains unenlarged, that is, so long as no adjective is added to it, can be applied to an almost countless number of things called by the general name of "house." But if I add to the noun the adjective "fourth," the noun so enlarged can be applied to only one house, viz. to that house which stands fourth in a certain row or terrace.

Observe that when we enlarge the meaning of "house" by adding "fourth," we do not alter the meaning of "house." "Fourth house" means all that "house" means, and more besides.

Shorter definition.—An adjective is a word used to qualify a noun.[1]

This shorter definition is intended to signify exactly the same thing as the longer one. On account of its shortness it is more convenient for parsing. Thus in parsing "fourth house" we can say that "fourth" is an adjective qualifying the noun "house."

Note.—Amongst adjectives we must not omit to include the Definite article *the* (a short form of *this*) and the Indefinite article *a* (a short form of *one*).

13. **Verb.**—This has been described already in §§ 2, 5.

Definition.—A verb is a word used for *saying* something about something else.

"Verb" is from Latin *verbum*, a word. A verb has been called pre-eminently "the word," because it is the chief word in a sentence. In fact, it is the most important kind of word in human speech. "James laughs": we might designate James by pointing to him with our finger; but we cannot express any fact about him, as "laughs," without using our voice and saying the word *laughs*.

14. **Preposition.**—Take such sentences as the following:—

(*a*) I put my hand *on* the table.
(*b*) A bird *in* the hand is worth two (birds) *in* the bush.
(*c*) He is opposed *to* severe measures.

In (*a*) the preposition *on* shows the relation between the thing denoted by *table* and the action denoted by "put." The hand might be held *above* the table, or *under* it, or *on* it. It is the preposition which defines the relation.

[1] Observe that *qualify* simply means *modify*. In grammar it means precisely the same thing that it does in ordinary language, and is not by any means limited to adjectives that express some quality or attribute.

In (*b*) the preposition *in* shows the relation between the thing denoted by the noun *bird* and the thing denoted by the noun *hand;* also between the things denoted by the noun *birds* and the thing denoted by the noun *bush.*

In (*c*) the preposition *to* shows the relation between the things denoted by *severe measures* and the quality (opposition) denoted by the word *opposed.*

Definition.—A preposition is a word used for showing in what relation one thing stands to another thing.

The noun or noun-equivalent that comes after a preposition is called its **Object.**

Note 1.—Avoid such definitions as the following:—

"A preposition is a word used before a noun or pronoun to show its relation to some other word in the sentence."

According to this, "a Jack in the box" does not mean that a Jack is in the box, but that the noun "Jack" is in the noun "box."

Nor is it enough to say that "a preposition connects a noun with a verb, an adjective, or other noun." In the phrase "time *and* tide," we have one noun connected with another noun; and in the sentence "men *are* mortal," we have a noun connected with an adjective by the copulative "are." Yet neither *and* nor *are* is a preposition.

Note 2.—When the relation between the two things named is not adequately expressed by a single preposition, two prepositions may be used for the purpose:—

The mouse crept out *from under* the floor.
The rabbit escaped by running *into* its hole.

15. Conjunction.—Take such examples as the following:—

(*a*) He is a humble-minded *and* contented man.
(*b*) We admire the character of a poor, *but* honest, man.
(*c*) That man is disliked, *because* he is ill-tempered.

In (*a*) the notion of humility expressed by *humble-minded* is connected (in the sense of addition) with the notion of contentment expressed by *contented.* The one notion is simply added to the other. The conjunction used for this purpose is *and.*

In (*b*) the notion of poverty expressed by *poor* is connected (in the sense of contrast) with the notion of honesty expressed by *honest.* The one notion is contrasted with the other. The conjunction used for this purpose is *but.*

In (*c*) the thought expressed by the sentence "he is ill-tempered" is connected (in the sense of cause or reason) with the thought expressed by the sentence "that man is disliked."[1] The one thought is given as the reason for the other.

[1] When the mind apprehends a single object, as "father," "son," "honesty," "poverty," the result is called a *notion;* and this is expressed

Definition.—A conjunction is a word used for showing in what relation one notion stands (in the mind of the speaker or writer) to another notion, or one thought to another thought.

Note 1.—A detail of the different relations expressed by conjunctions will be given hereafter. Meanwhile it may be pointed out that three different relations have been exemplified already—addition in example (*a*), contrast in (*b*), and causality in (*c*).

Note 2.—In parsing, it is convenient for the sake of brevity to say that "a conjunction joins words to words, and sentences to sentences." But this is not enough for the purposes of definition. Prepositions also join words, as "a bird *in* the hand." Some verbs, too, join words, as "time *is* money" (in fact, the verb *is* is called "copulative" for no other reason than that it couples or joins words). Some adverbs, too, like *where*, *when*, etc., join sentences, as "We found out *where* he was." Relative pronouns also join sentences, as "We have found the house *that* you were looking for"; and for this reason they are called conjunctive.

Note 3.—Prepositions and conjunctions have been bracketed sometimes as "connective words," and sometimes as "relational words." If there is any truth in what we have laid down, there is much more point in bracketing them as "relational" words than as "connective" ones. Both kinds of words express relations—prepositions a relation between one *thing* and another *thing*; conjunctions a relation between one *notion* and another *notion*, or between one *thought* and another *thought*.

16. **Adverb.**—What an adjective does for a noun or pronoun, an adverb does for any part of speech except a noun or pronoun: it enlarges or extends the meaning of a word and narrows its application. Take such sentences as the following:—

(*a*) *With verb.*—I *much* admire his industry.
(*b*) *With adjective.*—He is *deservedly* successful.
(*c*) *With preposition.*—The body floated *partly* above and *partly* below the water.
(*d*) *With conjunction.*—He was despised, *merely* because he was poor.
(*e*) *With other adverb.*—He writes *remarkably* well.

In (*a*) the verb "admire" is qualified by the adverb "much."

In (*b*) the adjective "successful" is qualified by the adverb "deservedly."

In (*c*) the preposition "above" is qualified by the adverb "partly"; and the preposition "below" by the same adverb.

In (*d*) the conjunction "because" is qualified by the adverb "merely."

---

by a single word or phrase. When the mind compares two notions and connects them by a Finite verb, the result is called a *thought;* and this is expressed by a sentence (Latin, *sententia*, a thought).

In (*e*) the adverb "well" is qualified by the adverb "remarkably."

Definition.—An adverb is a word that extends the meaning and narrows the application of any part of speech except a noun or pronoun.[1]

Note.—Example (*c*). Observe that in extending the meaning of "above" by the addition of "partly," we do not alter the meaning of "above." The phrase "partly above" expresses all that is implied in the preposition "above," and something more. It shows that the relation of above-ness denoted by "above" is not entire, but partial. The same remarks apply to the preposition "below."

Example (*d*). Here the meaning of the conjunction "because" is extended, not altered, by the adverb "merely." The phrase "merely because" expresses all that is implied in "because," and something more. It shows that the relation of cause denoted by the conjunction "because" is to be understood in a sense that excludes every other cause. If we change the order of the words and say, "He was merely despised, because he was poor," the meaning of the sentence is not the same: this would mean, "He was merely despised (not hated or attacked), because he was poor." Or, if we leave out the adverb "merely," the sense would again be different. The sentence would then imply that there may have been other reasons besides poverty for which he was despised.

17. Interjection.—All Parts of Speech except interjections have some grammatical connection with some other word in the sentence in which they occur. An interjection is the only part of speech that stands alone—isolated. It scarcely deserves to be called a part of speech; for it lies on the borderland of language, halfway between articulate speech and the inarticulate cries of animals. We must give it a name, however, because it is a *word;* for grammar takes account of every kind of word that occurs in human speech.

My son, *alas!* died yesterday.

Definition.—An interjection is a word thrown into a sentence to express some feeling of the mind, but forms no part of the construction of the sentence.

"Interjection" is from Latin *interjectus,* thrown between.

Note.—The meaning of an interjection might be expressed by a parenthetical sentence:—

My son (I am sorry to say) died yesterday.

Observe that a sentence substituted for an interjection is always

[1] In § 17 it is shown that an interjection is, properly speaking, not a Part of Speech. Hence no mention is made of interjections in this definition. An interjection, being absolute or isolated, cannot be qualified by any other word.

parenthetical. The sentence "I am sorry to say" is as completely isolated from the sentence "My son died yesterday" by the parenthesis as the interjection "alas!" is isolated from it by its own nature.

18. **Double Parts of Speech.**—Besides the eight Parts of Speech already described, there are four kinds of words which are double parts of speech, that is, two combined in one :—

(1) A **Participle.**—This is a verb and adjective combined.

A *retired* officer lives next door.

"Retired" is a verb, being part of the verb "retire." It is also an adjective, because it qualifies the noun "officer." Hence a participle may be called a verbal adjective.

(2) A **Gerund** or **Verbal Noun.**—This is a verb and noun combined.

I think of *retiring* soon from service.

"Retiring" is a verb, being part of the verb "retire." It is also a noun, because it is object to the preposition "of."

(3) An **Infinitive.**—This too is a verb and noun combined.

I wish *to return* that book.

Here "to return" is a verb, in the Infinitive mood. It is also a kind of noun, because it is the object to the Transitive verb "wish."

(4) **Relative Adverb.**—This is partly an adverb and partly a conjunction. It has hence been called a "Conjunctive adverb."

We shall be glad *when* the risk is over.

Here "when" is an adverb, because it qualifies the verb "is." It has also the character of a conjunction, because it connects the thought expressed by "we shall be glad" with the thought expressed by "the risk is over."

Exercise.

In the following sentences point out the Part of Speech in which each italicised word is used, and give your reason for saying that it belongs to one Part of Speech rather than to another :—

1. A square thing does not fit into a *round* hole. Draw a circle *round* a given centre. The flies are flying *round* and *round*. Men must go their daily *round* of duty. Vasco da Gama was the first to *round* the Cape of Good Hope.
2. The earth is very dry, and *needs* rain. He must *needs* know the reason of this. Our *needs* or wants are few.
3. I will wait for you at the *next* house. He stood *next* me in the class. Who came *next?*
4. We must *all* die some day. We lost our *all* on that day. The road was *all* covered with sand.
5. He returned *after* a week's absence. He returned *after* he had been absent for a week. The man died of fever, and his son died a few days *after*.

6. A beggar is standing *before* the gate. I never saw such a thing *before*. He took the book, *before* he had paid for it.

7. My book is a *better* one than yours. You are working *better* to-day. Do not despise your *betters*.

8. There is *but* one man present. Who *but* you would have made such a mistake. He is a man of common sense, *but* not learned in books.

9. He had *enough* to do. We have wages *enough* for three men.

10. *Half* measures do not succeed. One *half* of his task is now done. He was *half* dead with fear.

11. He has eaten *more* bread to-day than yesterday. *More* has been done than was expected. I like him *more* than I like you.

12. *Near* our house there is a fine tree. He is a *near* relative of mine. Stand *near*, while I whisper something into your ear.

13. He has wasted *much* time. I am *much* pleased with your conduct. You will not get *much* from me.

14. We should pity the sorrows of *others*. *Other* men besides you deserve pity.

15. You will *save* him if you try. All the men *save* one perished.

16. I have not seen him *since* Monday last. I took this house four weeks *since*. We shall trust you, *since* you were always honest.

17. I am not a student in *that* school. A student *that* works hard will get promotion. I heard *that* you were coming.

18. We must stop here a little *while*. *While* the cat is away, the mice play.

Section 2.—Classification of Phrases.

19. Phrase defined.—A phrase is a combination of words in which no Finite verb is either expressed or understood.

A phrase is therefore intermediate between a single word and a sentence.

20. Kinds of Phrases.—Phrases may be classified according to the parts of speech for which they are used as substitutes. There is no phrase which can be substituted for a pronoun, since a pronoun is a substitute word already (§ 11).

(*a*) *Noun-phrase:* one which does the work of a noun:—

How to do this is a difficult question.

(*b*) *Adjectival phrase:* one which does the work of an adjective:—

A bird *in the hand* is worth two (birds) *in the bush*.

(*c*) *Adverbial phrase:* one which does the work of an adverb:—

I shall wait *a few minutes*.
He shouted *at the top of his voice*.
The sun having set, they all retired.

(*d*) *Prepositional phrase:* one which does the work of a preposition:—

He went *on board* ship.

(*e*) *Conjunctional phrase:* one which does the work of a conjunction:—

In case we fail, we must try again.

(*f*) *Interjectional phrase:* one which does the work of an interjection:—

What a pity! For shame! Good gracious!

The result, then, is that any combination of words which can be substituted for some part of speech may be called a phrase; and we have seen that nouns, adjectives, adverbs, prepositions, conjunctions, and interjections may all be expressed by phrases.

The one exception is a Finite verb. Nothing but a Finite verb can do the work of a Finite verb,—which corroborates what is said in § 13, that a verb is the most important kind of word in human speech.

Exercise.

Show for what Parts of Speech the italicised phrases are used in the following sentences:—

1. I am sorry that he behaved *with so much rudeness.*
2. A sharp ride *on a spirited horse* is the best kind of exercise.
3. The beauties of nature are *beyond description.*
4. *Dinner being over*, let us now go into the next room.
5. He will be dismissed *in the event of* his doing such a thing again.
6. The young have to learn *how to profit by experience.*
7. He was not often *behind time.*
8. An English sailor had been shut up *for several years*, but he was set free *at the peace.*
9. Bind him *hand and foot* and take him away.
10. A man *in bad health* can seldom be happy.
11. He was not a man *to tell a lie.*
12. *The two chief points having been gained*, success is now certain.
13. He took medicine *in order that* he might recover.
14. He still feels tired, *notwithstanding that* he had ten hours' sleep.

Summary of Chapter II.

Parts of Speech: the different kinds of words that serve different purposes in a sentence (§ 9).

Noun: a word used for naming anything (§ 10).

Pronoun: a word used instead of a noun (§ 11).

Adjective: a word that enlarges the meaning and narrows the application of a noun (§ 12).

Verb: a word used for *saying* something about something else (§ 13).

Preposition: a word used for showing in what relation one thing stands to another thing (§ 14).

Conjunction: a word used for showing in what relation one notion stands to another notion, or one thought to another thought (§ 15).

Adverb: a word that extends the meaning and narrows the application of any part of speech except a noun or pronoun (§ 16).

Interjection: a word thrown into a sentence to express some feeling of the mind, but forming no part of the construction of the sentence (§ 17).

Double Part of Speech: a word in which the characters of two parts of speech are combined (§ 18).

Phrase: a combination of words in which no Finite verb is either expressed or understood (§ 19).

Noun-phrase: one which does the work of a noun (§ 20).

Adjectival phrase: one which does the work of an adjective (§ 20).

Adverbial phrase: one which does the work of an adverb (§ 20).

Prepositional phrase: one which does the work of a preposition (§ 20).

Conjunctional phrase: one which does the work of a conjunction (§ 20).

Interjectional phrase: one which does the work of an interjection (§ 20).

CHAPTER III.—NOUNS.

Section 1.—The Kinds of Nouns.

21. Nouns classified.—Nouns are of five different kinds:—

I. Concrete	Proper (one thing at a time) . .	1
	Common (any number of things) . .	2
	Collective (a group of things) . . .	3
	Material (what a thing is made of) . .	4
II. Abstract (quality, state, or action) . . .		5

22. A **Proper Noun** is a name for *one particular* thing as distinct from every other; as *James* (a person), *Kenilworth* (a book), *Paris* (a city), *France* (a country).

Note.—"Proper" (Lat. *proprius*) means "own." Thus a Proper name is "*own* name." It cannot be given to more than one thing at a time.

23. A **Common Noun** denotes no one thing in particular, but is *common to any number of things of the same kind;* as "man," "book," "country."

Thus, *man* does not point out any particular man, such as James, but can be used for any and every man. *Book* does not point out any particular book, such as *Kenilworth*, but can be used for any and every book. *Country* does not point out any particular country, such as *France*, but can be used for any country in any part of the world.

Note 1.—"Common" (Lat. *communis*) means "shared by several."

Things of the same kind, *i.e.* possessing some property in common, have an equal right to be called by the same name.

Note 2.—A Proper noun becomes a Common noun, when it is used in a descriptive or general sense :—

The *Czar* of Russia. The *Pharaohs* of Egypt.
He is the *Newton* (greatest astronomer) of the century.

24. A **Collective Noun** is a name for a *group of similar individuals*, the group being one complete whole.

For instance, there may be *many sheep* in a field, but only *one flock*. Here "sheep" is a Common noun, because it may stand for any and every sheep; but "flock" is a Collective noun, because it stands for all the sheep at once, and not for any one sheep taken separately.

Note 1.—A Collective Noun may be either Common or Proper :—

Thus the term "flock" may stand for many different flocks. But *Parliament*, *the House of Commons*, can stand for only one body.

Note 2.—A Noun of Multitude, since it denotes a specific group, must be classed as Collective; but with a difference.

(*a*) A Collective noun denotes *one undivided whole*; and hence the verb following is singular :—

The jury *consists* of twelve persons.

(*b*) A noun of Multitude denotes the *individuals* of the group; and hence the verb is plural, although the noun is singular :—

The jury (the men on the jury) *were* divided in their opinions.

25. A noun of **Material** is a name for some particular kind of *matter* or *substance*.

Thus "sheep" is a Common noun; but "mutton" (or the flesh of sheep) is a Material noun.

Note.—The same word can be a Material noun or a Common noun according to the sense :—

Fish live in water (*Com.*). *Fish* is good for food (*Mat.*).

26. An **Abstract Noun** denotes some *quality*, *state*, or *action*, apart from anything possessing the quality, etc.

Quality—Cleverness, height, humility, roguery, colour.
State—Poverty, manhood, bondage, pleasure, youth.
Action—Laughter, movement, flight, choice, revenge.

The four kinds of nouns first named are all **Concrete**; *i.e.* they denote *objects of sense*, viz. what can be seen, heard, touched, smelt, or tasted, or what can be perceived by the muscular sense, as weight, extension, etc. But an abstract noun relates to *qualities*, *states*, etc., which cannot be seen or touched, etc., and which are thought of *apart from* any object of sense.

For example: We know that a stone is *hard*. We also know that iron is *hard*. We also know that a brick is *hard*. We can therefore speak of *hardness* apart from stone, or iron, or brick, or any other object having the same quality. "Abstract" (Lat. *abstractus*) means "drawn off" (abstracted in thought) from the object. Hence *hardness* is an abstract noun; while *stone* or *brick* or *iron* is a concrete noun.

27. The same word may be an Abstract noun or a Common (*i.e.* Concrete) noun, according to the purpose for which it is used:—

(a) *Examples of Persons.*

Justice	1. Justice is a virtue	*Abstract*
	2. He is a justice of the peace . . .	*Concrete*
Beauty	1. She is admired for her beauty . . .	*Abstract*
	2. She is the beauty of the town . . .	*Concrete*
Authority	1. He has no authority	*Abstract*
	2. The best authorities differ . . .	*Concrete*
Nobility	1. I admire nobility of character . . .	*Abstract*
	2. He is one of the nobility	*Concrete*

(b) *Examples of Things.*

Judgment	1. He is a man of sound judgment . .	*Abstract*
	2. The magistrate passed a severe judgment	*Concrete*
Sight	1. Sight is a valuable faculty . . .	*Abstract*
	2. That was a fine sight	*Concrete*
Wonder	1. The news fills me with wonder . .	*Abstract*
	2. We have seen a wonder to-day . . .	*Concrete*
Kindness	1. Kindness is part of his character . .	*Abstract*
	2. He did me a great kindness . . .	*Concrete*

Note.—Sometimes we find that there is one form of adjective for an Abstract noun used as such, and another for the same Abstract noun used as Concrete or Common.

(1) *Industrious*, adjective of *industry* used as an Abstract noun.
(2) *Industrial*, adjective of *industry* used as a Common noun.

In (2) "industry" means some special kind of industry, as cotton-spinning. Thus "an industrial training" means a training which will prepare a man for some branch of industry, such as cotton-spinning. "An industrious training" would not express this. We can say "an industrious man," but not "an industrious training."

How Abstract Nouns are formed.

28. Abstract Nouns can be formed from Adjectives, or from Common nouns, or from Verbs:—

(a) *Abstract Nouns formed from Adjectives.*

Adj.	*Abstract Noun.*	*Adj.*	*Abstract Noun.*	*Adj.*	*Abstract Noun.*
Wise	wisdom	Prudent	prudence	Bitter	bitterness
Poor	poverty	Sweet	sweetness	Wide	width
High	height	Young	youth	Sole	solitude
Short	shortness	Proud	pride	Broad	breadth
Honest	honesty	Just	justice	Deep	depth
Dark	darkness	Great	greatness	True	truth
Long	length	Hot	heat	Cold	coldness
Brave	bravery	Sleepy	sleepiness	Humble	humility

(b) *Abstract Nouns formed from Common Nouns.*

Common Noun.	*Abstract Noun.*	*Common Noun.*	*Abstract Noun.*	*Common Noun.*	*Abstract Noun.*
Man	manhood	Agent	agency	Mother	motherhood
Child	childhood	Regent	regency	Rascal	rascality
Friend	friendship	King	kingship	Rogue	roguery
Boy	boyhood	Bond	bondage	Slave	slavery
Captain	captaincy	Hero	heroism	Infant	infancy
Priest	priesthood	Thief	theft	Owner	ownership

(c) *Abstract Nouns formed from Verbs.*

Verb.	*Abstract Noun.*	*Verb.*	*Abstract Noun.*	*Verb.*	*Abstract Noun.*
Serve	service	Relieve	relief	Seize	seizure
Live	life	Believe	belief	Laugh	laughter
Hate	hatred	Please	pleasure	Free	freedom
Obey	obedience	Advise	advice	Expect	expectation
Choose	choice	Defend	defence	Protect	protection
Move	motion	Judge	judgment	Think	thought
See	sight	Conceal	concealment		

Note.—All Verbal Nouns (§ 3 and § 18) ending in *-ing* are Abstract nouns :—

The *reading* of books is good for the mind.

(d) *Abstract Nouns of the same form as Verbs.*

Verb.	*Abstract Noun.*	*Verb.*	*Abstract Noun.*	*Verb.*	*Abstract Noun.*
Fear	fear	Fall	fall	Sob	sob
Hope	hope	Stay	stay	Laugh	laugh
Desire	desire	Stop	stop	Taste	taste
Regret	regret	Walk	walk	Ride	ride
Order	order	Run	run	Touch	touch
Move	move	Step	step	Love	love
Rise	rise	Cry	cry		

29. There are two ways in which a Proper, Material, or Abstract noun can be used as a Common noun—(*a*) by putting an article ("a" or "the") before it; (*b*) by putting it in the plural number.

Proper Noun.	*Common Nouns.*
Daniel was a learned Jew.	*A Daniel* come to judgment. There are more *Daniels* than one.
Material Noun.	
Apple is my favourite fruit.	Give me *the apple* in your hand. Give me one of your *apples*.
Abstract Noun.	
Justice is a noble quality.	He is *a justice* of the peace. There are four *justices* present.

SECTION 2.—GENDER.

30. Gender.—Nouns are now classified according to sex or absence of sex, and not, as once, by *form* or *declension* :—

(1) **Masculine**—*male* animals : *bull, horse, hog.*
(2) **Feminine**—*female* animals : *cow, mare, sow.*
(3) **Common**—of *either* sex : *parent, child.*
(4) **Neuter**—of *neither* sex : *box, flock, pain.*

Note 1.—It is only in the pronouns *he, she, it,* that gender according to *form* has survived.

Note 2.—When no account is taken of sex, we often speak of animals as neuter :—

The *child* is asleep : let *it* sleep on.
Have you a *horse :* will you let me ride *it !*

31. Modes of denoting Gender or Sex.—There are three different ways in which the gender (or sex) of living beings is indicated :—

1. *By a Change of Ending.*

Masculine.	*Feminine.*	*Masculine.*	*Feminine.*
Abbot	abbess	Marquis	marchioness
Actor	actress	Master	mistress
Author	authoress	Murderer	murderess
Duke	duchess	Negro	negress
Emperor	empress	Patron	patroness
Executor	executrix	Poet	poetess
Giant	giantess	Priest	priestess
God	goddess	Prince	princess
Heir	heiress	Prophet	prophetess
Hero	heroine	Shepherd	shepherdess
Host	hostess	Songster	songstress
Hunter	huntress	Testator	testatrix
Lad	lass	Tiger	tigress
Lion	lioness	Widower	widow

Note.—There are some Feminines that have no Masculines :—*blonde, brunette, dowager, dowdy, drab, prude, shrew, siren, termagant, vixen.* (But *vixen* was originally the Fem. of *fox.*)

2. *By a Change of Word.*

Masculine.	*Feminine.*	*Masculine.*	*Feminine.*
Bachelor	maid, spinster	Drake	duck
Boar	sow	Earl	countess
Boy	girl	Father	mother
Brother	sister	Friar (or monk)	nun
Buck	doe	Gander	goose
Bull	cow	Gentleman	lady
Bullock (or steer)	heifer	Hart	roe
Cock	hen	Horse	mare
Colt	filly	Husband	wife
Dog	bitch (or slut)	King	queen

Masculine.	*Feminine.*	*Masculine.*	*Feminine.*
Lord	lady	Sloven	slattern, slut
Man	woman	Son	daughter
Milter	spawner	Stag	hind
Nephew	niece	Uncle	aunt
Ram	ewe	Wizard	witch
Sir	madam		

3. *By placing a Word Before or After.*

Masculine.	*Feminine.*	*Masculine.*	*Feminine.*
Bride-groom	bride	He-goat	she-goat
Cock-sparrow	hen-sparrow	Land-lord	land-lady
Grand-father	grand-mother	Man-servant	maid-servant
Great-uncle	great-aunt	Pea-cock	pea-hen

4. *Nouns in the Common Gender;* i.e. *denoting either Sex.*

Baby—male or female.
Bird—cock or hen.
Calf—bullock or heifer.
Child—boy or girl.
Cousin—male or female.
Deer—stag or hind.
Fallow-deer—buck or doe.
Foal—colt or filly.
Fowl—cock or hen.
Friend—Enemy—male or female.
Monarch—king or queen.
Orphan—boy or girl without parents.
Parent—father or mother.
Person—man or woman.
Pig—boar or sow.
Pupil—boy or girl.
Relation—male or female.
Servant—man or maid.
Sheep—ram or ewe.
Student—boy or girl.
Teacher—master or mistress.

Note.—Some Masculines, as *colt, dog, horse,* and some Feminines, as *duck, goose,* are used to denote either sex, provided that no question arises as to whether the animal is male or female :—

A *goose* is a much bigger bird than a *duck.*

SECTION 3.—NUMBER.

32. When a Noun denotes *one* object, it is **Singular**. When it denotes *more than one,* it is **Plural**.

33. Proper, Material, and Abstract nouns have no Plural, unless they can be used as Common nouns :—

(*a*) **Proper** { *Egypt* is a country in Africa. (*Proper.*)
Many *Egypts* (=countries as large as Egypt) could be contained in India. (*Common.*)

(*b*) **Material** { *Tea* is a pleasant drink. (*Material.*)
The best *teas* (=kinds of tea). (*Common.*)

(*c*) **Abstract** { *Kindness* is part of his character. (*Abstract.*)
He did many *kindnesses* (=kind acts). (*Common.*)

34. The general rule for forming the Plural number of a noun is by adding *s* to the Singular :—

Singular.	*Plural.*	*Singular.*	*Plural.*
Hand	hand-*s*	House	house-*s*
Map	map-*s*	Stone	stone-*s*

But if the Noun ends in *s*, *x*, *sh*, or *ch*, the Plural is formed by adding *es* to the Singular :—

Singular.	*Plural.*	*Singular.*	*Plural.*
Glass	glass-*es*	Gash	gash-*es*
Gas	gas-*es*	Brush	brush-*es*
Tax	tax-*es*	Bench	bench-*es*
Box	box-*es*	Coach	coach-*es*

35. If the Noun ends in *y* and the *y* is preceded by a *consonant*, the Plural is formed by changing the *y* into *ies* :—

Singular.	*Plural.*	*Singular.*	*Plural.*
Duty	dut-*ies*	Army	arm-*ies*
Fly	fl-*ies*	Lady	lad-*ies*

But if the final *y* is preceded by a *vowel*, as in *ay*, *ey*, or *oy*, the Plural is formed by simply adding *s* to the Singular :—

Singular.	*Plural.*	*Singular.*	*Plural.*
Day	day-*s*	Monkey	monkey-*s*
Play	play-*s*	Toy	toy-*s*
Key	key-*s*	Boy	boy-*s*

Note.—In *colloquy* the *qu*=*kw* : so *y* becomes *ies*.

36. If the Noun ends in *o* and the *o* is preceded by a *consonant*, the Plural is generally (not always) formed by adding *es* to the Singular :—

Singular.	*Plural.*	*Singular.*	*Plural.*
Cargo	cargo-*es*	Volcano	volcano-*es*
Hero	hero-*es*	Potato	potato-*es*
Buffalo	buffalo-*es*	Echo	echo-*es*
Motto	motto-*es*	Negro	negro-*es*

Note.—The chief exceptions are :—*grotto, halo, memento, proviso, tiro, piano, canto, solo.*

But if the *o* is preceded by a *vowel*, the Plural is formed by simply adding *s* to the Singular :—

Singular.	*Plural.*	*Singular.*	*Plural.*
Folio	folio-*s*	Hindoo	Hindoo-*s*
Cameo	cameo-*s*	Bamboo	bamboo-*s*

37. If the Noun ends in *f* or *fe*, the Plural is generally formed by changing *f* or *fe* into *ves* :—

Singular.	*Plural.*	*Singular.*	*Plural.*
Loaf	loa-*ves*	Thief	thie-*ves*
Wife	wi-*ves*	Half	hal-*ves*
Wolf	wol-*ves*	Myself	oursel-*ves*
Knife	kni-*ves*	Shelf	shel-*ves*
Life	liv-*es*	Leaf	lea-*ves*
Calf	cal-*ves*	Sheaf	shea-*ves*

(*a*) Some Nouns ending in *f* form the Plural by adding *s* :—

Singular.	*Plural.*	*Singular.*	*Plural.*
Reef	reef-*s*	Dwarf	dwarf-*s*
Chief	chief-*s*	Turf	turf-*s*
Roof	roof-*s*	Cliff	cliff-*s*
Hoof	hoof-*s*	Gulf	gulf-*s*
Proof	proof-*s*	Grief	grief-*s*

(*b*) Three Nouns in *fe* form the Plural by adding *s* :—

Safe—safe-*s* ; strife—strife-*s* ; fife—fife-*s*.

38. Peculiar Plurals.—(*a*) Eight Nouns in common use form the Plural by a change of inside vowel :—

Singular.	*Plural.*	*Singular.*	*Plural.*
Man	m*e*n	Tooth	t*ee*th
Woman	wom*e*n	Louse	l*ice*
Foot	f*ee*t	Mouse	m*ice*
Goose	g*ee*se	Dormouse	dorm*ice*

(*b*) There are three Nouns which form the Plural in *en* :—

Ox—ox-*en* ; child—childr-*en* ; brother—brethr-*en*.

The word "cow" has two plurals—"cows" or "kine."

(*c*) Some Nouns have the same form in both numbers :—

Animals.—Deer, sheep, fish (rarely fishes), swine, grouse, salmon, trout, cod, heathen.

Collective numerals.—Yoke, brace, dozen, score, gross.

Measures of weight.—Stone, hundredweight.

(*d*) Some Nouns have no Singular :—

Annals	Gallows	Pincers	Victuals
Shears	Statistics	Scissors	Tidings
Bellows	Suds	Shambles	News
Tongs	Nuptials	Thanks	Means

Note.—In spite of the Plural form we say, "By *this* means," "*This* news is not true."

(*e*) Some Nouns, that take a Plural at ordinary times, use a Singular to express some specific quantity or number :—

A twelve-*month*. A three-*foot* rule. An eight-*day* clock. A six-*year* old horse. A fort-*night* (=fourteen nights). Forty *head* of cattle. Twelve *pound* weight. Ten *sail* of the line. A six-*penny* piece.

Note.—Such a phrase as "A hundred thousand men" does not come under this heading. Here "a hundred thousand" is a Collective noun in the Singular number, and the preposition "of" is understood after it.

(*f*) A Noun of Multitude, being plural already in sense (§ 24, *b*), has no need of a plural form :—

The *poultry* are doing well. These *cattle* are mine. These *vermin* do much harm. These *people* have come. No *gentry* live here.

(*g*) Foreign Plurals :—

Latin : Sing. in *-um ; agend-a, addend-a, dat-a, effluvi-a, errat-a.* Sing. in *-us ; alumn-i, foc-i, radi-i.* Sing. in *-a ; formul-æ.* From other Singulars ; *genera* (genus), *series* (series), *appendices* (appendix). **Greek** : Sing. in *-is ; bas-es, hypothes-es, parenthes-es.* Sing. in *-on ; phenomen-a, criteri-a.* **French** : *beaux, bureaux, messieurs, mesdames.* **Italian** : *banditti, dilettanti.* **Hebrew** : *cherubim, seraphim.*

(*h*) Compound Plurals. The principal word is pluralised :— *Step-sons, sons-in-law, hangers-on, maid-servants, courts-martial.*

(*i*) Double Plurals :—*Men-servants, lords-justices.*

Note.—For Plurals in special senses, see below pp. 176-8.

Section 4.—Case.

39. **Case defined.**—The *relation* in which a noun stands to some other word, or the *change of form* (if any) by which this relation is indicated, is called its **Case.**[1]

40. **Three Cases in modern English.**—These are the *Nominative*, the *Possessive*, and the *Objective.*

But the Possessive is the only case that is *now* indicated by a case-ending or *change of form.* The other cases have lost their case-endings, and are indicated only by grammatical relation.

Note.—A change of form is called an **inflexion.** All our noun-inflexions except (1) the plural, and (2) the possessive, are lost. The Feminine ending *-ess* is not an inflexion, but a suffix.

41. When a noun is used as the *subject* to a verb (§ 3), or for the sake of *address*, it is said to be in the **Nominative** case :—

Rain falls. (*Nominative of Subject.*)
Are you coming, my *friend?* (*Nominative of Address.*)

42. When a noun is the *object* to a verb (§ 6, *a*), or to a preposition (§ 14), it is said to be in the **Objective** case :—

The man killed a *rat.* (*Object to Verb.*)
The earth is moistened by *rain.* (*Obj. to Prep.*)

43. The **Possessive** case is so called, because it usually denotes the *possessor* or owner. It is formed by adding *'s* (called *apostrophe s*) to Singular nouns, and sometimes to Plural ones :—

Singular—man's. | *Plural*—men's.

Note 1.—The old inflexion for the Possessive case was *es.* When the *e* was omitted, as it now always is, the absence of the *e* was indicated by the comma or apostrophe ; as *moon, moones, moon's.*

---

[1] *Case* lit. means "falling" (Lat. *cas-us*). The Nom. was considered the upright or perpendicular, and the other cases were said to fall off to one side of it, and were hence called *oblique* or slanting. Since English nouns have lost every case-ending but one (the Possessive), the term "case" is etymologically inappropriate. We retain it, however, to denote grammatical relation as well as change of form.

Note 2.—There are three different senses in which this case can be used :—

(*a*) **Subjective** :—

England's power is very great. (*Possession.*)
A good son will repay his *father's* benefits. (*Origin.*)
Shakspeare's plays are excellent. (*Authorship, Agency.*)
His friendship (the friendship felt by him) is sincere. (*Subject.*)

(*b*) **Objective** (rather uncommon) :—

His friendship (friendship for him) must be given up.
Cæsar's murderers were conquered at Philippi.

(*c*) **Descriptive** (rather uncommon) :—

I'll break your *knave's* (=knavish) pate.—SHAKSPEARE.
The *mother's* (motherly) nature of Althæa.—LOWELL.
Her *woman's* heart, to which love was all, could at first scarcely comprehend the mystery.—MRS. CRAIK, *Ogilvies*, ch. l.

44. Omission of "s."—There are three kinds of instances in which the *s*, but not the apostrophe, is omitted :—

(*a*) After all plural nouns ending in *s;* as—

Horses' tails ; the *birds'* nests ; the *dogs'* kennels.

(*b*) Whenever the last syllable of a Singular noun begins and ends with *s;* as—

Moses' laws. (But we must say *Venus's* beauty ; *James's* hat, etc.)

(*c*) Whenever the last syllable of a Singular noun ends with *s* or *ce*, and the noun is followed by "sake" ; as—

Conscience' sake ; for *goodness'* sake. (But we must say—a *mouse's* skin ; *James's* smile.)

45. Rare use of Possessive.—The Possessive case was once used with any kind of noun ; but it is now restricted to such examples as those shown below :—

(1) Nouns denoting *persons* or other kind of *living thing;* as—

Henry's book ; a *man's* foot. (But we cannot say "a library's book," "the stocking's foot," since "library" and "stocking" are inanimate objects.)

A *cat's* tail ; a *horse's* head ; a *bird's* feathers.

(2) Nouns denoting *personified* things ; as—

Fortune's favourite ; *Sorrow's* tears ; *England's* heroes.

(3) Nouns denoting time, space, or weight ; as—

Time.—A *day's* journey ; a *month's* holiday ; three *weeks'* leave ; a *year's* absence ; at six *months'* sight ; three *days'* grace.
Space.—A *boat's* length ; a *hand's* breadth ; a *hair's* breadth ; a *razor's* edge ; a *stone's* throw ; a *needle's* point.
Weight.—A *pound's* weight ; a *ton's* weight.

(4) Nouns signifying certain dignified objects ; as—

The *court's* decree; the *sun's* rays; the *moon's* crescent; *nature's* works; the *earth's* axis; the *soul's* delight; *heaven's* will; the *law's* delays; *truth's* triumph; the *mind's* eye; the *ocean's* roar; *duty's* call; the *country's* good.

Let all the ends thou aim'st at be thy *country's*,
Thy *God's*, and *truth's*.—*Hen. VIII.* iii. 2.

Note.—The Possessive is also used in a few familiar phrases, in which it has been retained for the sake of shortness:—

Out of *harm's* way; at his *wit's* end; for *mercy's* sake; he did it to his *heart's* content; the *ship's* passengers; at his *fingers'* ends; he got to his *journey's* end; the *boat's* crew.

CHAPTER IV.—ADJECTIVES.

SECTION 1.—THE KINDS OF ADJECTIVES.

46. There are altogether seven different kinds of Adjectives:—

(1) **Proper**: describing a thing by some *Proper noun.*

(2) **Descriptive**: showing *of what quality* or *in what state* a thing is.

(3) **Quantitative**: showing *how much of* a thing is meant.

(4) **Numeral**: showing *how many* things or *in what order.*

(5) **Demonstrative**: showing *which* or *what* thing is meant.

(6) **Interrogative**: asking *which* or *what* thing is meant.

(7) **Distributive**: showing that things are taken *separately* or *in separate lots.*

Proper Adjectives.

47. These restrict the application of a noun to such persons or things as come within the scope of some Proper name:—

A *Portuguese* sailor = a sailor from Portugal.
The *Turkish* empire = the empire of the Turks.
The *English* language = the language of England.

Note.—Proper adjectives, like Proper nouns, may be used in a general sense; as, *French* leave (leave like that taken by the French); *British* pluck (pluck like that of a Briton).

Descriptive Adjectives:—Quality or State.

48. These restrict the application of a noun to such persons or things as possess the *quality* or *state* denoted by the adjective:—

A *brave* boy; a *sick* lion; a *tame* cat; a *large* field; a *black* horse.

Quantitative Adjectives:—Quantity or Degree.

49. These restrict the application of a noun to such things as are of the *quantity* or *degree* denoted by the adjective.

The only adjectives of this class are—*Much, little ; no ; some, any ; enough* or *sufficient ; all* or *whole, half.*

> He ate *much* (a large quantity of) bread.
> He ate *little* (a small quantity of) bread.
> A *half* loaf is better than *no* bread.
> He ate *some* (a certain quantity of) bread.
> He did not eat *any* (any quantity of) bread.
> He ate *enough* or *sufficient* bread.
> He ate *all* the (the *whole* quantity of) bread.

Note.—"No" is always followed by a noun, and is therefore an adjective. "None" is never followed by a noun, and is therefore a pronoun. It is a negative pronoun : see § 73.

Numeral Adjectives.

50. These restrict the application of a noun to such persons or things as are of the *number* or *serial order* denoted by the adjective.

Numeral Adjectives are subdivided into two main classes :—

I. Definite. II. Indefinite.

51. Definite numerals denote some *exact* number.

Those which show *how many* things there are (as one, two, three, four, etc.) are called **Cardinals.**

Those which show the *serial order* are called **Ordinals.**

Those which show *how often* a thing is *repeated* are called **Multiplicative.**

Cardinals.	*Ordinals.*	*Multiplicatives.*
One	first	one only, single
Two	second	twofold, double
Three	third	threefold, treble, triple
Four	fourth	fourfold, quadruple (four times one)
Six	sixth	sixfold (six times one)
Seven	seventh	sevenfold (seven times one)

52. Indefinite numerals denote number of some kind without saying precisely what the number is :—

All, some, enough, no or *none ; many, few ; several, sundry.*

All men are mortal.	*Some* men die young.
No men were present.	Ten men will be *enough.*
Many men are poor.	*Few* men are rich.
Several men came.	*Sundry* men went away.

A Definite numeral can be made Indefinite by placing the word *some* or *about* before it :—

> *Some* twenty men (=*about* twenty men, twenty men *more or less*) were present.

53. The words "some," "enough," "all," "no," are adjectives of *Number* or of *Quantity*, according to the noun following.

If the noun is Material or Abstract, the adjective is Quantitative. If the noun is Common, the adjective is Numeral :—

Quantitatives.	*Numerals.*
Much ; he had much bread.	*Many ;* he had many loaves.
Little ; he had little bread.	*Few ;* he had few loaves.
Enough ; he had enough bread.	*Enough ;* he had loaves enough.
Some ; he had some bread.	*Some ;* he had some loaves.
No ; he had no bread.	*No ;* he had no loaves.
All ; he had all the bread.	*All ;* he had all the loaves.
Any ; have you had any bread ?	*Any ;* did you bring any loaves ?

Demonstrative Adjectives.

54. These restrict the application of a noun to those persons or things that are intended to be *pointed out* by the adjective.

They are subdivided, like Numerals, into two classes :—

I. Definite. II. Indefinite.

When a person or thing is pointed out *exactly*, as "this man," the adjective is called a **Definite** Demonstrative.

When it is pointed out in a certain sense, but *not exactly*, it is called an **Indefinite** Demonstrative.

Definite.		*Indefinite.*	
Singular.	*Plural.*	*Singular.*	*Plural.*
The	the	A, an	*nil.*
This	these	One, any	any
That, yon, yonder	those, yon, yonder	A certain	certain
Such	such	Such and such	such and such
The same, or self-same	the same, or self-same	Some	some
The other	the other	Another, any other	other, any other

All purely Demonstrative adjectives are given in the above list.

Note.—In some books, however, the Ordinals (§ 51) are classed as Demonstratives, because they point a thing out by showing its place in a list or series. But it is better to call them Numerals, because they cannot show the place of a thing without showing its numerical order.

55. **Articles.**—"The" (short for *this, that*) is a Definite Demonstrative. "A" or "an" (short for *one*) is an Indefinite.

An is used before an open vowel, a silent *h*, or unaccented *h ;* as—

An apple ; *an h*eir ; *an h*onest man ; *an h*istorical fact.

A is used before a consonant, before *u* or *ew* or *eu* sounded as *yoo*, and before *one* sounded as *wun :*—

A kite ; *a* cart ; *a* bottle ; *a* useful thing ; *a* one-eyed man ; *a* European ; *a* ewer ; *an* unusual, but *a* unique case.

Interrogative Adjectives.

56. These restrict the application of a noun by asking a question :—

What book is that? *Which* book do you like best?

Note.—"What" has a general sense, "which" a selective one. "What" can also be used in an exclamatory sense, as "*What* folly!" It can also be used when no question is asked, as, "I do not know at *what* time he came."

Distributive Adjectives.

57. Distributive Adjectives show that the persons or things denoted by the noun are taken *singly*, or *in separate lots.* There are only four Adjectives of this class :—

(*a*) **Each.**—One of *two* or of any number *exceeding two* :—

The *two* men had *each* (man) a gun.
The *twenty* men had *each* (man) a gun.

(*b*) **Every.**—Never used of *two*. Denotes *each without exception* :—

Every man (out of the *twenty present*) had a gun.

"**Every six hours**" and similar expressions.—This means every *space of six hours*, six hours being taken collectively as *one* period :—

He came *every five hours* (=at the close of every space of five hours).

"**Every other.**"—This means *every second* or *each alternate* ; as—

He was attacked with fever *every other day* (=on every second day).

(*c*) **Either.**—(1) *One of two*, or (2) *each of two*,—that is, *both*.

(1) You can take *either* side ; that is, one side or the other.
(2) The river overflowed on *either* side ; that is, on both sides.

(*d*) **Neither.**—This is the negative of "either" :—

"You should take *neither* side" ; neither this nor that.

SECTION 2.—THE TWO USES OF ADJECTIVES.

58. There are two different ways in which an Adjective can be used—(*a*) the Attributive, and (*b*) the Predicative.[1]

(*a*) *Attributive use.*—An adjective is used attributively, when it qualifies its noun *directly*, so as to make a kind of compound noun. All true adjectives can be used attributively :—

A *lame* horse. A *noble* character. A *true* tale.

---

[1] We would not go so far, however, as to say (as Mr. Mason does in *English Grammar*, p. 37, § 87) "that all true adjectives can be used in both ways." A Distributive adjective cannot be used predicatively. For instance, we can say "every man," but we cannot say "man is every." Again, Quantitatives cannot in all cases be used predicatively. We can say "some bread," but we cannot say "bread is some."

Note.—When no noun is expressed, the adjective is used as a noun :—

A noble (=nobleman). The brave (=brave men). The true (=truth).

When an adjective assumes a noun-inflexion, it has become a real noun, and is not merely used as one :—

Nobles (=noblemen). Secrets (= secret things).

(*b*) *Predicative use.*—An adjective is used predicatively, when it qualifies its noun *indirectly*—through some verb going before :—

That horse went *lame*. His character is *noble*.

Section 3.—Comparison of Adjectives.

59. The degrees of comparison are three in number,—the Positive, the Comparative, and the Superlative.

The **Positive** denotes the simple quality ; as, "a *beautiful* horse."

The **Comparative** denotes a higher degree of the quality ; as, "a *more beautiful* horse." This is used when *two* things are compared.

The **Superlative** denotes the highest degree of the quality ; as, "the *most beautiful* horse." This is used when *one* thing is compared with *all other* things of the same kind.

60. In all adjectives of *more than two syllables*, and in most adjectives of two syllables, the Comparative is formed by adding "*more*" and the Superlative by adding "*most*," as in § 59.

61. But adjectives of one syllable and some adjectives of two can also form the Comparative by adding *er* or *r*, and the Superlative by adding *est* or *st*. This is the **inflexional** method.

(*a*) If the Positive ends in a consonant, *er* and *est* are added :—

Small	smaller	smallest
Great	greater	greatest
Thin	thinner	thinnest
Fat	fatter	fattest

(*b*) If the Positive ends in *e*, only *r* and *st* are added, and not *er* and *est* :—

Brave	braver	bravest
True	truer	truest

(*c*) If the Positive ends in *y*, and the *y* is preceded by a *consonant*, the *y* is changed into *i*, when *er* and *est* are added :—

Happy	happier	happiest
Dry	drier	driest

(*d*) If the *y* is preceded by a *vowel*, the *y* is not changed :—

Gay	gayer	gayest
Grey	greyer	greyest

62. Irregular Comparisons.—In the examples marked *

the Positive has had a Comp. and a Superl. allotted to it from some other root. These are defective rather than irregular.

Bad, ill, evil *	worse	worst
Fore	former, further	foremost, first, furthest
Good *	better	best
Hind	hinder	hindmost
Late	later, latter	latest, last
Little *	less	least
Much (quantity) *	more	most
Many (number) *	more	most
Nigh	nigher	nighest, next
Old	older, elder	oldest, eldest

63. There are five words which are adverbs in the Positive degree, but adjectives in the Comparative and Superlative :—

Far	farther	farthest
In	inner	innermost, inmost
Out	outer, utter	uttermost, utmost
Be-neath	nether	nethermost
Up	upper	uppermost

64. Latin Comparatives.—All of these end in *or*, and not in *er ;* and all are followed by *to* instead of *than :*—

Superior to, inferior to, anterior to, prior to, posterior to, senior to.

CHAPTER V.—PRONOUNS.

65. There are four different kinds of Pronouns : [1]—

(1) **Personal** ; as, *I*, *thou*, *he*, *she*, etc.

(2) **Demonstrative** ; as, *this*, *that*, *such*, *one*, etc.

(3) **Relative** or **Conjunctive** ; as, *which*, *who*, *that*, *as*, etc.

(4) **Interrogative** ; as, *who? which? what?*

---

[1] A different classification of Pronouns is given in Mason's *English Grammar*, p. 48, ed. 1891. After giving eight classes of Pronouns, he subdivides each class, wherever this is possible, into two columns, one for Substantive pronouns and the other for Adjective pronouns. Under adjective pronouns he includes Distributive and Demonstrative adjectives, which in this book have already been disposed of in the chapter on Adjectives. It is difficult to see how such adjectives as "every," "each," "some," "other," "any," etc., or, in fact, any adjective, can be correctly called a Pronoun. A Pronoun is a *substitute* word,—a word used *for* another word. But "every," "each," "some," "other," "any" are simply *qualifying* words. They are not *substitute* words. There are no other words for which they are used as substitutes, and therefore they are not pronouns. The same author has a class of pronouns which he calls **Indefinite**, and subdivides into Substantives (*one*, *aught*, *naught*) and Adjectives (*any*, *other*, *some*, *no*). We have already shown that the last four are not pronouns at all. *Aught* and *naught* are not pronouns either, because they are not *substitutes* for any other words. *One* is a pronoun in certain contexts, as shown below in § 73.

This classification excludes all words that are *adjectives*, and all words that are not *substitutes* for other words. It is shown in § 72 that *this, that, such* are not here adjectives, but substitutes for nouns.

Section 1.—Personal Pronouns.

66. The **Personal Pronouns** are so called, because they stand for the three persons, and have a different form for each.

(*a*) The First, which stands for the person *speaking*:—

I (*the person now speaking*) hope to win a prize this term.

(*b*) The Second, which stands for the person *spoken to*:—

You (*the person now spoken to*) should leave off this habit of idleness.

(*c*) The Third, which denotes the person or thing *spoken of*:—

He (*the person already mentioned*) did good work with his tutor.

67. Forms of Personal Pronouns.—Personal Pronouns have the same differences of gender, number, and case that nouns have.

I. *The First Person, Masculine or Feminine.*

Case.	Singular.	Plural.
Nominative . .	I	We
Possessive . .	My, mine	Our, ours
Objective . . .	Me	Us

II. *The Second Person, Masculine or Feminine.*

Case.	Singular.	Plural.
Nominative . .	Thou	Ye or you
Possessive . .	Thy, thine	Your, yours
Objective . . .	Thee	You

III. *The Third Person, of all Genders.*

Case.	Singular.			Plural.
	Masculine.	Feminine.	Neuter.	All Genders.
Nominative .	He	She	It	They
Possessive .	His	Her or hers	Its	Their or theirs
Objective .	Him	Her	It	Them

68. Two Forms of Possessive.—Most of the Personal Pronouns have two forms for the Possessive :—

	Singular.			Plural.		
First Form .	My	Thy	Her	Our	Your	Their
Second ,, .	Mine	Thine	Hers	Ours	Yours	Theirs

The first is used, when the Possessive is placed *before* its noun. It qualifies the noun like an adjective :—

This is *my* book. That is *their* house.

The second is used—(*a*) when it is separated from the qualified noun by a verb coming between ; (*b*) when the noun is not expressed ; (*c*) when the Possessive is preceded by "of" :—

(*a*) This book is *mine*. That house is *theirs*.
(*b*) My horse and *yours* (your horse) are both tired.
(*c*) That horse *of yours* is tired.

69. Reflexive or Emphatic Forms.—These are made by adding "self" in the Nom. or Obj. and "own" in the Possessive.

I. *The First Person.*

Case.	Singular.	Plural.
Nom. or Obj. . .	Myself	Ourselves
Possessive . .	My or mine own	Our own

II. *The Second Person.*

Case.	Singular.	Plural.
Nom. or Obj. . .	Thyself	Yourselves
Possessive . .	Thy or thine own	Your own

III. *The Third Person.*

Case.	Singular.			Plural.
	Masculine.	Feminine.	Neuter.	All Genders.
Nom. or Obj.	Himself	Herself	Itself	Themselves
Possessive .	His own	Her own	Its own	Their own

I hid *myself* (Reflexive). I *myself* saw it (Emphatic).

SECTION 2.—DEMONSTRATIVE PRONOUNS.

70. A **Demonstrative Pronoun** is one that *points to* some noun going before, and is used instead of it. This noun is called the Antecedent.

71. The chief pronouns of this class are :—*this, that, these, those; one, ones, none; such.*

The student will have observed that these words have appeared already in the list of Demonstrative *Adjectives.* Where, then, is the difference? This depends entirely on their use.

When they **qualify** *some noun expressed or understood, they are* **Adjectives.**

When they are **substitutes** *for some noun expressed or understood, they are* **Pronouns.**

(*a*) He came to my house *one* day.

Here *one* is an adjective (Indefinite Demonstrative) qualifying its noun "day."

(*b*) Your coat is black; mine is a white *one.*

Here *one* is a pronoun, because it is a substitute for the previously mentioned noun "coat," and is qualified by the adjective "white."

72. This, that, these, those.—The uses of these words as *pronouns,* and not as *adjectives,* are as follows :—

(*a*) When two nouns have been mentioned in a previous sentence or clause, "**this**" is a substitute for the *latter,* and "**that**" for the *former* :—

(1) Work and play are both necessary to health; *this* (=play) gives us rest, and *that* (=work) gives us energy.
(2) Dogs are more faithful animals than cats; *these* (=cats) attach themselves to places, and *those* (=dogs) to persons.

Observe that in the first of these sentences "*this*" does not specify *which* or *what* play is meant, and therefore it is not a Demonstrative Adjective. It is simply put as a *substitute* for the noun "play," and therefore it is a Demonstrative Pronoun.

A similar explanation holds good for the other example.

(*b*) The word "**that,**" together with its plural form "**those,**" is used as substitute for a single noun previously mentioned :—

(1) The air of hills is cooler than *that* (=the air) of plains.
(2) The houses of the rich are larger than *those* (=the houses) of the poor.

Observe the word "that" in the first example does not qualify the noun "air" by saying *which* air or *what* air, and therefore it is not an Adjective. It stands for "air" in general, and is a *substitute* for the noun "air"; and therefore it is a Pronoun.

(*c*) The words "**this**" or "**that**" can be used as substitutes for a *clause* or *sentence* previously mentioned :—

(1) I studied Greek and Latin when I was young, and *that* (=I studied Greek and Latin) at Oxford.

Here by using the pronoun "*that*" as a substitute for the sentence "I studied Greek and Latin," we not only avoid repeating this sentence a second time, but we give some emphasis to the words "at Oxford."

(2) Make the best use of your time at school ; *that*'s a wise boy.

Here "*that*" = "one who makes the best use of his time at school." All this repetition is avoided by using the pronoun "*that*" as a substitute for the implied sentence.

(3) You paid your debts ; and *this* (=the payment of your debts) is quite sufficient to prove your honesty.

73. One, ones, none.—When the antecedent noun is in the Singular number, we use "*one*"; but when the antecedent noun is Plural, we use "*ones*" :—

(1) He gained a prize last year ; but he did not gain *one* (=a prize) this term. (*Singular.*)

(2) There were six lazy boys and four industrious *ones* (=boys) in our class. (*Plural.*)

None (=*no one*) was originally used only as a Singular :—

None but the brave *deserves* the fair.—DRYDEN.

But "none" has also acquired a Plural meaning :—

None have gone away yet.

74. Such.—"Such" can be substituted for a noun in either number :—

(1) He is the judge appointed to hear this case, and as *such* (=as the appointed judge) you must not speak to him before the trial. (*Singular.*)

(2) Kings are constituted *such* (=kings) by law, and should be obeyed. (*Plural.*)

Examples for Practice.

Show whether the words printed in italics are Demonstrative **Adjectives** *or Demonstrative* **Pronouns** :—

This horse is stronger than *that*.

Health is of more value than money ; *this* cannot give such true happiness as *that*.

I prefer a white horse to a black *one*.

You will repent of this *one* day, when it is too late.

You have kept your promise ; *this* was all that I asked for.

The faithfulness of a dog is greater than *that* of a cat.

One Mr. B. helped his friend in need ; *that* was a true friend.

Return to your work, and *that* immediately.

Bring me *that* book, and leave *this* where it is.

The step you have taken is *one* of much risk.

Such a book as yours deserves to be well read.

Prosperous men are much exposed to flattery; for *such* alone can be made to pay for it.

Prosperous men are not always more happy than unlucky *ones*.

A pale light, like *that* of the rising moon, begins to fringe the horizon.

Will you ride *this* horse or *that?*

A stranger could not be received twice as *such* in the same house.

The plan you have chosen does not seem to me to be a wise *one*.

One man says *this*, another *that;* whom should I believe?

75. Indefinite Demonstrative Pronouns.—Sometimes Demonstrative Pronouns are used as substitutes, not for some noun previously mentioned, but for some noun understood or implied. These are Indefinite, because they have no antecedent.

All Indefinite pronouns are in the Third person. *I* and *you* cannot be indefinite, because we know who is speaking or who is spoken to.

(*a*) **They.**—This pronoun is sometimes used for *men in general*, or some person whose name is purposely concealed:—

They say that truth and honesty is the best policy.

(*b*) **One.**—Used in the sense of *any person* or *every person:*—

One should take care of *one's* health.

=*A man* (any and every man) should take care of *his* health.

Note 1.—Whenever "one" is the subject to a verb, it must be followed by "one" and not by "he." Thus we cannot say, "*one* must take care of *his* health."

Note 2.—When *they* and *one* are used as above, they are not true pronouns, because strictly speaking they are not substitute words. They are pronouns used as Common nouns.

(*c*) **It.**—In such sentences as the following, "*it*" is the subject to the verb, and the noun or other pronoun is the complement:—

Who is *it?* *It* is I. Is *it* you? No; *it* is he.

"*It*" gives **emphasis** to the noun or pronoun following:—

It was I who told you that. *It* is the men who work hardest, not the women. *It* was the queen who died yesterday. *It* is little things that chiefly disturb the mind.

SECTION 3.—RELATIVE OR CONJUNCTIVE PRONOUNS.

76. A **Relative Pronoun** not only refers to some noun going before (as a Demonstrative pronoun does), but it also *joins two sentences together* (which a Demonstrative pronoun does not do).

This is a good house; I live in *it*. (*Demonstrative Pronoun.*)

The house in *which* I live is a good one. (*Relative Pronoun.*)

77. Who, which.—These are declined as follows for Singular and Plural alike:—

Nom.	Who, . . .	which.
Poss.	Whose, . . .	(of which).
Obj.	Whom, . . .	which.

The forms *who*, *whose*, *whom* are used for persons only. The form *which* is used for things without life and for animals of any kind except men and women.

In poetry, and occasionally in prose, *whose* can be used as the Possessive form of *which*:—

The tree, under *whose* shade we are sitting.

78. Forms of Antecedent.—The antecedent may have the form of a noun, or any kind of noun-equivalent (§ 3 and § 204).

You have paid your debts, which (=the fact that you have paid your debts) is a clear proof of your honesty. (*Clause.*)

79. Antecedent understood.—When no antecedent is expressed, the neuter Relative takes the form of "**what**," while the Masculine and Feminine retain the form of "who."

(*a*) *Who* = *he who*, or *she who*, or *they who.*

Who (=he who) steals my purse, steals trash.—SHAKSPEARE.
Whom (=those persons whom) the gods love, die young.—*Proverb.*

(*b*) *What* = *the thing which*, or *the things which.*

I cannot tell you now *what* (=the thing which) then happened.
The laws are *what* (=the things which) you say they are.

(*c*) *So*, *ever*, or *soever* added to a Relative pronoun or to a Relative adverb gives the meaning of totality:—

Whosoever (=any and every person who) breaks this law will be punished, *wherever* (in any and every place where) he may live.

Note 1.—"**What**" has been called a "Compound Relative," because the antecedent is said to be contained in it. But this is not correct: for the antecedent is sometimes expressed, either (*a*) in a subsequent clause, or (*b*) immediately after the Relative itself:—

(*a*) *What* I tell you in darkness, *that* speak ye in the light.
(*b*) Take *what* (or *whatever*) *help* you can get.

Note 2.—Whenever the antecedent is placed after *what* or *which*, as in example (*b*), the *what* or *which* is not a *substitute* word, and therefore not a true pronoun, but an adjective (see § 56, *Note*).

Take *whichever book* (=that book of all books which) you prefer.

80. That.—The word "*that*" is often used for "who," "whom," or "which," but never for "whose":—

This is the house *that* (=which) Jack built.
The man *that* (=whom) we were looking for has come.

Note.—Whenever "that" is the object to a preposition, the preposition is invariably placed after the verb of its sentence, and never before its own object :—

The house *that* we live *in*.

81. **As.**—The word "as" can be used for a Relative pronoun, provided it is preceded by "such," or "as," or "the same." It may be in the Nominative or the Objective case, but not in the Possessive.

This is not *such* a good book *as* I expected.
As many men *as* came were caught.
Yours is not *the same* book *as* mine (is).

82. **But.**—The conjunction "but," *when some Demonstrative pronoun is understood after it*, is used in the sense of "who not" or "which not."

There was no one present, *but* saw (=but *he* saw=*who* did *not* see) the deed.

There is no vice so simple, *but* may (=but *it* may=*which* may *not*) become serious in time.

Note.—The student must avoid the common mistake of saying that *but* is a "negative relative." It is simply an Adversative conjunction with some Demonstrative pronoun understood after it. This pronoun is sometimes expressed, as in the common saying—

It never rains, *but it* pours.

The uses of Who and Which.

83. **Restrictive, Continuative.**—These words denote two distinct uses of "who" or "which":—

(*a*) *Restrict.*—The man *who lived there* died yesterday.
(*b*) *Contin.*—I have seen my friend, *who recognised* me at once.

In (*a*) the Relative clause does the work of an *adjective* to the noun "man," because it *restricts* the application of this noun to that particular man who is said to have "lived there" (see § 4).

In (*b*) the Relative clause "who recognised me at once" has no restrictive force on the noun "friend." It simply *continues* what was said in the previous clause :—"I found my friend, *and he* (=who) recognised me at once."

Note.—"*Who*," "*which*" in a restrictive sense are less commonly used than "*that*," which is invariably restrictive.

Section 4.—Interrogative Pronouns.

84. An **Interrogative Pronoun** is one that asks a question. It has been well called a pronoun in search of an antecedent.

Who spoke? (Nominative to the verb.)
Of *whom* did he speak? (Objective after preposition.)
What did he say? (Objective after verb "say.")
Whose book is that? (Possessive Case.)
Which of these boys will win the prize? (Selective.)

CHAPTER VI.—VERBS.

SECTION 1.—THE KINDS OF VERBS.

85. Verbs are subdivided into three main classes:—

Notional or Principal	Transitive	Class I.
	Intransitive	Class II.
Auxiliary		Class III.

An explanation of "Notional" is given in § 88, *Note.*

86. *A verb is* **Transitive**, *if the action does not stop with the doer, but passes from the doer to something else* (see § 6):—

(1) The man killed *a snake.*
(2) I do not know *whether he has come.*

The word or words denoting that person or thing, to which the action of the verb is directed, are called the **Object.**

87. *A verb is* **Intransitive**, *when the action stops with the doer, and does not pass from the doer to anything else* (§ 6):—

Men sleep to preserve life.

Sleep what? This is nonsense. No word or words can be placed as object to such a verb as "sleep."

88. An **Auxiliary** verb is one which (*a*) *helps* to form a tense, or a mood, of some Principal verb, and (*b*) *forgoes its own signification as a Principal verb* for that purpose:—

A merchant buys that he *may* sell.

Here *may* is not used either in its early sense of "power" or in its present sense of "permission." It helps to form a subjunctive.

I *have* come from home to-day.

Here *have* forgoes its proper signification—"possession," and helps the verb "come" to form a Present Perfect tense.

Note.—Principal verbs are called "Notional," because (unlike Auxiliaries) they express a notion or full meaning of their own.

SECTION 2.—TRANSITIVE VERBS.

89. Forms of Object.—There are seven forms at least.

(*a*) **Noun**:—The man killed a *snake* with his stick.
(*b*) **Pronoun**:—The man lifted *me* up out of the water.
(*c*) **Adj. used as Noun**:—He helped the *needy.*
(*d*) **Infinitive**:—He desires *to leave* us to-morrow.
(*e*) **Gerund**:—He disliked *sleeping* in the daytime.
(*f*) **Phrase**:—No one knew *how to make a beginning.*
(*g*) **Clause**:—We do not know *who has come.*

Note.—The Relative pronoun as object is often left out:—

The books (that) I bought have been lost.

90. The **Double Object.**—Some Transitive verbs take two objects, one denoting a *thing*, and the other a *person*.

The *thing* named is called the **Direct** object; the *person or other animal* named is called the **Indirect** (§ 6):—

I forgave him (*Indirect*) his faults (*Direct*).

The Indirect always stands first. If it is placed after the Direct, it is preceded by the preposition "*for*" or "*to*":—

He taught Euclid (*Direct*) to his sons (*Indirect*).

91. Factitive Verbs.[1]—Those Transitive verbs which take *one* object only, but still require some other word or words to make the predication *complete*, are called **Factitive** (§ 6).

The word or words so added are called the **Complement** (§ 6).

92. Forms of Complement.—There are at least eight.

	Subject.	*Verb.*	*Object.*	*Complement.*
Noun . .	They	made	him	king.
Possessive .	She	made	A.'s quarrel	her own.
Adjective .	The judge	set	the prisoner	free.
Participle .	They	found	her	still weeping.
Prep. with Object	This plot	filled	us all	with terror.
Infinitive .	I	like	a rascal	to be punished.
Adverb .	They	found	the man	asleep.
Clause .	We	have made	him	what he is.

Note.—The necessity of adding a Complement to certain verbs, to make the predication complete, can be seen at once from the example, "I like a rascal to be punished." If you merely say, "I like a rascal," you are saying the opposite to what you intended: for you do not like a rascal, but a rascal *to be punished*, or the *punishment* of a rascal.

93. Transitive Verbs used Intransitively.—There are two ways in which Transitives can become Intransitive:—

(*a*) When the verb is used in such a general sense that no object or objects are thought of in connection with it:—

Men *eat* to preserve life (Intr.). He never *eats* meat (Trans.).
A new-born child *sees*, but a kitten is born blind.
He *writes* well (Intr.). He *writes* a good letter (Trans.).

(*b*) When the Reflexive pronoun is omitted:—

He *drew* (himself) near me. He *made* (himself) merry.

---

[1] In books on Latin grammar the term "Factitive" is usually limited to those Transitive verbs that are followed by an adjective agreeing with the object, or by a noun in apposition with the object. In English grammar it is more convenient to extend the name to *all* Transitive verbs that require a complement in any form whatever.

The following are common examples of Transitive verbs which have acquired an Intransitive force by omitting the Reflexive pronoun :—

Transitive Verb.	*Intransitive Counterpart.*
Get you (yourself) gone.	*Get* out of my way.
Give him a penny.	The shoe *gives.*
He *obtained* a place.	This doctrine *obtained* (maintained itself) for a long time.
The fire *burnt* up the house.	He *burnt* with rage.
Do not *stop* me.	Let us *stop* here a little.
They *open* the doors at nine.	School *opens* at ten o'clock.
A man *breaks* stones with a hammer.	The day *breaks* at six.
The ox *drew* this cart.	He *drew* near to me.
Move away this stone.	*Move* on a little faster.
He *broke up* the meeting.	School *broke up* at three.
The mouse *steals* food.	The mouse *steals* into its hole.
They *bathed* the child.	Let us *bathe* here.
He *rolls* a ball down the hill.	The ball *rolls* down the hill.
He *burst* the door open.	The monsoon has *burst.*
Bad men *hide* their faults.	Bats *hide* during the day.
He *turned* me out of the room.	He *turned* to me and spoke.
They *drop* the boat into the water.	Rain *drops* from the sky.
They *keep* the boat on the left bank.	The boat *keeps* on the left bank.
He *sets* the school in order.	The sun *sets* at six P.M.
He *feeds* the horse on grain.	Many men *feed* on rice.
He *rested* his horse.	The horse *rested* in the stable.
He *lengthened* his journey.	The days begin to *lengthen.*
He *spread* his garment.	The mist *spreads* over the earth.
The shepherd *gathered* the sheep.	The sheep *gathered* round their shepherd.
The wind *dispersed* the clouds.	The clouds *have dispersed* from the sky.
He *closed* the business.	The day *closed* at six P.M.
The sun *melts* the snow.	The snow *melts* in the sun.
He *dashed* down the cup.	He *dashed* out of the room.
We must *widen* the road.	The road *widens* at this point.
Lift the box.	The fog *has lifted.*

SECTION 3.—INTRANSITIVE VERBS.

94. Of Complete Predication.—This is the name given to any Intransitive verb, which makes a complete sense by itself, and does not require a Complement :—

> Rivers *flow.* Winds *blow.* Horses *run,* or *walk,* or *graze,* or *lie down.* Birds *fly.* All animals *sleep.* All animals *die.*

95. Of Incomplete Predication.—This is the name given to those Intransitive verbs, which do not make a complete sense by themselves, but require a Complement to supply what the verb left unsaid (§ 6). Such verbs are more briefly called **Copulative**, because they couple one idea with another.

The Complement to Copulative verbs can be in the same eight forms as that to Factitive ones.

	Subject.	*Verb.*	*Complement.*
Noun . .	That beggar	turned out	a thief.
Possessive	This book	is	mine (§ 68, *a*), not James's.
Adjective .	The man	has fallen	sick.
Participle	The stag	continued	running and jumping.
Prep. with Object	That book	proved	of no use.
Infinitive	The flower	seems	to be fading.
Adverb .	The man	has fallen	asleep.
Clause .	The results	are	what we expected.

Note 1.—When the Complement comes after a Copulative verb, it is called a **Subjective Complement**, because it relates to the Subject.

But when it comes after a Factitive verb in the *Active* voice, it is called an **Objective Complement**, because it relates to the Object.

Note 2.—The same verb, whether Trans. or Intrans., may in different connections be either complete or incomplete predicates:—

{ The world *is* (exists) . . . . (*Comp.*)
{ The world *is round* . . . . (*Incomp.*)
{ They *made* a snow-man . . . (*Comp.*)
{ They *made* him *king* . . . (*Incomp.*)
{ The tree *is growing* . . . . (*Comp.*)
{ He *is growing strong* . . . (*Incomp.*)
{ The water *filled* the pipe . . (*Comp.*)
{ They *filled* the pipe *with water* . (*Incomp.*)

96. The Cognate Object.—An Intransitive verb, though it is never followed by a noun denoting an *outside* or foreign object, may sometimes be followed by a noun *already implied more or less in the verb itself*. ("Cognate" means "kindred.")

There are five different forms of Cognate object:—

(*a*) *Cognate noun formed directly from the verb.*

He laughed a hearty *laugh*.	He slept a sound *sleep*.
He died a sad *death*.	He prayed an earnest *prayer*.
He lived a long *life*.	He sighed a deep *sigh*.

(*b*) *Cognate noun of similar meaning.*

He went a long *way*.	He ran his own *course*.
He fought a hard *battle*.	It blows a brisk *gale*.
He struck a deady *blow*.	The bells ring a merry *peal*.

(*c*) *A noun descriptive of the Cognate noun understood.*

They shouted *applause* = they shouted a *shout* of applause.
He served his *apprenticeship* = he served his *service* as an apprentice.
He ran a great *risk* = he ran a *course* of great risk.

He played *the fool*=he played the *part* of a fool.
He looked *daggers* at me=he looked me a *look* of daggers.

(*d*) *An adjective qualifying the Cognate noun understood.*

He shouted his loudest (shout). He ran his fastest (run or pace).
He fought his best (fight). She sang her sweetest (song). He breathed his last (breath). He tried his hardest (trial or attempt).

(*e*) *Cognate noun expressed by "it."*

We must fight *it* (=the fight) out to the end.
Lord Angelo dukes *it* (=acts the part of a duke) well.—SHAKSPEARE.

97. **Reflexive Object.**—In older English, Intrans. verbs were often followed by a Personal pronoun, either reflexive or used reflexively, in the objective case. Examples still occur:—

Hie *thee* home. Fare *thee* well. Haste *thee* away. They sat *them* down. He over-ate *himself.* To over-sleep *oneself.* Vaulting ambition which o'erleaps *itself.*—SHAKSPEARE.

98. **Intransitive Verbs in Causal sense.**—An Intrans. verb, used in a causal sense, becomes Transitive.

Intransitive.	*Causal.*
The horse trotted out.	They trotted out the horse (=caused it to trot out).
Water boils.	He boils the water.
The prisoners walk out.	He walks out the prisoners.
A thorn ran into his hand.	He ran a thorn into his hand.
That horse will starve.	Do not starve the horse.
The bell rang twice.	Ring the bell.
The kite flew into the air.	He flew the kite.
The soldiers march out.	He marches out the soldiers.
Wheat grows in the field.	He grows wheat in the field.
The boat floated.	He floated the boat.
He talks hoarsely.	He talks himself hoarse (=he makes himself hoarse by talking).

99. There are a few Intransitive verbs, in which the causal sense is indicated by *some change of vowel.*

Intransitive.	*Transitive or Causal.*
The tree *falls.*	He *fells* the tree with an axe.
The sun will *rise* at six.	I cannot *raise* this box.
The cow *lies* on the grass.	The man *lays* down his coat.
We must not *sit* here.	He *set* the books in order.
He will *fare* well.	He will *ferry* me over.
The enemy *quails.*	He *quells* the enemy.

100. **Prepositional Verbs.**—An Intransitive verb can be made Transitive by adding a preposition to it. Such verbs are real Transitives, if they can be used in the Passive voice.

We *act on* this rule. (*Active.*)
This rule is *acted on* by us. (*Passive.*)
No one *relies on* his word. (*Active.*)
His word cannot be *relied on.* (*Passive.*)

Observe that when the verb is in the Passive voice, the *on* cannot be parsed as a preposition, since there is no object to it. It must therefore be parsed as part of the verb itself.

Note 1.—In prepositional verbs, the preposition is almost always placed after the verb; but "*with*" and "*over*" are often placed before it:—

He *withstood* (stood against, endured) the attack.
He was *overcome* (defeated) by the enemy.
The banks were *overflowed* (inundated) with water.
The field is *overgrown* (covered) with weeds.
The boundary has been *overstepped* (transgressed).

All these verbs, when they are used apart from the preposition, are Intransitive. It is the *preposition which makes them Transitive.*

Note 2.—It sometimes happens that the preposition after the Intransitive verb is not expressed, but the verb is none the less followed by an object:—

They *laughed* (at) *him* to scorn. He *looked* (at) *me* in the face.
Leonidas *fought* (against) *the Persians* at Thermopylæ.
I cannot *sit* (on) that horse.
I cannot *stand* (with-stand) your impertinence.

101. Summary.—There are thus two ways in which an Intransitive verb can become Transitive—(1) when it is used in a Causal sense (§ 98); (2) when it is connected with a preposition so closely that the verb, compounded with the preposition, can be made Passive (§ 100).

Similarly, there are two kinds of objects that can come after an Intransitive verb, although the verb itself continues to be Intransitive—(1) the Cognate object (§ 96); (2) the Reflexive or Personal object (§ 97).

SECTION 4.—AUXILIARY VERBS.

102. List of Auxiliary Verbs.—The Auxiliary verbs make up a very small class:—*have, be, shall, will, may, do*—only six, all told.

But their fewness is compensated by their usefulness; for no Transitive or Intransitive verb can be conjugated without them, except in two tenses, the Present and Past Indefinite.

Note 1.—*Have, be* are always followed by Participles. The other Auxiliaries are always followed by Infinitives.[1]

[1] The Infinitive that follows all the Auxiliaries except *be* and *have* might be parsed (if we wish to parse it separately) as the object to the Auxiliary verb going before: thus in "I shall go," *go* is object to the

Note 2.—Auxiliary verbs help not only Principal verbs, but one another. "I *shall have been* going"; here three Auxiliaries combine to form a single tense. *Shall* is followed by an Infinitive *have; have* is followed by a Participle *been*. The last Auxiliary "been" is then followed, as per rule in *Note* 1, by a Participle, "going."

Note 3.—*Can, ought,* and *must,* though Defective, are Principal verbs. *Let* is also a Principal verb. They are not Auxiliary—(*a*) because they do not help to form any tense, mood, or voice; and (*b*) because they do not discard their meanings as Notional verbs for auxiliary purposes. The Infinitive that follows is their object, as in the case of *shall, will, may, do.*

103. **Auxiliary and Principal.**—The same verb may be an Auxiliary at one time and a Principal at another:—

Have	I *had* a fine horse	(*Principal.*)
	I *had* gone away	(*Auxiliary.*)
Be	The earth *is* (exists). A horse *is* a quadruped	(*Principal.*)
	He *was* going. He *is* loved	(*Auxiliary.*)
Shall	You *shall* leave the house (Command, Authority)	(*Principal.*)
	I *shall* leave the house (Simple Futurity) .	(*Auxiliary.*)
Will	I *will* go to-day (Determination)	(*Principal.*)
	You *will* go to-day (Simple Futurity) . .	(*Auxiliary.*)
May	I *may* go (=am permitted to go)	(*Principal.*)
	He works that he *may* live (Purpose) . .	(*Auxiliary.*)
Do	You *did* that work well	(*Principal.*)
	You *did* indeed work hard	(*Auxiliary.*)

Note.—**Be** as a Principal verb has two uses, as below:—

(*a*) There *are* some who deny this . . (*Complete predication.*)
(*b*) This coat *is* of many colours . . (*Incomplete predication.*)

As an Auxiliary, it helps to form all tenses in Passive verbs, and all continuous tenses in Active ones.

Have as a Principal verb denotes possession:—"I *have* a watch." As an Auxiliary it helps to form all the Perfect tenses, in all the Moods, Active and Passive, of all verbs, Transitive and Intransitive.

Shall as a Principal verb denotes command; **should** denotes duty.

Thou *shalt* not steal. He *should* do it at once.

As an Auxiliary, "**shall**" helps to form the *first* person, Future, Indicative (§ 115), and "**should**" to form *any* person in the Subjunctive mood (§ 122):—"He worked hard lest he *should* fail."

Will as a Principal verb denotes intention, and **would** denotes habit.

I *will* never do such a thing again . . . . (*Intention.*)
The dog *would* come every day to the door . . (*Habit.*)

---

verb *shall*. This, at all events, is the way in which the Future tense came into existence. Nevertheless, we cannot consider the verb *shall* to be an ordinary Transitive. We must still call it an Auxiliary for two reasons—(1) because it helps to form a tense; (2) because it foregoes its own meaning for an auxiliary purpose. *Has*, when it is not an Auxiliary, is a full Transitive verb signifying "possesses." We cannot, however, parse it as a Transitive in "He *has* gone," Pres. Perf. tense.

As an Auxiliary, "**will**" helps to form the *second* and *third* persons Future (§ 115), Indicative, and "**would**" to form the same persons of the Subjunctive (§ 122).

May, might, as a Principal verb denotes permission or possibility.

You *may* now go. (*Permission.*) It *may* be true. (*Possibility.*)

As an Auxiliary, "**may**" expresses a wish, and "**may**" and "**might**" express a purpose;—both in the Subjunctive mood (§ 122).

Do, did.—On the Auxiliary uses, see below (§ 114 and § 119).

"**Do**" is also used as a **Pro-verb**, *i.e.* a *substitute* verb, and in this capacity it saves the repetition of some Principal verb going before; as, "I awoke at six A.M., and so *did* (=awoke) you"; "He worked more industriously than his brother *does* (=works)."

Section 5.—Active and Passive Voices.

104. A *Transitive* verb has two voices, the **Active** and the **Passive.**

In the Active voice the person or thing denoted by the Subject is said to *do something to* something else:—

Tom *kills* a snake. (Here Tom *does something to* a snake.)

In the Passive voice the person or thing is said to *suffer something from* something else:—

A snake *is killed* by Tom. (Here a snake *suffers something from* Tom.)

Note.—*Active* (from Latin "activus") means "doing." *Passive* (from Latin "passivus") means "suffering."

105. An *Intransitive* verb is not used in the Passive voice, unless it takes a Cognate object in the Active:—

The Athenians fought a hard battle at Marathon. (*Active.*)
A hard battle was fought by the Athenians at Marathon. (*Passive.*)

Here the subject "battle" does not really *suffer* anything. Nevertheless, the verb "fight," although it is Intransitive, can be conjugated all through the Passive voice in the *third* Person. It has no Passive forms, however, in the *first* and *second* Persons. In the third person it is conjugated throughout.

106. Retained Object.—Verbs that take *two* objects in the Active can still retain *one* in the Passive.

(*a*) The Indirect object of the Active verb; as—

Active Verb.	*Passive Verb.*
I forgave *him* his fault.	The fault was forgiven *him* by me.
We allowed *him* two pounds.	Two pounds were allowed *him* by us.

Or (*b*) the Direct object of the Active verb; as—

Active Verb.	*Passive Verb.*
I forgave him *his fault.*	He was forgiven *his fault* by me.
We allowed him *two pounds.*	He was allowed *two pounds* by us.

Note 1.—It has now been shown that there are five different kinds of objects which can be used with verbs :—

(1) **Direct** (with Trans. verbs).—He taught *Euclid* (§ 90).
(2) **Indirect** (with Trans. verbs).—He taught *his sons* Euclid (§ 90).
(3) **Retained** (with Pass. verbs).—His sons were taught *Euclid* (§ 106).
(4) **Cognate** (with Intrans. verbs).—The fever must run its *course* (§ 96).
(5) **Reflexive** (with Intrans. verbs).—He sat *himself* down (§ 97).

In (1), (3), and (4) the verbs are followed by a *Direct* object; in (2) and (5) by an *Indirect*. It should be also noted that in (3) the verb is Transitive without being Active, while in (4) it is Active without being Transitive.

Note 2.—Whenever a Factitive verb is changed from the Active voice to the Passive, the Objective Complement becomes Subjective.

Active : Comp. to Object.	*Passive : Comp. to Subject.*
They proclaimed him *king*.	He was proclaimed *king* by them.
They did not crown him *king*.	He was not crowned *king* by them.

107. Verbs Active in form, but Passive in sense.—Transitive verbs, Active, are sometimes used in a Passive sense.

(*a*) Verbs with a Complement :—

The stone *feels* rough (is rough when it is felt).
Honey *tastes* sweet (is sweet when it is tasted).
The milk *smells* sour (is sour when it is smelt).
Your blame *counts* for nothing (is worth nothing when it is counted).
Your composition *reads* well (sounds well when it is read).
The house *does* not *let* (is not taken when it is meant to be let).
The horse *does* not *sell* (is not taken when it is meant to be sold).
That cloth will *wear* thin (will become thin when it is worn).

(*b*) Verbs without a Complement :—

The house *is building* (=is in a state of being built).
The trumpets *are sounding* (=are being sounded).
The cannons *are firing* (=are being fired).
The drums *are beating* (=are being beaten).
The house *is finishing* (=is being finished).
The book *is printing* (=is being printed).
The cows *are milking* (=are being milked).

Note.—The generally received and best supported opinion regarding this construction is that what looks like a present participle is in reality a gerund, with the preposition *on* or *in* omitted.

This house was three years in *building* (Ger. or Verbal noun).

Others, however, think that it is a real Active participle used in a Passive sense, like the verbs in examples (*a*).[1]

---

[1] The word ending in *-ing* must certainly be a participle in such colloquialisms as "I want a button *sewing on.*" In such a sentence as "The wall is rapidly building," *building* must certainly be parsed as a participle, as otherwise the adverb *rapidly* could not be parsed.

SECTION 6.—MOODS AND TENSES, ACTIVE AND PASSIVE.

108. Moods.—Mood means the mode or manner in which an action is spoken of. There are three Finite moods (*i.e.* limited by number and person), and one Infinitive (not so limited).

(*a*) Three Finite moods :—

1. Indicative, the mood of **Assertion** or **Inquiry**.—*He comes.*
2. Imperative, the mood of **Command** or **Advice**.—*Come.*
3. Subjunctive, the mood of **Supposition**.—*If he come.*

(*b*) Infinitive mood . . . . *To come.*

109. Number and Person.—The number and person of a Finite verb depend upon the nature of its Subject.

Number
- If the subject is Singular, the verb must be Singular ; as, Rain *is* falling.
- If the subject is Plural, the verb must be Plural ; as, Raindrops *are* falling.

Person
- If the subject is in the First person, the verb must be in the First person ; as, I love. We come.
- If the subject is in the Second person, the verb must be in the Second person ; as, Thou lovest. You come.
- If the subject is in the Third person, the verb must be in the Third person ; as, He loves. The teacher *has* come.

Hence arises the following rule (which is called a Concord or Agreement) :—*A Finite verb must be in the same number and person as its Subject.*

110. Tense defined.—Tense is the form assumed by a verb (by means of inflexion or with the help of Auxiliaries) for indicating either (*a*) the *time* in which an event occurs, or (*b*) the *degree of completeness* ascribed to an event at the time of its occurrence.

As regards the question of time, the verb may tell you :—

(1) That an action *is done* in **Present** time ; as, "he *comes*."
(2) That it *was done* in **Past** time ; as, "he *came*."
(3) That it *will be done* in **Future** time ; as, "he *will come*."

111. To express the different degrees of completeness there are four different forms to each tense :—

I. **Indefinite** ; which denotes Present, Past, or Future time in its simplest form ; as, "I see," "I saw," "I shall see."

II. **Continuous** ; which denotes that the event (in Present, Past, or Future time) is still *continuing*, and is not yet completed ; as, "I am seeing," "I was seeing," "I shall be seeing."

Note.—This tense is sometimes called the **Imperfect**, because it denotes an event which is imperfect or not completed.

III. **Perfect**; which denotes that the event (in Present, Past, or Future time) is in a completed or *perfect* state; as, "I have seen," "I had seen," "I shall have seen."

IV. **Perfect Continuous**; which combines the meanings of the two preceding forms; as, "I have been seeing," "I had been seeing," "I shall have been seeing."

Complete Conjugation of a Verb in the Finite Moods.

In this scheme 1 stands for First person (*I*, *we*); 2 for Second person (*thou*, *you*); 3 for Third person (*he*, *she*, *it*, *they*). The non-Finite parts of a verb are shown in sections 10, 11, 12.

From the following scheme it will be seen that the only tenses formed by inflexion are two in number, viz. the Present Indefinite and the Past Indefinite, Active voice, in the Indicative and Subjunctive moods.

All the other tenses in the Active voice, and all the tenses in the Passive voice without any exception, are formed by means of Auxiliary verbs (§ 102).

A. Active Voice of Do.

I.—*Indicative Mood.*

Tense.		Singular. 1	2	3	Plural. 1 2 3
Present	*Indefinite*	do	doest or dost[1]	does	do
	Continuous	am doing	art doing	is doing	are doing
	Perfect	have done	hast done	has done	have done
	Perf. Cont.	have been doing	hast been doing	has been doing	have been doing
Past	*Indefinite*	did	didst	did	did
	Continuous	was doing	wast doing	was doing	were doing
	Perfect	had done	hadst done	had done	had done
	Perf. Cont.	had been doing	hadst been doing	had been doing	had been doing
Future	*Indefinite*	shall do	wilt do	will do	1. shall 2, 3. will — do
	Continuous	shall be doing	wilt be doing	will be doing	1. shall 2, 3. will — be doing
	Perfect	shall have done	wilt have done	will have done	1. shall 2, 3. will — have done
	Perf. Cont.	shall have been doing	wilt have been doing	will have been doing	1. shall 2, 3. will — have been doing

[1] When "*do*" is used as an Auxiliary (§ 103), the form is *dost*; when it is used as a Notional or Principal verb (§ 85), or as a Pro-verb (§ 103), the form is *doest*. In all other respects the auxiliary and the Principal forms are identical.

II.—*Subjunctive Mood.*

Tense.		Singular. 1	2	3	Plural. 1 2 3
Present	*Indefinite*	do	do	do	do
	Continuous	be doing	be doing	be doing	be doing
	Perfect	have done	have done	have done	have done
	Perf. Cont.	have been doing	have been doing	have been doing	have been doing
Simple Past	*Indefinite*		*(Same as Indicative)*		
	Continuous	were doing	wert doing	were doing	were doing
	Perfect		*(Same as Indicative)*		
	Perf. Cont.		*(Same as Indicative)*		
Compound Past	*Indefinite*[1]	should do	wouldst do	would do	1. should, 2, 3. would } do
	Continuous	should be doing	wouldst be doing	would be doing	1. should, 2, 3. would } be doing
	Perfect[2]	should have done	wouldst have done	would have done	1. should, 2, 3. would } have done
	Perf. Cont.	should have been doing	wouldst have been doing	would have been doing	1. should, 2, 3. would } have been doing

III.—*Imperative Mood.*

Present Singular 2. do (thou). *Plural* 2. do (ye or you).

B. Passive Voice of **See**.

This, if we omit the Past Participle "seen," gives a complete conjugation of the Finite moods of the verb "*to be.*"

I.—*Indicative Mood.*

Tense.		Singular. 1	2	3	Plural. 1 2 3
Present	*Indefinite*	am seen	art seen	is seen	are seen
	Continuous	am being seen	art being seen	is being seen	are being seen
	Perfect	have been seen	hast been seen	has been seen	have been seen
	Perf. Cont.		*(None)*		
Past	*Indefinite*	was seen	wast seen	was seen	were seen
	Continuous	was being seen	wast being seen	was being seen	were being see
	Perfect	had been seen	hadst been seen	had been seen	had been seen
	Perf. Cont.		*(None)*		
Future	*Indefinite*	shall be seen	wilt be seen	will be seen	1. shall, 2, 3. will } be seen
	Continuous		*(None)*		
	Perfect	shall have been seen	wilt have been seen	will have been seen	1. shall, 2, 3. will } have been seen
	Perf. Cont.		*(None)*		

[1] This tense, though it has the Past forms *should, would*, can be used to denote a conditional or contingent futurity, and hence it is sometimes called the Subjunctive future, answering to the Indicative future *shall, will*, "should" being substituted for "shall," and "would" for "will"—

I *shall* do this, if you *will* let me—*Indic. Future.*
I *should* do this, if you *would* let me—*Subjunct. Future.*

[2] On the other hand, the Perfect forms denote a conditional past, as is shown below in § 122 (3). The Perfect forms cannot be used in a future sense, but only in a past sense.

II.—*Subjunctive Mood.*

Tense.		Singular. 1	2	3	Plural. 1 2 3
Present	*Indefinite*	be seen	be seen	be seen	be seen
	Continuous		(*None*)		
	Perfect	have been seen	have been seen	have been seen	have been seen
	Perf. Cont.		(*None*)		
Simple Past	*Indefinite*	were seen	wert seen	were seen	were seen
	Continuous	were being seen	wert being seen	were being seen	were being seen
	Perfect		(*Same as Indicative*)		
	Perf. Cont.		(*None*)		
Compound Past	*Indefinite*	should be seen	wouldst be seen	would be seen	1. should, 2, 3. would } be seen
	Continuous		(*None*)		
	Perfect	should have been seen	wouldst have been seen	would have been seen	1. should, 2, 3. would } have been seen
	Perf. Cont.		(*None*)		

III.—*Imperative Mood.*

Present Singular 2. be (thou) seen. *Plural* 2. be (ye or you) seen.

Section 7.—Indicative Mood.

112. The Present Indefinite can be used to denote :—

(*a*) What is always and necessarily true :—

The sun *shines* by day and the moon by night.

(*b*) What is habitual in life or character :—

He *keeps* his promises. He *has* good health.

(*c*) What is present, if this is helped by the context :—

I *understand* what you *say*. The door *is* open.

(*d*) What is future, if this is helped by the context :—

When *do* you (=will you) start for Edinburgh ?

(*e*) What is past, provided that the event is known to be past. (This is called the Historic or Graphic Present.)

Baber now *leads* (=then led) his men through the Khyber Pass, and *enters* (=entered) the plains of India.

113. The Perfect tenses are used as follows :—

(1) The *Present* Perfect connects a past event in some sense or other *with present time* :—

The British Empire in India *has succeeded* to the Mogul.

The series of events by which the British Empire superseded the Mogul took place more than a century ago. The events are therefore long past. But the state of things arising out of these past events is *still present.* The British Empire *still exists.* Hence it is right to say "has succeeded."

Some Intransitive verbs (Transitive ones never), and especially those Intransitive verbs that signify going, coming, becoming, changing, etc., may use the Auxiliary **is** instead of *has*, and **was** instead of *had*:—

(*a*) The flower *is* faded. (*b*) The flower *has* faded.

In (*a*), however, the *state* of the flower (faded) is more prominently indicated; in (*b*) the *time* of the fading. So the two sentences are not quite equivalent.

(2) The *Past* Perfect (called also the Pluperfect) is never used, except when we wish to say that some action was either (*a*) completed, or (*b*) supposed to be completed, before another was commenced:—

(*a*) He *had been* ill two days, when the doctor was sent for. (*Fact.*)
(*b*) If I *had seen* him, I should have known him. (*Supposition.*)

(3) The *Future* Perfect denotes the completion of some event (*a*) in future time, (*b*) in past time:—

(*a*) He *will have reached* home before the rain sets in.
(*b*) You *will have heard* this news already; so I need not repeat it.

It seems like a contradiction to make a *Future* tense have reference to *Past* tense. But the future here implies an inference regarding something which is believed to have passed rather than past time itself. "You will have heard" means "I infer or believe that you have heard."

114. Do and **Did.**—The Present and Past Indefinite in the Active voice can also be formed by the Auxiliary "*do*" (§ 103).

Present Tense.

	Singular.	*Plural.*
1*st Person*	I do love	We do love
2*nd* ,,	Thou dost love	Ye or you do love
3*rd* ,,	He does love	They do love

Past Tense.

	Singular.	*Plural.*
1*st Person*	I did love	We did love
2*nd* ,,	Thou didst love	Ye or you did love
3*rd* ,,	He did love	They did love

This form is used for three different purposes:—

(*a*) For the sake of emphasis; as, "I *do* love," "I *did* love."

(*b*) For the sake of bringing in the word "not"; as, "I *do not* love" (which is better than saying "I love not"), "I *did not* love" (which is better than saying "I loved not").

(*c*) For the sake of asking a question; as, "*Does* he love?" "Why *did* he love?" "*Did* he not love?"

115. Shall and Will.—Beginners are sometimes puzzled to know when to use "*shall*" and when to use "*will*."

It should be understood that there are *three* senses in which the future tense can be used :—

(*a*) To express *merely future time*, and nothing more.
(*b*) To combine future time with an implied *command*.
(*c*) To combine future time with an implied *intention*.

(*a*) *Merely future time.*

When nothing but future time is intended—*mere futurity*, without any idea of command or intention being mixed up with it—*shall* must be used for the *First* person, and *will* for the *Second* and *Third* persons, as below :—

	Singular.	*Plural.*
1*st Person*	I *shall* go	We *shall* go
2*nd* ,,	Thou *wilt* go	You *will* go
3*rd* ,,	He *will* go	They *will* go

In these persons *shall* and *will* are strictly *tense-forming*, that is, Auxiliary verbs (see §§ 102, 103).

(*b*) *An Implied Command, Promise, or Threat.*

Whenever we desire to express, not merely future time, but some *command*, or *promise*, or *threat* in addition, *shall* is put for *will* in the Second and Third persons ;[1] as—

You *shall* be hanged (by some one's command).
You *shall* receive your prize to-morrow (promise).
If you do this, you *shall* be hanged (threat).

In these examples, the *shall* is not a tense-forming or Auxiliary verb, but a Principal or Notional one (see §§ 102, 103).

(*c*) *An Implied Intention.*

When the speaker wishes to express some intention of his own, then *will* is put for *shall* in the First person :[1]—

I *will* call on you to-day, and I *shall* then say good-bye.

Here *will* denotes the *intention* of calling, while *shall* denotes *merely future time*. Therefore *will* is a Principal verb, and *shall* is an Auxiliary.

Note.—In a command, promise, threat, or intention there is necessarily some sense of futurity. Nevertheless, the verb *shall* in all such contexts as (*b*) and *will* in such a context as (*c*) are in the

[1] In Old Eng. *sceal* (shall) means "I must," "I owe," "I am liable for" ; and this sense is maintained, wherever this verb is used in the Second and Third persons. *Will* in Old Eng. means to intend or desire ; and this sense is maintained, whenever this verb is used in the First person. But these senses are not maintained, when *shall* is used in the First person, and *will* in the Second and Third. The verbs have then become Auxiliary, that is, they have discarded their original meanings in order to help other verbs to express future time (§ 88).

Present tense, not in the Future. They are simply Notional verbs (Transitive) in the Present tense, and the Infinitive following is their object.

Section 8.—Imperative Mood.

116. The **Imperative** mood is used only in the Present tense, Second person : the Subject is seldom expressed.

Singular.	*Plural.*
Speak.	Speak.

117. To express our will in connection with the *First* or *Third* person we either (*a*) use the Transitive verb *let*, which is itself the Second person of the Imperative mood of the verb "to let," or (*b*) we employ the Subjunctive mood :—

	Singular.	*Plural.*
(*a*) 1*st Person*	Let me speak	Let us speak
3*rd* ,,	Let him speak	Let them speak

(*b*) Every soldier *kill* his prisoner.—Shakspeare.
Thither our path lies ; *wind we* up the height.—Browning.

The Third person of the Subjunctive occurs in the common phrases *suffice it* = "let it suffice" ; *so be it* = "so let it be."

Suffice it to say that all the prisoners were acquitted.

Note.—In such a construction as *Let me speak,* "speak" (Infin.) is the direct object to "let," and "me" the indirect.

118. The chief uses of the Imperative mood are to express (*a*) *command,* (*b*) *precept,* or (*c*) *entreaty* :—

(*a*) *Command* :—

Awake, arise, or *be* for ever fallen.—Milton.

(*b*) *Precept* or *Invitation* :—

Go to the ant, thou sluggard ; *consider* her ways and *be* wise. —*Old Testament.*

(*c*) *Entreaty* or *Prayer* :—

Give us this day our daily bread.—*Lord's Prayer.*

119. When the verb is negative, that is, prohibitive, the Imperative is now formed by the Auxiliary "*do.*" See § 114 (*b*).

Older Form.	*Present Form.*
Fear not.	*Do* not fear.
Taste not that food.	*Do* not taste that food.

Note.—Sometimes, even when the verb is affirmative, the Imperative is formed by "do," in order to give more emphasis to an entreaty. This, however, occurs only in colloquial English :—

Do help me to lift this box.

120. The Imperative mood is sometimes used to express a **Supposition** :—

Take care of the pence, and the pounds will take care of themselves (=If you take care of the pence, the pounds will, etc.).

121. Sometimes an Imperative is used **absolutely**; *i.e.* in isolation from the rest of the sentence :—

A large number of men, *say* a hundred, are working on the railroad.

Section 9.—Subjunctive Mood.

122. The Subjunctive mood expresses *a purpose*, *a wish*, *a condition*, or *a doubt*, anything rather than a fact.

(1) *A Purpose.*

In this case the verb in the Subjunctive mood is preceded by the conjunction *that* or *lest* (lest = that not). The Auxiliary verbs "*may*" and "*might*" are used after "*that*," and "*should*" after "*lest*."

	Indicative.	*Subjunctive: Purpose.*
Present or *Future*	I give you a prize, .	that you *may work* well again.
	I shall keep your book,	lest you *should lose* it. / that you *may* not *lose* it.
Past	I gave you a prize, .	that you *might work* well again.
	I kept your book, .	lest you *should lose* it. / that you *might* not *lose* it.

Note.—In the Tudor Period, and somewhat beyond it, the Subjunctive of purpose was commonly expressed in the Present Indefinite tense, without the help of the Auxiliary "may" :—

Love not sleep, lest thou *come* to poverty.—*Old Test.*

Speak to my brother, that he *divide* the inheritance with me. —*New Test.*

(2) *A Wish or Order.*

To express a wish or order, there are two forms of the Subjunctive that may be used : either (*a*) the simple form, without an Auxiliary ; or (*b*) the compound form, with the Auxiliary "*may*" :—

Thy kingdom *come*, thy will *be* done.
May he live long and see not the grave !
I wish that he *were* as clever as his sister.
Far *be* it from me to say anything false.
My sentence is that the prisoner *be hanged*.

(3) *Condition and its Consequence.*

When the verb expresses a *condition*, it is generally preceded by the conjunction "*if*." The verb denoting the *consequence* is expressed by the Auxiliary "*would*" in the Second and Third persons, and by "*should*" in the First :—

	First Sentence: Condition.	*Second Sentence: Consequence.*
Present or *Future*	If he *should meet* me,	he *would know* me at once.
	If I *were* in his place,	I *should pay* the money.
Past	If he *had met* me,	he *would have known* me.
	If I *had been* in his place,	I *should have paid* the money.

Sometimes the *if* is left out. In this case the *should*, or the *had*, or the *were* must be placed before its subject :—

Present or *Future*	*Should* he *meet* me,	he *would know* me at once.
	Were I in his place,	I *should pay* the money.
Past	*Had* he *met* me,	he *would have known* me.
	Had I *been* in his place,	I *should have paid* the money.

Sometimes the Conditional sentence is left out or understood, and only the Consequent sentence is expressed :—

He *would* never agree to that ("if you asked him," understood).
He *would* be very thankful to you for this kindness ("if you were to do him the kindness," understood).

(4) *A Doubt or Supposition.*

A verb in the Subjunctive mood, preceded by some conjunction or conjunctive pronoun, implies some *doubt* or *supposition* :—

I will not let thee go, *except* thou *bless* me.—*Old Test.*
Murder, *though* it *have* no tongue, will speak.
Whoever he *be*, he shall not go unpunished.

The conjunction is not always expressed :—

"*Come* weal, *come* woe, by Bruce's side,"
Replied the chief, "will Donald bide."—Scott.

Note.—The Subjunctive mood in some form or other is always used to express (1), (2), and (3). But to express (4) the Indicative is now often used instead of it. The Subjunctive, however, ought still to be used, whenever we express something that we know or believe to be either doubtful or contrary to the fact :—

If he *were* guilty (which I know he is not), I should never get over it.

Section 10.—Infinitive Mood.

123. The Infinitive may denote either Present or Past time :—

	Form.	*Active.*	*Passive.*
Present	*Indefinite* .	To send	To be sent
	Continuous .	To be sending	(*Wanting*)
Past	*Perfect* . .	To have sent	To have been sent
	Perf. Contin.	To have been sending	(*Wanting*)

Future time can be expressed only by some phrase; as, "to be about to send"; "to be going to send."

124. **The Perfect form of Infinitive.**—After verbs expressing wish, intention, duty, etc., the Perfect form of the Infin. is used, to show that the wish, etc., was not carried out :—

He intended *to have gone* (but something stopped him).
He would *have gone* (but he was not able).
He ought *to have gone* (but he neglected to do so).

It is a mistake, however, to use the Perfect Infinitive in any other connection. Thus we cannot say—

It was unkind of him *to have gone* without saying good-bye.

Here *to have gone* should be changed to "*to go.*"

His going (=to go) without saying good-bye was unkind.

Note.—After the verb "said," "known," "believed," "supposed," and such-like, the Perfect Infinitive is used to denote past time:—

He is said *to have gone*=It is said that he *went*.

125. Infinitive without "to."—The word "*to*" is usually, but not always, the sign of the Infinitive mood.

(*a*) Most of the verbs not followed by "*to*" occur in the following examples:—

I *hear* thee speak (to speak) of a better land.
I *saw* him take (to take) aim with his bow.
You *need* not send (to send) those books to me.
I *feel* the cold air strike (to strike) against my face.
He *dared* not say (to say) this in open day.
He *made* me come (to come) and sit (to sit) beside him.
I *let* him go (to go) back to his own house.
They *bade* me tell (to tell) them the right road.
We *watched* him go (to go) and come (to come).
We *beheld* the fish rise (to rise).
I have *known* him laugh (to laugh) for nothing.

(*b*) The "*to*" is also left out after Auxiliary and Defective verbs, as may be seen below:—

I shall *go*; I will *go*; I can *go*; I may *go*; I do *go*; I must *go*.
(But "I ought *to* go" is an exception.)

(*c*) The "*to*" is left out after *than* and *but*:—

He did nothing *but* laugh.
He did nothing else *than* laugh.

(*d*) The "*to*" is left out after certain phrases:—

You had better not *remain* here.
I had rather *take* this than that.

The Uses of the Infinitive Mood.

126. There are two main uses of the Infinitive mood:—

I. The Noun-Infinitive (also called Simple).
II. The Qualifying Infinitive (also called Gerundial).[1]

---

[1] The name Gerundial, though unfortunately it is now well established, is misleading. It implies that the Qualifying Infinitive has some connection with what we now call the Gerund or Verbal noun. In point of fact, it has no connection with it whatever, either historically or syntactically. They are as distinct in origin as they are in use. The one does

127. I. The Noun-Infinitive may be used in any way in which Nouns are used ; *i.e.* (*a*) as the Subject to a verb, (*b*) as the Object to a Transitive verb or to a Preposition, (*c*) as the Complement to a verb, or (*d*) as a form of exclamation :—

(*a*) Subject to a verb :—

To err is human ; *to forgive*, divine.

(*b*) Object to a Transitive verb or to a Preposition :—

A good man does not fear *to die*.
He was about (=near) *to die* (=death).

(*c*) Complement to a verb :—

He appears *to be* a wise man. (*Intrans.*)
We considered him *to be* the best in the class. (*Factit.*)

(*d*) As a form of **exclamation** :—

To think that he told so many lies !

II. The Qualifying Infinitive may be used in any way in which an adjective or adverb is used ; and sometimes it is used absolutely :—

(*a*) After a verb (here its use is adverbial) :—

He came *to see* (=for the purpose of seeing) the sport.
He wept *to see* (=at seeing) that shocking sight.

(*b*) After a noun (here its use is adjectival) :—

He hopes to be rewarded in the world *to come*.
Give him a chair *to sit* on.

Note.—The Qualifying Infin., when used with a noun, can be either attributive or predicative (§ 58) :—

A house *to let* (Attrib.). This house is *to let* (Predic.).

(*c*) After an adjective (here its use is adverbial) :—

He is quick *to hear* and slow *to speak*.

(*d*) Absolutely, for bringing in a **Parenthesis** :—

I am,—*to tell* you the truth,—quite tired of this work.
They were thunderstruck,—so *to speak*,—on hearing this news.

SECTION 11.—PARTICIPLES.

128. The forms of the different Participles are as follows :—

Transitive Verbs.

	Active Voice.	*Passive Voice.*
Present or Continuous	Loving	Being loved
Past Indefinite . .	(*Wanting*)	Loved
Past Perfect . .	Having loved	Having been loved

---

the work of an adjective or adverb, the other of a noun ; and so they have nothing at all in common. The Gerund so-called in *-ing* was never an Infinitive, and it is a great mistake to call it so.

Intransitive Verbs.

Present or Continuous . .	Fading
Past Indefinite . . .	Faded
Past Perfect . . .	Having faded

Note 1.—The form *loving* stands for both Present and Continuous participles. These are not the same in meaning :—

(*a*) *Hearing* this he was much surprised. (*Pres.*)
(*b*) He went away *sorrowing*. (*Cont.*)

In (*a*) the action is completed. In (*b*) it is continuous.

Note 2.—There is no Future Participle in English. Futurity can be expressed by the Qualifying Infinitive, as "the world *to come*," or by a periphrasis, as "about (*prep.*) to fall" (*Noun Infin.*), "going to see" (*Qual. Infin.*), "going to be beaten" (*Qual. Infin.*).

129. Double Character of Participles.—A Participle has two distinct functions, and can be defined as that part of a verb which may be used either (*a*) for helping to form a tense, or (*b*) as an adjective for qualifying some noun or noun-equivalent.

I. *As part of a tense.*

130. Many of the tenses of English verbs are formed with the help of the Past or Present Participle.

Thus all the tenses of the Passive voice are formed out of the verb "to be," followed by the Past Participle ; as, "I am loved," "I was loved," "I shall be loved."

Again, all the Continuous tenses in the Active voice are formed out of the verb "to be," followed by the Present Participle ; as, "I am loving, "I was loving," "I shall be loving."

Again, the Perfect tenses in the Active voice are formed out of the verb "to have," followed by the Past Participle ; as, "I have loved," "I had loved," "I shall have loved."

II. *As an Adjective.*[1]

131. A Participle, when it is not part of a tense, belongs to the class of Descriptive adjective (§ 48). Like other adjectives, it can (*a*) qualify a noun, (*b*) be qualified by an adverb, (*c*) admit of degrees of comparison, (*d*) be used as a noun :—

---

[1] To show how completely a Participle can assume the function of an adjective, there are instances in which it forgoes its verb-character altogether :—

Astonishing to any one. *Disturbing* to any one. *Surprising* to any one.

When the words italicised are used as verbs, they are Transitive, and do not allow the prep. *to* to come between them and their object. We could not say, "This astonishes *to* me, or disturbs *to* me, or surprises *to* me."

(*a*) *Being tired* of work, *the men* went home.
(*b*) The man was picked up in an *almost dying* state.
(*c*) This flower is *more faded* than that.
(*d*) Let *bygones* be *bygones*. (This kind of use is rare.)

132. Since a Participle is a verb as well as an adjective, it can take an Object, which may be of five different kinds (§ 106) :—

Having shot *the tiger*, he returned home. (*Direct Obj.*)
He is busy, teaching *his sons* Greek. (*Indirect Obj.*)
Having been taught *Greek*, he was a good scholar. (*Retained Obj.*)
We saw him fighting a hard *battle*. (*Cognate Obj.*)
Having sat *himself* down, he began to eat. (*Reflexive Obj.*)

133. **Past Indefinite.**—The use of such participles depends upon whether the verb is Transitive or Intransitive :—

(*a*) If the verb is *Transitive*, the Past Indefinite Participle is never used in the Active voice, but only in the Passive :—

This much-*praised* man proved to be a rogue.
Gold is a metal *dug* out of the earth.

(*b*) If the verb is *Intransitive*, the Past Indefinite is not used at all in most verbs. But whenever it is used (which depends entirely on custom), it must *precede* its noun, and not follow it :—

The *faded* rose. A *retired* officer. The *returned* soldier. The *fallen* city. The *risen* sun. A *withered* flower. A *departed* guest.

If the speaker or writer desires to place the Past Participle of an Intransitive verb *after* its noun, he must insert the Relative pronoun and change the participle into a Finite verb ; as—

The horse of Mr. A., *gone* to America, is for sale. (This is wrong. The sentence should be—"The horse of Mr. A., *who has gone* to America, is for sale.")

But the Past Participle of an Intransitive verb is sometimes put *after* its noun *in poetry* :—

A Daniel *come* to judgment.—SHAKSPEARE, *Mer. Venice.*
Toll for the brave—the brave that are no more,
All *sunk* beneath the wave, fast by their native shore.—COWPER.

Even in prose the Past Participle of an Intransitive verb is sometimes, *but very rarely*, placed after its noun :—

In times *past*=in times which have passed.
He is a man *descended* from a high family.

134. The Past Participle of verbs is sometimes used to express some *permanent habit*, *state*, or *character* :—

A well-*read* man=a man who has read much and read well.
A well-*behaved* man=a man whose habitual behaviour is good.
An out-*spoken* man=a man who habitually speaks out his mind.
A *retired* man=a man who dislikes appearing in public.
A *mistaken* man=one who errs by habit or in some specific case.

From this use of the Past Participle has arisen a large class of Adjectives, which are formed from nouns by adding "*ed*" to the end of the noun :—

An evil-*heart*-ed man. A *talent*-ed man. A *land*-ed proprietor. A long-*tail*-ed ape. A smooth-*skin*-ned cat. His *saint*-ed mother. A red-*colour*-ed rose. A rough-*face*-d youth. A *hood*-ed snake. A long-*leg*-ged spider. A purple-*crest*-ed helmet. A many-*page*-d book. A long-*arm*-ed monkey. A thickly-*wood*-ed hill. A noble-*mind*-ed man. A warm-*blood*-ed animal.

Section 12.—Gerunds and Verbal Nouns.

135. A **Gerund** has four forms—two for the Active voice and two for the Passive.

	Active.	*Passive.*
Present or Continuous	Loving	Being loved
Perfect . . .	Having loved	Having been loved

136. The *forms* of a Gerund, then, are the same as those of a Participle, and both are parts of a verb. What, then, is the difference? A Gerund is a kind of *Noun;* but a Participle is a kind of *Adjective.* So, in spite of the resemblance in *form*, they are quite distinct in *nature.*[1]

The reason of the resemblance in form is a matter of history. In Old English the *forms* of the Verbal Adjective and Verbal Noun were quite distinct. The suffix *-ing* originally belonged to the latter only.

Participle . .	*Writ-ende*, or *-inde*, or *-and.*
Verbal noun . .	*Writ-ung*, or *writ-ing* (both forms occur in Anglo-Saxon).

In later English the suffix *-inde* took the form of *-ing*, while *-ende* and *-and* died out; and *-ung* became obsolete. Hence we have now only one form instead of two for the two parts of speech :—

Participle	*Writing.*
Verbal noun	*Writing.*

137. Gerund defined.—A Gerund is that part of a verb which, if the verb is Intransitive, has the function of a noun only, but if the verb is Transitive, retains the function of a verb also, and can be followed by an object in the same way as if it were a Finite verb :—

Fond of *sleeping* . . . (*Noun-function only.*)
Fond of *hunting* foxes . . (*Noun- and verb-function combined.*)

In point of *function* there is no difference between a Gerund and an Infinitive. Either may be correctly defined as "that part of a verb

[1] In some books the Gerund is called a Participial noun. This name should be avoided, since a Noun is one part of speech and a Participle is another.

which names the action, without naming the doer.' Both are Abstract nouns. The difference between them is not in function, but in *form;* observe the suffix *-ing.* They differ also in syntactical usage; for a Gerund has case, and can be preceded or followed by any kind of preposition, and it can be preceded by the Def. art. *the;* the same cannot be said of Infinitives.

Subsequently the other forms of Gerund (sometimes called Compound), *being loved, having loved, having been loved,* were formed in modern English, on the analogy of corresponding participles.

138. Gerund as Noun.—Since a Gerund is a *kind of noun,* it may be the subject to some verb, or object to some verb, or complement to some verb, or object to some preposition; as—

Subject to a verb.—Sleeping is necessary to life.
Object to a verb.—He enjoyed *sleeping* in the open air.
Complement to a verb.—His almost constant habit was *sleeping.*
Object to a preposition.—He was fond of *sleeping.*

In the following sentences say whether the words noted below are Gerunds or Participles:—

The rice will grow well in the *coming* rains. We heard of his *coming* back to-day. Did you hear of his *having won* a prize? The boy *having won* a prize was much praised. She was fond of *being admired. Being admired* by all she was much pleased. The cow *having been killed* by a tiger yesterday could not be found. The boy was ashamed of *having been beaten* in class by his sister. I am tired of *doing* this work. *Doing* this work every day you will soon improve. *Spelling* is more difficult than *writing.* He was in the habit of *boasting* of his cleverness. A *boasting* man is much despised.

Note.—In such phrases as "a hunting whip," "a drinking fountain," the words *hunting* and *drinking* are Gerunds, not participles: "a whip for hunting," "a fountain for drinking." The Gerund or Verbal noun is here used as a substitute for an adjective; see § 180.

139. Gerund as a Verb.—Since the Gerund of a Transitive verb retains its verb-character (§ 137), the object by which it is followed may be of any of the five kinds shown in § 106, *Note.*

Direct (with Trans.).—He is clever at teaching *Euclid.*
Indirect (with Trans.).—He is clever at teaching *his sons* Euclid.
Retained (with Passive).—He is pleased at being taught *Euclid.*
Cognate (with Intrans.).—He is proud of having fought a good *fight.*
Reflexive (with Intrans.).—He is in the habit of oversleeping *himself.*

140. Gerund with Possessive.—A noun, when it is placed before a Gerund, should be in the Possessive case, provided it can be used in that case:—

He was displeased at the *barber's* not coming.

Avoid such constructions as the following:—

He was displeased at the *barber* not coming.
Would you mind *me* asking you a question?

Note.—Sometimes the letter "*a*" (an abbreviation of "*on*") is placed before a Gerund in a prepositional sense:—

This set him *a* (=on) *thinking*.

141. Gerundive use of Participles.—Such participles are not Gerunds, but participles used in a Gerundive sense:—

I depend on the wall *being built* immediately.

How are we to parse "being built" in such a connection? We must parse it as a participle; but it is not used as such in the ordinary way; for it does more than qualify the noun "wall." The sentence does not mean "I depend on the wall that was being built," or "the wall when it was being built"; but "I depend on the *wall-being-built* immediately," that is, "on the immediate *building of* the wall." There is therefore a Gerund or Verbal noun implied in the participle "being built," and hence it may be said that such participles are used Gerundively. (Dr. Abbott calls this the "Noun-use of the Participle." But he also uses the phrase "Gerundive use of Participles."—*How to Parse*, § 405, p. 235.)

142. A Verbal noun is the same thing at bottom as a Gerund, but a distinction has been drawn between them.[1]

A Verbal noun is preceded by the Definite article and followed by the preposition "*of*"; whereas a Gerund has no article preceding it and no preposition following it. The former construction is the original one. The latter is modern, and arose simply out of the omission of the preposition "of."[2]

(*a*) I am engaged in *the* careful reading *of* a book (*Verbal noun.*)
(*b*) I am engaged in carefully reading a book . (*Gerund.*)

In (*a*) "*reading*" is a *single* part of speech,—a noun and nothing more. In (*b*) "*reading*" is a double part of speech,—a noun and verb combined. Observe, too, that a Verbal noun is qualified by an **Adjective**, a gerund by an **Adverb**.

Note 1.—Sometimes the "*of*" is left out, even when there is a Definite article going before:—

---

[1] It has been said that "a word ending in *-ing* may be a participle, or an adjective, or a noun, or *a verb in the Infinitive mood*." For the last see Professor Earle's *Simple Grammar of English*, p. 241, where he calls it a "Flexional Infinitive," derived from the old Infinitive ending in *-en*; as "build-*en*," "build-*ing*." I cannot find any evidence for this theory, which he has borrowed, as he says, from Carlyle! The inflexion *-en* was dead by about 1500 A.D., and it died without leaving anything behind it. The noun-suffix *-ing* is as old as Anglo-Saxon. What we now call the Gerund has not sprung out of any Infinitive, but is simply the Verbal noun itself with the "*of*" omitted. See my *English Grammar Past and Present*, § 523, or *Historical English and Derivation*, § 148. That a word ending in *-ing* may be a participle or an adjective has been shown already; see § 131 and footnote. *It never is and it never was an Infinitive* of any kind whatever.

[2] Compare the omission of "*of*" in such phrases as "on board (of) ship," "inside or outside (of) the door," "a thousand (of) men."

The *giving* to the courts the power to review hard and unconscionable bargains will control the rest.—*Review of Reviews*, August 1898, p. 165.

Here there is no "*of*" after the word "giving." In such a construction we cannot distinguish between a Verbal noun and a Gerund.

Note 2.—The Abstract noun, which we call a Verbal noun or Gerund, can be used in a Concrete sense :—

I am pleased with my *surroundings*.
He went away with all his *belongings*.

Section 13.—The Strong and Weak Conjugations.

143. Strong and Weak.—Verbs are distinguished according to *function* into Transitive, Intransitive, and Auxiliary (§ 85). According to *form* or Conjugation, they are distinguished into **Strong** and **Weak**. (All our borrowed verbs are Weak.)

Note.—The names "Irregular" and "Regular" for Strong and Weak are misleading ; for in point of fact the Strong conjugation is, in its own way, not less regular than the Weak, besides being the older of the two. The name Irregular is reserved in this book for certain verbs mentioned below in § 147.

Tests of a Weak verb :—

(*a*) All verbs, whose Past tense ends in a *-d* or *-t*, which is not in the Present tense, are Weak :—

Live, live-*d*. Fan, fann-*ed*. Think, though-*t*. Sell, sol-*d*.

(*b*) All verbs, whose Past tense is formed by shortening (not changing) the vowel of the Present tense, are Weak :—

Bleed, bled. Shoot, shot. Lead, led. Light, lit or light-*ed*.

(*c*) All verbs, whose Past tense is the same as the Present, are Weak :—

Cut, cut. Hurt, hurt. Put, put. Rid, rid. Spread, spread.

Tests of a Strong verb :—

(*a*) All verbs, which form the Past tense by *changing* (not merely shortening) the inside vowel, and do *not* add on a final *-d* or *-t*, are Strong :—

Fight, fought (but "buy, bough-*t*" is Weak, because, after changing the inside vowel, it adds a final *-t*). Hold, held. Stand, stood.

(*b*) All verbs, which form the Past participle in *-en* or *-n*, are either wholly or partly Strong :—

Wholly.—Draw, drew, draw-*n*.
Shake, shook, shake-*n*.
Partly.—Saw, saw-*ed*, saw-*n*.
Cleave, clef-*t*, clov-*en*.

144. Lists of Strong Verbs.—The list of Mixed verbs given under Group III. exemplifies the tendency of Strong verbs to become Weak.

Group I. (*50 verbs*).—Final *-n* or *-en* retained in Past Participle.

Present Tense.	*Past Tense.*	*Past Part.*	*Present Tense.*	*Past Tense.*	*Past Part.*
Arise	arose	arisen	Hide	hid	*hidden, hid
Bear (produce)	bore	born	Know	knew	known
Bear (carry)	bore	borne	Lie	lay	lain
Beget	begot begat	begotten begot	Ride	rode	ridden
Bid	bade, bid	bidden, bid	Rise	rose	risen
Bind	bound	*bounden, bound	See	saw	seen
Bite	bit	bitten, bit	Shake	shook	shaken
Blow	blew	blown	Shrink	shrank	*shrunken, shrunk
Break	broke	broken	Sink	sank	*sunken, sunk
Chide	chid	chidden, chid	Slay	slew	slain
Choose	chose	chosen	Slide	slid	slidden, slid
Draw	drew	drawn	Smite	smote	smitten, smit
Drink	drank	*drunken, drunk	Speak	spoke	spoken
Drive	drove, drave	driven	Steal	stole	stolen
Eat	ate	eaten	Stride	strode	stridden
Fall	fell	fallen	Strike	struck	*stricken, struck
Fly	flew	flown	Strive	strove	striven
Forbear	forbore	forborne	Swear	swore	sworn
Forget	forgot	forgotten	Take	took	taken
Forsake	forsook	forsaken	Tear	tore	torn
Freeze	froze	frozen	Throw	threw	thrown
Get	got	*gotten, got	Tread	trod	trodden, trod
Give	gave	given	Wear	wore	worn
Go, wend	went	gone	Weave	wove	woven
Grow	grew	grown	Write	wrote	written

Note.—The seven participles marked * are now chiefly used as Verbal adjectives only, and not as parts of some tense :—

Verbal Adjective.	*Part of some Tense.*
Our *bounden* duty.	He was *bound* by his promise.
A *drunken* man.	He had *drunk* much wine.
A *sunken* ship.	The ship had *sunk* under the water.
A *stricken* deer.	The deer was *struck* with an arrow.
The *shrunken* stream.	The stream has *shrunk* in its bed.
Ill-*gotten* wealth.	He *got* his wealth by ill means.
A *hidden* meaning.	The meaning is *hid* or hidden.

Group II. (32 *verbs*).—Final *-n* or *-en* lost in Past Participle.

Present Tense.	*Past Tense.*	*Past Part.*	*Present Tense.*	*Past Tense.*	*Past Part.*
Abide	abode	abode	Sing	sang	sung
Awake	awoke	awoke	Sit	sat	sat
Become	became	become	Sling	slung	slung
Begin	began	begun	Slink	slunk	slunk
Behold	beheld,	beheld,	Spin	spun	spun
		beholden[1]	Spring	sprang	sprung
Cling	clung	clung	Stand	stood	stood
Come	came	come	Stick	stuck	stuck
Dig	dug	dug	Sting	stung	stung
Fight	fought	fought	Stink	stank	stunk
Find	found	found	String	strung	strung
Fling	flung	flung	Swim	swam	swum
Grind	ground	ground	Swing	swung	swung
Hold	held	held	Win	won	won
Ring	rang	rung	Wind	wound	wound
Run	ran	run	Wring	wrung	wrung
Shine	shone	shone			

Group III.—Mixed or Strong-Weak Verbs (28 *in number*).

Present Tense.	*Past Tense.*	*Past Participle.*
Beat	beat	beaten
Cleave (split)	clave, cleft	*cloven, cleft
Climb	clomb, climbed	climbed
Crow	crew, crowed	crowed, crown (rare)
Do	did	done
Grave	graved	*graven, graved
Hang[2]	hung, hanged	hung, hanged
Hew	hewed	*hewn, hewed
Lade	laded	laden
Melt	melted	*molten, melted
Mow	mowed	mown
Prove	proved	†proven, proved
Rive	rived	riven
Rot	rotted	*rotten, rotted
Saw	sawed	sawn
Seethe	seethed	*sodden, seethed
Sew	sewed	*sewn, sewed
Shape	shaped	†shapen, shaped
Shave	shaved	shaven
Shear	sheared	*shorn, sheared
Show	showed	shown
Sow	sowed	sown

[1] "Beholden" means "indebted."

[2] The Intransitive verb is conjugated in the Strong form only. The Transitive verb is conjugated in both forms. *Hanged* means "killed by hanging"; as, "The man was *hanged.*" *Hung* is used in a general sense; as "He *hung* up his coat."

Present Tense.	*Past Tense.*	*Past Participle.*
Stave	stove, staved	stove, staved
Strew	strewed	strewn or strown
Swell	swelled	swollen
Thrive	throve, thrived	thriven, thrived
Wash	washed	*washen, washed
Writhe	writhed	†writhen, writhed

Note 1.—The participles marked * are now chiefly used as Verbal adjectives, and not as parts of some tense :—

Verbal Adjective.	*Part of some Tense.*
A *graven* image.	The image was *engraved* with letters.
A *molten* image.	The image was *melted* with heat.
A *rotten* plank.	The plank was *rotted* by water.
The *sodden* flesh.	The flesh was *seethed* in hot water.
A well-*sewn* cloth.	I have *sewed* or *sewn* it.
Un-*washen* hands.	I have *washed* my hands.
A *shorn* lamb.	The lamb was *sheared* to-day.
A *hewn* log.	The log is *hewed* or *hewn*.

Note 2.—The participles marked † are now seldom seen except in poetry.

145. **Lists of Weak Verbs.**—The mode of adding the suffix of the Past tense is not uniform ; and the two rules given below should be observed :—

(1) If the verb ends in *e*, then *d* only is added ; as—

Live, *lived* (not *liveed*).
Clothe, *clothed* (not *clotheed*).

To this rule there is no exception.

(2) The final consonant is doubled before *ed*, provided (*a*) that the final consonant is *single*, (*b*) that it is *accented* or *monosyllabic*, (*c*) that it is preceded by a *single vowel* ; as—

Fan, *fanned* (not *faned*) ; *drop*, *dropped* (not *droped*).
Compel, *compelled* ; *control*, *controlled*.

But in a verb like *lengthen*, where the accent is not on the last syllable, the Past tense is *lengthened* ; in a verb like *boil*, where the vowel is not single, the Past sense is *boiled* ; and in a verb like *fold*, where the last consonant is not single, the Past tense is *folded*.

To this rule there are very few exceptions. One exception occurs in the final *l*. The final *l* is doubled, even when it is not accented ; as, travel, trav*elled* (not trav*eled*). But the final *l* is not doubled, if it has two vowels going before it ; as, *travail*, *travailed* (not *travailled*).

Group I.—Shortening of Inside Vowel : Past tense in **t**.

Present Tense.	*Past Tense.*	*Past Part.*	*Present Tense.*	*Past Tense.*	*Past Part.*
Creep	crept	crept	Sweep	swept	swept
Sleep	slept	slept	Keep	kept	kept

Present Tense.	*Past Tense.*	*Past Part.*	*Present Tense.*	*Past Tense.*	*Past Part.*
Weep	wept	wept	Smell	smelt	smelt
Burn	burnt	burnt	Spell	spelt	spelt
Deal (dēl)	dĕalt	dĕalt	Lean (lēn)	lēant or leaned	lēant or leaned
Dream (drēm)	drĕamt or dreamed	drĕamt or dreamed	Mean(mēn)	mĕant	mĕant
Dwell	dwelt	dwelt	Spill	spilt	spilt
Feel	felt	felt	Spoil	spoilt or spoiled	spoilt or spoiled
Kneel	knelt	knelt			

Exceptional Verbs.—Make, made, made. Have, had, had. Hear, heard, heard. Leave, left, left. Cleave, cleft, cleft. Lose, lost, lost. Shoe, shod, shod. Flee, fled, fled. Say, said, said. Lay, laid, laid. Pay, paid, paid.

Group II.—Changing of Inside Vowel.

Present Tense.	*Past Tense.*	*Past Part.*	*Present Tense.*	*Past Tense.*	*Past Part.*
Beseech	besought	besought	Work	wrought, worked	wrought, worked
Bring	brought	brought			
Buy	bought	bought	Owe	ought, owed	owed
Catch	caught	caught	Dare	durst or dared	dared
Seek	sought	sought	Can	could	(*Wanting*)
Sell	sold	sold	Shall	should	(*Wanting*)
Teach	taught	taught	Will	would	(*Wanting*)
Tell	told	told	May	might	(*Wanting*)
Think	thought	thought	Clothe	clad, clothed	clad, clothed

Group III.—Verbs ending in **d** *or* **t**.

Verbs ending in *d* or *t* in the Present tense have discarded the suffix of the Past tense, to avoid the repetition of *d* or *t*.

(*a*) Some verbs in this group have the three forms (Present tense, Past tense, and Past Participle) all exactly alike :—

Present Tense.	*Past Tense.*	*Past Part.*	*Present Tense.*	*Past Tense.*	*Past Part.*
Burst	burst	burst	Slit	slit	slit
Cast	cast	cast	Spit	spit or spat	spit
Cost	cost	cost			
Cut	cut	cut	Split	split	split
Hit	hit	hit	Spread	spread	spread
Hurt	hurt	hurt	Sweat	sweat	sweat
Let	let	let	Thrust	thrust	thrust
Put	put	put	Bet	bet	bet
Rid	rid	rid	Quit	quit or quitted	quit or quitted
Set	set	set			
Shed	shed	shed	Knit	knit or knitted	knit or knitted
Shred	shred	shred			
Shut	shut	shut			

Note.—"Spit" is a Weak verb, although it has a form *spat* for the Past tense. In Anglo-Saxon the Present had two forms also.

(*b*) Other verbs in this group end in *d* in the Present tense, but form the Past tense and Past Participle by changing *d* into *t*. (There are at least nine such verbs in English.)

Present Tense.	*Past Tense.*	*Past Part.*	*Present Tense.*	*Past Tense.*	*Past Part.*
Bend	bent	bent	Rend	rent	rent
Build	built	built	Send	sent	sent
Gild	gilt, gilded	gilt	Spend	spent	spent
Gird	girt, girded	girt	Wend	went	(*Wanting*)
Lend	lent	lent			

Exceptions:—end-ed, mend-ed, blend-ed or blent, defend-ed.

(*c*) Other verbs of this group have the three forms all alike, except that they shorten the vowel in the Past forms:—

Present Tense.	*Past Tense.*	*Past Part.*	*Present Tense.*	*Past Tense.*	*Past Part.*
Bleed	bled	bled	Lead	led	led
Breed	bred	bred	Read	re*a*d	re*a*d
Feed	fed	fed	Light	lit, lighted	lit, lighted
Speed	sped	sped	Shoot	shot	shot
Meet	met	met			

SECTION 14.—DEFECTIVE, IRREGULAR, AND IMPERSONAL VERBS.

146. Defective Verbs.—It has been shown that verbs can be classified (1) according to function into Notional (Trans. or Intrans.) and Auxiliary, see § 85; and (2) according to Conjugation or form into Strong and Weak, see § 143.

"Defective" does not constitute a separate class. This word merely means that a verb, whether Weak or Strong, is not conjugated in all its parts.

The verbs *shall*, *will*, *may*, *can* are defective, because they have no other forms besides that of the Past tense, viz. *should*, *would*, *might*, *could*.

The verbs *quoth*, *must*, *ought* are defective, because these are the only forms of tense in which they are now seen; and *quoth* is further defective, because it is never used in the Second person.

The verb *wit* is defective, because it is seen chiefly in the Infinitive mood, "*to wit*" (used only in legal documents.) (The Present *wot* and Past *wist* are almost obsolete.) The verb *worth* is defective, because it is seen only in the Subjunctive mood, as in the phrase "Woe *worth* (= be to) the day." The verbs *wont*, *hight*, *yclept* are defective, because these are now seen only as participles.

Anomalous is the name given to those verbs that are pieced together from parts of two or more Defective verbs; as, *am, was, been; go, went, gone.* The verb "to be" is a patchwork of three distinct roots, *es* (cf. Latin *es, est*), *béo* (cf. Latin *fi-o*), and *wes.*

147. Irregular Verbs.—The verbs *shall, will, may, can, wot, quoth* are irregular, because in the Third person Singular they do not take a final *s.*

For the same reason *dare* and *need* are irregular, whenever they are followed by an Infinitive without "to"; as, "He *dare* not go," "He *need* not go."

The Past tense *could* is irregular, because it has taken an intrusive *l*, in imitation of *should, would. Did* is an irregular Past tense of *do, made* of *make,* and *have* of *had. Made* has lost the medial *k*, and *had* the medial *v.*

148. Impersonal Verbs.—These take "it" for their Subject, and are followed by some Personal pronoun in the Objective case, which in Personal verbs would be the Subject in the Nom. case :—

It shames *me* to hear this = I am ashamed to hear this.
It repents *me* of my folly = I repent of my folly.
It behoves *me* to do this = I ought to do this.

There are three instances in which the *it* is omitted, and the pronoun is placed *before* the verb instead of after it :—

Methinks = it seems to me.
Meseems = it seems to me.
Melists = it seems to me, or it pleases me.

Note.—In Modern English there is no difference of spelling between *thinks* Impersonal and *think* Transitive. But in Old Eng. the former was *thync-an* (to seem) and the latter *thenc-an* (to think).

CHAPTER VII.—ADVERBS.

SECTION 1.—THE FUNCTIONS OF ADVERBS.

149. It has been shown already (§ 16) that an Adverb can qualify Prepositions and Conjunctions, as well as verbs, adjectives, and other adverbs.

(*a*) **Prepositions** :—

The bird flew *exactly over* the sleeper's head.
He paid the money *quite up* to date.
His abilities are *decidedly above* the average.
He was sitting *almost outside* the door.
He arrived *long before* the time.
He held his hand *partly on* and *partly off* the table.

(*b*) **Conjunctions** :—

A man is truly happy *only when* he is in sound health.
I dislike this weather *simply because* the air is too hot.

I wish to know *precisely how* it happened.
They locked the door *shortly before* the thieves came.
The watch was found *long after* the thieves had been caught.
He has been ill *ever since* he left us.

Note.—If for an adverb proper we substitute an adverbial phrase, we find that such a phrase can qualify a preposition or a conjunction in the same way as an adverb proper does :—

Preposition.—He arrived *a few hours after* midnight.
Conjunction.—He recovered *ten days after* he had been taken ill.

150. An Adverb can also qualify an entire sentence. *In this case it must stand first* :—

Unfortunately the thief was not caught.
Evidently you were much distressed at the news.

We could rewrite these sentences in the following form :—

It is unfortunate that the thief was not caught.
It was evident that you were much distressed.

151. *Adverbs do not qualify Nouns or Pronouns.* This is the work of adjectives.

The apparent exceptions to the above rule can all be explained :—

(*a*) I am *sincerely yours.* That book is *certainly mine.*

Here the words "yours" and "mine" are the Possessive forms of "you" and "I," and are therefore equivalent to *adjectives.*

(*b*) A by-path ; a fore-taste ; an out-house.

Here the adverbs do not qualify the several nouns, but are *compounded* with them, so that each compound makes a *single* word.

(*c*) In the following examples the adverb that precedes the noun does not qualify the noun, but some participle or adjective understood :—

The then king = the king then *reigning.*
The late king = the king lately *reigning.*
The above account = the account *given* above.
A far country = a country far *distant.*
An up mail = an up-*going* mail.

(*d*) In the following example the adverb "almost" or "quite" does not qualify the noun "drunkard," but the verb "is" :—

He is *almost* or *quite* a drunkard.

To say, "He is an almost or a quite drunkard," would be incorrect.

Note.—A slovenly practice is springing up, however, by which the adverb "quite" is made to qualify nouns :—

Quite a panic (= a serious panic) was caused.
They had *quite a run* (= a long run) of ill luck.

Section 2.—The Kinds of Adverbs.

152. Adverbs are subdivided into three distinct classes :—

I. Simple. II. Interrogative. III. Conjunctive.

153. Simple Adverbs.—These can be distinguished from one another according to their meaning :—

(1) **Time.**—He did this *before*, and you have done it *since*.

The chief adverbs of this class are :—*Now, then, before, since, ago, already, soon, presently, immediately, instantly, early, late*, etc.

(2) **Place.**—We must rest *here*, and not *there*.

The chief adverbs of this class are :—*Here, there ; hence, thence ; hither, thither ; in, out ; within, without ; above, below ; far, near.*

Note.—Sometimes *there* is merely introductory, and has no meaning of place :—

There is some one knocking at the door.

(3) **Number.**—He did this *once*, but he will not do it *again*.

The chief adverbs of this class are :—*Once, twice, thrice, again, seldom, never, sometimes, always, often, firstly, secondly, thirdly*, etc.

(4) **Description** (§ 46, 2).—He did his work *slowly*, but *surely*.

This class is very numerous. Most of them are formed by adding *-ly* to some adjective. But some do not end in *-ly* ; cf. *thus, so, well, ill, amiss, asleep*.

(5) **Quantity, Extent**, or **Degree.**—He is *almost*, but not *quite*, the cleverest boy in the class. He was *too* tired to go on.

To this class of adverb belong:—*Very, much, the, too, quite, almost, little, a little, rather, somewhat, half, partly, wholly, so*, etc.

Note.—The adverb "the" is quite distinct from the Definite article. It is an Adverb of Degree, derived from the Instrumental case (*thi*) of the Demonstrative, and is never used except before an adjective or adverb in the *Comparative* degree: "*the* more, *the* merrier."

(6) **Affirming** or **Denying.**—He did *not* come after all.

Yes, no, not, perhaps, probably, certainly, not at all, etc.

Note.—*Yes* and *no* are pro-sentence or substitute adverbs :—

(1) Did he come ? Yes (=He did come). *Affirm.*
(2) Did he come ? No (=He did not come). *Negat.*

In (1) *yes* is substitute for an affirmative sentence, and in (2) *no* is substitute for a negative sentence. As pro-nouns save the repetition of a noun, so these adverbs save the repetition of a sentence.

Note 1.—In some books a 7th class is added, viz. adverbs of Cause or Consequence :—*Therefore, then, consequently, because, for.* It appears, however, that these words do not exactly modify any word or words in a sentence, but are rather conjunctions combining the sense of one sentence with that of another by way of inference. They have therefore been included amongst Conjunctions in this book.

Note 2.—**Phrase-adverbs.**—Adverbs can be expressed by phrases (§ 19) as well as single words :—*now and then, to and fro, at present, by all means, up and down, how long? how far? now-a-days*, etc.

154. Interrogative Adverbs.—Used for asking questions:—

(*a*) **Time.**—*When* did he *come?* *How long* will he remain here?
(*b*) **Place.**—*Where* did he stop? *Whence* has he come? *Whither* is he going?
(*c*) **Number.**—*How often* did the dog bark?
(*d*) **Description** (manner, quality, or state).—*How* did he do this? *How* (in what state of health) is he to-day?
(*e*) **Quantity** or **Degree.**—*How far* (to what extent) was that report true?
(*f*) **Cause** or **Reason.**—*Why* did he do this? *Wherefore* did he go?

155. The adverbs "*how*" and "*what*" are sometimes used in an exclamatory sense:—

How kind of you to do that!
What a foolish fellow you are!

156. Conjunctive Adverbs.—These are the same in *form* as Interrogative adverbs; but instead of asking questions, they join sentences, being partly adverbs and partly conjunctions (§ 18).

(*a*) *The antecedent understood.*

This is *where* (=the place in which) we dwell.
Let me know *when* (=the time by which) you will come.

(*b*) *The antecedent expressed.*

This is the place *where* we dwell.
Let me know the time *when* you will come.

SECTION 3.—COMPARISON OF ADVERBS.

157. Adverbs of Quality have degrees of comparison, which are formed in the same way as those of adjectives:—

(*a*) If the Adverb is a word of *one* syllable, the Comparative is formed by adding *er* and the Superlative by adding *est*:—

Fast	faster	fastest	Loud	louder	loudest
Hard	harder	hardest	Late	later	latest or last
Near	nearer	nearest	Far	farther	farthest
Long	longer	longest	Rathe	rather	...

Till *rathe* (=early) she rose, half cheated in the thought.—TENNYSON.

(*b*) Some Adverbs have had a Comparative and Superlative allotted to them from another root:—

Well	better	best	Much	more	most
Ill or badly	worse	worst	Little	less	least

(*c*) Adverbs ending in *ly* form the Comparative by adding *more* and the Superlative by adding *most*:—

Wisely	more wisely	most wisely
Beautifully	more beautifully	most beautifully

Note.—The Adverb "*early*," however, has "*earlier*" for its Comparative.

Section 4.—Verbs Compounded with Adverbs.

158. A Verb is said to be compounded with an Adverb, when the two words are so habitually used together, that one is considered to be a part of the other.

Such Adverbs are almost always (except in poetry) placed *after* the verb; as "speak out," "rise up." Here the *out* should be parsed as part of the verb "speak"; and *up* as part of the verb "rise."

But in forming the corresponding noun, the adverb is put first:—

Verb.	*Noun.*
The crops will *come out* well.	The *outcome* was a good crop.
No profits will *come in*.	His *income* is small.
Cholera did not *break out*.	There was no *outbreak* of cholera.
He *set out* on his journey.	He had no trouble at the *outset*.

Similar instances are:—*Set off* (verb), *offset* (noun); *put out* (verb), *output* (noun); *fit out* (verb), *outfit* (noun); *shoot off* (verb), *offshoot* (noun); *spring off* (verb), *offspring* (noun); *shoot up* (verb), *upshot* (noun); *turn out* (verb), *outturn* (noun); *cast out* (verb), *outcast* (noun); *set on* (verb), *onset* (noun); *lay out* (verb), *outlay* (noun); *look out* (verb), *outlook* (noun); *draw in* (verb), *indraught* (noun); *let out* (verb), *outlet* (noun); *let in* (verb), *inlet* (noun).

Note.—"Set-off," "turn-out," and a few more are also used as nouns.

Section 5.—The Two Uses of Adverbs.

159. Adverbs, like Adjectives (see § 58), have two different uses, viz. (*a*) the Attributive, (*b*) the Predicative.

(*a*) *Attributive use.*—An Adverb is used attributively, when it qualifies in the ordinary way the word associated with it:—

He is *entirely wrong*. He *shouted loudly*. He *did* his work *very badly*. *Half through* the door. I dislike him *only because* he is lazy.

(*b*) *Predicative use.*—An Adverb is used predicatively, when it is made part of the Predicate of a sentence, or in other words, when it is used as the Complement of the verb going before it:[1]—

Subject.	*Verb.*	*Complement*, etc.
My son	is	*well* (in good health) to-day.
He	will be	*better* (in better health) soon.
He	was turned	*adrift* (to go where he could).
The two boys	are	much *alike* (like to each other).
The bear	was caught	*alive* (in a living state).
Those men	are	*aware* (conscious) of their faults.

[1] We cannot endorse what is said in Mason's *English Grammar*, p. 157, ed. 1891: "*An Adverb or adverbial phrase never forms the complement of a predicate.*" The examples given in the text show how very common the predicative or complementary use of Adverbs is.

Subject.	*Verb.*	*Complement*, etc.
The game	is	*over* (finished).
Some money	was	still *over* (remaining).
The results	are	*out* (published).
The stars	are	*out* (visible).
He	was heard	*out* (to the very end).
The bargain	is	*off* (cancelled).
The train	is	*off* (started).
He	is	*well off* (in good circumstances)
Our side	is	*in* (having their innings).
The late minister	is	*in* (holding office) again.

CHAPTER VIII.—PREPOSITIONS.

160. Kinds of Objects.—Besides nouns and pronouns, we sometimes have adverbs, Infinitives, phrases, and clauses as objects to a preposition :—

(*a*) *Adverbs* :—

We must be ready by *then* (=that time). By *far* the best.
He has worked hard from *then* to *now*.
He walks about from *here* to *there*.
I have heard of worse things being done before *now*.
Until *now* it has not ceased raining.
Many strange things may happen between *now* and *then*.
You must go at *once*. This will last for *ever*.

(*b*) *Infinitives ;* see § 127 (*b*) : (this construction is rare).

He was about *to die*.
He desired nothing but *to succeed*.

(*c*) *Phrases* :—

The day-spring from *on-high* hath visited us.
He has come from *beyond-the-seas*.
He did not return till *about-ten-days-afterwards*.
He did not see her till *within-a-few-weeks-of-his-death*.
These books are sold at *over-one-shilling* each.
I bought this for *under-half-its-value*.
He will not return till *after-the-holidays*.
The question of *how-to-do-this* is difficult.

(*d*) *Clauses* :—

This depends upon | whether-he-will-consent-or-not.
He told every one of | what-he-had-heard.
Go whenever you like except | that-you-must-not-go-in-the-rain.
In | that-he-died | he died unto sin once.—*New Testament*.

161. (*a*) **Omission of Object.**—There are two cases of this :—

Relative Pronoun.—The man (*whom* or *that*) we were looking for.
Demons. Pronoun.—A chair to sit on (*it*).

(*b*) **Omission of Preposition.**—This occurs chiefly with the prepositions *of* and *at* :—

(1) **Of**:—

On board (of) ship. A hundred (of) pounds. A many (=a multitude, of) tears (§ 38 (*e*), *Note*).

What we now call the Gerund in *-ing*, as "telling lies," has come into existence solely through the omission of "*of*" after the Verbal noun in *-ing;* as "telling of lies." (See § 142.)

(2) **At**: see § 100, *Note* 2:—

They laughed (at) him to scorn. He stared (at) me in the face. He looked (at) me in the face.

162. **Disguised Prepositions.**—"*On*" is changed into "*a*" in such phrases as "to go *a fishing*."

Similarly "*of*" can be changed into "*o*," as in "four o'clock," "Jack o' lantern," etc.

To the same class belong such phrases as the following:—

Flour sells at tenpence *a pound*.
He called to see me once *a week*.
He gave the men four shillings *a piece*.

The "a" *looks* so much like the Indefinite Article, that by a false analogy "the" is sometimes used in its place; as—

Flour sells at tenpence *the pound*.

163. **Than.**—This word has been used as a Preposition by the best English writers:—

No mightier than thyself or *me*	SHAKSPEARE.
A stone is heavy, and the sand weighty; but a fool's wrath is heavier than *them* both .	*Old Testament.*
She suffers hourly more than *me* . . .	SWIFT.
You are a much greater loser than *me* . .	*Ibid.*
Lined with giants deadlier than *them* all . .	POPE.
For thou art a girl as much brighter than *her* As he was a poet sublimer than *me* . . .	PRIOR.
Thou hast been wiser all the while than *me* .	SOUTHEY.
You know that I am, not less than *him*, a despiser of the multitude	GOLDSMITH.

She should look worse than *him*.—*Time*, July 1883, p. 83.

It struck me then that God knew better than *me*.—*Review of Reviews*, Aug. 1898, p. 126.

Even so far back as Caxton, the first English printer, we find *than* used as a preposition, followed by an objective case:—

For ther is nothyng more suspecte to evyl people than *them*, whom they know to be wyse and trewe.—*The Curial*, 4, 18.

These are not errors or solecisms of the illiterate. But in current books on Grammar the prepositional character of *than* is denied.[1]

---

[1] For example, in Mason's *English Grammar*, p. 177, ed. 1891, we are told that "no *syntactical* explanation can be given of the relative *whom* after *than*." The syntax, however, is very simple, if we parse *than* as a

Originally "than" was not a conjunction, but an adverb (another form of *then*). In modern English it has been further developed into a preposition, and has been used as such by good authors, and is still used. The best course to take is to parse it as a Conjunction, whenever it is possible to supply a Finite verb understood :—

No animal is larger than a whale.
No animal is larger than a whale (is large).

But in such constructions as the following "than" must still be parsed as a Preposition, because there is no Finite verb understood which could make it a Conjunction :—

	Kind of Object.
I will not take less than *ten shillings* . . . No one other than a *graduate* need apply [1] . .	*Noun.*
Here is my son, than *whom* a better does not exist	*Rel. Pron.*
He did nothing else than *laugh* . . .	*Noun-Infin.*
I will suffer myself rather than (that) *he should suffer* . . . . He got more *than* (what) he asked for . .	*Noun-clause.*
He has said so more than *once*	*Adverb* (§ 160, *a*).

164. But.—In such examples as the following "but" must be parsed as a Preposition. Otherwise it is a Conjunction :—

All *but* (except) one fulfilled their promises.
He was all *but* (=everything except) ruined. (Here "ruined" is an elliptical form of the Gerund "being ruined"; and this Gerund is the object of the preposition "but.")

---

preposition. There is ample analogy for the use of "than" as a preposition, besides ample authority. "Superior *to* mine" = "better *than* mine." If *to* is a preposition, why not *than*? The Scotch say, "He is taller *be* (=*by*) onie o' thaim." If *by* is a preposition, why not *than?* Again, there is the analogy of the French *que* (=than) followed by *lui* (Objective case) = "than *him.*"

[1] "No other than *he* need apply" is an exceptional phrase that proves nothing; cf. "but *he*" in "Whence all but *he* had fled" (Mrs. Hemans). In the sentence given, "No other than a graduate need apply," the phrase "other than" = different from, except, but. We cannot expand "than a graduate" into a clause containing a Finite verb, and hence *than* is a preposition. In some editions of Shakspeare we have the phrase "no other than *him*" :—

That you elect *no other* king than *him.*—1 *Hen. VI.* iv. 1, 4.

The editor who makes Shakspeare say "than *him*," evidently regards "than" as a preposition.

Sometimes the preposition *from* is used instead of *than* after "other":—

This is a far *other* tone *from* that
In which the Duke spoke eight, nine years ago.
COLERIDGE, *Piccolomini*, i. 12.

Mrs. Craik, in *The Ogilvies*, ch. x., uses *but* after *other*, where *but*, though undoubtedly a preposition, is followed by *he* :—

How could I hear such words from any other man *but he?*

But for your help (=except on account of your help=if you had not helped me) I should have been ruined. (Here the phrase "for your help" is object to the preposition.)

I cannot *but* fear (=I cannot do anything except fear) that you are ill. (Here the Noun-Infinitive "fear" is the object.)

CHAPTER IX.—CONJUNCTIONS.

165. According to the definition given in § 15, "a conjunction is a word used for showing in what relation one notion stands to another notion, or one thought to another thought."

As notions are expressed by single words or phrases, and thoughts by sentences or clauses, we can substitute a shorter, though less accurate, definition, which is more convenient for parsing and analysis,—"a conjunction joins one word to another word, or one sentence to another sentence." Conjunctions are subdivided into two main classes:—

I. **Co-ordinative**, which join sentences of co-ordinate (that is, of *equal*) rank, or words that stand in the same relation to some other word in the sentence.[1]

II. **Subordinative**, which join a *subordinate* or dependent sentence to a *principal* sentence (that is, to a sentence of *higher* rank).

SECTION 1.—CO-ORDINATIVE CONJUNCTIONS.

166. *Sentences are of* **Co-ordinate** *or* **equal** *rank, when one is not dependent on the other, nor enters at all into its construction.*

167. Sentences of equal rank can be related to one another in four different senses, and this gives rise to four different kinds of Co-ordinative Conjunctions:—

---

[1] Conjunctions for the most part join sentences, not words. We cannot, however, accept Mr. Mason's statement that "*and* is the single exception," the only instance of a conjunction which may join words; for in point of fact, *all* the Co-ordinative conjunctions can join *adjectives*.

(1) A captious *and* conceited man is not fit to review a book (*Cumulative.*)
(2) We admire the character of a poor, *but* honest man . (*Adversative.*)
(3) A drunk *or* mad Malay ran amuck yesterday . . (*Alternative.*)
(4) An iron (and) *therefore* durable box was procured . (*Illative.*)

In (1) the notion of self-conceit is added to that of captiousness. In (2) the notion of honesty is contrasted with that of poverty. In (3) the notion of madness is given as an alternative to that of drunkenness. In (4) the notion of durability is inferred from that of iron.

The Conjunction "*and*" will join *nouns* as well as adjectives. In this respect, and this only, it is unique:—

Youth *and* experience cannot exist together.

(*a*) **Cumulative.**—By these one thought is simply *added* to another :—*and*, *both* . . . *and*, *not only*, *but also*, *as well as* :—

He was *both* degraded *and* expelled.
He *as well as* you is guilty.

(*b*) **Alternative.**—By these a *choice* is offered between one thought and another :—*either* . . . *or*, *else*, *or*, *otherwise* :—

Leave the room, *or* take the consequences.
He was *neither* an idler *nor* a gambler.

(*c*) **Adversative.**—By these conjunctions one thought is *contrasted* with or set against another :—*but*, *still*, *yet*, *nevertheless*, *however* :—

He is very rich, *still* or *yet* or *but* he is not contented.

(*d*) **Illative.**—By these conjunctions one thought is *inferred* or proved from another :—*for*, *therefore*, *then*, *so then* :—

He was found guilty, and *therefore* he was hanged.
It is time to go ; let us start *then*.

SECTION 2.—SUBORDINATIVE CONJUNCTIONS.

168. One sentence is said to be *subordinate* to another, when it depends upon the other, that is, forms part of its construction, doing the work of a noun, adjective, or adverb.

That sentence on which the subordinate sentence depends is called the **Principal** sentence.

Principal.	*Conj.*	*Dependent.*	
I will read that book,	if	you advise me.	(*Adverb-clause.*)
We still hope	that	you may get well.	(*Noun-clause.*)

169. The chief modes of dependence are nine in number :—

(*a*) Apposition, (*b*) Causation, (*c*) Effect, (*d*) Purpose, (*e*) Condition, (*f*) Concession or Contrast, (*g*) Comparison, (*h*) Extent or Manner, (*i*) Time.

Apposition.—He made a promise, *that* he would soon return.
Causation.—I will do this, *because* or *as* or *since* you desire it.
Effect.—He talked so much *that* he made himself hoarse.
Purpose.—Men work *that* they may earn a living.
Condition.—I will do this, *if* I am allowed (=*unless* I am prevented).
Concession.—He was a contented man, *although* he was poor.
Comparison.—He is quite *as* clever *as* I am. (Equal degrees.)
,, He is more clever *than* I am. (Unequal degrees.)
Extent, *Manner.*—Men will reap *as* they sow.
Time.—He returned home *after* he had finished work.

170. As well as.—This conjunctional phrase is Co-ordinative in one sense and Subordinative in another :—

(*a*) *Co-ordinative.*—In adding one co-ordinate sentence to another, it gives emphasis to the *first* :—

He as well as you is guilty=
Not only you, but he also is guilty.

(b) *Subordinative:—*

Principal.	*Dependent.*
He does not write	as well as you do

=His writing is not as good as yours.

171. Though, but.—Both of these conjunctions (the first Subordinative, the second Co-ordinative) denote concession or contrast:—

(a) He is honest, *though* poor.
(b) He is poor, *but* honest.

These two sentences mean precisely the same thing, because in (a) "He is honest" is the *Principal* clause, and in (b) the Co-ordinate clause, "but he is honest," is more *emphatic* than the clause preceding it. Thus the Principal clause and the Emphatic clause are the same.

If, however, we rewrite the two sentences thus:—

(a) He is honest, though poor;
(b) He is honest, but poor,

the two sentences are not equivalent. The first emphasises the fact that he is honest in spite of his poverty. The second emphasises the fact that he is poor in spite of his honesty.

Conjunctive and Interrogative Adverbs.

172. It was explained in § 18 that a Conjunctive adverb is a *double* part of speech,—a conjunction and adverb combined in one:—*when, why, where, whence, how, whether.*

The same is true of Interrogative adverbs, when they are used as conjunctions:—

Let me ask you *how* you did this.

There is no difference in *form* between a Conjunctive and an Interrogative adverb. The former qualifies some noun expressed or understood in the Principal sentence. The latter is preceded by some verb that signifies *asking* or *inquiring.*

CHAPTER X.—INTERJECTIONS.

173. An Interjection is unlike every other Part of Speech, since it does not enter into the construction of a sentence.

It is merely an *exclamatory sound*, thrown into a sentence to denote some strong feeling or emotion (see § 17):—

Joy.—Hurrah! huzza!
Grief.—Oh! ah! alas! alack!
Amusement.—Ha! ha!
Approval.—Bravo!
Weariness.—Heigh-ho!
Attention.—Lo! hark! hush! hist!
Reproof.—Fie! fie!
Contempt or *ridicule*—Stuff! bosh! tut-tut! pooh! pish! pshaw! tush!
To call some one.—Ho! holloa!

174. There are certain moods of verbs and parts of speech which can be used for an exclamatory or Interjectional purpose:—

(*a*) *Noun-Infinitive.*—*To think* that he should have died! (§ 127, *d*).
(*b*) *Subjunctive.*—*Would* that I had gained that prize! (*Wish.*)
(*c*) *Imperative.*—*Hear! hear!* (*Applause.*)
(*d*) *Noun.*—Dreadful *sight!* Foolish *fellow!* *Fool!* *Dunce!*
(*e*) *Adjective* (with some noun understood).—*Strange!* *Shocking!*
(*f*) *Adverb.*—*How* very kind of you! *How* wonderful!
(*g*) *Pronoun.*—*What* a sad thing it is!
(*h*) *Conjunction.*—*If* I could only see him once more!

175. Sometimes in a rapid or exclamatory sentence an Auxiliary verb with its subject is left out, and only the main verb is expressed:—

Why dream and wait for him longer?—LONGFELLOW.
(=Why *dost thou* or why *do we* wait for him longer?)

CHAPTER XI.

THE SAME WORD USED AS DIFFERENT PARTS OF SPEECH.

A. *Indef. Article.* The sportsman shot *a* tiger.
Prep. He has gone *a*-hunting. They had three meals *a* day.

All. *Adj. of Quantity.* He ate *all* the bread.
Indef. Num. Adj. We must *all* die some day.
Adj. used as Noun. We lost our *all* on that day.
Adv. *All* bloodless lay the untrodden snow.

Any. *Adj. of Quantity.* Have you *any* bread?
Adv. of Qu. We must stop and rest before going *any* farther.
Indef. Num. Adjective. Did you bring *any* loaves?
Indef. Dem. Adjective. Take *any* book that you like best.

As. (*a*) *Conjunctive pronoun*:—
He is not such a fool *as* he looks.
As many men *as* came were caught.
Yours is not the same book *as* mine.

(*b*) *Conjunctive adverb* (or subordinative conjunction):—
Time. He trembled *as* (at what time) he spoke.
Manner. Do not act *as* (in what manner) he did.
State. He took it just *as* (in what state) it was.
Extent. He is not as (to that extent) clever *as* (to what extent) you are.
Hot *as* (to whatever extent) the sun is (=however hot the sun is), we must go out in it.
Reason. The air is now cool, *as* (for what reason or for the reason that) the rain has fallen.

(c) *In Elliptical Phrases:*—all of these imply "extent."
I condemn you *as* a judge (to what extent or so far as I am a judge), but *as* a man (to what extent I am a man) I pity you.
I will inquire again *as* to (to what extent the question relates to) that matter.
As regards this journey (to what extent the question regards this journey), we can now decide nothing.

Better. *Comp. Adj.* My book is a *better* one than yours.
Comp. Adv. You are working *better* to-day.
Adj. used as Noun. Do not despise your *betters.*

Both. *Def. Num. Adj.* *Both* the men have arrived.
Conj. Co-ord. He is *both* a fool and a knave.

But. *Adv.* There is *but* (only) one man present.
Prep. Who could have done this *but* (except) him?
I cannot *but* believe that you are lost. (I cannot believe anything *except* that, etc.)
Conj. Co-ord. He is a man of common sense, *but* not learned in books.
Conj. Subord. There was no one present, *but* (he) pitied (= who did not pity) the lame horse.
Perdition catch my soul, *but* I love thee.—Shakspeare. (May perdition catch my soul, *if* I do *not* love thee.)

Either. *Distrib. Adj.* He is ruined in *either* case.
Conj. Co-ord. He is *either* a fool or a knave.

Else. *Adv.* We could not catch any one *else.*
Conj. Co-ord. He has some real sorrow; *else* he would not weep as he does.

Enough. *Adj. of Quantity.* He has eaten *enough* bread.
Adj. of Number. We have *enough* loaves.
Adj. used as Noun. He had *enough* to do.

Half. *Adj. of Quantity.* *Half* measures do not succeed.
Adj. used as Noun. One *half* of his task is now done.
Adv. of Quantity. He was *half* dead with fear.

Little. *Adj. of Quality.* A *little* blow may give much pain.
Adj. of Quantity. He has eaten *a little* bread.
Adv. of Quantity. Let us wait here *a little.*
Adj. used as Noun. Man wants but *little* here below.

More. *Adj. of Quantity.* He eats *more* bread than you.
Adj. used as Noun. *More* is done than was expected.
Adv. of Quantity. I like him *more* than (I like) you.
Adj. of Number. *More* men came to-day than yesterday.
Adv. of Number. I saw him once *more.*

Much. *Adj. of Quantity.* He has wasted *much* time.
Adv. of Quantity. I am *much* pleased with your son.
Adj. used as Noun. You will not get *much* from me

Neither. *Adj. Distrib.* I agree with *neither* side.
Conj. Co-ord. *Neither* you nor I can do that.

Near. *Adv.* Stand *near,* while I speak to you.
Prep. There is a fine tree *near* our house.
Adj. He is a *near* relative of mine.

Needs. *Verb.* The earth is very dry and *needs* rain.
Adv. He must *needs* know the reason of this.
Noun. Our *needs* or wants are few.

One. *Def. Num. Adj.* There is but *one* shilling left.
Indef. Dem. Adj. He came here *one* day.
Indef. Dem. Pron. *One* is apt to waste *one's* time.
Def. Dem. Pron. Your horse is white; mine is a black *one.*

Only. *Adj.* The *only* dog I had was stolen.
Adv. I heard of this *only* yesterday.
Conj. Co-ord. Do what you like; *only* (=but whatever else you may do) keep silence.

Round. *Adj.* A square thing does not fit into a *round* hole.
Prep. Draw a circle *round* a given centre.
Adv. The flies are flying *round* and *round.*
Verb. Gama was the first to *round* the Cape of Good Hope.
Noun. Men must go their daily *round* of duty.

Since. *Prep.* I have not seen him *since* Monday last.
Adv. I took this house four weeks *since.*
Conj. Subord. We must trust you, *since* you are in earnest.

Single. *Verb.* *Single* out the best.
Adj. He is a *single* (unmarried) man.

Such. *Def. Dem. Adj.* He is not *such* a man *as* I expected.
Indef. Dem. Adj. He came to me on *such* a day.
Def. Dem. Pron. You are a coward; I am not *such.*

That. *Def. Dem. Adj.* I am no admirer of *that* book.
Def. Dem. Pron. The light of the sun is brighter than *that* of the moon.
Relat. Pron. The book *that* you gave me is lost.
Conj. { *Effect.* He aimed *so* well *that* he hit the mark.
Apposit. He heard (the news) *that* you had come.
Purpose. We must eat *that* we may live. }

Than. *Conj. Subord.* I like this more *than* (I like) that.
Prep. { These workmen, *than* whom I have never seen men more industrious, have left me.
He was fond of any drink other *than* wine. }

Then. *Adv. of Time.* He was better *then* than he is now.
Conj. Co-ord. I see, *then,* we ought to start at once.

The. *Def. Article.* *The* ass is a dull animal.
Adv. of Quantity. *The* more, the merrier.

Too. *Adv. of Quantity.* He is *too* fond of play.
Conj Co-ord. We *too* must expect to die some day.

Well. *Adv. of Quality.* He has done the work very *well.*
Adv. used as Noun. Leave *well* alone.
Conj. Co-ord. He has finished his work in time; *well,* I did not expect it of such a lazy man.

What. *Inter. Pron.* *What* did you say?
Rel. Pron. I do not know *what* you mean; § 79.
Indef. Demons. I tell you *what* (=something).
Adverb. *What* (=partly) with illness and *what* with losses, the poor man is almost ruined.

Yet. *Conj. Co-ord.* I have called; *yet* no one answers.
Adv. of Time. You may *yet* (=even now, still) find him.

CHAPTER XII.—SYNTAX AND PARSING.

Parsing Chart.

I. *Nouns.*

Kind of Noun.	Gender.	Number.	Case.
Concrete { Proper Common Collective Material Abstract	Masculine Feminine Common Neuter	Singular Plural	Nominative Possessive Objective

II. *Pronouns.*

Kind of Pronoun.	Gender.	Number.	Person.	Case.
Personal { Simple Reflexive Demons. { Definite Indefinite	Masculine Feminine Common Neuter	Singular Plural	1st 2nd 3rd	Nominative Possessive Objective
Conjunctive Interrogative	Agreeing (if Demonstrative or Conjunctive) in Gender, Number, and Person with its antecedent.			

III. *The Cases of Nouns or Pronouns.*

Nom. to Verb	*Obj.* to Verb Direct	*Obj.* in Apposition
,, as Compl. to Verb	,, ,, Indirect	,, to Preposition
,, in Apposition	,, ,, Retained	,, Adverbial
,, of Address	,, ,, Cognate	,, after certain Adjectives
,, Absolute	,, ,, Reflexive	,, Interjectional
Possessive	,, as Compl. to Verb	

IV. *Adjectives.*

The Kind of Adjective.		Degree.	Use.
Proper Descriptive Quantitative Interrogative Distributive	Numer. { Def. Indef. Demons. { Def. Indef.	Positive Comparative Superlative	Attributive Predicative

V. *Adverbs.*

Kind.	Degree.	Use.	Attributive Uses.
Simple Conjunctive Interrogative	Positive Comparative Superlative	Attributive Predicative	To qualify Verb ,, ,, Adjective ,, ,, Adverb ,, ,, Preposition ,, ,, Conjunction ,, ,, Sentence

VI. *Finite Verbs.*

Kind of Verb.	Conjug.	Voice.	Mood.	Tense.	Form of each Tense.
Trans. Intrans. Auxil.	Strong Weak Mixed	Active Passive	Indic. Imper. Subjunc.	Present Past Future	Indefinite Continuous Perfect Perf. Contin.

Number.	Person.	
Singular Plural	1st 2nd 3rd	Agreeing in Number and Person with its subject or subjects, expressed or understood.

VII. *Infinitive.*

Form.	(*a*) Use as Noun-Inf.	(*b*) Use as Qualifying Inf.
Indefinite Continuous Perfect Perf. Contin.	Subject to Verb Object to Verb Complement to Verb Object to Preposition Exclamatory	To qualify— ,, a Verb ,, a Noun { Attributively / Predicatively ,, an Adjective To introduce a Parenthesis

VIII. *Gerund.*

Form.	Voice.	Kind of Verb.
Present Perfect	Active Passive	Transitive Intransitive

IX. *Participle or Verbal Adjective.*

Form.	Voice.	Kind of Verb.	Use.
Present Past Perfect	Active Passive	Transitive Intransitive	Attributive Predicative { Complement / Absolute Gerundive

X. *Conjunctions.*

Co-ordinative.	Subordinative.

Some of the following rules have been incidentally given already in different places. They are here collected and summarised; and others not given before have been added, so as to make the account more complete.

176. Nominative case.—See No. III. of Parsing Chart.

(1) As Subject to a verb (see § 3 and § 41):—

I did this. *Rain* is falling. *You* are tired.

(2) As *Subjective* Complement to a verb (see § 95):—

I am *the man.* Cæsar was declared *emperor.*

Note.—An Infinitive can come between the verb and the noun:—

He appeared *to be* a wise man.

(3) In Apposition with a noun or pronoun (§ 4):—

John, *the carpenter*, has succeeded well in business.

(4) For purposes of Address (see § 41):—

How art thou fallen, *O Cæsar!*

(5) In the Absolute construction:—

(*a*) *With Participle*, in **past** or **present** sense:—

Off we start, he *remaining behind.*
Off we started, he *having given* the signal.

Note.—Without altering the sense, we could substitute the clause "while he remains behind" for the phrase "he remaining behind." In the absolute construction the noun or pronoun is in the Nominative case, because (as we see from this) it is *the Subject to the Finite verb that is implied in the Participle.*

(*b*) *With the Qualifying Infinitive*, in **future** sense:—

The caul was put up in a raffle, *the winner to pay* five shillings.—DICKENS, *David Copperfield.*

The estate has been divided between us, *you to have* two-thirds of it, and *I* one-third.

177. Possessive case.—See No. III. of Parsing Chart.

(*a*) A noun or pronoun in the Possessive case qualifies Nouns and Gerunds as an adjective would do :—

> *My* son. The *barber's* shop. The *tiger's* claw.—*Noun.*
> I was displeased at *his* going away without leave. } *Gerund*
> This was a plan of *your* contriving. } (§ 140).

(*b*) When two Possessive nouns are in apposition with each other, the apostrophe *s* is added either to the first or last, but not usually to both :—

> Herod married his *brother* Philip's wife.
> For the *queen's* sake, his sister.—BYRON.

(*c*) When two nouns are connected by "*and*," the apostrophe *s* is added to both to denote *separate* possession, and to the last only to denote *joint* possession :—

> *A.'s* and B.'s horses were sold yesterday.
> *A.* and B.'s horses were sold yesterday.

(*d*) A noun or pronoun in the Possessive case can be the Complement to a verb (see §§ 92, 95) :—

> That book is *mine*, not *James's.*

178. Objective case.—See No. III. of Parsing Chart.

(1) As Object to a verb, or in connection with some verb (§ 106, *Note*) :—

> (*a*) The master teaches *Euclid.* (*Direct.*)
> (*b*) He teaches *his sons* Euclid. (*Indirect.*)
> (*c*) His sons were taught *Euclid.* (*Retained.*)
> (*d*) The fever will run its *course.* (*Cognate.*)[1]
> (*e*) He sat *himself* down. (*Reflexive.*)

(2) As Objective Complement to a verb (§ 95) :—

> The citizens made him their *king.*

Note.—An Infinitive can come between the verb and the noun :—

> The people considered him *to be* a wise man.

(3) In Apposition with a noun or pronoun :—

> The people of England beheaded Charles I., their *king.*

(4) As Object to a preposition (§ 42) :—

> He fought against *me.* A house built on *sand.*

(5) Adverbial Objective :—called "Adverbial," because such phrases qualify words as an adverb would do :—

---

[1] It is maintained in Mason's *English Grammar*, p. 150, ed. 1891, that "the cognate objective should more properly be classed among the Adverbial Adjuncts," that is, as an Adverbial objective, see § 178 (5). This we cannot admit, because when the verb of the sentence is changed from Active to Passive, as "He fought a good fight," "A good fight was fought by him," the cognate object becomes the Subject; whereas, if the cognate object were adverbial, it would remain adverbial.

He lived ten *years* (Time). He walked ten *miles* (Space). This cost ten *shillings* (Price). That box weighs ten *pounds* (Weight). The air is a *trifle* hotter to-day (Degree). Bind him *hand* and *foot* (Attendant circumstance).

(6) Objective after the adjectives "like" or "unlike," "near," "next." (This has arisen from the omission of the preposition "*to*," which is still sometimes used after these adjectives):—

No man could bend the bow *like him*.
The house *nearest the grove* is the one that I prefer.

(7) Objective after Interjections or in exclamatory phrases:—

Oh unhappy *man!* Oh dear *me!*
Foolish *fellow!* to have wasted his time as he has done!

179. Two uses of Adjectives.—See No. IV. of Parsing Chart.

(*a*) Attributive use (§ 58):—

An *industrious* student will generally succeed.

(*b*) Predicative use (§ 58):—

He was *industrious*, and therefore he succeeded.

180. Noun or Gerund used as an Adjective.—It can be used attributively for an adjective, but not predicatively:—

A *village* watchman. *Drinking* water. A *bathing* place.

181. Adjective substituted for Adverb.—An adverb qualifying a *verb* can be changed into an adjective qualifying the *subject* to the verb. (More common in poetry than in prose.)

And *furious* every charger neighed.—CAMPBELL.
They neither toil nor spin, but *careless* grow.—THOMSON.
First they praised him *soft and low*.—TENNYSON.

Note 1.—When the adverb qualifies *any part of speech except a verb*, we cannot substitute an adjective for it. Thus we cannot say, "He is *immense* clever" for "He is *immensely* clever."

Note 2.—In poetry an adjective and adverb are sometimes coupled together by *and*.

Very *carefully* and *slow*.—TENNYSON.
Good gentlemen, look *fresh* and *merrily*.—SHAKSPEARE.

Here either one *-ly* is made to do duty for both adjectives; or the construction is mixed, the adjective qualifying the subject, and the adverb the verb.

182. Pronoun and Antecedent.—See Nos. II. and III. of Parsing Chart.

(*a*) A Pronoun is of the same person, number, and gender as the noun it stands for; but in case it depends upon its own sentence. (This is called a Concord or Agreement.)

After Cæsar was declared *emperor* (Nom.), they slew *him* (Obj.).
You must return the *book* (Objective), *which* (Nominative) was lent.

(*b*) A Conjunctive Pronoun, if it has two Antecedents not of the same person, agrees in person with the Antecedent *nearest to it* :—

You are the man who *is* (not *are*) chosen.

183. Two uses of Adverbs.—See No. V. of Parsing Chart.

(*a*) Attributive use (§ 159).

(1) *Adjective.*—He is *remarkably clever.*
(2) *Verb.*—*Act decisively,* if you act at all.
(3) *Other Adverb.*—He explained his views *remarkably well.*
(4) *Preposition.*—The sun stood *exactly over* our heads.
(5) *Conjunction.*—You may go *only if* you promise to return.
(6) *Sentence.*—*Fortunately,* all the thieves were caught (§ 150).

(*b*) Predicative use (§ 159).

(1) *Intrans. verb.*—The results will soon be *out* (=published).
(2) *Trans. verb.*—We have found him *out* (=in his true character).

184. Verb and Subject.—See No. VI. of Parsing Chart.

A Finite Verb must be in the same number and person as its Subject (§ 109). (This is another Concord or Agreement.)

Note.—Avoid such a mistake as "The man with his dog *have* just come." Such a mistake arises from confounding "*with*" with "*and.*"

185. Subjects not of the same Person.—(*a*) When two or more Subjects, not of the same Person, are joined by "*and,*" the verb is in the First person rather than the Second, and in the Second rather than the Third; and *the First person should be mentioned last* :—

James and I *are* (=we are) great friends.

(*b*) When two Subjects are joined by "*or*" or "*nor,*" the verb agrees in person with the Subject nearest to it :—

Either James or I *am* at the top of the class.
Either you or James *has* done it.
Neither James nor you *were* present.

It would be better, however, to repeat the verb for each Subject. The sentences would then be re-written as follows :—

Either James *is* at the top of the class, or I *am.*
Either you *have* done it, or James *has.*
Neither James *was* present, nor *were* you.

(*c*) When two Subjects are joined by "as well as," the verb agrees in number and person with the *first* one :—

My comrades as well as I myself *were* caught.

The reason of this rule is that "My comrades were caught" is the Principal clause, to which the other clause introduced by "as well as" is Co-ordinate (see § 170).

186. Two Singular Subjects with Plural Verb.—Two or

more Singular nouns, when they are joined by "*and*," require a verb in the Plural.

A man and his wife *have* come here asking for work.
Your horse and mine (=my horse) *are* both at the door.

To this rule there are a few exceptions :—

(*a*) If the two nouns joined by "*and*" refer to the same person or thing, the verb is Singular, and not Plural; as—

The great scholar and poet *is* dead.

Here "scholar" and "poet" refer to the same man, and the sentence might have been written :—

The man, who was a great scholar and a great poet, is dead.

Note.—When the article is mentioned *only once*, as in the sentence "*the* great scholar and poet," it stands for *both the nouns*. This shows that *only one* person (and not two) is intended, and that hence the verb must be singular.

But if the article is mentioned twice, as in the sentence "*the* scholar and *the* poet," then two distinct persons are intended, and the verb following must be in the plural number ; as—

The scholar and the poet *are* dead.

(*b*) If the two nouns joined by "*and*" are regarded as denoting *a single object or notion*, the verb is Singular; as—

Truth and honesty (=the practice of truth and honesty) *is* the best policy. Slow and steady *wins* the race.

(*c*) If the two nouns joined by "*and*" are qualified by a Distributive adjective (§ 57), the verb is Singular; as—

Every man and woman *is* gone. (This is really a condensed form of two sentences :—"Every man (is gone) and every woman is gone.")

(*d*) If the two Singular nouns are connected by *as well as*, the verb is Singular :—

James as well as John *has been* promoted. (This is really a condensed form of two sentences : "James has been promoted, as well as John has been promoted." See above, § 185, *c*.)

187. One Singular Subject with Plural Verb.—A noun of *Multitude* (see § 24, *Note* 2), since it implies plurality, is followed by a Plural verb :—

The jury (*i.e.* the individual jurors) *were* divided in *their* opinions.
The jury (as one body) selected *its* speaker.

188. Noun-Infinitive.—See No. VII. of Chart.

The Noun-Infinitive may be (*a*) the Subject to a verb, (*b*) the Object to a verb, (*c*) the Complement to a verb, (*d*) the Object to a preposition (although this is very uncommon), (*e*) a form of exclamation (see § 127, I.) :—

(*a*) *Subj. to Verb.*—*To sleep* is necessary to health.
(*b*) *Obj. to Verb.*—We desire *to improve.*
(*c*) *Compl. to Verb.*—He appears *to be clever.*
(*d*) *Obj. to Prepos.*—Your cow is about (=near) *to die* (=death).
(*e*) *Form of Exclam.*—*To think* that he should have deceived me!

189. Qualifying Infinitive.—See No. VII. of Chart.

The Qualifying Infinitive may be used—(*a*) to qualify a verb, in which case it does the work of an adverb; (*b*) to qualify a noun, in which case it does the work of an adjective; (*c*) to qualify an adjective, in which case it does the work of an adverb; (*d*) to introduce a parenthesis, in which case it is absolute (see § 127, II.):—

(*a*) *Verb.*—They went out *to see* the sport.
(*b*) *Noun* { A house *to let.* (*Attributive.*)
This house is *to let.* (*Predicative.*) }
(*c*) *Adjective.*—Be quick *to hear* and slow *to speak.*
(*d*) *Parenthesis.*—He is,—*to speak* plainly,—a thief.

Note.—In qualifying a *noun*, the Infinitive is sometimes used in the Passive voice. No rule, however, can be given as to when the Active voice is the more idiomatic and when the Passive:—

A man *to be admired.* (*Attributive.*)
That man is *to be admired.* (*Predicative.*)

190. Three uses of Participles.—See No. IX. of Chart.

(*a*) Attributive use (see § 58 for Adjectives):—

A *willing* horse. A *fallen* tree. A *withered* flower.

(*b*) Predicative use.—This may occur either (1) when the Participle is Complement to some verb (see § 58 again), or (2) when the Participle is used absolutely with some noun going before (see § 176, 5).

(1) { We found him *sleeping.* (*Object. Complem.*)
He became *alarmed.* (*Subject. Complem.*) }
(2) Our pace was slow, the horse *being tired.* (*Absolute.*)

Note 1.—That the Participle is predicative in the Absolute construction is clear from the fact that an absolute *phrase* can be easily rewritten in the form of a *clause*, in which a Finite verb is substituted for the Participle:—

{ Our pace was slow, the horse *being tired.*
Our pace was slow, *because* the horse *was tired.* }

Note 2.—When no noun or pronoun is expressed, the Participle is called an **Impersonal Absolute.**

Supposing this to be true, you are certainly guilty.

(*c*) Gerundive use (§ 141).—Here the Participle denotes

something that could be as well or better expressed by a Gerund or Verbal noun :—

{This prevented the letter *being sent* ;=
{This prevented *the sending of* the letter.

Note.—If we insert the preposition "*from*," "This prevented the letter *from* being sent," the form *being sent* is not a participle at all, but a Gerund or Verbal noun in the Passive voice. On this form see § 135.

191. Sequence of Tenses.—There are two main rules :—

I. A Past tense in the Principal sentence must be followed by a Past tense in the Dependent sentence :—

He *would* come, if you *wished* it.
He *succeeded*, because he *worked* hard.
He *worked* hard, that he *might* succeed.

Exceptions.—(1) If the verb in the Dependent sentence expresses some *universal* or *habitual* fact, it is in the Present tense :—

They *did* not know, that the earth *moves* round the sun.

(2) After "than" the verb can be in the Present or Future tense ; in fact, in any tense that expresses the sense intended :—

He *liked* you better than he *likes* me.
He *liked* you better than he *will like* me.

II. A Present or Future tense in the Principal sentence can be followed by any tense whatever in the Dependent sentence :—

I *know* that he *was* angry.
I *shall* soon get the letter that he *posted* yesterday.

Note on Concord and Government.

Syntax is sometimes subdivided under two main headings :—

I. Concord or Agreement. II. Government.

But this division is not of much use in our Syntax.

Concord or Agreement.

(1) The verb agrees with its subject in Number and Person (§ 184).

(2) The Demonstrative adjective "this" or "that" must be of the same number as the noun it qualifies. (These are the only two adjectives to which this Concord now applies.)

(3) A pronoun must be of the same Number, Gender, and Person as the noun it stands for. This is dealt with in § 182.

(4) A noun in apposition with a pronoun or other noun must be in the same case. This is shown in § 176 (3), § 177 (*b*), and § 178 (3).

Government.

Certain Verbs, two or three Adjectives, and all Prepositions govern a noun or pronoun in the Objective case.

CHAPTER XIII.—ANALYSIS IN DETAIL.

SECTION 1.—SENTENCES SIMPLE, COMPOUND, AND COMPLEX.

192. Simple Sentence.—A Simple sentence (Lat. *simplex*, single-fold) is one that has *only one Finite verb* expressed or understood.

Subject.	*Predicate.*
The merchant, having much property to sell,	*caused* all his goods to be conveyed on camels, there being no railway in that country.

In this sentence there are five different verbs, "having," "to sell," "caused," "to be conveyed," "being." Of these only one, viz. "caused," is *finite*. The sentence is therefore Simple.

193. Compound Sentence.—A compound sentence is one made up of two or more *Co-ordinate* clauses.

Co-ordinate clauses are joined together by the Co-ordinative conjunctions (§ 167).

(1) The sun rose with power, *and* the fog dispersed . . (*Cumulative.*)
(2) He called at my house, *but* I was not at home . (*Adversative.*)
(3) *Either* he must go *or* I (must go) . . . (*Alternative.*)
(4) He came back tired; *for* he had been out all day (*Illative.*)

In (1) one clause is simply added to another. In (2) one clause is contrasted with another. In (3) one clause is offered as an alternative to another. In (4) one clause is inferred from another.

Note.—When sentences are connected, not by any Co-ordinative conjunction, but merely by co-ordination of sense and by unity of construction, they are said to be **collateral** :—

The way was long; the wind was cold;
The minstrel was infirm and old;
The harp, his sole remaining joy,
Was carried by an orphan boy.—SCOTT.

194. The Conjunctive pronoun *who* or *which*, or a Conjunctive adverb, such as *where*, *when*, etc., provided its sense is continuative, and not restrictive (§ 83), may be used to connect Co-ordinate clauses :—

He went to London, *where* (=and there) he stayed ten days.

195. Complex Sentence.—A Complex sentence consists of a Principal clause (*i.e.* the clause containing the main *Finite verb* of the sentence) with one or more Subordinate clauses.

Complex	A merchant, who had much property to sell, *caused* all his goods to be conveyed on camels, as there was no railway in that country.
Simple	A merchant, having much property to sell, *caused* all his goods to be conveyed on camels, there being no railway in that country.

The latter sentence is evidently Simple, since there is only one Finite verb, *caused*. The former cannot be Simple, since it has three Finite verbs, *have, caused, was* (all Italicised). It cannot be Compound, because the clauses are not co-ordinate. It is therefore Complex, consisting of one Principal clause and two Subordinate ones.

195A. Compound and Complex mixed.—A Compound sentence can now be more fully defined than it was in § 193 :—

"A Compound sentence is one that is made up of two or more Co-ordinate *parts*."

Here the wider word *parts* has been substituted for the narrower word *clauses* given in § 193.

He seized the hill | and | occupied the strongest position that he found there.

This sentence is Compound, the first part being connected co-ordinately by *and* with the second part. The first part is a Simple sentence ; but the second part is Complex, consisting of a main clause, "he occupied the strongest position," and a Subordinate clause, "that he found there."

196. There are three kinds of Subordinate clauses—the Noun-clause, the Adjective-clause, and the Adverb-clause ; and these are defined as follows :—

I. *A Noun-clause is one which does the work of a noun in relation to some* **word** *in some other clause.*

II. *An Adjective-clause is one which does the work of an adjective in relation to some* **word** *in some other clause.*

III. *An Adverb-clause is one which does the work of an adverb in relation to some* **word** *in some other clause.*[1]

Note.—The same clause may be a Noun-clause in one context, an Adjective-clause in another, an Adverb-clause in another.

Where Moses was buried is still unknown.
—Noun-clause, subject to the verb "is."
No one has seen the place *where Moses was buried.*
—Adj.-clause, qualifying the noun "place."
Without knowing it the Arabs encamped *where Moses was buried.*
—Adverb-clause qualifying the verb "encamped."

---

[1] In these three definitions **word** has been printed in black type, because, in stating the kind of clause, it is necessary to state the word to which it relates. Mason's three definitions (*Eng. Grammar*, p. 160) merely say "in relation to *the rest of the sentence*." This is rather too vague for purposes of guidance.

I. *The Noun-clause.*

197. A Noun-clause is subject to all the liabilities and duties of a noun proper. It may therefore be the subject to a verb, the object to a verb, the object to a preposition, the complement to a verb, or in apposition to a noun :—

That he will come back soon is certain . . .	*Subject.*
I shall be glad to know *when you will return* .	*Obj. to verb.*
This will sell for *what it is worth*	*Obj. to prep.*
This is exactly *what I expected*	*Comp. to verb.*
The rumour *that he is sick* is false	*App. to noun.*

Note 1.—From the above examples it will be seen that a Noun-clause can be introduced either by the conjunction "*that*" or by a Conjunctive pronoun or by a Conjunctive adverb. Sometimes, however, the conjunction *that* is left out :—

It seems (that) he is not clever.

Note. 2.—A clause containing the very words used by a speaker is another form of Noun-clause :—

All that he said was, "*I have seen you before.*"

Here the italicised clause is the complement to the verb "was."

Examples of the Noun-clause.

I. *Pick out the Noun-clause in each of the following Examples and say whether it is the Subject to some Verb, or the Object to some Verb, or the Object to some Preposition, or the Complement to some Verb, or in Apposition to some noun expressed. Supply the Conjunction* "that" *wherever it has been left out :—*

1. No one knows when he will come, or whether he will come at all, or whether he is even alive.
2. How this came to pass is not known to any one.
3. What is sauce for the goose is sauce for the gander.
4. It is quite evident rain will fall to-day.
5. The Equator shows where days and nights are of equal length.
6. What is one man's meat is another man's poison.
7. You must know that the air is never quite at rest.
8. I think I shall never clearly understand this.
9. We heard the school would open in ten days' time.
10. The name "Volcano" indicates the belief of the ancient Greeks, that the burning hills of the Mediterranean were the workshops of the divine blacksmith, Vulcan.
11. Even a feather shows which way the wind is blowing.
12. Whatever faculty man has is improved by use.
13. The fool hath said in his heart, "There is no God."
14. "Know thyself," was the advice given us by a Greek sage.
15. He did not know that his father had been shot.
16. The fact that you have not signed your name to a letter shows that you lack moral courage.
17. It will be easily understood how useful even the simplest weapons were to the first dwellers on the earth.

18. The question first occurring to the mind of a savage is how is fire to be made.
19. Common-sense soon taught him that fire could be produced by rubbing two sticks together.
20. In chipping their flint weapons men must have seen that fire occasionally flashed out.
21. We learn from travellers that savages can produce fire in a few seconds.
22. He shouted out to the thief, "Leave this house."
23. We cannot rely on what he says.
24. It is quite evident you have made a mistake.
25. It was very unfortunate that you were taken ill.
26. He was a man of fine character except that he was rather timid.

II. *Expand each Simple Sentence into a Complex one containing a* **Noun-clause** *or* **clauses**:—

1. I was glad to hear of your having succeeded so well.
2. He is generally believed to have died of poison.
3. No one can tell the time of his coming.
4. One man's meat is another man's poison.
5. We have read of savages being able to produce fire by the friction of two pieces of wood.
6. He shouted to his neighbours to come to his help.
7. We can place no confidence in any of his words.
8. The fact of his having gone away without leaving us his address is a clear proof of the dishonesty of his intentions.
9. The usefulness of even the simplest weapons to men in the savage state will easily be understood.
10. His death at so young an age is much to be regretted.
11. We must hope for better times.
12. Tell me the time and place of your birth.
13. The verdict of the judge was in favour of the accused.
14. All his statements should be accepted.
15. They questioned the propriety of doing that.
16. The greatness of his labour could be seen from the result.
17. My departure will depend upon my getting leave.
18. He desired to know the nature of his offence.
19. The burial-place of Moses was never known to the Jews.
20. They explained to him the duty of confessing his fault.
21. He was reported to have lost most of his money.
22. We know the name of the writer of that letter.

II. *Adjective-clause.*

198. An Adjective-clause has but one function, viz. to qualify some noun or pronoun belonging to some other clause. In doing this it simply does the work of an adjective proper. Remember that the Conjunctive pronoun or Conjunctive adverb, by which an Adjective-clause is introduced, must have a Restrictive, not a Continuative, sense (§ 83); for if the sense is

Continuative, and not Restrictive, the sentence is Compound, not Complex (§ 194).

(1) We found it in the place *where* we had left it . *Complex.*
(2) We went to Brighton, *where* we spent a week . *Compound.*

In (1) the sentence is Complex, because the clause "where we had left it" qualifies the noun "place" as an adjective would do. *Where* is here Restrictive. In (2) the sentence is Compound, because the clause "where we spent a week" is merely Continuative,—co-ordinate with the preceding clause :—"We went to Brighton, *and* spent a week *there*."

Note.—The Conjunctive pronoun (when used in a Restrictive sense) is sometimes left out. (It is never left out when the sense is Continuative) :—

The food (that or which) he needed was sent.

I. *Pick out the Adjective-clause or clauses in each of the following examples, and point out the noun or pronoun qualified by it in some other clause. If the Conjunctive pronoun has been omitted anywhere, supply it :—*

1. Man has the power of making instruments, which bring into view stars, whose light has taken a thousand years to reach the earth.
2. The first thing that man needed was some sharp-edged tool.
3. The exact time when the theft was committed was never found out.
4. The man by whom the theft was committed has been caught.
5. The house we lived in has fallen down.
6. This is the same story that I heard ten years ago.
7. It's an ill wind that blows no one any good.
8. This is not such a book as I should have chosen.
9. He made his living by the presents he received from the men he served.
10. All that glitters is not gold.
11. In ponds, from which but a week before the wind blew clouds of dust, men now catch the re-animated fish.
12. A river is joined at places by tributaries that swell its waters.
13. Of what use is a knowledge of books to him who fails to practise virtue?
14. Fortune selects him for her lord, who reflects before acting.
15. Springs are fed by rain, which has percolated through the rocks or soil.
16. Nuncoomar prepared to die with that quiet fortitude with which the Bengalee, so backward, as a rule, in personal conflict, often encounters calamities for which there is no remedy.
17. I have seen the house where Shakspeare was born.
18. The plan you acted on has answered well.
19. They accepted every plan we proposed.
20. Surely the story you are telling me is not true.
21. Thrice is he armed that hath his quarrel just.
22. The night is long that never finds the day.

23. He travelled home by the way his father showed him.
24. There are times when every one feels a little sad.
25. Such men as are false to their friends should always be avoided.
26. I forgot to tell you the time when I shall return.

II. *Expand each Simple sentence into a Complex one containing an* **Adjective-clause** :—

1. Our present house suits us exactly.
2. This rule, the source of all our troubles, is disliked by every one.
3. That was a fault not to be forgiven.
4. The diamond field is not far from here.
5. He and his friend entered into a partnership binding themselves to incur equal risks.
6. Their explanation cannot be true.
7. The king took refuge in the fortress, being determined to make a last attempt in that place to save his kingdom.
8. The snow-line in India is about 20,000 feet high.
9. The troubles besetting him on all sides did not daunt him.
10. They soon forgot their past labours.
11. This spot, the first landing-place of the Pilgrim Fathers, is held to be sacred ground.
12. My leave-application has been dispatched.
13. Is this the way to learn your lessons?
14. A certain cholera-cure has not yet been found.
15. Egypt was one of the first countries to become civilised.
16. Death from snake-bite is of daily occurrence.
17. The benefits of his early training were thrown away.
18. That was the act of a coward.
19. Milton was the greatest poet in King Charles's reign.
20. These hills have never yet been trodden by the foot of man.

III. *The Adverb-clause.*

199. An Adverb-clause does the work of an adverb to some verb, adjective, or adverb belonging to some other clause.

An Adverb-clause can be introduced by any of the *Subordinative* conjunctions, or by the Conjunctive adverbs—*where*, *when*, *whether*, etc. :—

Principal Clause.	*Adverb-Clause.*	*Subord. Conjunc.*
He will succeed,	*because* he works hard	*Cause.*
He worked *so* hard,	*that* he was quite tired	*Effect.*
He took medicine	*that* he might get well	*Purpose.*
I will do this,	*if* I am allowed	*Condition.*
He is honest,	*although* he is poor	*Contrast.*
He likes you *more*	*than* (he likes) me	*Comparison.*
Men will reap	*as* they sow	*Extent or Manner.*
The tooth stopped aching	*when* the dentist came in	*Time.*

200. After the conjunctions *though*, *when*, *unless*, *till*, *if*, *whether . . . or*, and *while*, the Predicate-verb "**to be**" and its Subject are often omitted. These must be supplied in the Analysis.

Though (*he was*) much alarmed, he did not lose all hope.
He sprained his foot, while (*he was*) walking in the dark.
His opinion, whether (*it is*) right or wrong, does not concern me.

201. When an Adverb-clause is introduced by "**than**," its Finite Verb is not always expressed. It must then be borrowed *in the same tense* from the clause to which it is subordinate :—

He loves you better than (he loves) me.
He loves you better than I (love you).

202. The Conjunctive pronoun "**who**" or "**which**" makes an Adverb-clause, whenever it is substituted for a Subordinative conjunction signifying Cause or Purpose :—

Cause.—They should pardon my son, *who* (=*because he*) has never committed such a fault before.

Purpose.—A man was sent, *who* should deliver (=*that he* might deliver) the message.

Note.—The student can now therefore take note that four different kinds of clauses can be introduced by the pronoun "who" or "which" :—(1) A *Co-ordinate* clause, where the pronoun is used in a **Continuative** sense. This belongs to Compound sentences. (2) A *Noun*-clause, where no Antecedent to the pronoun is expressed. This belongs to Complex sentences. (3) An *Adjective*-clause, where the pronoun is used in a **Restrictive** sense. This belongs to Complex sentences. (4) An *Adverb*-clause, where the pronoun is used in the sense of **Cause** or **Purpose**. This also belongs to Complex sentences.

I. *Pick out the Adverb-clause or clauses in the following. Show what word or phrase is qualified by every such clause, and what Adverbial relation is denoted thereby :—*

1. He will succeed, because he has worked hard.
2. Men engage in some work, that they may earn a living.
3. He threatened to beat him, unless he confessed.
4. He was always honest, although he was poor.
5. This is not true, so far as I can tell.
6. He likes you as much as I do.
7. He tried for a long time before he succeeded.
8. Let us go to bed, as it is now late.
9. He walked with care, lest he should stumble.
10. I agree to this, provided you sign your name.
11. Though he punish me, yet will I trust in him.
12. He returned home, after he had finished the work.
13. Prove a friend, before you trust him.
14. When the cat's away, the mice will play.
15. He persevered so steadily, that he succeeded at last.
16. I will let off this man, who has been well punished already.
17. He sees very well, considering that he is sixty years of age.

18. I gave him a prize, that he might work harder next year.

19. They deserted their former associate, who had become poor and unfortunate.

20. As the tree falls, so will it lie.

21. Ever since we left the house, it has not ceased raining.

22. I should be glad to lend you that money, if I had as much in my own pocket.

23. Murder, though it have no tongue, will yet speak.

24. Unless you leave the house at once, I will send for a policeman.

25. A jackal, while prowling about the suburbs of a town, slipped into an indigo tank; and not being able to get out he laid himself down, so that he might be taken for dead.

26. Ambassadors were sent from Sparta, who should sue for peace.

II. *Expand each Simple sentence into a Complex one containing an* **Adverb-clause** *or* **clauses**:—

1. In the absence of any other helper, we must accept his aid.
2. The two chief points having been gained, success is now certain.
3. Owing to repeated failures, he made no further attempt.
4. The problem was too difficult to be solved.
5. He worked very well, to the astonishment of every one.
6. He fell under suspicion by becoming suddenly rich.
7. He worked hard for the purpose of gaining a prize.
8. Every precaution was taken against the failure of the plan.
9. He purposes to become rich by sticking steadily to his work.
10. Without leave from the master, we should not go out.
11. He would be very thankful to be relieved of all this trouble.
12. With or without his leave, I shall leave the room.
13. He would have been caught, but for his flight across the border.
14. Notwithstanding the heat of the sun we must go out.
15. In spite of all his riches, he is never contented.
16. For all his experience he is still incompetent.
17. The depth of the sea equals the height of the mountains.
18. With every man who came in, another went out.
19. Of all the boys in the class James is the most industrious.
20. Keep perfectly silent at peril of your lives.
21. Be it done unto thee according to thy belief.
22. The harvest will depend upon the sowing.
23. Nothing in my opinion will prosper under such a man.
24. He returned to duty immediately on the expiry of his leave.
25. With every cough he felt a good deal of pain.
26. In the performance of duty, no one should feel afraid.

Section 2.—Scheme of Analysis in Detail.

203. Scheme of Analysis.—The scheme of Analysis, given already in § 8, is here recapitulated to save reference:—

A man convinced against his will is of the same opinion still.

He made himself mean and of no reputation.

The second master of the school has been teaching my sons Euclid since Thursday last.

Whom the gods love die young.

I. Subject.		II. Predicate.			
			Completion of Finite Verb.		
Nominative or Equivalent.	Enlargement of Nominative.	Finite Verb.	Object. (1) Direct. (2) Indirect.	Complement.	Extension of Finite Verb.
1	2	3	4	5	6
man	(1) A (2) convinced against his will	is	...	of the same opinion	still.
He	...	made	himself	mean and of no reputation.	
master	(1) The (2) second (3) of the school	has been teaching	(1) *Direct* Euclid (2) *Indirect* my sons	...	since Thursday last.
Whom the gods love	...	die	...	...	young.

204. Nominative or its equivalent: see heading to col. 1. This is the chief part of the Subject, and when there is no enlargement, it is the only part. It is this that fixes the number and person of the Finite verb. Its most typical form is that of a noun or pronoun in the Nominative case. The following is a list of the various forms in which a Nominative or its equivalent can be expressed:[1]—

(1) **Noun.**—A *ship* went out to sea yesterday.
(2) **Adj. used as Noun.**—The *brave* are always respected.
(3) **Pronoun.**—*He* (some one previously named) has gone.
(4) **Noun-Infinitive.**—*To walk* regularly is good for health.
(5) **Gerund or Verbal noun.**—*Reading* is good for the mind.
(6) **Noun-phrase.**—*How to do this* is a difficult question.
(7) **Noun-clause.**—*Whom the gods love* die young.

Note.—Sometimes a sentence begins with "it," and the Nominative or its equivalent is mentioned after the verb: "*It* is easy to do this." Here the "it" is redundant, and may be left out in the analysis:—"To do this is easy."

[1] There is no need to commit this list of forms to memory. They are enumerated merely to show what the student may expect to find. The same remark applies to the lists in §§ 205-209.

205. Enlargement: see heading to col. 2. The most typical form is an Adjective. We call this "*enlargement*," because an adjective, according to the definition given in § 12, "is a word that *enlarges* the meaning of a noun and narrows its application."

The following is a list of the various forms in which an "enlargement" can be expressed:—

(1) **Adjective.**—*Just* men deserve to prosper.
(2) **Participle.**—A *fertilising* shower fell to-day.
(3) **Qualifying Infin.**—Water *to drink* is scarce in this place.
(4) **Possessive noun or pronoun.**—*Your* teacher has come.
(5) **Noun used as Adj.**—The *village* school opens at eight A.M.
(6) **Gerund used as Adj.**—*Drinking* water is scarce here.
(7) **Prep. with object.**[1]—A man *of virtue* does not tell lies.
(8) **Adverb with Def. article.**—*The then* king died suddenly.
(9) **Noun in Apposition.**—Charles, my *son*, has come.
(10) **Noun-clause in Appos.**—The rumour *that he was dead* is false.
(11) **Adjective-clause.**—The house *in which we live* has been sold.

206. Finite verb: see heading to col. 3. This is the chief part of the predicate, and, when the verb is Intransitive and of Complete predication (§ 6), it can be the only part; as, "Hogs *grunt*."

If the tense or mood of the Finite verb is formed, not by inflexion, but by the help of one of the six Auxiliary verbs (§ 102), remember that the Auxiliary verb and the Principal verb together make up the Finite verb, and must be mentioned together in column 3.

Subject.	Finite verb.	Object.
I	have been examining	the pictures.

But if the previous verb is not Auxiliary, as "*will*," for instance, when it occurs in the *first* person of the Future tense (§ 115), in such a sentence *will* alone makes the Finite verb, and the Noun-Infinitive that follows is its Object:—

Subject.	Finite verb.	Object.
I	will	see him to-morrow.

[1] In such a phrase as "a brute of a man," the "*of*" denotes apposition, "a man a brute," *i.e.* a brutish man, a man who is a brute. In such a phrase, therefore, the sense is analogous to (9), and not to (7).

207. Object, direct or indirect: see col. 4. The different forms in which a *Direct* object can be expressed are the same as those in which the Nominative can be expressed (§ 204) :—

(1) **Noun.**—The snake bit the *man*.
(2) **Adj. used as Noun.**—He satisfied the *public*.
(3) **Pronoun.**—My friend will not deceive *me*.
(4) **Noun-Infinitive.**—He deserves *to succeed*.
(5) **Gerund or Verbal noun.**—He likes *riding*.
(6) **Noun-phrase.**—We did not know *how to do it*.
(7) **Noun-clause.**—We do not know *who he is*.

There are only two forms in which an *Indirect* object can be expressed, viz. a noun denoting some person or other animal, or some personal pronoun :—

He gave *James* a book . . . . (*Trans. verb.*)
He overslept *himself* . . . . (*Intrans. verb.*)

208. Complement: see heading to col. 5. The following are the various forms in which a Complement can be expressed (§§ 92, 95) :—

(1) **Noun**	The citizens made him their *king*	(*Fact.*)
	That beggar turned out a *thief*	(*Cop.*)
(2) **Possessive**	She made A.'s quarrel *her own*	(*Fact.*)
	This book is *mine*, not *James's*.	(*Cop.*)
(3) **Adjective**	The judge set the prisoner *free*	(*Fact.*)
	The prisoner is now *free*	(*Cop.*)
(4) **Participle**	They found her *weeping*	(*Fact.*)
	He seemed much *pleased*	(*Cop.*)
(5) **Prep. with object**	I prefer a dog *to a cat*	(*Fact.*)
	He is *in a sad plight*	(*Cop.*)
(6) **Qualifying Infinitive**	I like a thief *to be punished*	(*Fact.*)
	This house is *to let*	(*Cop.*)
(7) **Adverb**	That noise sent him *asleep*	(*Fact.*)
	The man has fallen *asleep*	(*Cop.*)
(8) **Noun-clause**	We have made him *what he is*	(*Fact.*)
	The result is *what we expected*	(*Cop.*)

209. Extension: see heading to col. 6. The most typical form is an Adverb. We call this "*extension*," because an adverb, according to the definition given in § 16, "is a word that *extends* the meaning and narrows the application of any part of speech except a noun or pronoun."

Two points should be noticed : (1) In the analysis of sentences (not in parsing, which is a different kind of operation), extension applies *only to the Finite verb* of its own clause : if an adverb or adverb-equivalent belongs to any part of a sentence except the Finite verb, it must not be placed in column 6. (2) "Extension" means the same thing as "enlargement." But as one relates to the Finite verb, and the other to the Nominative or its equivalent, it is convenient in analysing sentences to give them separate names.

The following are the various forms in which "extension" can be expressed :—

(1) **Adverb.**—He slept *soundly.*
(2) **Prep. with object.**—He slept *for six hours.*
(3) **Adjective.**—He went away *sad.*
(4) **Participle.**—He went away *disappointed.*
(5) **Qualifying Infin.**—He came *to see* the horse.
(6) **Adverbial objective.**—Bind him *hand and foot.*
(7) **Absolute phrase.**—We all set off, *he remaining behind.*
(8) **Adverb-clause.**—We all set off, *while he remained behind.*

Note.—The student must not be surprised that in (3) an *adjective* is included among forms of extension, the typical form of which is an *adverb.* Analysis is not the same thing as parsing : there are three differences at least. (1) In analysis the unit to be dealt with is a sentence ; in parsing a single word. (2) Analysis deals with grammar on its logical side ; parsing on its syntactical. The word "sad," though it is an adjective in form and in syntax, is adverbial in function. In what manner or in what state of mind did he go away ? In a sad state. The word "sad" therefore qualifies the verb "went away" in just the same way as if it were expressed in the form "sadly." The same remark applies to the participle "disappointed" in the fourth sentence. (3) There are some words which can be parsed, but do not come within the framework of analysis at all ; such as an interjection, an exclamatory phrase, a nominative of address.

Section 3.—Degrees of Subordination.

210. Degrees of Subordination.—The following sentence may be taken as an example for analysis :—

One man in the audience, who was chief magistrate of the town and happened to be present, on seeing that the lion fawned on Androcles, when it was expected to tear him to pieces, called out with a loud voice, and ordered Androcles to explain how a savage beast could have so forgotten its innate disposition all of a sudden, that it became converted into a harmless animal, which chose to spare its intended victim rather than devour him.

Now, when we come to divide this sentence into its component clauses, we find, firstly, that it is a Compound sentence, consisting of two co-ordinate clauses connected by *and*, and secondly, that each of the co-ordinate clauses contains subordinate ones, the former containing three, and the latter four.

The two co-ordinate clauses, which are connected by *and* and make the sentence a Compound one, are marked by A and B.

(A) One man in the audience, (*a*) who was chief magistrate of the town (*b*) and happened to be present, on seeing (*x*) that the lion fawned on Androcles, (*y*) when it was expected to tear him to pieces, called out with a loud voice, (B) and ordered Androcles to explain (*a*) how a savage beast could have so forgotten its innate disposition all of a sudden, (*b*) that it became converted into a harmless animal, (*c*) which chose to spare its intended victim rather (*d*) than to devour him.

In (A) we see that clause (*a*) is an adjective-clause in the first degree, qualifying the noun "man"; clause (*b*) is co-ordinate to clause (*a*), and therefore a second adjective-clause to the noun "man"; clause (*x*) is a noun-clause in the first degree, object to the verb "seeing"; clause (*y*) is an adverb-clause in the second degree, qualifying the verb "fawned."

In (B) we see that clause (*a*) is a noun-clause in the first degree, object to the verb "explain"; clause (*b*) is an adverb-clause in the second degree, qualifying the verb "forgotten"; clause (*c*) is an adjective-clause in the third degree, qualifying the noun "animal"; and clause (*d*) is an adverb-clause in the fourth degree, qualifying the verb "chose."

The degree of subordination (as first, second, third, fourth, etc.), is shown by the number of lines drawn under the clause concerned.

211. Tabular form of Analysis.—Before beginning to analyse a sentence of many clauses in tabular form, it will be best to write it out with the clauses marked off in the manner shown in § 210. This will serve as a key to the tabulation, of which a complete example is given on page 106.

Words that are understood must be supplied: they can be shown in brackets in their proper column.

Words which do not come within the framework of analysis must be left out; as, for instance, an interjection, an exclamatory phrase, a noun used for purposes of address; see *Note* to § 209.

> This heavy rain, *alas!* has spoilt the harvest this year.
> The farmers, *poor fellows!* have lost heavily.
> *Friends, Romans, countrymen,* lend me your ears.

A **parenthetical sentence** cannot be considered a *clause* of the sentence into which it has been wedged.

> Mr. R. (so at least his friends say) will soon retire.

Here there are two distinct sentences to be analysed:—

> (1) Mr. R. will soon retire.
> (2) So at least his friends say.

Clause.	Kind of Clause.	Connective.	I. SUBJECT.		II. PREDICATE.			
			Nominative or Equivalent. 1	Enlargement of Nominative. 2	Finite Verb. 3	Completion of Finite Verb. Object. (1) *Direct.* (2) *Indirect.* 4	Completion of Finite Verb. Complement. 5	Extension of Finite Verb. 6
A. One man in the audience called out with a loud voice, on seeing that etc.	Principal.	..	man	(1) One (2) in the audience	called out	..	..	(1) with a loud voice, (2) on seeing that etc.
(*a*) who was chief magistrate of the town	Adj.-clause to "man" in A.	who	who	..	was	..	chief magistrate of the town	..
(*b*) and happened to be present,	Co-ord. to (*a*).	and	(who)	..	happened	..	to be present,	..
(*x*) that the lion fawned on Androcles,	Noun clause, object to "seeing."	that	lion	the	fawned on	Androcles,	..	..
(*y*) when it was expected to tear him to pieces,	Adv. clause, qualifying "fawned."	when	it	..	was expected	..	to tear him to pieces,	..
B. and ordered Androcles to explain	Principal, co-ord. to A.	and	(man)	..	ordered	Androcles	to explain etc.	..
(*a*) how a savage beast could have so forgotten its innate disposition all of a sudden.	Noun-clause object to "explain."	how	beast	(1) a (2) savage	could	have so forgotten its innate disposition all of a sudden,	..	..
(*b*) that it became converted into a harmless animal,	Adv.-clause to "have forgotten."	that	it	..	became	..	converted into a harmless animal,	..
(*c*) which chose to spare its intended victim	Adj.-clause to "animal."	which	which	..	chose	to spare its intended victim	..	rather than etc.
(*d*) rather than to devour him.	Adv. clause to "chose."	than	(it)	..	(chose)	to devour him.		

I.—*Examples in Parsing and Analysis.*

For parsing a word the student can follow the Parsing Chart given at the opening of chap. xii. The method there shown is as follows :—

I. **Noun.**—What kind (Proper, Common, Collective, Material, or Abstract)? What gender (Masc., Fem., or Neut.)? What number (Sing. or Plur.)? What case (Nom., Poss., or Obj.)? Why in such a case (see all possible reasons in Parsing Chart No. III.)?

II. **Pronoun.**—What kind (Pers., Dem., Conj., or Interr.)? What gender (depends on antecedent)? What number (depends on anteced.)? What person (depends on anteced.)? What case (depends on its own clause, see Parsing Chart No. III.).

IV. **Adjective.**—What kind (Proper, Descriptive, Quantit., Interr., Distrib., Numeral, or Demons.)? What degree of Comparison (Pos., Comp., or Superl.)? Which use (Attributive or Predicative)? What noun or pronoun does it qualify?

V. **Adverb.**—What kind (Simple, Conj., or Interr.)? What degree (Pos., Comp. or Superl.)? Which use (Attrib. or Predic.)? If Attrib., to qualify what word or words (Verb, Adj., Adv., Prep., Conj., or Sentence)? If Predic., complement to what verb?

VI. **Finite Verb.**—What kind (Transitive or Intransitive)? What Conjug. (Strong, Weak, or Mixed)? What voice? What mood? What tense? Agreeing with what subject? and therefore in what number (Singular or Plural)? and in what person (first, second, or third)?

VII. **Infinitive.**—What form (Indefinite, Continuous, Perfect, or Perf. Contin.)? Which Infin. (Noun-Infin. or Qualif. Infin.)? If Noun-Infin., in what connection? If Qual. Infin., in what connection?

VIII. **Gerund.**—What form (Pres. or Perf.)? What voice? What kind of verb? If Trans., governing what object?

IX. **Participle.**—What form (Pres., Past, or Perf.)? What voice? What kind of verb? If Trans., governing what object? What use (Attributive, Predicative, Absolute, or Gerundive)?

X. **Conjunction.**—What kind (Co-ordinative or Subordinative)? Joining what words or phrases, or what sentences?

Analyse the following sentences, and parse (with any explanation that may be necessary) the words printed in italics :—

1. By torch and trumpet *fast* arrayed,
Each horseman *drew* his *battle* blade,
And *furious* every charger neighed,
To join the dreadful revelry.—CAMPBELL.
2. Let *me hear what* you have *to say*.
3. *Week in*, *week out*, from morn till night,
You *may hear* his *bellows blow*.—LONGFELLOW.
4. On Linden, when the sun was *low*,
All bloodless lay the untrodden snow,
And dark as winter was the flow
Of Iser rolling rapidly.—CAMPBELL.
5. Perdition *catch* my soul, *but* I love thee.—SHAKSPEARE.
6. I cannot *but believe* that you are lost.
7. These men, *than* whom I have never known men more unwilling, have suddenly left me, *merely* because I asked them *to work* a *little* overtime on account of the orders *that* I unexpectedly received this *morning* from headquarters.
8. Toll for the *brave!*
Brave Kempenfelt is gone;
His *last* sea-fight *is fought*,
His work of glory *done*.—COWPER.
9. Cowards die many *times* before their death;
The *valiant only* taste of death *but* once.—SHAKSPEARE.
10. I now gave *over* any more thoughts of the ship, or of *getting* anything out of her, *except* what might *drive a*-shore from the wreck, *as* indeed divers pieces of her afterwards *did;* but those things were of small use to me.—*Robinson Crusoe*.
11. I like a rascal *to be punished*,[1] when I am quite sure that his guilt *has been proved* before a *jury who* had no prejudice against him, before they began *hearing* his case.
12. The reason *why* the seven stars are *no more than* seven is a pretty reason.—SHAKSPEARE.
13. *Just* so we have heard a baby, mounted on the shoulders of its father, *cry out*, "How *much* taller I am *than* papa!"—MACAULAY.
14. *There* is no despair so absolute as *that* which comes with the *first* moments of our first great sorrow, when we have not yet known *what* it is *to have suffered* and be healed, to have despaired and to have recovered hope.—G. ELIOT.
15. Music, when soft voices die,
Vibrates in the memory;
Odours, when sweet violets sicken,
Live within the sense they *quicken*.—SHELLEY.

---

[1] The explanation given in § 92 is that *to be punished* is the Infin. form of Complement; and this agrees with that given by Abbott in §§ 97 and 105 in *How to Parse*. Dr. Gow, however, in *Method of English*, p. 117, has expressed the view that *to be punished* (=punishment) is the Direct object to the verb "like," and "a rascal" (=for a rascal) the Indirect. Both views appear to be tenable; but on grounds of convenience I have adopted the former. It covers the ground of such a sentence as "I saw him come." This could scarcely be broken up into "I saw *come* (Direct object) for *him* (Indirect)."

16. Woe *worth* the chase, woe worth the day,
That cost thy *life*, my gallant *grey!*—SCOTT.

17. What must the king *do* now? Must he *submit?*
The king shall *do* it.—SHAKSPEARE.

18. At four o'clock P.M. we reached York, *which* is a fine old town dating back to the time of the Romans, though they called it by a different name, *that* I cannot now remember.

19. For *what* are men better than sheep and goats
That nourish a blind life within the brain,
If, knowing God, they lift not hands of prayer
Both for *themselves* and those who call them friend?
TENNYSON.

20. Our deeds shall *travel* with us from afar,
And what we have been makes us *what-we-are*.—G. ELIOT.

21. Because half a dozen grasshoppers under a fern make the field *ring* with their importunate chink, while thousands of great cattle, reposing beneath the shadow of the British oak, chew the cud and are silent, *pray do* not imagine that those who make the noise are the only inhabitants of the field.—BURKE.

22. For when the noble Cæsar saw him *stab*,
Ingratitude, more strong than traitors' arms,
Quite vanquish'd him: then *burst* his mighty heart;
And, in his mantle muffling *up* his face,
Even at the base of Pompey's statua,
Which all the *while* ran *blood*, great Cæsar fell.—SHAKSPEARE.

23. *Let me* now *tell you* that *every* six hours of study will be injurious to your health, unless you break the period with half an hour's *walk* in the open air or with some light form of recreation that *can give* relief to the brain.

24. He was proud, when I praised; he was submissive, when I reproved him; but he did never *love* me, and what he now mistakes for justice and kindness for me, is *but* the pleasant sensation *that* all persons feel at *revisiting* the scenes of their boyish hopes and fears, and the *seeing* on equal terms the man they were accustomed to look up *to* with reverence.

II.—*General Questions.*

1. When a Singular noun ends in an *s* sound, how is the Possessive sign affected? How is the Possessive expressed in plurals?

2. What are Weak verbs? Classify *bring*, *sing*, *take*, *seek*, *teach*, *set*, *bleed*, *eat* as Strong or Weak. Give reasons in each case.

3. Name all the Auxiliary verbs. Why are they so called? Distinguish them from every other class of verb.

4. Distinguish the uses of *but* in the following sentences:—

There is *but* one man present.
I cannot *but* believe that you are lost.
He is a clever man, *but* not learned in books.
There was no one present *but* pitied the lame horse.
He was all *but* ruined by that investment.

5. Explain and exemplify the difference between Extension and

Completion of a Finite verb, and between a Direct and an Indirect object.

6. Point out the grammatical difference between *the* in such a sentence as "He did his duty, and was *the* happier for it," and *the* in such a sentence as "He was *the* happier of the two."

7. Account for the resemblance in form between the Verbal noun and the Present Participle. Parse all the words ending in *-ing* in this sentence: "Darkling, we went singing on our way, with our walking-sticks in our hands, weary of toiling in town."

8. Show by what means Transitive verbs in English can be used intransitively and *vice versa*. Can Intransitive verbs be conjugated in the Passive voice? If so, to what extent?

9. Classify verbs of Incomplete predication, and exemplify the different forms that the Complement may assume with each class of verb.

10. What principle would you adopt in classifying nouns in English? Exemplify each class.

11. Exemplify the uses of the Qualifying or Gerundial Infinitive. Is there any connection in origin between this and what we now call a Gerund or Verbal noun?

12. Explain and exemplify the meaning of each of the Auxiliary verbs, when the said verbs are not used as Auxiliaries.

13. Under what circumstances are we debarred from parsing *than* as a conjunction? To what part of speech must we then assign it? Give examples.

14. Explain the points of resemblance and the points of difference between (*a*) adjectives and adverbs, (*b*) prepositions and conjunctions.

15. Explain and exemplify the terms *Impersonal verbs, Defective verbs, Irregular verbs, Auxiliary verbs, Factitive verbs, Copulative verbs.*

16. What is meant by the *case* of a noun? How did the word come to be used in such a sense?

17. How do we express simply futurity (1) in Finite verbs, (2) in the absolute construction? Give examples.

18. What form of the Indefinite article do you use before the words —*history, historical, European, usual, humble, ewe?* Give reasons.

19. Specify, with examples, the various meanings and uses of *one* in our language.

20. Give instances of the conversion of Abstract nouns into Concrete, Proper into Common, Material into Common.

21. Define a sentence. How would you deal with the following? (1) *go;* (2) *hence!* (3) *does it rain? yes; let us return.*

22. Explain and exemplify "*pro*-noun," "*pro*-verb," "*pro*-sentence."

23. Explain *finite* in the phrase "Finite verb." Mention those parts of a verb which are not finite.

24. Examine the following definitions of a preposition:—

> "A word used before a noun or pronoun to show its relation to some other word."
>
> "A word that connects a noun with a verb, an adjective, or other noun."

25. Give examples of the three main senses in which the Possessive

case can be used. To what class or classes of instances is the use of this case now restricted?

26. How would you distinguish between a Demonstrative adjective and a Demonstrative pronoun? Give examples.

27. Distinguish the uses of *as* in the following sentences:—

> Yours is not the same book *as* mine.
> He trembled *as* he spoke.
> Do not act *as* he did.
> Hot *as* the sun is, we must go out in it.
> I will inquire again *as* to that matter.
> *As* a judge I condemn you, *as* a man I pity you.

28. Describe and exemplify the different kinds of objects that can be used in connection with verbs.

29. Describe the main tests by which a Weak verb is distinguished from a Strong. Apply these tests to *hang, fight, read, beseech, see, saw, say, sow, sew, sue, sit, seethe, sell.*

30. Show how the distinction between Attributive and Predicative is applied to adjectives and Simple adverbs, and how that between Continuative and Restrictive is applied to Relative pronouns or Relative adverbs.

31. Exemplify the uses of (*a*) *though, but,* (*b*) *as well as,* as Co-ordinative or Subordinative conjunctions.

32. What exceptions are there to the rules (1) that two Singular subjects are followed by a Plural verb, (2) that one Singular subject is followed by a Singular verb?

33. Explain the cases of the words italicised below:[1]—

> (*a*) Knock *me* this gate and rap *me* well.—SHAKSPEARE.
> (*b*) Fare *thee* well. He overslept *himself.*
> (*c*) *Me*thinks. It likes *us* well (SHAKS.)
> (*d*) Woe worth *the day!* Woe is *me!*
> (*e*) I hope you will do *me* this favour.

III.—*Correct or justify the following.* (From London Matriculation Papers, Jan. 1879 to Jan. 1897).

1. I am verily a man who am a Jew.
2. Too great a variety of studies distract the mind.
3. Who do you speak to?
4. The river has overflown its banks.
5. Man never is, but always to be blest.
6. Neither our virtues or our vices are all our own.
7. If I were old enough to be married, I am old enough to manage my husband's house.
8. I am to blame, not you.
9. Art thou proud yet? Ay, that I am not thee.

---

[1] These are all now parsed as Objective cases. For (*b*) see § 97; for (*c*) see § 148; for (*e*) see § 90. In all of them the preposition *to* or *for* is understood. In Old English all these cases were Datives. The construction in (*a*) is still called the **Dative of Interest**: "Knock this gate *for* me and rap well *for* me." In (*d*) the prep. *to* is understood: "Woe happen *to* the day!"; "woe is *to* me" (Latin, *hei mihi*).

10. Whoever the king favours
The cardinal will find employment for.
11. Here you may see that visions are to dread.
12. Nothing but wailings was heard.
13. Neither of them are remarkable for precision.
14. I cannot tell if it be wise or no.
15. It must be confessed that a lampoon or a satire do not carry in them robbery or murder.—*Spectator.*
16. Whose own example strengthens all his laws,
And is himself the great sublime he draws.
17. They were both fond of one another.
18. Thersites's body is as good as Ajax, when neither are alive.
19. Thou art much older than thy looks.
20. There were no less than five persons concerned.
21. Recite the first six lines of *Paradise Lost.*
22. Neither he nor we are disengaged.
23. One of the best books that has been written on the subject.
24. I like it better than any.
25. And since I never dare to write
As funny as I can.
26. Laying the suspicion on some one, I know not who.
27. Well is him that hath found prudence!
28. Neither he nor I have any doubt of his success.
29. One of the best treatises that has been written on the subject.
30. I am one of those who cannot describe what I do not see.
31. The country was divided into counties, and the counties placed under magistrates.
32. Nobody ever put so much of themselves into their work.
33. He hath given away above half his fortune to the Lord knows who.
34. Friendships which we once hoped and believed would never grow cold.
35. Nepos answered him, Celsus replied, and neither of them were sparing of censures on each other.
36. Such are a few of the many paradoxes one would cite from his writings, and which are now before me.
37. The largest circulation of any Liberal newspaper.
38. Injustice springs only from three causes. . . . Neither of these can be found in a being wise, powerful, and benevolent.
39. This dedication may serve almost for any book that has, is, or shall be published.
40. In the best countries a rise in rents and wages has been found to go together.
41. He belongs to one caste, and the hewers of wood and drawers of water to another.
42. The second assault was met by Buckingham by a counter attack on the Earl of Bristol, whom he knew would be the chief witness against him.
43. And many a holy text around she strews,
That teach the rustic moralist to die.
44. This view has been maintained by one of the greatest writers that has appeared in this country.

45. The administration of so many various interests, and of districts so remote, demand no common capacity and vigour.

46. He having none but them, they having none but he.

47. Breaking a constitution by the very same errors that so many have been broke before.

48. They are not only the most charitable of any other nation, but most judicious in distinguishing the properest objects of compassion.

49. The part of this reed used by the Indians is from 10 to 11 feet long, and no tapering can be perceived, one end being as thick as another.

50. If he had writ one word by the next post, this had been just and civil.

51. Thou lovest, but ne'er knew love's sad satiety.

52. *Macbeth.* There's blood upon thy face.
Murd. 'Tis Banquo's then.
Macb. 'Tis better thee without than he within.

53. This is he, my master said,
Despised the fair Athenian maid.

54. Luckily the monks have recently given away a couple of dogs which were returned to them, or the breed would have been lost.

55. It was the most amiable, although the least dignified, of all the party squabbles by which it had been preceded.

56. Having perceived the weakness of his poems, they now reappear to us under new titles.

57. Neither you nor I am right.

58. I am one of those who cannot describe what I feel.

59. Whom they were I really cannot specify.

60. Whom do you say that I am?

61. His is a poem, one of the completest works that exists in any language.

62. He was shot by a secretary under notice to quit, with whom he was finding fault,—very fortunately without effect.

63. It is characteristic of them to appear but to one person, and he the most likely to be deluded.

64. I think it may assist the reader by placing them before him in chronological order.

65. Few people learn anything that is worth learning easily.

66. My resolution is to spare no expense in education; it is a bad calculation, because it is the only advantage over which circumstances have no control.

67. Image after image, phrase after phrase, starts out vivid, harsh, and emphatic.

68. Books that we can at a glance carry off what is in them are worse than useless for discipline.

69. He preferred to know the worst than to dream the best.

70. Humanity seldom or ever shows itself in inferior minds.

71. You have already been informed of the sale of Ford's theatre, where Mr. Lincoln was assassinated, for religious purposes.

72. The Moor, seizing a bolster, full of rage and jealousy, smothers her.

73. Nor do I know any one with whom I can converse more pleasantly or I would prefer as my companion.

74. They drowned the black and white kittens.
75. The then Ministry were in favour of the bill.
76. The people is one; they have all one language.
77. George and myself went up the mountain together.
78. The Duke of Wellington is one of those who never interfere with matters over which he has no control.
79. Her voice was ever soft, gentle, and low; an excellent thing in woman.
80. Peter the Hermit's diet was abstemious, his prayers long and fervent.
81. I shall have great pleasure in accepting your invitation.
82. Each of the girls went to their separate rooms to rest and calm themselves.
83. Being early killed, I sent a party in search of his mangled body.

IV.—*Direct and Indirect Narration, with Examples.*

A speech is said to be in *Direct* Narration, when the very words used by the speaker are repeated without any change; in *Indirect*, when the words are given with some change of construction.

In Indirect Narration the verbs are bound by the same rules as those given in § 191 for the Sequence of Tenses.

Thus by Rule I., when the reporting or principal verb is in the Past tense, the Present tense in the reported speech must be changed into its corresponding Past form. Thus we change:—

Shall	into	*should*	*See*	into	*saw*
Will	,,	*would*	*Is seeing*	,,	*was seeing.*
May	,,	*might*	*Has seen*	,,	*had seen*
Can	,,	*could*	*Has been seeing*	,,	*had been seeing*

Observe also that when the Present tense is changed into the Past by Rule I., an adjective or adverb expressing *nearness* is similarly changed into one expressing *distance.* Thus we change:—

Now	into	*then*	*To-day*	into	*that day*
This or *these*	,,	*that* or *those*	*To-morrow*	,,	*next day*
Hither	,,	*thither*	*Yesterday*	,,	*the previous day*
Here	,,	*there*	*Last night*	,,	*the previous night*
Hence	,,	*thence*	*Ago*	,,	*before*
Thus	,,	*so*			

1. **Direct.**—"What *is this* strange outcry?" said Socrates; "I *sent* the women away mainly in order that they might not offend in *this* way; for I *have heard* that a man should die in peace. *Be* quiet then and *have* patience."

Indirect.—Socrates *inquired* of them what *that* strange outcry *was.* He *reminded* them that he *had sent* the women away mainly in order that they might not offend in *that* way; for he *had heard* that a man should die in peace. He *begged* them therefore *to be* quiet and *have* patience.

2. **Direct.**—The teacher became angry with the student and *said*, "Why *have* you again *disturbed* the class in *this* way? I *have told* you before, that when I *am speaking*, you should be silent. *Leave* the room, and *do not return* again *to-day*."

Indirect.—The teacher became angry with the student and *inquired* of him why he *had* again *disturbed* the class in *that* way. He *reminded* him that he *had told* him before that he (the student) should be silent when he (the master) *was speaking*. He *ordered* him therefore *to leave* the room, and *forbade* him *to return* again *that* day.

(1) *Convert the following sentences from Direct to Indirect:*—

1. We said to him, "The weather is stormy, and the way is long."
2. He said to us, "The carriage has come, and we shall start soon."
3. The teacher told us, "The prize will be presented to-morrow."
4. He said to me, "The rain has been falling since daybreak, and you cannot go."
5. We said to him, "Your fault will be pardoned, if you confess it."
6. He said to me, "I am glad to tell you that you are pardoned."
7. He said, "The man has started, but he has not yet come."
8. We heard him say, "I will agree to what you propose, if you sign this."
9. He said to me, "You are mistaken; you will not go to-day."
10. John said to me, "I shall leave this place, as soon as I can."
11. John said to me, "You will be tired before you arrive."
12. John said, "Our friend arrived yesterday, but will go to-day."
13. My son exclaimed, "Some one has taken the book I was reading."
14. He made a promise, "I will come, if I can."
15. He said, "I have been very ill, but am now better."
16. Pilate replied to the Jews, "What I have written, I have written."
17. He said to me, "You are guilty, and I am innocent."
18. They said, "The boy is hiding in the place where we left him."
19. They said, "The boy will soon be found; and we will bring him."
20. And Reuben said unto them, "Shed no blood; cast Joseph into this pit that is in the wilderness, but lay no hand upon him."—*Old Testament.*
21. And Judah said unto his brethren, "What profit is it, if we slay our brother and conceal his blood? Come, let us sell him to the Ishmaelites, and let not our hand be upon him; for he is our brother and our flesh."—*Old Testament.*
22. Joseph said to James, "I can tell you what strikes me as the most useful machine in the world." James replied, "Can you, Joseph? I should like to hear of it. What is it used for?"

23. "What do you mean?" asked the man; "how can a rope be used for binding flour?" "A rope may be used for anything," replied the man, "when I do not wish to lend it."

24. A rich man once said to his poorer brother, "Why do you not enter the service of the king, so that you may be relieved of the baseness of labour?"

25. Finding no remedy, he said to himself, "It is better to die than to live in such misery as I am compelled to suffer from a master who treats me and always has treated me so unkindly."

26. And they said one to another, "We are verily guilty concerning our brother, in that we saw the distress of his soul, when he besought us, and we would not hear: therefore is this distress come upon us." —*Old Testament.*

27. The violent man said, "What violence have I done? What anger have I been guilty of?" Then the others laughed and said to him, "Why should we speak? You have given us ocular proof of your violent temper."

28. The robber said to Alexander, "I am thy captive: I must hear what thou art pleased to say, and endure what thou art pleased to inflict. But my soul is unconquered; and if I reply at all to thy reproaches, I will reply to thee like a free man."

29. "You are old, Father William," the young man cried,
"The locks that are left you are grey;
You are hale, Father William, a hale old man;
Now tell me the reason, I pray."

30. "I am sorry indeed," replied the king, "that my vessel is already chosen; and I cannot therefore sail with the son of the man who served my father."—DICKENS.

31. He cried to them in agony, "Row back at any risk! I cannot bear to leave her behind to be drowned."—DICKENS.

32. He made a promise to the king's surgeon, saying:—"Bleed the king to death with this lancet, and I will give you a thousand pieces of gold; and when I ascend the throne, you shall be my chief minister."

(2) *Convert the following sentences from Indirect to Direct:—*

1. He made them understand that he would soon return.
2. He told them that he had been robbed of the book which he had bought.
3. He said that he was very sorry for the fault he had committed.
4. They all said to him that he deserved to be pardoned.
5. They affirmed that he was the best worker they had seen.
6. He admitted that he had not worked so hard as we had done.
7. He heard them say that he did not deserve the prize.
8. He promised them that he would do it as soon as he could.
9. They said that he deserved their thanks for all he had done.
10. All who heard this said that he was speaking the truth.
11. He said that he had been three years in jail, and yet was innocent.
12. They told him they would never believe what he said.
13. He replied that he would prove what he had said to be true.

14. My brother told me that he had been reading all day.

15. My father told me that I was wrong and would be fined.

16. I replied that if my fault was proved I would pay the fine.

17. I admitted that I had acted foolishly in what I had done.

18. Damon, before his execution, requested but one favour from Dionysius, which was that he might be permitted to visit his wife and children, who were at that time a considerable distance from him, and he promised faithfully to return on the day appointed.

19. This Dionysius refused to grant, unless some person could be found who would consent to suffer death in his stead, if he did not perform his promise and return by the appointed time.

20. In a short speech Pythias told the surrounding multitude that his dear friend, Damon, would soon arrive; but he hoped not before his own death had saved a life so dear as Damon's was to his family, his friends, and his country.

21. He sent his compliments to Francis, Clavering, and Monson, and charged them to protect Raja Guru Das, who was about to become the head of the Brahmans of Bengal.

22. The governor of the town then called out with a loud voice, and ordered Androcles to explain to them how a savage and hungry lion could thus in a moment have forgotten its innate disposition, and be converted all of a sudden into a harmless animal.

23. Androcles then explained to them that that very lion, which was standing before them, had been his friend and partner in the woods, and had for that reason spared his life, as they now saw.

24. Socrates then suggested to Glaucon that the entire abolition of the guards which he (Glaucon) recommended could not remedy the evils which he desired to remove, and he inquired of Glaucon whether he knew by personal examination that the guards did their work as badly as he imagined.

25. When he reached home, his father asked him where his ship was and what had become of his merchandise. The son in reply told him what had happened,—how he had given up his vessel with its cargo, and had taken in exchange the slaves and set them free, and how he had consented to take this girl back with him and make her his wife.

26. When they asked Thales what thing in the world had the best claim to be called universal, he replied that Hope had the best claim to be so called, because Hope remained with those who had nothing else left.

27. When Solon and Periander were sitting together over their cups, Periander, finding that Solon was more silent than usual, asked him whether he was silent for want of words or because he was a fool. Solon told him in reply that no fool could be silent over his cups.

PART II.—COMPOSITION: FORCE AND PROPRIETY OF DICTION.

CHAPTER XIV.

Punctuation, or the Right Use of Stops.

212. Punctuation divides one sentence or one part of a sentence from another, to help the reader's eye. Much confusion is caused by using wrong stops, or by putting them in wrong places, or by leaving them out where they are wanted. Punctuation is therefore an element in composition.

To take a very simple example, there is a vast difference in meaning between the two following sentences:—

May I be promoted?
May I be promoted!

And this difference turns, not upon the grammatical construction, nor upon the order of the words, nor (if the sentences are read aloud) upon the modulation of the voice, but solely on the punctuation.

213. The names and forms of the different points, stops, or marks are the following:—

Comma, indicated by	,	Note of exclamation, indicated by	!
Semicolon, indicated by	;	Brackets, indicated by	() or []
Colon, indicated by	:	Dash, indicated by	—
Full stop or period, indicated by	.	Hyphen, indicated by	-
Note of Interrogation, indicated by	?	Inverted commas, indicated by	“ ”
Apostrophe, indicated by	'		

The Comma.

214. The shortest pause in the sense or voice is represented by a comma. Its chief uses in a **simple** sentence are the following:—

(*a*) Between nouns or pronouns in apposition; as—

Alexander, the *son* of Philip, *king* of Macedon.

(*b*) Between two or more words of the same Part of Speech :—

A dull, heavy sound was heard. (*Adjectives.*)
Greece, Italy, and Spain are peninsulas of Europe. (*Nouns.*)
We should live soberly, prudently, and industriously. (*Adverbs.*)
Steam propels, elevates, saws, prints, threshes, etc. (*Verbs.*)

(*c*) After the Nominative of address :—

Friends, Romans, countrymen, lend me your ears.

(*d*) Before and after an absolute construction or words interpolated in the middle of a quotation :—

The sun having set, we all went home.
"Leave the room," said he, "and do not come back."

(*e*) When words of the same class or rank go together in pairs, each pair is separated by a comma :—

By night or by day, at home or abroad, asleep or awake, he is a constant source of anxiety to his parents.

(*f*) After an adverbial phrase at the commencement of a sentence. (Here, however, the use of the comma is optional.)

In fact, his poetry is no better than prose.

(*g*) Before and after a participial phrase, provided that the participle might be expanded into a sentence, and is not used in a merely qualifying sense :—

Cæsar, having defeated the Gauls, led his army into Britain. (Here "having defeated" means "after he had defeated.")
Convinced of the accuracy of his facts, he stuck to his opinion. (Here "convinced" means "because he was convinced.")

But when the participle merely qualifies the noun as an adjective would do, no comma need be used :—

A dog lying asleep on a public road is likely to be run over.
A man convinced against his will is of the same opinion still.

(*h*) Explanatory phrases are separated by commas :—

The field was oblong, 60 yards in length, 40 in breadth.

(*i*) Before and after Qualifying Infinitives, when these are used in an explanatory or parenthetical sense :—

I am, to tell you the truth, thoroughly sick of work.
To sum up, the man was accused of three offences.

(*j*) To introduce the words actually or apparently used by a speaker. The sentence so quoted must begin with a capital :—

What I say unto you, I say unto all, Watch.—*New Testament.*
The question is, What shall we do with it?

(*k*) To mark the omission and save the repetition of a verb :—

My regiment is bound for India ; yours, for Gibraltar.

215. (*a*) In a **compound** sentence the co-ordinate clauses, when expressed at full length, are separated by a comma :—

His vanity is greater than his ignorance, and what he lacks in knowledge is supplied by impudence.

But when the two sentences are not expressed at full length and have the same Subject, the comma is omitted :—

I made haste and caught him.
I took up a stone and threw it at the mad dog.

(*b*) If the conjunction is omitted between Co-ordinate clauses, these must be separated (1) by a comma, when they are short; or (2) by a semicolon, when they are long :—

(1) Steam propels, elevates, lowers, pumps, drains, pulls, etc.
(2) Between fame and true honour there is much difference : the former is a blind applause ; the latter is an internal and more silent homage.

216. In **complex** sentences the following are the main rules regarding the use of commas :—

(*a*) A Noun-clause is not separated by a comma from the word to which it stands in grammatical relation :—

It is generally allowed that the art of teaching is difficult.
No one knows when he will come.
His pardon depends upon whether he will confess his fault or not.

But two or more Noun-clauses must be separated by commas, when they stand in the same relation to the same word :—

No one knows when he will come, or whether he will come at all, or whether he is even alive.
Who he was, or why he came, or what he intends to do, will all be found out in time.

(*b*) An Adjective-clause is not separated from its noun or pronoun, unless it is rather lengthy :—

The man *we saw* yesterday has come again to-day.
The man, *who reflects carefully before acting*, is more likely to be successful than one, *who thoughtlessly takes a leap in the dark*.

(*c*) An Adverb-clause is separated from the Principal clause :—

He will succeed, because he works hard.
I will gladly do this, if I am allowed.

The comma is never omitted, unless the Adverb-clause is either very short or expressed elliptically :—

He likes you better than me.
Send me word before you start.

Insert commas, where necessary, in the following sentences :—

The triple alliance consists of Germany Austria and Italy. My son so far from being blamed for his conduct was commended and even rewarded. The roof of the house having caught fire the inmates fled and remained outside the house until the fire was put out. Towns villages and hamlets were all alike attacked with the epidemic of cholera. I shall be happy to make the attempt that you speak of, if I am permitted. From morning till noon from noon to evening from evening to midnight this same grief never leaves him. Early this morning when we had just left the house we met the man that we had been looking for. He found as I expected he would that the house he had lately purchased was a bad one. What was the cause of so much grief to him was never known to any of us. I hope my friend that you will come and spend at least a week with us. He has now grown so old that he spends most of his time in sleeping taking his food or sitting in an easy-chair. I remain my dear sir yours faithfully William Matthews. I shall not leave home for business unless you set the example. Example as the proverb says is the sincerest form of precept. To tell you the plain truth I should be glad to retire from business altogether considering that I am now past sixty years of age and have a son to succeed me. The boatman shouted to a man on shore throw out the rope. A snake sleeping in the grass will bite if any one treads upon it. The prisoner having been convicted of the crime of which he was accused must make up his mind to suffer the penalty. The building is a noble structure of red brick and comprises a reading-room a library a room for writing letters and a room for refreshments. It is quite true that this fine building was erected by private subscriptions. In fact of all that was subscribed L. gave the largest amount in cash but M. was not less liberal because he gave the land on which the building was erected. A dog barking at nothing is a nuisance.

The Semicolon.

217. A **Semicolon** indicates a longer pause than what is indicated by a comma. Its chief uses are as follows :—

(*a*) To separate *longer* Co-ordinate clauses (see § 215, *b*). A longer pause gives greater emphasis to each clause in the series, as it gives the mind more time to dwell on each of them separately :—

> Honesty of purpose in worldly affairs has many advantages over deceit. It is a safer way of dealing with men ; it is an easier mode of despatching business ; it inspires men with greater confidence ; it acquires more and more confidence in itself, while deceit becomes more and more diffident.

(*b*) To divide clauses, which are connected by some Alternative or Illative conjunction. (Here a greater pause is required, because the mind requires a little more time to perceive the alternative or the inference) :—

> I met him as he was leaving his house ; *otherwise* I should not have known where he lived.
>
> I refused to do what he asked me to do ; *for* I was convinced that he had been misinformed of the facts.

The Colon.

218. Colon: The main uses of the colon are the following:—

(*a*) To introduce an additional remark in explanation or in confirmation of a previous one:—

> Strive above all things, in whatever station of life you may be, to preserve health: there is no happiness in life without it.

(*b*) To introduce a quotation: usually followed by a dash:—

> Then Peter stood forth and said:—"Of a truth I perceive that God is no respecter of persons," etc.

(*c*) To introduce or to sum up a series of Co-ordinate clauses. Here, too, the colon is followed by a dash:—

> You must now hear what I have to say about the uses of iron:—we sleep on iron; we travel on iron; we float on iron; we plough the fields with iron; we shoot with iron; we chop down trees with iron:—in fact, there is scarcely anything that we can do without the help of this wonderful metal.

(*d*) To introduce an enumeration of particulars:—

> Send me the following articles:—a pen, a brush, a pencil, a portfolio, and some fine-pointed nibs.

Insert commas, colons, or semicolons, where necessary, in the following sentences:—

1. According to an old belief if a sick man sneezes it is a sure sign of recovery but when a man is going on a journey or about to commence some business should any one about him sneeze the sneeze indicates that the object in which he is interested will not be accomplished.

2. In Rome the army was the nation no citizen could take office unless he had served in ten campaigns.

3. The drill was unremitting at all times so long as a man continued to be a soldier when the troops were in winter quarters sheds were erected in which the soldiers fenced with swords buttoned at the points or hurled javelins also buttoned at the points at one another.

4. The Carthaginian army was composed entirely of mercenary troops Africa Spain and Gaul were their recruiting grounds and these countries were an inexhaustible treasury of warriors as long as the money lasted which the recruits received as pay.

5. While I was still wondering at my sudden deliverance a man came suddenly forward and said my good sir there is nothing to be surprised at I was sent h[illegible] find you and rescue you from these robbers well I have succe[illegible]nding you and so I have accomplished what I was sent for as you now see.

6. Whenever you hesitate about beginning to do something which must be done eventually remember the maxim a thing begun is half done.

The Full Stop or Period.

219. The **Full Stop** or **Period** indicates the close of a complete sentence. The sentence following must invariably be commenced with a capital letter. (See Note at close of Chapter.)

The full stop is also used after abbreviations; as, A.D. (for Anno Domini); B.L. (for Bachelor of Law); Bart. (for Baronet); the Hon. (for the Honourable).

But if the last letter is given, the stop is sometimes not used; as, Dr Jones, Mr Clark, Mrs Jones, Messrs Scott and Sons.

Inverted Commas.

220. **Inverted Commas** are used for indicating the beginning and end of a quotation, or of the actual words used by a speaker:—

> The councillors stood up, and with one voice exclaimed:—"Death before dishonour."
>
> "Wine is a mocker," said the wise king.

To introduce a quotation within a quotation, a single comma is used at either end:—

> "What did they say to you?" inquired the man.
>
> "They gave me," he answered, "strict orders, 'That gate is not to be opened under any circumstances whatever.'"

Note of exclamation.

221. A **Note of Exclamation** is used after words or sentences which express emotion:—

> How are the mighty fallen in the midst of the battle! I am distressed for thee, my brother Jonathan!
>
> "Land ahead!" shouted the delighted crew.

The Apostrophe.

222. The **Apostrophe** (') is inserted to show that some letter or letters have been omitted:—

> The Hon'ble (for *Honourable*); e'en (for *even*); 'tis (for *it is*); ta'en (for *taken*); don't (for *do not*); shan't (for *shall not*); won't (for *will not*); tho' (for *though*); an ox's head (for *oxes head*); and all other instances of the Possessive case.

Note of Interrogation.

223. A **Note of Interrogation** is used after sentences which ask questions. The sentence following must be commenced with a capital:—

> Where was he born? When did he die?

Insert the proper stops and capitals, where necessary, in the following sentences:—

Whats the matter Thomas, ist that old pain of yours again no its not that at all said he but something a good deal better would you believe it my poor old uncle is dead and he has left me five thousand pounds that was very good of him she replied but its come too late why he inquired because she answered you are now old and broken in health what a pity it is that he did not die twenty years ago or give you the money while he was still alive.

Dashes.

224. The **Dash** has five main uses :—

(*a*) To mark a break or abrupt turn in a sentence :—

> Here lies the great—false marble where ?
> Nothing but sordid dust lies here.

(*b*) To mark words in apposition or in explanation :—

> They plucked the seated hills with all their loads—
> Rocks, waters, woods—and by the shaggy tops
> Uplifting bore them in their hands.—*Paradise Lost.*

(*c*) To insert a parenthesis. Here *two* dashes are required.

At the age of ten—such is the power of genius—he could read Greek with facility.

(*d*) To resume a scattered subject :—

> Health, friends, position,—all are gone.

(*e*) To indicate a hesitating or faltering speech :—

> I—er—I—that is,—I don't care.

Brackets.

225. **Brackets** are used like a couple of dashes in (*c*), as just explained, for inserting a parenthesis.

At the age of ten (such is the power of genius) he could read Greek.

Brackets are also used for introducing humorous or ironical side-speeches :—

> I gave all I had (twopence) to that noble cause.

The Hyphen.

226. A **Hyphen** is used for joining the parts of a compound word ; as "bathing-place." It is a shorter line than the Dash.

A hyphen is also used to indicate syllabic division (see note at close of this chapter) ; as "for-mer-ly."

Insert a dash, hyphen, or brackets, wherever necessary, in the following sentences, and add any other appropriate stops :—

England and Russia the two greatest empires on the face of the earth have no real cause of enmity. I could tell you all about my but perhaps you have heard enough by this time. My dog such is the power of jealousy attacked its rival whenever they met. This is very uphill work. If you read without spectacles and I believe you can be so good as to read out the contents of this letter. When I took my degree (and this was twelve years ago) I had good prospects before me. I will never—but I need not finish my sentence—for you know already what I was going to say.

Diæresis.

227. Diæresis (separation) consists of two dots placed over the second of two vowels, to show that the two vowels are to be sounded separately :—

Coöperation = co-operation.

Asterisks.

228. Asterisks denote that some words or clauses have been omitted :—

The Jews * * * * * had to pay heavy taxes to the Norman kings.

Note on Syllabic Division.

Syllabic division, to which allusion is made in § 226, assists pronunciation. It is therefore ruled by accentuation, and not, as has been sometimes maintained, by etymology. "Word-division has nothing to do with etymology. From a practical point of view *im′-pu-dence* is right, being based on true phonetic principles, *i.e.* on the spoken language. It is only when we take the word to pieces that we discover that it is formed from *im-* (for *in*), the base *pud*, and the suffix *-ence*. The spoken language has *pe-ruse′* at one moment, and *pe-ru′-sal* at another. It rightly regards ease of utterance, and nothing else" (Skeat).

It may be added that syllabic division by etymology is impracticable for two reasons: (1) the component parts of a word are sometimes so mixed together as to be indistinguishable; cf. *monkey* (2 syll.), from Old Ital. *moniccio* (4 syll.); (2) the etymologies of words can be known only to those few persons who have studied the subject, whereas all men should know how a word ought to be sounded; cf. *banqu-et* (lit. little bench), which is divided phonetically as *ban′-quet.*

La-ment′, lam′-en-ta′-ble. At′-om, a-tom′-ic. At′-tri-bute (noun), at-trib′-ute (verb). Or′-tho-dox, or-thog′-ra-phy. Pro-vide′, prov′-i-dence. Tel′-e-gram, te-leg′-ra-phy. Ex-pect′, ex′-pec-ta′-tion. Me-chan′-ic, mech′-a-nism. Do-min′-ion, dom′-i-nant. Fi′-nite, fin′-ish. Ta′-ble, tab′-let. Nu′-me-ral, nu-mer′-i-cal. O′-cean, o′-ce-an′-ic.

The terminations *-cial*, *-cious*, *-cean*, *-sion*, *-gion*, *-tion*, *-tial*, *-tious*, since they are sounded as one syllable, should not be divided into two :—

So′-cial, o′-cean, le′-sion, le′-gion, con′-scious, mo′-tion, par′-tial, cap′-tious, fi-nan′-cial.

But in such words as the following the termination *-ion* or *-ious* has to be detached from the preceding consonant, in order to throw the accent on the consonant:—

Re-lig'-ion, con-trit'-ion, prec'-ious, con-dit'-ion, o-pin'-ion, on'-ion, ver-mil'-ion, de-cis'-ion.

Note on the Use of Capitals.

Capitals are used for the first letter of a sentence following a full stop (§ 219); for the first letter of a sentence following a note of interrogation (§ 223); for the first letter of proper names; for the first letter of the names of days and months; for the first letter of the name of the Deity; for the pronoun "I"; for the first letter of every line of poetry; for the first letters of titles of honour or office; for the first letter of a quoted speech or sentence (see § 214 (*j*) and § 220); for the interjection "O" or "Oh."

In a technical treatise, such as one on Architecture, Photography, Grammar, etc., when a technical term is first introduced and defined, it is usual to print the first letter of every such term in a Capital. As the work proceeds, the use of the Capital may be continued or not at the option of the writer.

CHAPTER XV.—THE NORMAL ORDER OF WORDS.

229. The Rule of Proximity.—The cardinal rule regarding the order of words or phrases is this:—*things which are to be thought of together must be mentioned together.* This has been called the "Rule of Proximity." [1]

In a language like ours which has lost nearly all its inflexions, we usually have nothing but the position of a word to show with what other word or words its sense is to be connected. Observe the faulty order in the following:—

A piano is for sale by a lady about to cross the Channel in an oak case with carved legs.

He blew out his brains after bidding his wife good-bye with a gun.

Erected to the memory of John Phillips accidentally shot as a mark of affection by his brother.

The University of London Commissioners.—*Daily Telegraph*, 6th August 1898. (Say, The London University Commissioners.)

The above is a reproduction of the magnificent picture by the celebrated French artist Benjamin Constant, representing the interior of a carpet bazaar in Tangiers, now in the possession

[1] Bain's *Composition and Rhetoric*, p. 1.

of Messrs. Treloar and Sons, Ludgate Hill.—*Black and White*, 6th August 1898, p. 191.

In an inflected language, like Latin for example, the order of words is of less importance, because the sense is shown by the endings. The following words cannot have more than one meaning. The inflexions leave no choice.

Brut*us* et Cassi*us* Cæsar*em* interfec*erunt*.

The same five words, when translated into English without reference to their Latin inflexions, will give six different senses:—(1) "Brutus slew Cassius and Cæsar," (2) "Cæsar slew Brutus and Cassius," (3) "Cassius slew Cæsar and Brutus," (4) "Brutus and Cassius slew Cæsar," (5) "Cæsar and Brutus slew Cassius," (6) "Cæsar and Cassius slew Brutus."

All that we have to say in this chapter about "the normal order of words" in English consists of the various applications of the Rule of Proximity.

Nouns.

230. Nouns must be placed as near as possible to the nouns or pronouns with which they are connected in sense:—

(1) The death is announced of Dr. Scott, the joint-author with Dr. Liddell of the well-known Greek dictionary.

The only good point in the order of these words is that "joint-author" is placed close to "Dr. Scott," with which it is in apposition. This does not, however, redeem the sentence from clumsiness; for the noun "Scott" ought not to be separated from the noun "death," nor the noun "dictionary" from the noun "author." The sentence might be rewritten thus:—

We regret to announce the death of Dr. Scott, who with Dr. Liddell was the joint-author of the well-known Greek dictionary.

(2) As the leading and consistent champion of the oppressed, I trust you will permit me in your columns to advocate the cause of humanity towards helpless animals.—*To the Editor of the "Daily Telegraph,"* 6th Jan. 1898.

This sentence can be put right by changing "*I trust you will*" to "*you will, I trust.*" As it stands, the noun "champion" is wrongly placed in apposition with the pronoun "I."

Adjectives and Participles.

231. Attributive use.—When an adjective is used attributively (§ 58), it should as a rule be placed *before* the noun that it is intended to qualify:—

A *just* man. *Bright* prospects. *This* rose. *Other* roses.

There is a vast difference between an "English village" and "village English"; and it is the qualifying or adjectival word standing first that decides the meaning. In such examples as the following, however, the position of the adjective is exceptional:—

(*a*) If the adjective is enlarged by some qualifying phrase, it must be placed *after* its noun, to avoid a breach of the "rule of proximity":—

A matter too *urgent* to be put off any longer.

We could not separate *matter* from *urgent* by saying:—

A too urgent to be put off any longer matter.

(*b*) If several adjectives qualify a single noun, it often sounds better to place them *after* the noun than before it:—

God is the maker of all things *visible and invisible, animate and inanimate.*

(*c*) There are certain stock phrases, in which it has become idiomatic (chiefly through the influence of French) to place the adjective after its noun:—

The body *politic.* Malice *prepense.* Heir *apparent.* Lords *Temporal and Spiritual.* Notary *public.* Knight *errant.* Governor *General.* Bishop *elect.* The sum *total.* Point *blank* (the white or blank spot in the centre of a target). Letters *patent.* Price *current.* Lord *paramount.* Durance *vile.* Court *martial*, etc.

Note.—The adjective *alone*, as "he alone," is always placed after the noun or pronoun that it qualifies.

232. Predicative use.—When an adjective is used predicatively (§ 58), it is placed after its noun:—

All men are *mortal.* He lay *dead* on the ground. He became *very rich.* He was left *rich* by his father. (*Subjective Complement*, § 95.)

My father left me *poor*, but *well educated.* The judge declared him *guilty.* (*Objective Complement*, § 95.)

The difference in meaning between the two following sentences hinges on the position of the word "public":—

He made *public* confessions. (*Attrib. use.*)
He made his confessions *public.* (*Predic. use.*)

233. Sometimes an adjective (§ 209, 3) is used instead of an adverb to qualify the predicate-verb of the sentence. In this case it must be placed as near as possible *after* the verb that it qualifies, as in example (*a*) given below:—

(*a*) I can do it *alone.*
(*b*) I *alone* can do it.

Observe that the sense of each sentence depends entirely on the position of the adjective "alone."

(*c*) He bought the material *cheap*.
(*d*) He bought *cheap* material.

In (*c*) "cheap" must be *parsed* as an adjective qualifying the noun "material"; but in point of meaning it qualifies the verb "bought" and signifies "at a low price." The first sentence means that he bought good material at less than the market-price; the second, that he bought inferior material at the market-price.

Adverbs.

234. If the word to be qualified is an Adjective, or an Adverb, or a Preposition, or a Conjunction, the qualifying Adverb is placed immediately *before it*:—

Adjective.—We are *half* pleased and *half* sorry.
Adverb.—He stood *far* apart from me.
Preposition.—He arrived *long* before the time.
Conjunction.—This is *precisely* how it happened.

Note.—But "enough" is placed *after* the adjective that it qualifies, because it is followed by a phrase:—

Your pay is good *enough* for your work.

235. If the Verb to be qualified is *Intransitive*, the Adverb, unless it is one of Time, is placed immediately *after* it:—

He *always* laughed *heartily* at a good joke.
He *never* spoke *boastfully* about his own merits.
He *often* wept *bitterly* on passing that tomb.
He *sometimes* slept *soundly* in my house.
He *seldom* slept *well* in any house but his own.

236. If the Verb to be qualified is *Transitive*, the qualifying Adverb must not be allowed to separate the verb and its object.

The Adverb must therefore be placed either *before the Verb* or (which is rather more common) *after the Object.*

He bore his losses *cheerfully*.
He *briefly* explained his meaning.

But if the Object is qualified by a clause, or consists of a good many words, the adverb may come between the verb and its object:—

He rewarded *liberally* all those who had served him well.

But this is scarcely so idiomatic as, "He liberally rewarded," etc.

237. An Adverb is often placed *between* the Auxiliary verb and the Principal verb (whether Transitive or Intransitive):—

The wind has *suddenly* risen. I have *quite* understood you.

The Negative adverb "*not*" is always placed between the Auxiliary verb and the Principal verb:—

We have *not* seen him since Monday last.

238. An Adverb is placed first in a sentence—(*a*) when it qualifies *the whole sentence*, (*b*) when it is emphatic.

Rewrite the following pairs of sentences, so as to show how the sense depends on the position of the Adverb :—

{ *Happily* he did not die. { *At length* he wrote to her.
{ He did not die *happily*. { He wrote to her *at length*.

239. Divided Infinitives.—An adverb should not be placed between the "to" and the Infinitive. The custom is springing up, but it is not sanctioned by the usage of any good writers :—

I feel it my duty to plainly inform you, etc.
I feel it my duty to inform you plainly, etc.

240. Only.—This adverb must be placed immediately before the word that it is intended to qualify :—

(*a*) *Only* he promised to read the first chapter of that book.

Here "only" is an Adjective, and not an Adverb ; and it qualifies the pronoun "he." *He alone* would be more suitable than *only he*.

He alone, and no one else, promised to read the first chapter, etc.

(*b*) He *only* promised to read the first chapter of that book.

Here "only" is an Adverb qualifying the verb "promised" ; and the meaning is that he merely or only promised, but did not perform the promise.

(*c*) He promised *only* to read the first chapter of that book.

That is, he did not promise to study, analyse, or remember, but *only to read*. Here "only" is an Adverb qualifying the verb "read."

(*d*) He promised to read *only* the first chapter of that book.

That is, he promised to read nothing more than the *first* chapter. Here "only" is an Adverb qualifying the adjective "the first."

(*e*) He promised to read the first chapter of that book *only* (or, *only* of that book).

That is, he promised to read the first chapter of no other book but that. Here "only" is an Adverb qualifying the phrase "of that book."

Note.—At the beginning of a sentence, *only* can have the force of *but* :—

Go wherever you like ; *only* do not stop here.

Subject and Object.

241. The Subject usually precedes its verb ; but the following exceptions should be noted :—

(*a*) When the verb is Intransitive, and is preceded by the introductory adverb "there" ; see § 153 (2).

On the whole *there* is nothing to prove his guilt.

(*b*) When the verb is used for asking a question :—

At what hour in the morning does *he* get up ?

(*c*) When the verb is in the Imperative mood :—

Go *ye* into all the world, and preach the gospel to every creature.

(*d*) To express a wish or a condition :—

Wish { Long live *the king*.
May *he* never again come inside this house.

Condition { Should *he* meet me, he would know me at once.
Had *he* met me, he would have known me.

242. If the Object to a verb is expressed by a Conjunctive pronoun, or is qualified by an Interrogative, it is placed before the verb instead of after it :—

The house *that* we occupy suits us well. (*Conjunctive.*)
What kind of book do you like best? (*Interrogative.*)

243. If the Object is qualified by an Adjective-clause, it may be separated from its verb by an adverbial phrase :—

The captain took *with a thankful heart* the good things which the firm provided.

Nobler and loftier emotions lit up *with a generous enthusiasm* the hearts of men who had heavy sacrifices still to make.

If the italicised phrases were placed at the end of the sentence, the sense would be either obscured or radically altered.

Pronoun and Antecedent.

244. A Conjunctive pronoun or Conjunctive adverb must always be placed as close as possible to its antecedent :—

(1) I have read Plato's writings, who succeeded Socrates.

Here it would have been better to say "the writings *of Plato, who* succeeded," etc.

(2) It is the system, not the individual, which I condemn.

The clause *which I condemn* should be written after *system*.

(3) I now come to one of the objections to free trade, which has never yet been answered.

The sentence can be rewritten thus, "Among the objections to free trade, I now come to one which has never yet been answered."

245. Demonstrative and Conjunctive pronouns should not, as a rule, be mentioned until the Antecedent has been mentioned.

Avoid such an order of words as the following :—

Before we pay *them*, let us see what work *the men* have done.

The proper arrangement would be :—

Before we pay *the men*, let us see what work *they* have done.

Preposition and Object.

246. In prose (not always in poetry) the preposition is placed immediately before its Object. But the following exceptions occur in prose also :—

(*a*) When the Object is "whom," "which," or "what," the preposition *may be* placed last in the sentence and its Object first:—

That is the man *whom* we were looking *for*. (*Conjunctive.*)
Which of these chairs did you sit *on?* (*Interrogative.*)

(*b*) When the Object is the Conjunctive pronoun "that," the preposition *must be* put last:—

This is the man *that* we were looking *for*.

Prepositions.

247. A Preposition must be placed immediately after the word with which it is intended to be construed:—

Books authorised by teachers as fit for use.
Books authorised as fit for use by teachers.

The meaning of each sentence turns entirely upon the position of the phrase *by teachers.*

Correlative Conjunctions.

248. When Conjunctions are used correlatively, that is, in pairs, each member of the pair must invariably be connected with words *of the same part of speech* or *of the same function.*

(1) *Not . . . but*:—

A wise physician endeavours *not* to cure diseases, *but* to prevent them. (*Infinitive mood.*)
Objections were raised *not* to his having spent the money, *but* to his having done so without leave. (*Preposition.*)

(2) *Not only . . . but also* or *but*:—

All his work was done *not only* with zeal, *but also* with judgment. (*Preposition.*)
He was *not only* sad, but *disgusted.* (*Adjective and Participle.*)
This *not only* amused, *but* enlightened them. (*Verb.*)

(3) *Not more . . . than*:—

I am *not more* amused, *than* surprised. (*Participle.*)

(4) *Both . . . and*:—

He is thoroughly tired out *both* in mind *and* in body. (*Preposition.*)

(5) *Either . . . or*, *neither . . . nor*:—

They have worked *either* stupidly *or* lazily. (*Adverb.*)
This wall was built *either* crookedly *or* of bad material. (*Adverb and Adverb-phrase.*)
Neither James *nor* I saw it. (*Noun and Pronoun.*)

Exercise.

Rewrite or rearrange the following sentences in such a way as to remove any impropriety that may exist in the order of the words:—

1. The chair cost ten shillings on which he sat.
2. He shot the mad dog after driving it out of the house with a gun.
3. A gang of robbers entered the house at night armed from head to foot.
4. He is an undoubted man of honesty, and yet persons accused him of cheating who ought to have known him better.
5. This tablet was erected to the memory of a faithful dog that was accidentally shot as a mark of respect.
6. He left the house where he had slept next morning mounted on a horse.
7. He repeated these lines after he had read them only once with perfect accuracy.
8. The judge saw more clearly that the man was innocent than the jury did.
9. The girl was conveyed from the house where she had just been married in a carriage and pair.
10. They found the house on the top of a hill where they wished to spend the night.
11. It is believed that they are most desirous of keeping up this practice who profit most by it.
12. There was a small house on the side of the mountain, out of which came a black slave.
13. The magistrate passed too severe a sentence, being young and inexperienced.
14. English is not only difficult to read, but also to speak.
15. Such were the Centaurs of Ixion's race,
Who a bright cloud for Juno did embrace.
16. The general ordered indignantly the deserters to be shot.
17. I only like a pear when it is ripe.
18. He wisely did this because he was ordered, not because he liked it.
19. Northern India is bounded by the Himalaya mountains, with at their base a very thick jungle.
20. The natives of the other islands only knew how to divide time by the sun and moon, whereas these had acquired some knowledge of the stars.
21. They are as ready, nay more ready, to apply these things to their right uses than we are.
22. I soon arrived at the mansion of my friend, guarded by a huge mastiff that flew at me.
23. He cannot be said to have died prematurely whose work was finished, nor does he deserve to be lamented who died so full of honours.—SOUTHEY.
24. Sir Morton Peto spoke of the notion that the national debt might be repudiated with absolute contempt.
25. An unquestioned man of genius.
26. I am neither an ascetic in theory or practice.
27. Her success is neither the result of system nor strategy.
28. I never remember to have felt an event more deeply than Horner's death.
29. His last journey was to Cannes, whence he was never destined to return.

30. No one has been able to deny that there is a connection between virtue and vice on the one hand and happiness and misery on the other.—*Saturday Review*. 2nd Sept. 1865.

31. All goes on well at Winchester, the attention and attendance gradually deepening and increasing.

32. Since several thoughts may be natural which are low and grovelling, an epic poet should not only avoid such sentiments as are unnatural or affected, but also such as are mean and vulgar.—*Spectator*, No. 279.

33. This shipping is to a great extent now the product of German yards, which have developed rapidly to suit the requirements every day increasing of local shipbuilding.—*Daily Tel.*, 27th Jan. 1898.

34. There are not meanwhile critics wanting here who assign this victory as regards moral and political supremacy in China to Russia. —*Berlin Telegram, Daily Tel.*, 5th Feb. 1898.

35. The sitting closed definitely at five o'clock without the matter which had brought so many together having been practically entered upon.—*Daily Tel.*, 8th Feb. 1898.

36. The death occurred last week in Madrid of Mr. W. Macpherson, formerly British Vice-Consul at Seville.—*Times Weekly*, 11th Feb. 1898.

37. The captain took the good things which the gods provided with thankful good-humour.

38. His daily custom is to tell anecdotes which amuse or excite the company after dinner.

39. Othello seizing a bolster, full of rage and jealousy, smothers Desdemona.

40. Some paintings by lady artists, well worthy of inspection, will be exhibited to-morrow.

41. The daughter of a civil officer retired from India, brought up in England, seeks employment.

42. Lost, a walking-stick belonging to a gentleman, with a curiously shaped head.

43. Here the train made a halt to take in water, which lasted only for a few minutes.

44. He wept in passing that tomb often.

45. Do you take the medicine that I send you regularly?

46. In all scientific books it is necessary to clearly define the technical terms employed.

47. I never remember to have spent a more agreeable visit.

48. Zedekiah was sent captive to Babylon, from which he was never destined to return.

49. His body was found floating lifeless on the water at a short distance from where the boat was upset by a fisherman.

50. No one is entitled to form or express an opinion on the relations between Nelson and Lady Hamilton, or on the parentage of Horatia, who has not carefully studied the letters to be found in this invaluable collection.—*Times Weekly*. 4th March 1898.

51. It will be a war on sea, instead of land, largely, and we do not know much about sea warfare of late years.—Quoted in *Daily Tel.*, 15th April 1898.

52. Right from the birth of a Spanish monarch he is subject to an

etiquette the most pronounced.—*Cassell's Family Magazine*, Jan. 1897, p. 149.

53. For this person to accuse us of want of knowledge can only create amusement in the minds of those who have studied the views and know the facts as I have and do.—*Middlesex County Times*, 30th April 1898.

54. We may well ask what is the use of it, if parallel action in shipbuilding is not accompanied by energetic action in diplomacy? —*Homeward Mail*, 25th July 1898.

55. With regard to the Ottoman bank, the government, in case of its leaving Cyprus, would undertake some measures to replace it.—*Report of Mr. Chamberlain's Speech*, 9th August 1898.

CHAPTER XVI.—INVERSION OF THE NORMAL ORDER: EMPHASIS.

249. Inversion of Normal Order.—In the last chapter we showed what is the normal order of words in a sentence. We have now to show how emphasis may be given to a word by placing it out of the normal order. A word so placed excites surprise, and thereby attracts more attention. But no inversion must be made, if it obscures the meaning or offends the ear.

(1) The Object placed before its verb instead of after it:—

Direct object:—

Silver and gold have I none; but *such as I have* give I unto thee: in the name of Jesus of Nazareth, arise and walk.—*Acts* iii. 6.

If *heaven* I cannot summon to my prayer,
Hell will I move, and try mine interest there.
DRYDEN'S *Virgil*.

The sorrow for the dead is the only sorrow from which we refuse to be divorced. *Every other wound* we seek to heal, *every other affliction* to forget; but *this wound* we consider it a duty to keep open, *this affliction* we cherish and brood over in solitude. —WASHINGTON IRVING.

Indirect object:—

They held their peace, and glorified God, saying, Then *to the Gentiles also* hath God granted repentance unto life.—*Acts* xi. 18.

(2) The Complement placed before its verb instead of after it:—

On Linden, when the sun was low,
All bloodless lay the untrodden snow,
And *dark* as winter was the flow
Of Iser rolling rapidly.—CAMPBELL.

Great is Diana of the Ephesians.—*Acts* xix. 28.

Immense is the attention that the government in France is devoting to the Zola trial.—*Daily Tel.*, 16th Feb. 1898.

Fallen, fallen is Babylon, the great city.[1]—*Rev.* xviii. 2.

(3) Adverb or Adverbial phrase placed first :—

Not at once was language adequate to receive or take up into itself the ideas that were asking for expression.—JOWETT.

On these two commandments hang all the law and the prophets.—*Matt.* xxii. 40.

In thy presence is fulness of joy ; *at thy right hand* there are pleasures for evermore.—*Psalms* xvi. 11.

(4) The Verb placed first (rare except in poetry) :—

Every man has left behind him influences for good or evil that will never exhaust themselves. It may be his fireside, it may be a kingdom ; it may be a village or a great nation ; but *act* he does, ceaselessly and for ever.—CUMMING.

Flashed all their sabres bare,
Flashed as they turned in air.—TENNYSON.

(5) Adverb with verb placed first :—

Thus came into prominence what are called sacred and profane knowledge : *thus came into the presence of each other* two opposing parties, one relying on reason, the other on revelation. —DRAPER.

Then burst his mighty heart.—SHAKSPEARE.

Up goes my grave Impudence to the maid.—*Tatler.*

(6) Adjective or Adjectival phrase placed after its noun :—

I appeal from Philip *drunk* to Philip *sober*.
Alfred *the Great*. Pliny *the Elder*. Pliny *the Younger*.

I will talk of things *heavenly* or things *earthly ;* things *moral* or things *evangelical ;* things *sacred* or things *profane ;* things *past* or things *to come ;* things *foreign* or things *at home ;* things *essential* or things *circumstantial ;* provided that all be done to our profit.—BUNYAN.

I love thee, Cassio,
But nevermore be officer *of mine.*—SHAKSPEARE.

250. Emphatic Positions.—The middle of a sentence is less emphatic than the beginning, and the beginning in most cases is less emphatic than the end.

---

[1] This is the rendering given in the Revised Translation, 1885. In the translation of 1611 the wording is far less pointed.

Babylon is fallen, is fallen, that great city.

Compare what Horace puts into the mouth of Hannibal :—

Occidit, occidit,
Spes omnis et fortuna nostri
Nominis, Asdrubale interempto.—Ode iv. 4, 70.

"Fallen, fallen are all our hopes and our fortune ; for Hasdrubal is slain."

(*a*) *The beginning.*—If we take a word out of its normal order in order to place it first, the emphasis that it acquires arises partly from the surprise excited by its unusual position, and partly from the prominence that naturally belongs to the initial word. This has been exemplified already in § 249.

The subject of a sentence is usually placed first, because that is its normal order. In this position it possesses a certain degree of prominence, because it names the person or thing about which the assertion is made.

Romulus, according to the ancient legend, founded Rome.

If that degree of prominence, however, happens not to be sufficient, additional emphasis can be given to the subject "Romulus" by placing it last:—

Rome, according to the ancient legend, was founded by Romulus.
The founder of Rome, according to the ancient legend, was Romulus.

(*b*) *The end.*—The end of a sentence is more emphatic than the beginning, because one's mind is held in suspense till we know the closing circumstance, and our interest is aroused to know what that circumstance is. This is called the PRINCIPLE OF SUSPENSE.

(1) Add to your faith *virtue;* and to virtue *knowledge;* and to knowledge *temperance;* and to temperance *patience;* and to patience *godliness;* and to godliness *brotherly kindness;* and to brotherly kindness *charity.*—2 *Peter* i. 5-7.

(2) Knowing that you are very inquisitive after everything that is curious in nature, I will wait on you *in the dusk of the evening with my show upon my back.*—*Spectator*, No. 271.

Here the emphatic phrases, the first of which shows the time of coming, and the second the purpose of coming, are rightly placed last.

Corollary.—If we do not wish a word to be emphatic, we must avoid placing it in an emphatic position.

That all members of the same household should live together in peace is necessary.
He, deserted by his friends and pursued by his enemies, fled from the country.

The undue emphasis given in one sentence to the word "necessary," and in the other to "he" can be avoided by altering their positions:—

It is necessary that all members of the same household should live together in peace.
Deserted by his friends, and pursued by his enemies, he fled from the country.

251. Correlative Conjunctions and Phrases.—Conjunctions and phrases which go in pairs add to the energy of a sentence, because the first one keeps the mind in suspense (§ 250, *b*) till the second one has been mentioned :—

Either—or	Partly—partly	On the one hand—on the other hand
Neither—nor	In the first place—in the second place	Though—yet
Not only—but also	On this side—on that side	As—so
Both—and	Here—there	Indeed—but
If—then	Not—but	

(1) The use of language is to conceal the thoughts.

To emphasise *conceal*, we could say :—"The use of language is not to express, but to conceal the thoughts."

(2) I regard the prospects of peace with confidence.

To emphasise *confidence* we could say :—"I regard the prospects of peace not only with hope, but with confidence."

(3) He is both a fool and a knave.

To emphasise *fool* we should say :—"He is not only a knave, but also a fool" ; or, "He is a fool as well as a knave." To emphasise *knave*, we should say :—"He is not only a fool, but also a knave" ; or "He is a knave as well as a fool."

252. Emphasis by Repetition.—Emphasis is sometimes added to a word by repeating it, or by adding some other word almost synonymous. Repetition, when it adds force, is "not like a bird flapping its wings uselessly in the air, but like a blacksmith repeating his blows on an anvil" (Nichol).

If I were an American, as I am an Englishman, I never would lay down my arms, *never—never—never.*—BURKE.

Christ being raised from the dead dieth no more ; *death hath no more dominion over him.*—*New Test.*

Our language abounds in phrases, in which words of the same or almost the same meaning go in pairs.

They were driven out *bag and baggage.* He works only by *fits and starts.* His progress is by *leaps and bounds.* He was *fair and square* in all his dealings. Words full of *fire and fury.* He is a stickler for *forms and ceremonies.* He is *free and easy* in his manners. His presence is *gall and wormwood* to me. Where are my *goods and chattels?* He took to it *heart and soul.* He is very *high and mighty.* Turned out of *house and home.* To all *intents and purposes.* Eager for the *loaves and fishes* of office. He would not yield one *jot or tittle.* His will is *null and void.* Over *head and ears* in debt. The *pains and penalties* of the law. He arrived *safe and sound.* All *stuff and nonsense.* *Time and tide* wait for no man. If you do this, *well and good.* This is my *will and pleasure.* He worked with *might and main.* Drenched *through and through.* *First and foremost* be truthful.

253. "It is," "it was."—These introductory phrases are much used for giving prominence to the word that the writer wishes to emphasise (see § 75, *c*).

(1) Romulus, according to the ancient legend, founded Rome.

If "Romulus" is not sufficiently emphatic as it stands, we could say:—"*It was* Romulus who, according to the ancient legend, founded Rome."

(2) Cicero admired Pompey.

These words stand in their normal order, and one is not more emphatic than the other. Each in turn might be emphasised as follows:—"It was Cicero who admired Pompey;" "It was admiration, not blame, that Cicero expressed for Pompey;" "It was Pompey whom Cicero admired."

254. Conjunctions and Prepositions repeated.—If we wish to give equal emphasis to each word in a series of particulars, we can do so by repeating the conjunctions or prepositions before each of them instead of mentioning it once only before the first or last.

Now, brethren, if I come unto you speaking with tongues, what shall I profit you, except I shall speak to you *either by* revelation, *or by* knowledge, *or by* prophesying, *or by* doctrine?—1 *Cor.* xiv. 6.

The latter part of this sentence would sound very feeble in comparison if it stood thus:—"Except I shall speak to you by revelation, knowledge, prophesying, or doctrine."

255. Recapitulation of Clauses.—A series of subjects or clauses can be recapitulated by the use of pronouns like "these" or "such"; and this adds to the energy of the sentence.

Intellect, imagination, power of expression, humour, taste, truth to life, and truth to human nature,—*these* are not the qualities which to-day make a writer popular."—*Fort. Rev.*, Feb. 1898, p. 280.

The storm had passed, the sun was shining on the green leaves of the trees; the stream was dancing around the rocks; the birds hopped about him as they chirped with their cheerful notes;—*such* were the pleasant scenes and sounds that welcomed the wanderer back to his home.

256. Antithesis.—Antithesis means "setting one word against another," like balancing opposite things against each other in a pair of scales. The balance of form and sound not only pleases the ear, but is an aid to memory, as we may gather from its frequent use in proverbs, and in the best-remembered sayings of great authors:—"It never rains, but it pours;" "A bird in the hand is worth two in the bush;" "Evil communications corrupt good manners;" "The Sabbath was made for man, not man for the Sabbath."

> God, who at sundry times and in divers manners, spake in time past unto the fathers by the prophets, hath in these last days spoken unto us by his Son, whom he hath appointed heir of all things, by whom also he made the worlds.—*Hebrews* i. 1, 2.

The antithesis of this finely balanced sentence is marred in the Revised Version of 1885, where it is made to run as follows:—

> God, having of old time spoken unto the fathers in the prophets by divers portions and in divers manners, hath at the end of these days spoken unto us in his Son, whom he appointed heir of all things, through whom also he made the worlds.

Exercises.

I. *Rearrange, or if necessary supplement or rewrite, the following sentences so as to throw the emphasis on certain words as directed:—*

1. I am not sure he said that. (Emphasise (1) *sure*, (2) *he*, (3) *said*, (4) *that*, (5) *I*.)
2. They brought home her dead warrior. (Emphasise *home*.)
3. No man hath greater love than this. (Emphasise *greater love*.)
4. Consummate men of business are almost as rare as great poets, and perhaps rarer than veritable saints and martyrs.—HELPS. (Emphasise *rare* and *rarer*.)
5. The battle of Hastings was fought in 1066. (Emphasise (1) *the battle of Hastings*, (2) *in 1066*.)
6. A greater mistake was never made. (Emphasise *never*.)
7. Thou didst not anoint mine head with oil.—*New Testament*. (Emphasise *mine head with oil*.)
8. The wind blows keen, and the night is coming on. (Emphasise *keen*.)
9. If I have told you earthly things, and ye believe not, how shall ye believe if I tell you of heavenly things. (Emphasise *earthly* and *heavenly*.)
10. When all were seated, a noise was suddenly heard outside. (Emphasise *suddenly*.)
11. Moses led the children of Israel out of Egypt. (Emphasise (1) *Moses*, (2) *the children of Israel*, (3) *Egypt*.)
12. The reign of Constantine marks the epoch of the transformation of Christianity from a religion into a political system. (Emphasise *the reign of Constantine*.)
13. All classes of the population did not with equal rapidity adopt monotheistic views. (Emphasise (1) *not with equal rapidity*, (2) *all classes of the population*.)
14. All parties in the Roman commonwealth concurred in appointing Quintus Fabius to the command of the Roman forces against Hannibal. (Emphasise (1) *all parties*, (2) *Quintus Fabius*, (3) *concurred*.)
15. Nature conciliates and forms the mind of man to his condition. —GOLDSMITH. (Emphasise *mind*.)

II. *Give some additional point to the following sentences by a change of order, or by a change of words, or by any other means*:—

1. Which of you by taking thought can add one cubit to his stature? (cf. *Matt.* vi. 27 with *Luke* xii. 25).

2. The government prosecuted Watson for high treason and were defeated; had they indicted him for aggravated assault, they would have obtained a conviction.

3. The authors of a revolution are not like those whom the revolution produces.

4. Tully was the first who observed that friendship improves happiness and abates misery by the doubling of our joy and dividing of our grief; a thought in which he has been followed by all the essayers upon friendship, that have written since his time.—*Spectator*, No. 68.

5. A clever magistrate would see whether a witness was deliberately lying a great deal better than a stupid jury.

6. The air last night condensed the vapour into white particles, but was not cold enough to turn them into actual hoar-frost.

7. Nothing in this war threatened our interests more than the interests of other countries.

8. A coxcomb, flushed with victories over the fair young creatures whom he has deceived, will protest and vow he never thought of matrimony, and wonder talking civilly could be so strangely misinterpreted.—*Spectator*, No. 288.

9. Nor is the reason that has led to the establishment of this moral law difficult to be discerned.

10. In our search after God and contemplation of Him our wisdom doth consist; in our worship and obedience to Him our religion doth consist; in both of them our happiness doth consist.

11. It is not without a degree of patient attention, greater than the generality are willing to bestow, though not greater than the object deserves, that the habit can be acquired of examining and judging of our own conduct with the same accuracy and impartiality as that of another.

12. Every man calleth that which pleaseth and is delightful to himself good, and that evil which displeaseth him.

13. Our Berlin correspondent telegraphs that in diplomatic circles there confidence is placed in no reports about the Chinese loan.—*Daily Telegraph*, 8th Feb. 1898.

14. In the last few hours that preceded his death he was only able to make a few audible sounds, and no one understood them.

15. In this evil world guilt has a better chance than misfortune of being treated with indulgence.

16. He that tells a lie is not sensible how great a task he undertakes; for he must invent twenty more to maintain one.

CHAPTER XVII.—STRUCTURE OF SENTENCES.

257. Rule of Proximity.—Subordinate clauses are subject to the Rule of Proximity (§ 229) to the same extent as the various parts of speech and the corresponding phrases. A construction which violates this principle is called by the French *construction louche*, "a squinting construction"; or to adopt the more homely English phrase, "One eye is fixed on the kettle, while the other is looking up the chimney."

(*a*) *Noun-clause.*—A Noun-clause must be placed as close as possible to the verb or noun to which it belongs by grammatical relation :—

> Mr. J. S. Chapple points out in reference to our remark last week, that, with the exception of Sir G. Scott, no other architect of our time has erected a cathedral, that Mr. W. Burgess erected St. Fin Barré's Cathedral at Cork in the year 1862.—*Church Times*, 23rd Dec. 1897.

The chief fault of this slovenly sentence lies in the fact that it separates the object from its verb by a block of twenty-five words, and this without any necessity whatever. The sentence could easily have been arranged as follows :—

> In reference to our remark last week that, with the exception of Sir G. Scott, no architect of our time has erected a cathedral, Mr. J. S. Chapple points out that Mr. W. Burgess, etc.

(*b*) *Adverb-clause.*—An Adverb-clause must be placed as close as possible to the word that it qualifies :—

> He imprudently put all his money in that concern, as the event showed.

The adverbial clause "as the event showed" is intended to qualify and explain the adverb *imprudently*, and should therefore be placed immediately after it.

> Imprudently, as the event showed, he put all his money in that concern.

To take another example :—

> All this is meant to open the eyes of the Chinese, and to cause them to accept each and every claim that we make upon them as soon as possible.—*Daily Telegraph*, 3rd Jan. 1898.

The clause or phrase *as soon as possible* should have been placed immediately after the verb *accept*, since it is not intended to qualify the verb *make*.

(*c*) *Adjective-clause.*—The position of such clauses is determined by the rule laid down in § 244, that a Conjunctive pronoun or Conjunctive adverb must be placed as close as possible to its Antecedent.

258. **Rule of Priority.**—The Rule of Proximity is supplemented by another—the Rule of Priority.[1] According to this rule, qualifying clauses should, as far as possible, precede the clause or words to which they are subordinate.

---

[1] Bain's *Rhetoric and Composition*, p. 1.

The principle underlying this rule is that the mind of the reader is by this means *kept in suspense* (see § 250, *b*). His interest is aroused to know what is coming, and when it does come, it comes with the greater force. The final or principal clause thus receives the emphasis that it ought to have.

(1) *Ghost.* If ever thou didst thy dear father love,
Hamlet. O heaven!
Ghost. Avenge his foul and most unnatural murder.

Observe how the effect of this dialogue would have been marred, if the order of the clauses had been reversed. Observe, too, how the interest of Hamlet has been awakened by the suspensive influence of the conditional clause. This is shown by the exclamation, "O heaven!"

(2) Though I speak with the tongues of men and of angels, and have not charity, I am become as sounding brass, or a tinkling cymbal.—1 *Cor.* xiii. 1.

Compare with this well-arranged sentence the following extract from Bacon, in which the limiting clause is awkwardly put last:—

A crowd is not company, and faces are but a gallery of pictures, and talk but a tinkling cymbal, where there is no love.

259. Qualifying Phrases.—What is true of subordinate clauses is no less true of qualifying phrases also. These, for the sake of their *suspensory influence*, should, whenever the idiom of our language allows it, be placed before, and not after, the word that they qualify.

A man who has mortgaged his estate up to almost its full value has, *to all intents and purposes,* ceased to be the owner of it.

This is very much better than saying, "Has ceased to be the owner of it to all intents and purposes."

In the following sentence[1] the Rule of Priority and that of Proximity are both neglected:—

With this small force the general determined to attack the foe, flushed with recent victory and rendered negligent by success.

The proper collocation would be as follows:—

Flushed with recent victory and rendered negligent by success, the general determined with this small force to attack the foe.

260. Sentences Periodic or Loose.—In point of structure sentences have been subdivided into two main classes—the Periodic and the Loose.

A Periodic sentence (called also a Period) is one that keeps the meaning in suspense and is not grammatically complete until the close.

[1] Quoted from Abbott's *How to Write Clearly,* p. 31.

A Loose sentence is one that continues running on after grammatical completeness has been reached, and when we think the sentence has come to an end. The distinction applies to simple sentences no less than to complex ones.[1]

Loose.	*Periodic.*
(1) We came to our journey's end at last, ‖ with no small difficulty, after much fatigue, through deep roads and in bad weather.	(1) At last, with no small difficulty and after much fatigue, we came, through deep roads and in bad weather, to our journey's end.
(2) This was forbidden by good taste ‖ as well as by judgment.	(2) This was forbidden *both* by good taste and by judgment.
(3) This disposition saves him from offending his opponents, ‖ and also from alienating his supporters.	(3) This disposition saves him from offending his opponents *on the one hand*, and from alienating his supporters on the other.
(4) He kept himself alive with the fish he caught, ‖ or with the goats he shot.	(4) He kept himself alive *either* with the fish he caught or with the goats he shot.
(5) The world is not eternal, ‖ nor is it the result of chance.	(5) The world is *neither* eternal, nor the result of chance.
(6) The Romans consider religion a part of virtue, ‖ the Jews virtue a part of religion.	(6) *While* the Romans consider religion a part of virtue, the Jews, *on the contrary*, consider virtue a part of religion.
(7) His actions were frequently criticised, ‖ but his character was above criticism.	(7) *Though* his actions were frequently criticised, his character was above criticism.
(8) His word may be as good as his bond, ‖ but we have still to ask how good his bond is.	(8) *Granting that* his word is as good as his bond, we have still to ask how good his bond is.

In the examples given on the left side of the table, the double stroke shows where the sentence could have stopped without leaving any sense of incompleteness in the mind of the reader. Up to that point the sentence is a Period. In the examples given on the right side, the word or phrase, by which the interest of the reader is held in suspense and the sentence changed from Loose to Periodic, is indicated by italics.

The distinguishing mark of a Period, then, is that *the mind is kept in suspense* (§ 250) until the sentence comes to an end. From the above examples it will be seen that suspense can be produced in four different ways at least, and there may be more :—

---

[1] The table of examples is quoted from Carpenter's *Exercises in Rhetoric* (Macmillan and Co., New York, 1894), p. 99. This author refers to Hill's *Principles of Rhetoric*, p. 153. I find, however, that the first, the fourth, and the sixth examples are from Whately's *Rhetoric*, p. 206.

(*a*) By putting adverbial or qualifying phrases before, and not after, the word that they are intended to qualify, as in example (1), (see § 259).

(*b*) By using correlative words and phrases, as in examples (2), (3), (4), (5). See remarks in § 251.

(*c*) By putting subordinate clauses before the main clause, as in examples (6) and (7), (see § 258).

(*d*) By using participial phrases, and making them precede the subject of the sentence, as in example (8).

261. Advantages of the Period.—In point of energy the Period has in most cases the advantage over Loose sentences. When we meet with qualifying clauses or phrases, our tendency is to look forwards rather than backwards. Our interest is thus roused to know what is coming. The Loose sentence is less stimulating and often disappointing. "An unexpected continuation of a sentence, which the reader had supposed to be concluded, is apt to produce in the mind a sensation of being disagreeably balked, analogous to the unpleasant jar which is felt when, in ascending or descending a flight of stairs, we meet with one step more than we had expected" (Whately).

> Shaftesbury's strength lay in reasoning and sentiment more than in description, however much his descriptions have been admired.[1]

When this Loose sentence has been converted into a Period, the reader will at once perceive how much the energy is increased.

> However much Shaftesbury's descriptions have been admired, his strength lay not so much in description as in reasoning and sentiment.

262. Occasional Inconvenience of the Period.—On the other hand, the Loose sentence, though its name implies something of reproach, is at times very useful, and many sentences would be spoilt rather than improved by an attempt to coerce them into Periods.

> (1) As the sun at this time of the year sets as early as four o'clock, we had better start at once, if we are to get to our journey's end in daylight.

Here the rhythm is improved by placing the principal clause between the two subordinate clauses that qualify it. Moreover, the first subordinate clause does not give a full explanation of the reason for starting at once, and hence the second one does not come as "a disagreeable surprise."

[1] Bain's *Rhetoric and Composition*, p. 55.

(2) Through great, low-lying fields of golden grain, over which the evening breezes swept with impetuous speed, blending the radiant yellow of the corn and the bright blood-red of the poppies in a glorious arabesque of gold and green and scarlet, the river stole.[1]

This sentence exemplifies the abuse of the Periodic style. The sentence would be greatly improved by commencing with "the river stole." Undue emphasis is given to the word "stole" by placing it last.

A Period may be so clumsily constructed that, in spite of the Periodic character being sustained to the very close, the reader's attention is never once roused. The following is an example :—

The reflections of such men are so delicate upon all occurrences which they are concerned in, that they should be exposed to more than ordinary infamy and punishment for offending against such quick admonitions as their own souls give them, and blunting the fine edge of their minds in such a manner that they are no more shocked at vice and folly than men of slower capacities.—*Spectator*, No. 6.

263. Rule of Unity.—Every clause or other part of a sentence should be made subservient to the unfolding of one leading thought. This is called the Rule of Unity. If several leading thoughts are thrown together, the sentence containing them should be distributed into as many separate sentences as there are leading thoughts. In point of grammatical accuracy, the string of thoughts may be "as coherent as a string of sausages ; but sausages to be eaten must be separated" (Hodgson).

(1) On looking back (at the House of Commons as it was thirty or forty years ago), I do think that in the past, in spite of angry controversy, there was not the vulgar personality which is now sometimes heard *with regret*.—*Fort. Rev.*, Feb. 1898, p. 250.

The Unity of this sentence is marred by the two last words. The sentence should have ended with "heard." The regret expressed is irrelevant. Moreover, it renders the sentence ambiguous ; for it might mean that vulgar personality is not always, but only sometimes, to be regretted. It might also mean that the angry controversies of a former day were not to be regretted, only the vulgar personality of the present day. There would be no breach of Unity and no consequent ambiguity, if the last clause were reworded thus : "which (we regret to say) is now sometimes heard."

(2) But now we must admit the shortcomings, the fallacies, the defects, as no less essential elements in forming a sound judgment as to whether the seer and artist were so united in him as to justify the claim first put in by himself and afterwards

[1] Carpenter's *Exercises in Rhetoric*, p. 103.

maintained by his sect to a place beside the few great poets, who exalt men's minds and give a right direction and safe outlet to the passions through the imagination, while insensibly helping them towards balance of character and serenity of judgment by stimulating their sense of proportion, form, and the nice adjustment of means to ends.[1]—LOWELL, *Among my Books.*

In all this jungle of words there seem to be at least two leading questions: (1) What are the claims of some one to be ranked among the few great poets? (2) What are the characteristics of a great poet? If this supposition is correct, there ought to be two sentences at least, which might be stated as follows:—

If we wish to form a sound judgment as to whether the seer and (the) artist were so united in him as to justify the claim, first put in by himself and afterwards maintained by his sect, to a place among the few great poets of our nation, his shortcomings, fallacies, and defects must be taken into account no less than his merits. By "great poets" we mean those men of exceptional genius who exalt men's minds and give a right direction and safe outlet to the passions through the imagination, while insensibly helping, etc., of means to ends.

Even now the second sentence is very ungainly. The first one is guilty of the omission of "the" before "artist." We have inserted "the" to save the sentence from being ungrammatical (see § 186, *a*).

264. Use of Parentheses.—A *short* parenthesis, if it is needed for explanatory purposes or to express a passing comment, may be admitted, but not otherwise. A *long* parenthesis constitutes too glaring a breach of Unity, and is not admissible on any terms.

Short parenthesis: admissible.

This gentleman (for I found he was treated as such by his audience) was entertaining a whole table of listeners with the project of an opera.—*Spectator*, No. 31.

By that one act a final stamp was given, not to Russian "policy." —that is far too limited an expression,—but to Russian evolution in Asia.—*Blackwood's Magazine*, Feb. 1898.

Long parenthesis: inadmissible.

This ill-favoured fraternity consists of a president and twelve fellows, the choice of which (?) is not confined by patent to any particular foundation (as St. John's men would have the world believe and have therefore erected a separate society within themselves), but liberty is left to elect from any school in Great Britain, provided the candidates be within the rules of the club as set forth in a table entitled the Act of Deformity, a clause or two of which I shall transmit to you.—*Spectator*, No 17.

[1] Hodgson's *Errors in English*, p. 186.

Exercises.

I.—*Convert the following Loose sentences into Periods*:—

1. She was a phantom of delight,
When first she gleamed upon my sight.

2. Murder has no tongue, but it will speak.

3. The responsibility of managing such a large business was more than he could bear, as he had not been trained in book-keeping and office-accounts.

4. English may claim to be called the universal language, if any language deserves to be so called.

5. The order of nobility was exceedingly numerous in France before the outbreak of the Revolution, since all the children of a nobleman belonged to the class of their father, and the class was continually increased by the creation of new nobles.

6. Little good will be effected, notwithstanding the exertions that public-spirited individuals may make to dispel the ignorance and raise the moral tone of the lower orders, without the cordial co-operation of the government.

7. During his long imprisonment he was harassed with many bitter reflections, deprived of the consolations of friendship by the cruelty of the tyrant.

8. There was nothing out of place inside the house or outside.

9. William the Conqueror laid waste a tract of thirty square leagues in Hampshire, to make space for the New Forest, as it is still called.

10. On that occasion the men in the street behaved in a very unruly manner, and it was found necessary to read the Riot Act.

11. He has many irons in the fire and his affairs are getting into disorder.

12. I found all the shops closed next morning, as I went down the street.

13. We no longer understand the language of our stage, insomuch that I have often been afraid, when I have seen our Italian performers chattering in the vehemence of action, that they have been calling us names and abusing us among themselves.—*Spectator*, No. 18.

II. *Reconstruct the following sentences so as to enforce the rule of Proximity, or the rule of Priority, or the rule of Unity. If no rearrangement is considered necessary, give your reason*:—

1. He returned to England in 1839, and next year he was persuaded to enter Parliament, but he soon lost his seat, and then he retired, and resumed his literary studies, and died suddenly in 1849.

2. To cut a long story short, I pulled the labouring oar for a few years, and saw every class of business, and earned money enough to keep me, till I found myself man enough to sail my own ship, and I stayed in Parliament Street for forty years.—*Fortnightly Review*, Feb. 1898, p. 240.

3. The improved revenue is due to a steady and uniform increase in demand for the products of the company, as will be gathered from the statement that sales for the thirteen and one-third months just

completed exceed by 88·15 per cent the sales of the twelve months ended 30th June 1896.—*Daily Telegraph*, 1st Feb. 1898.

4. Mrs. Jennings entered the drawing-room where Elinor was sitting by herself, with an air of such hurrying importance as prepared her to hear something wonderful.—MISS AUSTEN.

5. I may, however, again state that the security was ample, and that I urged upon the Foreign Office that there were the strongest reasons in the interest of British trade and commerce, and of the position and influence of Great Britain in China, for the government most seriously considering the proposal.—*Daily Telegraph*, 7th Jan. 1898.

6. The very landlord's agent, who has been giving you all the landlord side of the question, when you come to the subject of evictions, breaks away and becomes an Irishman.

7. As a man must have no slavish fears and apprehensions hanging upon his mind, who will indulge the flights of fancy or speculation, and push his researches into the abstruse corners of truth, so it is necessary for him to have about him a competency of all the conveniences of life.—*Spectator*, No. 287.

8. Besides poverty and want there are other reasons that debase the minds of men who live under slavery, though I look on this as the principal.—*Spectator*, No. 287.

9. The prospect of being guillotined seemed to be singularly disagreeable to him, though he had helped a multitude of people to find that road out of the world with the utmost composure.

10. To the future of the agricultural labourer he looks forward with confidence, if the labourer will only be true to himself.—*Times Weekly*, 21st Dec. 1898.

11. Neither I nor they should wear handcuffs and see the inside of a jail, if I could help it.—JOSEPH ARCH.

12. In Prussia, nothing goes down with the public, that is to say, there is no independence of action or judgment, unless the crown or the government leads the way.—*Daily Telegraph*, 28th Jan. 1898.

13. It would, in my opinion, be scarcely possible to spend the public money for a better or more patriotic purpose, provided the movement is kept strictly undenominational.—LORD ROBERTS, 4th Feb. 1898.

14. Cutting our way through the undergrowth, we crept and clambered down the slippery slopes, till we reached the bottom of the glen and came to a moss-covered rock, from which a tiny spring issues and has made a pool below.—*The Niger Sources*, TROTTER.

15. And it is also pleasant to have heard Lord Lyndhurst, when ninety years of age, the son of Copley Fielding, who was born at Boston, U.S.A., an English subject before the Independence of America, speaking on a Canadian question, and his voice ringing as clearly as a bell.—*Fortnightly Review*, Feb. 1898, p. 250.

16. The political morality of the nation was undermined in the reign of Queen Anne by the corrupt practices of the court and the ministers, and not, as has been asserted, by the quarrels between Whigs and Tories, which involved some degree at least of political principle.

17. After a smooth and on the whole enjoyable voyage, the last

part of which was through the cooler air of the Arabian Sea, we landed at Bombay, which is still suffering from the plague.

18. It is not without a degree of patient attention and persevering diligence greater than the generality are willing to bestow, though not greater than the object deserves, that the habit can be acquired of examining and judging of our own conduct with the same accuracy and impartiality as that of another.

19. Close upon two-thirds of the present work are devoted to the writer's earlier career in the northern hemisphere, and of the remainder, two chapters tell of his visits to Europe during his colonial career, although his public life in Europe extended only from 1836 to 1855, while his colonial career occupied close upon a quarter of a century. But the proportion is not perhaps ill-adjusted. —*Times Weekly*, 11th Feb. 1898, p. 92.

20. Natural historians tells us that no fruit grows originally among us, besides hips and haws, acorns and pig-nuts, with other delicacies of the like nature. —ADDISON.

21. At the same time, it was impossible to disprove the fact that there was a large body of lay public opinion in Ireland drawn from that section of the Catholics who could send their sons to a University, who were suffering a very serious educational disability.—*Mr. Lecky's Speech*, 17th Feb. 1898.

22. Mr. Ph. protested against people in the provinces, who, when they wanted a recreation ground, had themselves to pay for it, being taxed for the maintenance of the Royal Parks, which were really pleasure grounds for Londoners.—*Daily Telegraph*, 19th April 1898.

23. What! That there should be a return to fanaticism, an attempt to light up a religious war in this epoch of ours, one hundred years after the Revolution, in the heart of our great Paris, in the days of democracy, of universal toleration, at the very time when there is an immense movement being made everywhere towards equality, justice, and fraternity!—ZOLA.

24. The working of democratic institutions means one long training in enlightened altruism, one continual weighing of those larger experiences on which all successful conduct of social life depends, not of the advantage of the particular act to the particular individual at the particular moment.—WEBB, *Studies in Democracy*.

25. The will, in the testator's own handwriting, bears date 4th November 1871, of the Rev. Charles L. Dodgson (Lewis Carroll), student of Christ Church, Oxford, author of *Alice in Wonderland* and other works, who died at the Chestnuts, Guildford, on January 14th last, aged sixty-five years.—*Daily Telegraph*, 17th May 1898.

26. In the first place, there will be a derangement of business, which had just begun to emerge from a long and ruinous depression, which must affect most deeply every legitimate industry and employment that belongs to a time of peace.—Quoted in *Daily Telegraph*, 15th April 1898.

CHAPTER XVIII.—PURITY OF DICTION.

265. Purity defined.—When we speak of "pure air," "pure gold," or "pure water," we mean air, gold, or water that has been cleared of all extraneous matter. Similarly, when we speak of "pure language," we mean language that has been cleared of all extraneous words and phrases. In this definition any word or phrase that does not belong to *reputable*, *national*, and *present* use is considered "extraneous."

Lord Chesterfield, in writing to his son, gave him the following advice regarding the choice of words:—"The first thing you should attend to is to speak whatever language you do speak in its greatest purity and according to the rules of grammar; for we must never offend against grammar, nor make use of words that are *not really words*."

Not really words—as the dross in ore is not really metal. The dross of language consists of the following kinds of extraneous matter:—

(1) Vulgarisms,—words or phrases that should be avoided even in conversation; such words are not "reputable."

(2) Colloquialisms,—words or phrases admissible in conversation, but not "reputable" enough for use in written composition, except in the dialogues of novels or in correspondence between friends and equals.

(3) Provincialisms,—words confined to some particular province or locality, and used chiefly by the lower classes; these cannot be considered either "national" or "reputable."

(4) Technical words,—used in professional or didactic manuals, but not used in general literature, and not generally understood; such words are "reputable" among the specialists who understand them, but they are not "national."

(5) Obsolete words,—such words are barred by the rule of Purity, because they are not "present"; and they are not "national," because they are not generally understood.

(6) Foreign words,—appropriate in their own language, but not naturalised in ours; such words are obviously not "national."

(7) Newly-coined words,—candidates for becoming "national," "reputable," and "present," but not established so far, and perhaps not deserving to become so.

Note.—Purity carried to an excess is called *purism*. Thus Macaulay says of Fox:—"He purified his language with a scrupulosity unknown to any purist."

266. Vulgarisms.—It may be difficult to draw the line between Vulgarisms, *i.e.* words or phrases to be avoided at all times, and Colloquialisms, *i.e.* words or phrases admissible in dialogue or in correspondence between friends and equals.

Such words or phrases as the following we place among the former class :—

Kid for "child." *That angry* for "so angry." *You bet* for "you may bet anything you like." *Awfully* for "very." *He don't* for "he doesn't). *Too utterly utter*. *Quite plenty* for "amply sufficient." *Kick the bucket* for "die." To *sleep* five persons and *eat* ten ("find sleeping-room for five and table-room for ten").

267. Colloquialisms need not be exemplified at length. When used at the proper time and place, they are considered to give zest to conversation. Others use them, because they will not take the trouble to think of the proper words. Others use them very sparingly or not at all. The safest example to follow is the last.

Peckish for "hungry." To be *sat upon* for "blamed," "censured." *Do the handsome thing* for "act a liberal or generous part." *Dance attendance* for "go backwards and forwards to meet some one, who takes his own time for seeing you." *Boss* for "head man." *Fluke* for "lucky stroke." *Out of sheer cussedness* for "without any reasonable purpose." *Masher* for "lady-killer." *Put on the haw-haw* for "assume an air of great personal importance." *End in smoke* for "have no tangible result," "come to nothing," etc. *Jiffy* for "instant."

268. Provincialisms.—Our earlier literature was in three markedly distinct dialects,—the Northern, the Midland, and the Southern. Provincialisms that have come down from dialects are *old* English rather than *bad* English. For instance, if we happen to hear *vixen* still used by rustics for the female of *fox*, or *stag* for the male of any animal, even of a *duck*, or *ourn* for *ours*, or *childern* for *children*, this is merely a survival of correct language, which has become antiquated and provincial.

The poems of Burns, and the dialogues in some of Scott's novels, are among the most recent specimens of the Northern dialect. The Lincolnshire dialect (chiefly Northern) is seen in Tennyson's *Northern Farmer;* the Southern in Barnes's *Dorsetshire Poems;* Cockney dialect in some of the conversations in Dickens's novels.

269. Technical Terms.—Such terms are avoided by good writers, if the book is intended for general, and not professional, readers. "I have often wondered," says Addison, "how Mr. Dryden could translate a passage out of Virgil after the following manner :—

Tack to the larboard and stand off to sea,
Veer starboard sea and land.

"Milton makes use of 'larboard' in the same manner. When he is upon building, he mentions Doric pillars, pilasters, cornice, frieze, architrave. When he talks of heavenly bodies, you meet with 'ecliptic and eccentric, the trepidation, stars dropping from the zenith, rays culminating from the equator': to which might be added many instances of the like kind in several other arts and sciences."—*Spectator*, No. 297.

Tennyson, in his allusions to geology, is more guarded; he does not talk of the Ichthyosaurus:—

> A *monstrous eft* was of old the lord and master of earth.
> *Dragons of the prime*,
> That tare each other in their slime,
> Were mellow music match'd with him.

270. Obsolete Words.—Here we must distinguish between poetry, which retains old words, and prose, which discards them:—

> Entered then into the church the Reverend teacher;
> Father he *hight*, and he was in the parish.—LONGFELLOW.
> But come, thou goddess, fair and free,
> In heaven *yclept* Euphrosynë.—MILTON.
> No mean recompense it brings to your *behoof*.—*Ibid.*
> Bring the *rathe* primrose, that forsaken dies.—*Ibid.*
> *Beholden, phantasy, poesy, belike.*

Impersonal verbs are becoming more and more scarce even in poetry. Our more recent poets appear to avoid them.

> It *irks* me. It *repents* me. It *likes* me. It *yearns* me not (*Hen. V.* iv. 3, 26). It would *pity* any living eye (*Faërie Queene*, 1, 6, 43). So *like* you, sir (*Cymb.* ii. 3, 59). Where it *thinks* best unto your royal self (*Rich. III.* iii. 1, 63).

Sometimes a whole class of words will disappear. For instance, we once had several words beginning with the negative prefix *wan*. All of these except *wan-ton*, "undisciplined," would now be considered "impurities," because they are obsolete, and there is no need to revive them.

> *Wanhope* (despair); *wanthrift* (extravagance); *wanluck* or *wanhap* (misfortune); *wanlust* (indifference); *wanwit* (folly); *wangrace* (wickedness); *wantrust* (diffidence); *wantruth* (falsehood); *wanchance* (ill-luck).

271. Foreign Words and Phrases.—It is a mark of affectation to use exotic French words, when English ones exist to express the sense:—

> *Amour propre* (self-respect); *à la mode* (according to fashion); *à l'ordinaire* (in the ordinary way); *à propos* (with reference to); *arrière pensée* (mental reservation); *au fait* (up to the mark); *au reste* (besides); *autre droit* (another's right); *bête noire* (black beast, bug-bear); *bon soir* (good evening); *bon voyage*

(good journey); *bon jour* (good day); *bouleversement* (catastrophe); *émeute* (a riot); *congé* (dismissal); *belles lettres* (literature); *tout ensemble* (aggregate); *cortège* (train of attendants); *fracas* (brawl), etc.

But there are some Latin and Greek words that are well established, and could not easily be spared :—

Sine die (without a day, no day being fixed); *ad interim* (for the meantime, provisionally); *ad nauseam* (to an extent that causes disgust); *alias* (assumed name); *alibi* (elsewhere); *ibid.* (short for *ibidem* "in the same author"); *alma mater* (lit. "benign mother"); *a priori* (from the cause to the effect); *a posteriori* (from the effect to the cause); *ad hominem* (a personal argument; lit. "to the person"); *effluvia* (bad smells); *phenomena* (facts worthy of observation); *criterion* (test); *analysis* (breaking up into parts); *ceteris paribus* (other things being equal); *in statu quo* (as before); *caveat* (let him beware); *ex officio* (in virtue of his office); *ultra vires* (beyond his jurisdiction); *de jure* (by right); *de facto* (in point of fact), etc.

272. Newly-coined Words.—When new thoughts or new situations arise, new words must be found to express them, if none exist already. But the attempt sometimes made to expel long-established words of Romanic or Greek origin, "in order to make room for Teutonic ghosts," is ridiculous. A few examples of such ghosts are taken from a book on English Grammar,[1] which the author terms "Speechcraft," *Grammar* having been banished on account of its foreign origin :—

Fore-say (preface); *speech-lore* (philology); *speech-strain* (emphasis); *word-strain* (accent); *matterly* (concrete); *unmatterly* (abstract); *one-head thing-names* (proper names); *sundriness* (difference); *rank-words* (ordinals); *mark-word* (article); *onely* (Singular); *somely* (Plural); *out-showing mark-words* (Demonstrative adjectives); *mark-words of suchness* (Adjectives of Quality); *pitches of suchness* (Degrees of Comparison), etc.

Some curious words like the following are occasionally seen; but there is no need of them, and it is not safe to use them :—

Enthuse (a bad coinage from "enthusiasm"); *divagation* (deviation); *seldomcy* (coined by Trench, and accepted by no one); *denigration* (blackening the character of a man); *illaudable* (reprehensible); *evidence* (as a verb); *averagely; gentlemanhood; preventative* (apparently a blunder for "preventive"); *donate* (to give); *deontology* (science of duty, coined by Bentham), etc.

The following, however, have been accepted, because they were wanted :—

[1] *Speechcraft*, by Rev. W. Barnes, 1878.

After-witted (one who does not think of a thing till it is too late); *unionist* (a political title); *altruist* (one who upholds the principle of living for others); *scientist* (one who believes in nothing that is supernatural); *aloofness* (a distant attitude); *objective* (the point to which anything is directed); *cable* (verb, to telegraph by a submarine cable); *wire* (verb, to send a telegram); *exploit* (verb, to make the utmost use of); *boycott* (verb, to refuse to trade with); *mellay* (adapted by Tennyson from Fr. *melée*, a confused and disorderly conflict).

Exercise.

Point out any words in the following examples that seem to be opposed to Purity, and substitute suitable words in their places:—

1. The decline of Izzet Bey's influence over the Sultan receives new impulsion from the flight of his son, who was recently summoned from Paris, etc.—*Times Weekly*, 4th Feb. 1898.
2. The illustrations add to the handsome appearance of the volume, and perhaps to some extent supply its raison d'être.—*Times Weekly*, 4th Feb. 1898.
3. Even his famous mot about ambassadors is only a hasty and youthful epigram.—*Times Weekly*, 4th Feb. 1898.
4. He spent four years in the office of a very small firm of solicitors, whose clientèle were almost exclusively peers, country gentlemen, and people of high position.—*Fortnightly Review*, Feb. 1898, p. 240.
5. Not all the information of all the pundits in the British Museum would enable him to sell books, if he neglected, etc.—*Fortnightly Review*, Feb. 1898, p. 258.
6. She must be asked if she did not give the soubriquet of Demi-Dieu to Captain de Lallemaud.—*Daily Telegraph*, 8th Feb. 1898.
7. They propagate the wildest and most inaccurate rumours, but always appealing to the fanaticism of their entourage.—*Daily Telegraph*, 8th Feb. 1898.
8. Mr. Archer remarked that where our theatres were not disguised as gin palaces, they were sandwiched between them.—*Daily Telegraph*, 8th Feb. 1898.
9. Nor is it necessary to refer in detail to the attacks upon the Egyptian policy of the government: if ever there was a chose jugée, it is this.—*Daily Telegraph*, 9th Feb. 1898, p. 9.
10. Since the war between China and Japan, it seemed desirable that Germany should have a point d'appui in China for safeguarding her interests.—*Speech from Berlin*, 9th Feb. 1898.
11. People were shaking their fists at the fictionist, and cries were raised of "Throw him into the river."—*Daily Telegraph*, 9th Feb. 1898.
12. It is not every one who will take the same view that she herself does of her "mediumistic gifts."—*Times Weekly*, 11th Feb. 1898, p. 92.
13. Severe moralists have lately been exercised about the increased admiration, etc.—*Daily Telegraph*, 14th Feb. 1898, p. 9.
14. Quinine is a palliative, but not a preventative, of fever.
15. This remark was followed by a rencontre described as trifling on the official, but violent on the Nationalist, side.—*Daily Telegraph*, 25th Feb. 1898.

CHAPTER XIX.—PROPRIETY OF DICTION

273. **Propriety defined.**—Propriety of language means the using of words (1) in their proper senses, (2) in proper connections:—

(1) I doubt that he is ineligible on the score of age.

Here *doubt* is used for *fear*. This is an impropriety, because "doubt" does not signify "fear."

(2) His life was shaking in the balance.

Here the impropriety consists in using the verb *shake* in a context from which it is debarred by idiom. The verb should have been "trembling." The grammar is correct, and every word is used in its proper sense. But the connection is wrong.

Any sense or connection of words may be considered **proper** that has the *concurrent* authority of standard writers, who have lived near enough to our own time to be regarded as safe guides for present usage.

Note 1.—We are obliged to add the word *concurrent*, because a blunder made by a standard author does not justify even the humblest writer in following a bad example. For instance, Byron's expression "There let him *lay*," for "There let him *lie*," is none the less an impropriety because it is used by a first-rate poet like Byron, who lived near our own time. Again, such a phrase as "the *seldom* use" cannot be tolerated, though it has the authority of an eminent scholar like the late Archbishop Trench.

Note 2.—We are also obliged to add the limitation "who have lived near enough to our own time," etc. Our language has not been changeless for the last four centuries, or even for the last two centuries. Words have in some instances acquired new meanings, and phrases have acquired new forms. Some words have died out, others have come in or have been revived.[1] A writer, if he wishes to keep clear of "improprieties," must conform to *present* usage. There are many modes of expression in Shakspeare and Milton, and even in so recent a writer as Addison, which cannot now be imitated with impunity.

SECTION 1.—COMMON ERRORS IN THE USE OF COMMON WORDS.

274.—Under this heading we have placed a miscellaneous collection of words and usages about which some persons are liable to make mistakes.

---

[1] Thus Campbell, who wrote less than 150 years ago, says that "all writers of any name have now ceased to use *behest, tribulation, self-same*" (*Philosophy of Rhetoric*, p. 171). Evidently these words have been revived since his time; for they are now in "present," "reputable," and "national" use.

Nouns.

(1) **Concrete, Abstract.**—If a noun can be used in either sense (see § 27), take care to use it in one sense only within the *same sentence*:—

> He is a man of clear judgment; but as regards this case I still think it was too severe for the offence. (For *it* say *his sentence*, or *his verdict*. *It* is here improper, because it stands for "judgment" in a concrete sense, whereas in the former clause "judgment" is used in an abstract sense.)

(2) **Collective** nouns must not be associated with adjectives that imply individual attributes, nor with verbs that imply individual action:—

> The average population of England is tall. (For *average population of England* say *the average Englishman* or *most Englishmen.*)
>
> Mankind seeks for happiness in both worlds. (For *mankind* say *most men* or *men in general.*)

(3) **Abstract** nouns must not be pluralised without authority (§ 29):—

> Leave off such stupidities. (For *stupidities* say *acts of stupidity.*)

(4) **Possessive Case.**—Be careful how you use this case with nouns denoting anything inanimate or not personified (see § 45):—

> Beware of life's shortness.
> Look at this letter's signature.
> } For the Possessive form substitute "of."

(5) **Apostrophe "s."**—If the apostrophe "*s*" is given to the ear, it should also be given to the eye. In other words, it must be written as it is pronounced:—

> Epps' cocoa. (Write *Epps's* for *Epps'*.)

(6) **Plurals in a Special Sense.**—On this point see appendix to this chapter.

Pronouns.

(7) **We, I.**—If *we* is substituted for *I*, avoid coupling it with a singular noun:—

> We did things in a much better way, when we were manager. (Either change *we* to *I*, or change *were manager* to *held the office of manager.*)

(8) **I.**—Take care to place the first personal pronoun last, if it appears in company with other nouns or pronouns:—

> I and Herbert return to school to-morrow. (For *I and Herbert* write *Herbert and I.*)

(9) **Them.**—Avoid using this Demonstrative pronoun as if it were a Demonstrative adjective:—

> Leave them books alone. (For *them* say *these* or *those.*)

(10) **Myself**, etc.—A Reflexive pronoun cannot be the subject to a verb :—

In October last George and myself spent ten days at Hampton Court. (For *myself* say *I* or *I myself.*)

(11) **They.**—This is less suitable than "those" as an antecedent to "who" :—

They who have large private means need not for that reason lead an idle life. (For *they* write *those.*)

(12) **One**, as an Indefinite Demonstrative pronoun. This must not be followed by "he," "his," or "him," since a Definite Demonstrative cannot have an Indefinite for its antecedent :—

One must not be too confident of his own success. (For *his* write *one's.*)

(13) **My, our, your, his, her, their.**—The use of these Possessive pronouns as antecedents to a Relative, though defensible and used occasionally by good writers, is not common and had better be avoided :—

The more accurately we search into the human mind, the stronger traces we everywhere find of His wisdom who made it.—BURKE. (For *His wisdom* write *the wisdom of Him.*)

(14) **Who, which** (as subjects to a verb).—These must not be omitted like "whom," "which" (objects) :—

I had several men in my ship died of calentures.—SWIFT. (Insert *who* before *died.*)

(15) **Which, whom, that** (objects to a verb).—When one of these words is the connective between two rather long clauses, it is better not to leave it out :—

The action for libel recently brought in the City Magistrates' Court by Miss ———, a nurse, against Mr. ———, in respect of a letter the latter had written to a relative who was being nursed by the plaintiff, terminated in favour of the defendant. —*Daily Telegraph.* (Insert *which* or *that* after *a letter.*)

(16) **Which.**—If this word stands for two different cases in the same sentence, it must be mentioned twice, once for each case :—

This is a point which is very important, and all men acknowledge to be so. (Insert *which* after *and.*)

(17) **Which, that.**—In a restrictive or limiting sense, "who" or "which" is less suitable than "that" (see § 83, *Note*):—

This is the house which Jack built. (Say *that.*)

(18) **Same.**—After "same" use *as* or *that* for the following Relative, not *who* or *which* (see § 81) :—

This is the same man who came yesterday. (Say *that.*)

(19) **As.**—Avoid the vulgarism of using *as* for "who" or "which" or "that," unless it is preceded by "such" or "same":—

This is not the book as I bought. (For *as* say *that.*)

(20) **And which.**—These words must not be used to introduce a Relative clause, unless another Relative clause similarly introduced by *which* has been expressed already:—

It is a doctrine not very easily adapted to his habitual creed, and which drops out of his mind whenever, etc. (Insert *which is* after *doctrine*, and leave out *which* after *and.*)

Note.—The second *which* is unnecessary in such a sentence as that here given, because it stands for the same case as the first one. A second *which* is necessary only when it is in a different case; see (16).

Adjectives.

(21) **A, an.**—Observe the invariable rule, that the *n* of *an* must be written if it is pronounced, but not otherwise (see § 55).

A clock is an useful thing.
He is an one-eyed man. } For *an* write *a.*

That is not a hotel.
A historical record. } For *a* write *an.*

Note.—In the last two examples the *h* is silent, or so nearly silent as to be inaudible, because the syllable following is accented.

(22) **A, the.**—Take care to repeat the article after *and*, when a separate person or thing is introduced by *and* (see § 186, *a, Note*):—

The styles of a poet and historian are not the same. (Insert *an* after *and.*)

Note.—The sentence would be further improved by adding *respectively* after *historian.*

(23) **Other.**—Take care to use this word with a Comparative, and to abstain from using it with a Superlative:—

He is more learned than any person now living. (Insert *other* before *person.*)

Of all other scholars he is the most accurate. (Omit *other.*)

(24) **Each other, one another.**—Remember that the first is used for two things, and the second for more than two:—

His knees smote one against another.—*Dan.* v. 6. (For *one against another* say *against each other*, or *the one against the other.*)

(25) **Other . . . but.**—Avoid using the preposition *but* after *other*:—

He had no other object but to get his money. (For *but* say *than*, which is appropriate, since "other" is etymologically a Comparative adjective; or omit *other.*)

(26) **Few, little.**—Remember that these are implied negatives (= not many, not much), unless they are preceded by *a* :—

Few men escaped, and these were rewarded. (Insert *a* before *few.*)
Little hope remained, but that was soon disappointed. (Insert *a* before *little.*)

Also remember that "*few*" denotes number, and "*little*" quantity or degree.

To-day there is less than eight hours of full daylight. (For *is less* say *are fewer*).

(27) **Any, either.**—Observe that *either* is used for two things, and *any* for more than two :—

He was first groom, then coachman, then stable-boy ; and he did not do well in either capacity. (For *either* say *any.*)

(28) **Comparatives.**—Use the Comparative in preference to the Superlative, when two things are referred to :—

This picture is the best of the two. (For *best* say *better.*)

(29) **Comparatives in -or.**—Avoid using "than" after Latin comparatives in *-or* :—

His work is superior and deserves to be better paid than yours. (Say *superior to yours and deserves to be better paid.*)

(30) **Like.**—Avoid the vulgarism of using this adjective as if it were a conjunction :—

A timid, nervous child like Martin was. (Say *as* or *such as* for *like*, or put *what* after *like.*)

Verbs.

(31) **Shall, will.**—Remember that these are Principal verbs in some persons and Auxiliaries in others (see § 103 and § 115)

I will be drowned ; nobody shall save me. (Let *shall* and *will* change places.)
Will I accompany you ? (For *will* say *shall.*)

(32) **Present, Past.**—Avoid putting an Historic Present (§ 112, *e*) in the same sentence with a Past Indefinite.

While the governor is thus quietly kept in bonds, the prisoners were triumphantly paraded through the streets. (For *is* say *was*, or change *were* to *are.*)

(33) **Perfect Infinitive.**—Use the Perfect form, when you wish to show that some expectation, supposition, or desire *was not realised* (§ 124). Use it also after the verb "said" in the Passive voice, when you wish to express *past time* (§ 124, *Note*). In all other connections use the Present form :—

They, supposing him *to have been* in the company, went a day's journey.—*Luke* ii. 44. (Correct.)

But for his illness he would *have come*. (Correct.)
I should like *to have seen* him. (Correct.)
I intended *to have seen* him, and I succeeded. (Wrong.)
(In the last line change "*to have seen*" to "*to see*.")
He is said *to have been* once an honest man. (Correct.)

(34) **Infinitive, Gerund.**—The Noun-infinitive and the Verbal noun or Gerund are equivalent in sense, both being equivalent to Abstract nouns. But if the verb or other word going before requires a preposition, the Infinitive (with few exceptions) must not be used :—

He persisted to say this. (Change to *in saying*.)
I insisted to have my fee paid. (Say *on having*.)
I am confident to win. (Say *of winning*.)
I assisted to do this. (Say *in doing*.)
Disqualified to compete. (Say *from competing*.)

In some few contexts, however, the Infinitive is more idiomatic than the Gerund, even though the word going before usually requires a preposition :—

I have a great desire of seeing you. (Say *to see*.)

(35) **Gerundial or Qualifying Infinitive.**—When this is used to qualify an *adjective*, the Active voice is more common than the Passive :—

The road, on account of robbers, was difficult to be passed. (For *to be passed* write *to pass*.)

(36) **Two Direct Objects to the same verb.**—If the same verb does not suit one of the two objects mentioned, add a second verb which suits the other :—

Very few of the Sultans of Turkey have enjoyed a life of peace or a natural death. (After *or* insert *died*.)

(37) **One Auxiliary with two Principal verbs.**—Repeat the Auxiliary, if the voice of the two Principal verbs is not the same :—

The growth of tobacco has been established in India for the last 300 years and overspread the country. (Insert *has* before *overspread*.)

(38) **Two Auxiliaries with one Principal verb.**—When two Auxiliaries are used with the same Principal verb, take care to use the Principal verb in two forms, if one form is not sufficient :—

I never have, and I never will, accuse a man falsely. (After *have* insert *accused*, and cancel the comma after *will*.)

(39) **Mixed use of verbs.**—Repeat the full form of the tense

in each clause, if the use of the verb is not the same in two successive clauses:—

> Happily we have not and could not have seen a repetition of the scandalous scenes which took place at the Assize Court.—*Times Weekly*, 8th April 1898, p. 213.

The sentence should begin, "Happily we have not *seen*," etc. The "*seen*" must be inserted. In the first clause "have seen" is the Present Perfect tense, *Indicative* mood; in the second clause "have seen" is the Perfect *Infinitive*, object to the verb *could*.

Adverbs.

(40) **Quite.**—(*a*) Avoid the impropriety of using this adverb as if it were an adjective and competent to qualify nouns. "Quite" means "perfectly," "entirely," and should not be used in any other sense or for any use other than adverbial:—

> Quite an item. (*A considerable item.*)
> Quite a place. (*An important place.*)
> Quite a sensation. (*A startling sensation.*)

(*b*) Avoid the impropriety of using this adverb in the sense of "very":—

> Quite a unique and interesting document has been published here. —*Daily Telegraph*, 13th Jan. 1898.

(*Quite unique* is nonsense; for there cannot be degrees of uniqueness. Erase *quite* and insert *very* between *and* and *interesting.*)

(41) **Since, ago.**—These adverbs mean "from the present time reckoning backwards." They must always be preceded by a verb in the Past Indefinite tense:—

> My house has fallen down two weeks since. (Say *fell.*)

Note.—For the conjunctional use of *since*, see below (48).

(42) **That.**—Avoid the vulgarism of using *that* as if it were an adverb signifying "so."

> I am that tired that I can scarcely walk. (Say *so tired.*)

(43) **Scarcely, hardly.**—Avoid the vulgarism of using a negative with these adverbs.

> I don't hardly know how to answer you. (Omit *don't.*)

Prepositions.

(44) **Sequence of Prepositions.**—Take care that nouns, adjectives, verbs, and adverbs are followed by the right preposition, that is, the preposition required by idiom and by the sense:—

> The three brothers divided the estate between them. (Say *amongst.* "Between" can be said of only two things.)
> China's resistance of Japan was vain. (Say *to.*)

A sad picture was presented before our sight. (Say *to.*)
All the examples can be reduced under three heads. (Say *to.*)
Marred, as you see, with traitors.—SHAKSPEARE. (Say *by.*)
I have no sympathy for his opinions. (Say *with.*)
A testimonial of my industry. (Say *to.*)
M'Arthur's history treats only with his own time. (Say *of.*)
I do not concur with that. (Say *with you in that.*)
Dutch is of the same origin with Anglo-Saxon. (Say *as.*)
I prevailed with him to let me go. (Say *on.*)
I never interfere with other men's affairs. (Say *in.*)
I never interfere in other people. (Say *with.*)
This is not the question which we were contending. (Add *about.*)
His style is characterised with verbiage. (Say *by.*)

(45) **One preposition for two.**—If one preposition is not fit to do the work of two, fill up the gap with one that is fit:—

This fact did not add but detract from his merits. (Put *to* after *add;* we cannot say *add from.*)

(46) **Than.**—This must not be used after "different," nor after "prefer," nor after "scarcely":—

His ideas are different than those of the majority. (Say *from.*)
He had scarcely gone than a letter was brought in. (For *scarcely* say *no sooner,* or change *than* to *when.*)
I prefer to do this than that. (Say *doing this to doing that.*)

(47) **Except, without, against.**—Avoid the vulgarism of using these as conjunctions. (This is no longer allowed. Their former use as conjunctions was through the absorption of *that* or some other conjunction, which introduced a Noun-clause):—

Except ye repent. (Say *unless.*)
Without you apologise. (Say *unless.*)
Have it ready against I come. (Say *my coming.*)

Conjunctions.

(48) **Since.**—This word, when used as a conjunction, must be preceded by a Present Perfect tense and followed by a Past Indefinite:—

Two years passed since my father has died. (Say *have passed* for *passed,* and *died* for *has died.*)

(49) **Not only . . . but also.**—Take care that the first of these is followed by *the same part of speech* as the second (§ 248):—

He not only built a house, but also a stable. (Put *not only* before *a house.*)

(50) **Both . . . and.**—If a preposition occurs after *both,* repeat it after *and:*—

Excess of any kind is bad both for mind and body. (Insert *for* before *body,* or else say *for both mind and body.*)

(51) **Than . . . as.**—*As* will not do duty for *than* as well as for itself:—

My prospects are no better, and not even as good, as they were before. (Say *my prospects are no better than they were before, and not even as good.*)

(52) **That.**—This must not be used as a general hack, to save the repetition of *when, though, if, whether, unless,* etc. It is, however, a common trick with careless writers to misuse it in this way.[1]

If I do not speak of them, it is because they do not come within my subject, and not that they are lightly esteemed by me. (For *that* say *because.*)

(53) **As.**—Avoid the vulgarism of using *as* for *that* to introduce a noun-clause.

I do not know as I need say anything more. (Say *that.*)

(54) **And that.**—If this is used for introducing a noun-clause, take care that it is preceded by another noun-clause which also begins with *that.* When the first *that* has been mentioned, a second one need not be repeated unless the subject to the verb is changed.

(*a*) I fancied I should get on well by degrees and that I had a good chance of ultimate success. (Insert *that* after *fancied*, and omit *that I* in the subsequent clause.)

(*b*) There seemed to be some hope of his recovery and that he would live to make a fresh effort. (For *of his recovery* say *that he would recover*, and omit *that he would* in the subsequent clause.)

(*c*) Physicians declare lung-disease to be difficult to cure in England, and that the patient must go to a more equable climate. (Say *that lung disease is difficult*, etc. Here *that* must be repeated in the second clause, because the subject is changed.)

(55) **Though, but.**—Remember that *though* is a subordinative conjunction, while *but* is a co-ordinative one, and therefore more emphatic (see § 171).

He is an honest man, but poor; and honesty is always rewarded. (The context shows that in the first clause the emphasis is on the word *honest*. Hence *but* must be changed to *though.*)

(56) **Whether . . . whether.**—When contradictory alternatives are offered by a couple of verbs, repeat the word *whether*; otherwise simply say *or*:—

---

[1] A collection of authenticated examples is given in Hodgson's *Errors in English*, pp. 120, 121.

(1) I beg to ask whether our minister at Pekin has protested against, or in any way recognised, the claims made by the German minister and consul.—*House of Commons*, 10th August 1898. (Insert *whether he has* after *or*.)

(2) I beg to ask whether our minister has protested against or in any way opposed the claims, etc. (This is correct, because protesting against and opposing, though not synonymous, are not contradictory.)

(57) **Or.**—When the noun following *or* is contrasted with the noun preceding it, put an article or a preposition, if possible, before the second noun :—

Has he gained a prize or scholarship? (Insert *a* before *scholarship.*)

Tell me whether he influenced you with promises or threats. (Insert *with* before *threats.*)

Exercise.

Correct any improprieties that may be found in the following sentences :—

1. The creed of Zoroaster assumes the coexistence of a malevolent and benevolent principle, which divide the sovereignty of the world between them.
2. The failure of the spring and autumn harvest in 1897 led to a serious famine in India that year.
3. Is that house in the distance a hospital or a hotel?
4. He mistook James' hat for his own.
5. Sir Roger was saying last night that he was of opinion none but men of fine parts deserve to be hung.—*Spectator*, No. 6.

Note.—For correction of this, see page 66, Note 2.

6. A coxcomb, flushed with many of these infamous victories (over young women), shall say he is sorry for the poor fools, protest and vow he never thought of matrimony.—*Spectator*, No. 288.
7. The jury summoned to attend the court was a clever body of men.
8. Mazzini did more for the emancipation of his country than any living man of his own time.
9. The squadron consisted of about 200 men, and divided the booty among themselves after the victory.
10. A masterly genius does not care what men say of him.
11. I heard the multitude's shout.
12. The stamina of a plant consists of the anther and filament.
13. The violences of a mob must be suppressed.
14. Bring them books down from the shelf.
15. No one as yet had exhibited the structure of the human kidneys, Vesalius having only examined them in dogs.—HALLAM.
16. The claim to inspiration, which is made for these persons and they would not perhaps claim for themselves, cannot be proved.
17. There were very few passengers who escaped without serious injury. (Why is this sentence ambiguous? remove the ambiguity.)
18. In Palestine at the time of Christ the three chief sects were

the Pharisees, the Sadducees, and the Essenes; and they thoroughly disliked each other.

19. My readers too have the satisfaction to find that there is no rank or degree among them who have not their representation in this club.—*Spectator*, No. 34.

20. You shall seldom find a dull fellow of good education, but if he happens to have any leisure upon his hands, will turn his head to one of those two amusements for all fools of eminence—politics or poetry.—*Spectator*, No. 43.

21. Your Englishman is just as serious in his amusements as in any act of his life.

22. I prefer a profitable occupation and which I can look back upon afterwards without regret.

23. There is no popular *Life of Oliver Cromwell* in print; those by Guizot and Carlyle being too bulky for general use.

24. I have read of a man who was very rich, but he considered himself poor all the same.

25. On a subject in which the feelings of others are entitled to respect, one must keep his thoughts to himself.

26. How do you distinguish between a poet and orator, and what is there in common between them?

27. I have few things more to talk about, but I have no time now; you shall hear them to-morrow.

28. "A little knowledge is a dangerous thing," says Pope; but with all due deference to Pope, even little knowledge is better than none.

29. My friend sent me a pair of turkeys to choose from; but I returned them with thanks, and told him I did not want any of them.

30. Several neighbouring gentlemen contributed works, for which they had either given commissions direct to our most distinguished artists, or had purchased them during this exhibition at the Royal Academy.

31. You will perceive that this is the same horse which yourself possessed four years ago.

32. I do not think that the Squire and myself ever had better sport together than we had that day.

33. On comparing his gun with mine, they pronounced his to be the best.

34. In selecting this house in preference to any others, I had no other object but to get the one that was nearest the railway station.

35. In commerce it often happens that they who have abilities want capital, and they who have capital want abilities.

36. Were he still disposed to go there, my purse shall be open to him.

37. I shall have great pleasure in accepting your invitation.

38. If he has been the cause of all this trouble, it would weigh heavily on his conscience.

39. I have lived ten years of my life in Canada, but left it for good and all two years ago.

40. I never have and never will attack a man for speculative opinions.—Buckle.

41. Quite an innovation in the mode of dressing the hair has come into fashion this year.

42. My almost drunkenness of heart.—BYRON.

43. My success or otherwise will be communicated to me by post this evening.

44. From my point of view Grote is a greater historian than Gibbon, though his style is much less grand.

45. I really believe that except to doctors and clergymen, and the very few intimate friends who have seen me frequently, even my state of extremity has been doubted.—MISS MITFORD.

46. In his translation of the *Iliad*, Pope has sometimes given us a picture of a very different kind than what Homer intended.

47. It was in this situation of affairs that Hastings was made Governor-General of India.

48. Breaking a constitution by the very same errors, that so many have been broken before.—SWIFT.

49. The trees have cast their leaves a month ago.

50. I will not let thee go, except thou bless me.—*Gen.* xxxii. 26.

51. He not only gave them his advice, but a good deal of pecuniary help besides.

52. It is contrary both to justice and common sense to do such a thing as that.

53. This building is both superior in size and more suitable in design than any other town-hall that I have seen.

54. No one ever worked more regularly or so carefully as he.

55. We decidedly prefer reading the *Swiss Family Robinson* at this moment than the rather characterless *Masterman Ready*.—MISS YONGE.

56. The modern Germans are fond of metaphysics like the ancient Athenians were.

57. But scarce were they hidden away, I declare,
Than the giant came in with a curious air.—TOM HOOD.

58. I am not that fond of my books that I like to stay in the house reading them all the afternoon.

59. I consider him to be very clever, and that he will do great credit to his teachers.

60. If any such rash project were attempted and that any serious trouble came of it, the fault would be yours, not mine.

61. I pass over this subject in silence, because it does not come within my present purpose, and not that I feel at all incompetent to deal with it.

62. He is an industrious boy, but naturally rather dull, and industry is almost always rewarded in the long run.

63. Whether this conflagration was the work of an incendiary, or that some one employed by the firm was guilty of carelessness, will never be ascertained.

64. This statement was repeated and carefully impressed upon the audience.

65. The man as came here yesterday went away to-day.

66. That operation was first performed on rabbits; it is now performed with success on the human family.

67. It is interesting to observe the various substitutes for paper before its invention.

68. The virtuous and the vile, the learned and ignorant, the temperate and debauched, all give and return the jest.—BROWN'S *Characteristics*.

69. This bold statement of fact will be sufficient to show that the permanency of the Yukon goldfields is established beyond peradventure.—*Liverpool Daily Post*, 29th Jan. 1898.

70. How should I look to have any part of my desire herein satisfied, unless myself be careful to satisfy the like desire which is in other men?—HOOKER.

71. Air, when carefully tested, is found to contain something else than nitrogen and oxygen.—GEIKIE.

72. The misreading of a person's character is an error rather difficult to be avoided.

73. He is as likely to make a good living for himself as his brothers have done.

74. Driving down the street, his horse ran off, and he was thrown out.

75. There have been three famous talkers in Great Britain, either of whom would illustrate what I say about dogmatists well enough for my purpose.—HOLMES.

76. We already possess four times as great a trade with China as every other nation put together.—*Report of G. Balfour's Speech*, 4th Feb. 1898.

77. The Zulu chief, Dinizulu, after some years of exile in St. Helena, has now been reinstated, to rank as a hereditary chief.—*Daily Telegraph*, 8th Feb. 1898.

78. France has obtained a firm footing at Tonkin; England is settled at Hong-Kong for some time past; Russia is at the Amoor; and even Spain, and Portugal, and Holland have their resting-places in East Asia.—*Daily Telegraph*, 8th Feb. 1898.

79. No one would accuse the representative of an English newspaper as an Irishman desirous of exaggerating the distress and grievances of his country.—*Dillon's Speech*, 10th Feb. 1898.

80. Quite a record gallop fell to the Whaddon Chase from Wing, where Lord Orkney kept open house.—*Daily Tel.* 10th Feb. 1898.

81. We were no sooner sat down, but after having looked upon me a little while, she said, etc.—*Spectator*, No. 7.

82. It is difficult to imagine a rougher experience than that involved by his attempt to carry out the adventurous project of reaching Paris from New York by land.—*Times Weekly*, 11th Feb. 1898, p. 92.

83. It (the work of Abbé Dubois) records the impressions of an acute and a patient observer of the actual life of the Hindus.—*Times Weekly*, 11th Feb. 1898, p. 92.

84. The predicate of a sentence always is or contains a verb.

85. Few of his friends except myself knew of his being in the kingdom.

86. The public and private good are so far from being inconsistent that they promote one another.

87. He regretted that the pupil-teacher did not prevent the boys

from writing so fast, as he noticed that is done in the absence of such immediate supervision as the master, otherwise engaged, would have prevented.

88. Men and women who have no object or aim than amusement. —*Daily Telegraph*, 16th Feb. 1898, p. 8.

89. Though these nine warships were built in different dockyards, the design of the whole nine is the same, with slight differences in points of detail.—*Daily Telegraph*, 16th Feb. 1898, p. 9.

90. Bounteous harvests in the Punjaub and in the wheat lands of the River Plate are expected to furnish supplies from the Southern Hemisphere to the extent of about 5,000,000 quarters, etc.—*Daily Telegraph*, 29th April 1898.

91. Mr. Gladstone was able to sit for a short while in an easy-chair on the small lawn by the side of the house, which is charmingly sheltered by quite a small pine forest.—*Daily Tel.*, 22nd March 1898.

92. I shall leave this house at once without you put it in proper repair.

93. You will have to get that lesson by heart like I did.

94. He preferred to take a sweep-crossing than beg his bread from door to door.

95. The army liked their quarters so well, that neither officers nor soldiers was in any degree willing to quit them till they should be thoroughly refreshed.—CLARENDON.

96. The recent fighting has led many people to reconsider the whole question of the relations between the Cape, the Imperial Government, and the natives.—*Review of Reviews*, Feb. 1898, p. 147.

97. I am anxious for the time when he will talk as much nonsense to me as I have to him.—W. S. LANDOR.

98. From this coalition, and not from the spirit of its own laws and institutions, he attributed the harsh and ungenerous treatment of our fallen enemy, Napoleon Buonaparte.—MRS. FLETCHER.

99. The position of the Cabinet is exceedingly difficult between the danger of foreign and civil war, either of which may be precipitated by a simple error.—*Telegram from Madrid*, 14th April 1898.

100. The image and name of Goethe occurs to us at once when we try to evoke the man of most perfect brain who ever existed.—*Fortnightly Review*, May 1898, p. 766.

101. The condition of Mr. Gladstone, who is without pain, is not quite so favourable.—*Daily Telegraph*, 21st April 1898.

102. The nurses for the Spanish Royal family are always chosen from the peasantry of Asturias; a large number are sent for, and from them the most handsome of the province is finally selected.—*Cassell's Family Magazine*, Jan. 1898, p. 152.

103. By that time he will have come in contact with some of the most gifted genius of the earth.—*Ibid.* p. 158.

104. Here is a specimen from *Hamlet* which illustrates the unmethodical character conversation will assume when a principal interlocutor is pursuing a private train of thought with intense eagerness. —ABBOTT AND SEELEY, *English Lessons for English Readers*, p. 231.

105. The whole question is accordingly remitted to a committee, the composition of which has already been announced in our columns,

who will consider and report upon with all convenient speed the proposals of the Government of India.—*Times*, 3rd May 1898.

106. Chung Chih Tung, Viceroy of Nankin, a thorough Chinaman, a Progressive, though disliking foreigners, but who has the unique distinction of being absolutely honest and incorruptible, has engaged German instructors for his army.—*Daily Tel.*, 19th April 1898.

107. He gathered that the Government were not altogether satisfied with each other.—MORLEY, quoted in *Daily Tel.*, 23rd June 1898.

108. Throughout the whole of the north-east of the Soudan trade and industry are reviving surely, but no doubt slowly.—Sir M. HICKS-BEACH, quoted in *Daily Telegraph*, 28th June 1898.

109. How could I hear such words, how could I meet such looks, from any other man but he?—MRS. CRAIK, *The Ogilvies*, ch. x.

110. No one is more fully alive than himself to the heavy burden of his responsibilities.—*Standard*, 11th August 1898, p. 4.

111. These agents should be authorised to (and capable of) discussing industrial questions, and of availing themselves of the best markets.—*Daily Telegraph*, 15th August 1898, p. 2.

112. At any other time, and in any other person, such an exhibition might have been conducive of pity.—*Windsor Magazine*, August 1898, p. 258.

113. The adulteration of food generally occurs in some wholesome form. Margarine is an excellent food substance, though it is not butter; the potato is very nourishing, but it should not be found in bread.—*Daily Telegraph*, 27th August 1898.

114. Would not a man of far inferior abilities than Bismarck have become cognisant from that moment of France's exact power of resistance?—*Fortnightly Review*, September 1898, p. 407.

SECTION 2.—WORDS USED IN WRONG SENSES OR WRONG CONNECTIONS.

275. Under this heading we have given, chiefly in alphabetical order, some examples of words that have within recent times been used in senses that do not belong to them, or in contexts, from which they are debarred by current idiom.

When the use of a word in a wrong sense has become so general that the acquired meaning is as commonly recognised as the proper one, it is doubtful whether we can still call this an Impropriety. It is much to be regretted, however, that words should be handled in this slovenly fashion; for our language gains nothing in wealth by the process, while it loses much in precision. To take a few examples:—

(1) When he (Napoleon III.) was brought before the court in Paris, he *demeaned* himself with a dignity which diminished the childish absurdity and the ridiculous details of his attempt at Boulogne.—*Daily Telegraph*, 2nd Feb. 1898.

Here *demean* is used in its proper sense. It is derived from old French *démener*, to conduct, guide, or manage; and it is from this source that we get our noun *demeanour*, which signifies bearing, manner. Now, however, the phrase "demean oneself" is more commonly used in the sense of "lower oneself," owing perhaps to an absurd etymology which derived the word from Latin *de*, down, and English *mean*, base.

(2) Free trade equalises advantages, making the advantage of each the *advantage* of all.[1]—ZINCKE.

This makes a good balance; but the words taken literally contain a contradiction. The italicised *advantage* is made to mean "benefit," "profit,"—a sense in which the word is often loosely used. But the first "advantage" is used in its proper sense, viz. a step in advance. It would be impossible for all men to be in advance of one another.

(3) This is the theory, but how are we to *replace* the Emperor, when he has been *displaced* by such an event as Waterloo or Sedan? —HOMERTON.

Here *replace* is correctly used in the sense of "restore to his place," "put back," "reinstate"; and this is what the etymology of the word implies. Nevertheless, the word "replace" has come to be used in the sense of "displace," "take the place of," "supersede," and the blunder has become so common that it attracts no attention.

(4) In the Attic commonwealth it was the *privilege* of every citizen to address the people.—SWIFT.

The italicised word taken in its proper sense involves a contradiction with "every." A privilege means a law or right in *favour of some particular person or class*. This cannot be the right "of *every* one." Yet the word privilege is now loosely used for any kind of right that can exist.

(5) The confession that he made begins at the wrong end, and is thus literally *preposterous*, in the sense of putting that first which ought to be last.

The word *preposterous* is now loosely used in the sense of "absurd," in which sense it was not wanted, and should have been condemned as an Impropriety. Hence, when any one now uses the word in its proper sense of something being put first which ought to have been put last, he is obliged to explain himself by adding "literally," "in the sense of putting that first which ought to be last." It is much to be regretted that through the carelessness of writers our language has practically lost this expressive word.

276. Fixed Character of Phrases.—One great peculiarity about phrases is that they are fixed; that is, any change in the order of words or in the words themselves would amount to an "impropriety."

Thus we can say that a man is "*saturated* with selfishness," but not "*soaked* in selfishness"; or that a house is "*pulled* down," but not "*drawn* down"; or that a prophecy "*came* true," but not "*became* true"; or that some one's life was "cut *short*," but not "cut *brief*"; or that a tax "falls *heavy*," but not "falls *burdensome*";

[1] Hodgson's *Errors in English*, p. 3.

or that a country is "*laid* waste," but not "*placed* waste"; or that a matter is "*carried* to extremes," but not "*put* to extremes"; or that some one's fate "*trembled* in the balance," but not "*shook* in the balance"; or that men "made *merry*," but not "made *joyful*"; or that they "*mustered* strong," but not "*collected* strong"; or that they "played some one *false*," but not "played him *deceitful*"; or that they "*put* a thing right," but not "*placed* it right"; or that money "*runs* short," but not "*flies* short"; or that men "*steer* clear of a danger," but not "*swim* or *ride* clear"; or that some one "*stops* short," but not "*stays* short"; or that some one "*casts* his eyes" upon a thing, but not "*throws* his eyes"; or that some one is "struck *dumb*," but not "struck *mute*"; or that a man "thinks *fit*" to do a thing, but not "thinks *suitable*" to do it.

Exercise.[1]

Put correct words or phrases for those italicised below, and show in what their impropriety consists. If you see no impropriety, give your reasons:—

1. His writings did not meet with a very general *acceptation*.
2. If both were to *aggravate* their parents, as my brother and sister do mine, etc.—RICHARDSON.
3. My decided preference is for the fourth and last of these *alternatives*.—GLADSTONE.
4. An *ancient* man, strangely habited, asked for quarters.—SCOTT.
5. Lest a sudden peace should *appreciate* the money.—RAMSAY.
6. They have *approached* the Education Department for some purpose in which their interests are concerned.
7. In a few hours above thirty thousand men left his standard and returned to their ordinary *avocations*.—MACAULAY.
8. Though the intentions of any person should be ever so *beneficent*, yet if they fail in producing their effect, his merit seems imperfect.—BENTHAM.
9. The only danger that attends the multiplicity of publications is that some of them may be *calculated* to injure rather than benefit society.—GOLDSMITH.
10. Brodie made a scrawl on paper only to be equalled by the *calligraphy* of Elliotson.—CLARKE.
11. In the *capacious* recesses of his mind.—BANCROFT.
12. Mr. Bright *attacked* in parliament the ruinous expense of the army, and *claimed* that the young officers, with their scarlet and gold, were kept mainly for the amusement of the young ladies of the aristocracy.—*Fortnightly Review*, Feb. 1898, p. 243.
13. We must look higher for the *climax* of earthly good.—TAYLOR.
14. We *commence* judges ourselves.—COLERIDGE.
15. When the actual motions of the heavens are calculated in the best possible way, the process is difficult and *complex*.—WHEWELL.

---

[1] Out of the 123 examples here given, about 20 have been selected from Hodgson's *Errors in English.*

16. To persist in neglecting to have a child vaccinated is a breach of parental duty which nothing should be permitted to *condone.*—*Times*, 5th April 1878.

17. The compactness of the parts resting together doth much *confer* to the strength of the union.—GLANVILL.

18. *Congenital* lameness caused by a fall from the nurse's arms.

19. I have *constantly* seen one bull kill six or seven horses, and have heard of one that has killed as many as seventeen.—H. J. ROSE.

20. It contributed a good deal to confirm me in the *contemptible* idea I always entertained of Cellarius.—GIBBON.

21. He that is of a merry heart hath a *continual* feast.—*Proverbs* xv. 15.

22. In short, the facts are as nearly as possible the precise *converse* in every respect of what the press states.—*Morning Star*, 19th March 1866.

23. He accepted all these tales with a *credible* mind.

24. Next morning a severe frost set in which lasted ten days, and my field of turnips was absolutely *decimated.* Scarce a root was left untouched.—*Scotsman*, 19th Dec. 1859.

25. Her son would *demean* himself by a marriage with an artist's daughter.—THACKERAY.

26. A difference between them and another *description* of public creditors.—HAMILTON.

27. The school of Rousseau idealised the natural man and regarded all social influence as *deteriorating* from his original purity.—*Contemporary Review*, May 1879.

28. The printing of my letters is left entirely at your *disposition.*

29. I *doubt* some foul play.—SHAKSPEARE.

30. The balminess of the atmosphere occasioned by the *effluvia* of the gulf stream.

31. Their *eldest* historians are of suspected credit.—STILLINGFLEET.

32. His mission was to *eliminate* religion of all such and kindred rubbish.—CARRUTHERS.

33. It is our duty to *endeavour* the recovery of these beneficial subjects.—LORD CHATHAM.

34. His body behind the head becomes broad, from whence it is again *extenuated* all the way to the tail.—GREW.

35. With a reluctance not unnatural in a *female.*

36. We need not go any *further* in this subject.—*Edinburgh Review*, Jan. 1842.

37. Her *future* life was virtuous and fortunate.—CHAMBERS.

38. A *Herculanean* task.

39. Nature has impressed upon some animals deformity and *horror.*—*Spectator.*

40. The bodies were so charred that *identity* was impossible.

41. These perplexities require *illumination.*

42. Never was my life in such fearful *imminence.*—GILCHRIST.

43. He was a very curious *individual.*

44. If Persia had invaded Greece at this critical time, Greece would have fallen almost *infallibly.*—GROTE.

45. The French put Marshal Bazaine into prison, because they suspected his *infidelity.*

46. *Innate* depravity, due to early training and general recklessness of life.—A. GRIFFITHS.

47. He was a man of *insatiable* energy.

48. Most of our mistakes arise from the neglect to *interrogate* facts.

49. He has shown throughout a *large* amount of patience.

50. Have you heard the *last* news?

51. Dapple had to *lay* down on all fours before the lad could bestride him.—DASENT.

52. He repeated without hesitation a *lengthened* passage from one of the eclogues of Virgil.—KILLAN.

53. A regiment contains not *less* than 800 men.

54. He is a man of *limited* income.

55. A. *made use of* the same inaccuracy as B.

56. *Mutual* enmities are said to cement friendship.

57. What a *nice* story we heard yesterday!

58. In his youth he was a *novitiate* of the Franciscan order.

59. In such circumstances we are to procure leave to omit the *observation* of the rule.—JER. TAYLOR.

60. The rapid stream had *overflown* its narrow banks.—BLACK.

61. At one o'clock we *partook of* lunch at the hotel.

62. He did not examine the wound till after the death of the *party*.—*Letters of Junius.*

63. The great difficulty of *permeating* the masses with sound ideas is the prevalent lack of elementary education.—JER. HEAD.

64. He thinks very highly of the *perspicuity* of his son's mind.

65. The plains of Tartary are *pervaded* by nomad hordes.

66. It is not so easy to mould the formed character of an adult as the *plastic* mind of a child.

67. The evidence furnished by this witness is very *precarious.*

68. It needed no ghost from the grave to *predicate* even then the success of the young D'Israeli in public life.—MADDEN.

69. We must take note of their defects as well as of their *qualities.*

70. He lent me a *quantity* of books.

71. The *question* proposed by Lord Beaconsfield was successfully opposed.

72. He could not *retrieve* his friend from the false notion that had possessed him.

73. That sight prompted him to *risibility.*

74. A *small* alteration of the stops will make the sentence quite clear.

75. His retirement from public life was *spontaneous.*

76. Our interest in Persia is *synonymous* with that of the Persians themselves.—A. ARNOLD.

77. His recovery from that illness *transpired* in a shorter space of time than any one expected.

78. The *veracity* of the Gospel narrative is unquestionable.

79. A *verbal* agreement is less binding than a written one.

80. His character is *undeniable.*

81. He is much *addicted* to the study of mathematics.

82. A man of evil life and *soaked* with selfishness.

83. The salt tax falls more *burdensome* on the poor than on the rich.

84. I *apprehend* that much good will result.

85. I feel sure that this fact *portends* some good.
86. He was the first to *break the news* of that happy event.
87. He received his full share of praise for the procedure in which he had been *implicated*.
88. He *pocketed* the praise so cordially given to him.
89. He *richly* deserved the reward they gave him.
90. To do what he bid was an act of *sheer* benevolence.
91. He is *utterly* fit for the duties that he has undertaken.
92. A *bevy* of gentlemen appeared on the scene.
93. He arrived at nine o'clock in *broad* moonlight.
94. The opinion that he expressed on the merits of the case was a foregone *inference*.
95. It is not fair in a trial to put a leading *inquiry* to a witness.
96. That is a moot *question*.
97. The two men fought in single *conflict*.
98. Our *standing navy* is much greater than our standing army.
99. Your house is scarcely a stone's *fling* from ours.
100. He is a *sworn enemy* of mine.
101. He also worked on most important public business, sitting as chairman of the Indian Railways Committee, a long and important investigation.—*Fortnightly Review*, Feb. 1898, p. 252.
102. After he had suffered great poverty and want, honest old George Stevenson and George Bidder *conspired* with others and made an annuity for him.—*Fortnightly Review*, Feb. 1898, p. 247.
103. He was an *advanced middle-aged* man of very large dimensions.—*Fortnightly Review*, Feb. 1898, p. 237.
104. An important decision was *rendered* by the judges.
105. How the new constitution will turn out for Crete in all its details, and who will have the pleasure of ruling this interesting island, can only be supremely *indifferent* to us.—*Daily Telegraph*, 9th Feb. 1898.
106. Millais, on the other hand, with a *perspicuity* rare in so young a man, regarded the movement as a school in which he would find the discipline that he felt he needed.—*Fortnightly Review*, Feb. 1898, p. 193.
107. A wicked and probably *unveracious* story is told of a critic who said, etc.—*Fortnightly Review*, Feb. 1898, p. 194.
108. Only the individual who has had practically to confront this problem can adequately appreciate its difficulties and perplexities; and if it *presents a not swiftly conquerable solution* to an educated person, to a defenceless and inexperienced girl it is little less than hopelessly *unattainable*.—*Fortnightly Review*, Feb. 1898, p. 202.
109. It is not for the *likes* of us Saxons and West Britons to formulate the measure, etc.—*Review of Reviews*, Jan. 1898, p. 9.
110. It is announced that the directors of the Crystal Palace have under consideration a definite scheme for the *purchase* of the property at Sydenham.—*Daily Telegraph*, 11th Feb. 1898, p. 6.
111. These obscurities will be *unravelled* shortly.
112. Must I submit to all this injury with *impunity*?
113. He gives me a *lot* of trouble.
114. All this happened while I was *stopping* away from home.
115. We have received news of great *import*.

116. Take care to part your hair in the *centre.*

117. On that subject he was *literally* out at sea.

118. They are meant no doubt to make the wrongdoer suffer in his *proper* person.[1]—*Daily Telegraph*, 16th Feb. 1898.

119. His plea for unity among Irishmen was *underlined* by the audience with repeated applause.—*Daily Telegraph*, 17th Feb. 1898.

120. German goods have taken possession of markets which were but recently *innocent* of their existence.—*Nineteenth Century*, Feb. 1898.

121. The writer deals this time with the question of *crude* materials. —*Review of Reviews*, Feb. 1898, p. 143.

122. It was summer all over Upper India, a season so entirely different from its *congener* in the British Isles.—*Mariam*, p. 2.

123. Spain stands convicted of a horrible crime, the Maine *disaster*, and we owe it to ourselves to vindicate the victims of the explosion from the charge that they were *dead* by their own hands, and to see that the perpetrators should not go *unwhipped* by justice. —*Speech delivered in Congress*, 14th April 1898.

APPENDIX TO CHAPTER XIX.—PLURALS IN SPECIAL SENSES.

(*a*) Two forms of Plural, each with a separate meaning :—

Brother	Brothers,	*sons of the same mother.*
	Brethren,	*members of the same society.*
Cherub	Cherubim,	*angels of a certain rank.*
	Cherubs,	*images or models of a cherub.*
Cloth	Cloths,	*kinds or pieces of cloth* (Distributive).
	Clothes,	*articles of dress* (Collective).
Cow	Cows,	*individual cows* (Distributive).
	Kine,	*cattle* (Collective).
Die	Dies,	*stamps for coining* (Distributive).
	Dice,	*small cubes used in games* (Collective).
Genius	Geniuses,	*men of genius or talent.*
	Genii,	*fabulous spirits of the air.*
Index	Indexes,	*tables of contents.*
	Indices,	*signs used in algebra.*
Pea	Peas,	(Distributive).
	Pease,	(Collective).
Penny	Pennies,	=*penny-pieces* (Distributive).
	Pence,	(sometimes Collective).[2]
Staff	Staves,	*sticks or poles.*
	Staffs,	*departments in the army.*
Stamen	Stamens,	*male organs of flowers* (Distributive).
	Stamina,	*endurance, vigour,* lit. *threads* (Collective).
Shot	Shot,	*little balls discharged from a gun.*
	Shots,	*discharges ; as, "he had two shots."*

[1] This is a misleading translation of the Latin phrase *in propriâ personâ.*

[2] Hence *six-pence* has a Collective sense, denoting a single coin, which makes the noun appear to be Singular, so that we say *a sixpence* (Singular), *sixpences* (Plural).

(*b*) Different senses of Singular and Plural :—

Singular.	Plural.
Advice, counsel.	*Advices*, information.
Air, atmosphere.	*Airs*, demeanour.
Ban, a curse (under a *ban*).	*Banns*, announcement (*banns* of marriage).
Beef, flesh of ox.	*Beeves*, cattle, bulls and cows.
Compass, range or extent.	*Compasses*, an instrument.
Copper, a metal.	*Coppers*, pennies.
Domino, a kind of mask.	*Dominoes*, the game so-called.
Force, strength or energy.	*Forces*, army.
Good, benefit.	*Goods*, movable property.
Iron, a metal.	*Irons*, fetters made of iron.
Minute, of time.	*Minutes*, of a meeting.
Physic, medicine.	*Physics*, natural science.
Return, coming back.	*Returns*, statistics.
Salt, seasoning substance.	*Salts*, smelling salts.
Sand, a kind of matter.	*Sands*, a tract of sandy land.
Vapour, invisible steam.	*Vapours*, dejection.
Vesper, evening.	*Vespers*, evening prayers.
Water, the element.	*Waters*, springs.

(*c*) Two meanings in the Plural against one in the Singular :—

Singular.		Plural.	
Colour,	colour.	*Colours*	1. Kinds of colour. 2. *Flag of regiment.*
Custom,	habit.	*Customs*	1. Habits. 2. *Toll* or *tax.*
Element,	simple substance.	*Elements*	1. Simple substances. 2. *Conditions of the air.*
Effect,	result.	*Effects*	1. Results. 2. *Goods and chattels.*
Letter,	1. Of alphabet. 2. Epistle.	*Letters*	1. Of alphabet. 2. *Epistles.* 3. *Learning.*
Manner,	mode or way.	*Manners*	1. Modes, ways. 2. *Behaviour.*
Number,	as in counting.	*Numbers*	1. As in counting. 2. *Poetry.*
Pain,	suffering.	*Pains*	1. Sufferings. 2. *Trouble, care.*
Part,	portion.	*Parts*	1. Portions. 2. *Abilities.*
Premise,	a statement or proposition.	*Premises*	1. Propositions. 2. *Buildings.*
Quarter,	a fourth part.	*Quarters*	1. Fourth parts. 2. *Lodgings.*
Spectacle,	anything seen.	*Spectacles*	1. Things seen. 2. *Eye-glasses.*

(*d*) Two meanings in the Singular against one in the Plural :—

	Singular.		*Plural.*
Abuse	1. Wrong use. 2. Reproaches.	*Abuses,*	wrong uses.
Foot	1. Part of body. 2. Infantry.	*Feet,*	parts of body.
Horse	1. A quadruped. 2. Cavalry.	*Horses,*	quadrupeds.
Issue	1. Result. 2. Offspring.	*Issues,*	results.
Light	1. A lamp. 2. Radiance.	*Lights,*	lamps.
People	1. A nation. 2. Persons.	*Peoples,*	nations.
Powder	1. A medicinal mixture. 2. Gunpowder.	*Powders,*	medicinal mixtures.
Practice	1. Habitual act. 2. Professional connection.	*Practices,*	habitual acts.
Stone	1. A piece of rock. 2. Fourteen pounds.	*Stones,*	pieces of rock.
Wood	1. A forest. 2. Timber.	*Woods,*	forests.

CHAPTER XX.—PERSPICUITY OR CLEARNESS OF DICTION.

277. Perspicuity.—Most of what has been said hitherto about punctuation, the normal order of words, inversion of the normal order, the structure of sentences, purity of diction, and propriety of diction, leads up to the subject of clearness or perspicuity; and much that we shall have to say about simplicity or ease of diction, and about brevity or terseness of diction leads up to the same subject. Of all qualities of style the one that is of most general use is Perspicuity; for if the writer does not make himself understood, he writes to no purpose.

"By perspicuity," says Quintilian, "care is taken, not that the reader *may* understand, if he will, but that he *must* understand, whether he will or not."

The original and once the only sense of the word "perspicuity" was "transparency,"—transparency of the medium through which objects can be seen. Afterwards, by a vigorous metaphor, it came to be applied, and was eventually restricted, to *transparency of language,*—language being the medium through which the thought or image intended by the writer can be seen by the reader, as light is the medium through which objects can be seen by the eye.

SECTION 1.—GRAMMATICAL PRECAUTIONS.

278. Among the grammatical devices conducive to perspicuity the following deserve attention :—

(*a*) Repeat the Subject, if there is any fear of a wrong subject being construed with the next verb :—

He is endeavouring to help some friends, who are very grateful for his assistance, and (*he*) will not allow any one else to help them.

If the *he* had not been repeated, the word "who" might naturally have been considered the subject to the verb "will allow"; and this would have completely altered the sense. All ambiguity is removed by repeating "*he.*"

(*b*) Repeat a Preposition, if the nouns governed by it are at some distance apart :—

(1) As soon as he had the power, he took vengeance on all those persons, who had injured his friends and relatives, and especially (*on*) his cousin John.

If the *on* had not been repeated, the reader would certainly have considered that "cousin John" was intended to be an object to the verb "injured."

(2) The concessions by China of Kiao-chau to Germany, and (of) Port Arthur and Ta-lien-wan to Russia, for terms of years, belong to a new development, etc.—*Times Weekly*, 8th April 1898.

The repetition of "*of*" (not given in the original) before "Port Arthur" improves the perspicuity. Cancel comma after *Germany*.

(*c*) Repeat a Conjunction, if the verbs depending on it are at some distance apart :—

Some persons have maintained that Julius Cæsar did not destroy the republican constitution of Rome for the sake of making himself emperor; (*that*) the republic had, in fact, been destroyed already by the ambitious citizens who preceded him; and (*that*) he merely stepped into a position which had been left open for him by force of circumstances.

If the conjunction "*that*" is not repeated, the two last sentences might be taken to express the writer's own opinion, and not that of "some persons" referred to in the first sentence.

(*d*) Repeat an Auxiliary verb, when the Principal verbs are far enough apart to give rise to ambiguity :—

My powers, such as they were, had been cultivated at Oxford from the age of nineteen, when I was still young enough to be moulded into the shape that my advisers considered best for me, and (*had been*) trained to the study of science in preference to that of ancient philosophy.

Unless the auxiliary "*had been*" is repeated, the word "trained" would naturally be regarded as the sequel to the word "moulded."

(*e*) Repeat the Verb or use the pro-verb *do* after the conjunctions "than" and "as," if the omission of the verb would cause any ambiguity :—

The Presbyterians of Scotland disliked the Independents led by Cromwell as heartily as (*did*) the Royalists.

The Presbyterians of Scotland disliked the Independents led by Cromwell more heartily than the Royalists (*did*).

The ambiguity of both sentences is removed by using the pro-verb "*did.*"

(*f*) Antecedent clauses must not be mixed up with consequent ones :—

The prosperity of England will decline, if she loses her command of the sea, and other countries step into her place.

Does the last clause go with the consequent or with the antecedent? Begin with the antecedent or conditional clause first in any case, and then the sentence may be rewritten in two different ways, whichever meaning the writer may have intended :—

(1) If England loses her command of the sea, her prosperity will decline and other countries step into her place.

(2) If England loses her command of the sea and other countries step into her place, her prosperity will decline.

(*g*) Infinitives dependent on one word must not be mixed up with Infinitives dependent on another :—

He decided *to* take his daughter with him to the British Museum *to* see the Assyrian monuments and *to* compare these with the researches of Layard and Rawlinson.

This sentence might be rewritten so as to make at least three different senses :—

(1) He decided to go with his daughter to the British Museum that she might see the Assyrian monuments and compare these with, etc.

(2) He decided to take his daughter to the British Museum that they might see the Assyrian monuments and compare these with, etc.

(3) He decided to take his daughter with him to the British Museum that she might see the Assyrian monuments, and (he decided) to compare these, etc.

Section 2.—The Obscure.

279. Defective Expression.—Elliptical phrases or idioms, provided they are in current use and are generally understood, are unobjectionable. For instance, there is no lack of perspicuity in the sentence, "Do all you can," because the omission of the Relative pronoun as object to a verb, though unknown in other modern languages, is common in English. The same cannot be said, however, of ellipses that result from over-brevity or from rapidity of thought followed by carelessness of diction :—

(1) He is inspired with a true sense of that function, when chosen from a regard to the interests of piety and virtue.—*Guardian*, No. 13.

A function cannot be a sense or sentiment. The wording should have been "a true sense of the dignity, or of the importance, of that function."

(2) You ought to contemn all the wit in the world against you.—*Guardian*, No. 53.

The writer means "all the wit that can be employed against you."

(3) He talks all the way upstairs to a visit.—*Spectator*, No. 2.

The writer perhaps means, "He talks all the way as he goes upstairs to pay a visit."

(4) Arbitrary power I look upon as a greater evil than anarchy itself, as much as a savage is a happier state of life than a slave at the oar.—*Sentiments of a Church of England Man.*

Neither a savage nor a slave can be called a state of life. The writer means "the life of a savage is happier than that of a slave."

(5) This courage among the adversaries of the court was inspired into them by various incidents, for every one of which the ministers, or, if that was the case, the minister alone is to answer.—*Free Thoughts on the Present State of Affairs.*

If that was the case! He means, "if there was but one minister."

(6) Never let the glory of our nation, who made France tremble, and yet has the gentleness to be unable to bear opposition from the meanest of his own countrymen, be calumniated in so insolent a manner, etc.—*Guardian*, No. 53.

By "the glory of our nation," he means "the man who was the glory of our nation,"—a fact that is by no means obvious on first reading.

(7) His chapters on these themes, or the commercial prospects of Siberia, are the pleasantest in his book.—*Daily Telegraph*, 25th Jan. 1898.

The writer means apparently "or *those on* the commercial prospects," etc.

(8) The ship was insured for a voyage from Cassis to Constantinople with cement.—*Syren and Shipping*, 9th Feb. 1898.

It looks at first as if the ship was insured with cement. The sentence should be worded: "The ship, with a cargo of cement, was insured," etc.

280. Bad Arrangement of Words.—The rules for the order of words, phrases, and clauses, with examples of their violation, have been given already in Chapters xv. and xvii. A few more examples may be given here, in illustration of the subject of obscurity :—

(1) It contained a warrant for conducting me and my retinue to Traldragdubb or Trildrogdrib, for it is pronounced both ways, as near as I can remember, by a party of ten horse.—SWIFT.

The phrase *by a party of ten horse* must be construed with the gerund "conducting," and should therefore be placed after the word "retinue."

(2) I perceived it had been scoured with half an eye.—*Guardian*, No. 10.

The phrase *with half an eye* must be construed with the verb "perceived." The sentence should therefore be arranged as follows: "With half an eye I perceived it had been scoured"; or "I perceived with half an eye *that*," etc.

(3) The young man did not want natural talents; but the father of him was a coxcomb, who affected being a fine gentleman so unmercifully, that he could not endure in his sight, or the frequent mention of one who was his son, growing into manhood and thrusting him out of the gay world.—*Spectator*, No. 496, T.

The confused construction, together with the vile application of the word "unmercifully," is such that this sentence might with equal justice be ranked under solecism, impropriety, or obscurity (Campbell).

281. Using the same Word in different Senses.—The same word should not be repeated in the same sentence, unless it is used in the same sense and in the same part of speech:—

(1) Any reasons of doubt, which he may have in this case, would have been reasons of doubt in the case of other men, who may give *more*, but cannot give *more* evident, signs of thought than their fellow-creatures.—BOLINGBROKE, Essay 1, Sect. 9.

Here the first "more" is the Comparative degree of "many." It should be changed to "more numerous," to match the phrase "more evident"; or "more evident" might be changed to "clearer."

(2) One may have an air (demeanour) *which* proceeds from a just sufficiency and knowledge of the matter before him, *which* may naturally produce some motions of his head and body, *which* might become the bench better than the bar.—*Guardian*, No. 13.

Here *which* is repeated three times, each time with a different antecedent. This is tantamount to using the same word in three different senses in the same sentence.

(3) *They* were persons of such moderate intellects, even before *they* were impaired by *their* passions.

The first *they* refers to "persons," and the second to "intellects." *Their* refers back again to "persons."

282. Uncertain Reference of Pronouns.—Pronouns must not be used in such a way as to cause any doubt about what noun they stand for:—

(1) Such were the centaurs of Ixion's race,
Who a bright cloud for Juno did embrace.—DENHAM.

What is the antecedent to *who?*

(2) There are other examples of the same kind, which cannot be brought without the utmost horror, because it is supposed impiously, against principles as self-evident as any of those necessary truths, which are *such* of all knowledge, that the Supreme Being commands by one law what He forbids by another.—BOLINGBROKE.

What word does *such* here stand for?

(3) When a man considers the state of his own mind, he will find that the best defence against vice is preserving the worthiest part of his own spirit pure from any great offence against *it*.—*Guardian*, No. 19.

What does *it* (the last word in the sentence) refer to?

Note 1.—There is no uncertainty of reference, if the pronoun relates to a principal word, such as the subject of a verb or the object to one:—

But I shall leave this subject to your management, and question not but you will throw *it* into such light as shall at once, etc. —*Spectator*, No. 628.

Here *it* relates to "subject," and not to the nearer word "management," for two reasons—(1) because "subject" is a chief word, while "management" is a subsidiary one; (2) because the rhythm of the sentence requires that the verb "throw" shall have the same object as the verb "leave."

Note 2.—If there is no other way of avoiding ambiguity, it is better to repeat the noun, as in the following example:—

The lad cannot leave his father: for if he should leave his father, *his father* would die.—*Gen.* xliv. 22.

283. **Words changed without Change of Meaning.**—When words are changed, not to alter the sense, but merely to save a repetition of the same sound, they must not be set against each other antithetically, as if they were intended to be understood in different senses:—

Scarlet rhododendrons 60 feet in *height* are surrounded by trees 200 feet in *elevation*.[1]

Here *height* and *elevation*, though apparently balanced against each other by way of anthithesis or contrast, are intended to mean exactly the same thing. Instead of 200 *feet in elevation* we could say *that reach to a height of* 200 *feet*.

SECTION 3.—THE DOUBLE MEANING.

284. **Equivocal Words and Phrases.**—Our language abounds, as most other languages do, in equivocal words; and there is no harm in using them, so long as the sense is clear from

---

[1] Bain's *Rhetoric and Composition*, p. 247.

the context. Thus, if some one says that "he rents his house at fifty pounds a year," no one would suppose that he means pounds in troy-weight or pounds in avoirdupois. Sometimes, however, the context fails to give the requisite clue, or gives it so imperfectly, that the reader is forced to read the sentence twice and reflect a little upon its contents, before he can be quite sure that he has understood it. Whenever an author's style exacts such reflection from his reader, he has committed an offence against perspicuity.

There is no part of speech which, if used incautiously, is not susceptible of a double meaning :—

(a) *Prepositions* :—

(1) I am persuaded, that neither death, nor life . . . shall be able to separate us from the love *of* God.—*Romans* viii. 38.

Does this mean God's love to us, or our love to God ?

(2) A little after the reformation *of* Luther.—SWIFT.

The natural meaning of the words "reformation of Luther" occurs to the mind much more readily than the intended meaning, "reformation *by* Luther."

(3) If I cannot be commended *for* the beauty of my style, I hope I may be pardoned *for* its brevity.

Here the preposition "for" is used in two different senses: the first "for" means "on account of," while the second "for" means "in consideration of." What the author intended to express (but the meaning is not as obvious as it should have been) is, that the brevity of his style may be taken as a set-off to its want of beauty..

(b) *Conjunctions* :—

(1) They were both much more ancient among the Persians than Zoroaster *or* Zerdusht.

Or is here equivocal. The mention of *both* suggests that the writer names two distinct persons by Zoroaster or Zerdusht, by way of balance. It is not every reader who would know that *or* is here used to denote an alternative spelling of the same name. All ambiguity can be removed by inserting the parenthesis "(*as he is also called*)" after *or*. On other means of avoiding the ambiguity of *or*, see § 274 (57).

(2) I did not sing yesterday *as* I wished.

Owing to the ambiguity of *as*, this sentence may give opposite senses: either "I did sing yesterday, but not in the manner that I wished," or "I did not sing yesterday, though I wished to have done so."

(3) And *seeing* dreams are caused by the distemper of the inward parts of the body, etc.

It requires something of an effort to find out that *seeing* here is equivalent to *seeing that* or *since*,—a conjunction. not a participle.

(c) *Pronouns*:—

She united the great body of the people in *her* and their common interest.

Is *her* here Objective or Possessive? The sense would have been clear at a glance, if the author had said "in *their and her* common interest."

(d) *Nouns*:—

(1) Your Majesty has lost all hopes of any future excises by their *consumption*.—*Guardian*, No. 52.

"Consumption" might be either Active or Passive. The sense appears to be "all hopes of levying any future excises on what they shall consume." But this is anything but obvious.

(2) A man who has lost his eyesight has *in one sense* less consciousness.

The words italicised might mean either "in one organ of sense" (eye-sight) or "in one respect." Which is it?

(e) *Verbs*:—

I have long since learned to like nothing but what you *do*.—*Spectator*, No. 627.

Is *do* here a pro-verb (§ 103) to save the repetition of *like*, or is it a notional verb (§ 88, *Note*) signifying "perform"?

(f) *Adjectives*:—

He has a *certain* claim to a share in that property.

Does *certain* here mean "undoubted," or is it merely an Indefinite Demonstrative adjective? (see § 54).

(g) *Phrases*:—

Your character of universal guardian, joined to the concern you ought to have for the cause of virtue and religion, assure[1] me that you will not think that clergymen, when injured, have *the least* right to your protection.—*Guardian*, No. 80.

He aimed at *nothing less than* the crown.

I will *have mercy*, and not sacrifice.—*Matt*. ix. 13.

He writes *as well as* you. (The sense is ambiguous, because *as well as* may be either Co-ordinative or Sub-ordinative; § 170.)

Much conversation was going on *about me*.

The counsel for the defence spoke *before the judge*.

Fish can scarcely be got now *at any rate*.

I grieve much *for his loss*.

There seems to be no limit *to the scolding of the housekeeper*.

285. Ambiguous Construction.—Such ambiguities arise, not from the equivocal character of a word or a phrase, but from the careless arrangement or careless omission of words:—

(1) Solomon, the son of David, who built the temple of Jerusalem, was the richest monarch that ever reigned over the Israelites.

[1] Observe that here the grammar is wrong.

Is "Solomon" the antecedent to *who*, or is "David"? According to the rule given in § 244 the antecedent should be "David," but the writer means "Solomon."

(2) I know that *all words which* are signs of complex ideas furnish matter of mistake and cavil.—BOLINGBROKE.

Is *which* here used in a Restrictive or in merely a Continuative sense? If the former, "all words" should be changed to "all *those* words," or *that* should be substituted for *which* (see § 83).

(3) God heapeth favours on His servants ever liberal and faithful.

Do the adjectives *liberal and faithful* refer to God or to His servants? If to the former, say, "God, ever liberal and faithful, heapeth," etc.

(4) The ecclesiastical and secular powers concurred in that measure. The high and mighty states of Holland are against us.

The second sentence is quite correct, because the same "states" are both "high and mighty." But are we to understand that the epithets "ecclesiastical and secular" relate to the same powers or to different powers? The careless omission of *the* before "secular" would compel us, if we did not happen to know better, to understand the phrase in the former sense. This is an instance of "impropriety" leading to a misunderstanding of the sense; see § 274 (22).

(5) And thus the son the fervent sire addressed.
POPE'S *Odyssey*, Book xix.

Did the son address the father, or the father the son? We prefer to consider "son" the subject to the verb, because it stands first. The sense, however, would have been much clearer if the poet had said "*his* fervent sire" instead of "*the* fervent sire."

(6) At least my own private letters leave room for a politician, well versed in matters of this nature, to suspect as much, as a penetrating friend of mine tells me.—*Spectator*, No. 43.

Here, except for the comma after *much*, the ambiguity of the sentence as it stands would be insoluble. All doubt would have been removed, if the author had observed the Rule of Proximity given in § 257. The sentence would then run as follows: "At least my own private letters, as a penetrating friend of mine tells me, leave room," etc.

(7) I beseech you, sir, to inform these fellows, that they have not the spleen, because they cannot talk without the help of a glass, or convey their meaning to each other without the interposition of clouds.—*Spectator*, No. 53.

Is *because* intended to qualify the verb "beseech," or the verb "inform," or the verb "have," or the negative verb "have not"?

(8) He has by some strange magic arrived at the value of half a plumb, as the citizens call a hundred thousand pounds.—*Tatler*, No. 40.

Does this mean that a hundred thousand pounds was denoted by a plumb, or by half a plumb?

Exercise.

Rewrite the following sentences, so as to make each of them more perspicuous than it is in its present form; or if more than one meaning is possible, express each meaning more distinctly. If no ambiguity exists, give your reason for thinking so:—

1. Providence, my son, has given you strength of body and cleverness of mind; but instead of this you waste your time in frivolity and idleness.

2. The workmen decided to come to terms with their employers, but to ask for the same wages as before, and accept as much less as they possibly could.

3. Allahabad, one of the principal cities in Northern India, is situated between the junction of the Jumna and the Ganges.

4. I prefer doing this to that.

5. Looking at his own warm overcoat, he could not help wishing that he could cover the poor, whom he saw shivering around him, with the same.

6. The farmstead was always the wooden white-painted house, of which the small country towns are composed.

7. A river adds much beauty to natural scenery; but a mountain is the thing that carries grandeur in its idea.

8. I doubt the application of the German military system to England.

9. Lisias promised his father never to abandon his friends.

10. A box-tree was planted between each plane-tree.

11. The insincerity of Charles I. was suspected by his people, and with good reason.

12. Both sides confidently predicted victory for their candidate, and up to the time when the last vote was recorded, it was difficult to decide whether victory lay with Conservatives or Liberals.—*Daily Telegraph*, 13th Jan. 1898.

13. This prevents their attending enough to what is in the Bible, and makes them battle for what is not in the Bible, but they have put it there.—M. ARNOLD.

14. Had I but served my God with half the zeal
I served my king, he would not in mine age
Have left me naked to mine enemies.—SHAKSPEARE.

15. Young Itylus, his parent's darling joy,
Whom chance misled the mother to destroy.
POPE'S *Odyssey*, Book xix.

16. I will spend a hundred or two pounds rather than be enslaved. —SWIFT.

17. My Christian and surname begin and end with the same letters.—*Spectator*, No. 505.

18. It has not a word but what the author religiously thinks in it.—*Guardian*, No. 4.

19. Mr. Dryden makes a very handsome observation on Ovid's writing a letter from Dido to Æneas, in the following words.—*Spectator*, No. 62.

20. As it is necessary to have the head clear as well as the com-

plexion, to be perfect in this part of learning, I rarely mingle with the men, but frequent the tea-tables of the ladies.—*Guardian*, No. 10.

21. All orders not issued by the managing director must not be attended to.

22. The history of Natal during the past year has been, except for agricultural depression caused by rinderpest and locusts, the happy history of a colony which has none.—*Times Weekly*, 7th Jan. 1898.

23. To a barbarous and inhuman wit there cannot be a greater gratification than to stir up sorrow in the heart of a private person by secret charges, at the same time that he remains unseen and undiscovered.—*Spectator*, No. 23.

24. I must confess that we live in an age, wherein a few empty blusterers carry away the praise of speaking, while a crowd of fellows overstocked with knowledge are run down by them; I say overstocked, because they certainly are so as to their service to mankind, if from their very store they raise to themselves ideas of respect and greatness of the occasion, and I know not what, to disable themselves from explaining their thoughts.—*Spectator*, No. 484.

25. The German Mercantile Marine has, since 1871, more than trebled its capabilities; and since 1880 has more than doubled them. —*Daily Telegraph*, 27th Jan. 1898, p. 9.

26. The more faulty we consider the protective system to which Germany, in common with all the other Great Powers of Europe except Great Britain and the United States of America, adheres, the more surprising is the progress recorded.—*Daily Telegraph*, 27th Jan. 1898, p. 8.

27. Mr. B—— has issued invitations for a full-dress parliamentary dinner, and Lord ——, his colleague, has issued invitations for a full-dress banquet.

28. No one has now any idea of how the Powers will deal with the question of the evacuation of Thessaly, as it is certain that the Porte will not quietly abandon the only fertile province of Greece, if the selection of Prince George of Greece (for the governorship of Crete) is forced upon him.—*Daily Telegraph*, 28th Jan. 1898.

29. It is out of the question that Germany and Austria will join in measures of force against Turkey.—*Daily Telegraph*, 2nd Feb. 1898.

30. His (Hudson's) fall was like the crash of a cliff. He who had been slapping noble lords on the back and the king of his Company, was left a wreck on the shore, and deserted by all who had battened on him.—*Fortnightly Review*, Feb. 1898, p. 247.

31. In view of recent changes, and especially since the war between China and Japan, it seemed desirable that Germany should have a seaport there for safeguarding her interests.—*Speech from Berlin*, 9th Feb. 1898.

32. The hopes of parents are blighted, if their children are indolent, and the money spent on them is wasted.

33. He is a great admirer of the artist who painted that picture and lives in Brompton.

34. We have just heard that the two boys leave school at the end of next week, and hope that they will not return to the same school again.

35. Geddes is now one of the bright points of the world which lies in darkness, to which my spirit will often turn for light.—N. MACLEOD.

36. There is probably no one of this generation who bestows any thought upon the problems of history and politics, who will not acknowledge his indebtedness to Mr. Carlyle.—*Times*, 18th Nov. 1870.

37. They forget to consult, and, as far as they are not vicious, conform to the tastes, feelings, habits of those whose happiness they would promote, and think only of their own.—W. J. Fox.

38. Lord Chelmsford is put on his trial for an alleged mistake in the disposition of troops in war, and why not a police officer who has placed a young man's life in peril, and who but for public energy would have been executed?—W. E. Stutter.

39. Sir Morton Peto spoke of the notion that the national debt might be repudiated with absolute contempt.—*Spectator*, 18th Nov. 1855.

40. Seldom has there been any great revolt of unskilled labour which attracted so much attention throughout the world, and which was fought out under circumstances of such constant peril of violence, which was brought to a close with so clean a sheet.—*Review of Reviews*, Feb. 1898, p. 127.

41. Antony was not less desirous of destroying the conspirators than his officers.

42. The amount which we annually devote to increasing our navy is, roughly speaking, identical with that expended by France, Russia, and Germany.—*Daily Telegraph*, 22nd April 1898.

43. The political demands of the party in power in Madrid have made it necessary for the political life of that party to resist in every form every attempt upon the part of the Cubans to secure their liberties, and to resist all attempts of other countries to assert them. —*Fortnightly Review*, June 1898, p. 858.

44. Fresh attempts should be made to give shelter to a harbour by laying out not a few large, but a large number of small, floating breakwaters.—*Geograph. Journal*, May 1898.

45. By a narrow majority the Australian Federal Convention has reversed its decision making it compulsory for the Federation to take over the debts of the individual states.—*Daily Telegraph*, 3rd Mar. 1898.

46. It was part of the work of Alfred the Great to create little by little the love of country in place of the old love of tribe. He might, like the King of Mercia, have fled to Rome and religious life; in fact, he fought them for nine long years, growing every year weaker.—*Times Weekly*, 25th Feb. 1898.

47. The trial resulted in the binding over of the two boys who were charged with the stealing and the acquittal of the man who was charged with receiving.—*Daily Telegraph*, 8th August 1898.

CHAPTER XXI.—SIMPLICITY OR EASE OF DICTION.

286. Simplicity described.—Simplicity of diction means the use of plain and easy words in preference to uncommon, affected, or difficult ones. The following description of the merits of simplicity is worth quoting:—

> It is by means of familiar words that style takes hold of the reader and gets possession of him. It is by means of these that great thoughts get currency and pass for true metal, like gold and silver which have had a recognised stamp put upon them. They beget confidence in the man who, in order to make his thoughts more clearly perceived, uses them; for people feel that such an employment of the language of common life betokens a man who knows that life and its concerns, and who keeps himself in contact with them. Besides, these words make a style frank and easy. They show that an author has long made the thought or the feeling expressed his mental food; that he has so assimilated them and familiarised them, that the most common expressions suffice him in order to express ideas which have become every-day ideas to him by the length of time they have been in his mind. And lastly, what one says in such words looks more true; for of all the words in use none are so clear as those which we call common words, and clearness is so eminently one of the characteristics of truth, that often it even passes for truth itself.—JOUBERT, *quoted in Arnold's "Essays on Criticism."*

An affected loftiness of style, *i.e.* a style the opposite to simple, has been called "euphuism" from a book named *Euphues* by Lyly (A.D. 1579).

287. Long Words and Periphrases.—Fine writing to express ordinary facts is a vulgarism,—the mark of an ill-informed mind, that seeks to hide its emptiness under big words and phrases, like the drum in the fable, that gave a booming sound, but was found on inspection to be hollow within. Nothing is gained by saying *in all human probability* for "most likely" or "most probably"; *lunar effulgence* for "moonlight"; *the tender passion* or *the amorous affection* for "love"; *pharmaceutical chemist* for "apothecary"; *caudal appendage* for "tail"; *the nasal organ* for "nose"; *skilful agriculturist* for "good farmer" or "good husbandman"; *partake of lunch* for "take lunch" or "lunch" (verb); *inebriate* or *dipsomaniac* for "drunkard"; *minatory expressions* for "threats"; *ruminating* for "chewing the cud"; *location* for "site"; *tonsorial artist* for "barber" or "hair-cutter"; *expression* for "word"; *adumbrate* for "foreshadow"; *to donate* for "to present" or "give"; *culinary department* for "kitchen"; *maternal relative* for "mother"; *the lower extremities* for "legs" or "feet"; *potables* for "drinkables"; *arcana* for "secrets"; *pedagogue* for "teacher"; *impeccable* for "faultless"; *germane* for "relevant" or "allied"; *infructuous* for "fruitless," "barren of results"; *apologue* for "fable"; *the sacred edifice* for "the church"; *the* *sacred day of hebdomadal rest* for "Sunday"; *animadversion* for "blame" or "censure"; *vituperation* for "abuse"; *exacerbate* for "embitter"; *multitudinous* for "manifold"; *incarnadine* for "dye red"; *evangel* for "gospel"; *contumacy* for "obstinacy"; *exemplar* for "model"; *cleptomaniac* for "thief"; *eventuate* for "come to pass"; *circumambient air* for "surrounding air"; *disembogues its waters* for "empties its waters"; *metamorphosis* for "change"; *precipitate* for "throw down," etc.

288. Hackneyed allusions and quotations.—It is better to give persons and things their plain names than to express them by allusions or quotations, which are hackneyed, pointless, or irrelevant. A writer adds nothing either to the clearness of his sentences, or (if this be his object) to his reputation for learning, by saying *the father of history* for "Herodotus"; *the blind old bard* for "Homer"; *the sublime author of "Paradise Lost"* for "Milton"; *the swan of Avon* for "Shakspeare"; *the Stagirite* for "Aristotle"; *the father of ecclesiastical history* for "Eusebius"; *the first Christian emperor* for "Constantine the Great"; *the apostle of the circumcision* for "St. Peter"; *the great lexicographer* for "Johnson"; *the bard of Mantua* for "Virgil"; *the queen of the night* or *the crescent satellite of the earth* for "the moon"; *the glorious lamp of day* for "the sun"; *the fragrant weed* for "tobacco"; *the cup that cheers but not inebriates* for "tea"; *more honoured in the breach than the observance* for "better avoided"; *the seven-hilled city* or *the eternal city* for "Rome"; *the modern Babylon* for "London"; *the land of Prester John* for "Abyssinia"; *Caledonia stern and wild* for "Scotland"; *few and far between* for "rare"; *plods his weary way* for "plods"; *the green-eyed monster* for "jealousy"; *'durance vile* for "imprisonment"; *the altar of Hymen* for "marriage"; *training the young idea to shoot* for "teaching"; *the gentle art of Izaac Walton* for "angling" or "fishing"; *a disciple of Bacchus* for "drunkard," etc.

Campbell's fine lines on Poland lose some of their effect through his calling Poland by the far-fetched and little-known ancient name of "Sarmatia":—

> O bloodiest picture in the book of Time!
> *Sarmatia* fell unwept, without a crime.
>
> *Pleasures of Hope.*

289. Simple facts to be told in simple terms.—A narrative loses much of its effect, if it is not told in words that express the natural feelings of the writer. Dr. Johnson, in the course of his tour to the Hebrides, expressed himself as follows in a letter to a friend :—

> When we were taken upstairs, a dirty fellow bounced out of the bed on which one of us was to lie.

But in the "Journal" that he prepared for the press, the same incident is dished up for the public in the pompous terms quoted below :—

> Out of one of the couches on which we were to repose there started up at our entrance a man as black as a Cyclops from the forge.

The same writer, when asked for his opinion on the comedy called the *Rehearsal*, said without any restraint or premeditation :

> It has not wit enough to keep it sweet.

Then, correcting himself, he added in more formal, but less effective, terms :

> It has not vitality enough to preserve it from putrefaction.

290. Simplicity marred by a clash of negatives.—When two or more negatives come together in the same sentence, we cannot easily catch their combined effect. "No men are immortal" is not so easily grasped as its more simple equivalent "All men are mortal." [1]

(1) There can be no doubt that nothing will be done.

Write :—It is certain that nothing will be done.

(2) I doubt whether the reverse be not the case.

Write :—I scarcely think so, or I doubt it.

(3) If we cannot recall at pleasure a single idea, we are not less unable to recall a whole train of ideas.

Write :—If we cannot recall a single idea, we are equally or more at a loss to recall a whole train of ideas.

(4) The loss of blood destroys strength.

This is less easily taken in by the mind than the more positive form—"Blood is the source of strength."

(5) Do not do to others what you would not wish them to do to you.—Confucius.

This is less direct than, "Do unto others as you would be done by."

291. Simplicity sometimes unsuitable.—A simple and direct statement is sometimes avoided for the sake of euphemism. Thus Cicero, to avoid saying that Milo's servants *killed* Clodius, employs the following periphrasis :—

> They did that which every master would have wished his servants to do in such an emergency.—*Pro Milone.*

[1] Bain's *Rhetoric and Composition*, Part I. p. 256.

Sometimes a periphrasis is used in preference to a single word, because it suits the argument or sustains the gravity of the subject better than a single word or a short sentence could do :—

(1) Shall not the judge of all the earth do right?

Here "the judge of all the earth" is a circumlocution for God; and the context is well served by using it.

(2) The very source and fount of day
Is dashed with wandering isles of night.—TENNYSON.

A roundabout, but impressive, way of saying that even the sun has spots.

Simplify the following sentences. If no simplicity is required in any case, give your reason :—

1. He breathed his last in indigent circumstances.
2. At ten P.M. the fatal noose was adjusted to the criminal's neck, and he was launched into eternity.
3. A vast concourse of people collected to witness the event.
4. Votes were taken by members exhibiting their hands above the heads of dissentients.
5. The rider was precipitated from his horse, but he met with no serious injury.
6. Your meaning does not come within my comprehension.
7. They called into immediate requisition the services of the physician who was accustomed to attend the family.
8. "I am under the impression," said Mr. Micawber, "that your peregrinations in this metropolis have not as yet been extensive, and that you might have some difficulty in penetrating the arcana of the Modern Babylon in the direction of the City Road,—in short," said Mr. Micawber, in another burst of confidence, "that you might lose yourself.—I shall be happy to call this evening, and install you in the knowledge of the nearest way."—DICKENS.
9. The contest of boats terminated in a victory to our crew.
10. I enjoy a post-prandial nap in a chair made for ease of posture.
11. An unwise man, if he is possessed of means, soon parts company with them.
12. Clouds of passion which might obfuscate the intellects of meaner females.—SCOTT.
13. She was tripping it on the light fantastic toe most of last night.
14. The actual cost of the barrages at Assouan and Assirt (in Egypt) will be £2,000,000.—*Daily Telegraph*, 24th Feb. 1898.
15. Sarah Bernhardt is recuperating from the operation she underwent a week ago.—*Ibid.* 25th Feb. 1898.
16. Nature seemed to tremble under the fierce rays of the incandescent luminary.—*Mariam*, p. 2.
17. During the month the hebdomadal figures of the fatalities directly due to this undoubted scourge (influenza) have been 43, then 40, followed by 73, and now 88.—*Daily Telegraph*, 2nd Feb. 1898.

18. What I was proposing to do was to facilitate the granting of municipalities to communities that are deserving of that honour. But it is no way germane to such proceedings that I should strike off that County Council which was the object of legislation ten years ago.—LORD SALISBURY, 3rd Feb. 1898.

19. Mr. Wheeler introduced an old friend, and brought up the apologue of the body and its members.—LORD SALISBURY, 3rd Feb. 1898.

20. This happy consummation was adumbrated last night at a social gathering of the London Spiritualist Alliance.—*Daily Telegraph*, 8th Feb. 1898.

21. He has vanished with the order of things in which he existed: his lamp cannot be relumed.—*Fortnightly Review*, Feb. 1898, p. 259.

22. The railway officials did not like to turn the station into an abattoir.—*Daily Telegraph*, 8th Feb. 1898.

23. We learn without immoderate surprise that there is reason to apprehend the breakdown of the negotiations for a Chinese loan.—*Times Weekly*, 11th Feb. 1898.

24. The sartorial art is quite as difficult as the culinary.

25. Experienced members of the feathered tribe are not entrapped with husks of corn.

26. In Queensland the Labour party has antagonised even the more advanced portions of the community.—*Review of Reviews*, Jan. 1898, p. 86.

27. The ballot-box is no longer the panacea which it appeared in the eyes of the multitude only twenty years ago.—*Review of Reviews*, Jan. 1898, p. 6.

28. This is not a time for twiddling our thumbs over the banalities of worn-out factions.—*Review of Reviews*, Jan. 1898, p. 7.

29. Having lately conversed much with the fair sex on the subject of your speculations (which since their appearance in public have been the chief exercise of the female loquacious faculty), I found the fair ones possessed with a dissatisfaction at your prefixing Greek mottoes to the frontispiece of your late papers.—STEELE, *Spectator*, No. 296.

30. All the ill offices and defamatory whispers, which take their birth from domestics, would be prevented, if this charity could be made universal: it would create endearing dependencies; and the obligation would have a paternal air in the master, who would be relieved from much care and anxiety from the gratitude and diligence of an humble friend attending him as his servant.—STEELE, *Spectator*, No. 294.

31. His incessant vigilance for the promotion of piety disposed him to look with distrust upon all metaphysical systems of theology and all schemes of virtue and happiness purely rational; and therefore it was not long before he was persuaded that the positions of Pope, as they terminated for the most part in natural religion, were intended to draw mankind away from revelation, and to represent the whole course of things as a necessary concatenation of indissoluble fatality; and it is undeniable that in many passages a religious eye may easily discover expressions not very favourable to morals or to liberty.—JOHNSON'S *Life of Pope*.

32. The peruser of Swift wants little previous knowledge: it will be sufficient that he is acquainted with common words and common things; he has neither to mount elevations nor to explore profundities.—JOHNSON'S *Life of Swift.*

CHAPTER XXII.—BREVITY OR TERSENESS OF DICTION.

292. **Brevity.**—It has been shown in § 252 that occasions may arise, in which repetition adds force to a sentence. As a general rule, however, brevity gives as much force to a sentence as diffuseness takes from it. A word that does no good does harm. "If a thought can be expressed in five words, there is a waste of strength in employing ten" (Bain). Attention given to superfluous words represents a loss of attention that might have been given to the matter.

China must go forwards or go to pieces.

This short sentence is more pointed than the following, and it contains as much:—

China must bring herself up to date and adopt the methods and appliances of modern science, or submit to seeing her territory divided among the different nations of Europe.

293. I. **The Choice of Words.**—The most obvious, and yet the most difficult, mode of attaining brevity is to choose such words as express the greatest amount of meaning in the smallest space. This is the language of proverbs. The best known quotations from distinguished authors are usually those that say the most in the fewest words:—

Thou knowest that Joab shed the blood of war in peace.—1 *Kings* ii. 5.

The virtuous woman eateth not the bread of idleness.—*Prov.* xxxi. 27.

Man is the only animal that blushes, or that needs to blush.—MARK TWAIN.

Nor love thy life, nor hate; but what thou livest
Live well; how long or short permit to Heaven.—*Par. Lost.*

The power of fortune is confessed by the miserable; the happy ascribe all their success to merit.—SWIFT.

The desire of the slothful man killeth him; for his hands refuse to labour.—*Proverbs* xxi. 25.

The progress of civilisation has been from status to contract.—MAINE.

The slothful hideth his hand in his bosom; it grieveth him to bring it again to his mouth.—*Proverbs* xxvi. 15.

There are several safeguards against temptation, but the surest is cowardice.—MARK TWAIN.

I am too proud to be vain.—SWIFT.
A grief too deep for tears.—SHELLEY.
Ring out the feud of rich and poor.—TENNYSON.

(The short phrase "the feud of rich and poor" covers the ground of two of the great social questions of the day—the conflicts of labour and capital, the jealousies of class-feeling.)

294. II. Grammatical Devices.—In the examples given below, the words enclosed in brackets show the longer form, in which the sentence may be supposed to have been expressed prior to condensation:—

(1) Using Abstract nouns for clauses:—

The *boldness* of Gama's manner (=Gama's manner was so bold that it) alarmed the King of Calicut, and made him submit to the Portuguese demands.

Mr. Casaubon's words had been quite reasonable; yet they had given her a vague, instantaneous sense of *aloofness* on his part (=that his thoughts and pursuits were not in sympathy with her own).—GEORGE ELIOT.

(2) Condensing two sentences into one by means of apposition:—

Vasco da Gama, the celebrated Portuguese admiral (=was a celebrated Portuguese admiral, and) was the first to round the Cape of Good Hope.

He put all his prisoners to death—a cruel and barbarous act (=which was a cruel, etc.).

(3) Condensing two Co-ordinate sentences into one by using a participle or by omitting one of the verbs:—

Cæsar, having now completed the conquest of Gaul, determined (=had now completed the conquest of Gaul, and so he determined) to invade Britain.

Hannibal led his forces over the Alps into the plains (=and entered the plains) of Italy.

(4) Placing a noun before another noun or before an adjective, to avoid a periphrasis:—

Eye-service (=service done when there is some one to see it, but not otherwise).

Penny-wise and pound-foolish (=saving a slight expense, to incur a much heavier one in the long run).

Hat-box (a box for carrying a hat).

(5) Using an adjective to express what would otherwise have to be expressed by a phrase or clause:—

Colonial Office (the office in which the affairs of the Colonies are administered).

The Liberal policy (the policy of the Liberal party).

Physical science (the science that treats of physics).

The evidence of language is irrefragable (=so conclusive that nothing can shake it).—MAX MÜLLER.

(6) Substituting a participle for a Subordinate clause:—

Pursued (=because he was pursued) on all sides, he was forced to surrender at last.
Slow rises worth by poverty depressed.—POPE.
(When it is depressed by poverty.)
The shepherd, having counted (=after he had counted) the sheep, left the field.

(7) Stating a fact by implication, instead of stating it explicitly and at full length:—

The spread of England's power to new continents is largely due to the adventurous spirit of her people.

This is shorter than saying:—

The people of England are of an adventurous spirit, and this is one of the chief causes that have led to the spread of her power to new continents.

(8) Giving a noun the form of a participle to avoid using a phrase:—

Landed aristocracy (owning large estates of land).
A gifted man (a man of unusual gifts or ability).
A strong-minded woman (a woman of unusual courage).
A one-eyed horse (a horse with only one eye).

(9) Forming Compound words (see further details in Chap. xxiv.):—

Geography is a mind-expanding subject (=a subject that expands the mind).
Red-hot (=so hot as to become red in colour).

(10) The use of prefixes and suffixes:—

His conduct was un-man-ly (=unworthy of a man).
His conduct was woman-ish (=worthy of a woman, but not worthy of a man).
He is a dull-ard (more than usually dull).
An ex-judge (a man who was once a judge).
An examin-ee (a person undergoing examination).
Absentee-ism (the habit of not living on one's estate).
Christen-dom (the aggregate of nations professing the Christian faith).
Critic-aster (an unworthy and incompetent critic).—SWINBURNE.
Grievance-monger (one who makes a habit of complaining about some grievance).
To beauti-fy (to make beautiful). To dark-en (to make dark).

295. Offences against Brevity.—The four chief offences against brevity are—(1) tautology, (2) pleonasm or redundancy, (3) verbosity, and (4) prolixity.

(1) **Tautology.**—This consists in employing superfluous

words in the same grammatical relation.[1] In the following examples the superfluous words are those enclosed in brackets :—

In the Attic commonwealth it was the privilege (and birthright) of every citizen (and poet) to rail (aloud and) in public.—SWIFT.

Integrity hath many advantages over dissimulation (and deceit): it is much the (plainer and) easier, much the safer (and more secure) way of dealing in the world; it has less of trouble (and difficulty), of entanglement (and perplexity), of danger (and hazard) in it; it is the shortest (and nearest) way to our end (carrying us thither in a straight line), and will hold out (and last) longest.—TILLOTSON.

Note.—Cases may arise, however, in which tautology is useful. Its usefulness as an aid to *impressiveness* has been shown already in § 252. It may also be an aid to *perspicuity*, when the full meaning cannot be expressed by a single word, as in the three following examples :—

(1) The *tribes* and *castes* of India.—SHERRING.

Neither of the italicised words expresses all that is wanted; for there are tribes which are not strictly castes, and castes which are not strictly tribes. The two words are not quite synonymous. It is therefore necessary to mention both.

(2) Oh happiness! our being's *end* and *aim!*
Good, pleasure, ease, content, whate'er thy name.—POPE.

Different shades of meaning are expressed in *end* and *aim;* also in *good, pleasure, ease, content.*

(3) As science makes progress in any *subject-matter*, poetry recedes from it.—NEWMAN.

The word *subject* is used in such a variety of senses that the word *matter* has been tacked on to it to prevent what in certain connections would be an ambiguity.

(2) **Redundancy** or **Pleonasm.**—This consists in employing superfluous words that are not in the same grammatical relation. Wherever it is possible, the superfluous words in the following examples are shown in brackets :—

He had the (entire) monopoly of the whole trade.
He (voluntarily) offered to stand security.
I must decline (to accept) your offer.
The judge ordered that the property be restored (again) to its rightful owners.
He has made a (new) discovery.
Charles V. of Spain and Francis I. of France (mutually) encouraged each other to extirpate the heretics.
I went home full of (a great many) serious reflections.—*Guardian*, No. 34.

---

[1] This definition of Tautology has been adopted from Bain's *Rhetoric and Composition*, and some of the examples under this head have been selected from the same source.

If he happens to have any leisure (upon his hands).—*Spectator*, No. 43.

The everlasting club treats all other clubs with (an eye of) contempt.—*Spectator*, No. 73.

Flavia, who is the mamma, has all the charms and desires of youth still (about her).—*Spectator*, No. 206.

Let them throw as much (foul) dirt at me as they please.—*Craftsman*, No. 232.

Let *observation* with extensive *view*
Survey mankind from China to Peru.—JOHNSON.

How many are there, by whom these *tidings* of good *news* were never heard?—BOLINGBROKE.

The dawn is overcast; (the morning lowers;
And heavily in clouds brings in the day.)—ADDISON.

In the late Franco-German war it is difficult to say who were the (first) aggressors.

Over-expression is not only a loss to energy, but by leading to wrong suggestion, may become a bar to perspicuity:—

A square is a four-sided figure having all its sides equal (and parallel) and all its angles right angles.

The words *and parallel* must not be added; for they might suggest that the sides of a right-angled figure could be equal without being parallel.

(3) **Verbosity.**—This consists in using a multiplicity of words, by the weight of which the sentiment, far from being strengthened, is like David in Saul's armour, encumbered and oppressed:—

For seeing those things which are equal must needs have all one measure, if I cannot but wish to receive all good, even as much at every man's hand as any man can wish unto his own soul, how should I look to have any part of my desire herein satisfied, unless myself be careful to satisfy the like desire which is in other men?—HOOKER.

This is a very languid and clumsy way of saying:

I cannot expect to have my own desires satisfied, if I pay no need to those of other men.

Or we might quote the terse couplet of Pope:—

His safety must his liberty restrain:
All join to guard what each desires to gain.

(4) **Prolixity.**—A tedious style clogged with twaddling details, amongst which it is not easy to catch the main point at a glance, is said to be *prolix*,—a fault quite distinct from wordiness or verbosity. In prolixity it is not redundancy of words that harasses the reader, but the enumeration of unnecessary facts:—

(1) On hearing this news he got off his chair, went out of the room, took down his hat, brushed it, put on his greatcoat, went

round to the stable, saddled his horse, mounted, and, after giving a few directions to the cook, rode off into the town.

A prolix way of saying:—

On hearing this news he rode off at once into the town.

(2) Last year a paper was brought here from England called a dialogue between the Archbishop of Canterbury and Mr. Higgins, which we ordered to be burnt by the common hangman, as it well deserved, though we have no more to do with His Grace of Canterbury than you have with the Archbishop of Dublin, whom you tamely suffer to be abused openly and by name by that paltry scoundrel of an observator; and lately upon an affair wherein he had no concern, I mean the business of the missionary of Drogheda, wherein our excellent prelate was engaged and did nothing but according to law and discretion.—SWIFT.

What can we make of such a sentence as this? A number of paltry details strung together in any order without any point or purpose.

296. Short Sentence between two Long Ones.—It is often expedient to wedge a short and pithy sentence in between two long ones, especially if these are in antithesis to each other. In such a case the little word *but* is hardly sufficient to express the transition from one bulky sentence to another:—

Without force or opposition, chivalry subdued the fierceness of pride and power; it obliged sovereigns to submit to the soft collar of social esteem, compelled stern authority to submit to elegance, and gave a dominating vanquisher of laws to be subdued by manners. *But now all this is to be changed.* All the pleasing illusions which made power gentle and obedience liberal, which harmonised the different shades of life, and which by a bland assimilation incorporated into politics the sentiments that beautify and soften private society, are to be dissolved by this new conquering empire of light and reason. *All the decent drapery of life is to be rudely torn off.* All the superannuated ideas furnished from the wardrobe of a moral imagination, which the heart owns and the understanding ratifies, as necessary to cover the defects of our naked shivering nature and to raise it to dignity in our own estimation, are to be exploded as a ridiculous, absurd, and antiquated fashion.—BURKE.

297. Over-brevity.—"I labour to be brief," said Horace, "and become obscure." Perspicuity should be the first consideration, and this must not be sacrificed to brevity:—

Lady Ellesmere. Without translating, gentlemen must not talk Latin, nor smoke, nor swear, in the presence of ladies.

Ellesmere. She thinks now she has been very epigrammatic. The men may swear, if they translate it? The commonest form of muddlement in sentences is occasioned by the endeavour to be brief. You apply two or three nominatives to one verb, or two or three verbs to one nominative, which do not agree together, if you look at them separately. What she did mean was,—that in the presence of ladies men must not smoke without permission, must not swear at all, and must not quote Latin without translating it.—HELPS's *Realmah*.

298. Condensation.—In condensing a sentence, take care that the shortened sentence expresses precisely the same point as the original:—

I have been told that, if a man that was born blind could obtain to have his sight for but only one hour, during his whole life, and should, at the first opening of his eyes, fix his sight upon the sun when it was in its full glory, either at the rising or setting of it, he would be so transported and amazed, and so admire the glory of it, that he would not willingly turn his eyes from that first ravishing object, to behold all the other various beauties this world could present to him.[1]—IZAAC WALTON.

This has been abridged as follows:—

It is said that, if a man born blind could obtain his sight for but one hour, the glory of the sunset or the sunrise, should he happen to behold it, would entrance him beyond all the other beauties of the world.

This abridgment, however, appears to miss the point. It implies that, after comparing the glory of the sunset or the sunrise with the other beautiful objects of the world, he would be more entranced by the sunset or sunrise than by anything else; whereas Izaac Walton's meaning seems to be that he would not take the trouble even to look at anything else. We should therefore condense the passage in the following way:—

I have been told that, if a man born blind could obtain his sight for but one hour, and should happen to fix his first gaze upon the rising or the setting sun, he would be so transported by the brilliancy of that one spectacle, that he would have no curiosity to see any of the other beauties that this world could present to him.

Exercises.

I. *Eliminate any superfluous words that you may find in the following; if you find nothing superfluous, give your reason:*—

1. He instituted a strict investigation and inquiry into the circumstances attending the bankruptcy of that insolvent firm.
2. Less time is required for this business, but more must be given to that.

---

[1] Bain's *Rhetoric and Composition*, p. 39. The abridged version which we have quoted, and which we do not consider an equivalent, is by the same author. Izaac Walton, it may be here noted, should have inserted *the* before the word "setting"; see § 274 (57).

3. The meeting gave one unanimous vote in favour of re-electing him as their chairman.

4. It was the universal opinion of all who saw him that he looked none the worse after his prolonged and obstinate attack of fever.

5. The literature of England should be studied in chronological order, beginning with the most ancient books and coming down gradually to the most recent.

6. Lampoons and satires, that are written with wit and spirit, are like poisoned darts, which not only inflict a wound, but make it incurable.—*Spectator*, No. 23.

7. This week is in a manner set apart and dedicated to serious thoughts.—*Spectator*, No. 23.

8. The immediate reason which led Louis XIV. to convoke the Assembly of 1682, was in order to strengthen his hands in the contest he was carrying on with Pope Innocent XI.

9. The highest actual bid for your horse was £15, but I did not let it go at that price, which I considered much too low.

10. Without a logical head a critic is perpetually puzzled and perplexed amidst his own blunders, mistakes the sense of those he would confute, or, if he chances to think right, does not know how to convey his thoughts to another with clearness and perspicuity.—*Spectator*, No. 291.

11. Payment of a dividend for the past half-year, at the rate of 20 per cent per annum, making 20 per cent for the year, is recommended by the directors of the Machinery Trust, Limited.—*Daily Telegraph*, 29th Jan. 1898.

12. There cannot be a greater gratification to a barbarous and inhuman wit, than to expose whole families to derision, while the traducer remains unseen and undiscovered.—*Spectator*, No. 23.

13. The matter being thus reduced within clearly-defined limits, and prepared for business-like discussion, it was submitted to the deliberations of a committee of Imperial and Colonial delegates.—*Times Weekly*, 21st Jan. 1898, p. 34.

14. It was her firm belief that to the coldness, the independence, and the want of the adoring faculty generally in women, were due the sole causes of matrimonial disagreement.—MRS. LYNN LINTON.

15. I am persuaded that if we go further we shall fare worse, and the longer we go on, the more heavily we shall suffer.—SIR JOHN LUBBOCK.

16. I trust the session of 1898 will not pass without something being done to place our West-Indian Colonies in a position and condition which shall ensure for them the best possible industrial prosperity.—*Fortnightly Review*, Feb. 1898, p. 320.

17. These responsibilities, these obligations, these duties can be adequately, effectively, and economically fulfilled on the lines that I have indicated.—*Fortnightly Review*, Feb. 1898, p. 320.

18. Never did Atticus succeed better in gaining the universal love and esteem of all men.—*Spectator*, No. 467.

19. A quite unique compliment was paid to the navy.—*Daily Telegraph*, 14th Feb. 1898.

II. *Condense the following sentences, or correct over-brevity, if you find any:—*

1. In defiance of all this, they make their selection in favour of the deplorable cheerlessness and dreariness of their own apartment to the airy, spacious, well-warmed wards of a hospital.—AYTOUN.

2. To talk to a man of moral corruption to elevate himself by contemplating the abstract conception of holiness, is somewhat a similar absurdity as to ask a man born blind to admire the beauty of colour.—*Contemporary Review*, July 1869, p. 404.

3. The truth of it is, there is nothing in history which is so improving to the reader as those accounts which we meet with of the deaths of eminent persons, and of their behaviour in that dreadful season.—*Spectator*, No. 289.

4. Whatever it can be clearly seen that parents ought to do or forbear for the interests of children, the law is warranted, if it is able, in compelling to be done or forborne, and is generally bound to do so.—J. S. MILL.

5. The results of administrative economy in the eastern colonies (of Australia) have made themselves felt with satisfactory effect.—*Times Weekly*, 7th Jan. 1898.

6. These orders being illegal, they are generally communicated verbally.—J. S. MILL.

7. During our stay in town one young man had his cheek cut open; another his under-lip nearly taken off; a third his scalp cut in two; and a fourth the tip of his nose so thoroughly excised that the end of his nasal organ lay upon the ground.—HENRY MAYHEW.

8. In all human probability England will maintain her present commercial supremacy over other nations, if a greater degree of attention is paid than heretofore to the demands of technical education.

9. The avenue to commercial prosperity between England and China has always passed through the treaty ports.

10. There was a Parliamentary surrender at discretion to stop further inquiry and save the plotters, big and little, from condign and most deserved punishment.—*Recollections of O'Connell.*

11. At the Royal Academy there is what we may call a full measure of pictures—a measure pressed down and overflowing; at the New Gallery a rather meagre "special selection" of Rossettis, upon what principle made it is difficult to say.—*Fortnightly Review*, Feb. 1898, p. 189.

12. The greater number of the works produced by the Pre-Raphaelite brotherhood were not strongly medieval in feeling.—*Fortnightly Review*, Feb. 1898, p. 194.

13. A severe and tyrannical exercise of power must become a matter of necessary policy with kings, when their subjects are imbued with such principles as justify and authorise rebellion.

14. Proposals having for their object to secure increased strength and efficiency in the army, and for amending the present conditions of military service, will be submitted to you.—*Queen's Speech*, 8th Feb. 1898.

15. The guinea places were better filled than the half-guinea, and not a jot better.

16. De —— had a painful complaint, which, sometimes keeping him awake, made him sleep perhaps, when it did come, the deeper.—DE QUINCEY.

17. It is a remarkable fact, that though probably there were more writers of Provençal poetry during these two centuries than there ever were in a similar period in any other land, they have not left a single masterpiece: they have vanished and made no sign.—R. S. WATSON.

18. In another column there appears an article discussing the influence conflict between the United States and Spain would have on British commerce.—*Daily Telegraph*, 18th April 1898.

19. We have now to think as we never before had of keeping old customers and attracting new.—*Times Weekly*, 25th Feb. 1898.

20. In the great railway, which is being constructed not so much in the interests of trade as in civilisation, he sees nothing but foolish expenditure.—*Report of Mr. Curzon's Speech in "Times Weekly,"* 4th March 1898.

CHAPTER XXIII.—ELEGANCE OF DICTION.

299. What is required by Elegance.—Elegance or beauty of diction requires two things—(1) "that all homely and coarse words or phrases shall be avoided, even at the expense of brevity; (2) that in respect of the sound of sentences there shall be a smooth and easy flow of words" (Whately).[1]

300. Refinement of Diction.—Elegance in the first sense, *i.e.* the avoidance of coarse words and phrases, is secured—(*a*) sometimes by circumlocution (§ 373); (*b*) sometimes by using a less common word, which, though it expresses the same thing, appears to express it in a less offensive form, because it is less common; (*c*) sometimes by the decent obscurity of a foreign word or phrase, as in example (2):—

(1) An uglier phrase was now coming on the stage; I mean what is now the national oath of England.

(2) *Effluvia*, a Latin Plural noun, used to avoid the word "stinks."

301. Smoothness of Diction: Euphony.—This kind of elegance is generally called euphony,—that quality of style which pleases the ear. The writer himself must have a good ear, if he wishes to know what will please the ear of his readers. A few hints, however, are herewith offered for guidance:—

(1) Avoid ending a sentence with a short and pointless word:—

The walls of the fortress, battered with guns from the ships and artillery from the shore for a space of eight hours, *fell*. (Write, "were razed to the ground.")

(2) Avoid using two constructions, when it is possible to use one:—

[1] Whately's *Rhetoric*, Part III. chap. iii. p. 213.

They suspected that he had been bribed and given an unjust sentence. (Here there is an abrupt and misleading transition from the Passive voice to the Active. Write: "They suspected that he had received a bribe and given an unjust sentence.")

(3) Avoid using the same form of participle more than once in the same clause or phrase:—

Yesterday the vestry of St. George, Hanover Square, decided to seal the memorial to be presented to the Duke of Devonshire, *praying* for the introduction of a bill in the next session of Parliament *providing* for the creation of metropolitan municipalities.—*Daily Telegraph*, 21st Jan. 1898. (Write, "which should provide for the creation.")

(4) Avoid using the same word twice in a different connection:—

To enable us to make the *necessary* arrangements, it is *necessary* for us to hear not later than noon on Friday, 21st current.—*Daily Telegraph*, 20th Jan. 1898. (Write "requisite" for the first "necessary.")

(5) Avoid using the same word twice in different senses:—

He *means* to take advice as to the best *means* of testing the fact. (Write "method" or "mode" for the second "means," or "intends" for the first one.)

We (the writer) will now explain how *we* (men in general) are led into making such a mistake.

(6) Avoid using words of nearly the same sound within a short interval, unless the play upon words is intentional:—

The action for libel brought by Miss ——, a nurse, against Mr. ——, in respect of a *letter* the *latter* had written to a relative, terminated in favour of the defendant.—*Daily Telegraph*, 27th Jan. 1898. (Write "which he" for "the latter.")

If all local authorities *affected acted* in the same manner, ratepayers might receive some benefit from unity.—*Daily Telegraph*, 8th Feb. 1898. (Write "concerned" for "affected.")

(7) Avoid mixing Present participles too freely with Verbal nouns, as the frequent repetition of *-ing* not only has a bad sound, but may lead to some confusion in the mind of the reader:—

The Epistle to the Hebrews, *bearing* in its title a special form of address, is yet universal in its drift, as *designing* to convince all mankind of the necessity of *seeking* for happiness in a future life and *avoiding* all things *leading* men to sin. (Write: "The epistle to the Hebrews, though it bears in its title a special form of address, is yet universal in its drift, as its aim is to convince all mankind of the necessity of seeking for happiness in a future life and avoiding everything that may lead men to sin.)

(8) Avoid using a string of Relatives in the same sentence :—

The doctrine in question only appears a paradox, because it has usually been so expressed as apparently to contradict these well-known facts ; *which*, however, were equally well known to the authors of the doctrine, *who* therefore could only have adopted from inadvertence any form of expression *which* could to a candid person appear inconsistent with it.—J. S. Mill. (Write "the said facts" for the first "which.")

Few, indeed, are those *who* still linger among us *who* took an active part in the great movement of 1848.—*Review of Reviews*, April 1898, p. 343.

(9) Avoid using adverbs close together for qualifying different words, if they can be separated without loss of idiom :—

In fact, those who study such matters *closely, already*, I think, perceive the tentative beginnings, etc.—*Fortnightly Review*, Feb. 1898, p. 261. (Write, "perceive already, I think.")

(10) Avoid using verbs in different tenses without necessity :—

The lion *roared* to a false note, and then *rates* the jackals for yelping in unison.—*Daily Telegraph*, 5th Feb. 1898.

(11) Adverbs or adverbial phrases that qualify the same word should be separated by some intervening word, if the construction admits of it :—

He, *at four o'clock p.m., in spite of his contract, obstinately and with some acrimony declared* that he would not work another hour. (Write : "At four o'clock P.M. he, in spite of his contract, declared obstinately and with some acrimony that he would not work another hour.")

(12) Avoid awkward constructions to which the ear is not accustomed :—

Flying visits to settlements of Finns, Poles, Bohemians, and Russians, located along the Northern Pacific, *disclosed them to have attained* a degree of Americanisation, etc.—*Harper's Magazine*, Feb. 1898. (Write, "disclosed the fact that these foreign settlers had attained," etc.)

302. Play upon Words.—Euphony as well as point is sometimes produced by repeating the same words in a different meaning or in a different relation :—

Evil (=evil consequences) be to him that evil thinks (=imputes misconduct).

Bad (=unlucky) accidents happen to bad (=unskilful) players.

The right (*noun*) divine of kings to govern wrong (*adj.*).—Pope.

These are all practical and practicable measures.—*Fortnightly Review*, Feb. 1898, p. 317.

If the ministers had comprehended as much as they apprehended, they would have saved the nation a good deal of money.—*Pulteney's Speech.*

I comprehend that gentleman, though I do not apprehend him.—*Walpole's Reply.*

When our vices leave us, we flatter ourselves that we have left our vices.—*French Proverb.*

When reason is against a man, he will be against reason.—*Proverb.*

He who never changes his mind has no mind to change.—*Ibid.*

Playing upon words, if this adds nothing either to force or clearness, produces not euphony, but a jingle. The following lines in *Paradise Lost* have been condemned by a distinguished critic:[1]—

> And brought into the world a world of woe.
> This tempted our attempt and wrought our fall.
> At one slight bound high overleapt all bound.

Exercise.

Improve the euphony of the following sentences:—

1. This brings me to the question—the most important of all—of the final aims of British policy in the Far East.—*Fortnightly Review*, Feb. 1898, p. 329.

2. So it is that I must be forced to get home partly by stealth and partly by force.—SWIFT.

3. I look upon it as my duty, so far as good health enabled me and as long as I keep within the bounds of truth, of duty, and of decency, to do, etc.—SWIFT.

4. Buildings should not be put up unless in conformity with the bye-laws, unless we wish to encourage the jerry-builder.—*Middlesex County Times*, 23rd July 1898.

5. Two great sins, one of omission and the other of commission, were committed by him.

6. Far and wide the plain of the Vardu softened by a delicate blue haze, and in the extreme distance a thread of silver light—the Gulf of Salonica—stretches.

7. That Pre-Raphaelism was not, any more than any other, the school in which the doctrine of art for art's sake was being forced upon its students, may be conceded.—*Fortnightly Review*, Feb. 1898, p. 196.

8. Of the western provinces which obeyed the Cæsars, Britain was the last that was conquered, while they (the Cæsars) gave it away before any other province.

9. Wit should be used as a shield for defence, rather than as a sword to wound others.

10. Knowledge in one of its senses is synonymous with sensation.

11. If the profession of anything is good for anything, practice is better.

12. It is a remarkable fact that some of the most remarkable men in ancient times combined warlike pursuits with political ambition.

13. The blessings of fortune are the lowest; the next are the

[1] Addison takes exception to such "jingle" in *Spectator*, No. 297.

bodily advantages of strength and health; but the superlative blessings, in fine, are those of the mind.

14. A. came here daily; every other man came every other day.

15. Innumerable failures occur every day in the numerous careers of life.

16. As one peruses the accounts, as they are issued, the outlook seems to be very serious.

17. We should cease persisting in trying to put a quart into a pint pot.—*Review of Reviews.*

18. Your not having hitherto paid the tithe, should such be the case, and the fact that the sum you are now called upon to pay does not rateably correspond with any previous payment made by you, cannot be raised as an objection.—*Tithe-collector's Notice.*

19. The friendless state that he was in, and that he wished to die, made every one pity him.

20. Accident having opened a new and most congenial career to him, and having become a great favourite of, and of much use to, Mr. Nash, he ultimately accompanied his patron to London.—C. J. MATHEWS.

21. Perhaps we might venture to add, that it is hardly explicable, except as a portrait drawn by a skilful hand guided by love, and by love intensified by the consciousness of some impassable barrier.—LESLIE STEPHEN.

22. We believe the freedom and happiness of a people are not the result of their political institutions, but that their political institutions are, in a great degree, the result of their own temper and aspiration.—PARNELL.

23. I have a book printed at Antwerp, and which was once possessed by Adam Smith.

24. Burns is a handy man with his fists, and maintains, after long experience, that he would prefer to rely on the clenched hand to defend himself in a mêlée to any weapon yet invented.—*Review of Reviews*, Feb. 1898, p. 129.

25. Mr. J. H. C. said that there had been innumerable instances of bribery in the Guardians' Boards, leading to their supersession by the Government by paid guardians.—*Daily Telegraph*, 28th Apr. 1898.

26. It is the men who have bridged the ocean with the steamship, who have tunnelled the mountains and severed the isthmus, who have made the empire.—*Ibid.* p. 130.

27. Notwithstanding his illness, and that he had lost nearly all his money, he still kept the business going, hoping for better times.

28. Prince Ferdinand of Bulgaria, who since the murder of M. Stambuloff, from which time the relations between Austria and Bulgaria changed considerably for the worse, has not appeared at the Vienna Court, was received in a long audience to-day at noon by the Emperor.—*Daily Telegraph*, 8th March 1898.

29. The first suggestion I would make is that usurers all over the country, who trade under false names and pretend to be banks, and issue circulars and prospectuses which are false and fraudulent, and who use these names for the purpose of securing contracts with borrowers in order to defraud them by a system of usury, should be dealt with.—*Evidence of Sir G. Lewis*, 11th March 1898.

30. The first thing the usurers do is to see who are the relatives of the young borrower. In the S. C. case we had a man whose bills were discounted because a nobleman took them to them.—*Ibid.*

31. Our ministers cannot understand that England is sick of the parish pump and sickest of all of the Manchester school.—*Review of Reviews*, April 1898, p. 354.

32. The Americans are perhaps sincere in saying that the United States are not contemplating seizing Cuba in order to annex it.—*Times Weekly*, 6th May 1898, p. 276.

33. In 1874, though not then prepared to advocate the disestablishment of the Scotch Church, though he admitted an established church in a minority is an anomaly, he yet strenuously opposed when the Church Patronage Scotland Bill was before Parliament to invest this Church with powers never before entrusted to an ecclesiastical body.—*Middlesex County Times*, 4th June 1898.

34. The step was only decided upon at the very last moment; indeed, for reasons upon which it is unnecessary to dwell, it had appeared but a few hours previously utterly and absolutely impossible that it could be taken before to-day at the earliest.—*Daily Telegraph*, 16th June 1898, p. 7.

35. With a ministry without any authority any sudden course of action may be looked for.—*Daily Telegraph*, 23rd June 1898, p. 9.

36. When a person has attracted to himself by an elevated moral bond several other persons, when he dies, it always happens that the survivors, often divided up to that time by rivalries, beget a strong friendship the one for the other.—*Translation from* RENAN'S "*Apostles.*"

37. This army is incapable because of sickness of marching anywhere except to the transports.—*Telegram quoted in "Daily Telegraph,"* 8th August 1898.

38. The rest of the evening was devoted to voting away the nation's money, etc.—*Standard*, 9th August 1898.

39. The Carlists possessed an army of their own, now disbanded, but many of whose officers would expect to be reinstated in their former positions.—*Fortnightly Review*, 1st August 1898.

40. He discourses more or less discursively upon the various changes, etc.—*Review of Reviews*, August 1898, p. 165.

41. If there is one thing that strikes one more than another, it is His Majesty's ardent desire for peace.—*Times*, 31st August 1898.

PART III.—ENLARGEMENT OF VOCABULARY: FIGURES OF SPEECH.

CHAPTER XXIV.—ENLARGEMENT BY COMPOSITION.

303. Sources of Enlargement.—Besides the borrowing of foreign words (which in English make up about two-thirds of the vocabulary), there are at least eight home-sources from which the vocabulary has been or can yet be enlarged :—

(1) Provincial or local words becoming national: (rather rare). A few examples are given below :—

Pony, gruesome, canny, feckless, force (waterfall), glint, gloaming, (all from Scotland). Fun (a slang word in Dr. Johnson's time). Tory (an Irish word for "bog-trotter," first used in a political sense in 1679). Whig (short for "whiggamor," a Scotch word for "driver"; first used in a political sense in 1679).

(2) Proper names acquiring a general sense: (not uncommon). Older examples are numerous; as *milliner* (a man of Milan); *lumber-room* (a room where the Lombard brokers stowed away their pledges). The following examples are recent :—

A gladstone bag. To lynch (from an American judge named Lynch). A davy-lamp (from the inventor). To boycott (from a Captain Boycott, so treated in Ireland). To bowdlerise (to expurgate; from Bowdler's expurgated edition of Shakspeare). A hansom cab (from the inventor).

(3) Revival of obsolete words: (rare) :—

Love-some (Tennyson). Burgeon (Scott). Holts (the wooded tops of hills—Tennyson). Sough (the whistling of wind through trees). Over-lord (suzerain—Freeman). Worsen (to make worse—Southey, Gladstone). Aloofness (George Eliot).

(4) Doublets: words derived from the same original elements, but possessing different forms, to each of which there is a different meaning. In our vocabulary we have at least four hundred

and thirty words which have one or more different forms with differentiated meanings :—

Wile, guile. Antic, antique. Chance, cadence. Aptitude, attitude. Prune, plum. Bank, bench. Gabble, jabber. Brown, bruin. Etiquette, ticket.

(5) Compound words : described in the present chapter.

(6) The use of prefixes and suffixes ; see Chapter xxv.

(7) The use of metaphors }
(8) The use of metonymy } see Chapter xxvi.

304. Compounds.—When two or more words are joined together, the word so formed is called a *Compound ;* as *ink-pot*, *drinking-water*, *cod-liver-oil.*

Compound words are subdivided into—

I. **Unrelated**, or those in which the Simple words are not connected together by any grammatical relation. (These have been also called Juxta-positional.)

II. **Related,** or those in which there is some grammatical relation between the component words. (These have been also called Syntactical.)

SECTION 1.—UNRELATED OR JUXTA-POSITIONAL COMPOUNDS.

305. In all compounds of this class the word that stands *first* defines the one that stands second :—

Thus "*horse-race*" means that kind of race which is run by *horses*, and not by boats or by men or by anything else. But "*race-horse*" means that kind of horse which is used for *racing*, and not for ordinary riding, or for drawing a carriage.

In a triple compound, as "*cod-liver-oil*," the same rule holds good : here *cod* qualifies *liver*, and *cod-liver* qualifies *oil.*

306. Compound Nouns can be formed as follows :—

(1) A noun preceded by another noun :—

Oil-lamp, lamp-oil ; ear-ring, ring-finger ; rail-way, way-side.

(2) A noun preceded by a Gerund :—

Cooking-stove, looking-glass, drinking-water, bathing-place.

Note.—The *-ing* is not always used ; as in *wash-house*, not *washing-house ; grind-stone*, not *grinding-stone*, etc.

(3) A noun preceded by an adverb :—

By-word, by-path, under-tone, under-wood, up-land, in-land.

307. Compound Adjectives can be formed as follows :—

(1) An adjective preceded by a noun, denoting—

(*a*) *Some point of resemblance :*—

Snow-white (=white like snow) blood-red, coal-black, sky-blue.

(b) *Some point of reference:—*

Air-tight (=tight against air), fire-proof, head-strong, heart-broken, book-learned, top-heavy, colour-blind, blood-thirsty.

(c) *The cause or source of the quality:—*

Home-sick (=sick for home), purse-proud, heaven-born.

(d) *The extent or measure of the quality:—*

Skin-deep (=deep as the skin), world-wide, breast-high, life-long.

(2) A noun (with suffix *-ed*) preceded by a noun:—

Chicken-hearted, hook-nosed, ox-tailed, web-footed, cow-houghed.

(3) An adjective or participle preceded by an adjective:—

Red-hot, dark-brown, bright-blue, dead-alive, luke-warm.

308. Compound Verbs can be formed as follows:—

(1) A verb preceded by a noun:—

Hen-peck, brow-beat, top-dress, back-bite, hood-wink, way-lay.

(2) A verb preceded by an adjective:—

Safe-guard, rough-hew, white-wash, rough-shoe, dumb-founder.

Section 2.—Related or Syntactical Compounds.

309. Compound Nouns can be formed as follows:—

(1) A verb Transitive followed by its Object:—

A tell-tale (one who tells tales), a cut-throat, a pick-pocket.

(2) A verb Transitive (with suffix *-er* or *-ing*) preceded by its Object:—

Shoe-maker, tax-payer; engine-driving, house-building, etc.

Note.—The "*er*" and the "*ing*" are not always used, as in *tooth-pick*, not *tooth-picker; blood-shed*, not *blood-shedding*.

(3) A verb qualified by an adverb:—

(a) *When the adverb precedes the verb:—*

An out-turn, an out-look, an out-fit, an up-start, an in-let.

(b) *When the adverb is placed after the verb:—*

A run-away, a cast-away, a break-down, a break-up, a fare-well.

Note.—Some compounds of this class have two forms: *set-off* or *off-set; turn-out* or *out-turn; look-out* or *out-look*.

(4) A noun qualified by an adjective:—

A noble-man, a half-penny, a mad-man, a sweet-heart, mid-day.

(5) A noun qualified by a participle:—

(a) *Present Participle:—*

Humming-bird, loving-kindness, spinning-top, finishing-stroke.

Note.—the "*ing*" is not always used; as in *screech-owl*, not *screech-ing-owl; glow-worm*, not *glowing-worm*.

(*b*) *A verb with the force of a Past or Passive participle*:—

Hump-back = humped-back ; lock-jaw = locked-jaw.

(6) A noun qualified by a Possessive noun :—

Sales-man (for sale's-man), bats-man, oars-man, Tuesday, kins-man, herds-man, crafts-man, bees-wax, states-man, sports-man.

Note 1.—In some compounds the apostrophe is retained before the *s* :—*stone's-throw, king's-bench, cat's-paw, heart's-ease, land's-end.* The noun *spokes-man* has been formed by a false analogy.

Note 2.—The following compounds, since the first noun is not Possessive, are of the Unrelated or Juxta-positional class :—*boat-man, sea-man, oil-man, wood-man, cart-man, plough-man*, etc.

(7) A noun in apposition with a noun or pronoun :—

Washer-woman ; he-goat, she-goat ; man-servant, maid-servant.

310. Compound Adjectives can be formed as follows :—

(1) A noun preceded and qualified by an adjective :—

Evil-hearted, hot-headed, long-tailed, one-sided, red-coloured.

(2) A noun as object to the Pres. part. of a Trans. verb :—

A *heart-rending* sight ; a *time-serving* man ; a *soul-stirring* story.

(3) A noun as object to some preposition :—

An *over-land* (over the land) journey ; an *underhand* trick.

311. Verbs can be compounded with adverbs :—

(*a*) When the adverb precedes the verb : (uncommon) :—

Back-slide, cross-question, over-awe, under-state, with-hold.

(*b*) When the verb precedes the adverb. This is very common. The two words are written separately; as *turn out, come on*, etc. (But in *don* (= do on), *doff* (= do off) they are compounded.)

312. Phrase Compounds.—Such compounds are sometimes used as nouns, and sometimes as adjectives :—

Forget-me-not (noun); hand-and-glove (friends that fit each other as closely as hand and glove) ; man-of-war ; would-be (adj. used for one who intended to be or do something, but was stopped); barrister-at-law ; note-of-hand ; ticket-of-leave ; Jack-o'-lantern ; hole-and-corner (adj. clandestine) ; son-in-law ; four-in-hand ; spic-and-span new (lit. spike and spoon new ; new as a nail or spike just made, or a spoon (chip) just cut).

313. Spelling of Compounds.—In words of two or more syllables the accent is usually thrown back on the first syllable, and in many cases this has the effect of altering the spelling:—

Bon-fire from *bone-fire.* *Hus-band* from *house-band* (lit. house-dweller). *Hus-sif* or *hus-sy* from *house-wife.* *Nos-tril* from *nose-thril.* *Star-board* from *steer-board.* *Tad-pole* from *toad-poll.* *Fort-night* from *four-teen-night.* *Suf-folk* from *South-folk.* *Fur-long* from *furrow-long.* *Sus-sex* from *South-sex*, etc.

In some words, however, the change of sound produced in this first syllable by the accent is not accompanied by any change in the spelling:—

Black-guard. Cup-board. Break-fast. Two-pence, three-pence, four-pence, five-pence. Row-lock (sounded as *rullock*).

CHAPTER XXV.—ENLARGEMENT BY PREFIXES AND SUFFIXES.

314. Prefixes, Suffixes, Affixes.—A prefix (Lat. *præ*, "before") is a particle placed at the beginning of a stem; a suffix (Lat. *sub*, "after") is a particle placed at the end of one. The name "affix" (Lat. *ad*, added to either side) may be given to either. (Some writers use "*affix*" for "*suffix*." It is more convenient, however, to have a word like "affix," which with etymological propriety can stand for either "suffix" or "prefix.")

Prefixes alter the meanings of words, while suffixes alter their functions.

There is a radical difference of meaning between *teach* and *unteach; bid* and *for-bid; con-vert* and *sub-vert; pro-ceed, pre-cede, suc-ceed, ac-cede, se-cede, con-cede, ex-ceed, inter-cede*, and *re-cede*.

On the other hand, suffixes form nouns, adjectives, verbs, and adverbs, and hence they change the function of a word, that is, they make it of one part of speech or another. Thus the stem *dark* becomes a noun in *dark-ness*, a verb in *dark-en*, and an adverb in *dark-ling* and *dark-ly*.

315. Sources of Affixes.—The sources from which our affixes have come are three in number:—

I. Teutonic (which consists of Anglo-Saxon forms, together with a few Norse, Frisian, and Dutch ones).
II. Romanic (which includes Latin, French, and Italian).
III. Greek (partly direct, partly through French or Latin).

Our Teutonic affixes have been sometimes called "English." The name "Teutonic," however, appears to be preferable for two reasons. (*a*) If by "English" we are to understand Anglo-Saxon, some of our Teutonic affixes are not of English origin; for instance the *-kin* of "firkin" and the *-scape* of "landscape" are Dutch; the *un-* of "unto" is Frisian; the *-sk* of "bask" and "busk" is Norse, having been imported by the Danes. (*b*) *All* affixes, which have become naturalised in our language, whatever their origin may have been, are now entitled to be called "English." Our vocabulary abounds in hybrids; that is,

Teutonic stems with Romanic or Greek affixes, and *vice versa.* "Cottager," for example, is made up of three elements: (1) the Norse word *cot* (still in common use) furnishes the stem; (2) the first suffix *-age* is Romanic, having come to us from Latin through French; (3) the second suffix *-er* might be either from Anglo-Saxon *ere*, an agent or doer, or from Latin *-arius*, French *-aire*, *-ier*, or *-er*, which also denotes agent or person. The suffix *-ery* in "fish-ery" is itself a hybrid, made up of the Teutonic *-er*, as in "fish-er," and the Romanic *y*, as in "famil-y," "stud-y."

Section 1.—Teutonic Prefixes.

316. A- (*on, in*): *a*-bed, *a*-shore, *a*-sleep, *a*-way, *a*-stir, *a*-float.

A- (*off, up, from*): *a*-rise, *a*-wake, *a*-fresh, *a*-light, *a*-rouse, *a*-new. *Intensive*:—*a*-maze, *a*-weary, *a*-shamed, *a*(*c*)-cursed, *a*(*c*)-knowledge.

After-: *after*-wards, *after*-witted, *after*-thought.

Al- (*all*): *al*-one, *l*-one, *al*-most, *al*-so, *al*-ready, *al*-together.

At- (*to*): *at*-one, *at*-onement, *a*-do (for *at*-do).

Be- (*by*): (1) It forms Transitive verbs out of nouns or adjectives: *be*-calm, *be*-dew, *be*-friend, *be*-fit, *be*-numb, *be*-guile, *be*-fool, *be*-night.

(2) It forms Transitive verbs out of Intransitive: *be*-moan, *be*-speak.

(3) It gives an intensive force to verbs: *be*-daub, *be*-smear, *be*-seech, *be*-get, *be*-stir, *be*-sprinkle, *be*-stow, *be*-take, *be*-deck.

(4) It forms a part of some nouns, adverbs, and prepositions: *be*-half, *be*-quest, *be*-low, *be*-neath, *be*-sides, *b*-ut, *be*-fore, *be*-tween (twain).

Note.—In the word "*be*-head" the "be" has a privative sense.

By- (*on the side*): *by*-path, *by*-word, *by*-stander, *by*-election.

For- (*thoroughness*): *for*-bear, *for*-lorn.

For- (*privative* or *depreciatory*): *for*-swear, *for*-get, *for*-bid, *for*-sake.

Fore- (*before*): *fore*-cast, *fore*-tell, *fore*-see, *fore*-head, *fore*-lock, *fore*-thought, *fore*-runner, *fore*-stall, *fore*-man, *fore*-ground, *fore*-leg.

Forth-: *forth*-coming, *forth*-with.

Fro- (*from*): *fro*-ward (opp. to *to*-ward).

Gain- (*against*): *gain*-say (speak or say against).

In-: *in*-to, *in*-sight, *in*-land, *in*-let, *in*-mate, *in*-come.

Mis- (*wrongly*): *mis*-deed, *mis*-lead, *mis*-take, *mis*-judge, *mis*-lay.

N- (*negative*): *n*-one, *n*-either, *n*-ever, *n*-or, *n*-illy willy.

Off- (*of* or *off*): *off*-ing, *off*-spring, *of*-fal, *off*-shoot.

On-: *on*-set, *on*-slaught.

Out-, **ut-**: *out*-cast, *out*-side, *out*-landish, *out*-look, *out*-come, *out*-let, *out*-break, *out*-post, *out*-house, *out*-cry; *ut*-ter, *ut*-most.

It makes Intransitive verbs Transitive: *out*-live (=live beyond), *out*-run (=run ahead of), *out*-shine (surpass in brightness), *out*-vote (=defeat by votes), *out*-weigh (=surpass in weight).

Over- (*above, beyond*): *over*-eat, *over*-*flow*, *over*-hear, *over*-coat, *over*-charge, *over*-step, *over*-awe, *over*-look, *o*r-lop (for *over*-lop).

Thorough-, **through-**: *thorough*-fare, *through*-out, *through*-ticket.

To- (*to*, *for*): *to*-day, *to*-night, *to*-gether, *to*-ward, un-*to*-ward, *to*-morrow.

Twi- (*double*): *twi*-n, *twi*-ce, *twi*-light, *twi*-ne.

Un- (*not*): *un*-truth, *un*-real, *un*-wise, *un*-told, *un*-ripe.

Un- (*back*, *reversal*): *un*-bolt, *un*-tie, *un*-lock, *un*-twine, *un*-do.

Note.—In the word "*un*-loose," the "*un*" is merely intensive.

Un- (*up to*): *un*-to, *un*-til.

Under: *under*-go, *under*-stand, *under*-hand, *under*-ling, *under*-neath, *under*-mine, *under*-sell, *under*-take.

Note.—This prefix also denotes deficiency, or too little: *under*-paid, *under*-fed, *under*-valued, etc.

Up-: *up*-right, *up*-ward, *up*-on, *up*-lands, *up*-hold, *up*-shot.

Well- (*in good state*): *wel*-fare, *wel*-come.

With- (*against*, *back*): *with*-draw, *with*-hold, *with*-stand.

Note.—In *with*-drawing room, the *with* has been dropped.

Section 2.—Teutonic Suffixes.

Nouns.

317. An **Agent** or **Doer**:—

-er, **-ar**, **-or**: bak-*er*, do-*er*, li-*ar*, tail-*or*, sail-*or*, cloth-i-*er*, court-i-*er*, law-y-*er*, saw-y-*er*.

-ster (fem.): spin-*ster*. It is not Feminine, but merely marks the agent in song-*ster*, malt-*ster*, trick-*ster*, young-*ster*, huck-*ster*.

-en (fem.): vix-*en*, formerly the feminine of "fox"; now denotes a cunning and spiteful woman.

-herd (*keeper*): shep-*herd*, swine-*herd*, cow-*herd*, neat-*herd*.

-man (*person*): wo-*man*, post-*man*, fish-er-*man* (double suffix).

-monger (*dealer*): ballad-*monger*, coster-*monger*, iron-*monger*.

-nd (*old ending of present participle*); fie-*nd*, frie-*nd*, erra-*nd*, wi-*nd*, husba-*nd*.

-ter, **-ther**, **-der**: daugh-*ter*, fa-*ther*, mo-*ther*, spi-*der* (spin-der), ru(d)-*der* (from *row*).

-wife (*woman*): fish-wife, mid-*wife*.

-wright (*workman*): ship-*wright*, wheel-*wright*, cart-*wright*.

318. Abstract Nouns, marking *state*, *action*, *condition*.

-craft: witch-*craft*, priest-*craft*, handi-*craft*.

-dom: wis-*dom*, king-*dom*, free-*dom*, martyr-*dom*, serf-*dom*.

-hood, **-head**: god-*head*; man-*hood*, child-*hood*, neighbour-*hood*, mother-*hood*, widow-*hood*.

-ing: learn-*ing*, writ-*ing*, walk-*ing*.

-ledge, **-lock**: know-*ledge*, wed-*lock*.

-ness: good-*ness*, holi-*ness*, wit-*ness* (from *wis* or *wit*).

-red: hat-*red*, kind-*red*.

-red (*reckoning*): hund-*red*.

-ric: bishop-*ric*. (This denotes jurisdiction.)

-ship, **-scape**: friend-*ship*, lord-*ship*, wor-*ship*; land-*scape*.

-ter: laugh-*ter*, slaugh-*ter* (from *slay*).

-th: heal-*th*, steal-*th*, bread-*th*, dep-*th*, wid-*th*, tru-*th*, leng-*th*.

-t or **-d**: heigh-*t*, sigh-*t*; dee-*d* (from *do*), cu-*d* (from *chew*).

319. Diminutives :—

-el, -l, -le : sack, satch-*el* ; corn, kern-*el* ; scythe, sick-*le* ; nave, nav-*el* ; spark, spark-*le* ; speck, speck-*le* ; freak, freck-*le* ; fow-*l*, hai-*l*.

Note.—In the following words these suffixes denote the means or result of some action :—shov-*el* (a thing to shove with), gird-*le*, spind-*le* from *spin*, shutt-*le* from *shoot*, hand-*le*, thimb-*le* from *thumb*, sadd-*le* from *sit*, sett-*le* from *sit* or *set*, bund-*le* from *bind*.

-en : chick-*en* (from *cock*), kitt-*en* (allied to *cat*), maid-*en*.

-ie, -y : bird-*ie*, lass-*ie*, bab-*y*, dadd-*y*, Will-*ie*, Ann-*ie*, mann-*i-kin*, lamb-*i-kin*. (Endearment.) The last two are double diminutives.

-ing : farth-*ing*, tith-*ing*, shill-*ing*, whit-*ing*, wild-*ing*.

-kin : lamb-*kin*, fir-*kin*, Peter-*kin* or Per-*kin*, nap-*kin*, bump-*kin*.

-ling : duck-*ling*, gos-*ling*, dar-*ling*, strip-*ling*, suck-*ling*, seed-*ling*.

-ock : hill-*ock*, bull-*ock*, padd-*ock* (from *park*), humm-*ock* (*hump*).

320. Miscellaneous :—

-en, -on (*that which acts*) : hav-*en* (have), mai-*n* (may), wag-*on*, wai-*n* (weigh).

-fare (*going*) : war-*fare*, thorough-*fare*, wel-*fare*, chaf-*fer* (cheap fare).

-lock, -lic (*plant*) : hem-*lock*, house-*leek*, gar-*lic*.

-stead (*place*) : home-*stead*, bed-*stead*, in-*stead* of, Hamp-*stead*.

-tree (*sawn timber*) : axle-*tree*, roof-*tree*.

321. *Adjectives.*

-ed (*form of Past Part.*) : wretch-*ed*, letter-*ed*, land-*ed*, gift-*ed*, ragg-*ed*.

-en (*made of*) : wood-*en*, braz-*en*, earth-*en*, silk-*en*, wax-*en*.

-en (*Past Part.*) : drunk-*en*, hew-*n*, op-*en* (that which is *up*).

-ern (*direction to*) : east-*ern*, north-*ern*, etc.

-fast (*firm*) : stead-*fast*, shame-*faced* (for shame-*fast*).

-fold (*repeated*) : two-*fold*, mani-*fold*, hundred-*fold*.

-ful (*full of*) : fear-*ful*, play-*ful*, hope-*ful*, wil-*ful*, truth-*ful*.

-ish (*somewhat like*) : girl-*ish*, whit-*ish*, self-*ish*, brut-*ish*, snobb-*ish*, wolf-*ish*, pal-*ish*, snapp-*ish*. (This suffix often implies contempt.)

-ish (*nationality*) : Engl-*ish*, Span-*ish*, Turk-*ish*, Fren-*ch* (Frank-*ish*).

-less (*without*) : shame-*less*, house-*less*, hope-*less*, cease-*less*, sleep-*less*, cause-*less*, resist-*less*, worth-*less*.

-like : god-*like*, war-*like*, lady-*like*, business-*like*.

-ly (*like*) : god-*ly*, love-*ly*, king-*ly*, sick-*ly*, kind-*ly*, friend-*ly*.

-most (*superl.*) : fore-*most*, in-*most*, ut-*most*, hind-*most*, etc.

-ow, -w : call-*ow*, fall-*ow*, mell-*ow* ; fe-*w*, ra-*w*, slo-*w*, tr-*ue*.

-some (*full of, inclined to*) : game-*some*, win-*some*, burden-*some*, trouble-*some*, hand-*some*, frolic-*some*, quarrel-*some*.

-teen, -ty (*ten*) : nine-*teen*, twen-*ty*, thir-*teen*, etc.

-th (*order*) : six-*th*, seven-*th*, etc.

-ther (*comparative*) : far-*ther*, fur-*ther*, whe-*ther*, o-*ther*.

-ward (*turning to*) : fro-*ward*, south-*ward*, down-*ward*, for-*ward*, way-*ward*, heaven-*ward*, home-*ward*.

-y (*pertaining to, abounding in*) : hill-*y*, storm-*y*, bush-*y*, rock-*y*, wooll-*y*, smok-*y*, wood-*y*, trust-*y*, feather-*y*.

322. *Adverbs.*

-ling, -long (*-wise, manner*) : head-*long*, dark-*ling*, side-*long*.

-ly (*like*) : sad-*ly*, careful-*ly*, bad-*ly*, on-*ly*.

-meal (*division*) : piece-*meal*, inch-*meal*, limb-*meal* (Shaks.).

-n : whe-*n*, the-*n*-ce, he-*n*-ce. (There are two suffixes in *thence, hence*. For the second one see **-s, -ce** below.)

-om : seld-*om*, whil-*om*. (This was once a Dative case-ending.)

-re : whe-*re*, the-*re*, he-*re*.

-s, -ce : need-s, twi-*ce*, beside-*s*, el-*se*, on-*ce* (sign of Possessive).

-ther : whi-*ther*, thi-*ther*, hi-*ther*.

-ward, -wards (*turning to*) : for-*ward*, up-*wards*, down-*wards*.

N.B.—The adv. is usually formed by "*wards*"; the adj. by "*ward*."

-way, -ways : al-*ways*, straight-*way*, any-*way*, no-*way*.

-wise (*manner, mode*) : other-*wise*, no-*wise*, like-*wise*.

Verbs.

323. Frequentative (sometimes in augmentative sense) :—

-er : ling-*er* from long, flutt-*er* from flit, falt-*er* from fail, clamb-*er* from climb, shimm-*er* from shine, glitt-*er* from glint, sputt-*er* from spout, hank-*er* from hang, spatt-*er* from spot.

-k : tal-*k* from tell (questioned by some), har-*k* from hear, stal-*k*.

-le, -l : dibb-*le*, spark-*le*, start-*le*, knee-*l*, crack-*le*, shuff-*le*, cack-*le*, wrigg-*le*, pratt-*le*, dazz-*le*, draw-*l*, nibb-*le*, sniv-*el* (from sniff).

-on, -om, -m : bloss-*om* from blow, glea-*m* from glow, sea-*m* from sew, reck-*on*, blaz-*on*.

324. Causative or Factitive :—

-en : fatt-*en*, short-*en*, length-*en*, gladd-*en*, black-*en*, thick-*en*.

-se : clean-*se*, rin-*se*, glimp-*se* (Rare).

-le : start-*le* (start), jost-*le* (joust), stif-*le* (stiff).

SECTION 3.—ROMANIC PREFIXES.

325. A-, ab-, abs- (*away from*) : *ab*-hor, *ab*-use, *ab*-surd, *ab*-normal, *abs*-tract, *abs*-ent, *abs*-cond, *abs*-tain ; *a*-vert, *a*-vo-cation.

Ad- (*to*) : By assimilation *ac-*, *af-*, *ag-*, *al-*, *an-*, *ap-*, *ar-*, *as-*, *at-*.

ad-vice, *ad*-join, *ad*-monish, *ad*-ore, *ad*-here, *ad*-opt.

ac-custom, *ac*-cept, *ac*-cede, *ac*-cent, *ac*-cuse, *ac*-quire.

af-flict, *af*-fix, *af*-fection, *af*-filiate, *af*-fable, *af*-firm.

ag-grieve, *ag*-gravate, *ag*-gregate, *ag*-gressor, *ag*-grandise.

al-lege, *al*-lot, *al*-lure, *al*-low, *al*-lay, *al*-leviate.

an-nounce, *an*-nex, *an*-noy, *an*-nul, *an*-nihilate.

ap-proach, *ap*-pear, *ap*-peal, *ap*-point, *ap*-pease, *ap*-pal.

ar-rive, *ar*-rears, *ar*-rest, *ar*-rogant, *ar*-ray, *ar*-range.

a-spect, *a*-scribe, *a*-spire : (here the *d* has been lost).

as-sent, *as*-sert, *as*-sume, *as*-certain, *as*-sail, *as*-sets.

at-tend, *at*-tain, *at*-tract, *at*-tach, *at*-tempt, *at*-tack.

Ambi-, amb-, am- (*around*) : *ambi*-dexterous, *amb*-ition, *am*-putate.

Ante-, anti- (*before*) : *ante*-chamber, *ante*-cedent, *anti*-cipate.

Bene- (*well*) : *bene*-fit, *bene*-volent, *bene*-diction, hence *ben*-ison.

Bi-, bis-, bin- : *bi*-ped, *bis*-cuit, *bi*-sect, *bi*-ennial, *bin*-ocular.

Circum-, circu- (*around*) : *circum*-ference, *circu*-it, *circum*-stance.

Com-, con-, co- (*with*): by assimilation, *col*, *cor*, *cog*, etc.
Com-pete, *com*-bat, *com*-merce, *com*-pact, *com*-mand, *com*-ply.
Con-tend, *con*-trive, *con*-flict, *con*-cur, *con*-fluence, *con*-sonant.
Co-alesce, *co*-heir, *co*-habit, *co*-eternal, *co*-exist, *co*-here.
Col-lapse, *col*-lege, *col*-lect, *col*-league, *col*-lision, *col*-lateral.
Cor-rupt, *cor*-rect, *cor*-rode, *cor*-respond, *cor*-roborate.
Cog-nate, *cog*-nizance, *cog*-nition.
Coun-sel, *coun*-cil, *coun*-tenance.

Contra-, contro-, counter- (*against*): *contra*-dict, *counter*-act, *contra*-st, *contro*-versy, *counter*-feit, *counter*-part, *counter*-sign.

De- (*down*): *de*-scend, *de*-grade, *de*-crease, *de*-jected (down-cast).
,, (*reversal*): *de*-camp, *de*-throne, *de*-tach, *de*-plete, *de*-odorise.
,, (*astray*): *de*-viate, *de*-lude, *de*-face.
,, (*intensive*): *de*-liver, *de*-clare, *de*-file, *de*-fend, *de*-fraud.

Note.—*De* (down) and *ad* (up) are sometimes contrasted :—*de*-preciate, *ap*-preciate; *de*-scend, *a*-scend; *de*-clivity, *ac*-clivity. Sometimes *de* is used in contrast with *en* or *in* :—*de*-throne, *en*-throne; *de*-camp, *en*-camp; *de*-cline, *in*-cline.

Dis-, di-, dif- (*asunder*, *not*): *dis*-honour, *dis*-please, *dis*-ease, *dis*-locate, *dis*-like: *di*-verse, *di*-gest, *dif*-fer, *dif*-ficult.
,, (*reversal*): *dis*-close, *dis*-mount, *dis*-arm, *dis*-appear, *dis*-continue, *dis*-enchant, *dis*-illusion, *dis*-franchise.
,, (*intensive*): *di*-minish, *di*-rect, *dis*-annul, *dis*-sever.

Ex-, e-, ef- (*out of, from*): *ex*-alt, *e*-lect, *ex*-pel, *ex*-amine, *e*-ducate; *ef*-fort, *ef*-fulgence, *ef*-fervesce; *ex*-king, dethroned king.

Extra (*beyond*): *extra*-ordinary, *extra*-work, *stra*-nger.

In-, en-, em- (*in, into, on*): *in*-vert, *in*-vade, *im*-pose, *im*-press, *im*-pute, *il*-lusion, *ir*-ruption, *ir*-rigate, *en*-tice, *em*-ploy, *em*-brace, *em*-bark, *em*-barrass. *In*-close or *en*-close, *in*-dorse or *en*-dorse, *in*-quire or *en*-quire, *in*-trust or *en*-trust, *in*-twine or *en*-twine, *in*-circle or *en*-circle, *im*-bitter or *em*-bitter.

Note.—This prefix, placed before a noun or adjective, makes a Transitive verb :—*en*-dear, *en*-rich, *en*-large, *en*-slave, *en*-title, *em*-body, *im*-peril, *en*-danger.

In- (*not*): *in*-firm, *in*-fant (*not speaking*), *ig*-noble, *il*-legal, *im*-pious, *ir*-regular, *ir*-rational, *ig*-nominy, *il*-literate, *im*-passive.

Note.—The Latin "in" and the Teutonic "un" are so much alike, that some words are spelt both ways :—*in*-frequent or *un*-frequent, *in*-cautious or *un*-cautious, *in*-stable or *un*-stable.

Inter-, intro-, enter- (*within*): *inter*-course, *inter*-preter, *inter*-rupt, *inter*-pose, *intro*-duce, *intro*-spection, *enter*-tain, *enter*-prise, *intel*-lect.

Juxta- (*near*): *juxta*-position.

Male-, mal- (*ill, badly*): *male*-factor; *mal*-treat, *mal*-ignant.

Mis- (from Lat. *minus*, less): *mis*-chief, *mis*-creant, *mis*-nomer.

Ne-, neg-: *ne*-farious, *neg*-lect, *neg*-ative.

Non- (*not*): *non*-sense, *non*-existent, *non*-age, *non*-compliance.

Note.—"Non" is much less emphatic than "in" or "un." Compare "*non*-christian" and "*un*-christian"; "*non*-professional" and "*un*-professional." *Non*-sense and *non*-entity are exceptional.

Ob- (*in front of, against*): *ob*-ject, *ob*-stinate, *oc*-cupy, *oc*-casion, *of*-fer, *of*-fend, *op*-pose, *op*-press, *os*-tensible, *o*-mit.

Per-, pel- (*through*): *per*-force, *per*-spire, *per*-form, *pel*-lucid.

Note.—*Per*, like the Teutonic *for*, sometimes passes from the notion of *thoroughness* to that of going *too far* or *in a wrong direction*:—

Per-vert, *per*-sist, *per*-jure, *per*-fidy, *per*-ish, *per*-dition.

Pene- (*almost*): *pen*-insula, *pen*-ultimate.

Post- (*after*): *post*-date, *post*-script, *post*-pone, *post*-humous.

Pre- (*before*): *pre*-dict, *pre*-caution, *pre*-pare, *pre*-judice.

Preter- (*beyond*): *preter*-natural, *preter*-ite.

Pro-, por-, pol-, pur- (*forth*): *pro*-ject, *pro*-pose, *pro*-noun, *pro*-mise, *por*-tend, *pol*-lute, *pur*-pose, *pur*-sue, *pur*-port, *pur*-loin.

Quasi- (*pretence*): a *quasi*-judge (a sham or pretended judge).

Quondam- (*formerly*): a *quondam*-judge (a former judge).

Re-, red- (*back, again*): *re*-join, *re*-act, *re*-new, *red*-eem, *red*-ound, *red*-undant.

Note.—The insertion of a hyphen alters the meaning. Compare "recover" and "re-cover"; "rejoin" and "re-join"; "redress" and "re-dress"; "reform" and "re-form"; "recollect" and "re-collect"; "recount" and "re-count"; "return" and "re-turn."

Retro- (*backward*): *retro*-spect, *retro*-grade, *retro*-cession.

Se-, sed- (*apart*): *se*-clude, *se*-parate, *sed*-ition, *se*-cret, *se*-cure.

Semi-, demi- (*half*): *semi*-circle; *demi*-god, *demi*-official.

Sine- (*without*): *sine*-cure.

Sub- (*under, after*): *sub*-ject, *suc*-cour, *suc*-cess, *suf*-fer, *suf*-fice, *sug*-gest, *sub*-committee, *sus*-tain, *sus*-pend, *sup*-port, *sur*-reptitious.

Note.—In words like "*sub*-tropical" the "sub" means "rather." In "*sub*-judge" it denotes lower rank. In *sub*-marine (under the sea) and *sub*-terranean (under the earth) the "sub" is prepositional.

Subter- (*beneath*): *subter*-fuge.

Super-, sur- (*above, over, beyond*): *super*-structure, *super*-ficial; *sur*-face, *sur*-pass, *sur*-vive, *sur*-charge, *sur*-feit, *sur*-mount.

Trans-, tra- (*across*): *trans*-figure, *trans*-gress, *trans*-form, *trans*-it, *trans*-mit, *trans*-late, *trans*-parent, *tra*-verse, *tra*-dition, *tra*-duce.

Tri- (*three*): *tri*-angle, *tri*-lateral, *tri*-nity.

Ultra- (*beyond*): *ultra*-liberal (very liberal, adverbial sense), *ultra*-marine (beyond the sea, prepositional sense).

Un-, uni- (*one*): *un*-animous, *uni*-form, *uni*-corn.

Vice-, vis- (*instead of*): *vice*-regent, *vis*-count, *vice*-roy.

326. *Disguised Prefixes (Latin or French).*

Ante- (*before*): *an*-cestor for *ante*-cessor.

Bi- (*twice*): *ba*-lance.

Con-, co- (*together*): *cus*-tom, *cur*-ry (verb), *co*-ver, *co*-venant, *co*-unt (verb and noun), *cou*-ch, *co*-st.

Dis-, di- (*apart*): *des*-cant, *des*-patch, *de*-feat, *de*-luge, *s*-pend.

Ex-, e- (*out*): *a*-mend (but *e*-mendation), *a*-bash, *a*-fraid, *a*-ward, *as*-tonish, *es*-cape, *es*-cheat, *es*-say, *is*-sue, *s*-ample, *s*-carce, *s*-corch.

Extra- (*outside*): *stra*-nge, *stra*-nger. (Stem formed from prefix.)

In- (*not*): *en*-emy (hence adj. *in*-imical), *an*-oint.

Intra- (*within*): *entr*-ails. (Here the prefix is made the stem.)

Juxta- (*near*) : joust, jost-le. (The prefix is made the stem.)
Non- (*not*) : *um*-pire (old French, *nom*-per).
Per- (*through*) : *par*-don, *par*-amount, *par*-son, *pil*-grim.
Post- (*after*) : *pu*-ny (Fr. *puis*-né, Lat. *post*-natus).
Pre- (*before*) : *pre*-ach, *pro*-vost.
Re- (*back*) : *ren*-der, *r*-ansom, *r*-ally, *ru*-nagate (*re*-negatus).
Retro- (*back*) : *rear*-guard.
Sub- (*under*) : *so*-journ, *sud*-den, *s*-ombre (*sub* or *ex* umbrâ).
Super- (*above*) : *sopr*-ano, *sover*-eign (older spelling, *sovr*-an).
Trans- (*across*) : *tres*-pass, *tre*-ason, *tra*-ffic.
Ultra- (*beyond*) : *outr*-age. (Here the prefix is made the stem.)

SECTION 4.—ROMANIC SUFFIXES.

Nouns.

327. Agent :—

-ain, **-en**, **-an** : capt-*ain*, chieft-*ain*, guardi-*an*, citiz-*en*, librari-*an*.
-ant : merch-*ant*, serv-*ant*, brig-*and*, confid-*ant*, depend-*ant*.
-ard, **-art** : cow-*ard*, wiz-*ard*, drunk-*ard*, slugg-*ard*, bragg-*art*.
-ary, **-ar**, **-aire** : dignit-*ary*, mission-*ary*, secret-*ary*; vic-*ar*, schol-*ar*; million-*aire*, doctrin-*aire*.
-ate : candid-*ate*, advoc-*ate*, cur-*ate*, prim-*ate*.
-ee, **-y** : trust-*ee*, devot-*ee*, pay-*ee*; deput-*y*, jur-*y*, lev-*y*, attorn-*ey*.

Note.—These words have a *Passive* signification. Thus "trust-*ee*" means one who is trusted: "jur-*y*" means one who is sworn. But there is no Passive meaning in the words "absent-*ee*" (one who is absent), "refug-*ee*" (one who has taken refuge).

-eer, **-ier** : engin-*eer*, auction-*eer*, volunt-*eer*; sold-*ier*, financ-*ier*.
-ent : stud-*ent*, presid-*ent*, pati-*ent*, rod-*ent*.
-ess (fem.) : song-str-*ess*, poet-*ess*, tigr-*ess*, lion-*ess*.
-ine, **-in** : libert-*ine*, gobl-*in*, cous-*in*, pilgr-*im*.
-ive, **-iff** : capt-*ive*, fugit-*ive*, nat-*ive*, plaint-*iff*, cait-*iff*, bail-*iff*.
-on : fel-*on*, glutt-*on*, mas-*on*, sculli-*on*, drag-*on*.
-our, **-eur**, **-or**, **-er** : savi-*our*, emper-*or*, govern-*or*, preach-*er*, robb-*er*, act-*or*, doct-*or*, monit-*or*, cens-*or*, ancest-*or*, amat-*eur*, connoiss-*eur*.

328. Abstract Nouns :—

-acy, **-cy** : priv-*acy*, accur-*acy*, intric-*acy*, secre-*cy*, bankrupt-*cy*.
-age : bond-*age*, cour-*age*, hom-*age*, marri-*age*, pilgrim-*age*.
Cost of action : post-*age*, freight-*age*, broker-*age*, halt-*age*.
Result of action : break-*age*, leak-*age*, mess-*age*, pill-*age*.
Agent : person-*age* (a person of importance).
-al, **-als** : refus-*al*, propos-*al*, tri-*al*, nupti-*als*, credent-*ials*.
-ance, **-ence** : disturb-*ance*, endur-*ance*, repent-*ance*; obedi-*ence*, innoc-*ence*, abs-*ence*, pres-*ence*, depend-*ence*, dilig-*ence*, pati-*ence*.
-ancy, **-ency** : const-*ancy*, brilli-*ancy*, ten-*ancy*; excell-*ency*, reg-*ency*, urg-*ency*, frequ-*ency*, insolv-*ency*, emerg-*ency*, innoc-*ency*.
-el, **-le**, **-ele** : quarr-*el*, sequ-*el*, tut-*el*-age, client-*ele*, cand-*le*.
-ess, **-ice**, **-ise** : serv-*ice*, larg-*ess*, rich-*es*, prow-*ess*, merchand-*ise*, exerc-*ise*, just-*ice*, pract-*ice*, coward-*ice*, avar-*ice*, not-*ice*.
-eur : grand-*eur*, liqu-*eur*. (The last is not an abstract noun.)
-ity, **-ty** : fals-*ity*, real-*ity*; cruel-*ty*, frail-*ty*, boun-*ty*, un-*ity*.
-lence : pesti-*lence*, vio-*lence*, viru-*lence*, turbu-*lence*, opu-*lence*.

-ment: conceal-*ment*, enchant-*ment*, nourish-*ment*, nutri-*ment*.

-mony: cere-*mony*, acri-*mony*, matri-*mony*, testi-*mony*.

-our, -or: fav-*our*, hon-*our*, err-*or*, langu-*or*, col-*our*.

-ry, -ery: chival-*ry*, poet-*ry*; slav-*ery*, treach-*ery*, cook-*ery*.

-sion: conver-*sion*, cohe-*sion*, occa-*sion*, compul-*sion*, proces-*sion*, illu-*sion*, man-*sion*, colli-*sion*, confu-*sion*, admis-*sion*.

-tion, -son, -som: benedic-*tion*, beni-*son*; po-*tion*, poi-*son*; redemp-*tion*, ran-*som*; ora-*tion*, ori-*son*; tradi-*tion*, trea-*son*.

tude: longi-*tude*, apti-*tude*, alti-*tude*, multi-*tude*, servi-*tude*.

-ure: creat-*ure*, verd-*ure*, meas-*ure*, vest-*ure*, seiz-*ure*, agricult-*ure*.

-y: harmon-*y*, stud-*y*, victor-*y*, miser-*y*, industr-*y*, env-*y*.

329. Collectives; Nouns of Place:—

-ade: colonn-*ade*, balustr-*ade*, cavalc-*ade*, brig-*ade*, crus-*ade*.

-age: assembl-*age*, plum-*age*, foli-*age*, vill-*age*, hermit-*age*, cott-*age*.

-ary, -arium: libr-*ary*, gran-*ary*, semin-*ary*, sanctu-*ary*, gloss-*ary*, diction-*ary*; sanit-*arium*, aqu-*arium*.

-ery, -ry: machin-*ery*, caval-*ry*, jewel-*ry*, gent-*ry*, tenant-*ry*, infant-*ry*, station-*ery*, shrubb-*ery*, bak-*ery*, cemet-*ery*, spic-*ery*, rock-*ery*.

-ory: fact-*ory*, dormit-*ory*, arm-*ory*, territ-*ory*, observat-*ory*.

330. Diminutives:—

-aster: poet-*aster*, ole-*aster*, pil-*aster*.

-el, -le, -elle: dams-*el*, cast-*le*, mod-*el*, citad-*el*, mors-*el*, parc-*el*, bagat-*elle*. (Fem-*ale* from Fr. fem-*elle*, Latin fem-*ella*.)

-et, -let: lock-*et*, lanc-*et*, pock-*et*, tick-*et*, turr-*et*, coron-*et*, thick-*et*; brace-*let*, stream-*let*, brook-*let*, leaf-*let*, rivu-*let*, ring-*let*, root-*let*.

-ette: etiqu-*ette*, statu-*ette*, cigar-*ette*, wagon-*ette*, brun-*ette*.

-icle, -cule: art-*icle*, part-*icle*, animal-*cule*, curr-*icle*, curr-*iculum*, cut-*icle*, corpus-*cle*, pinna-*cle*, cod-*icil*, domi-*cile*.

-ot: fag-*ot*, chari-*ot*, parr-*ot*, magg-*ot*, ball-*ot*, piv-*ot*.

ule: glob-*ule*, pill-*ule*, nod-*ule*, caps-*ule*.

331. Miscellaneous:—

-ace: popul-*ace*, pinn-*ace*, men-*ace*, pal-*ace*, sp-*ace*, grim-*ace*.

-and, -end: vi-*and* or vi-*ands*, leg-*end*, divid-*end*, rever-*end*.

-cre, -chre: lu-*cre*, sepul-*chre*, massa-*cre* (formed in imitation).

-en, -om, -n: ali-*en*, ven-*om*, chai-*n*.

-ern: tav-*ern*, cav-*ern*, lect-*ern*, lant-*ern*, cist-*ern*.

-ic, -k, -ge: fabr-*ic*, rust-*ic*, mus-*ic*; cler-*k*, sil-*k*; ser-*ge*.

-il, -ile, -le: pup-*il*, imbec-*ile*, sea-*l*, ais-*le*, quadr-*ille*, bac-*illus*.

-in: marg-*in*, orig-*in*, virg-*in*.

-o: studi-*o*, grott-*o*, incognit-*o*.

-oon, -one (*augmentative*): ball-*oon*, bass-*oon*, tromb-*one*.

-ter, -tre: clois-*ter*, thea-*tre*, lus-*tre*, spec-*tre*, fil-*ter*, mons-*ter*.

332. *Adjectives.*

-acious: ten-*acious*, loqu-*acious*, mend-*acious*, cap-*acious*.

-al: loy-*al*, leg-*al*, roy-*al*, reg-*al*, equ-*al*, mort-*al*, vit-*al*.

-an, -ane, -ain: hum-*an*, hum-*ane*; cert-*ain*; pag-*an*, Rom-*an*.

-aneous: simult-*aneous*, instant-*aneous*, contempor-*aneous*.

-ant, -ent: vac-*ant*, indign-*ant*, ramp-*ant*, pati-*ent*, innoc-*ent*, curr-*ent*, confid-*ent*, tru-*ant*, vagr-*ant*.

Note.—When *-ant* and *-ent* are seen in pairs of words, as "confid-*ant*, confid-*ent*," "depend-*ant*, depend-*ent*," the latter is an adjective and the former is a noun.

-ar : sol-*ar*, lun-*ar*, regul-*ar*, singul-*ar*, vulg-*ar*, vernacul-*ar*.

-ary, **-arious**, **-arian** : contr-*ary*, ordin-*ary*, necess-*ary*, tempor-*ary*, solit-*ary*; nef-*arious*, greg-*arious*; agr-*arian*, humanit-*arian*.

-ate : fortun-*ate*, separ-*ate*, desol-*ate*, priv-*ate*, accur-*ate*.

-ble, **-able** : sta-*ble*, fee-*ble*, terri-*ble*; mov-*able*, laugh-*able*, eat-*able* (edi-*ble*), service-*able*, lov-*able*, drink-*able*. (*Passive* sense.)

-ble, **-ple** : dou-*ble*, tre-*ble*; sim-*ple*, tri-*ple*. (Signifies "fold.")

-eel, **-il**, **-le** : gent-*cel*, gent-*le*, civ-*il*, fra-*il*, cru-*el*, subt-*le*.

-erious : delet-*erious*.

-escent : conval-*escent*, efferv-*escent*, incand-*escent*, adol-*escent*.

-ese : Chin-*ese*, Malt-*ese*, Burm-*ese*, Siam-*ese*, Portugu-*ese*, Geno-*ese*.

-esque : pictur-*esque*, grot-*esque*, burl-*esque*.

-ete, **-eet** : compl-*ete*, obsol-*ete*, discr-*ete*, discr-*eet*.

-fic : terri-*fic*, horri-*fic*, beati-*fic*, sopori-*fic*, honori-*fic*. (*Active* sense.)

-ian : Austral-*ian*, Ind-*ian*, Christ-*ian*.

-ic, **-ique** : publ-*ic*, rust-*ic*; un-*ique*, obl-*ique*, ant-*ique*.

-id : ac-*id*, pall-*id*, squal-*id*, rig-*id*, plac-*id*, morb-*id*.

-ile : serv-*ile*, frag-*ile*, doc-*ile*, puer-*ile*, fac-*ile*, juven-*ile*.

-ine : div-*ine*, infant-*ine*, leon-*ine*, can-*ine*, clandest-*ine*.

-ite : oppos-*ite*, favour-*ite*, exquis-*ite*.

-ive : act-*ive*, capt-*ive*, sport-*ive*, relat-*ive*, nat-*ive*, posit-*ive*.

-lent : pesti-*lent*, vio-*lent*, turbu-*lent*, fraudu-*lent*, corpu-*lent*.

-monious : sancti-*monious*, queri-*monious*, cere-*monious*.

-ory, **-orious** : compuls-*ory*, transit-*ory*, curs-*ory*, dilat-*ory*; lab-*orious*, cens-*orious*. (Generally in an *Active* sense.)

-ose, **-ous** : verb-*ose*, joc-*ose*; monstr-*ous*, danger-*ous*, glori-*ous*, ponder-*ous*, dexter-*ous*, courte-*ous*.

-und, **-ond** : rubic-*und*, morib-*und*, vagab-*ond*.

-urn : tacit-*urn*, aub-*urn*.

-y : test-*y*, mass-*y*, hast-*y*, joll-*y*.

333. *Verbs.*

-ate : agit-*ate*, captiv-*ate*, moder-*ate*, stimul-*ate*, cre-*ate*.

-esce : efferv-*esce*, coal-*esce*, acqui-*esce*. (Growing or becoming.)

-fy : magni-*fy*, signi-*fy*, simpli-*fy*, modi-*fy*, terri-*fy*. (*Transitive.*)

-ish : fin-*ish*, nour-*ish*, pun-*ish*, publ-*ish*, van-*ish*.

-ite, **-it** : exped-*ite*, cred-*it*, mer-*it*, inhab-*it*.

-y : marr-*y*, sall-*y*, carr-*y*.

Section 5.—Greek Prefixes.

334. Amphi- (*about*, *on both sides*) : *amphi*-theatre, *amphi*-bious.

An-, **am-**, **a-** (*not*, *without*; like Teutonic *un-* or Romanic *in-*) : *an*-archy, *a*-theism, *a*-pathy, *am*-brosial, *a*-trophy, *an*-omalous.

Ana-, **an-** (*up to*, *again*) : *ana*-tomy, *ana*-logy, *ana*-lysis, *an*-eurism.

Anti-, **ant-** (*against*) : *anti*-podes, *anti*-pathy, *ant*-agonist.

Apo-, **aph-** (*from*) : *apo*-logy, *apo*-state, *apo*-strophe, *aph*-orism.

Arch-, **archi-** (*chief*, *head*) : *arch*-heretic, *arch*-enemy ; *archi*-tect.

Auto-, **auth-** (*self*) : *auto*-graph, *auto*-biography ; *auth*-entic.

Cata-, **cath-**, **cat-** (*down*): *cata*-ract, *cath*-edral, *cata*-strophe, *cat*-echism.
Dia- (*through*): *dia*-meter, *dia*-logue, *dia*-dem, *dia*-gonal.
Di- (*in two*): *di*-ssyllable, *di*-phthong, *di*-lemma.
Dys- (*ill*): *dys*-peptic, *dys*-entery.
Ec-, **ex-** (*out, from*): *ex*-odus, *ec*-centric, *ec*-lipse, *ec*-logue.
En- (*in*): *en*-thusiasm, *em*-phasis, *el*-lipsis, *en*-comium.
Endo- (*within*): *endo*-gamous, *endo*-genous.
Epi-, **eph-**, **ep-** (*upon*): *epi*-gram, *ep*-och, *epi*-taph, *eph*-emeral, *epi*-stle.
Exo- (*without*): *exo*-gamous, *exo*-tic
Eu-, **ev-** (*well*): *eu*-phony, *eu*-phemism, *ev*-angelist.
Hemi- (*half*): *hemi*-sphere.
Hepta-, **hept-** (*seven*): *hepta*-gon, *hept*-archy.
Hetero- (*different*): *hetero*-dox, *hetero*-geneous.
Hex- (*six*): *hex*-a-meter, *hex*-a-gon.
Homo-, **hom-** (*same*): *homo*-geneous, *hom*-onym.
Hyper- (*above*): *hyper*-bole, *hyper*-critical (critical to a fault).
Hypo-, **hyph-** (*under*): *hypo*-crite, *hypo*-thesis, *hyp*-hen.
Meta-, **meth-**, **met-** (*after, substitution*): *meta*-phor, *meth*-od, *met*-onymy.
Mono-, **mon-** (*single, alone*): *mono*-graph, *mon*-archy, *mon*-astery, *mon*-k.
Pan-, **panto-** (*all*): *pan*-theist, *pan*-oply, *pan*-orama, *panto*-mime.
Para-, **par-** (*beside*): *para*-phrase, *para*-ble, *par*-allel, *para*-site.
Penta- (*five*): *penta*-meter, *penta*-polis.
Peri- (*around*): *peri*-meter, *peri*-phrasis, *peri*-od.
Poly- (*many*): *poly*-syllable, *poly*-theist, *poly*-glot.
Pro- (*before*): *pro*-gramme, *pro*-logue, *pro*-phet, *pro*-boscis.
Pseudo-, **pseud-** (*false*): *pseudo*-critic, *pseud*-onym.
Syn- (*with*): *syn*-thesis, *syn*-tax, *sym*-pathy, *syl*-lable, *sys*-tem.
Tele- (*afar*): *tele*-graph, *tele*-phone, *tele*-gram.
Tri- (*thrice, or three*): *tri*-pod, *tri*-syllable, *tri*-sect.

335. *Latin and Greek equivalent Prefixes.*

Latin.	*Greek.*	*Meaning.*
Ambi-, amb-iguous	**Amphi-**, amphi-bious	On both sides
Ab-, ab-solute	**Apo-**, apo-logy	From
Ex-amine	**Ec-**, ec-stasy	Out of
In-, in-spection	**En-**, **Em-**, em-phasis	Into, in
Semi-, **demi-**, demi-god	**Hemi-**, hemi-sphere	Half
Super-, supervise	**Hyper-**, hyper-bole	Above
Sub-, sub-stantive	**Hypo-**, hypo-thesis	Under
Pro-, pro-portion	**Pro-**, pro-phet	Before or for
Tri-, tri-angle	**Tri-**, tri-pod	Thrice

Section 6.—Greek Suffixes.

Nouns.

336. **Agent**:—

-ac: mani-*ac*, demoni-*ac*.
-ant: gi-*ant*, adam-*ant*, eleph-*ant*.
-ast: enthusi-*ast*, iconocl-*ast*, gymn-*ast*, encomi-*ast*.

-ic : heret-*ic*, scept-*ic*, crit-*ic*, cler-*ic* (=clerk).
-ist : dent-*ist*, the-*ist*, egot-*ist*, alarm-*ist*, extrem-*ist*, optim-*ist*.
-ite : Israel-*ite*, erem-*ite* or herm-*it*, anchor-*ite* or anchor-*et*.
-ot : patri-*ot*, zeal-*ot*, idi-*ot* (big-*ot*, doubtful).
-te, **-t** : prophe-*t*, poe-*t*, plane-*t*, aposta-*te*, come-*t*.

337. Abstract Nouns :—

-asm : enthusi-*asm*, pleon-*asm*, sarc-*asm*, ch-*asm*.
-ic, **-ics** : log-*ic*, mag-*ic*, mus-*ic*; eth-*ics*, mathemat-*ics*, polit-*ics*.
-ism : patriot-*ism*, barbar-*ism*, magnet-*ism*, the-*ism*, critic-*ism*.
-sis, **-sy**, **-se** : drop-*sy*, pal-*sy*; paraly-*sis*, ba-*sis*; eclip-*se*, ellip-*se*.
-y : monarch-*y*, philosoph-*y*, democrac-*y*, energ-*y*.
-ysm : catacl-*ysm*, parox-*ysm*.

338. Diminutives :—

-isk : aster-*isk*, obel-*isk*, basil-*isk*.

339. Miscellaneous :—

-ad, **-id** : myri-*ad*, dec-*ade*, mon-*ad*, Ili-*ad*, Æne-*id*.
-m, **-mme** : theore-*m*, proble-*m*, telegra-*m*, progra-*mme*, cli-*me*, cli-*m*-ate.
-oid : anthrop-*oid*, negr-*oid*, metall-*oid*, tabl-*oid*.
-ter, **-tre** : cen-*tre*, me-*tre*, diame-*ter*, scep-*tre*.

340. *Adjectives.*

-astic : pleon-*astic*, ecclesi-*astic*, sarc-*astic*, dr-*astic*.
-ic : dramat-*ic*, cosm-*ic*, com-*ic*, trag-*ic*, polit-*ic*, authent-*ic*.
-istic : eulog-*istic*, evangel-*istic*, patr-*istic*.

341. *Verbs.*

-ise : civil-*ise*, scrutin-*ise*, fertil-*ise*, real-*ise*, theor-*ise*.

342. *Some General Results.*

(*a*) Affixes denoting a *moderate* degree of some quality :—

-ish, Teutonic : black-*ish* (rather black), sweet-*ish* (rather sweet).
-ly, Teutonic : clean-*ly* (disposed to be clean), sick-*ly* (liable to be sick).
Sub-, Romanic : *sub*-acid (rather acid), *sub*-tropical (slightly tropical).

(*b*) Suffixes denoting a *high* degree of some quality :—

-ful, Teutonic : plenti-*ful*, wonder-*ful*, taste-*ful*, truth-*ful*.
-ous, **-ose**, Romanic : verb-*ose*, numer-*ous*, fam-*ous*, odi-*ous*.

Note.—The equivalence of these suffixes is seen from the fact that the same stem sometimes takes both forms :—

Plenti-*ful*, plente-*ous*. Beauti-*ful*, beaute-*ous*. Bounti-*ful*, bounte-*ous*. Piti-*ful*, pite-*ous*. Joy-*ful*, joy-*ous*. Grace-*ful*, graci-*ous*.

(*c*) Prefixes denoting the undoing of something done :—

Un-, Teutonic : *un*-bolt, *un*-tie, *un*-lock, *un*-fold.
De-, Romanic : *de*-throne, *de*-camp, *de*-tach.
Dis-, or **di-**, Romanic : *dis*-mount, *dis*-appear, *dis*-arm.

(*d*) Affixes denoting a negative :—

For-, Teutonic : *for*-bid.
-less, Teutonic : hap-*less*, law-*less*, hope-*less*.
N-, Teutonic : *n*-one, *n*-ever, *n*-either, *n*-or.
Un-, Teutonic : *un*-happy, *un*-safe, *un*-ready.
Dis-, **di**-, Romanic : *dis*-quiet (opposite to quiet), *dif*-ficult (not easy), *dif*-fident (not confident), *dis*-honour.
In-, Romanic : *in*-human, *ir*-regular, *im*-moral, *il*-legible.
Ne-, **neg**-, **non**-, Romanic : *ne*-farious, *neg*-lect, *non*-sense.
A-, or **an**-, Greek : *a*-pathy, *an*-archy, *am*-brosial.

(*e*) Suffixes indicating the Feminine gender :—

-ster, Teutonic : spin-*ster*. (Only one word.)
-en, Teutonic : vix-*en*. (Only one word.)
-ess, Romanic : lion-*ess*, temptr-*ess*, tigr-*ess*.

(*f*) Prefixes indicating something bad :—

Mis-, Teutonic (from *miss*) : *mis*-take, *mis*-deed, *mis*-hap.
Male-, **mal**-, Romanic : *male*-factor, *mal*-treat.
Mis-, Romanic (from *minus*) : *mis*-use, *mis*-fortune.
Dys-, Greek : *dys*-entery, *dys*-pepsia.

(*g*) Prefixes indicating something good :—

Well-, Teutonic : *wel*-fare, *wel*-come, *well*-being.
Bene-, Romanic : *bene*-volent, *bene*-fit, *bene*-diction.
Eu-, Greek : *eu*-phemism, *ev*-angelist, *eu*-phony.

(*h*) Affixes for forming Transitive verbs :—

Be-, Teutonic : *be*-friend, *be*-calm, *be*-moan, *be*-little.
-en, Teutonic : dark-*en*, length-*en*, hast-*en*, lik-*en*.
-le, Teutonic : start-*le*, jost-*le*, stif-*le*.
-se, Teutonic : clean-*se*, rin-*se*, glimp-*se*.
-fy, Romanic : magni-*fy*, modi-*fy*, stupe-*fy*.
In-, **en**-, Romanic : *im*-peril, *en*-dear, *em*- or *im*-bitter.
-ise, Greek : human-*ise*, brutal-*ise*, galvan-*ise*.

(*i*) Suffixes having a depreciatory force :—

Teutonic for forming Nouns :—
-craft : priest-*craft*, state-*craft*, witch-*craft*.
-erel, **-rel** : mong-*rel*, dogg-*erel*, dott-*erel*, wast-*rel*.
-ling : hire-*ling*, ground-*ling*, under-*ling*, world-*ling*, weak-*ling*.
-monger : ballad-*monger*, crotchet-*monger*, grievance-*monger*.
-ster : trick-*ster*, young-*ster*, rhyme-*ster*.

Romanic for forming Nouns :—
-ard : cow-*ard*, drunk-*ard*, slugg-*ard*, dot-*ard*.
-aster : poet-*aster*, critic-*aster*.

Teutonic for forming Adjectives :—
-ish : Rom-*ish*, woman-*ish*, child-*ish*, baby-*ish*, upp-*ish*, slav-*ish*.

Romanic for forming Adjectives :—
-ile : puer-*ile* (child-*ish*), infant-*ile* (baby-*ish*), serv-*ile* (slav-*ish*).

(*j*) Suffixes having an augmentative force :—

Teutonic :—
-er (frequentative verb) : sputt-*er*, be-spatt-*er*, wand-*er*, etc.
-le (freq. verb) : dabb-*le*, grumb-*le*, wagg-*le*, etc.

Romanic :—
-ard (excess to a fault) : blizz-*ard*, lagg-*ard*, drunk-*ard*.
-oon, **-one** (augment. noun) : ball-*oon*, bass-*oon*, tromb-*one*.

(*k*) Suffixes denoting patronymics :—

Teutonic :—
-ing : Vik-*ing*, k-*ing* (A.S. cyn-*ing*), Brown-*ing*, Mann-*ing*.
-kin : Peter-*kin* (hence Per-*kin*), Sim-*kin* (Simon-*kin*), Wil-*kin*-s.
-son : Ander-*son*, Collin-*son*, David-*son*.

I. *Write short sentences illustrating the difference of meaning in each of the following pairs of Abstract nouns formed with different suffixes :—*

(*a*) *Teutonic suffixes :—*

Dearth, dearness.
Drought, dryness.
Hardness, hardihood.
Sleight, slyness.
Sloth, slowness.
Truth, trueness.
Witness, wisdom.

(*b*) *Romanic suffixes :—*

Acquitt-ance, acquitt-al.
Appar-it-ion, appear-ance.
Benefact-ion, benefic-ence.
Committ-al, commiss-ion.
Compos-ure, compos-it-ion.
Content-ment, content-ion.
Continu-ance, continu-at-ion.
Creat-ure, creat-ion.
Degener-at-ion, degener-ac-y.
Depart-ment, depart-ure.
Destin-y, destin-at-ion.
Dispos-al, dispos-it-ion.
Eject-ment, eject-ion.
Expos-ure, expos-it-ion.
Fixt-ure, fix-ity.
Fract-ure, fract-ion, frag-ment.
Impost-ure, impos-it-ion.
Impress-ment, impress-ion.
Intim-at-ion, intim-ac-y.
Luxury, luxuriance.
Observ-ance, observ-at-ion.
Post-ure, posit-ion.
Propos-al, propos-it-ion.
Protest-er, protest-ant.
Serv-i-tude, serv-ice.
Signific-ance, signific-at-ion.
Stat-ure, stat-ion.
Tempera-ment, tempera-ture.
Vac-ancy, vac-at-ion.

(*c*) *Romanic and Teutonic suffixes :—*

Appropriate-ness, appropriat-ion.
Apt-ness, apt-i-tude.
Close-ness, close-ure.
Complete-ness, complet-ion.
Direct-ion, direct-ness.
Distinct-ness, distinct-ion.
Exact-ness, exact-ion.
False-hood, fals-ity, false-ness.
Human-ity, humane-ness.
Ingenu-ity, ingenu-ous-ness.
Just-ness, just-ice.
Lax-ity, lax-ness.
Pall-or, pale-ness.
Proced-ure, proceed-ing.
Quiet-ude, quiet-ness.
Remiss-ness, remiss-ion.
Secure-ness, secur-ity.
Till-age, til-th.

(*d*) *Greek and Romanic suffixes*:—

Barbar-ism, barbar-ity.
Commun-ism, commun-ity.
Fatal-ism, fatal-ity.
Formal-ism, formal-ity.
Vulgar-ism, vulgar-ity.

II. *Show by an example the difference of meaning, if any, in each of the following pairs of adjectives formed with different suffixes*:—

Beneficial, beneficent.
Ceremonious, ceremonial.
Childlike, childish.
Comic, comical.
Comprehensive, comprehensible.
Congenial, congenital.
Contemptible, contemptuous.
Continual, continuous.
Corporate, corporal.
Credible, creditable.
Definite, definitive.
Dramatic, dramatical.
Elemental, elementary.
Exceptional, exceptionable.
Expedient, expeditious.
Godlike, godly.
Illusive, illusory.
Imaginary, imaginative.
Imperial, imperious.
Industrial, industrious.
Ingenious, ingenuous.
Innocent, innocuous.
Judicial, judicious.
Luxurious, luxuriant.
Masterly, masterful.
Momentary, momentous.
Notable, notorious.
Official, officious.
Ordinal, ordinary.
Permissive, permissible.
Politic, political.
Popular, populous.
Respective, respectful.
Reverend, reverent.
Sanatory, sanitary.
Sensitive, sensible.
Sensual, sensuous.
Silvery, silvern.
Spirituous, spiritual.
Temporal, temporary.
Tragic, tragical.
Transit-ory, transit-ional.
Verbal, verbose.
Virtual, virtuous.

III. *Substitute a single word (an adjective) for the words printed below in italics*:—

(*a*) This writing is *such as cannot be read*.
(*b*) The plan you mention *cannot be put into practice*.
(*c*) He is *one who cannot according to the rules be elected*.
(*d*) That herb is *fit to be eaten*.
(*e*) The colour is *beyond my perception*.
(*f*) You are *liable to be called to account* for your actions.
(*g*) The plan you propose is *open to objections*.
(*h*) That word is *no longer in use*.
(*i*) This is a bird *of passage*.
(*j*) Your office is *one for which no salary is paid*.
(*k*) His motive was merely *to get some money*.
(*l*) His position was *beyond all hope of improvement*.
(*m*) His manners are *more like those of a woman than of a man*.
(*n*) He is *one who takes no trouble* about his work.
(*o*) His style is *too full of words*.
(*p*) He is *inclined to find fault*.
(*q*) A wolf is an animal *that cannot be tamed*.
(*r*) That problem is *one which is never likely to be solved*.
(*s*) His character *has an evil reputation*.

(*t*) The use of opium is *likely to do much injury.*
(*u*) That impression is *too vivid ever to be effaced.*
(*v*) He is *unable to pay his debts.*

IV. *To each of the verbs, nouns, or adjectives given below, add some Abstract suffix or suffixes:—*

Serve, coward, right, grand, err, miser, apt, victor, acrid, just, merchant, trick, pass, seize, try, judge, compel, admit, patron, repent, regent, bankrupt, accurate, poor, rely, captive, fragile, facile, felon, sole, assist, scarce, secret, defy, father, real.

V. *Form Diminutive nouns out of the following by adding to each of them its appropriate Diminutive suffix:—*

Animal, code, pouch, brook, poet, cigar, vase, lance, globe, mode, pill, bill, car, cellar, statue, part, song, sign, table, home, wagon, hump, park, maid, cut, lamb, hill, change, bird, lad, scythe, corn.

VI. *Point out the six different senses of the suffix* "**age**" *as exemplified in the following words:—*

Herbage, hermitage, courage, postage, breakage, personage.

VII. *Describe the uses of the suffix* "**-en**" *as exemplified in the following words:—*

Maiden, flaxen, vixen, fatten, drunken, kitten, alien, rotten, golden, oxen, haven.

VIII. *In the following sentences, the meaning of the word to which* "**re-**" *has been prefixed depends upon whether a hyphen has or has not been placed between the prefix and the verbal root. Substitute some other verb or phrase in each sentence:—*

(1) { I have never remarked this before.
The box must be re-marked.

(2) { My losses were soon recovered.
The chairs must be re-covered.

(3) { He has rejoined his post.
He has re-joined the two planks.

(4) { Their wrongs were soon redressed.
The doll must be re-dressed.

(5) { His character was reformed.
The classes were re-formed.

(6) { I cannot recollect this.
You must re-collect all the coins that have been lost.

(7) { I will not recount my sorrows.
You had better re-count all these coins.

(8) { You must return that book.
Having turned the verse into prose, he re-turned the prose into verse.

(9) { This has been reserved for future use.
The summons, which he could not then receive, must be re-served upon him.

(10) { A. went out of office and was replaced by B.
A. has been re-placed in his appointment.

IX. *Define and distinguish the three meanings of the prefix* "**sub-**" *in the following words:—*

(*a*) Sub-terranean, sub-montane; (*b*) sub-acid, sub-tropical; (*c*) sub-judge, sub-deputy.

X. *Show the difference of meaning implied in the following words by the prefix* "**non-**" *and the prefix* "**in-**" *or* "**un-**"*:—*

(*a*) Non-active, inactive; (*b*) non-effective, ineffective; (*c*) non-Christian, unchristian; (*d*) non-famous, infamous; (*e*) non-professional, unprofessional; (*f*) non-judicial, unjudicial.

XI. *Form sentences showing the difference of meaning between—*

Confidant, confident; dependant, dependent; pendant, pendent; plaintive, plaintiff.

XII. *Show what prefixes are disguised in the following words:—*

Cost, essay (trial), spend, pilgrim, sudden, sovereign, outrage, trespass, sojourn, umpire, entrails, deluge, ancestor, balance, anoint, sombre, provost, runagate, puny.

XIII. *Distinguish the suffixes in each of the following pairs:—*

Hatred, hundred; hemlock, wedlock; learning, farthing; freckle, spindle; seedling, darkling; friend, reverend.

XIV. *Distinguish the suffix* "**-ther**" *in each of the following:—*

Other, father, hither.

XV. *Distinguish the prefix* "**a**" *in each of the following:—*

Aspect, apathy, avert, afresh, afloat, arise, ado, amend.

XVI. *Separate the stem from the affixes (prefixes or suffixes) of the following words, and the affixes from each other:—*

Undenominationalism, valetudinarian, unsophisticated, renegade, instrumentality, disproportionate, talkativeness, protestantism, absenteeism, accidentally, miscreant, indentures, intoxicate, interest, intellectual, demonetise, telephone, introspection, captivate, insignificant, homogeneous, inaccessible, procedure, likelihood.

CHAPTER XXVI.—FIGURES OF RHETORIC.

343. Figure of Speech defined.—A Figure of Speech or Rhetoric is a deviation from the plain and ordinary use of words with a view to increasing or specialising the effect.

Thus we can say, "There are six *pillars* on either side of this colonnade." Here the word *pillars* is used in its ordinary and literal sense.

Again, we can say, "This law is one of the *pillars* of the common-wealth." Here *pillar* is used in a figurative or non-literal sense, and signifies "main support."

344. Figures of Speech classified.—The three main classes of figures have their origin in the three chief faculties of the human intellect, viz. (1) comparison or the perception of resemblance, (2) discrimination or the perception of difference, and (3) association or the impression of contiguity.[1]

I. When *like* objects come under our notice, we are struck with the resemblance. The figures named Simile, Metaphor, and Allegory are based on similarity or resemblance. These figures constitute Class I.

II. When *unlike* objects come under our notice, we are struck with the difference. The figures named Antithesis, Epigram, and the Condensed Sentence are based on contrast or difference. These constitute Class II.

III. When two impressions *occurring together* become permanently associated in the mind, the thought of the one calls up the thought of the other, as a storm suggests shipwreck, wealth suggests gold, etc. This is called the law of Contiguity, and is the foundation of memory or the retentive faculty. The figures of speech named Metonymy, Synecdoche, and the Transferred Epithet are based upon Contiguity. These constitute Class III.

Besides the above, there is a Fourth Class consisting of miscellaneous figures, which though not based on any one faculty like the three classes just named, involve some deviation from the ordinary use of words, and are therefore rightly included among Figures of Speech.

Class I.—Figures based on Resemblance.

345. Simile: lit. "a thing like" (neuter of Latin *similis*, like).—A simile is the explicit statement of some point of resemblance conceived to exist between two things, *that differ in other respects.*

Observe, in the simile and in all other figures based upon resemblance, the comparison is, not between things of the same kind, but between things *of different kinds.* Thus there is no figure, if we compare a camel with a dromedary, but only when, for example, we compare it with a ship and call it "the ship of the desert." Again, there is no simile if we compare Burke with

[1] Bain's *Rhetoric and Composition*, Part I. p. 135.

Cicero, Napoleon with Alexander, or the Russian Empire with the Roman Empire. These are all good parallels. But, as the comparisons are *literal*—that is, between objects *of the same kind* —there is nothing figurative about them.

> Errors, *like* straws, upon the surface flow;
> He that would search for pearls must dive below.—DRYDEN.
>
> The tribes (on the North-west frontier of India) hung upon the flanks of our retreating columns *like* wasps.—*Review of Reviews*, Jan. 1898, p. 5.
>
> They flourished the interests of the national defence, *like* a Medusa's head, to frighten off the men.—*Daily Telegraph*, 24th Feb. 1898.

A simile is especially effective, when some *abstract* thought or series of thoughts is illustrated by means of some *concrete* parallel. Keats, having read several translations of Homer into English verse, and not being satisfied with any of them, found a new world suddenly opened out before him on seeing the translation by Chapman (A.D. 1598), and expressed his feelings under the following simile:—

> Then felt I like some watcher of the skies,
> When a new planet swims into his ken;
> Or like stout Cortez, when with eagle eyes
> He stared at the Pacific,—and all his men
> Looked at each other with a wild surmise,—
> Silent, upon a peak in Darien.

From such examples as the above it will be seen that a simile is usually introduced by some words, such as *like*, *as*, *as—so*, which draw attention to the likeness. But this is not necessary. All that is necessary to the simile is that both sides of the comparison shall be distinctly stated:—

> Whenever I hear the member for N—— speak about East Africa, I am reminded of one of those mirrors in which we see everything upside down, and in which things are presented in a topsy-turvy condition.—*Mr. Curzon's Speech*, 4th March 1898.
>
> The repose of repletion may not be a very heroic attitude to a great nation like the English; but even a lion sleeps after a full meal.—*Review of Reviews*, Jan. 1898, p. 8.

346. Metaphor: lit. a transfer (Gr. *meta*, across; *phor-e*, carrying).—A metaphor is a *potential* or *implied* simile. In a simile both sides of the comparison are distinctly stated; whereas in a metaphor one side is stated, but not the other. Thus when we say, "He *curbs* his passion," we mean that he restrains his passion, as a man would curb a restless horse. If both sides of the comparison were to be given, this is how the simile would be expressed.

Our eldest son is the *star* (brightest member) of the family.
His rash policy let loose the *dogs* of war.
Hold fast to the *anchor* of faith.
The news you bring is a *dagger* to my heart.
The town was *stormed* after a long siege.
He was fond of *blowing* his own *trumpet* (praising himself).
He *swam* bravely against the *tide* of popular applause.
Can'st thou not minister to a mind diseased,
Pluck from the memory a *rooted* sorrow?—SHAKSPEARE.

347. *Personal Metaphors.*—A metaphor is personal, when it speaks of inanimate objects as if they were living.

A *treacherous* calm; a *sullen* sky; a *frowning* rock; *pitiless* cold; *cruel* heat; a *learned* age; the *thirsty* ground; a *virgin* soil.

Every hedge was *conscious* of more than what the representations of enamoured swains admit of.—*Tatler.*

The *childhood* of the world; the *anger* of the tempest; the *deceitfulness* of riches. Wine is a *mocker.*

Oh *mother* Ida, many-fountained Ida,
Dear mother Ida, hearken ere I die.—TENNYSON.

Our *unwearied* and *unsubsidised* allies, the waves.—STEAD.

When empire in its *childhood* first appears,
A watchful fate o'ersees its *tender years.*—DRYDEN.

Everything *smiled* on him. Familiarity *breeds* contempt.

Perhaps the vale
Relents awhile to the reflected ray.—THOMSON.

The *voice* of thy brother's blood *crieth* unto me from the ground.—Gen. iv. 10.

Weary wave and *dying* blast
Sob and *moan* along the shore;
And all is peace at last.

348. *Sustained Metaphors.*—The resemblance expressed by a metaphor is usually limited to a single point. Occasionally, however, a metaphor can be sustained through a series of kindred images.

Let us (since life can little else supply
But just to look about us and to die)
Expatiate free o'er all the scene of man,
A mighty *maze,* but not without a *plan;*
A *wild,* where *weeds and flowers* promiscuous *shoot;*
A *garden* tempting with forbidden *fruit,*
Together let us beat the ample *field,*
Try what the *open,* what the *covert* yield;
The *latent tracks,* the *giddy heights* explore
Of those who blindly creep or sightless soar.—POPE.

We believe that the *embers* of municipal patriotism have never ceased to *burn* and *glow* in these smaller communities, into which, by historical and physical necessity, London has been divided. We will do nothing to *quench these embers.* Rather we will *tend* them and *fan* them, until over the whole of those communities they have shed an equal and a vivifying *light* and *warmth*.—*Duke of Devonshire's Speech*, 15th February 1898.

349. *Confusion of Metaphors.*—Metaphors borrowed from more than one source must not be combined in the same phrase or clause. The mixing of metaphors, far from increasing the effect, weakens it by the sense of incongruity that it excites.

Savoy and Nice, the *keys* of Italy and the *citadel* in her hands to *bridle* Switzerland, are in that consolidation of the French power.—BURKE.

He is understood to have expressed the belief that the true policy for the Liberal party to pursue was to *launch a campaign* against the House of Lords.—*Daily Telegraph*.

Traders should once and for all abandon the hope that the province of Yunnan is a *rich mine* only waiting to be *tapped*.—*Cont. Review*, February 1898.

Nothing can save China but a *radical right-about-face* on the part of the British Foreign Office.—*Review of Reviews*, February 1898, p. 148.

There are *phrases* of *music* that go home to the *centre* of our being, and five minutes' dwelling on them at sunrise will give a *keynote* that will *sound* for the day, the *morning bath* of the mind.—*National Review*, February 1898.

In cases of this kind the Stock Market, which is considerably more liable to fits of *panic* than to *phlegmatic* indifference or foolish optimism, is the safest political *thermometer*.—*Daily Telegraph*, 25th February 1898.

It is but cold comfort to know that reason must in the end prevail over superstition, and that a religion *grafted* upon science will *come to the birth* by the slow but sure processes of evolution. —*Times Weekly*, 4th March 1898.

350. *Succession without confusion.*—We may, however, have a succession of metaphors without confusion.

(1) I *bridle* in my struggling muse with pain,
That longs to *launch* into a bolder *strain*.—ADDISON.

(2) At length Erasmus, that great honoured name
(The glory of the priesthood and the shame),
Stemmed the wild *torrent* of a barbarous age,
And *drove* those holy Vandals off the *stage*.—POPE.

We consider (1) an instance of confusion, and (2) an instance of succession without confusion. Ex. (1) is a *confusion* of metaphor for two reasons—(*a*) because an adjective clause, being a syntactical part of the main clause (§ 195), is not entitled to employ a metaphor distinct from that employed by the main clause; and (*b*) because the adjective clause itself contains two distinct metaphors. On the other hand, we consider (2) a *succession*, not a confusion, of metaphors, because the fourth line is a co-ordinate, not a subordinate, clause, and is therefore entitled to employ its own metaphor independently of the other.

The following is a striking example of a succession of co-ordinate metaphors, each of which is in apposition with a single noun, "sleep," and could easily be expanded into a co-ordinate clause.

> Macbeth doth murder sleep, the innocent sleep,
> Sleep that knits up the ravelled sleave of care,
> The death of each day's life, sore labour's bath,
> Balm of hurt minds, great nature's second course,
> Chief nourisher in life's feast.—*Macbeth*, ii. 2.

351. *Appropriateness of Metaphor.*—A far-fetched metaphor defeats its own object; for instead of setting a point in a clearer light by the comparison, it makes it darker. On the other hand, a metaphor is especially appropriate and forcible when the comparison is backed by some fact of a kindred character:—

(1) For seven weeks he tramped, a workless worker, the *stony-hearted* streets of London.—*Review of Reviews*, Feb. 1898.

(2) We believe the integrity of China is most likely to be secured by throwing the country open to the commerce of the world instead of closing it up, so to speak, in *water-tight compartments.*—*Mr. Curzon's Speech*, 2nd March 1898.

Here the provinces of China, closed against foreign commerce, are compared to "water-tight compartments." The comparison is doubly apt, because the only access to these provinces at present is by water, viz. the treaty-ports and the mouths of the great inland rivers.

(3) Mr. Bright condemned the ruinous expense of the army, and maintained that the young officers with their scarlet and gold were kept up mainly for the amusement of the young ladies of the aristocracy; and he added, "And these young ladies pet the robin red-breast, who is the most quarrelsome and disreputable of birds,—simply because he wears a red waistcoat."—*Fortnightly Review*, February 1898, p. 243.

(4) My hon. friend is a spinner of long yarns of low quality. (Applied in a double sense to the late Mr. Bright, a cotton-spinner by trade, and a distinguished speaker in the House of Commons.)

(5) Where wert thou, mighty Mother, when he lay,—
When thy son lay pierced by the shaft that flies
In darkness?—SHELLEY'S *Adonais*, 9-12.

Adonais is Keats, the poet, whose premature death is mourned by Shelley. The metaphor of death as "the arrow that flieth by day," "the pestilence that walketh in darkness" (Ps. xci.) is rendered doubly appropriate by the fact that the immediate cause of his death was said to be a malignant attack written by an anonymous reviewer.

352. *Metaphors based on history, fable, parable,* etc.—Metaphors may be drawn not only from resemblances of objects, but from resemblances of situation, and these may be taken from history, or fable, or parable, or proverb. Every one is familiar with such phrases as "hiding one's light under a bushel," "the lion lying down with the lamb" (parables from the Bible); "to wash one's hands of a thing" (Pilate's action in the prætorium); "cutting one's coat according to the cloth," "letting sleeping dogs lie," "swapping horses in crossing a stream," "putting the cart before the horse" (proverbs).

The lion roared to a false note and then rated the jackals for yelping in unison. (Fable of jackal in lion's hide.)—*Daily Telegraph*, 5th February 1898.

The interests of Great Britain had to be defended in language that should steer safely between the Scylla of weakness and the Charybdis of arrogance. (The fabled whirlpools in the Straits of Messina.)—*Ibid.* 2nd March 1898.

The Hon. H. B. with his green cutaway coat and brass buttons had an annual tilt in favour of the ballot. (Don Quixote having a tilt at a windmill.)—*Fort. Review*, February 1898, p. 245.

The western labyrinth of hills serves as an invaluable mural barrier of Hindostan. (The "labyrinth" is borrowed from the famous building at Arsinoe in Egypt; and "the mural barrier" from the Great Wall of China.)—*Review of Reviews*, Jan. 1898.

Mr. L., writing in the *Fortnightly*, takes up his parable against Lord Salisbury. (Balaam and Balak.)—*Ibid.* Feb. 1898.

The English, when they are lavishing their derision against the Kaiser and his brother, should remember that they are living in glass houses and ought not to throw stones. (Proverb.)—*Ibid.* January 1898.

He received his baptism of fire in the Crimea. (Name for spiritual baptism in New Testament.)—*Daily Telegraph*, 4th March 1898.

It would be disreputable to allude to the Most Serene, Mighty, Beloved Emperor as the drunken Helot of English Jingoism. (The Spartan custom of making the Helots drunk as a caution to Spartan citizens.)—*Review of Reviews*, Jan. 1898.

You have burnt your ships, and must go forward or perish.—(Agathocles of Syracuse, as soon as he landed at Carthage, burnt his ships so as to render return impossible.)

353. **Allegory, Fable, Parable.**—These are the same at bottom, and, like metaphors, are based upon resemblance.

An Allegory is a tale consisting of a series of incidents analogous to another series of incidents, which it is intended to illustrate. The object of such a tale is to exemplify and enforce some moral truth; as in Bunyan's *Pilgrim's Progress.*

A Parable is a short allegory, as the Sower, the Ten Virgins, the Prodigal Son, the Grain of Mustard Seed, the Lost Sheep, etc. In the Old Testament the parable of the Ewe Lamb was intended to bring King David to a sense of his guilt by putting a parallel case before him; and it succeeded.

The Fables of classical literature, in which birds and beasts are made to think, speak, and act like men, all teach some moral, as allegory and parable do.

Class II.—Figures based on Contrast or Difference.

354. **Antithesis.**—"It is a first principle of the human mind, that we are affected only *by change of impression*. Among the many consequences of this law is the efficacy of contrast in verbal composition" (Bain).[1]

We cannot use the commonest word, say "weak" for example, without inwardly contrasting it with "strong." Barring proper names, which are mere marks or tokens, and interjections, which are mere sounds, there is not a word in our language, or in fact in any language, which does not imply some other word or words with which it is contrasted in meaning. This law is so universal, that in ordinary speech it is sufficient to mention one word, such as "weak," without adding its negative form "not-strong."

Sometimes, however, it is expedient, "for the sake of increasing or specialising the effect," to mention both of the contrasted terms; and as this is a departure "from the ordinary use of words," we call it a Figure of Speech. (See definition in § 343.)

Antithesis is a Greek word signifying "setting against"; that is, setting one word against another.

He can *bribe*, but he cannot *seduce*; he can *buy*, but he cannot *gain*; he can *lie*, but he cannot *deceive*.

A *friend* exaggerates a man's *virtues*, an *enemy* his *crimes*.

Between fame and true honour there is much difference; the former is *a blind* and *noisy applause*; the latter is an *internal and more silent homage*.

As Cæsar loved me, I weep for him; as he was fortunate, I rejoice at it; as he was valiant, I honour him; but, as he was ambitious, I slew him. There is tears for his love; joy for his fortune; honour for his valour; and death for his ambition.—SHAKSPEARE.

Though deep, yet clear; though gentle, yet not dull;
Strong without rage; without o'erflowing full.—DENHAM.

There is everywhere a perceptible reaction in favour of government by the capable as opposed to government by the counting of noses.—*Review of Reviews*, Jan. 1898, p. 6.

Themistocles, being asked whether he would choose to marry his

[1] *Rhetoric and Composition*, Part I. p. 196.

daughter to an indigent man of merit, or to a worthless man of wealth, replied: "I would prefer a man without wealth to wealth without a man."—*Spectator*, No. 372.

Antithesis should not be sacrificed to brevity. Compare the following, and see which of the two is the more pointed :—

(*a*) The *posthumous* fame of Buddha is far greater than what accrued to him during his life.

(*b*) The fame *which has gathered round the name of Buddha since his death* far exceeds that which accrued to him during his life.

Observe that in (*b*) not only is one clause balanced against another, but the Present Perfect tense "has gathered" is contrasted with the Past Indefinite "accrued."

355. Epigram: lit. an inscription (a Greek word, *epigramma*), the name given by the Greeks to a short piece of verse inscribed on a public monument. Brevity is still one of the distinguishing marks of epigram. But the word has been made to denote any kind of pointed saying, and especially one in which the words appear to be contrasted, or at least to contain some kind of incongruity. It is therefore based upon the perception of difference, and is closely allied to Antithesis.

"The epigram is an apparent contradiction in language, which, by causing a temporary shock, rouses our attention to some important meaning underneath" (Bain).

The *child* is *father* of the man.—WORDSWORTH.
By *merit* raised to that *bad* eminence.—MILTON.
Loveliness
Needs not the foreign aid of ornament,
But is, when *unadorned*, *adorned* the most.—THOMSON.
Conspicuous by its *absence*.—DISRAELI.
In the midst of *life* we are in *death*.—*Proverb.*
He lived a life of *active idleness.*
'Tis all thy *business*, *business* how to shun.—POPE.
Art lies in concealing *art*.—*Latin Proverb.*
Fame is the spur that the clear spirit doth raise
(That last *infirmity* of *noble* minds)
To scorn delights and live laborious days.—MILTON.
Ambition first sprung from your blest abodes,
The *glorious fault* of angels and of gods.—POPE.
He who lives *without folly* is not so *wise* as he imagines.—*Proverb.*
Affected *simplicity* is refined *artfulness*.—*Proverb.*
A *workless workman* (a man seeking for work and not finding it).
To *damn* with faint *praise*.
Indecision is sometimes a *decisive* kind of action.—*Review of Reviews.*
Another such *victory*, and we are *undone*.—*Saying of Pyrrhus.*
Beware the *fury* of a *patient* man.—DRYDEN.

A *favourite* has *no friend.*—GRAY.
I protest by that glorying in you which I have in Christ Jesus our Lord, I *die daily.*—1 Cor. xv. 31.
Defend me from my *friends.*—*Proverb.*
Silence is sometimes more *eloquent* than words.
Owe no man anything but to love one another.—*New Testament.*
Murder, though it have no *tongue*, will yet *speak.*
A rule more *honoured* in the *breach* than the observance.
Great wits will sometimes *gloriously offend*,
And *rise* to *faults* which critics dare not mend.—POPE.
His *honour* rooted in *dishonour* stood,
And *faith unfaithful* kept him *falsely true.*—TENNYSON.

The following phrases, all of common occurrence, can be classed under the heading of epigrammatic: *White* lie, *solemn* trifling, a *silent* rebuke, *masterly* inactivity, an *open* secret, a *tedious* amusement, a *pious* fraud, *noble* revenge, *expressive* silence, *shabby* genteel.

356. **Pun.**—In this figure the incongruity consists in using the same word in different senses. The figure is used chiefly for purposes of humour :—

The leopard changes his spots, as often as he goes from one spot to another.
Is life worth living? That depends on the liver.

Ben Battle was a soldier bold
And used to war's alarms;
But a cannon ball shot off his legs,
So he laid down his arms.—HOOD.

The figure is sometimes, however, used seriously. In such instances there is a play upon words not amounting to a pun; § 302.

Home-keeping youth have ever homely wits.—SHAKSPEARE.
Bad accidents happen to bad players.
Evil be to him that evil thinks.
The right divine of kings to govern wrong.—POPE.

In three of these examples the repeated word (*home, bad, evil*), is used in a different sense in the same sentence. In the remaining example there is almost a pun on the word *right*. It is really a noun signifying "lawful power or prerogative," but it is made to look like an adjective used as the opposite to "wrong," a real adjective.

357. **The Condensed Sentence.**—This figure consists in bringing together under one verb or in one enumeration ideas so different, that we should ordinarily give a distinct clause or an entirely distinct sentence to each of them.

The Russian grandees came to Elizabeth's court dropping pearls and vermin.—MACAULAY.
She dropped a tear and her pocket-handkerchief.—DICKENS.
Smelling of musk and of insolence.—TENNYSON.

Corsica is an island swarming with bandits and bandicoots.

There used to be in Paris under the ancient regime a few women of brilliant talents, who violated all the common duties of life and gave very pleasant little suppers. Among these supped and sinned Madame D'Epinay.—MORLEY.

It is by the goodness of God that we have possession of three unspeakably precious things,—freedom of speech, freedom of conscience, and the prudence of using neither.—MARK TWAIN.

Napoleon was equally great in directing a battle or in regulating the length of a ballet-girl's skirts.—*Daily Telegraph*, 9th Feb. 1898.

Class III.—Figures based on Contiguity.

358. **Metonymy**: lit. "a change of name" (Gr. *meta*, change; *onoma*, name).—This figure consists in describing a thing by some *accompaniment* or *significant adjunct*, instead of naming the thing itself. When the sign is such as to strike the imagination more vividly than what it stands for, the language gains in impressiveness.

(*a*) *The symbol for the person or thing symbolised*:—

He succeeded to the *crown* (=royal office).
He is too fond of *red tape* (=official routine).
From the *cradle* to the *grave* (=from childhood to death).
Leather (=shoe-making) pays better than learning.
Grey hairs (=old age or old men) should be respected.
Show deference to the *chair* (=the chairman's ruling).
Brought to the *hammer* (=put up to auction).
Backstairs (=secret, intriguing) influence.
Promoted to the *bench* (=the office of judge).
The *woolsack* (=the seat, and hence the office, of Lord Chancellor).
Called to the *bar* (=made a barrister).

> Bluff Harry broke into the spence
> And turned the *cowls* (monks) adrift.—TENNYSON.

A 'bus driver, summoned for delaying his 'bus, pleaded that he was hailed by a *fare* who subsequently changed his mind. —*Daily Telegraph*, 9th March 1898.

(*b*) *The instrument for the agent*:—

The *pen* has more influence than the *sword*.
Give every man thine *ear*, but few thy *voice*.
He is a good *hand* at composition.
To carry *fire* and *sword* (=a desolating war) into a country.
The *tongue* of slander is never silent.
Taliessin is our fullest *throat* of song.—TENNYSON.

The "resident commissioner" will be the *eyes* and *ears*, and to a limited extent the *voice*, of the High Commissioner.—*Times Weekly*, 4th March 1898.

How shall we attract men to the *colours* (=the army)?

In India trade preceded the *flag*, and the function of the *flag* is to protect trade.—*Daily Telegraph*, 25th Feb. 1898.

Sceptre and *crown*
Must tumble down,
And in the dust be equal made
With the poor crooked *scythe* and *spade.*—JAMES SHIRLEY.

(That is, kings must die as well as peasants).

(*c*) *The container for the thing contained*:—

He drank the *cup* (=the contents of the cup).
He is too fond of the *bottle* (=the liquor in the bottle).
The *kettle* (=water in the kettle) boils.
The conquerors smote the *city* (=inhabitants of the city).
Going over to *Rome* (=the Church centred in Rome).
He keeps a fine *stable* (=fine horses).
The *gallery* (=spectators in the gallery) loudly applauded.
The power of the *purse* (=the money in the purse).
Oxford (=the Oxford crew) won the last boat-race.
England does not desire war with *Russia.*
He keeps a sumptuous *table* (=viands on the table).

(*d*) *The effect for the cause*:—

A favourable *speed*
Ruffle thy mirrored mast.—TENNYSON, *In Memoriam.*

(Here *speed* is put for *wind*, the cause of speed.)

He desperate takes the *death*
With sudden plunge.—THOMSON.

(Here the *death* is the angler's hook seized by the fish.)

O for a beaker full of the *warm south!*—KEATS.

(Here wine is described by the *warm south*, that is, the warm sun of the south, which ripens the grape from which the wine is produced. This is a metonymy three deep.)

(*e*) *The maker for the thing made; the place for the thing*:—

They have *Moses* and the *prophets.*—*New Testament.*
I have never read *Homer* (=the poems of Homer.)
This is a common phrase in *Tennyson.*
I am not fond of *Euclid* (=geometry).
The miner went without his *Davy* (=the safety lamp invented by Sir Humphry Davy).
Look it out in *Bradshaw* (=time-table by Bradshaw).
I am fond of old *china* (=crockery made in China).
A book bound in *morocco* (=leather of Morocco).
We have several Turners (=pictures by Turner).
You have a beautiful *canary.*
A little *cayenne* will improve the flavour.

(*f*) *The name of a passion for the object of the passion*:—

She is coming, my *life*, my *fate.*—TENNYSON.
For Lycidas, your *sorrow*, is not dead.—MILTON.

At length Erasmus, that great honoured name,
The *glory* of the priesthood and the *shame.*—POPE.

The *sigh* of her secret soul (the person sighed for).—OSSIAN.
The Lord is my *strength* and my *song*, and is become my *salvation.*—*Old Testament.*

Soul of the age!
The *applause*, *delight*, and *wonder* of our stage!
My Shakspeare rise!—BEN JONSON.
The people's *prayer*, the glad diviner's *theme*,
The young men's *vision*, and the old men's *dream*.

(The italicised words are all applied by Dryden to the Duke of Monmouth.)

359. Syn-ec-do-che: lit. "the understanding of one thing simultaneously with another" (a Greek word transliterated into English).—This figure is distinguished from Metonymy by the fact that the sign, which is made to represent the thing signified, may be any kind of symbol except an *accompaniment*, this last being the exclusive property of Metonymy. Perhaps, however, the best way to distinguish these two figures is as follows:—

In synecdoche one name is substituted for another, whose meaning is more or less *cognate* with its own.

In metonymy one name is substituted for another, whose meaning is wholly *foreign* to itself.

(*a*) *The less general put for the more general.*—The more general the term is, the fainter is the picture; the more special the term, the more vivid the picture. Hence, if a writer desires to be impressive, he should employ words as particular and determinate in sense as the scope of the subject will allow:—

They *sank* as *lead* in the mighty waters.—Exodus xv. 10.

Consider the *lilies* how they grow: they *toil* not, they *spin* not; and yet I say unto you that *Solomon* in all his glory was not arrayed like one of these.—Luke xii. 27.

The kiss *snatched* hasty from the *sidelong* maid,
On purpose guardless.—THOMSON, *Winter*.

All *hands* employed, the royal work grows warm.—DRYDEN.

Return to her? and fifty men dismissed?
No, rather I abjure all *roofs*, and choose
To be a comrade with the *wolf* and *owl*.—SHAKSPEARE, *King Lear*.

A *sail* was descried in the distance.

For seven weeks he *tramped*, a workless worker, the stony-hearted streets of London.—*Review of Reviews*, Feb. 1898, p. 124.

Moralise capital! you might as well propose to moralise a *boa constrictor* or tame a *tiger*.—*Ibid.*

Do men gather *grapes* of *thorns*, or *figs* of *thistles*?—*New Testament*.

That maiden's blood
Is as unchristian as a *leopard's*.—GEORGE ELIOT, *Spanish Gipsy*.

(*b*) *An individual for a class.*—A well-known individual is sometimes made to represent a class: in this way a Proper noun becomes a Common noun, see § 23, *Note* 2. Even when a Proper noun is not so used, a general statement is made much more forcible, if it is illustrated by a good individual example:—

A *Daniel* (very wise judge) come to judgment.—SHAKSPEARE.
Smooth *Jacob* still robs homely *Esau*.—BROWNING.
He's *Judas* to a tittle, that man is.—*Ibid.*
"That" was the real *Saturn* of the Genealogy.[1]—MASSON.

I would have such a fellow whipped for o'erdoing
Termagant; it out-*Herods Herod*.—SHAKSPEARE.

Sternhold himself he out-*Sternholded*.—SWIFT.
To *gorgonise* (to turn into stone by a glance of the eye).—TENNYSON.
You call ours harassing legislation: of course all progressive governments are harassing legislators: doubtless when Moses brought down the law from Sinai, many stout Conservatives present thought the ten commandments harassing legislation. —BRIGHT'S *Speeches*.

(*c*) *The more general for the less general.*—As the usual tendency of general words is to weaken the effect rather than to strengthen it (see remarks under (*a*)), this form of Synecdoche is rather uncommon:—

We say *vessel* for "ship"; *measure* for "dance" or for "poetry"; the smiling *year* for the smiling "season," spring or summer; the Christian *world* for the Christian Church as a whole; *liquor* for intoxicating drink; *action* for "battle"; *company* for a "commercial firm."

Sometimes a very general term is used by way of contempt:—

A poor *creature*. A wretched *individual*. A *thing* of shreds and patches.

Sometimes a very general term is used to avoid a more particular one, which we do not like to mention:—

Thus we say *deceased* or *departed* or *gone to rest* for "dead"; *elevated* for "tipsy"; *if any thing should happen to him* for "if he should die"; *plain* for "ugly," etc.

(*d*) *The concrete for the abstract:*—

There is a mixture of *the tiger* and *the ape* in the character of a Frenchman.—VOLTAIRE.

I do the most that friendship can,
I hate *the Viceroy*, love *the man*.—SWIFT.
An English muse is touched with generous woe,
And in the unhappy man forgets *the foe*.—ADDISON.

A tyrant's power in rigour is expressed,
The father yearns in the true prince's breast.—DRYDEN.
A healthy lad, and carried in his cheeks
Two steady *roses* that were five years old.

[1] The author is here comparing the antiquity of the conjunctive pronouns "who," "that," "which," "what." He declares "that" to be the Saturn or great ancestor of all, *i.e.* the earliest form of Relative.

(e) *The abstract for the concrete:* see § 27:—

All the *rank* and *fashion* came out to see the sight.
The *authorities* put an end to the tumult.
Pecksniff is one of the *characters* created by Dickens.
Grace and *loveliness, wit* and *learning* were assembled in that meeting.
Up goes my grave *Impudence* to the maid.—*Tatler.*

The same figure appears in such phrases as, *His Majesty* for "king," *her ladyship* for "lady," *his lordship* for "lord," *His Excellency* for "governor" or "viceroy," *His Holiness* for "pope," *His Grace* for "archbishop," a *justice* of the peace for "judge," etc.

(f) *The part for a whole:*—

A fleet of fifty *sail* (=ships).
Pin money (a lady's dress allowance).
How beautiful upon the mountains are the *feet* of him that bringeth good tidings.—*Old Testament.*
He is a very good *hand* at cricket.
A man of seventy *winters.*[1]

(g) *The material for the thing made:*—

A foeman worthy of his *steel* (=sword).
The speaking *marble* (=statue of marble).
He was buried under this *stone* (=tablet of stone).
He was bound in *irons* (=fetters made of *iron*).
Have you any *coppers?* (=pence made of copper).
Silver and *gold* (=money) have I none.—*New Testament.*

360. Transferred Epithet.—This is a third kind of figure based on Contiguity. When two impressions are associated together in the mind, an epithet that properly belongs to one only is transferred to the other. One of the commonest, though not the only, application of this figure is when some personal quality (§ 347) is transferred to something inanimate:—

He lay all night on a *sleepless* pillow.
The prisoner was placed in the *condemned* cell.
Melissa shook her *doubtful* curls.—TENNYSON.
The long-*tormented* air.—*Ibid.*
And bells made *Catholic* the trembling air.—GEORGE ELIOT.
A lackey presented an *obsequious* cup of coffee.—CARLYLE.
And *drowsy* tinklings lull the distant fold.—GRAY.

Such phrases as the following are common:—A *virtuous* indignation; a *happy* time; an *unlucky* remark; a *foolish* observation; a *learned* book; a *criminal* court; the *Colonial* Office; the *Foreign* Office; *easy* circumstances; a *fat* incumbency; a *cheap* market; a

---

[1] We are now justified perhaps in calling this an example of Synecdoche. But in A.S. the word *winter* meant "year," and this use of the word seems to have never wholly died out.

weary journey; *melancholy* news; *weary* romances; an *eloquent* speech; *hysterical* appeals; *brutal* threats; the *smiling* morn; a *furious* wave; the *angry* ocean; a *prattling* brook; the *dimpling* waves; the *blushing* rose; the *laughing* harvest; the *raving* tempest; an *inexorable* law; a *busy* life; a *dishonest* calling, etc.

Class IV.—Miscellaneous Figures.

361. **Innuendo**: lit. "by making a nod" (Latin word, but often wrongly spelt in English as *inuendo*).—This figure consists in hinting a thing without plainly saying it:—

There are two times in a man's life when he should not speculate:—when he cannot afford it, and when he can. (That is, Never speculate at all.)—MARK TWAIN.

The principal difference between a cat and a lie is that a cat has only nine lives.—*Ibid.*

I do not consult physicians; for I hope to die without them.—SIR W. TEMPLE.

He had a number of coins of the Roman emperors, and a good many more of the later English kings.—FULLER.

There is never a good champagne year, unless there is a good apple crop in Normandy.—LORD PALMERSTON.

We need not pry too deeply into the motives which actuated Li-Hung-Chang in disregarding the interests of his country: Russia does not employ an auditor-general.—*Daily Telegraph*, 9th September 1898.

362. **Irony**: lit. "dissimulation" (a Greek word, *eironeia*).—A mode of speech, in which the writer or speaker says the opposite to what he means, but does not intend or expect his words to be taken in their literal sense.

An argument to prove that the abolition of Christianity may, as things now stand, be attended with some inconveniences, and perhaps not produce the many good effects proposed thereby.—SWIFT.

The Holy Alliance (Russia, Prussia, Austria) was minded to stretch the arm of its Christian charity across the Atlantic and put republicanism down in the western hemisphere as well as in its own.—GOLDWIN SMITH, *United Kingdom*, ii. 324.

Sarcasm.—In sarcasm a man does not, as in irony, say the opposite to what he means. He says what he means, but says it in a way that implies ridicule, disapproval, or contempt.

If ideas were innate, it would save much trouble to many worthy persons.—LOCKE.

Mr. Ewart annually brought forward a motion against capital punishment, and so far succeeded that, according to ordinary parlance, it requires some ingenuity to get hung[1] now, if there is a fair loophole for the Home Office to creep through.—*Fortnightly Review*, Feb. 1898, p. 245.

[1] This word should have been *hanged*, not *hung*. See p. 66, Note 2.

363. Interrogation.—Usually, when we ask a question, we do so for the sake of getting an answer. Whenever we do this, we are using language "in the plain and ordinary way," and there is no Figure of Rhetoric involved in the process.

There are, however, at least two kinds of instances in which Interrogation is used as a rhetorical device: (*a*) when the speaker or writer, having asked a question, leaves the hearer or reader to answer it for himself—an indirect mode of affirming or denying, which is sometimes more forcible than direct assertion; (*b*) when a question is asked for purposes of exposition; here the teacher or writer directs attention to a point by putting it in the form of a question to be solved; having done this, he propounds his own answer. Hence school-manuals are sometimes written in this form.

(*a*) *For purposes of persuasion*:—

Can the Ethiopian change his skin, or the leopard his spots?—*Old Testament.*

For the body is not one member, but many. If the foot shall say, Because I am not the hand, I am not of the body; is it therefore not of the body? And if the ear shall say, Because I am not the eye, I am not of the body; is it therefore not of the body? If the whole body were an eye, where were the hearing? If the whole were hearing, where were the smelling? —1 *Cor.* xii. 14-17.

(*b*) *For purposes of exposition*:—

What is this world in the high scale of the Almighty's workmanship? A mere shred which, though scattered into nothing, would leave the universe of God one entire scene of greatness and of majesty.—CHALMERS.

The same figure can also be used in soliloquy, as when a person puts a question to himself and gives his own answer:—

Will all great Neptune's ocean wash this blood
Clean from my hand? No: this my hand will rather
The multitudinous seas incarnadine,
Making the green one red.—*Macbeth.*

364. Exclamation.—What an Interjection is in grammar, Exclamation is in rhetoric. It is a mode of expressing some strong emotion without describing it in set terms. By this means the speaker or writer hopes to communicate the same feeling to the mind of the hearer or reader:—

O, what a fall was there, my countrymen!
Then you, and I, and all of us fell down,
Whilst bloody treason flourish'd over us!—SHAKSPEARE.

But she is in her grave, and oh!
The difference to me!—WORDSWORTH.

They (the earliest Christians) were there in their secluded world, clothed internally with light in the kingdom of God, their Father; but without them what a hell!—RENAN.

How art thou fallen from heaven, O Lucifer, son of the morning! how art thou cut down to the ground, which didst weaken the nations!—*Isaiah* xiv. 12.

365. **Personification.**—This figure consists in ascribing life and any property of life to things inanimate; see § 347.

> Fair *Science* frowned not on his humble birth,
> But *Melancholy* marked him for her own.—GRAY.

Note.—An extreme form of this figure is called the **Pathetic Fallacy**, by which external objects are made to sympathise in all the emotions of the agent, feeling exactly as he does, and hearing and understanding what he says to them. When Cromwell was dying, a furious storm was raging outside, "as if in sympathy," says Hallam, "with the mighty soul that was passing away from the earth." In Tennyson's *Maud* the rose, the lily, the larkspur, the passion-flower, etc., are as eager as the lover himself to hear or see the maiden come out from the ballroom to meet him "at the gate, alone."

366. **A-pos-tro-phe**: lit. "turning away" (a Greek word, transliterated into Roman character).—By this figure the speaker or writer suddenly breaks off from the tenor of his speech or narrative, and addresses in the second person some person or thing, whether absent or present. If something inanimate is addressed, it is personified. If some dead person is addressed, he is addressed as if he were alive.

Unhappy man![1] and must you be swept into the grave, unnoticed and unnumbered, and no friendly tear be shed for your sufferings, or mingled with your dust?—ROBERT HALL.

> Frailty, thy name is woman!—SHAKSPEARE.

> Hast thou a charm to stay the morning star
> In his steep course? So long he seems to pause
> On thy bald awful head, O Sovran Blanc!—COLERIDGE.

> Departed spirits of the mighty dead,
> Ye that at Marathon and Leuctra bled!—CAMPBELL.

367. **Vision.**—By this figure the writer or speaker, in relating something past, or describing some anticipated future, employs the *present* tense instead of the *past* or *future*, and thus makes it appear as if the event were actually passing before his eyes. The same figure can be used for describing something neither past nor future, but purely imaginary.

(*a*) *Some past event.* This is called the Historic Present (§ 112, *e*).

The sack and carnage of Delhi lasted from three o'clock in the morning until three in the afternoon. The streets echo with

[1] This was said in reference to the wounded in war.

the shouts of brutal soldiery and with the cries and shrieks of the inhabitants. The atmosphere reeks with blood. Houses are set on fire, and hundreds perish in the flames. Husbands kill their wives, and then destroy themselves. Women throw themselves into the wells. Children are slaughtered without mercy, and infants are cut to pieces at their mothers' breasts.—WHEELER's *India*.

(*b*) *Some anticipated future*:—

I see and behold this great city, the ornament of the earth and the capital of all nations, suddenly involved in one conflagration. I see before me the slaughtered heaps of citizens lying unburied in the midst of the ruined country. The furious countenance of Cethegus rises to my view, while with a savage joy he is triumphing in your miseries.—CICERO.

(*c*) *Something imaginary*:—

What beckoning ghost along the moonlight shade
Invites my steps, and points to yonder glade?
'Tis she. But why that bleeding bosom gored?
Why dimly gleams the visionary sword?—POPE.

Is this a dagger which I see before me,
The handle toward my hand? Come, let me clutch thee.
I have thee not, and yet I see thee still.
Art thou not, fatal vision, sensible
To feeling as to sight? or art thou but
A dagger of the mind; a false creation,
Proceeding from the heat-oppressed brain?—SHAKSPEARE.

These lines describe the "vision" seen by Macbeth, just before he entered the chamber of Duncan to murder him.

368. **Climax, Anti-climax**.—It adds much to the impressiveness of a sentence or group of sentences, if the mind of the reader is made to ascend from a lower thought to a higher by successive steps; for it is as difficult for the mind to grasp a final issue by a single step, as for the body to ascend a ladder by a single rung.

In a climax (Greek word for "ladder") the first part of a sentence prepares the mind for the middle, and the middle for the end:—

It is an outrage to bind a Roman citizen; to scourge him is an atrocious crime; to put him to death is almost a parricide; but to crucify him, what shall I call it?—CICERO, *Contra Verrem*.

His reason had been outraged at Lourdes; his illusions were dissipated in Rome; his shaken faith comes to utter shipwreck in Paris.—*Times Weekly*, 4th March 1898.

The opposite process, by which the thought descends from a higher level to a lower, is called **Anti-climax** or **Bathos** (Greek for "depth"). This may be done intentionally,—for point, humour, or any other purpose,—or it may be done through an inadvertence, in which case the effect will be feeble or even ludicrous :—

> Here thou, great Anna, whom three realms obey,
> Dost sometimes counsel take, and sometimes tea.—POPE.

> The autocrat of Russia possesses more power than any other man on earth, but he cannot stop a sneeze.—MARK TWAIN.

The following is an example of inadvertence, where the strong word "necessity" is followed by the weaker word "desirability" :—

> It would seem almost superfluous to point out the propriety, and necessity, and desirability of appointing female officers.—*Fortnightly Review*, Feb. 1898, p. 282.

369. Hy-per-bo-le (a Greek word of four syllables, signifying exaggeration).—This is usually a fault. But when it is resorted to for the sake of heightening the effect, and provided that the departure from truth does not offend one's sense of the truthful, it is a recognised Figure of Speech :—

> They were swifter than eagles, they were stronger than lions.—*David's Lament for Saul and Jonathan.*

> All the perfumes of Arabia will not sweeten this little hand.—SHAKSPEARE (Lady Macbeth).

> That execrable sum of all villanies, commonly called the Slave Trade.—WESLEY.

> My dust would hear her and beat,
> Had I lain for a century dead;
> Would start and tremble under her feet,
> And blossom in purple and red.—TENNYSON, *Maud.*

Such examples as the following appear, however, to be extravagant and artificial :—

> The sky shrunk upward with unusual dread,
> And trembling Tiber dived beneath his bed.—DRYDEN.

> I saw their chief, tall as a rock of ice; his spear, the blasted fir; his shield, the rising moon; he sat on the shore, like a cloud of mist on a hill.—OSSIAN.

370. Repetition.—Another mode of giving expression to intense feeling or conviction is by repeating the principal word, or adding equivalent words (§ 252). Repetition, when it is used with no rhetorical effect, that is, when it is a fault in composition, is called Tautology or Pleonasm (§ 295) :—

> He sung Darius great and good,
> Fallen, fallen, fallen, fallen,
> Fallen from his high estate,
> And weltering in his blood.—DRYDEN.

Faithful found
Among the faithless, faithful only he.
MILTON, *Par. Lost.*

And like a rat without a tail,
I'll do, I'll do, and I'll do.
SHAKSPEARE, *Macbeth.*

You cannot, sir, take from me anything that I would more willingly part withal, except my life, except my life, except my life.—SHAKSPEARE, *Hamlet.*

Alone, alone, all, all alone,
Alone on a wide, wide sea.
COLERIDGE, *Ancient Mariner.*

So runs my dream; but what am I?
An infant crying in the night,
An infant crying for the light,
And with no language but a cry!
TENNYSON, *In Memoriam.*

A multiplicity of words meaning the same, or almost the same, thing can be used to intensify the effect:—

How weary, stale, flat, and unprofitable,
Seem to me all the uses of this world!—SHAKSPEARE.
But now I'm cabined, cribbed, confined.—*Ibid.*
All is little, and low, and mean among us.—BOLINGBROKE.
A man of sorrows, and acquainted with grief.—*Old Test.*
Surely he hath borne our griefs, and carried our sorrows.—*Ibid.*
What is man, that thou art mindful of him? or the son of man, that thou visitest him?—*Ibid.*

371. **Lit-o-tes** (a Greek word signifying plainness, simplicity). The name is now given to that figure of speech by which we place a negative before some word, to indicate a strong affirmative in the opposite direction:—

He is no *dullard* (=decidedly clever).
A citizen of *no mean* (=a distinguished) city.—*New Test.*

Note.—By this figure such words as "infamous," "unprofessional," "unchristian," etc., all of which have merely negative prefixes, have acquired a strongly affirmative sense in the opposite direction, (see § 325, under **Non**).

372. **Euphemism** (Gr. *eu*, well; and *phemi*, I speak). By this figure we speak in gentle and favourable terms of some person, object, or event which is ordinarily seen in a less pleasing light (§ 291):—

China is a country where you often get different accounts of the same thing (=where many lies are told).—*Lord Salisbury's Speech.*

He kneeled down, and cried with a loud voice, Lord, lay not this sin to their charge. And, when he had said this, he fell asleep.—Death of Stephen, *Acts* vii. 60.

Discord fell on the music of his soul; the sweet sounds and wandering lights departed from him; yet he wore no less a loving face, although he was so broken-hearted.—E. B. BROWNING, *Cowper's Madness.*

373. Circumlocution: "saying a thing in a roundabout way" instead of saying it at once. This figure may be used either for poetic ornament, as in example (1); or for giving greater prominence to a thought, as in example (2); or for Euphemism, as in example (3); or for humour, as in example (4):—

(1) The sightless couriers of the air (=the winds).—SHAKSPEARE.

(2) The very source and fount of day (=the sun).
Is flecked with wandering isles of night.—TENNYSON.

(3) She declared that neither she nor her husband was suffering from the domination of stimulant (=was tipsy).—*Daily Telegraph,* 9th March 1898.

(4) The driver of the engine played a sweet symphony with the steam whistle, then he caused it to whoop wildly, and finally made the steam hiss and puff like Vesuvius in a state of eruption; but all was in vain, the cow still held the line.—*Ibid.*

374. Alliteration.—The repetition of the same letter or syllable at the beginning of two or more words:—

*Ru*in seize thee, *ru*thless king!—GRAY.
A *st*rong man *st*ruggling with the *st*orms of fate.—ADDISON.
*Gl*ittering through the *gl*oomy *gl*ades.—POPE.
A *l*oad of *l*earning *l*umbering in his head.—*Ibid.*
*D*eep in a *d*ungeon was the captive cast,
*D*eprived of *d*ay, and held in *f*etters *f*ast.—DRYDEN.
Our *d*readful *m*arches to *d*elightful *m*easures.—SHAKSPEARE.
The *m*audlin prince of *m*ournful sonneteers.—BYRON.
*W*ilful *w*aste makes *w*oeful *w*ant.—*Proverb.*

375. Sense suggested by sound: Onomatopœia.—An impression can sometimes be strengthened, if "the sound," as Pope says, "is made an echo to the sense." This device is more commonly used in poetry than in prose; yet it is common in prose also. In fact, we have a considerable number of words whose origin is clearly imitative. "A drum," says Smollett, "is not inaptly so called, from the noise and emptiness of the entertainment."

We still for the most part recognise the imitative intent of such words as the *clucking* of hens, *cackling* of geese, *gobbling* of turkeys, *quacking* of ducks, *croaking* of frogs, *cawing* of rooks, *cooing* of doves, *hooting* of owls, *booming* of bitterns, *chirping* of sparrows, *twittering* of swallows, *chattering* of pies or monkeys, *neighing* or *winnying* of horses, *purring* or *mewing* of cats, *yelping, howling, growling, snarling* of dogs, *grunting* or *squealing* of hogs, *bellowing* of bulls, *lowing* of oxen, *bleating* of sheep, *baaing* of lambs."—*Preface to "Wedgwood's Dictionary."*

On the same principle, authors have sometimes used words in such a way that their sound may seem to suggest the sense :—

(1) *Grate* on their *scrannel* pipes of wretched straw.—MILTON.

(2) Alarm-guns *booming* through the midnight air.—W. IRVING.

At eve the beetle *boometh*
Athwart the thicket lone.—TENNYSON.

Hence a sudden and rapid advance of some article of commerce, accompanied with noisy excitement and hollowness of substance, has been called a *boom.*

(3) So he with difficulty and labour hard
Moved on, with difficulty and labour he.—MILTON.

Here the difficulty of scanning the first line, with the repetition of the same words in the second, suggests the difficulty with which Satan, by repeated efforts, made his way through Chaos to our earth.

(4) All unawares,
Fluttering his pennons vain, *plumb down* he drops
Ten thousand fathom deep.—MILTON.

Here the precipitate descent of Satan is suggested by the sound of the second line.

(5) R*end* with treme*nd*ous sound your ears as*under*
With *gun*, d*rum*, t*rum*pet, bl*under*buss, and th*under*.—POPE.

(6) Eternal wrath
Burnt after them to the *bottomless pit.*—MILTON.

Here the sudden drop of the accentuation at the close of the second line, where an accent is indispensable to the metre, suggests the sudden and precipitate fall of the rebellious angels from heaven to hell.

CHAPTER XXVII.—ENLARGEMENT OF VOCABULARY BY METAPHOR AND METONYMY.

376. Decay of Metaphors.—We may detect three different stages in the life of metaphors. It is only by the last two,—both of which are stages of decay,—that the vocabulary of a language is enlarged.

(1) In the first stage the word or words still have a purely figurative signification. In using them the only thought that strikes us is the similarity (in some particular point) between the two things compared, and we are fully conscious all the while that we are employing a figure of speech.

Any member of the Viceroyal Council (in India), who proposes any extension of British sovereignty among the hills, should do so *with a rope round his neck.*—*Review of Reviews*, Jan. 1898, p. 8.

Clearly the first thing is the maintenance of the navy, without which we are merely a *huge plum pudding ready for the spoons of our hungry neighbours.*—*Ibid.* p. 9.

The young man about London or Paris was branded as *a fanged, but handless, spider, that sucks indeed and stings, but cannot spin,*—this with an intensified sibilation, which made the whole sentence a hiss.—*Century Magazine*, Feb. 1898.

After a brief discussion the House *sailed smoothly and quietly into the shallow and becalmed* waters of the Supplementary Estimates.—*Daily Telegraph*, 25th Feb. 1898.

(2) In the second stage the signification of the word is divided between the literal and the figurative. The original or literal meaning is still there; but the figurative has become so familiar that we are only partially conscious that any such figure exists. In this stage the decay of the metaphor has begun, and possibly it may go no further.

The *point* of a needle (*lit.*).	I differ with you on that *point* (*fig.*).
Draw a straight *line* (*lit.*).	A clear *line* of argument (*fig.*).
His *height* is six feet (*lit.*).	It was the *height* of rudeness (*fig.*).
A *smooth* surface (*lit.*).	A *smooth* tongue (*fig.*).
The *key* to a lock (*lit.*).	The *key* to a problem (*fig.*).

(3) In the third stage the original or literal meaning has gone quite out of use, and nothing but the figurative remains. In fact, the figurative has become the literal. This is the final stage of decay to which a metaphor can come. (It is conceivable, however, that this acquired literal sense might itself some day acquire a metaphorical sense and be eventually ousted by it like its predecessor.)

Perspicuity, at first "transparency of medium"; now "clearness of diction."

Melancholy, at first "black bile"; now "low spirits."

Ardour, at first "physical heat"; now "enthusiasm," "zeal."

Cynosure, at first "dog's tail," a constellation; now "a centre of attraction."

Acuteness, at first "sharpness of edge"; now "quickness of mind."

It is not till a metaphor has *decayed*, either in whole or in part, that it can be said to *enlarge* the vocabulary of a language. Even then it is not a new word added to the vocabulary, but an old word invested with a new sense. If the language gains nothing in quantity, it gains much in quality, that is, in expressiveness. For instance, the limitation of the word "perspicuity" to the sense of "transparency *of diction*" is a distinct gain, so long as the word "transparency" is available for other connections.

"Perspicuity" is more expressive than "clearness," because the latter word can be applied to many kinds of things besides diction.

Whether any given word has reached the final, or is only passing through the earlier, stage of decay is a point on which different opinions might be held. Some persons, for instance, might still be to some extent conscious of using a figure of speech in the word "ardour," while to others "zeal" might seem to be the only literal meaning that the word ever had.

377. **Nouns**: figurative uses, that have become literal:—

A *ray* of hope. A *shade* of doubt. A *flash* of wit. An *outburst* of temper. The *fire* of passion. A *gleam* of delight. The *light* of knowledge. A *flight* of fancy. A *spark* of humour. The *gloom* of despair. The *wreck* of his hopes. The *spur* of ambition. The *torments* of jealousy. The *reins* of office. The *anger* of the tempest. The *feast* of reason. The *tide* of democracy. The *fall* of empires. In the *sunset* of his years. His prosperity is on the *decline* (going down). His reputation is on the *wane*. The *pangs* of remorse. The *sting* of conscience. The *impulse* (driving on) of revenge. The *motive* (moving power) of fear. The wish was *father* to the thought. The *decadence* (falling down or falling off) of that firm.

Hand: literally the bodily organ so called:—

To be *hand and glove* with a person (to be on terms of friendship as close as a hand is to a glove). The *hand* of a clock (because it points). A horse fourteen *hands* high (a hand's breadth). On all *hands* (on all sides, because the hand is on the side). The Protestants were then on the winning *hand* (side, Milton). He was their *right-hand* man (most useful co-operator).

Foot: literally the bodily organ so called:—

Things are now on a good *footing* (basis). The *foot* (base) of the mountain. The *foot* of a table (that on which the table rests). The *foot* (lowest part, fag-end) of a procession. A four-*foot* rule (measure of length). An Iambic *foot* (a measure in prosody). To put one's *foot* down (make a resolute resistance). To put the best *foot* foremost (to do one's best and lose no time about it). To set on *foot* (start, set in motion). To trample under *foot* (spurn, oppress).

Body: literally the physical structure as opposed to mind:—

Rivers that run up into the *body* (mainland) of Italy (Addison). A *body* (band) of troops. A *body* (system or collection) of laws. A *body* (mass) of cold air (Huxley). This wine has no *body* (substance). The *body* (nave) of a church. The *body* politic (the state).

Branch: literally what grows from a tree:—

The *branch* of a river. The *branch* of an antler. The *branch* of a chandelier. The *branch* of a railway. The *branch* of a subject (as geometry is a *branch* of mathematics). The younger *branch* of a family. They were exterminated *root and branch* (totally).

Root: lit. the underground portion of a plant:—

The *root* of a tooth (the part inside the gum). The *root* of a nail. The *root* of a cancer. The love of money is the *root* (source, main cause) of all evil. The *root* (ancestral origin) of a family. The *root* (original elements) of a word. The *roots* (lowest parts) of mountains (Southey). Square *root*, cube *root* (in arithmetic). That opinion struck *root* (took a firm hold on the mind).

Stream: lit. a current of water :—

A *stream* of air. A *stream* of lava from a volcano. A *stream* of light. A *stream* of words. A *stream* of sand. The *stream* (continuous acts) of benevolence. A *stream* of eloquence. The *stream* of emigration.

Air: lit. the fluid which we breathe :—

The keen, the wholesome *air* (surrounding influence) of poverty (Wordsworth). An *air* (melody) in music. A lofty *air* (demeanour). He gives himself *airs* (gives full vent to his conceit).

Face: lit. the countenance, visage :—

The *face* of a clock. The *faces* of a cube. The *face* of a type. We put a good *face* on it. He had the *face* (effrontery) to do this. To fly in the *face* of danger. The *face* of a gun. The *face* of a compass.

Arm: lit. a limb of the human body :—

The *arm* (branch) of a tree. An *arm* (inlet) of the sea. The *arm* of a chair. The *arm* (strength, might) of the law. To hold *at arm's length* (keep at a distance).

Head: lit. that part of the body which is supported by the neck :—

The *head* of a pin. The *head* of a cabbage. A river has a *head*, where it *heads* among the highlands. An army, a school, a sect has its *head*. A class has its *head*. The *head*-student of a class; the *head*-master of a school. The *head* of a coin. A sermon has its *heads*, as subdivided by the different *headings*. Let us hear no more on that *head*. A sore comes to a *head*. We give a horse his *head*, when we let it go as fast as it likes. This beer has a good *head* on. They sailed up to the *head* of the bay. I cannot make *head* or tail of what he says. That was the *head* and front of his offence.

378. Adjectives: figurative uses, that are now literal :—

Brazen impudence; *brazen*-faced (shameless); a *stony* heart; a *rosy* complexion; a *lame* (halting, inefficient) excuse; *snowy* (as white as snow) locks; a *fiery* (violent) temper; *fiery* speech; *burning* passion; an *angry* sore; a *piercing* wind; a *brilliant* piece of eloquence; a *stormy* discussion; a *weighty* argument; a *crystal* stream; a *transparent* falsehood; a *groundless* excuse; a well-*laid* plan; a *treacherous* calm; a *sullen* sky; a *frowning* rock, etc.

Golden (literally made of gold).—A *golden* harvest; the *golden* grain; *golden* hair; a *golden* opportunity; a *golden* sunset; *golden* silence; a *golden* rainfall; he won *golden* opinions; the *golden* mean; the *golden* age; the *golden* rule—"Do to others as you would be done by"; a *golden* wedding. (All these metaphors are based either on the colour or on the value of gold. "Golden" has so entirely lost its literal sense, that we are now obliged to say "a *gold* watch," not "a *golden* watch.")

Iron (as adjective; literally made of iron).—*Iron* (unflinching) courage; *iron* (unyielding) firmness; an *iron* (inflexible) will; an *iron* (very strong) constitution; an *iron* (dark) grey. (These metaphors are based on the hardness, solidity, or colour of the metal.)

Dead (literally, inanimate, that from which life has departed).—A *dead* language (no longer spoken); faith without works is *dead*, being alone (*New Test.*); *dead* (inert) matter; he is a *dead* shot (never fails to hit); a *dead* (unalterable) certainty; a *dead* (motionless) calm; a *dead* (totally unconscious) sleep; he is *dead* (callous) to all sense of honour; the *dead* (most silent hours) of night; a *dead* (unchanging) level; a *dead* weight (a weight which cannot help to raise itself); a *dead*-lock (a stoppage which cannot be removed); a *dead* (irrecoverable) loss; a *dead* ball (one that is excluded from the rest of the game); *dead* (unproductive) capital; a *dead* heat (a race without results); *dead* (spiritless) colouring; he made a *dead* set (determined attack) at me; he was *dead* against my proposal (opposed to it unconditionally); *dead*-alive (alive, but without vitality).

Light (literally, what can be easily lifted, not heavy).—A *light* affliction; a *light* heart; *light* food (easy of digestion); a troop of *light* horse (lightly armed); a *light* touch on the piano; a *light* coin (clipped, below the standard weight); a *light* (sandy) soil.

Simple (literally "single-fold," "one at a time").—A *simple* (plain, unadorned) dress; *simple* (unmitigated) rubbish; *simple-minded* (genuine); *simple* (unaffected) manners; a *simple* (direct) statement); *simple* (plain) diet; a *simple* (lowly, unpretentious) husbandman; a *simple* sentence (with only one Finite verb); a *simple* body (an atom, indivisible, ultimate); a *simple* equation (with only one unknown quantity); *simple* interest (not compound).

379. Verbs: figurative uses, that have become literal:—

To *employ* means; to *contract* habits; to *carry* a matter to extremes; to *cast* one's eyes on a thing; to *prosecute* studies; to *pass over* in silence; to *gain* celebrity; to *pocket* an insult; to *pick* a quarrel; to *curry* favour; to *harbour* malice; to *cultivate* an acquaintance; to *indulge* in hopes; to *take* offence; to *play* the fool; to *put* a question; to *triumph* over difficulties; to *stick* to a point; to *draw up* a scheme; to *pursue* a subject, etc.

Strike (literally, to hit a thing with some force).—They shall *strike* (throw) the blood on the two side posts (*Exodus* xii. 7). To *strike* (stamp) coin from metal. The tree has *struck* root (thrust it into the ground). The drums *strike* up (begin to play) a march. A new idea has *struck* me (occurred to me). To *strike* (lower) sail. We *struck* (unpitched, took down) our tents. The men have *struck* (left off) work. To *strike* a match (ignite it by concussion). To *strike* (make or ratify by joining hands) a bargain. They *struck* (hit upon) the trail. The clock *struck* (sounded the hour of) twelve. This *strikes* (impresses) me as strange. He *struck* (entered suddenly) into the conversation. A man well *stricken* (advanced) in years.

Catch (literally, to seize anything in motion, with the effect of holding it).—To *catch* him in his words (entangle him; *Mark* xii. 13). To *catch* a tune (seize with the mind); to *catch* an argument; to *catch* a meaning. The house *caught* fire; to *catch* cold, *catch* measles. To *catch* one asleep (come upon unexpectedly). To *catch* a train (reach it in time). To *catch* one's eye (attract notice). To *catch* one up (interrupt any one captiously, while in the act of speaking; or to overtake some one in front).

Break (literally, to sever by fracture, divide by violence; as to *break* a seal, to *break* a lock, to *break* a chain, to *break* a window).—To *break* the news (disclose or lay open for the first time; especially ill news). To *break* (transgress or violate) a law. To *break* (interrupt) silence. The French cavalry were not able to *break* the British squares (throw into disorder). His health has been much *broken* (impaired). To *break* a colt (train it for work). To *break* down (crush) opposition. To *break* one of a habit (make him leave it off). He *broke* through the enemy's lines. To *break* up house (give it up entirely). The ladder that he fell against *broke* (lessened the violence of) the fall. To *break* a fast (take food after a long interval). To *break* new ground (open it out for the first time; to enter upon some new project). That grief *broke* his heart (overwhelmed him with grief). To *break* a lance (engage in a contest). To *break* the ice (introduce a new subject).

Intransitive uses.—The day begins to *break* (dawn). Measles *broke* out. The coach *broke* down. I am afraid he will *break* (become bankrupt). The bank *broke* (became insolvent). The horse *broke* into a galop. The school—the frost—has *broken* up. His partner *broke* with him (dissolved partnership).

Cut (literally, to make incision with a sharp edge).—That sneer *cut* (wounded) him to the quick. He was not *cut* out (suited by temperament) for a lawyer. One line *cuts* (passes through) another at right angles. He *cut* me (refused to recognise me). He *cut* (gave up) the profession. To *cut* a strange figure (show oneself in a strange character). To *cut* down (reduce) expenses. He was *cut* off (died) in the height of his career. To *cut* a person short (suddenly stop him from speaking). The child is *cutting* its teeth (thrusting them through the gums). To *cut* the cards (divide the pack).

Run (literally, the action of running, used of men and other animals).—To *run* into debt. He *runs* on (continues talking) from one subject to another. Rivers *run* into the sea. The fire *ran* through the forest. Her blood *ran* cold. Iron ores *run* (melt) freely in the fire. This train *runs* to York. The mill *runs* (is at work) six days in the week. The engine *runs* day and night. The road *runs* (has a direction) east and west. His plans *run* counter to mine. The sentence *runs* thus (is worded thus). The plant is *running* to seed. Colours *run* (do not remain fixed) in the washing. The lease has ninety years to *run* (continue in force). A *running* sore (one that continues to discharge matter). The ship *ran* (moved swiftly) before the wind. To *run* down a coast (sail along it). The money has *run* out (has all been spent). The cup *runs* over (is so full that the contents overflow). He *ran* through his money (spent it all rapidly).

Transitive uses.—To *run* a thread into a needle's eye. To *run* a nail into one's foot. They *ran* the ship aground. To *run* a railway (cause it to be made) through a country. To *run* (incur) a risk. To *run* an hotel (keep it at work). To *run* a blockade (get through it without being caught). To *run* a man down (disparage, traduce). He *ran* him hard (very nearly caught him up). To *run* up a bill or a house (cause it to rise rapidly).

380. Prepositions.—There is scarcely any part of speech that has lent itself more readily to metaphorical usage than prepositions. Their first and literal use was to express relations in *space;* they were next applied metaphorically to relations in *time;* and then gradually to many other kinds of relations.

About (on + by + out): lit. just on the outside of, very near in point of locality; as, "he has a comforter *about* his neck"; "have you any money *about* you?" *Metaphorical uses.*—It is *about* seven o'clock (nearness of time); he is *about* to be married (nearness of state); he went *about* his work in earnest (occupation); I have heard *about* it (concerning).

Above (on + by + up): lit. in a higher place; as, "the head is *above* the neck." *Metaphorical uses.*—He stayed with us *above* a week (longer in time); *above* a hundred (more in number or amount); he is *above* such meanness (better or higher in quality).

After: lit. backwards or behind in place; as, "I will enter *after* you." *Metaphorical uses.*—He arrived *after* dark (sequence in time); *after* all you have told me I am convinced (sequence in effect); he is seeking *after* wealth (sequence in pursuit); he takes *after* his father (sequence in imitation); *after* all the advice given him, he did the very opposite (sequence in contrast).

Against: lit. opposition of place; as, "he is leaning *against* the wall." *Metaphorical uses.*—*Against* my interest (aim or purpose); *against* the day of battle (in preparation for); four pupils have left *against* three last term (in comparison with).

At: lit. the locality of an action or thing, the point reached or desired; as, "he is not *at* home"; "the dog sprang *at* him." *Metaphorical uses.*—*At* four o'clock (time); *at* his ease (state); *at* a certain price (value); he plays well *at* cricket (sphere of action); stand up *at* the given signal (time and consequence combined). Do this *at* your convenience (time and state combined).

Before (by + fore): lit. in front of, the opposite to "after" or "behind"; as, "he stands *before* the door." *Metaphorical uses.*—The train starts *before* ten A.M. (priority in time); death before dishonour (priority in quality, preference).

Behind (by + hind): lit. at the back of (in the relation of space); as, "the dog runs *behind* its master." *Metaphorical uses.*—The train is *behind* time (lateness); there is a smile *behind* his frown (disguise, concealment).

Below (by + low): lit. in a lower place, opposite to "above"; as, "he stands *below* me in class." *Metaphorical uses.*—The number was *below* ten (less than); his attainments are *below* yours (inferior in quality).

Beneath (by + neath): lit. in a lower position; as, "he sat *beneath* the shade." *Metaphorical use.*—His conduct is *beneath* contempt (inferior in quality, not even worth despising).

Beside, besides (by + side): lit. at the side of (in the relation of place); as, "he is *beside* you (at your side)." *Metaphorical uses.*—That remark is *beside* the question (near the question, but not in it;

irrelevancy); *besides* advising, he gave them money (in addition to). (The difference of sense attached to *beside* and *besides* respectively is a mere matter of idiom.)

By: lit. proximity in space, "close to"; as, "come and sit *by* me"; "he lives *by* himself," that is, with no one near but himself, alone. *Metaphorical uses.*—Get up *by* sunrise (time); he did his duty *by* his children (towards); he was treated well *by* me (agency); seize him *by* the neck (instrument or point of action); cleverer than A. *by* a good deal (amount); sold *by* the bushel (unit of measurement); he swore *by* heaven (adjuration).

For: lit. in front of, hence direction; as, "he started *for* home." *Metaphorical uses.*—Imprisoned *for* life (time, duration); *for* what offence was he punished (cause or reason); *for* all his learning he has no sense (in spite of); he sold his horse *for* a small sum (exchange); he fought hard *for* his friends (in behalf of); do not translate word *for* word (conformity); this is not fit *for* food (purpose).

From: lit. the opposite to "by," "at," or "to": remoteness, distance, implying either rest or motion; as, "he is *from* home," "he had gone *from* home." *Metaphorical uses.*—*From* morning to night (time); sprung *from* noble ancestors (origin); *from* all we hear he is mad (inference); this was done *from* spite (motive); a wise man is easily known *from* a fool (discrimination); he is going *from* bad to worse (change of condition).

Of: lit. separation or movement from something, but at a near distance; as, "within a few miles *of* the town." *Metaphorical uses.*—He died *of* fever (cause); he comes *of* a high family (source); deprived *of* his appointment (removal); a man *of* strong will (quality); a box *of* books (contents); a box made *of* leather (material); the house *of* his father (possession); a sum of forty pounds (apposition); I never heard *of* it (concerning); lame *of* one leg (point of reference); he gave us *of* his best (partition); the love *of* parents (subject); the love *of* parents (object); hated *of* all men (agency).

On: lit. rest on the outside of a thing; as, "I place my hand *on* the table." *Metaphorical uses.*—*On* Saturday last (time); he lives *on* his father (dependence); *on* these terms (condition or basis); an attack *on* my house (direction); *on* that subject (concerning).

In: lit. rest in the interior of anything; as, "he is not in the house." *Metaphorical uses.*—*In* a bad temper, *in* motion (state); he will come back *in* an hour (at the end of an hour, time).

Over: lit. above or beyond anything in space; as, "the sun shines *over* the earth," "his house is *over* the way." *Metaphorical uses.*—He was absent *over* two weeks (beyond in time); he is placed *over* me (authority); he has been promoted *over* my head (precedence)

Through: lit. across the interior of anything; as, "bore a hole *through* that plank." *Metaphorical uses.*—He worked hard all *through* the term (duration of time); he has passed *through* many troubles (state, circumstances); *through* your help I succeeded (cause); all this was done *through* envy (motive).

To: lit. motion towards anything in space; as, "he returned *to* his country." *Metaphorical uses.*—*To*-night (time); *to* all appearances (conformity, adaptation); three *to* one (proportion); they fought *to* the last man (limit); *to* their great surprise (effect); he came *to* see us (purpose; Gerund. Infin.).

Under: lit. situation beneath something; as, "he sat *under* the tree." *Metaphorical uses.*—The house is *under* repairs (condition); *under* these circumstances (subjection); he travelled *under* the guise of a monk (concealment).

With: lit. nearness in space; as, "he lives *with* his mother." *Metaphorically* it denotes nearness in a friendly, hostile, or neutral sense:—His views accord *with* mine (agreement); he gets up *with* the sun (nearness in time); one king fought *with* another (nearness in hostility, opposition); I have parted *with* my servant (separation); I do this *with* pleasure (concomitant circumstance); he is popular *with* his pupils (reference); *with* all his wealth he is not contented (in spite of); shot *with* a gun (instrument); treated *with* respect (manner).

381. Metaphors limited to a particular point.—If we expect a metaphor to hold good through a series of resemblances, we are certain to be disappointed. A resemblance is limited to one particular point at a time; and if the metaphor serves to set this point in a clear light, it has answered the purpose of enlarging the vocabulary.

For instance, we say of a river that it has its *head* in the highlands from which it springs. But we call its extremity its *mouth* (not *feet*), because that is the opening through which sea-water is poured into its channel. The channel of a river is called its *bed;* yet the river is said to *run* in its channel. The tributaries of a river are called its *feeders;* yet these enter the river at its *sides*, not at its *mouth*, as it would do if the metaphor were preserved. These again are at one time called *branches*, as of a tree; at another, *arms*, as of a man. Each of these metaphors suits its own purpose; and they must not be expected to have any consistency with one another.

382. Metaphors indispensable.—The importance of metaphors is best seen in the fact that many of our ideas cannot be put into words without them. Few, if any, of our mental operations or faculties can be expressed except by words that originally denoted something sensible or non-mental.

Thus *perception* originally meant taking hold of; *conception*, laying hold of with both hands, or on all sides; *apprehension*, seizing or grasping with the hand; *recollection*, gathering things together again; *inspiration*, breathing into; *imagination*, drawing a visible picture; *deliberation*, weighing in a pair of scales; *emotion*, moving out or being moved out; *expression*, squeezing out; *sagacity*, quickness of scent; *acuteness*, sharpness of edge; *suspense*, hanging up; *penetration*, making a hole through a thing; *motive*, that which produces motion, etc.

Many of the technical terms in music have been furnished by metaphors; as, *scale* (lit. a ladder), *chromatic* (lit. what gives colour), *key* (lit. what turns a lock), *key-note*, *sharp*, *flat*.

383. Enlargement of Vocabulary by Metonymy.—Metonymy, like metaphor, to a smaller, but still an appreciable, extent has helped to enlarge our vocabulary. In metonymy, as in metaphor, it is the *decay* of the figure that invests the word with a new literal meaning. In both words the first syllable is from Greek *meta*, which signifies change, transfer, substitution,—the transfer in the case of metaphor being based on Similarity, in that of metonymy on Contiguity (§ 344). We speak of the *legs* of a chair or of a bed, because their uses are similar to those of the legs of animals. This is Metaphor, based on Resemblance. On the other hand, we speak of the *back* and *seat* of a chair, because they are associated in the mind with the back and seat of a person using the chair, and we speak of the *head* and *foot* of a bed, because they are associated in the mind with the head and foot of the sleeper. This is Metonymy, based on Contiguity. No one, when he speaks of the back and seat of a chair, or of the head and foot of a bed, is conscious that he is using a figure of speech. The figure has decayed; the names that were once figurative are now literal.

Original meaning.	*Transferred meaning.*
Style: a thing to write with	manner of composition.
Rubric: words printed red	directions contained in the words.
Guinea: on the west coast of Africa	a coin of Guinea gold.
Fare: what is paid for conveyance	the passenger who pays it.
China: on the south-east of Asia	the crockery made there.
Security: safety	what is deposited for safety.
Army: a multitude of armed men	the military profession.
Navy: a multitude of ships	the naval profession.
Force: energy, strength	a band of soldiers.
Foot: part of the body	infantry.
Horse: a four-legged animal	cavalry.
Uniform: of the same form	official costume.
Court: chamber of justice	the presiding judge.
Brief: (adj.) concisely worded	(noun) statement of a client's case.
Porte: gate of the Sultan's palace	the Sultan and his ministers.
Urbane: belonging to a city	courteous, polite.
Rustic: belonging to the country	uncultivated, unrefined.

Exercises.

I. (*a*) *Point out the literal meaning of the italicised words in the following sentences.* (*b*) *Expand each metaphor into a simile.*

1. The *attitude* of England has been defensive throughout.
2. That opinion is *based* on facts, not fancies.

3. There is something very unpractical in *beating* about the *bush*, instead of coming to the point at once.

4. The Indian post office will soon *bid* for a first place among the postal administrations of the globe.—*Times Weekly*, 4th March 1898.

5. All his hopes were *blighted.*

6. By closing the ports, they aimed a deadly *blow* at British commerce.

7. Any statement of policy that he might draw up would, in its promulgation, *blow* his policy *into the air.*—*Review of Reviews*, Jan. 1898.

8. To expect anything from the Chinese is beyond the *bounds* of reason or of hope.

9. Trade-unionism has acquired a hold on every *branch* of industry.

10. While congratulating him on the excellence of his speech, I must condole with him on the badness of his *brief.*

11. Our military system has *broken down.*

12. Kindness makes him *brim* over with gratitude.

13. Let us enjoy a *brush* across the country.

14. She was admired for her *bushy* eyebrows.

15. He *played* his *cards* so well that he was taken into partnership.

16. The defects of his style were that he spoke with a certain *choppiness* and *jerkiness.*

17. It is a dangerous thing for a writer to *coin* new words.

18. This year has witnessed the *collapse* of the representative system at Vienna.

19. This symptom lends *colour* to the prevailing belief.

20. The mention of life-boats *conjures* up painful recollections.

21. This would be *courting* almost certain ruin.

22. His efforts were *crowned* with success.

23. Proverbs are homely precepts in which the wisdom of many centuries has been *crystallised.*

24. Obsequious men take their *cue* from their patrons.

25. It is simply the scandal of the Panama Canal *disguised* under the name of the African railways.—*Times Weekly*, 4th March 1898.

26. The footsteps of debt are always *dogged* by crime.

27. We cannot go on *drifting* like this any longer with impunity.

28. Trade-unionism is *driving* trade out of the country.

29. He always has a capable man at his *elbow.*

30. In common with most *epidemics,* frequency has more than once deprived a war-*fever* of its malignancy.—*Daily Telegraph*, 25th Feb. 1898.

31. Belief is *extinct* in France, and with good reason.

32. War-fever is at once a popular political *stimulant* and a lucrative financial expedient.—*Daily Telegraph*, 25th Feb. 1898.

33. Facts which come out during the present trial throw a *flood* of light upon this question.—*Ibid.*

34. Three gaudy standards *flout* the pale blue sky.—BYRON.

35. Love is *founded* on esteem,—the only foundation which can make the passion last.—*Times Weekly*, 4th March 1898

36. He felt a genial *glow* of satisfaction.

37. He had not the capacity to *grasp* abstract truths.
38. All this was done under the *guise* of friendship.
39. This is what places a *gulf* between the two authors.
40. Mr. F——, who represents the meat-trade, has been *hammering* away at Mr. W——, who represents the War Office.
41. The prolonged strike in the engineering trade *played* havoc with British industry.
42. Their political *horizon* has been enlarged.
43. There is nothing so welcome and so *infectious* as the spirit of fun.
44. Unreality was the *key-note* of the attack upon the Indian frontier policy last night.—*Daily Telegraph*, 15th Feb. 1898.
45. The civilisation of West Africa will be postponed, if the white races engaged in the task devote their time and their energies to *jostling* one another.—*Ibid.*
46. The ranks of the aristocracy include a *leaven* of clever and public-spirited men.
47. If Germany retains that position, Russia must get *level* with her by taking some other.
48. There was no chance of *light* being thrown on the case.
49. He *handled* the subject with remarkable lucidity.
50. The parliamentary *machine* is hopelessly blocked.
51. We now build *mammoth* vessels of 12,000 to 14,000 tons.
52. Plans are rapidly *maturing* for a resumption of hostilities.
53. The characters of the young are more easily *moulded.*
54. For years past the difficulty of legislating at Westminster has been the *nightmare* of our practical men.
55. The citizens of the United States are now at *the parting of the ways:* the decisive step must be taken now or never.
56. Gunboats are *patrolling* the Nile near Metemmeh.
57. He is remarkable for the *perspicuity* of his style.
58. I cannot *pin* my faith on that notion.
59. The Oceania was the *pioneer* steamship of the Star line.
60. This post he still held, when he was suddenly *pitchforked* into the Ministry of Foreign Affairs.
61. He *plumed* himself on his skill at cricket.
62. An insensate policy has *plunged* us into this disastrous campaign.
63. He protested against this *puffing* of a particular machine.
64. Zola would deny his mission, if he shrank from probing to the *quick* the highest of social sores.—*Times Weekly*, 4th March 1898.
65. Above all, they objected to the policy which they hoped was now going to receive its *quietus.*—*Daily Telegraph*, 15th Feb. 1898.
66. We must provide *remedies* for our foolish policy, before it is too late.
67. The military court *rode rough-shod* over the fundamental principles of civil law.
68. The question is now *ripe* for settlement.
69. Question-time in the House started with a *ripple* of laughter.
70. If some *roads* to success are closed, others must be taken.
71. Herein lies the *root* of the question.
72. Some 25,000 more men, *roughly* speaking, including those sanctioned last year, are required.

73. A *rupture* with France, if it can be avoided, is inexpedient.

74. The paramount power in Europe can afford to be indulgent to her *satellites.*

75. Zola's "Paris" is a *scathing* satire professedly founded on fact.

76. He is a conservative of the old *school.*

77. In India it is difficult to check the *scourge* of malarial fever.

78. That was a very *shady* transaction.

79. The faith of the people in the people has been rudely *shaken.*

80. My ideas have now assumed a definite *shape.*

81. To relieve the distress caused by the Balfour *smash.*

82. War, whatever its issue, would inevitably *spell* ruin to their country.

83. Among the men present he *spotted* the culprit.

84. He took the unusual *step* of changing his profession.

85. Civilisation has advanced with rapid *strides* in Japan.

86. A more *striking* example could hardly be named.

87. To tamper with free trade is a confession of failure crowned by *suicide.*—*Review of Reviews*, Jan. 1898, p. 9.

88. He made *sweeping* charges.

89. The safest political *thermometer* in this case is the stock-market.—*Daily Telegraph*, 25th Feb. 1898.

90. Sir E. A. —— B. *thundered,* and Sir W. L. joked.—*Ibid.*

91. An empire won by the sword and held by the sword must at times pay the *toll* of the sword.—*Ibid.*

92. They are the most loyal of men, when their hearts are *touched.*

93. The news announced in the Lords *trickled* rapidly down to the Lower House the same evening.

94. We cannot allow any foreign power to *trade* so far on our known love of peace as to extort unreasonable concessions.

95. The sentence passed on Zola is a *triumph* for fanaticism.

96. This is not a moment for *twiddling our thumbs* over trifles.

97. Class has been oppressed by class, and capital is the *tyrant* of labour.

98. A competence is *vital* to contentment.

99. Every man is a *volume,* if you know how to read him.

100. Our correspondent says that the *war* of rates between the Canadian Pacific Railway and its rivals is creating great interest.—*Times Weekly*, 25th Feb.

101. After the reign of the Puritans the *whirligig* of time brought its revenge by the corrupt and debased reign of the second Charles.

102. Hitherto the two *wings* of the Unionist party have worked well together.

103. A good idea of how great a man he was may be gained at the cost of a good deal of *winnowing.*—*Fortnightly Review,* Jan. 1898, p. 7.

104. He is a man of *home-spun* wit.

II. *Write short sentences illustrating the use of metaphors connected with the following subjects* :—

1. *Metals.*—Gold, silver, brass, lead, dross, mine.

2. *Building.*—Edify, construction, foundation, pillar, corner-stone, door, wall, floor, back-stairs, tower (verb).

3. *Parts of a door.*—Key, lock, unlock, hinge, bolt.

4. *Machinery.*—Pivot, screw, safety-valve, engine.
5. *Trade.*—Bargain, discount, shop, stock.
6. *Cookery.*—Concoct, hash, boil.
7. *Mathematics.*—Square (verb), count on, miscalculate, discount, reckon.
8. *Horticulture.*—Root, tap-root, branch, flowers, florid, weed out, prune, engraft, bloom, flourish, fade, rosy, cultivate, season, fruit, ripe, stem, plant, germ.
9. *Agriculture.*—Field, plough (verb), sow, seed, hedge, sift, chaff, harvest, crop, fertile, reap, plant.
10. *Navigation.*—Anchor, sheet-anchor, steer, pilot, harbour, helm.
11. *Temperature.*—Cold, warm, lukewarm, hot, boiling.
12. *Dimensions.*—Solid, breadth, depth, superficial, straight, crooked.
13. *Sense of touch.*—Smooth, rough, hard, soft, polished, slippery, blunt, sharp, flat.
14. *Sense of taste.*—Sweet, sour, bitter, acrimonious, nauseous.
15. *Sense of sight.*—Light, dark, colour, clear, dim, gloomy, obscure, lucid.
16. *Sense of sound.*—Discord, harmony.
17. *Natural scenery.*—Fountain, torrent, ocean, vista, mountain, forest, desert (noun).
18. *The sky.*—Star, planet, satellite, comet, meteor, cloud, thunder.
19. *War.*—Conflict, combat (verb), alarm, trumpet, defeat, triumph, peace.
20. *Bodily organs*, etc.—Pulse, vein, artery, heart, legs, neck, foot, mouth, eye, tongue, hand, sinews, brow, thumb.
21. *Bodily condition.*—Blind, lame, health, energy, weakness, fever, atrophy, hunger, thirst, youth, childhood, tired, sick.

PART IV.—PROSE AND POETRY.

CHAPTER XXVIII.—MAIN DIVISIONS OF PROSE-COMPOSITION.

384. Prose, Poetry.—Poetry (from Latin *poet-a*, Greek *poiēt-es*, a maker or originator) is distinguished from prose (Latin *prosa*, for *prorsa* or *proversa*, turned forward, unchecked) by the restraints of metre and by certain peculiarities of thought and diction to be described hereafter. All composition comes under one or other of these great headings. The present chapter deals with prose only.

385. Two modes of classifying Prose.—In attempting to draw up a scheme showing the main divisions of prose-composition, we may make either *matter* or *form* the basis of the classification. We propose in this chapter to classify the main divisions under both headings, taking the former one first.

Section 1.—Classification according to Matter.

386. Subjects of Prose-composition.—Prose-compositions may be divided into A, Technical or non-Literary; and B, Non-Technical or Literary.

Literary prose may be further subdivided under the eight headings of History, Biography, Description, Reflection, Fiction, Persuasion, Censure, and Humour.

Technical composition deals with those branches of study that concern the specialist, but do not interest the general reader. It is therefore classed as non-Literary. Its one aim is to instruct—to impart any such information in art, science, philosophy, law, language, or theology as the inquirer may need for his particular calling or for some department of research in which he is personally interested.

Non-Technical composition, like the preceding, may have an instructional aim. But even when it has, it never stops there. If it seeks to instruct, it also seeks to entertain—to combine pleasure with profit. It is therefore literary to the same extent that the other is non-literary.[1]

History deals with *events* of interest, **Biography** with *persons* of interest, and **Description** with *objects* of interest.

Historical literature relates the life (or some period of the life) of a nation; biography the whole life of an individual. Their provinces overlap, if the person whose private life is told was one who left his mark on the history of his own time.

Descriptive literature deals with natural scenery, natural history on its less scientific side, cities, countries, industries, weapons, customs, superstitions, etc. Books of travel contribute very largely to this class of literature, and are the most typical representatives of the class.

Reflective composition does not deal primarily either with events of interest, or with persons of interest, or with objects of interest; but rather with such thoughts and feelings as may be suggested by the study of any of these. Criticisms and reviews

---

[1] This chapter, we find, covers substantially the same ground as Part IV., "Selection and Arrangement," in *English Lessons for English People*, by Abbott and Seeley. Our own classification had been mapped out before this Part IV. was seen. It may, therefore, be of some use to the student to see how far the one fits in with the other.

In the book referred to, composition is divided into I. Scientific, and II. Non-Scientific. Non-Scientific is then subdivided under four different headings, viz. (1) Conversation, (2) Oratory, (3) Didactic, (4) Imaginative, including Poetry. "Scientific" presumably answers to what we have called Technical; the term "Technical," however, includes not Science only, but the various arts and the various branches of law, language, philosophy, and theology. "Conversation" does not come into the present classification at all; we have placed it among the *forms* of composition in section 2. "Oratory" covers the very same ground as what we have called the literature of Persuasion: the ground is the same, because the word "oratory," as the authors explain in p. 218, is meant to include *all* forms of pleading, and not merely speeches or oratory proper. "Didactic," as we gather from the remarks and comments given by the authors in different places, covers the same ground as our History, Biography, Description, and Reflection,—the aim of which is didactic as well as literary. "Imaginative" covers the same ground as our Fiction, except that we have not included Poetry: (this we have discussed in a separate chapter, and on a basis of its own). The two schemes, therefore, run upon almost parallel lines.

No niche, however, appears to have been provided in the scheme under reference for our seventh and eighth divisions, viz. Censure (or Satire), and Humour. These seem to be deserving of a place in the list, since each has a peculiar function of its own, and is represented in all the cultivated languages, ancient and modern, by a considerable, though less valuable, amount of literature.

of books belong to this class. Sermons that appeal to men's devotional feelings, or are intended to influence their general conduct (as distinct from those that are intended to incite men to some particular act, such as subscribing to some charity), come under this heading. Commemorative speeches in honour of the dead, since they give expression to thoughts and feelings more than to anything else, fall into the same class.

The literature of **Fiction** differs from all the kinds of composition that have been hitherto named. In works of History, Biography, Description, or Reflection, the writer is limited to *facts*, and his aim is to instruct the reader as well as to please him, the instructional element being the more essential of the two. But the chief, and sometimes the only, aim of Fiction is to please the imagination, instruction (if it comes in at all) being only an accessory. This class of literature comprises allegory, romances, novels, idylls, and fairy tales. Such books, as we have said, may be and sometimes are written with a practical purpose. But if they are not interesting and give no pleasure, no one reads them. Men will read fact for the sake of fact, but they will not read fiction for the sake of fiction. The giving of pleasure is therefore the main, and sometimes the only, characteristic of works of this class.

The literature of **Persuasion** does not aim either to instruct or to please (though incidentally it may do both), but to incite men to do some particular act, as to vote for some candidate at an election, to acquit or condemn some accused person, to pass some law, to subscribe to some charity, etc. If we were asked to describe the kinds of subjects that Persuasive literature deals with in order to gain its particular end, "action," we should sum them up under a single word, "motives."

The literature of **Censure** consists of satire, the reproof of individuals or communities, exposure of abuses, political invective, etc. Its aim, if this is sincerely acted on, is to correct and reform evil of any kind. But the occasional virulence of its tone makes one feel that it is sometimes inspired by an indignation other than what is purely virtuous.

The literature of **Humour** deals with any such points in the manners, actions, appearance, and sayings of men (real or fictitious) as are likely to excite laughter. Amusement, not ridicule (for ridicule is one of the keenest weapons of satire), is its only aim. The comic drama is a large contributor to this class of composition, and is, on the whole, its best representative.

The scheme then stands as follows; but it will, of course, be understood that one kind of composition often overlaps another :—

A. **Technical** composition (non-literary) : aim—to instruct. Subject-matter—the various arts, the various sciences, the various branches of law, philosophy, language, or theology.

B. Non-Technical composition (literary) :—

I. **History** : aim—to instruct and also to please. Subject—the events that mark the life of nations, institutions, etc.

II. **Biography** : aim—the same as that of History. Subject—the private life and personal character of individuals.

III. **Description** : aim—the same as I. and II. Subject—natural scenery, objects and places of interest, travels, etc.

IV. **Reflection** : aim—to stimulate thought and feeling in some specific direction. Criticisms of books, reflections on men and manners, devotional treatises, sermons intended to influence men's general conduct.

V. **Fiction** : aim—to please the imagination. Allegory, romances, novels, idylls, and fairy tales.

VI. **Persuasion** : aim—to incite men to do some particular act. Popular addresses, political pamphlets, forensic and parliamentary speeches, sermons in aid of some charity, etc.

VII. **Censure** : aim—to correct and reform. Satire, the censure of individuals or communities, political invective.

VIII. **Humour** : aim—to excite laughter. The comic drama, and any other kind of literature intended chiefly for amusement.

Note.—We may point out in passing how these several kinds of prose-composition are exemplified in current journalism :—

Technical composition is seen in the numerous weekly or monthly journals on special subjects, such as Engineering, Architecture, Building, Mining, Music, Education, Natural Science, etc.

History (that is, contemporary history) is told by the daily papers in the latest telegrams or news about Home, Colonial, and Foreign affairs, or about the proceedings of public men at home and abroad.

Biography.—On the death of any distinguished person, the papers usually give us a short account of his life.

Descriptive composition is exemplified in the accounts given of some sea-side resort, or some place of interest, or some concert, or some dramatical performance, or some exhibition of paintings, or the ceremony of opening some new institution, or some political gathering.

Reflective writing is exemplified in the leading articles, in which the editor expresses his comments on some passing event or his anticipations regarding the near future ; or in the criticisms of books that appear in the monthly and quarterly journals.

Fiction is represented by some short story, or by some novel that is published by instalments in any of the numerous periodicals.

Oratory or persuasive composition is exemplified every day in the reports of speeches delivered in courts of justice, or in parliament, or in political gatherings outside parliament.

Censorial composition is seen in the rebukes administered to public men, or in the exposure of abuses.

Humorous composition is seen in those papers that are devoted entirely to this class of subject.

Thus all kinds of prose-composition, if our classification is exhaustive, are represented in current journalism. What is true of journalistic literature in particular is true of the national literature as a whole.

387. **Technical Composition.**—This, as its name implies, cannot dispense with the use of technical terms; and this is one of the causes that place it outside the range of general literature; for in such literature the use of technical terms is an offence against purity (§ 269). It would be a mistake, however, to suppose that technical composition, though classed as non-literary, gives no scope for the exercise of literary tact. A writer who has the art of stating his facts clearly and forcibly, selecting his materials well, arranging them judiciously, and testing his statements by well-chosen examples, has a much better chance of being read with attention and profit than one who, though equally accurate and complete, is deficient in these qualities. There is as much art in handling a subject effectively in writing as there is in teaching it effectively by word of mouth.

Technical composition is seen in three different varieties—(*a*) The formal exposition of theory and fact; (*b*) The history of inventions and discoveries; (*c*) Controversy or argumentation.

388. **History.**—The name "history" is from a Greek word which means "inquiry." This is a part, and a very important part, of its meaning still; for inquiry or research into facts is the chief quality that distinguishes Historical literature from Imaginative or Fiction. The points on which an historian has to be especially guarded are the following:—

(1) To separate fact from legend. It is chiefly in dealing with *early* periods that this precaution has to be exercised. The history of almost every country, modern as well as ancient, begins with traditions handed down orally from an age when events were not recorded by men living at or near the time of their alleged occurrence.[1] It has been said of Hume, the first great historian of England, that he relates "legendary and half-

[1] It was not till Sir George Cornewall Lewis brought out (in 1855) his *Enquiry into the Credibility of Early Roman History* that the canons of historical evidence, so far as early periods are concerned, were established. According to him nothing can be accepted as historical which does not rest on *written and almost contemporary* testimony. Grote was the first to take advantage of this canon; he divides his subject into Part I. Legendary Greece, and Part II. Historical Greece.

mythological stories with the same air of belief as the well-authenticated events of recent times,—a fault pardonable enough in Herodotus or Livy, but less venial in a writer who ought to have applied his powerful critical faculty to the sifting of truth from tradition" (Shaw).

(2) To eliminate and discard unnecessary details. Prolixity as a fault in composition has been described already in § 295 (4). It is a fault against which an historian, if he has a great multitude of facts to choose from, should be especially guarded. Details which throw no light on the main events, or on the motives of the principal actors, or on the character of the age, are not merely superfluous, but obstructive; for they obstruct the reader's endeavour to follow the main thread of the narrative. "Macaulay remarks of Orme, the historian of British India, that in one volume he allots on an average a closely printed quarto page to the events of every forty-eight hours. It may be questioned whether in the later volumes of Macaulay's own history too much space is not given to parliamentary disputes which have lost their interest in a century and a half" (Abbott and Seeley). In contemporary historians we must expect greater prolixity than in those who write of earlier periods; for a keener interest is taken in occurrences that are still recent, and time has not yet shown which events will have most interest and importance for posterity. Kinglake's *Crimean War* covers eight big volumes, one of which is devoted to a single battle. Future historians of the Victorian age will probably dismiss this battle with a page or two.

(3) To give greater prominence to the more important facts. The importance of one fact above another depends mainly on its *consequences*. In human affairs one event springs out of another, as in the physical world an effect springs from a cause. Admiral Byng's defeat of the Spanish navy off Cape Passaro was as decisive in its way as Drake's defeat of the Armada; yet in comparative importance they stand very wide apart; for the one led to no result in particular, while the other represented the triumph of the reformed religion and the rescue of England from the iron heel of Spain. The Crimean war will not fill much space in future histories, as time has already shown that every object for which the Crimea was invaded has been frustrated, and that Turkey was not worth fighting for.

(4) To divide a long period into parts. If the history is one that covers a long period of time, its subdivision into parts

is of great help to the reader's conception of the main events, besides adding much to the interest of the narrative. Here, again, it is the relative importance of events that fixes the landmarks. Taking English history as a whole, few persons (we think) would hesitate to close the first great period with the Norman Conquest,[1] and the second with the Reformation.[2] If each of the three great periods is to be further separated into smaller ones, the first or pre-Norman might be subdivided by King Alfred's defeat of the Danes in A.D. 879, which saved England from a relapse into barbarism; the second or pre-Reformation period by the battle of Lewes, A.D. 1264, which led to the first summoning of Commons to Parliament; and the third by the Revolution of 1688,[3] which in this country decided for ever the question of absolute or limited monarchy. Different writers may, of course, adopt different modes of division, and this will largely depend on the purpose for which they write.

The mental faculties chiefly employed in the composition of history are (*a*) judgment or discrimination for the sifting of evidence, and (*b*) the imaginative faculty for realising past events as if they were present, and putting oneself in the place of the principal actors. Imagination, or the power to realise a situation not one's own, is quite as necessary to an historian as to a novelist or even to a poet. A writer who fails to catch the spirit of the age to which his narrative relates, however accurate and impartial he may be in compiling the facts and expounding the events, is not an historian in the full sense of the term. "Our view of every transaction, especially one that is remote in time and place, will necessarily be imperfect and generally incorrect, unless it embrace something more than a bare outline of the occurrences; unless we have before the mind a lively idea of the scenes in which the events took place, the habits of thought and feelings of the actors, and all the circumstances connected with the transaction; unless, in short, we can in a considerable degree transport ourselves out of our own age

[1] This is the division actually followed by Freeman, who brings his *Early History of England* to a close with the defeat of Harold, and commences a new work with the Norman Conquest.

[2] Froude commences his *History of England* with the fall of Cardinal Wolsey, which was immediately followed by Henry VIII.'s secession from Rome.

[3] Macaulay's *History of England* begins with James II., who was deposed (after a reign of three years and a half) in the Revolution of 1688.

and country and persons, and imagine ourselves to be the agents or spectators" (Whately).

389. Biography.—In the sifting of evidence, giving of greater prominence to the more important facts, suppressing of unnecessary details,[1] and separating one portion of a life from another, the methods of the biographer are analogous to those of the historian. The difference lies in the subject and in the style.

Subject.—In biography the aim of the writer is to delineate personal character and describe an individual career, not, as in history, to exhibit great events, or great national movements, or the outcome of large courses of policy. Biography is private history teaching by example. An uneventful biography can therefore be quite as interesting, and sometimes more instructive, than one that is full of striking incidents. There is no plot-interest in the recently published *Life of Tennyson* such as we find, for example, in Moore's *Life of Byron*; yet the one can be read with quite as much interest as the other, and certainly with more profit.

Style.—Dignity of language is more suitable to history; simplicity to biography. *The Decline and Fall of the Roman Empire*—the grandest panorama in the history of mankind—is told by Gibbon in the loftiest style that our language admits of. On the other hand, an easy and familiar style, such as that described in § 286, is peculiarly appropriate to biography or personal history. If a writer has thoroughly mastered the character and career of the person whose life he relates, a style that is "frank and easy" is certain to carry the reader with him.

Impartiality is as great a merit in a biographer as in an historian. "If it [the life of an author] is written from the point of view of an admirer, nay, of a disciple, that is right; but then the disciple must be also a critic, a man of letters, not, as too often happens, some relation or friend with no qualification for his task except affection for his author" (Matthew Arnold). Boswell's *Life of Johnson* (the earliest model of biography in our literature) shows how the qualities of a disciple can be combined with those of a man of letters.

390. Description.—Under this heading we place that kind of composition which describes *objects*, as distinct from history or biography, which relates *events*, public or private. The same

[1] Among unnecessary details we should include those letters that are not worth preserving, and clog the reader's attention to no purpose.

faculties are not employed in description as in history. What research or the sifting of evidence is to the historian, observation is to the describer. One collects his facts from what he reads; the other from what he sees and hears.

As models of Descriptive composition, all written within the Victorian age, we might name Wordsworth's *Greece* (lately re-edited and brought up to date), Ruskin's *Stones of Venice* (one of the finest descriptive works in our language), Stanley's *Sinai and Palestine*, and Wallace's *Russia*. All these were the result of observation and travel; all describe countries and places of world-wide interest, make frequent allusions to history, and give graphic descriptions of natural scenery. All are written with consummate literary skill.

391. Reflection.—What Matthew Arnold says about "criticism" may be taken to apply to Reflective literature as a whole. He defines it to be "*a disinterested endeavour to learn and propagate the best that is known and thought in the world*" (*Essays on Criticism*, p. 38). So much importance did he attach to this definition, that he printed it in italics, as we have done. Examples:—Smiles's treatises on "Character," "Self-Help," "Duty," "Thrift"; Helps's "Friends in Council," "Companions of my Solitude"; Coleridge's "Aids to Reflection"; Baxter's "Saints' Everlasting Rest" (1687), a devotional treatise still read with eagerness in all parts of the British empire.

The distinctive character of this kind of literature is seen from the habit that has lately sprung up of selecting and publishing in a separate volume extracts from distinguished writers. Thus we have *The Wit and Wisdom* of Sydney Smith; *Wise, Witty, and Tender Sayings* of George Eliot; *Daily Thoughts* selected from the writings of Charles Kingsley. The *Book of Thoughts* consists of the favourite passages in prose and verse, upon which the late Mr. Bright used to stimulate and refresh his mind during his stirring and useful career.

Reflective composition, dealing as it does with general principles, about which opinions may differ, is sometimes forced to resort to argumentation. In such a case a judicious writer is careful (1) to adopt a moderate tone in stating his own side of the question; (2) to do full justice to the side from which he differs. The same precautions apply to the historian and biographer also, if, as may easily happen, some debateable question should arise in the course of the narrative. In instructional literature of all kinds a combative or oratorical attitude defeats its own object; for, instead of carrying conviction, it provokes opposition and excites distrust. "When the reader sees a case made out too clearly, he has time to suspect that the opposite case has been suppressed, and will not give full confidence to his author, unless he finds the opposite case exhibited with scrupulous and anxious candour. Macaulay sometimes fails to convince in consequence of his forgetting this rule, and of trying to *overwhelm* his opponent in the rhetorical fashion" (Abbott and Seeley).

392. **Fiction.**—Imaginative composition differs from all that have been described hitherto, since it deals with fiction, not with fact. Its aim is not to instruct the mind of the reader, but to please his imagination. If instruction is admitted at all, it is admitted only as an accessory.

Imaginative composition may be distinguished into (1) Allegory, including parable and fable, (2) Romances, (3) Novels, (4) Idylls, (5) Fairy Tales.

(1) *Allegory, Parable, Fable.*—In these, as the student is aware from § 353, the story is intended to have a double sense,—one illustrating the other by analogy,—whereas in every other kind of fiction it has only one. To every allegory, parable, or fable there is a moral, and hence this kind of fiction has more of the instructional element than any other:—

> The cock and fox the fool and knave imply;
> The truth is moral, though the tale a lie.—DRYDEN.

Examples: *Pilgrim's Progress*, by John Bunyan (1628-88); *Gulliver's Travels* and *Tale of a Tub*, by Swift; *Æsop's Fables*. Allegorical creations have no chance of becoming popular, unless the truth that lies behind them is apparent at a glance and is already well established in popular conviction. The presence of these conditions in *Pilgrim's Progress* accounts for its unfailing popularity.

(2) *Romances.*—A romance is a tale that turns chiefly on adventure. The interest of the story lies, not in the delineation of character, but in the striking nature of the incidents. In *Robinson Crusoe*, the earliest romance in our literature (by Daniel Defoe, 1661-1731), the hero has no peculiarity of character that would distinguish him from any other man who can show pluck and common-sense under unusual difficulties.

(3) *Novels.*—A novel is a tale that turns chiefly on manners and

character. Richardson (1689-1761) was the founder of this kind of fiction, as Defoe was of romance. In such writings personal character is shown less by startling adventures than by trivial incidents. "The chief incidents in Jane Austen's novels are meetings in shops, or at balls or picnics; and much the same may be said of Thackeray's novels. In Thackeray it is remarkable that he avoids the great incidents that fall in his way, and confines himself to tracing the domestic consequences of them. In *Vanity Fair*, for example, the novelist stays at Brussels, while the battle of Waterloo is being fought" (Abbott and Seeley).

Note.—Romance and novel have now become very much mixed in our literature. Scott, the greatest master of romance in our language, seldom or never fails to delineate personal character, notwithstanding the prominence that he gives to scenes of warlike and other dangerous or exciting adventure.

(4) *Idylls.*—An idyll is a tale (sometimes only a dialogue) describing the simple scenes and pursuits of country life. The earliest idyll that appeared in our literature was the *Vicar of Wakefield*, by Goldsmith, published in 1766. The story, however, in some of its parts takes us away into scenes that are far removed from rustic simplicity; and these mar its consistency of design. A more perfect idyll is *Silas Marner*, by George Eliot, to which we might add parts of *Adam Bede* by the same authoress. *Arcadia*, by Sir Philip Sidney (1554-86) can hardly be called a national idyll, as it is based on Italian models.

(5) *Fairy Tales.*—Among the most recent examples are Kingsley's *Water Babies*, and *Alice in Wonderland* and *Alice through a Looking-Glass*, by Lewis Carroll (C. L. Dodgson).

393. *Intermixture of fact and fiction.*—Imaginative literature has not always kept clear of Historical, notwithstanding the great gulf that lies between them in point of aim and purpose.

In ancient times, when the speeches of statesmen were not recorded, historians both in Greece and Rome were in the habit of composing speeches, which they put into the mouths of statesmen as if they had been actually delivered. This was a convenient way of making a statesman expound his own policy, and it added vivacity to the narrative. This mixture of fiction with history is not now tolerated.

But romancists have introduced another kind of mixture, peculiar to their own craft; and to this no objection has yet been raised. In what are called "historical" novels or romances, historical incidents and persons are blended as parts of the same story with fictitious ones; and the blending is done with so much literary tact, that the reader is thrown upon his own resources to find out what is history and what is fiction. The soliloquy that Scott puts into the mouth of Cromwell at the sight of King Charles's portrait comes so naturally into the story, that more than one reader has taken it for genuine. Similarly, Defoe's *Journal of the Great Plague of London*,—which journal is supposed to have been kept by a London shopkeeper,—has been quoted as if it were an historical document. It was Defoe who set the first example of this mixing of romance with history.

Note.—There are two different ways in which the mixing of history and fiction has been carried out. In Bulwer-Lytton (and the same may be said of Kingsley) history is put in the foreground, and fiction is merely an accessory. Examples: *Harold, the Last of the Saxons; Rienzi, the Last of the Tribunes; The Last of the Barons.* In Scott, however, the main actors and events in the story are fictitious, and the historical ones come in as it were by accident. Thus *Quentin Durward* describes the career of a young Scotchman of rank who plays an extraordinary, but wholly fictitious, part in the disputes between Louis XI., King of France, and Charles the Bold, Duke of Burgundy. In fact, Scott does not scruple to alter dates, if it suits his purpose. Thus in the novel just named, as he explains in a note, "the murder of the Bishop of Liege has been antedated by fifteen years, for reasons which the reader of romances will easily appreciate."

394. Persuasion.—Persuasion is the art of influencing the will of another by means of words, and leading him to do some particular act advocated by the speaker or writer. The typical form of this kind of composition is that of a speech or sermon addressed to an audience. But other forms are used. Pamphlets, articles in magazines, and whole books are written to advocate particular measures. In an official document urging the adoption of some new project or policy the only form used is that of a letter.

Oratory, or extempore speaking, is unwritten composition. The conditions of success depend on manner, style, and argument.

(*a*) *Manner.*—A manner that indicates assurance, sincerity, and faith is always effective. This kind of manner carries weight even in conversation, much more so in large assemblies of men. Speeches or sermons delivered with the help of notes or read out from a manuscript are less impressive than addresses which, though they may have been carefully prepared beforehand, seem to the audience to be the unpremeditated outpourings of the speaker's soul. One reason why speeches appear less forcible when they are read than when they are heard is that in reading them we lose the effect of the teacher's manner and the contagion that it spreads through an assembly of listeners.

(*b*) *Style.*—In oratory a simple and natural style is more effective than one that is elaborate and polished. The speeches of Burke are the most remarkable in our literature for richness and ingenuity of style; but in the House of Commons they were not much listened to. They are more fit to be read than heard.

The two great qualities of style that a speaker is concerned in are perspicuity and force. Perspicuity is the first essential; but as an audience may be inattentive, impatient, or even dull of understanding, force is necessary also.

Force is produced by antithesis (§ 354), occasional epigram (§ 355), and the various other devices explained in Chapter xxvi. A short sentence interposed between long ones (§ 296) gives time for the hearer to collect his thoughts. Another rhetorical device is the frequent reassertion (§ 370), in various different forms or aspects, of the point on which most emphasis is laid. A simile or metaphor that conveys the pith of an abstract argument by a concrete image is not easily forgotten, and helps the listener to grasp what the speaker desires to enforce (see § 345). A terse phrase is often very effective. Some forty years ago a proposal was made to establish constituencies which should represent learned societies, the various arts, professions, and sciences. The short condemnatory phrase that Bright applied to them, "fancy-franchise," took hold of the public mind at once, and did more to discredit the scheme than many lengthy speeches. In marshalling and arranging facts or arguments, Climax (§ 368) is a valuable expedient: "the mind, no less than the eye, cannot so well take in and do justice to any vast object at a single glance, as by successive approaches and repeated comparisons" (Whately). Facility in the use of such devices can be acquired only by practice: *poeta nascitur, orator fit*, "a poet is born, an orator is made." It is now well known that the late Mr. Bright took great trouble in preparing his speeches, and wrote down some of his most telling phrases before he delivered them.

(*c*) *Argument.*—"It is the characteristic of oratory that it must be understood at once and produce all its effects at once, since it attempts to influence a decision that is near at hand" (Abbott and Seeley). The speaker must therefore use great caution both in the selection and in the arrangement of his facts.

In the *selection* of his facts he will take care to be one-sided; that is, he will exclude or explain away whatever is likely to tell against the decision that he desires to produce, and enlarge upon everything that will tell in favour of it. Again, he will avoid subtle arguments that cannot be grasped as soon as they are heard, reflections that are above the ordinary level of intelligence, and points of view with which the bulk of the audience are less familiar than himself.

For the *arrangement* of facts and arguments no absolute rules can be laid down. Much depends upon the occasion, and upon the character of the audience.

If the speaker is conscious before he begins that the audience is for the most part in sympathy with him, he can state his conclusion at once, and produce his facts and arguments in support of it. A long statement of facts, without any preliminary explanation of their purpose or of the inference to be drawn from them, is wearisome and perplexing.

If the audience is against him, he must state his conclusion, not first, but last, and bring his hearers gradually round to it, by urging one consideration after another. "It is a short way," says Swift, "to obtain the reputation of a wise and reasonable man, whenever any one tells you his opinion, to agree with him." It is related of Cobden that in one of his speeches in favour of free trade the meeting at first hooted him down and would not even grant him a hearing; but by agreeing with them in certain points which they held in common, he gradually brought them round to his own view, and was heartily cheered before he had finished. A parallel example is afforded by the speech which Shakspeare puts into the mouth of Mark Antony over the corpse of Julius Cæsar. The multitude had just been led, by the earnest appeals that Brutus had made to their pride as free citizens of the Roman republic, to approve of the assassination of Julius Cæsar, by whom their rights as Roman citizens had been destroyed. Mark Antony had therefore a difficult part to play. He begins by appearing to agree with the audience, disowns any intention of "praising Cæsar," and admits more than once that Brutus is "an honourable man." Having thus obtained a hearing, he begins to correct their judgment of Cæsar, shows that Cæsar respected their rights, and finally so exasperates them that they seize lighted torches and run off to Brutus's house to set fire to it.

395. Censure.—The aim of this kind of literature is to

expose abuses, censure individuals or societies, and redress wrongs of every kind. Political invective, such as *Junius' Letters*, belongs to this class. As an orator selects whatever will further the ends of persuasion, so a satirist selects whatever will damage the person or the cause that he attacks, and give pain to the offender. He enlarges upon the evil side, and says nothing about the good. The arts of rhetoric on which he chiefly relies, whenever he does not resort to direct vituperation, are innuendo and irony (see examples given in §§ 361, 362).

Censure has rarely been administered without acrimony, and its motives have seldom been purely virtuous. Of Swift (1667-1745), our most distinguished satirist in prose, it has been said: "He is like the Indian savage, who, in torturing his captive at the stake, cares little how much he wounds and harms himself, so long as he can make his victim writhe; or like the street ruffian, who, in throwing mud at his victim, is indifferent to the mud that may stick to his own fingers" (Shaw).

396. Humour.—Under this heading we have placed the last division of literary prose. Humour, which provokes mirth, is not to be confounded with ridicule, which gives pain. The latter is one of the keenest weapons of satire.

Humorous literature is seen in two different forms,—Comedy, Narrative. In the former there is always some kind of plot, in the latter not always. In both, however, the plot, that is, the outline of the story, is as ridiculous as the dialogues and the actors,—unlike the plot of a novel, which is intended to be probable, or at least conceivable.

(*a*) *Comedy.*—We have placed this first, because it came first in the order of time. In the Elizabethan age the line between tragedy and comedy was not sharply drawn. Thus in *Macbeth* the comic scene of the hell-porter is introduced in the most tragical crisis of the play,—the murder of Duncan; and in *Hamlet* we have the comic scene of the grave-digger in the midst of the pathetic scene of the burial of Ophelia. Most of Shakspeare's so-called comedies, such as the *Tempest* and the *Merchant of Venice*, are not what we now mean by comedies, but romantic or idyllic dramas with comic scenes interspersed.

Prose, not verse, is the language of comedy. The two comic scenes just referred to in *Macbeth* and *Hamlet* are entirely in prose, all other parts of the plays named being in metre. Similarly, in the neutral dramas the comic scenes are in prose, the more serious ones in metre. Again, in the "historical" plays, Jack Cade in *Henry VI.* and Falstaff in *Henry IV.* talk, not in metre, but in prose.

(*b*) *Narrative.*—Humorous narrative did not appear in our literature before the Restoration. It began with the new turn that Comedy then took; and the same authors sometimes contributed to both.

As an example of a narrative with a plot, we may mention the *Pickwick Papers* by Dickens, which can hardly be called a novel, as the Pickwick Club, on which the story is based, is itself as ridiculous as the chief actors, and will not bear the test of probability. The greatest of living humorists is Mr. Clemens, popularly known as Mark Twain, author of *Innocents Abroad*, *New Pilgrim's Progress*, *More Tramps Abroad*, etc. His narratives have little or no plot.

SECTION 2.—CLASSIFICATION ACCORDING TO FORM.

397. **Four forms of Prose-composition.**—There are four different forms of prose-composition,—Conversation, Letter-writing, Speech-making, Narration.

398. **Conversation.**—Conversation as a form of literary composition may be of three different kinds,—Imitative, Expository, Dramatic.

(1) *Imitative.*—It is imitative, when it is made to resemble the kind of conversation that takes place in ordinary life. This is seen chiefly in works of fiction, as these are largely of an imitative character. Those novelists who make the imitation of nature the secret of their art, cause their actors to talk in a manner suited to their respective characters and ranks. Thus Scott introduces countrymen, who use homely phrases in the Highland dialect. Dickens puts a pompous style into the mouth of the arrogant Dombey; a provincial dialect into the mouths of Sam Weller and Mark Tapley; a euphemistic or plausible style into the mouth of the hypocrite, Pecksniff; a euphuistic or showy style (§ 286) into the mouth of the empty-headed Micawber.

Examples of the art of polite conversation occur sometimes in books that are not works of fiction; as in Hazlitt's *Table Talk*, and Helps's *Friends in Council* and *Realmah.* Such conversation is desultory and unmethodical on principle, and it excludes subjects that cannot be expressed in short speeches or apprehended without mental effort.

(2) *Expository.*—The most celebrated example is that of *Plato's Dialogues*, which have been translated from the original Greek into most modern languages. In our own literature we have Coleridge's *Table Talk* collected in his "Literary Remains," and *Imaginary Conversations* (between Literary men and Statesmen) by Landor. The form of dialogue, as the example of Plato showed, is as suitable for the discussion of serious subjects as it is of light ones. A writer can sometimes state the different sides of a question more pointedly by an informal dialogue than he can by formal exposition.

(3) *Dramatic.*—In dramatic composition the whole of the story, excepting the short directions given to the stage manager, is told in the conversations of the *dramatis personæ*. In serious dramas the dialogue is usually given in metre, in comedy in prose (§ 396).

399. Letter-writing.—There are few kinds of subjects that have not been dealt with in the epistolary form.

"History" is represented by Goldsmith's *History of England*, which is told in the form of letters from a nobleman to his son. Despatches sent by an officer in command of an expedition to the Secretary of State for War are contemporary history told in the form of official correspondence.

"Biography" is represented by the letters actually written by the person whose life is told. Such letters are of the nature of autobiography.

"Description" is represented by the celebrated *Paston Letters* (1424-1506), consisting of a thousand letters of the Paston family in Norfolk, which throw much light on the state of the country and the manners of England in the fifteenth century. White's *Natural History of Selborne* is given in a series of letters addressed to a couple of friends. Lady Mary Montagu's travels over Europe to the East and her residence in Constantinople are all told in the form of *Letters*, the name under which her celebrated book was published in 1763.

"Reflection" is represented in *Letters to his Son*, containing advice on behaviour, mode of life, dress, etc., by Lord Chesterfield (1694-1773); in *Letters to Sir William Windham*, in defence of his political conduct, and *Letters on the Study and Use of History*, by Bolingbroke (1678-1751); in *Letters from a Citizen of the World*, by Goldsmith; in *Letters on Toleration*, by Locke; in *Letter on a Regicide Peace*, by Burke; and in Lord Selborne's *Letters to his Son on Religion* (1898).

"Fiction."—All Richardson's novels were composed in the form of letters, and his example was followed by Rousseau in the composition of his celebrated *Nouvelle Héloïse.* Smollett's *Humphrey Clinker* and Scott's *Redgauntlet* are written entirely in the same form.

"Satire."—Such composition appears in the epistolary form in *Drapier's Letters*, by Swift; *Junius' Letters*, by an unknown author (§ 395); and Ruskin's *Fors Clavigera*, a series of letters addressed to British working-men.

400. Speech-making.—This has two literary uses—Persuasive and Reflective.

Persuasive.—This is exemplified in the pleadings addressed by a barrister to a jury or judge; in speeches made in parliament advocating some particular measure; in the speeches made by a candidate for parliamentary election; in sermons addressed to a congregation, urging them to do some particular act, such as subscribing to some charity. Persuasion is the function of oratory proper.

Reflective.—This is exemplified in a judge's charge to a jury, in which he sums up the issues of a case that has just been heard; in public addresses, in which a statesman reviews or justifies his recent political acts or explains the policy of his party; in sermons intended to influence men's general conduct, or to stimulate devotion, or to commemorate the events of some sacred anniversary; in panegyrical addresses intended to honour the memory of some dead person.

Oratory of the Persuasive kind can be imitated in epic poetry, as in the debates in hell described in Book II. of *Paradise Lost;* in the drama, as in the speeches put into the mouths of Brutus and Antony in *Julius Cæsar;* and in novels, as in the electioneering speech delivered by Felix Holt, the Radical, in the novel so named. It was imitated, too, by Milton in *Areopagitica*, in which he uses the form of a speech addressed to the "High Court of Parliament" for advocating the unconditional freedom of the press. In ancient times (see § 393) it was imitated by historians, who put speeches made by themselves into the mouths of statesmen and rulers.

401. Narration.—Every kind of subject can be expressed in the form of continuous narrative, and excepting in the 6th kind (persuasive, see § 394) it is the form most commonly used.

CHAPTER XXIX.—PROSODY AND POETIC DICTION.

SECTION 1.—PROSODY.

402. Prosody (Gr. *pros-odia*, lit. a song sung to an instrument) treats of the laws of metre. It might be called "the grammar of verse."

403. Rhythm (Gr. *rhuthmos*, measured flow or motion) is "the musical flow of language." This is produced for the most part by a well-balanced recurrence of pauses and accents.

Rhythm has been elsewhere defined "a principle of proportion introduced into language."[1] This definition is practically equivalent to our own, though perhaps it scarcely gives enough prominence to *sound*. It is only a practised reader who can perceive "the proportion of language" without reading the composition aloud.

Rhythm is not confined to verse. It is quite as necessary to an orator as to a poet; and there is scarcely any kind of prose, of which the attractiveness is not increased by the recurrence of pauses and accents at suitable intervals.

404. Rime (A.S. *rím*, "number," misspelt as *rhyme* from a supposed connection with Gr. *rhuthmos*) is a repetition of the same sound at the *ends* of two or more lines. The effect of rime, however, is not produced, unless the lines succeed one another immediately or near enough for the resemblance of sound to strike the ear. Monosyllabic rimes are always accented.

Note 1.—A rime is usually of *one* syllable. But rimes can also be in two or more syllables, provided that the first syllable is accented and the rest are unaccented; as, *motion, ocean; behaviour, saviour*. Double rimes in French, and sometimes in English, are called female or feminine, while a single rime is called a male. Double and treble rimes are more commonly used in comic poetry:—

> To hear them rail at honest *Sunderland*,
> And rashly blame the realm of *Blunderland*.—POPE.

Note 2.—A monosyllabic rime is *perfect* under three conditions: (1) the vowel or vowels, whatever the spelling may be, must produce precisely the same effect on the ear; (2) if any consonant or consonants *follow* the riming vowel or vowels, these (whatever the spelling may be) must produce precisely the same effect; (3) the consonant that *precedes* the rime must, to prevent monotony, produce a *different* effect on the ear. Thus *hair* and *fair* are perfect rimes, because the three conditions just stated are all satisfied. But *bear* and *fear* are not perfect rimes, because the vowel-sounds, though not very different, are not quite the same. Again, *fare* and *af-fair* are not perfect rimes, because the riming vowel is preceded by the same consonant. Again, ap-*peased*, re-*leased* are not perfect rimes, because

---

[1] Abbott and Seeley's *English Lessons for English People*, p. 143.

the final consonants in the former have the sound of *zd*, while those in the latter have the sound of *st*.

When the rime is dissyllabic or polysyllabic, every syllable except the first must begin with the same consonant; cf. *Sunderland*, *Blunderland*, un-*fortunate*, im-*portunate*.

Note 3.—Rime is a matter of the ear, and not of the eye. Sight-rimes, such as *love* and *grove*, *farm* and *warm*, *home* and *some*, *path* and *hath*, are not rimes at all. On the other hand, *fight* is a true rime to *indict*, *dawn* to *morn*, *fourth* to *cloth*, *fire* to *higher*, *hour* to *power*, *there* to *air*, *colonel* to in-*fernal*. Pronunciation, not spelling, is the only test of a rime.

405. Assonance (Lat. *ad* + *sonant-ia* verba).—This term is applied to words which rime in the vowel or vowels, but not in the consonant or consonants following. It is therefore a very imperfect kind of rime; as, *slumber*, *blunder*; *same*, *cane*. A specimen of Assonance, in imitation of a Spanish ballad, occurs in the *Spanish Gypsy* by George Eliot:—

> Maiden, crowned with glossy blackness,
> Lithe as panther forest-roaming,
> Long-armed naiad, when she dances,
> On a stream of ether floating.

406. Alliteration (Lat. *ad* + *litera*).—When two or more words begin with the same vowel, or the same consonant, or the same syllable, this is called alliteration (§ 374). It is *initial* riming as distinct from *end*-riming.

> *R*uin seize thee, *r*uthless king!—GRAY.

Note.—All our earliest poetry was alliterative. The last great specimen of such poetry in our literature is *Piers the Plowman*, by William Langland, born in A.D. 1332. The poem is written in lines of ten to twelve syllables. The following is a specimen:—

> In a somer *s*eson, when *s*oft was the *s*onne,
> I *sh*ope me in *sh*roudës, as I a *sh*epe were.

407. Cæsura (a Latin word denoting "a cut"). In Latin prosody this meant the "cut" or division of a foot somewhere near the middle of the line, the cut being followed by a pause of the voice in reading the line aloud. In English prosody cæsura means merely the *pause* of the voice, by which lines of eight or more syllables are usually divided, when they are read aloud; and this pause may occur either at the end or in the middle of a foot. (For the meaning of "foot" see below, § 409.) Rhythm greatly depends on the position of the cæsura.

In the following example the figure against each line shows the number of feet (with or without a half foot) preceding each cæsura. When a comma or other stop occurs in the same place as the cæsura, the rhythm of the line is helped by the sense;

but a pause or cæsura can be made independently of punctuation, if the rhythm of the line is improved thereby. Sometimes a line has no cæsura; that is, neither the rhythm nor the sense of the line requires that any pause should be made in reading or repeating the line aloud:—

3½ Of man's first disobedience || and the fruit
3 Of that forbidden tree, || whose mortal taste
Brought death into the world and all our woe
2½ With loss of Eden, || till one greater Man
1½ Restore us || and regain the blissful seat,
2 Sing, Heavenly Muse, || that on the secret top, etc.

MILTON.

Observe that monotony is avoided and the rhythm of the lines enhanced by varying the place of the cæsura.

Observe also that the third line does not suggest any cæsura.

408. Metre (Gr. "measure") is "rhythm reduced to law." It depends on two factors:—

(*a*) The accentuation of syllables.

(*b*) The number of *accented* syllables to a line.

Note.—**Quantity** means the amount of time required for pronouncing a syllable distinctly. In Latin prosody syllables were subdivided by quantity into Long and Short. In English versification, however, quantity is of no importance. It is entirely subordinated to accent.

Then tore′ | with blood′- | y tal′- | on the′ | rent plain′.—BYRON.

Here the short syllable *the* is made as long as possible for the sake of giving an accent, and the long syllable *rent* is made as short as possible for the sake of removing one.

409. A specific combination of accented and unaccented syllables is called a **foot**. The number of syllables to a foot may be either two or three, but it cannot be less than two or more than three, and *one of these must be accented.*

(*a*) An **Iambus** consists of one unaccented and one accented syllable. This is the commonest of all our feet.

Ap-pear′, be-sides′, at-tack′, sup-ply′.

(*b*) A **Trochee** consists of one accented and one unaccented syllable. Not so common as the Iambus.

Ho′-ly, up′-per, grand′-eur, fail′-ing.

(*c*) An **Anapæst** consists of two unaccented syllables followed by an accented one. Rather uncommon.

Col-on-nade′, re-ap-pear′, on a hill′.

(*d*) A **Dactyl** consists of one accented syllable, followed by two unaccented ones. Very rare.

Mes′-sen-ger, mer′-ri-ly, prop′-er-ty, in′-fa-mous.

Note 1.—A fifth kind of foot is sometimes added, called an **Amphi-**

brach, consisting of an accented syllable between two unaccented ones; as *re-venge′-ful*, *a-maz′-ing*. The following line from Campbell may be quoted as an example:—

There came′ to | the beach′ a | poor ex′-ile | of E′-rin.

It would be easy, however, to subdivide the line into anapæsts by making the first foot an Iambus, which is common in anapæstic metre:—

There came′ | to the beach′ | a poor ex′- | ile of E′-rin,

in which *Erin* is a double rime.

But the following lines contain amphibrachs, which cannot be resolved into anapæsts:—

Most friend′-ship | is feign′-ing,
Most lov′-ing | mere fol′-ly;
Then heigh′-ho | the hol′-ly,
This life′ is | most jol′-ly.—SHAKSPEARE.

Note 2.—A sixth kind of foot, long and consisting of two accented syllables, is sometimes added. In Latin prosody this foot is called a **Spondee**. But in English prosody no such foot is recognised, since theoretically there cannot be more than one accent to an English foot. Sometimes, however, two accented syllables are placed together for the artificial purpose of making the sound of the line suggestive of the sense (§ 375):—

When A′- | jax strives′ | *some* rock's′ | *vast* weight′ | to throw′,
The line′ | *too* la′- | bours and′ | the words′ | *move* slow′.

Note 3.—The names of all the feet are derived from Greek. *Iambus* means "aiming at," "attacking," so called because this foot was first used in Satire. *Trochee* means "running," so called because it is a rapid measure. *Dactyl* means "finger," so called because, like the parts of a finger, it consists of one long followed by two shorts. *Anapæst* means "thrown back," because this foot is a dactyl reversed. *Spondee* means "pertaining to libations," so called because, when libations were poured out on an altar, slow and solemn melodies were used. *Amphibrach* means "short at both sides," so called because this foot consists of one long syllable enclosed by two short ones.

410. To **scan** a line (Lat. *scan*-d-ere, to climb) is to divide it into its several feet, and say *what kind* of feet they are, and *how many* of them there are. Lines of two feet are called *dimeters*; of three, *trimeters*; of four, *tetrameters*; of five, *pentameters*; of six, *hexameters*. In Tennyson's *Locksley Hall* we have an example of *octometers* (8 feet). In scanning a line the following precautions should be noted:—

(*a*) The number of feet to a line depends on the number of *accented* syllables, not on the total number of syllables (§ 408).

(*b*) An accented monosyllable at the beginning of a line is sometimes made to do duty for an entire Iambic foot:—

Stay′, | the king′ | hath thrown′ | his war′- | der down′.—SHAKS.
(*Iambic pentameter*, 5 feet.)

(*c*) In the Trochaic and Dactylic metres, an accented monosyllable at the end of a line counts as an entire foot, though in the former this foot is short of one unaccented syllable, and in the latter of two :—

Life′ is | but′ an | em′-pty | dream′.—LONGFELLOW.
(*Trochaic tetrameter*, 4 feet.)

Com′-rades, | leave′ me | here′ a | lit′-tle, | while′ as | yet′ 'tis |
ear′-ly | morn′.—TENNYSON (*Trochaic octometer*, 8 feet.)

Mer′-rily, | mer′-rily | shall′ I live | now′,
Un′-der the | blos′-som that | hangs′ on the | bough′.—SHAKS.
(*Dactylic tetrameter*, 4 feet.)

(*d*) Metres are not always perfectly carried out. In an Iambic line the first foot is sometimes a Trochee instead of an Iambus. In the Anapæstic metre, Iambic feet are sometimes put for Anapæsts, and this in any part of the line :—

Daugh′-ter | of God′ | and man′, | ac-com′- | plished Eve′.—MILTON.
(*Iambic pentameter*, 5 feet.)

Not a drum′ | was heard′, | not a fu′- | neral note′.
(*Anapæstic tetrameter*, 4 feet.)

(*e*) In scanning a line, two short syllables coming together can be counted as one for the sake of the metre :—

Wing″d with | red light′- | ning and′ | impet′- | *uous* rage′,
The mul′- | ti-tud′- | *inous* sea′ | incarn′- | adine′.

(*f*) Two open vowels belonging to different words can be slurred, so as to be fused together and pronounced as one :—

Impressed′ | th*e* *e*fful′- | gence of′ | his glo′- | r*y* *a*bides′.
By her′- | ald's voice′ | explained′ ; | the hol′- | l*ow* *a*byss′,
Abom′- | ina′- | b*le*, *u*nut′- | tera′- | b*le*, *a*nd worse′.
T*o* *in*sult′ | the poor′ | or beau′- | ty in′ | distress′.
May I′ | express′ | th*ee* *u*nblamed′, | since God′ | is light′.

411. Blank Verse.—"Blank" means unrimed. This is much used in Epic and Dramatic verse, and generally in Iambic pentameters. This is the noblest of all verse. It is the most difficult to write effectively, though it seems the easiest.

See example of Epic blank verse quoted from *Paradise Lost* in §407 under **Cæsura.**

In Longfellow's *Hiawatha* we have a solitary example of blank verse in Trochaic tetrameters:—

Then′ the | lit′-tle | Hi′-a- | wa′-tha
Learned′ of | ev′-ery | bird′ the | lan′-guage.

Occasionally we have blank verse in Dactylic dimeters :—

Can′-non to | right′ of them,
Can′-non to | left′ of them,
Can′-non in | front′ of them.—TENNYSON.

Some attempts have been made to introduce Classical (Latin and Greek) metres into English. This is another kind of blank verse. The best examples of Latin hexameters are Longfellow's *Evangeline* and Kingsley's *Andromeda* :—

> This' is the | for'-est pri- | mev'-al, the | mur'-mu-ring | pines',
> and the | hem'-lock.—LONGFELLOW.

Special Metres and Stanzas.

412. **The Heroic Couplet.**—In this metre lines consisting of five Iambic feet rime together in pairs.

This is called "Heroic" because it has been much used in translating Epic or Heroic poetry ; as in Dryden's translation of Virgil, and Pope's Homer.

This metre is sometimes varied by a **triplet**, in which the third line (called an Alexandrine) can have *six* Iambic feet instead of five :—

> The sacred lake of Trivia from afar,
> The Veline fountains, and sulphureous Nar,
> Shake at the baleful blast, the signal of the war.—DRYDEN.

413. **The Sonnet.**—Borrowed from Italy. It consists of fourteen Iambic pentameters, of which the first eight lines are called the *octave*, and the last six the *sestette*. The Italian octave (followed by Milton) has *two* rimes, in the order of *abba*, *abba* ; the octave in Shakspeare's sonnets has *four* rimes, in the order of *abab*, *cdcd*. The sestette has either two or three rimes, and their order is various.

414. **Ottava Rima.**—Borrowed from Italy. Each stanza consists of eight Iambic pentameters. The letters *a*, *b*, *c* show the system of riming. (The word *ottava* means "octave.")

> *a* 'Tis sweet to hear the watch-dog's honest bark
> *b* Bay deep-mouthed welcome as we near our home ;
> *a* 'Tis sweet to know there is an eye will mark
> *b* Our coming, and look brighter when we come ;
> *a* 'Tis sweet to be awakened by the lark,
> *b* Or lulled by falling waters ; sweet the hum
> *c* Of bees, the voice of girls, the song of birds,
> *c* The lisp of children and their earliest words.—BYRON.

415. **The Spenserian Stanza.**—Called Spenserian from its originator, Spenser, who used it in writing *The Faërie Queene.*

> *a* Roll on', | thou deep' | and dark'- | blue O'- | cean, roll,
> *b* Ten thou'- | sand fleets' | sweep o'- | ver thee' | in vain :
> *a* Man marks' | the earth' | with ru'- | in ; his' | control
> *b* Stops with' | the shore' ; | upon' | the wa - | tery main
> *b* The wrecks' | are all' | thy deed' ; | nor doth | remain
> *c* A shad'- | ow of' | man's rav'- | age save' | his own,
> *b* When for' | a mo'- | ment like' | a drop' | of rain

c He sinks′ | into′ | thy depths′ | with bub′- | bling groan,
c Without′ | a grave′, | unknelled′, | uncof′- | fined, and′ | unknown.
BYRON.

The ninth and last line, which in this metre always consists of six feet instead of five, is called an Alexandrine, like the third line in heroic triplets (§ 412).

416. The Metre of "In Memoriam."—This consists of a four-line stanza in which each line contains four Iambic feet, the fourth line riming with the first, and the third with the second. This metre was not, as is often supposed, originated by Tennyson. It was used by Sandys in his metrical paraphrase of the Psalms, A.D. 1636 :—

What profit can my blood afford,
When I shall to the grave descend ?
Can senseless dust thy praise extend ?
Can death thy living truth record ?—*Psalm* xxx. 9.

417. Stanzas (Ital. *stanza*, Old Ital. *stantia*, so called from the stop or pause at the end of it). All stanzas are in rimed, not in blank, verse.

A stanza of three lines is called a **Triplet**, as in Tennyson's *Two Voices*, in which each line consists of an Iambic tetrameter ; the third line is not an Alexandrine.

Whatev′- | er cra′- | zy sor′- | row saith′,
No life′ | that breathes′ | with hu′- | man breath
Has ev′- | er tru′- | ly longed′ | for death′.

A stanza of four lines is called a **Quatrain** (Fr. *quatre*, Lat. *quatuor*, four). Of such stanzas the most common examples are —(1) the **Ballad** metre, as in *Chevy Chase ;* and (2) the **Elegiac** metre, as in Gray's *Elegy*. In both of these the rimes alternate —in the former a tetrameter with a trimeter ; in the latter a pentameter with a pentameter. The stanza used in *In Memoriam* is another kind of quatrain ; see § 416.

A stanza of six lines is called a **Sextant**, in which the rimes may occur in the following orders :—(1) *a*, *b*, *a*, *b*, *a*, *b ;* (2) *a*, *a*, *b*, *c*, *c*, *b ;* (3) *a*, *b*, *a*, *b*, *c*, *c*.

A stanza of eight lines is called an **Octave** ; but it is best known under the name of Ottava Rima (Ital. sounded as *ottàva reema*, Lat. *octavus*, eighth) ; see § 414.

A stanza of nine lines is the Spenserian ; see § 415.

SECTION 2.—POETIC DICTION.

418. Prose, Poetry.—Poetry is distinguished from prose not only by the possession of metre, but by certain peculiarities of diction and of thought. The most prosaic matter may be expressed in the most prosaic language, and yet in the most perfect metre; the metre does not make either the matter or the language poetical.

> Something had happened wrong about a bill,
> Which was not drawn with sound commercial skill;
> So, to amend it, I was told to go
> And seek the firm of Clutterbuck and Co.—CRABBE.

419. Poetic Diction.—The chief peculiarities are the following:—

(1) *The use of archaic or less common words.*—Poetry pays little or no attention to changes in current speech. At the same time it likes to distinguish itself from prose. It therefore avoids common words, and retains words that were used by former poets, after they have gone out of general use:—

Nouns.—Poetry often uses *swine* for *pigs; swain* for *peasant* or *husbandman; billow* for *wave; main* for *sea* or *ocean; maid* or *damsel* for *girl; nuptials* for *marriage; vale* for *valley; steed* or *charger* for *horse; ire* for *anger; woe* for *sorrow* or *misery; thrall* for *distress; might* for *strength; marge* for *margin; spouse* for *wife; numbers* for *verse* or *metre; bower* for *summer-house; quest* for *search; guile* for *deceit; bliss* for *happiness; bane* for *poison* or *mischief; ken* for *perception; troth* for *veracity* or *faithfulness; chanticleer* for *cock; combat* for *battle; goblet* for *cup; aught* for *anything; naught* for *nothing; eve* for *evening; meed* for *reward; morn* for *morning; mead* for *meadow; realm* for *kingdom; scribe* for *writer; victor* for *conqueror; foe* or *foeman* for *enemy; yeoman* for *peasant* or *husbandman; tilth* for *tillage* or *agriculture*, etc.

Adjectives.—Poetry often uses *lone* or *lonesome* for *lonely; drear* for *dreary; dread* for *dreadful; lovesome* for *lovely; intrepid* or *dauntless* for *brave; yon* for *yonder; rapt* for *delighted; hallowed* for *holy; baleful* for *pernicious; doleful* for *sorrowful; artless* for *innocent; hapless* for *unlucky; lowly* for *low* or *humble; forlorn* for *distressed*; *sylvan* for *woody; sequestered* for *retired; joyless* for *unhappy; jocund* for *merry; aweary* for *weary; stilly* for *still; reckless* for *careless; bootless* for *unprofitable; ingrate* for *ungrateful; recreant* for *unfaithful; mute* for *silent; darksome* for *dark; quenchless* for *inextinguishable; fond* for *foolish; wrathful* for *angry; dire* for *dreadful*, etc.

Adverbs.—Poetry often uses *scarce* for *scarcely; haply* for *perhaps*; *sore* for *sorely; oft* for *often; erst* or *whilom* for *formerly; of yore* or *of old* for *in ancient times; scantly* for *scantily; anon* for *at once; amain* for *violently* or *suddenly; hard by* for *close* or *very near; full* for *very*, as in "full many a gem," etc.; *right* for *very* or *precisely*, as in "right against the eastern gate" (Milton).

Verbs.—Poetry often uses *quit* for *leave; wax* for *grow: quoth* for *said; list* for *listen; sojourn* for *lodge* or *dwell; trow* for *believe: tarry* for *remain* or *stay; hearken* for *hear* or *attend; obscure* for *darken; fare* for *walk; vanquish* for *conquer; quaff* for *drink luxuriously; cleave* for *stick; hie* or *speed* for *hasten; smite* for *hit* or *strike*. *-Est* and *-eth* are still commonly used for the second and third persons respectively. The older or Strong forms of Past tenses are used in preference to the modern or Weak ones; as *wrought* for *worked; bade* for *bid; begat* for *begot; clove* for *cleft; crew* for *crowed; drave* for *drove; throve* for *thrived; clomb* for *climbed; stove* for *staved; clad* for *clothed.*

Conjunctions.—Poetry often uses *what though* or *albeit* for *although; ere* or *or ere* for *before; nathless* for *nevertheless; an if* for *if.*

(2) *Omission of words required by Prose.*—Two purposes are served by such omissions: the metre is preserved, and the diction is made less like that of prose:—

Example	Omitted
The brink of (the) haunted stream Creeping like (a) snail unwillingly to school	*Article.*
(He) who steals my purse steals trash Lives there (the man) who loves his pain?	*Noun or Pronoun.*
For is there aught in sleep (that) can charm the wise? 'Tis distance (that) lends enchantment to the view	*Relative as Subject to a Verb.*
Mean though I am, (I am) not wholly so Happy (is) the man, whose wish and care, etc. To whom thus Adam (spoke)	*Finite Verb.*
Soldier rest, thy warfare (being) o'er, etc. My ramble (being) ended, I returned	*Participle.*
He knew himself (how) to sing Permit (that) I marshal thee the way	*Conjunction.*
He mourned (for) no recreant friend Through the dear might of Him that walked (on) the waves Despair and anguish fled (from) the struggling soul	*Preposition.*

In poetry a verb is often used alone, where in prose it would have an Auxiliary verb attached to it:—

Long *die* thy happy days before thy death!
(*May* thy happy days die, etc.)
This day *be* bread and peace my lot!
(*May* peace and bread be, etc.)
Gives not the hawthorn bush as sweet a shade?
(*Does* it not *give*, etc.)
Tell me not in mournful numbers.
(*Do* not tell me, etc.)
He goes to do what I *had done*, if, etc.
(What I *should have* done, if, etc.)

(3) *The use of uncommon constructions:*—

(*a*) An Adjective substituted for an Adverb (see § 181):—

First they praised him *soft* and *low*.—TENNYSON.
The green trees whispered *low* and *mild*.—LONGFELLOW.

(*b*) Positive adverb in *-ly* changed to Comparative in *-lier*:—

You have taken it *wiselier* than I meant you should.—SHAKSPEARE.
Destroyers *rightlier* called the plagues of men.—MILTON.

Strange friend, past, present, and to be;
Loved deep*lier*, dark*lier* understood.—TENNYSON.

Note.—This form of the Comparative adverb occurs, however, in the familiar word "earlier," which can be either an adverb or an adjective.

(*c*) Superfluous employment of a pronoun:—

My banks—*they* are furnished with bees.—SHENSTONE.
They tremble—the sustaining crags.—TENNYSON.
The smith a mighty man is *he*.—LONGFELLOW.

(*d*) An epithet (adjective) used as a noun:—

Below the chestnuts, when their buds
Were glistening to the breezy *blue* (=sky).—TENNYSON.
The dread *vast* (=expanse) of night.—MILTON.
The palpable *obscure* (=darkness).—*Ibid.*
The kindling *azure* (=sky).—THOMSON.

(*e*) The formation of new compound words:—

The *always-wind-obeying* deep.—SHAKSPEARE.
Or in the *violet-embroidered* vale.—MILTON.
Proxy-wedded with a bootless calf.—TENNYSON.
Before the *crimson-circled* star.—*Ibid.*

(*f*) A freer use of Reflexive objects after Intransitive verbs (§ 97):—

Then Satan first knew pain,
And *writhed him* to and fro.—MILTON.
The shepherd *hied him* home.

(*g*) Possessive case of noun used for an adjective (§ 43, *c*):—

Pity and *woman's* (=womanly) compassion.—LONGFELLOW.
The *mother's* (=motherly) nature of Althea.—LOWELL.

(*h*) The Simple form of Personal pronoun for the Reflexive:—

I thought *me* (=myself) richer than the Persian king.
BEN JONSON.
How close she veils *her* (=herself) round.—KEBLE.

(*i*) The use of "and" in an Interrogative sentence, to express a passionate sense of grief:—

And art thou cold and lowly laid.—SCOTT.
And wilt thou weep, when I am low?—BYRON.

(4) *Change in the regular order of words.*—The same two purposes are hereby served as before; see above (2):—

(*a*) Adjective placed after its noun, instead of before it:—

Or where the gorgeous East with richest hand
Showers on her kings *barbaric* pearl and gold.—MILTON.

(*b*) Subject placed after its verb, and object before it:—

No *hive* hast *thou* of hoarded sweets.

(*c*) Preposition placed after its noun instead of before it:—

Where echo walks steep hills *among.*

(*d*) Infinitive placed before the Finite verb, instead of after it:—

When first thy sire *to send* on earth,
Virtue, his darling child, designed.—GRAY.

(*e*) Adverb placed before its verb, instead of after it:—

Up springs from yonder tangled thorn
A stag more white than mountain snow.—SCOTT.

(*f*) Complement placed before its verb, instead of after it:—

Grieved though thou art, forbear the rash design.

(*g*) Use of *or* for *either*, and *nor* for *neither*:—

Remote, unfriended, melancholy, slow,
Or by the lazy Scheld or wandering Po.—GOLDSMITH.
Nor grief nor pain shall break my rest.

(5) *The use of adjectives or participles instead of clauses.* This is done for the sake of terseness. Poetry does not patronise Relatives and Conjunctions so freely as prose does.

(1) He can't combine each well *proportioned* part.

That is, he cannot make the different parts proportionate to each other and then combine them into a symmetrical whole.

(2) See that your *polished* arms be primed with care.—COWPER.

That is, see that your arms (or weapons) are well polished and primed with care.

(3) Forth goes the woodman, leaving unconcerned
The *cheerful* haunts of men.—COWPER.

Here "cheerful" means "*however cheerful they may be.*"

(4) From his *slack* hand the garland wreathed for Eve
Down dropped, and all the faded roses shed.—MILTON.

Here "slack" stands for "which had become slack."

(5) But he who hurts a *harmless* neighbour's peace,
Insults *fallen* worth or beauty in distress.—POPE.

Here "harmless" stands for "though he is harmless," and "fallen" for "*when* it is fallen."

(6) From *loveless* youth to *unrespected* age
No passion gratified except her rage.—POPE.

Her youth was devoid of love, the peculiar grace of youth; and her old age was devoid of respect, the peculiar privilege of age; she gratified no passion except her evil temper.

(7) The jay, the rook, the daw,
And each harsh pipe, discordant *heard alone*,
Aid the full concert.—THOMSON.

Here *heard alone* means "when it is heard alone."

Note.—In paraphrasing poetry into prose (if this questionable practice is to be encouraged) one of the first things to be done is to convert such adjectives or participles as those quoted above into verbs, adding such Relatives or Conjunctions as may be necessary.

(6) *The use of epithets for the sake of ornament.*—This peculiarity is in keeping with the chief aim of poetry, which is to please rather than to instruct. An epithet is *ornamental* (without being useful), when it does not contribute to the sense :—

The breezy call of *incense-breathing* morn,
  The swallow twittering from its *straw-built* shed,
The cock's shrill clarion, and the echoing horn,
  No more shall rouse them from their lowly bed.—GRAY.

Here the epithets "breezy," "twittering," "shrill," and "echoing" are all conducive to the sense ; but *incense-breathing* and *straw-built* serve no purpose other than that of ornament.

Ornamental epithets are italicised in the following :—

(1) Oh mother Ida, *many-fountain'd* Ida,
  Dear mother Ida, harken ere I die.—TENNYSON.
(2) Then answer made the *bold* Sir Bedivere.—*Ibid.*

In the following the italicised epithets are essential :—

As shines the moon in *clouded* skies,
She in her *poor* attire was seen.

The *golden* harvest ; the *swift* stag ; the *tawny* lion ; the *briny* deep ; the *mighty* deep, etc., are all stock phrases common in poetry. The epithets are merely ornamental.

Note.—In paraphrasing poetry into prose the student should take care to give greater prominence to the essential than to the ornamental epithets, or leave the latter out altogether.

(7) *The use of graphic or picturesque language.*—This peculiarity, too, arises from the desire to please. Language is graphic or picturesque, when it calls up some image to the mind by dwelling on the particular rather than on the general or abstract.

Arise, my love, my fair, and come away ; for, lo ! the winter is past, the rain is over and gone, the flowers appear on the earth ; the time of the singing of birds is come, and the voice of the turtle is heard in our land ; the fig tree putteth forth her green figs ; and the vines with the tender grapes perfume the air. Arise, my love, my fair, and come away.—*The Song of Solomon.*

420. **Paraphrasing from Poetry to Prose.**—"Poetry is not distinguished from Prose by superior beauty of thought or of expression, but is *a distinct kind* of composition ; and they produce, when each is excellent in its own way, *distinct kinds of pleasure*" (Whately). If we break up the metrical structure of a piece of poetry, we find it inflated and bombastic prose. If

we remove this defect by altering the words, we find it better prose than before; but still it is not good prose. The fact that the same style which gave pleasure in one kind of composition proves offensive in the other shows that poetry and prose are not mutually convertible without injury to both (condensed from Whately).

If these views are borne out by experience, then the practice of paraphrasing poetry into prose should not be encouraged.

CHAPTER XXX.—MAIN DIVISIONS OF POETRY.

421. **Different kinds of Poetry.**—Poetry can be classified, according to *subject*, on lines analogous to those of prose. We will take the divisions in the same order as that given in Chapter xxviii. The reader must not expect the analogy to be quite complete: it is near enough, however, to form the basis of a classification.

422. **Technical.**—In poetry this is called "Didactic." It consists of instruction set forth in verse, and embellished as far as possible with poetic ornament and illustrative anecdotes. Technical subjects, being of a non-literary character, are not suited to poetry; and no attempt at writing such poetry has been made since the beginning of the nineteenth century. It is now quite out of fashion, and perhaps will never come into fashion again.

"As science makes progress in any subject-matter, poetry recedes from it" (Newman). To the same effect Coleridge, in his *Table Talk*, contends that "the real antithesis of poetry is not prose, but science."

Dryden's *Religio Laici* (a defence of the Anglican Church against dissenters), 1682. Pope's *Essay on Criticism* and *Moral Essays* (1688-1744). Somerville's *Chase* (1692-1742). Armstrong's *Art of Preserving Health*, 1744. Dyer's *Fleece*, 1757. Green's *Spleen* (1696-1737). Falconer's *Shipwreck*, 1762. Grainger's *Sugar-cane*. Philips's *Cider*.

423. **History.**—Under this heading we have (*a*) the Epic poem, (*b*) the Historical drama, (*c*) the Historical lyric.

(*a*) *Epic poetry.*—"The epic poem treats of one great complex action in a grand style, and with fulness of detail" (Arnold).

Two more points, it seems to us, must be added to make this definition complete. (1) An epic is told mainly in the form of *narration*. If this point is not added, an epic poem might be confounded with an historical drama, in which the action of the story is told by dialogue. (2) The "great complex action" of an epic, though possibly embellished with a few fictitious details and episodes, must be historical, or at least it must be believed to be historical, and fraught with important consequences either to the race as a whole or to some particular nation. Let us examine this second point a little more closely:—

Homer's *Iliad:* the exploits of Achilles and other great heroes at the siege of Troy. Most of the Greek states traced the origin of their history to these heroes, whose existence no one doubted.

Virgil's *Æneid:* the foundation of Rome by Æneas, the Trojan hero, and the commencement of the quarrel between Rome and Carthage, as prefigured by that between Æneas and Queen Dido.

Lucan's *Pharsalia:* the defeat of Pompey the Great by Julius Cæsar. This poem follows authenticated history very closely.

Tasso's *Jerusalem Delivered:* the rescue of the holy city from the Turks by the Crusaders. Though there is a great deal of romantic fiction in this poem, the groundwork is historical, and of very wide interest.

Milton's *Paradise Lost:* the wars in heaven, the coming of Satan into the earth, the origin of heathen idolatries, the fall of Adam and Eve and their expulsion from Paradise.

Camoen's *Lusiad:* the discovery by Vasco da Gama of the passage to India and Southern Asia *via* the Cape of Good Hope.

Voltaire's *Henriade,* 1724: the history of the French king, Henry IV. (1553-1610).

The true Epic, therefore, has an historical intention. It is well known that Milton intended at one time to make King Arthur and his Knights the subject of an epic. But sharing, as he himself says, the common doubt of most writers as to "who King Arthur was, and whether any such reigned in history," he rejected the *Round Table* as a subject in favour of the Loss of Paradise. Tennyson has treated the Arthurian legends from an allegorical, not an historical, standpoint (page 300, footnote); and he calls them by the more modest title, *Idylls of the King.*

We have no great *national* epic. Milton's epic is not for his own nation only, but for the whole human race. His hero is neither Adam nor Satan, but Providence; and the aim of his epic, as he tells us, is to "justify the ways of God to men."

Doubt has been expressed as to whether we are likely to have any more epics in our literature. "The critical spirit which is now applied to history makes epic poetry more than ever difficult. Whether future poets will succeed in treating real history in the epic manner, renouncing the right of invention entirely, but still finding scope in the selection, interpretation, and appreciation of incidents according to their historical importance, may be left an open question. Carlyle has tried this in his *History of the French Revolution*, which resembles an epic poem more than any other work of this age" (Abbott and Seeley).

Certainly the critical spirit in which history is now studied is adverse to the composition of epic poetry, just as the scientific spirit of the present age is adverse to didactic poetry (§ 422). Yet we do not see why an epic poet of the future should "renounce the right of invention entirely," so long as the same right is conceded to writers of romance (§ 393). We should say that Kingsley's *Hereward the Wake* and Bulwer-Lytton's *Last of the Saxons* and *Last of the Barons* were fit subjects for national epics, and might have reached that standard, had the gifted authors devoted themselves to poetry instead of prose. If Macaulay's splendid fragment, the *Armada*, had been completed in the stately, yet spirited, metre,[1] the fulness of detail, and the lofty patriotic spirit with which it was commenced, we should have had a national epic that would probably be read after his *Essays* and *History* are forgotten.

(*b*) *The historical drama.*—Of such drama the "histories" of Shakspeare (as they are called, to distinguish them from his tragedies and comedies) furnish the best example.

In Roman history we have Shakspeare's *Julius Cæsar; Antony and Cleopatra; Coriolanus.* In English history, *King John; Henry IV.*, Parts I. II.; *Henry V.; Henry VI.*, Parts I. II. III.; *Richard II.; Richard III.; Henry VIII.* (ten dramas). English history in Shakspeare's time was still a tradition. Evidence had not been sifted, nor had events been narrated with historical exactness. It was therefore easier for Shakspeare to dramatise English history than it has been to his successors in the same field.

The best dramas (based on English history) since Shakspeare's time are those by Tennyson, viz. *Queen Mary, Harold,* and *Becket,* in all of which the poet adheres very closely to history.

(*c*) *Historical lyrics.*—Our literature possesses some lyrics that are purely historical, and others that are partly so.

Purely historical: Cowper's *Wreck of the Royal George* (1731-1800); Wolfe's *Burial of Sir John Moore,* 1817; Campbell's *Battle of the Baltic* and *Hohenlinden* (1777-1844); Tennyson's *Revenge, Charge of the Light Brigade,* and battle-scenes in the *Ode on the Duke of Wellington's Funeral.* It is noteworthy that these poems, though strictly historical, are among the very best lyrics in our language.

---

[1] The metre of the *Armada* is the long Iambic line in seven feet. The same metre is used with excellent effect in Chapman's translation of the *Iliad,* and in Morris's translation of the *Æneid.*

Partly historical: Cowper's *Ode on Queen Boadicea;* Gray's *Bard.* In both cases history is told by a prophecy put into the mouth of a Welsh bard.

424. Biography.—So far as we are aware, there is nothing analagous to this in our poetic literature. The best delineations (so far as we know) of private character in metre will be found in Crabbe's poems. But these poems are not of a high order. Private life is not a suitable subject for poetry.

425. Description.—Here our poetic literature is well represented.

Drayton's *Polyolbion* (1563-1631): a topographical and descriptive poem, in which the poet traverses the whole surface of his native land,—county by county, hill by hill, rivulet by rivulet. Milton's *L'Allegro* and *Il Penseroso.* Denham's *Cooper's Hill* (1615-68). Pope's *Windsor Forest* (1688-1744). Addison's *Letter from Italy* (1672-1719). Thomson's *Seasons* (1700-48). Goldsmith's *Traveller* and *Deserted Village* (1728-74). Shenstone's *Schoolmistress* (1714-63). Crabbe's *Village, The Borough, Parish Register* (1754-1832). Rogers's *Italy,* 1822. Byron's *Childe Harold* (1788-1824). Wordsworth's *Evening Walk, Descriptive Sketches* (1770-1850).

426. Reflection.—Poems of this character may be roughly classified into (*a*) longer poems, (*b*) elegies and other shorter poems, (*c*) sonnets, (*d*) songs.

(*a*) *Longer poems.*—Young's *Night Thoughts on Life, Death, and Immortality* (1681-1765). Pope's *Essay on Man.* Akenside's *Pleasures of Imagination* (1721-70). Cowper's *Table Talk, Tirocinium, The Task* (1731-1800). Johnson's *Vanity of Human Wishes* (1709-84). Shelley's *Alastor* (1792-1822). Campbell's *Pleasures of Hope* (1777-1844). Rogers's *Pleasures of Memory* (1763-1855). Wordsworth's *Excursion* (1770-1850). Tennyson's *In Memoriam.*

(*b*) *Elegies and other shorter poems.*—Spenser's *Tears of the Muses* (1553-99). Milton's *Hymn on the Nativity,* and *Lycidas.* Pope's *Elegy on an Unfortunate Lady.* Thomson's *Rule Britannia* (1700-48). Gray's *Ode on the Prospect of Eton, Progress of Poesy, Ode to Adversity, Elegy written in a Country Churchyard* (1716-71). Collins's *Ode on the Passions, Verses to the Memory of Thomson* (1721-59). Cowper's *Shrubbery, Slave's Complaint, On the Receipt of his Mother's Picture, The Dog and the Water-Lily, The Castaway* (1731-1800). Burns's *Cottar's Saturday Night, The Mountain Daisy, Turning up a Mouse's Nest with the Plough* (1759-96). Southey's *Holly Tree* (1774-1843). Wordsworth's *Ode to Duty, On Immortality* (1770-1850). Byron's *Hebrew Melodies, Prisoner of Chillon, Lament of Tasso* (1788-1824). Keats's *Ode on a Grecian Urn* and *Ode to a Nightingale* (1796-1821). Shelley's *Adonais, Ode to a Skylark* (1792-1822). Mrs. Hemans's *Graves of a Household, The Homes of England* (1793-1835). Tennyson's *Two Voices.* Longfellow's *Poems on Slavery, Psalm of Life.*

(*c*) *Sonnets.*—A sonnet generally expresses a single thought or reflection, on some subject connected with love, sorrow, patriotism history, etc. The best sonnets in our language are by Wyatt (1503-42), Surrey (1517-47), Sidney (1554-86), Shakspeare, Milton, Wordsworth, and Martin Tupper.

(*d*) *Songs.*—Short rythmical pieces, in stanzas, intended to be accompanied by music. Moore's *Irish Melodies* is simply a collection of songs composed by him to suit Irish airs.

427. **Fiction.**—This is represented in poetry by (*a*) Allegory, (*b*) Romance, Legend, or Tale, (*c*) Ballads, (*d*) Idylls or Pastorals.

(*a*) *Allegory.* — Spenser's *Faery Queen* (1553-99). Quarles's *Divine Emblems* (1592-1644). Dryden's *Hind and Panther.* Gay's *Fables* (1688-1732). Parnell's *Hermit* (1679-1718). Mandeville's *Fable of the Bees* (1670-1733). Thomson's *Castle of Indolence* (1700-48).

(*b*) *Romance, Legend, or Tale.*—Narrative poetry of this character is well represented in our literature. The first example was set by Chaucer, whose *Canterbury Tales* have scarcely been surpassed. In more recent times we have Beattie's *Minstrel* (1735-1803). Scott's *Lay of the Last Minstrel, Lady of the Lake, Rokeby, Marmion, Lord of the Isles* (1771-1832). Byron's *The Gaiour, Bride of Abydos, Corsair, Lara, Siege of Corinth,* and others (1788-1824). Moore's *Lalla Rookh* (1779-1852). Shelley's *Revolt of Islam, Hellas,* and the *Witch of Atlas* (1792-1822). Campbell's *Gertrude of Wyoming,* 1809. Keats's *Endymion,* 1818. Wordsworth's *White Doe of Rylstone,* 1815. Coleridge's *Christabel* and *Ancient Mariner* (1772-1834). Mrs. Browning's *Aurora Leigh,* 1856. Macaulay's *Lays of Ancient Rome* (legendary) (1800-59). George Eliot's *Spanish Gipsy* (told chiefly in dramatic form, but not intended to be acted). Tennyson's *Princess, Maud.* Robert Browning's *The Ring and the Book.* Whittier's *Narrative and Legendary Poems.* Longfellow's *Evangeline* and *Hiawatha.* Tennyson's *Idylls of the King.*[1]

Romance and Legend are often told in dramatic form, that is, in the form of dialogue as distinct from that of narrative. This, too, is largely represented in our literature.

(*c*) *Ballads.*—Ballads or short metrical romances preceded the longer romances just described. It was Percy's revival of ballads, under the name of *Reliques of Ancient Poetry* (1728-1811), that created a taste for romantic poetry. Next we have Scott's ballads of the *Border Minstrelsy;* Wordsworth's *Lyrical Ballads;* Southey's *Ballads of the Rhine.* The short ballad metre is very similar to that adopted by Scott in his longer romances named under (*b*).

(*d*) *Idylls and Pastorals.*—Spenser's *Shepherd's Calendar,* a series of pastorals divided into twelve parts or months, is the greatest pastoral poem in our language. Pope's *Pastorals,* 1705. Gay's *Shep-*

---

[1] The story of these *Idylls* is not a mere narrative of romantic adventure. Tennyson himself considers it to be partly an allegory :—

An old imperfect tale,
New-old, and shadowing Sense at war with Soul
Rather than that gray king, whose name, a ghost,
Streams like a cloud, etc.

herd's Week. Collins's *Eclogues*. Shenstone's *Pastorals*. Wordsworth's *Michael*, and Tennyson's *Enoch Arden* (both idylls or tales of rustic life).

Idylls are sometimes in dramatic form, as Shakspeare's *As You Like It*, Jonson's *Sad Shepherd*, Beaumont and Fletcher's *Faithful Shepherdess*, and Milton's *Comus*.

428. **Persuasion.**—We have no department of poetry corresponding to oratory in prose. Speeches, however, do occur in poetry, as the Debates in Hell described in *Paradise Lost*, Book ii., and the speeches of Brutus and Antony over the body of Julius Cæsar.

429. **Censure.**—In poetry this is called Satire. It barely admits of poetic treatment: there is nothing in the thought that raises it above ordinary prose. The poetic element, if there is one, lies in the metre and the diction. No metrical satires have been written within the nineteenth century.

Donne's *Satires*, in imitation of Horace and Juvenal (1573-1631). Hall's *Virgidemiarum* (consisting of what he calls "toothless" satires and "biting" satires, 1574-1656). Dryden's *MacFlecknoe* (aimed at his rival, Shadwell), and *Absalom and Achitophel*, a political satire aimed at the Duke of Buckingham and others. Pope's *Dunciad*, the Iliad of the Dunces, an ill-natured and malicious invective against contemporary authors. Johnson's *London*, an insincere satire against London life, in imitation of Juvenal's satire against Rome. Churchill's *Rosciad*, a political satire (1731-64). Byron's *English Bards and Scotch Reviewers*, aimed at contemporary poets and at the editor of the *Edinburgh Review*, who had attacked him. Gifford's *Baviad* and *Mæviad*, and metrical translations of Juvenal's *Satires* (1757-1826).

430. **Humour.**—Humorous poetry is well represented in our literature. It has often been associated with Satire. If the ridicule is more humorous than corrective or spiteful, we class it with the former.

Skelton's *Booke of Philip Sparrow* (1529), describing how a sparrow was buried with the ritual of the Roman Church; the *Booke of Colin Clout*, in ridicule of Wolsey. Butler's *Hudibras* (1612-80), a burlesque poem, more humorous than satirical, aimed at the Puritans. Pope's *Rape of the Lock*, a mock-heroic, the most poetical tale of the humorous class in our literature. Gay's *Trivia, or the Art of Walking the Streets of London*, a mock-didactic poem. Cowper's ballad of *John Gilpin*. Hood's *Whims and Oddities* (1799-1845). *The Ingoldsby Legends*.

431. **Names of different kinds of Poetry.**—We will conclude with giving some account of the names given to the different kinds of poetical composition.

Epic: from Greek *epik-os*, that which pertains to "words"

(Gr. *epos*, a word). Heroic legends told in metrical language were originally recited, not written; hence such poems were called "words." An epic is always a long poem. Its subject is historical, or what was believed to be so (§ 423).

Lyric: from Gr. *lurik-os*, adapted to the lyre. A lyric is always short: it expresses *one* incident, situation, or emotion. Its subjects are love, battle-scenes, patriotism, banqueting. A more dignified kind of lyric is called an Ode (lit. song); as Dryden's Ode on *Alexander's Feast*, or Cowper's on *Queen Boadicea.*

Dramatic: from Gr. *dramatik-os*, that which pertains to action or acting.

Note 1.—Thus in the name "Epic" the idea of recitation is prominent; in "Lyric" the music; and in "Dramatic" the acting.

Note 2.—The word "Lyric" is now loosely used for almost any kind of short poem. Originally it meant an ode expressing the emotions of the poet himself. This is still the proper meaning of "Lyric." The metre may be either regular or irregular.

Idyll: from Gr. *eidullion*, lit. a little picture, a short descriptive poem. Gradually, however, it came to be limited to short poems describing rustic life, with or without rustic incident.

Note.—Tennyson's use of *idyll* in the title *Idylls of the King* is peculiar. He appears to have gone back to the etymological use of the Greek *eidullion*, which the ancient Greeks did not limit to rustic life. The *Idylls of the King* are anything but rustic.

Pastoral: from Lat. *pastor*, a shepherd. Pastorals, like idylls, describe rural life; but such poems usually consist of conversations between shepherds about their love-affairs, their losses, the state of their flocks, etc.

Elegy: from Gr. *elegeion*, an "*elegos*" or lament told in metre. The name is given to mournful or any other kind of serious poetry, as Gray's *Elegy in a Country Churchyard*, Shelley's *Adonais* (on the death of Keats). Tennyson's *In Memoriam* is a prolonged elegy, in memory of Arthur Hallam.

Ballad: from Old French *balade* (Low Latin *ballare*, to dance); lit. a dancing song. It now means a short legendary tale, told in a light and rapid metre, and fit for recitation; example, *Chevy Chase.* Macaulay's *Lays of Ancient Rome* are enlarged ballads, as Tennyson's *In Memoriam* is an enlarged elegy.

Romance: the word was originally applied to the legends of popular heroes, told in medieval verse. It is now applied to any tale of striking adventure, with or without a legendary basis, whether told in prose or verse. Scott's metrical romances, such as *Rokeby*, are very like enlarged ballads, and are told in the rapid ballad-metre.

Satire: Lat. *satira*, *satura*, from *satura lanx*, a dish full of mixed foods, a medley (Skeat).

Didactic: from Gr. *didaktik-os*, instructional.

Sonnet: from Fr. *sonnet*, Ital. *sonetto*, lit. "a little strain." A short poem limited to the exposition of a single thought or sentiment, that may be amatory, reflective, patriotic, or of any other kind.

Blank verse: unrimed verse, borrowed from Italian. First used by the Earl of Surrey, who translated Virgil's *Æneid* Books II. and IV., into this kind of metre. It was Christopher Marlowe who in 1587 first used it for the drama, in his play *Tamburlaine*. Milton speaks contemptuously of rime, "the invention of a barbarous age, to set off wretched matter and lame metre." "True metre," he says, "consists in apt numbers, fit quantity of syllables, and the sense variously drawn out from one line to another." Among the best specimens of Blank Verse in our literature are Shakspeare's dramas, Milton's epic, Thomson's *Seasons*, Keats's *Hyperion*, Tennyson's *Idylls of the King*, and George Eliot's *Spanish Gypsy*.

PART V.—HISTORY OF THE LANGUAGE.

CHAPTER XXXI.—ORIGIN AND GROWTH OF ENGLISH.

SECTION 1.—ENGLISH AND COGNATE LANGUAGES.

432. Celtic.—Before the English invaded and occupied Britain, the language spoken by the native tribes—the Britons—consisted of various dialects of Celtic, remains of which are still traceable in the Cymric or Welsh, the language of Wales, and in the Gaelic of the Highlands of Scotland. The Manx dialect of the Isle of Man and the Erse of Ireland belong to the same family—the Celtic.

Latin.—When Britain was annexed to the Roman empire, A.D. 43, Latin was the language of the ruling class, and during the last two centuries of the Roman occupation it was the language of the Church also. A form of Latin was beginning to be spoken by the native Celts; and this, had the Romans remained, would in time have overspread the island. But after A.D. 409, when the Romans finally left the country, all traces of the Latin language, and nearly all traces of the Celtic also, were swept away by a race of heathen, who, coming from the mouths of the Rhine, the Weser, and the Elbe, swarmed into Britain, bringing their own language with them. These invaders were the English, a race of Low-Germans, *i.e.* Germans inhabiting the low-lying lands facing the North Sea between Belgium and Denmark.

English.—In the order of time this was the third language spoken in Britain. It has not only overspread the British Isles, but is now the dominant language in North America, Australia, New Zealand, India, Burma, and South Africa, and is beginning to be spoken by the natives in Egypt and in several parts of China and Japan. The name "*Ænglisc*" (English) was originally confined to the dialect spoken by the Angles,—the tribe that occupied Northumbria. As this was the first of the new dialects that formed a literature of its own, the name was gradually extended to all the other Low-German dialects spoken in Britain, to distinguish them from *Læden* (Latin), which after the conversion of the Low-German tribes to Christianity had again become the language of the Church.

433. The Aryan family of languages.—The three languages named already, together with certain other languages to be named below, all belong to a larger group called the Aryan; and this is subdivided into East-Aryan and West-Aryan :—

East-Aryan :—

Sanskrit, and the neo-Sanskrit languages of India.
Persian : the old and modern languages of Persia.
Armenian, ancient and modern.

West-Aryan :—

Greek, ancient and modern.
Romanic : Latin and the neo-Latin languages of Europe (**French**, Spanish, Portuguese, Italian, and Roumanian).
Slavonic : the languages (ancient and modern) of Russia, Poland, Bohemia, Bulgaria, and Servia.
Lettic : the languages spoken in Lithuania and in the Baltic provinces of Russia and Germany.
Teutonic : Low-German (including English) ; High-German.

434. The Teutonic family.—Teutonic (from Lat. *Teutonicus*, a corruption of German *Deutsch*, which we have Anglicised to *Dutch*) is thus a division of the West-Aryan group, and this again is subdivided into Low-German and High-German.

High-German, the official and literary language of the German empire (called High, because it first sprang up in the higher parts of Germany, *i.e.* those farthest removed from the sea), is an offshoot from Low-German, that is, the language of the low-lands facing the North Sea. High-German was Low-German once, and did not begin to exist as a separate branch until after the beginning of the eighth century A.D. In Germany itself, but not elsewhere, it is now the more important branch of the two.

Low-German includes:—(1) the Gothic or South-eastern group, of which fragments are still preserved in the translation of parts of the Bible by Ulphilas, A.D. 350; (2) the Scandinavian or North-eastern group, or more briefly the Scandian,—the languages of Sweden, Norway, and Denmark ; (3) the Western group,—Saxon, Friesic, Flemish, Dutch. It was out of a mixture of the two groups last named that the English Language was formed.

SECTION 2.—OLD ENGLISH.

435. Periods in the growth of English.—The growth of English has been subdivided into three main periods, to each of which approximate dates have been assigned,—approximate, because changes in language cannot be other than gradual and continuous :—

I. Old English ; from A.D. 450 to about 1200.
II. Middle English ; from A.D. 1200 to about 1500.
III. Modern English ; from A.D. 1500 to the present time.

Old English has been called the period of *full* endings, Mid. Eng. of *levelled* endings, and Mod. Eng. of *lost* endings :—

Old	leorn-*ian*	món-*a*	sun-*ne*	sun-*u*	stán-*as*
Mid.	lern-*en*	mon-*e*	sun-*ne*	sun-*e*	ston-*es*
Mod.	learn	moon	sun	son	stones

By *levelled* endings is meant that the vowels *a*, *o*, *u* are all levelled or assimilated to *e*. By *lost* endings is meant that none, or only a very few, of them have remained, and these few have usually become non-syllabic. Thus *stán-as* (two syllables) has become *stones*, one syllable ; and *luf-o-de* or *luf-o-den* (three syllables) has become *loved* (one syllable).

436. Dialects of Old English.—Old English consisted of three main dialects :—

(1) The **Northumbrian**, covering the whole tract north of the river Humber up to the Highlands of Scotland. It is represented at the present day by the dialects of Northumberland and Lowland Scotch, and less perfectly by those of Yorkshire and Lincolnshire. This was imported by a Scandinavian tribe called *Angles*, who came from what is now known as the Duchy of Schleswig. Although it gave its name *Ænglisc* (English) to all the other Low-German dialects spoken in Britain (§ 432), it is least like the standard English of the present day. Its Scandian character has stuck to it through all vicissitudes ; and the marked peculiarities that still cling to the Scotch and Northumberland dialects are due to their Scandinavian origin.

Note.—One of the marked peculiarities of this dialect is the retention of its original gutturals. Thus Northerners to this day say *kirk*, *brig*, *rig*, while Midlanders and Southerners say *church*, *bridge*, *ridge*.

(2) The **Mercian** dialect, spoken between the Humber and the Thames, the great ancestor of Modern English. This, according to the last researches, was imported by Frisian tribes,

who spoke Friesic on the Continent, and dwelt on the coast-lands between the Ems and the Elbe. To this day the Friesic dialect is more like English than any other continental language. It was more closely allied to the dialect of the Saxons than to the Scandinavian dialects of the Angles and Danes. It was called *Mercian* from Mercia, the name of the powerful kingdom which the Frisians founded in the heart of Great Britain.

(3) The **Wessex** dialect, spoken south of the Thames. This was imported by *Saxon* tribes from the Continent, who before they came into Britain inhabited the lower coast-lands of the Rhine. The dialect was called "Wessex" (just as the midland dialect was called "Mercian"), from the kingdom in which it was spoken. The subjects of Alfred the Great were called "West-Saxons," or Wessex men; and hence their dialect also was called Wessex. *Now*, however, the name by which this dialect is best known is that of "Anglo-Saxon,"—a name given to it by some scholars of the sixteenth century, who wished to revive the language of Alfred the Great, and knew of no better name to give to it. It was never called by this name, however, either by Alfred the Great himself or by any of his successors.

Note.—The name "Anglo-Saxon" is misleading. The Saxon or Wessex dialect was quite distinct from the Angle or Scandinavian dialect. Compare the rustic dialects spoken to this day south of the Thames with those spoken north of the Humber: and that will show how very different they were in their origin. The best interpretation to put upon the word "Anglo-Saxon" is to say that "Anglo-Saxon" means the Saxon dialect spoken in England as distinct from the Saxon dialect spoken on the Continent. With this interpretation the name "Anglo-Saxon" will convey a useful meaning.

437. Mixed character of Old English.—English, then, even in its oldest period, was not a single Teutonic dialect, but the sum of at least three Teutonic dialects,—a Scandinavian dialect (the Angle) in the north, a Frisian dialect (the Mercian) in the centre, and a Saxon dialect (the Wessex) in the south.

We are apt to speak of the Wessex dialect (misnamed "Anglo-Saxon") as if it covered the whole ground of Old English. This is a mistake. The Wessex dialect is merely a third part of Old English, not the whole of it. There are instances in which it fails to give any clue to the origin of modern English words. For instance, the word "*are*" is not derived from A.S. or Wessex "*sindon*," but from the Mercian "*ărun*," which was itself borrowed from the Northumbrian dialect.

The reason why we look to Anglo-Saxon rather than to Mercian and Northumbrian for the origin of most of our Teutonic words, is that a large part of the Anglo-Saxon literature has been preserved, while most of the other two literatures has been lost. We do so, therefore, from necessity, not from choice. If we had our choice, we should go to the Mercian or Midland dialect, from which modern English has chiefly sprung.

438. Old and Modern English compared.—Old English is distinguished from Modern by two chief characteristics.

(*a*) It was in the main a *Synthetical* language, *i.e.* it had a large number of inflexions, which modern English has discarded. "Synthesis" means "putting together," "adding on." A language is said to be in the Synthetical stage, when it expresses the grammatical relations of words by adding some inflexion to the stems of nouns, adjectives, pronouns, and verbs. A language that discards such endings as much as possible, and in their place makes a freer use of prepositions and other auxiliary words, is said to be in the Analytical stage. This is the character of Modern English.

(*b*) It was in the main a *pure* language: that is, it contained very few words not of Teutonic origin; whereas modern English is very mixed, more than half of its vocabulary being non-Teutonic. Layamon's *Brut*, though it was not completed till a century and a half after the Norman Conquest, and contains some 56,000 lines, has scarcely 150 French words in it. The number of Latin words amounted to less than 200; and the number of Celtic borrowings did not come to 15.

(1) God blets-*o-de* Noe and his sun-*a*, and cwæth hem tó:
(*God blessed Noah and his sons, and quoth them to:*
Weax-*ath* and bé-*oth* gemenigfil-*de* and á-fyll-*ath* th-*á* eorth-*an*.
Wax (ye) *and be* (ye) *manifolded and fill* (ye) *the earth.*)

(2) God bless-ed Noah and his son-s, and said unto them, Be fruitful and multiply, and replenish the earth.

Observe that in (1) every word (barring the Hebrew name *Noe*) is Teutonic; whereas in (2) there are two Romanic words, *multiply* and *replenish*, and one Hybrid or mixed word, *fruitful*. Observe also that in (1) the verbs, adjectives, and nouns have inflexions, which modern English has discarded.

439. Continuity of English.—The name "English," taken in its widest sense, denotes the language used by the English people from their first settlement in Britain up to the present time, in whatever parts of the world they may have settled since. It has been growing for the last 1400 years, and is now so unlike its earliest forms that most persons would probably find it harder to learn Anglo-Saxon than to learn French. Yet we must call Anglo-Saxon a form of English, unless we are prepared to deny the name of Englishman to Alfred the Great; for that was the language that he wrote and spoke. Moreover, there are many words that have never altered their form within the historical period, such as *corn*, *lamb*, *nest*, *ram*, *wind*, *hand*, *spell*, *his*, *him*, *word*, *in*, *bill* (axe), *twist*, *bed*, *gold*, *can*, *blind*, *storm*, *is*, *winter*, which were so spelt in the seventh century.

440. Periods of Anglo-Saxon.—The Mercian and the Northumbrian literatures are too fragmentary to admit of anything like a subdivision into periods. On the other hand, the Anglo-Saxon literature has, through the influence of Alfred the Great, been so well preserved, that two great periods, followed by a transitional one, can be traced:—

	A.D. A.D.
Early A.S. (the language of Alfred) . . .	700- 900
Late A.S. (the language of Ælfric) . . .	900-1100
Transitional Period (the language of Layamon) .	1100-1200

Alfred the Great, born in 849, superintended the translation from Latin into Saxon of the *History of the World* by Orosius, the *Church History* by Bede, the *Consolations of Philosophy* by Boethius, and the *Pastorals* of St. Gregory. He also superintended the compilation of the early portions of the *Old English Chronicle*.

Ælfric wrote a collection of *Homilies* and other works; and Layamon was author of the poem called *Brut*, on the kings of Britain (alluded to in § 438, *b*).

SECTION 3.—MIDDLE ENGLISH.

441. Character of Middle English.—In its Middle period, 1200-1500 A.D., the English language went through three kinds of change.

(*a*) The Mercian, or, as we should now call it, the Midland, dialect became eventually dominant, taking the place of the Wessex or Southern, which up to the Norman Conquest, and for about two centuries later, had been in the first rank.

(*b*) Many of the vowel-sounds were changed; many of the old inflexions were lost; and all that were not lost were levelled (§ 435); form-words, viz. prepositions and auxiliary verbs, were more freely used; many Strong verbs became Weak.

(*c*) A very great addition was made to the vocabulary. A

large number of French words, which for about 200 years had been used only by the clergy and the upper classes and in the law-courts, filtrated at last into the native speech, and became permanently fixed as part of our English vocabulary. The absorption of all this French facilitated the introduction of fresh relays of Latin, which throughout the Middle Ages continued to be the language of the learned and of the church.

442. Tests of the three Dialects.—Two marks of distinction between the three dialects may be here mentioned. (1) The ending of the Present Indicative plural: the Northern dialect had *-es*, as "sing-*es*" (we, you, or they sing); the Midland had *-en* or *-e*, as "sing-*en*" or "sing-*e*" (we, you, or they sing); the Southern had *-eth*, as "sing-*eth*" (we, you, or they sing). (2) The ending of the Pres. Part.: the Northern had *-and*, as "sing-*and*" (singing); the Midland had *-ende*, as "sing-*ende*" (singing); the Southern had *-inde*, as "sing-*inde*" (singing).

Both points are important. In (1) the final *-en* or *-e* of the Midland dialect fell off at the close of the Middle period, leaving only the stem of the verb, such as "*sing*," for the plural form of the Pres. Indic., the very form that we have now. In (2) the final *-inde* of the Southern dialect superseded the *-ende* of the Midland, and became itself converted to *-ing*, the very form that we now possess of the Pres. Participle.

443. Supremacy of the Midland dialect.—The rivalry between the three dialects, which lasted till about 1400 A.D., ended with the triumph of the Midland, or rather with that of the East-Midland, the area of which included the important cities of London, Oxford, and Cambridge,—London, the seat of commerce and of government; Oxford and Cambridge, the two great national seats of learning. In towns like Oxford, Cambridge, and London all dialects met; and hence the Midland dialect has borrowed from both the others. Thus the phrase "they are" is of Northern origin; the phrase "he hath" is of Southern. The Midland adopted both.

"The Mercians," says Trevisa, A.D. 1387, "who are men of the middle of England, being as it were partners with the extremities, better understand the side-languages, Northern and Southern, than Northern and Southern understand each other."

Other reasons for the ascendancy of the Midland dialect were the following:—(1) It was the dialect in which the *Old English*

Chronicle, that had been written in the Wessex dialect up to the time of the Norman Conquest, was completed up to the year 1154,—the death of Stephen. In 1258 A.D. it was the dialect used by Henry III. in his proclamation for summoning a parliament from all the counties of England. It was the dialect used by Wycliff, the first translator of the Bible into the popular speech; and by Chaucer, himself a Londoner, who raised English poetry to a height of excellence that has hardly been surpassed since. (2) When Caxton introduced printing into England in 1477, the Midland dialect was the only one that he patronised. The Midland dialect thus became the literary speech of the nation. Until this standard had been established the different local varieties were dialects of co-equal rank. But when a standard speech had been formed, the dialects or local varieties fell into a lower rank, and were regarded as the speech of the unlearned.

Note.—The degradation of the Southern dialect was rapid and sudden. It ceased to be used for literary purposes after 1400. Not so the Northern dialect, which in the Scotch lowlands at least was represented by a distinguished line of poets from 1422 to 1555, viz. James I. (of Scotland), Henryson, Dunbar, Gavin Douglas, and Lyndsay. Burns is the last great poet who wrote in this dialect.

444. Danish influence on the Northern dialect.—The Danes were of the same stock as the Angles,—Scandinavian. Their geographical position in Europe led them, as it had led the Angles about 500 years before, to take the shortest cut across the North Sea into Britain; and this necessarily landed them in the country north of the Humber. The settlement of the Danes in the north of England and in the Scotch Lowlands had a marked effect on the Northumbrian or Northern dialect. By about 1250 A.D. this dialect had become almost as flexionless as modern English. Since the stems of the words were the same with the Angles as with the Danes, the two tribes could understand each other better by dropping their inflexions than by retaining them. Thus out of the Anglian "sun-*u*" and the Danish "sun-*r*" the more simple word "sun-*e*" (now changed to "sun") was formed. The same kind of process is now going forward in the United States, where German immigrants, settled among English-speaking people, find it convenient to strip their German words of their inflexions, so as to adapt them more easily to English speech.

445. Danish influence on the Midland dialect.—The

incursions of the Danes were by no means limited to the country north of the Humber. Their conquest of East Anglia and the greater part of Mercia must have materially affected the Midland dialect, from which our modern English has mainly sprung.

The following are examples of words in very common use, all of which were borrowed by the Midland from the Northern dialect :—

Same.—This took the place of the Southern *thilke.*

Are.—This took the place of the Southern *sindon.*

They, their, them.—These superseded the Southern *hi, heora, hem,* the old plurals of *he.*

Till.—This preposition is of Scandinavian origin, and was unknown to the Anglo-Saxon or Wessex dialect.

Note.—The words *that, ours, yours,* and *she* have also been ascribed to Northern influence. But this is a mistake. The first three are Anglo-Saxon, and *scæ̂* (the earliest form of *she*) is pure Midland ; for it has been found in the later chapters of the *Old English Chronicle,* that were written in Peterborough, in the East-Midland dialect (see § 443).

446. The Norman Conquest.—The Norman Conquest, which took place about 180 years after Alfred the Great had defeated the Danes and compelled them to accept his terms for the division of the island, had much more extensive consequences. The Normans or Northmen were themselves of Danish or Norse origin, and therefore, like the Danes, cousins of the English. But it happened that before their conquest of England they had lived for five or six generations on the north-west coast of France, where they forgot their mother tongue, and became French in speech. This speech they brought with them to England ; and for at least a century and a half after the Conquest it was doubtful which of the two languages, French or English, would ultimately triumph. They kept sullenly apart all those years, refusing to intermingle,—English being still the language of the masses, and French (or rather the Norman dialect of French) that of the ruling class—the Court, the aristocracy, the legal profession, and to some extent the priesthood. The large poem of 56,000 lines, known as Layamon's *Brut* (§ 438, *b*), contains scarcely any words of French origin ; and this was not completed before the year 1205.

It was not till after 1300 that French words began to be incorporated in English *in large numbers.* But by this time English had made itself the daily speech of the upper classes, as it always had been of the lower, while French was going more and more out of daily use. The incorporation, when it did come, was very complete. Such words as *grace*, *peace*, *fame*, *beef*, *ease* (all of French origin) appear now to be as much a part of our original language as *kindness*, *rest*, *shame*, *ox*, *care*, all of which are native words that were in common use in the time of Alfred. Verbs were borrowed as freely as nouns and adjectives, which proves that the two languages had completely coalesced.

447. Triumph of English over French.—The triumph of the English language over the French was marked by the following events. In 1204 the loss of Normandy, by separating England from France, broke the connection between the French and the Anglo-Norman aristocracies. In 1215 a combination of English and Norman barons forced King John to sign the Magna Charta. In 1258 English was officially used for the first time since the Conquest, in the celebrated proclamation used in the name of Henry III. for summoning a parliament of *barons* from all parts of England; which shows that French had ceased to be the only language spoken and read by the Anglo-Norman nobles. In 1349, three years after the victory at Crecy, it was ruled that Latin should be no longer taught in England through the medium of French. In 1362 it was ruled that all pleadings in the law-courts should be conducted in English, for the reason (as stated in the preamble to the Act), "that French has become much unknown in the realm." We may safely say that by the year 1400 French was not much spoken in England. A vast English literature had sprung up in the interim, which was as popular in the halls of nobles as in the humbler dwellings of knights and burgesses.

448. French Influence on English Grammar.—The only influence of French on English grammar was to accelerate the change from Synthetical to Analytical: it did for the Midland and Southern dialects what the Danish language had already done for the Northern (§ 444). We say *accelerate* designedly; for the change would have come in any case, though possibly neither so rapidly nor so completely as it did, without the help of French. Symptoms of the change had shown themselves clearly enough before French influence had begun to work, and even to some extent before the Conquest. In Layamon's *Brut*, which shows no signs of French influence and contains *very few* words of French origin, the "levelled" inflexions of the Middle period begin to be seen side by side with the full inflexions of Old

English. The growing tendency of English was to strengthen the accent on the *first* syllable, so that the last syllable, containing the inflexion, was slurred over or lightly sounded. Thus, forms like *nam-a* (name), *sun-u* (son), became *nam-e*, *sun-e*. In the same way all unaccented vowels in the final syllable excepting *i* were "levelled" (§ 435) or assimilated to *e*, so that *-an*, *-as*, *-ath*, *-on*, *-od* became *-en*, *-es*, *-eth*, *-en*, and *-ed*. Adjectives of French origin seldom took English inflexions, which helped English adjectives to discard theirs.

449. **English Grammar exclusively Teutonic.**—The grammatical structure of our language was as strictly Teutonic by the close of the Middle period as it had been before the Conquest, notwithstanding the shock that it had received in the interim. The Teutonic elements are noted below:—

(*a*) *Grammatical forms*:—

(1) Noun-inflexions; the possessive *-'s*, plural in *-en*, plural in *-s*.

(2) All pronoun-inflexions.

(3) All verb-inflexions; the personal endings *-st*, *-th*, and *-s*; tense endings *-d* and *-t*; participial endings *-en* and *-ing*; gerundial ending *-ing*.

(4) Adjective suffixes *-er* and *-est* marking degrees of comparison; and the auxiliary words *more* and *most* used for the same purpose.

(5) All the suffixes used for forming adverbs, and many of those used for forming verbs.

(*b*) *Grammatical words*:—

(1) All nouns forming the Plural by vowel-change.

(2) Almost all nouns having the same form for the Plural as for the Singular.

(3) All the pronouns,—Personal, Demonstrative, Relative, and Interrogative.

(4) All the Demonstrative adjectives,—*the*, *this*, *that*, *other*, *such*, etc.

(5) All the Numerals except *second*, *dozen*, *million*, *billion*, *trillion*.

(6) All the Distributive adjectives.

(7) All adjectives of irregular comparison.

(8) All Strong verbs (except *strive* and possibly one or two more).

(9) All Weak verbs, excepting *catch*, that have different vowels in the Pres. and Past tenses.

(10) All Auxiliary verbs.

(11) All Defective and Anomalous verbs.

(12) The old Causative verbs, viz. those formed by vowel-change.

(13) Almost all the prepositions.

(14) Almost all the conjunctions.

(15) Most of the adverbs of Time and Place.

(16) All pronominal adverbs.

It is easy to make sentences on ordinary subjects without using a single word of French or Latin origin. But it is very difficult to make the shortest English sentence out of French or

Latin words, and wherever such words are used, they are forced to submit to all the duties and liabilities of English ones.

450. French Influence on the English Vocabulary.—The Norman Conquest established in England a foreign court, a foreign aristocracy, and a foreign hierarchy. The French language, in its Norman dialect, became for a time the only polite medium of intercourse. The native tongue, at first despised as the language of a subject race, was left for a time to the use of boors and serfs. Words denoting the commonest and most familiar objects,[1] such as the elements, the seasons, divisions of time, natural scenery, soils and metals, the closest kinds of kinship, parts of a house, food and clothing, agricultural implements and processes, trees and plants, quadrupeds, birds, water animals, insects, parts of the body, actions and postures, etc., are to this day, in a large number of instances (though not by any means exclusively), of Teutonic origin.

A few generations after the Conquest, when English began to be used for general literature in the place of French, most of the terms at hand to express ideas above those of daily life were to be found in the French of the privileged and learned classes, who, for the past two centuries, had had the chief control of art, science, and law. Hence each successive literary effort of the reviving English tongue shows a large adoption of French words to supply the place of the forgotten native ones. Thus in general literature we have *ancestors* for *fore-elders*, *beauty* for *fair-hood*, *caution* for *fore-wit*, *conscience* for *in-wit*, *library* for *book-hoard*, *obstructive* for *hinder-some*, *remorse* for *ayen-bite* (=again-bite), *astronomy* for *star-cræft*, *arithmetic* for *rím-cræft*, *agriculture* for *feld-tilth*, etc.

---

[1] But it is possible to underrate the influence of French in furnishing names even for common and familiar objects. Elements: *air* is French. Seasons: *autumn* is Latin. Divisions of time: *hour*, *minute*, *second* are French. Natural scenery: *valley*, *mountain*, *gravel*, *river*, *torrent*, *fountain* are French. Kinship: *uncle*, *aunt*, *nephew*, *niece* are French; and *grandfather*, *grandmother* are half French. Parts of a house: *brick*, *lintel*, *storey*, *attic*, *ceiling*, *tile*, etc., are French; and *door-post* is half French. Food: *beef*, *mutton*, *veal*, *venison*, etc., are French. Clothing: *gown*, *coat*, *chemise*, *trousers*, etc., are French. Agricultural implements: *hatchet*, *hoe*, *coulter* are French. Agricultural processes: "*turn the soil*," *manure*, *fruit*, *herb*, *vegetable*, *cole*, *cauli-flower*, *cabbage*, *grain*, *granary*, *stable*, *car* are French. Trees and plants: *damson*, *chestnut*, *almond*, *laurel*, *bay*, *mustard*, etc., are French. Colours: *blue*, *violet*, *lake*, *crimson*, *carmine*, *mauve* are French.

Another effect of French on the English vocabulary was to give it a dualistic or *bilingual* character. Thus nouns or adjectives often go in pairs; as *foe, enemy; hostile, inimical; home, domicile; homely, domestic; unlikely, improbable; bold, courageous,* etc. Sometimes a Romanic adjective is given to a Teutonic noun; as *bovine, ox; oval, egg; human, man,* etc. Verbs, too, often go in pairs; as *cast out, eject; be, exist; buy back, redeem,* etc.

451. Other Results of French Influence.—To French influence combined with Latin we owe certain other effects besides those already named :—

(*a*) *Word-building.*—We owe to this influence a very large number of prefixes and suffixes, many of which are still in living use for forming new words. Our Romanic suffixes are even more numerous than our Teutonic ones. The French fem. suffix *-ess* superseded the Teutonic *-ster.* We have also many hybrid words, in which Teutonic and Romanic elements are compounded; as *cott-age* (from Anglian *cot,* "hut," + *age,* Fr. suffix). Our language thus gained in wealth as much as it lost in purity.

(*b*) *Spelling.*—The chief, perhaps the only, harm that French did to our language was to disturb the phonetic spelling that it possessed in its earliest form. It is to French that we owe the unnecessary compound *qu* (the function of which was served equally well by our own *cw* in A.S.), the sibilant sound of *c* before the vowels *e* and *i*, the sound of *g* as *j* before the same vowels, and the use of the letter *i* as a consonant to denote the sound now expressed by *j*. Thus almost all words containing a *j* are of French or other foreign origin.

Note.—Among the effects commonly ascribed to French influence, it is said that our language has lost the power of forming new compounds. This oft-repeated statement is a pure fallacy. Tennyson coins whenever he likes: cf. *proxy-wedded, crimson-circled, slow-arching, heavy-shotted, hammock-shroud, hundred-throated,* etc. We form fewer compounds than we once did, because we have less occasion to do so, not because we cannot. Our vocabulary has been so enriched by borrowings, that words usually exist to express the ideas we want. Other coinages by Tennyson are the following :—*breaker-beaten, flesh-fallen, gloomy-gladed, lady-laden, mock-meek, rain-rotten, tongue-torn, work-wan, slowly-mellowing, hollower-bellowing,* etc. "Cod-liver-oil" was coined the moment the name was wanted. Cf. "Hand-in-hand-fire-and-life-Insurance-Society"; this is one large compound, though the hyphens between the words are omitted to save the trouble of writing them.

SECTION 4.—MODERN ENGLISH.

452. Commencement of the Modern Period.—The period of Modern English begins somewhere about A.D. 1500, or a little later. The commencement of this period was preceded or accompanied by several great events, which, in other countries besides England, mark the commencement of Modern as distinct from Medieval history. The art of printing was introduced into England in 1477 by Caxton, who learnt it from the Dutch. Columbus discovered the West Indies in 1492, which led to the discovery of the American continent soon after. Vasco de Gama rounded the Cape of Good Hope in 1497, which brought Southern Asia in touch for the first time with the western nations of Europe. The Renaissance or Revival of Learning opened up new fields of research; and in 1497 Erasmus, the Dutchman, one of the foremost champions of the new learning, visited England, and took up his residence here for a time. Greek began to be studied for the first time in the English Universities. Luther had just begun to lecture in Germany, when Henry VII., the first of our Tudor kings, died on 21st April A.D. 1509.

453. Characteristics of Modern English.—The Modern form of English is distinguished from those that preceded it by two main characteristics:—

(a) Our language has now become almost entirely *analytical*; as analytical, in fact, as it is ever likely to be, and more so than any other Teutonic language. Final *e*, which in the Middle period was syllabic, has either disappeared or is retained to give length to the preceding vowel. The plural and possessive suffixes of nouns have ceased to be syllabic, except when the preceding consonant happens to be of such a kind as to compel the sounding of the final *-es*. Ben Jonson, the dramatist, who wrote a treatise on English grammar, lamented the loss of the plural suffix *-en* in verbs (see § 442, where it is shown that *-en* was the Plural inflexion of the Midland dialect). But the lamentation was in vain; for the suffix had gone beyond recovery. The fact that this suffix, together with the suffix *e* (levelled from *a*, *o*, *u*, see § 435), disappeared *after* Norman-French had ceased to operate, and not while it was still dominant, shows that the tendency to discard inflexions was inherent in the language itself, and was merely accelerated, not produced, by foreign influences.

(b) The Modern period is marked by a large number of new

borrowings, and these from a great variety of sources. The study of Greek, introduced into England with the revival of learning, led to the influx of a considerable number of Greek words, in addition to such as had been previously borrowed through the medium of Latin. "Surrey, Wiat, and others introduced a knowledge of Italian literature, which soon had a great effect, especially on the drama. Several Italian words came in through this and other influences, either directly or through the medium of French. The discoveries of Columbus and the opening up of the New World brought us into contact with Spanish, and many names of things obtained from the West Indies came to us in a Spanish form. The English victories in India, beginning with the battle of Plassy in 1757, made us acquainted with numerous East Indian words; and English maritime adventure has brought us words from nearly all parts of the world. During the resistance of the Netherlands to Spain, in the time of Elizabeth, English borrowed several words from Dutch: it was not uncommon for English volunteers to go over to Holland to aid in the repulse of the Spaniards. English has also borrowed, chiefly in very recent times, from German, and even from remote continental languages, including Russian, and even Turkish and Hungarian. In fact, there are few languages from which we have failed to borrow words either directly or indirectly. It often requires a little patience to discover from what foreign language a word has been borrowed, and at what period. It is some help to remember that most of the words taken from remote and somewhat unlikely sources have been borrowed during the Modern period, *i.e.* since 1500" (Skeat).

454. Subdivisions of the Modern Period.—The Modern period can be subdivided into three stages or periods:—

I. Tudor English, from about 1500 to 1625, the date of the death of James I. Speaking roughly, its literature may be called that of the sixteenth century, though it goes some twenty-five years beyond it.

II. The English of the remainder of the seventeenth century, which comes to an end with Dryden, who died in A.D. 1700. The language of Milton abounds in Latinisms and other idioms, which are not now admissible. The age of Dryden is marked by a large number of borrowings from Modern French, a good deal of which is not even yet fully assimilated. It is also marked by the thorough establishment for the first time of "*its*" as the Possessive form of "*it.*"

III. The remaining period up to the present day. One main difference between the two centuries represented by I. and II. on the one hand, and the two which have succeeded it on the other, is that "the former is the period of experiment and comparative licence both in the importation of new words and in the formation of idioms and grammatical constructions. The latter period, on the other hand, is marked by selection and organisation" (Sweet). The grammar of Shakspeare is in some points so unlike that of the present day that it has been found necessary for a modern scholar (Dr. Abbott) to publish a "Shakspearian Grammar" explaining its peculiarities. The forms and inflexions used by Shakspeare and his contemporaries are, however, strictly modern.

455. Decay of Dialects.—In Old and Middle English we were forced to recognise three distinct literary dialects,—the Anglian, the Mercian, and the Wessex in the Old period, answering to the Northern, the Midland, and the Southern in the Middle period.

In Modern English, owing to the complete ascendancy of the Midland dialect, which before the close of the Middle period had left no rivals in the field, we recognise only one language, viz. that of Modern English literature.

Provincial dialects still exist in different parts of England. We may still hear *housen* for *houses* in Wiltshire and Dorsetshire, *brig* for *bridge* in some parts of Yorkshire. But such dialects are no longer literary, or are revived merely as literary curiosities, as in Barnes's *Dorsetshire Poems*, or Tennyson's "Northern Farmer" in imitation of the Lincolnshire dialect.

The only English dialect that survived for some time longer in literary form was what we now call Lowland Scotch, though this is really nothing but a modern form of the old Northern dialect (see § 436). Burns's poetry is mostly written in this dialect, and is its best modern representative.

CHAPTER XXXII.—BORROWINGS.

SECTION 1.—CELTIC.

456. Fewness of Celtic borrowings.—The Celtic borrowings were *very few*, much fewer than has been supposed. Those Britons who were not killed or ousted by the invading English were so completely conquered, that they had every motive for acquiring the new speech and forgetting their own. We are not even sure whether the bulk of them still spoke Celtic; for many had come to speak a rustic kind of Latin, as in Gaul.

Most of the words supposed to have been borrowed by English from Celtic, and still quoted as Celtic in some books, are now known to have been borrowed the other way; as *bake, basket, cart, cradle, down* (hill), *put, slough, lad, lass, loop, boast*, etc.

Celtic appears in a few geographical names and a few names of objects :—

(*a*) *Geographical names* :—*Avon* (river); *exe, axe* (river; cf. Ex-eter, Ax-minster); *aber* (mouth of river; cf. Aber-deen); *car* (castle; cf. Car-lisle); *llan* (sacred enclosure; cf. Llan-daff); *combe* (hollow in a hill-side; cf. Ilfra-combe); *strath* (broad valley; cf. Strath-clyde); *pen* or *ben* (mountain; cf. Pen-rith, Ben-Nevis); *inch* (island; cf. Inch-cape).

(*b*) *Names of objects* :—

(1) Before the Conquest :—*brock* (a badger), *crock* (hence *crockery*), *dun* (brown), *taper* (?) (a small wax candle). (Number of words very small.)

(2) After the Conquest, from about 1250 A.D. :—*bald, bog* (quagmire), *brag, brat, bump, clock* (orig. a bell), *crag* (rock), *cub* (whelp), *curd* (of milk), *nook, plod, rub, skip, prop* (support), *ribbon*. (Many of these, however, are doubtful.)

(3) From Welsh :—*cam* (crooked, *Shaks.*), *cromlech* (stone monument), *Druid, flannel, gag* (stop the mouth), *gull* (sea-bird), *hassock* (footstool), *hawk* (clear the throat), *lag* (slack, backward), *toss* (to throw), *bard* (poet).

(4) From Scotch :—*cairn, clan, claymore* (kind of sword), *galloway* (small horse), *gillie* (a boy, page), *pibroch* (martial tune), *plaid, reel* (Highland dance), *whisky*.

(5) From Irish :—*brogue* (wooden shoe), *colleen* (a little girl), *fun, mug* (cup), *shamrock* (a trefoil), *shanty* (small mean dwelling), *tory* (a hostile pursuer, first used in a political sense in 1680).

Section 2.—Danish or Later Scandian.

457. Danish borrowings.—Danish words were used in current speech long before 1250; but it was not till about 1250 or later that many of them were brought into literary use. In those days not one Saxon or Dane in a thousand could read or write, and hence changes were thoroughly established in popular speech long before they showed themselves in writing. The Danish verb "call" appears, however, in the *Battle of Maldon*, an A.S. poem written in A.D. 993. The verb "cast" appears in a Homily written in 1230. These are among the earliest examples of Danish borrowings of *verbs*.

Danish words have a tendency to resist palatalisation,—that is, the conversion of the gutturals *k* or *g* to the corresponding palatals *ch*, *j*, or *y*. Many of our words beginning with *sk*, such as *skill*, *skin*, are Danish. The suffix *-sk*, as in *bu-sk* (prepare oneself), *ba-sk* (orig. to bathe oneself) is exclusively Danish, and is still used in Icelandic.

(1) Nouns of Danish origin :—*tarn* (pool), *stag*, *hustings*, *bark* (of tree), *brink*, *beck* (brook), *bulk* (size), *cleft*, *cur*, *egg*, *fell* (hill), *fellow* (*felági*, partner), *geysir*, *harbour*, *husband*, *kid*, *leg*, *raft*, *reindeer*, *sister*, *skirt*, *sky*, *slaughter*, *trust*, *tryst*, *window*, *wing*.

(2) Verbs of Danish origin :—*bait*, *bask*, *busk*, *call*, *cast*, *dash*, *die*, *drip*, *droop*, *gasp*, *glint*, *glimmer*, *irk* (hence *irk-some*), *are* (Third plur. of *am*), *bark*, *raise*, *rouse*, *rush*, *skim*, *smelt*, *smile*, *take*, *thrive*, *wag*, *wail*, *whirl*, *rive*, *thrive*, etc.

(3) Adjectives and adverbs :—*both*, *bound* (for some journey), *harsh*, *ill*, *irksome*, *loose*, *same*, *scant*, *sleek*, *sly*, *their* (Poss. Pronoun), *tight*, *ugly*, *weak*, etc.

(4) *Patronymics*.—The A.S. suffix for forming patronymics is *-ing*, as *Hard-ing*, *Mann-ing*, etc. The Scandian or Danish suffix is *-son*, as *Ander-son*, *Eric-son*, *Collin-son*, *Swain-son*, *Robert-son*, *David-son*, *Thom-son*, etc.

(5) Prepositions :—*till*, *fro* (a doublet of A.S. *from* or *fram*), *a* for *on* in *aloft*, etc.

(6) Pronouns :—*they*, *them*, *their*.

SECTION 3.—DUTCH.

458. Two sets of Dutch borrowings.—(*a*) In the time of Edward III. a large number of Dutch weavers were induced to settle in England, especially in Norfolk, Suffolk, Essex, and Kent. The dialects that they brought with them (Old Frisian and Old Dutch) had much in common with that brought by Frisians and Saxons many centuries before. (*b*) In the reign of Elizabeth, English soldiers, who went out to Holland as volunteers to assist the Dutch against the Duke of Parma, brought home a good many Dutch words with them. After the fall of Antwerp, about a third of its merchants and manufacturers settled on the banks of the Thames, and Dutch sailors at the same time brought some new nautical terms.

(*a*) *First borrowings* :—

(1) Words connected with weaving or the sale of woven goods :—*Botch* (to repair, patch), *brake* (machine for breaking hemp), *curl* (crimple), *lash* (to join a piece and make a seam), *spool* (a reel to wind yarn on), *tuck*, *groat*, *hawker*, *huckster*, *lack* (orig. blemish).

(2) Other words in common use :—*cough*, *mud*, *muddle*, *nag*, *fop*, *loll*, *luck*, *rabble*, *scoff*, *scold*, *slot* (bolt), *slender*, *slight*, *sprout*, *tub*, *tug*, *wiseacre* (Dutch *wijs-segger*, a wise sayer, a sooth-sayer).

(*b*) *Second borrowings*:—

(1) Naval words:[1]—*deck* (of a ship), *freebooter* (pirate or sea-robber), *hoise* or *hoist*, *hold* (of a ship), *hoy* (a small vessel), *hull* (of a ship), *skipper* (mariner), *yacht*, *boom* (pole), *cruise*, *sloop*.

(2) Trade words:—*cope* (orig. to bargain with; cf. *cheap*), *dollar*, *gilder*, *hogshead* (Dutch *oxhoofd*), *holland* (Dutch linen), *ravel* (to unweave or entangle).

(3) Words picked up by volunteers, etc.:—*boor* (Dutch peasant), *burgomaster* (lit. town-master), *canakin*, *frolic*, *fumble*, *glib* (smooth, voluble), *jeer*, *leaguer* (a camp; cf. be-*leaguer*, *lair*, *lie*), *loiter*, *landscape*, *manakin*, *mop*, *mope*, *rover*, *ruffle*, *sniff*, *sutler*, *toy*, *trick*, *slope*, *fop*, *wagon*, etc.

(4) A few words connected with painting,[2] such as *easel*, *landscape*, *lay-figure* (Dutch *lee*-man, a jointed model of the human body that may be put up in any attitude).

Note 1.—Some very recent Dutch borrowings have come to us from the Boers in South Africa:—*laager* (a camp), *kraal* (a collection of huts within a stockade), *trek* or *treck* (to migrate with waggons drawn by oxen).

Note 2.—The diminutive suffix *-kin*, as in *bump-kin*, *mana-kin*, *manni-kin*, is usually Dutch, in which it had the form of *-ken*. The suffix *scape* occurring in *landscape* is from Dutch *schap* (shape).

Section 4.—Latin.

459. Latin borrowings distinct from French.—Since French is little else than a modern form of Latin, it has been usual to put the Latin and French borrowings together, and to arrange them in the following periods:—

First Period, A.D. 43-410:—borrowings traced to the Roman occupation of Britain or picked up on the Continent: *all Latin*.

Second Period, A.D. 596-1066:—words borrowed during and after the conversion of our ancestors to Christianity: *all Latin*.

Third Period, A.D. 1066-1480:—words borrowed on and after the Norman Conquest till the accession of Henry VII., the commencement of Modern History: *all French*.

Fourth Period, from A.D. 1480:—words borrowed during and after the great intellectual movement known as the Renaissance or Revival of learning: *all Latin*.

The arrangement is faulty, because shoals of Latin borrowings came in within the third period, and shoals of French ones within the fourth. Moreover, there was a special class of French

---

[1] It must not be supposed, however, that *all*, or even the majority, of our naval terms are from Dutch. Others are Romanic, Scandian, or Anglo-Saxon. Romanic: *anchor*, *vessel*, *navy*, *navigate*, *flotilla*, *careen*, *gally*, *hulk*, *prow*, *port*, *mariner*, *poop*, *mizzen*-(mast). Scandian: *lee*, *harbour*, *raft*. Anglo-Saxon: *ship*, *oar*, *seaman*, *sail*, *mast*, *steer*, *stern*, *helm*, *keel*, *fleet*, *yard*.

[2] On art terms borrowed from Italian, see § 471, (1), (*a*).

borrowings in the time of Charles II., of which no account is taken in the above arrangement.

The plan followed in this chapter is to keep the French and the Latin borrowings apart, and to subdivide each aggregate into separate periods of its own.[1] We shall take the Latin borrowings first, as the earliest of these were fixed in English, even before the French language had begun to exist.

The first two periods in the new arrangement tally, as will now be shown, with the first two in the old.

460. I. First Period: pre-Christian, up to A.D. 596.—These borrowings, about ten in number, may have been picked up on the Continent by the English before they landed in Britain; but some could easily have been learnt in Britain itself from the conquered natives.

Caster, Chester: A.S. *ceaster*, Lat. *castrum*, camp or fortified place; seen only in geographical names:—*Chester*, *Caster*, *Caistor*.

Coln: Lat. *colonia*, settlement:—Lin-*coln*, *Colne*, *Col*-chester.

Mile: A.S. *mīl*, Lat. *mille* (*passuum*), a thousand paces.

Pine (verb): A.S. *pīn*, Lat. *pœn-a*; cf. Eng. *pain*, *pun*-ish-ment.

Pool: A.S. *pól*, Welsh *pwll*, Lat. *padul*-is, a marsh.

Port: A.S. *port*, Lat. *port*-us, a harbour; cf. *Por*-chester.

Street: A.S. *strǣt*, Mercian *strēt*, Lat. *strāta* (*via*), a paved road.

Wall: A.S. *weall*, Mercian *wall*, Lat. *uall*-um, a rampart.

Wick, wich: A.S. *wīc*, Lat. *uic*-us, a town or village; seen only in geographical names: *Wick*-ham, *Wig*-ton, etc.

Wine: A.S. *wīn*, Lat. *uin*-um.

461. II. Second Period: pre-Norman, A.D. 597-1066.—In A.D. 597 St. Augustine with a band of forty monks landed in Kent to teach Roman Christianity to the heathen English. The number of Latin borrowings arising from this event amounts to less than 200.

(1) Church terms of Latin origin:—*altar*, *candle*, *chalice*, *cowl*, *creed*, *cup*, *disciple*, *font*, *mass* (sacrifice), *nun*, *shrine*, *shrive*, etc.

Church terms of Greek or Hebrew origin borrowed through Latin:—*alms*, *angel*, *anthem*, *amen*, *apostle*, *bishop*, *canon*, *Christ*, *church*, *clerk*, *deacon*, *devil*, *martyr*, *minster*, *monk*, *paschal*, *pope*, *priest*, *psalm*, *school*, *stole*, etc.

(2) Trade words, articles of commerce, etc.:—*beet* (beetroot), *box* (chest), *cap*, *cheese*, *fan*, *fork*, *kettle*, *linen*, *mat*, *mint*, *mul*-(berry), *pease* (Lat. *pis*-um, from which a false singular *pea* has been formed), *pear*, *penny*, *poppy*, *pound*, *sock*, *spend* (Lat. *dis-pend*-ere), *ton*, *tun*, etc.

(3) Miscellaneous:—*ass*, *belt*, *box* (tree), *castle*, *chalk*, *coulter* (of a

[1] The arrangement observed in this chapter is in accordance with that shown in Professor Skeat's *Principles of English Etymology*, series i. and ii.

plough), *fever*, *fiddle*, *fennel*, *hemp*, *kiln* (Lat. *culina*), *kitchen* (Lat. *coquina*), *lake*, *lobster*, *mill*, *mount-ain*, *noon* (Lat. *nona hora*, the ninth hour), *pan*, *pillow*, *pine* (tree), *pipe*, *pit*, *pole*, *post*, *prime*, *punt*, *shambles*, *sickle*, *sole* (of foot), *tile* (Lat. *tegul*-a), *tunic*, *turtle*-(dove), *verse*, *dish* (A.S. *disc*, Lat. *disc*-us), etc.

462. III. **Third Period: pre-Classical or pre-Renaissance, A.D. 1066-1485.**—The Norman Conquest, which took place in 1066, and was the means of making about half our vocabulary French two or three centuries later, gave a great impetus to the study of Latin, from which French itself is mainly derived.

It must be remembered, too, that during the Middle Ages, as Craik observes, "Latin was the language of all the learned professions, of law and physic as well as of divinity in all their grades. It was in Latin that the teachers in the Universities (many of whom in England were foreigners) delivered their prelections in all the sciences."

Words borrowed direct from Latin, as the following examples show, are more like the original Latin than the early French borrowings (A.D. 1066 to about 1350):—

Ab-brevi-ate (Latin *brevis*; cf. Fr. *abridge*). *Ab-negat-ion* (Lat. *neg-*, *negat-*; cf. Fr. "de-*ny*"). *Ac-quiesce* (Lat. *-quiesc-ere*; cf. Fr. *ac-quit*). *Ac-quire* (Lat. *quær-ere*; cf. Fr. "con-*quer*"). *Ad-judic-ate* (Lat. *judic-*, *judicat-*; cf. Fr. "*ad-judge*"). *Ag-grav-ate* (Lat. *grav-*, *gravat-*; cf. Fr. "*ag-grieve*"). *Al-levi-ate* (Lat. *levis*, light; cf. Fr. "re-*lieve*"). *Ap-preci-ate* (Lat. *pretium*, price; cf. Fr. "*ap-praise*"). *Ap-prehend* (Lat. *prehend-*; cf. Fr. "*ap-prise*"). *Ap-proxim-ate* (Lat. *proximus*; cf. Fr. "*ap-proach*," from Lat. *prope*, near). *Dis-simul-ate* (Lat. *simul-*, *simulat-*, to pretend; cf. Fr. "*dis-semble*"). *Bene-diction* (cf. Fr. *benison*). *Male-diction* (cf. Fr. *malison*). *Cad-ence* (cf. Fr. *chance*), etc.

One of the borrowings of this period, *autumn*, has superseded *harvest*, which in A.S. denoted the season (of autumn), and is now made to denote the fruits of the season.

The great difference between the Latin borrowings of Period II. and those of Period III. is that the former were adapted to Saxon models, and the latter to French ones.

463. IV. **Fourth Period, from A.D. 1480.**—The tendency to Latinise our speech received a new and very powerful impulse from the Revival of *classical* learning, Greek and Latin.

A writer in Queen Elizabeth's time condemns such innovations as the following, though all but the last three have held their ground:—*audacious*, *compatible*, *egregious*, *despicable*, *destruction*, *homicide*, *obsequious*, *ponderous*, *portentous*, *prodigious*, *attemptat*, *facundity*, *implete*.

Among the rejected words the following will serve as examples:—

torve, tetric, cecity, fastide, trutinate, immanity, scelestick, pervicacy, stramineous, lepid, sufflaminate, facinorous, immorigerous, stultiloquy, mulierosity, coaxation, ludibundness,[1] etc.

It has been estimated that the total number of words which we have borrowed immediately from Latin, and not through the medium of French, is considerably above 2400.[2]

SECTION 5.—FRENCH.

464. Three sets of French borrowings.—There are *three* different sets of French borrowings, as against the four of Latin.

I. "Words of **Anglo-French** origin, that came into the language before 1350, and belong to the good old stock, being of equal value and use with the words of native origin." It was the Norman Conquest in 1066 that set this stream flowing in force, and led to the formation, in England itself, of a separate French dialect, which has been called "Anglo-French" (§ 466).

II. "Words of **Central** (or Parisian) French origin, imported chiefly between 1350 and 1660, the date of the accession of Charles II."

III. "**Late French** words (of Parisian origin), introduced into the language since 1660 or thereabouts. They are on the whole of far less value than those in the two former classes" (Skeat).[3]

Note.—It has been asserted by very high authorities that there was a set of French borrowings which *preceded* the Norman Conquest (see article by Kluge in *Englische Studien*, vol. xxi. p. 334):—*bat, capon, castle, cat* (North Fr.), *catchpoll* (in late A.S. *cæcepol*), *false, mantle, market, proud, pride, purse, rock, sot, targe, trail, turn.* All these appear in late A.S., and are traceable to a French origin.

465. Popular and Learned.—The former belong chiefly to Class I., the latter (to a large extent) to Classes II. and III.

(*a*) "Popular" French words are such as grew up orally in ancient Gaul from the intercourse of Roman soldiers and settlers with the Gauls or *people* of the province; and hence they are called *popular*—"lingua Romana popularis"—lip-Latin, and not book-Latin. Such words are a good deal changed from the original Latin speech.

(*b*) "Learned" French words are such as were borrowed by French writers from the study of Latin books, and not from lip-

[1] Trench's *English Past and Present*, ed. 1877, pp. 102-110.
[2] Skeat's *Princ. Eng. Etym.* series ii. p. 250.
[3] *Ibid.* series ii. chap. ix.

Latin. They are merely Latin words slightly altered and put into a French dress. Central or Parisian French enriched itself with a large stock of such words. Among our "Learned" words some were borrowed direct from Latin itself, others from literary French. In the following list, which is by no means exhaustive, we put the "Learned" word first, because its connection with Latin or literary French is more easily traced. Historically, however, the "Popular" form of the word came first.

Abbreviate, abridge.	Dignity, dainty.	Penitence, penance.
Aggravate, aggrieve.	Dilate, delay.	Piety, pity.
Allocate, allow.	Diurnal, journal.	Portico, porch.
Antique, antic.	Errant, arrant.	Potion, poison.
Appreciate, appraise.	Example, sample.	Predicate, preach.
Assimilate, assemble.	Fabric, forge.	Probe, proof.
Benediction, benison.	Fact, feat.	Prolong, purloin.
Cadence, chance.	Faction, fashion.	Propose, purpose.
Calumny, challenge.	Fidelity, fealty.	Prosecute, pursue.
Canal, channel, kennel.	Fragile, frail.	Provide, purvey.
Cancer, canker.	Granary, garner.	Prune, plum.
Cant, chant.	Hospital, hotel.	Quiet, quite.
Capital, chattel.	Illumine, limn.	Redemption, ransom.
Captive, caitiff.	Indict, indite.	Reprove, reprieve.
Castigate, chastise.	Invidious, envious.	Respect, respite.
Castle, chateau.	(In)vite, vie.	Rote, route, rut.
Cave, cage.	Locus, lieu.	Secure, sure.
Collect, coil, cull.	Locust, lobster.	Senior, sir, sire.
Collocate, couch.	Major, mayor.	Separate, sever.
Complacent, complaisant.	Malediction, malison.	Spirit, sprite.
Complete, comply.	Memory, memoir.	Status, estate.
Comprehend, comprise.	Native, naive.	Strict, straight.
Compute, count.	Obedience, obeisance.	Tract, trait.
Conception, conceit.	Oration, orison.	Tradition, treason.
Conduct, conduit.	Pallid, pale.	Triumph, trump.
Deposit, depôt.	Par, pair, peer.	Vast, waste.
Describe, descry.	Patron, pattern.	Verb, word.
Desiderate, desire.	Pauper, poor.	Vocal, vowel.

466. I. **Anglo-French borrowings**, up to about A.D. 1350. —These are called Anglo-French, as distinct from those of every other French dialect, because this dialect was *developed in England independently of foreign influence.*

Our Anglo-French words are on the whole quite as necessary to our language as our Anglo-Saxon ones. The word *hour*, for example, is indispensable, because A.S. *tíd* (= tide), which also meant "hour," is now used to denote the ebb and flow of the sea. Again, *second* is indispensable as the ordinal for "two," because A.S. *óðer* (= other, lit. "second") has become useful in other ways. Cf. Lat. *autumn* and A.S. *harvest* in § 462.

(*a*) Titles, offices, etc. :—*duke*, *marquis*, *baron*, *constable*, *count*, *lieutenant*, *mayor*, *prince*, *viscount*, *emperor*, *vicar*, *dean*, *canon*, *chancellor*, etc.

(*b*) Feudalism and war, etc. :—*aid*, *cavalry*, *banner*, *battle*, *captain*, *fealty*, *lance*, *realm*, *armour*, *arms*, *fief*, *escutcheon*, *homage*, *vassal*, *serjeant*, *serf*, *trumpet*, etc.

(*c*) Law : *attorney*, *barrister*, *damages*, *felony*, *larceny*, *fine*, *judge*, *jury*, *justice*, *estate*, *fee*, *plea*, *plead*, *plaintiff*, *defendant*, *assize*, *prison*, *suit*, *summons*, etc.

(*d*) Government : *people*, *parliament*, *crown*, *reign*, *treaty*, *council*, *cabinet*, *court*, *minister*, etc.

(*e*) Church : *friar*, *relic*, *tonsure*, *ceremony*, *baptism*, *Bible*, *prayer*, *preach*, *lesson*, *cloister*, *penance*, *homily*, *sermon*, etc.

(*f*) Hunting : *course*, *covert*, *falcon*, *leveret*, *quarry*, *rabbit*, *venison* (hunted flesh), *catch*, *chase*.

(*g*) Cookery : *beef*, *veal*, *pork*, *mutton*, *pullet*, *boil*, *roast*, *broil*, *salmon*, *sausage*, etc.

(*h*) Abstract terms : *sense*, *honour*, *glory*, *fame*, *colour*, *dignity*, *chivalry*, *piety*, *art*, *science*, *nature*, etc.

(*i*) Relationship : *aunt*, *cousin*, *spouse*, *parent*, *uncle*, *nephew*, *niece*.

Note.—Most terms expressing very close relationship are, however, Teutonic ; such as *son*, *daughter*, *father*, *mother*. Hybrids like *grandfather*, *grandmother* help to show how completely the two languages were blended.

467. II. **Central French borrowings**, from A.D. 1350 to about 1660.—By the middle of the fourteenth century, when English was the only language spoken, and Anglo-French had almost ceased to affect our vocabulary, we had begun to borrow from literary French, that is, the French derived from book-Latin, and not that derived, as old French was, from lip-Latin.

Specimens of Central French borrowings found in Chaucer :—

Cadence (Lat. *cadentia*, Anglo-French *chance*), *poetry*, *advertence*, *agony*, *annex*, *ascendant*, *casual*, *complexion*, *composition*, *conservative*, *cordial*, *duration*, *existence*, *fructify*, *oracle*, *persuasion*, *reprehend*, *triumph*, *urn*, *volume*, *vulgar*,[1] etc.

Specimens in Lydgate, fifteenth century :—*adulation*, *ambiguity*, *artificer*, *combine*, *condign*, *chronicle*, *deception*, *decoction*, *demure*, *dissent*, *doublet*, *encourage*, *fraudulent*, *hospitality*, *immutable*, *inclination*, *influence*, *inspection*, etc.

The French borrowings of this period were not all book-words. Some were names of products imported into England through France by way of Calais. The following examples are given in their modern English spelling :—

Sugar, *almonds*, *spicery*, *vermilion*, *figs*, *raisins*, *saffron*, *ivory*, *pepper*, *ginger*, *liquorice*, *sulphur*, *incense*, *pæony*, *anise*, *dates*, *chestnuts*, *olive oil*, *rice*, *turpentine*, *cotton*, *canvas*, *fustian*, etc.

---

[1] Skeat's *Princ. Eng. Etym.* series ii. p. 153.

468. III. **Late French borrowings,** from A.D. 1660.—The borrowings of this period differ from those that preceded it in three respects at least—(1) They contain scarcely any *verbs*, which shows that Modern French is to Modern English an exotic, and not a true graft; (2) they have in many instances retained the Modern French system of accentuating the last syllable, whereas the older borrowings followed the English method of throwing the accent back on the first; cf. *cap'-tain* (Old French), *cam-paign'* (Modern French); (3) they have in many instances preserved the Modern French method of pronouncing vowels and consonants; compare for example *rage* (Old French) with *rouge* (= rōōzh, Modern French). Old French, on the contrary, was pronounced in nearly the same way as English was at the time of its incorporation.

An affected preference for everything French came into fashion with Charles II., whose vicious reign of twenty-five years corrupted the language no less than the morals of his country. The poet Dryden (1631-1700), from a desire to please the Court, fell in with the prevailing fashion, as when he needlessly substituted the French *fraicheur* for the English *freshness*:—

> Hither in summer evenings you repair
> To taste the *fraicheur* of the purer air.

The following are a few examples of the borrowings of this period:—*adroit, brunette, cadet, cajole, campaign, caprice, caress, festoon, grimace, guitar, harangue, intrigue, grotesque.*

Section 6.—Greek.

469. Continuity of Greek borrowings.—Greek shares with Latin, though to a much smaller degree, the distinction of having been a continuous source of supply from the fifth century down to the present day.

All Greek borrowings up to the Revival of Greek learning (which for England may be dated from A.D. 1540) reached us at second or third hand through Latin or French.

Since 1540 some Greek words have been borrowed direct from Greek, and are especially so borrowed at the present day, when new words are wanted for some new fact or object in art or science. Others have been borrowed through Latin or French, as before, or through Italian, Spanish, Arabic, Portuguese, or Dutch.

470. Specimens of Greek borrowings:—

(*a*) Out of the Latin borrowings (rather less than 200) of the Second Period (§ 461), at least one-third were Greek before they became Latin:—

Alms (A.S. *ælmesse*, Gr. *eleēmos-yne*); anthem (A.S. *antefn*, Gr. *anti-phona*); angel (Gr. *angel-os*); apostle (Gr. *apostol-os*); bishop (A.S. *biscop*, Gr. *episcop-os*); chest (Gr. *kist-e*); Christ (Gr. *Christ-os*); church or kirk (A.S. *cyric-e*, Gr. *kuriak-a*); clerk (Gr. *cleric-os*); devil (A.S. *déofol*, Gr. *diabol-os*); dish (A.S. *disc*, Gr. *disc-os*), etc.

(*b*) Greek borrowings that have come through French, having first passed into Latin:—

Blame (Fr. *blasm-er*, Lat. *blasphem-are*, Gr. *blasphem-ein*); currants (Fr. *raisins de Corinthe*, Gr. *Corinth-os*); dropsy (Fr. *hy-dropisie*, Gr. *hydropisis*); fancy (Fr. *fantasie*, Gr. *phantasia*); frenzy (Fr. *frenaisie*, Gr. *phrenesis*); govern (Fr. *govern-er*, Gr. *kubern-ān*); graft (Fr. *graffe*, Gr. *graph-ein*); ink (Fr. *enque*, Gr. *en-caust-on*); place (Fr. *place*, Gr. *plat-eia*); slander (Fr. *esclandre*, Gr. *scandal-on*); surgeon (Fr. *chirurgien*, Gr. *cheir-urg-eon*); palsy (Fr. *paralysie*, Gr. *para-lysis*); al-chemy (Arab. article *al*: Gr. *chemeia*, mingling).

(*c*) Greek borrowings that have come from Greek direct:—

Analysis, hydrophobia, monopolist, telephone, anthology, demology, zoo-logy, tele-gram, epi-dem-ic, epi-lepsy, epicure, utopia, æsthetic, cosmetic, cosmo-polite, etc.

(*d*) Hybrids:—

Con-trive (Lat. prefix *con-*; Old Fr. *trov-er*, to find; Gr. *trop-os*, a turn, revolving); re-trieve (Lat. prefix *re-*, base the same as the preceding); in-toxic-ate (Lat. prefix *in-*, Gr. stem *toxic-on*, poison, Lat. suffix *-ate*), etc.

Verbs of Greek origin are rare. But a very large number of verbs have been formed with the Greek suffix *-ize* or *-ise*, which can be freely attached to stems of any origin whatever.[1]

SECTION 7.—MODERN BORROWINGS: MISCELLANEOUS.

471. Modern borrowings.—Under this heading we include the various sources not already named, from which new words came into English within the modern period of our language,—that is, after A.D. 1500.

(1) *Italian.*—The Renaissance or Revival of Learning, which originated in Italy, led to a study of Italian literature. Dante, Tasso, Ariosto, and Petrarch were all translated into English. The poems of Surrey, Wyatt, Spenser, and Milton all show an intimate acquaintance with Italian. In the reigns of the Tudors

[1] The spelling *-ise* is French; but this was altered to *-ize* by pedants, who knew Greek, but forgot that *-ise* came to us through Fr. *-iser*.

Italian was as necessary to every courtier as French was in the time of Charles II. The Ottava Rima, Blank Verse, and the Sonnet all came from Italy. The scenes of seven of Shakspeare's plays are laid in Italy. The tide receded with the establishment of the Commonwealth, and was entirely thrown back by the overwhelming taste for French, that set in with the accession of Charles II.

One word, and possibly two more, came from Italy at a very early period. *Pilgrim* occurs in Layamon's *Brut*, spelt as *pilegrim*, from Italian *pellegrino*. Another word is *roam*, probably derived from *Rome*, to which pilgrimages were made by Englishmen from the time of Alfred the Great to that of Chaucer's *Wife of Bath*. *Ducat*, a Venetian word, occurs in Chaucer.

(*a*) Direct from Italian :—

Balcony (It. *balcone*, a stage); bandit (It. *bandito*, outlawed); canto ; comply (It. *complire*, Lat. *complere*) ; contraband (Lat. *contra*, against, *bannum*, a decree) ; ditto (a thing already said, from Lat. *dictum*, said) ; duel ; duet ; monkey (It. *monicchio*) ; gusto (Lat. *gust-us*, taste) ; fresco (of the same root as *fresh*) ; milliner (a dealer in *Milan* goods) ; isolate (It. *isolato*, detached) ; imbroglio ; grotto ; portico ; quota ; rebuff, etc.

Note.—We are indebted to Italian for many of our terms in music, poetry, and painting :—

Music :—concert, sonata, spinet, fugue, breve, duet, contralto, opera, piano, prima donna, quartet, quintet, solo, soprano, trio, canzonet, tremolo, falsetto, etc.

Poetry :—canto, sonnet, stanza, improvise, octava rima.

Painting :—miniature, profile, vista, model, palette, pastel, mezzotinto, amber, etc. (On painting terms derived from Dutch, see § 458, *b*.)

(*b*) Through French :—

Alert (It. *all' erta*, on the watch) ; arcade ; artisan ; bank-rupt (It. *banco*, *rotto*, afterwards changed to Lat. *rupta*) ; brusque (It. *brusco*) ; bust (It. *busto*) ; caprice (It. *cappriccio*, a whim) ; canteen (It. *cantina*, a cellar) ; cartoon (It. *cartone*, Lat. *charta*) ; cavalcade (It. *cavalcata*, a troop of horsemen) ; cascade (It. *cascata*, a waterfall), etc.

(2) *Spanish.*—Our borrowings from Spain were not due to a study of Spanish literature, but to our commercial and political relations with Spain, and to the descriptions of the country and her colonies furnished by English travellers. Spanish borrowings are almost as numerous as Italian. The *al-* prefixed to some Spanish nouns is the Arabic article, *al*.

(*a*) Direct from Spanish :—

Alligator (*al ligarto*, a lizard) ; armada (armed fleet) ; booby (*bobo*, a blockhead); buffalo; canoe (West Indian); cargo; cigar; armadillo (the little armed one, an animal); cork (*corcho*, Lat. *corticem*, bark); domino; don; filibuster (Sp. *filibuster;* corruption of Dutch *vrijbuiter*, Eng. freebooter); peccadillo (dim. of *pecado*, a sin), etc.

(*b*) Through French :—

Bizarre; calenture; cask (Fr. *casque*, Ital. *casco*); castanets (of the same root as *chestnut*); escalade; garble; parade (*parada*, a show); risk (*risco*, a steep rock), etc.

(3) *Portuguese.*—About four dozen words :—

Albatross, albino, apricot, caste (Indian trade-guild), corvette (small frigate), firm (mercantile association), lingo (language), marmalade, molasses, parasol, tank (cf. Lat. *stagnum*, a pool of standing water), fetish (Lat. *factitius*, artificial).

(4) *German:* that is, the High-German (see § 434). Only about twenty-four all told; and all of these are scientific and technical terms, except the following :—

Landau (a kind of carriage), meerschaum, mesmerise, plunder, poodle, swindler, waltz, zinc, carouse (through Fr. *carous*, Germ. *gar-aus*, lit. "quite out," a bumper drunk right off).

(5) *Russian* or *Slavonic:* rather fewer than the German :—

Knout, mammoth, argosy, mazurka (Polish dance), sable (an animal), rouble, polka, slave, steppe, vampire, czar.

(6) *Persian* :—

Bazaar, bezique (a game), caravan, divan, orange (*P. naring*), check or cheque, chess, dervish, exchequer, hazard, jackal, jasmine, jujube (through French), lemon, lilac, etc.

(7) *Sanskrit* :—

Banyan (a kind of tree), camphor, chintz, crimson, ginger, hemp, indigo, jungle, loot (to plunder), etc.

(8) *Hindustáni* (Northern India) :—

Bangle (a ring bracelet), chutny (a kind of pickle), dacoit (highway robber), topee (a sunshade for the head).

(9) *Hebrew* :—

Balsam (cf. older form *balm*, through French), alphabet (through Greek), amen, bedlam (mad-house, corruption of *Bethlehem*), cinnamon, cherub, cider (through French), maudlin (corruption of *Magdalene*), jubilee, jockey (corruption of *jackey*, dim. of *Jack*, Hebrew *Jac-ob*), hallelujah (*halelú jáh*, praise ye God), seraph (coined from the plural *seraphim*), shekel, etc.

(10) *Syriac* :—

Abbess, abbot, abbey (all from *abba*, father), damask (from *Damascus*), damson (a Damascene plum), muslin (from the town *Mosul*), mammon (riches), Messiah (anointed), etc.

(11) *Arabic:* rather numerous; some have come from the Levantine trade through Greek or Italian; others by way of

Spain, in which country the Arab-speaking Moors were dominant for about 700 years; others less directly by way of France.

Admiral (spelt by Milton as *ammiral;* Arab. *amir*, prince, with suffix *-al*, which may have arisen in various ways; see *New Eng. Dict.*), alcove (a recess), algebra, Arabesque, arsenal, artichoke, assassin, caliph, caraway (seed), cipher, coffee, cotton, garbage, garble, nadir, zenith, etc.

(12) *Turkish* :—

Bey (provincial governor), horde, bosh (nonsense), ottoman (from *Ottoman*, founder of the Turkish empire), yataghan (a dagger-like sword), janizary, and a few more.

(13) *Dravidian* (Southern India) :—

Teak (a kind of timber), bandicoot, mungoose, curry, cheroot, cooly (labourer), mango (kind of fruit), tope (mango-orchard), pariah (out-caste), and a few more.

(14) *Malay* :—

Bamboo, caddy (small tea-chest), cockatoo, gong, mangrove, ourang-outang, paddy (rice), rattan (cane), sago, upas (a (fabled) poisonous tree), amuck (as in the phrase "to run amuck." Dryden treats the *a* as an article, and uses the phrase "to run *an* Indian muck." The noun *mucker* for *muck* is well fixed in colloquial speech).

(15) *Chinese* :—

China (in the sense of porcelain), tea (Ch. *tsa, chá;* the last, though not used in England, is universally used in India, where it became current through the Portuguese), nankeen (a kind of cloth, from *Nankin*).

(16) *Thibetan* :—

Lama (Buddhist high priest at Llassa), yak (Thib. ox).

(17) *Australian* :—

Boomerang, kangaroo, paramatta (so called from the place).

(18) *Polynesian* :—

Taboo (a prohibition), tattoo.

(19) *Egyptian* :—

Behemoth, sack (hence dim. *satchel*, and *sack-cloth*), gum, gipsy, ibis, oäsis, paper (*papyrus*).

(20) *North African* :—

Barb (a horse), morocco (from the country), fez (Moorish cap).

(21) *West African* :—

Canary, chimpanzee, guinea, gorilla, yam (sweet potato).

(22) *North American* :—

Caucus (perhaps, one who urges on; now, a preliminary meeting for a political purpose), moose, skunk, squaw, tobacco, tomahawk, totem (ancestral symbol), wigwam (Indian hut), opossum, raccoon.

(23) *Mexican* :—

Cocoa (orig. *cacao*), chocolate, copal, jalap, tomato.

(24) *Peruvian* :—

Alpaca, coca (whence cocaine), condor, guano, llama, pampa (a wide grassy plain in South America; cf. *prairie* in North America, and *steppe* in Russia), jerked beef (corruption of *charqui*, raw meat cut up into strips and dried in the sun), puma.

CHAPTER XXXIII.—NOTES ON AFFIXES AND ACCIDENCE.

SECTION 1.—ORIGIN OF TEUTONIC AFFIXES.

472. The study of Affixes.—There are two points of view from which prefixes and suffixes can be studied :—(1) the enlargement of the vocabulary, dealt with already in Chapter xxv.; (2) the etymology of words, which includes the origin of the affixes themselves.

Our language, as the reader is aware, contains three different sets of affixes,—the Teutonic, the Romanic, and the Greek. The last two (see §§ 325-341) appear in our language in much the same forms as those by which they were known in their original tongues,—the Latin, the neo-Latin, and the Greek. On the other hand, most of our Teutonic affixes appear in a form which is much less easily recognised, since Anglo-Saxon is less generally known than Latin or Greek. The present section, therefore, gives some account of the origin of our Teutonic affixes.

473. Prefixes.—These are distinguished into Separable, viz. those which can be used as independent words; and Inseparable, those which are now seen only as prefixes.

A. Separable :—(the A.S. *æ* had the sound of *a* in *rat*).

After-, A.S. *æft*, *æfter*, preposition and adverb : *after*-wards.
Al-, l-, A.S. *eal*, all, adjective : *al*-one, *l*-one, *al*-ready.
At-, A.S. *æt*, at, preposition : *at*-one, *at*-one-ment.
By-, A.S. *bi*, by, preposition and adverb : *by*-path.
Fore-, A.S. *fore*, in front, preposition and adverb : *fore*-tell.
Forth-, A.S. *forth*, adverb : *forth*-coming.
Fro-, Norse *frá*, from : *fro*-ward.
In-, A.S. *in*, in, preposition : *in*-sight, *in*-land.
Mis-, A.S. and Norse *mis*, wrongly, adverb : *mis*-deed (A.S. *mis-dǽd*).
Off-, A.S. *of*, of or off, preposition : *off*-spring, *off*-ing.
On-, A.S. *on*, on, preposition : *on*-wards, *on*-set.

Out-, **ut-**, A.S. *út*, out, adverb: *out*-side, *ut*-most.
Over-, A.S. *ofer*, over, preposition: *over*-whelm.
Through-, **thorough-**, A.S. *thurh*, through, prep.: *thorough*-fare.
To-, A.S. *tó*, to, preposition: *to*-day (A.S. *tó dæge*, for the day).
Under-, A.S. *under*, beneath, preposition: *under*-let.
Up-, A.S. *up*, up, adverb: *up*-lands.
Wel-, **well-**, A.S. *wel*, well, adverb: *wel*-fare.
With-, A.S. *with*, against, by, near, prep.: *with*-stand.

B. Inseparable :—

A-, A.S. *of*: *a*-down (A.S. *of-dune*, off a hill or dune).
A-, A.S. *on*: *a*-light (verb, A.S. *on-liht-an*, to light on).
A- or **an-**, A.S. *and* (against): *an*-swer (A.S. *and-swer-ian*, to swear or speak back), *a*-long (A.S. *and-lang*).
A-, A.S. *án* (one): *a*-ught (A.S. *á-wiht*, one thing).
A-, A.S. *á* (intensive): *a*-rise (A.S. *á-rís-an*).
A-, A.S. *æt* (at): *a*-do (for *at*-do, Northern dialect).
A-, A.S. *ge*: a(f)-ford (A.S. *ge-forth-ian*, to further).
Be-, A.S. *be* (by): *be*-hoof (A.S. *be-hóf*, advantage).
E-, A.S. *ge*, which became *i-*, *e-*: *e*-nough (A.S. *ge-nóg*).
For-, A.S. *for* (intensive): *for*-lorn (A.S. *for-loren*).
Gain-, A.S. *gegn* (against): *gain*-say (the only word left).
N-, A.S. *ne* (not): *n*-aught (A.S. *n-á-wiht*, nothing).
Or-, A.S. *or* (out): *or*-deal (A.S. *or-dél*, a dealing out).
Twi-, A.S. *twi* (double): *twi*-light, a doubtful light.
Un-, A.S. *un* (reversal): *un*-lock, to reverse the locking.
Un-, Frisian *und*: *un*-to, for *und*-to; *un*-til, for *und*-til.
Y-, A.S. *ge*: *y*-clept, *y*-wis (wrongly changed to *I wis*).

474. Noun-forming Suffixes.

A. Separable, or formerly Separable :—

-craft, A.S. *cræft* (skill): hand-i-*craft*.
-dom, A.S. *dóm* (jurisdiction): wis-*dom*.
-fare, A.S. *far-u* (journey): thorough-*fare*, chap-*fer* (cheap fare)
-herd, A.S. *heorde* (keeper): shep-*herd*, swine-*herd*.
-hood, **-head**, A.S. *hád* (state): man-*hood*, maiden-*head*.
-ledge, *lác-an* (to play, verb): know-*ledge* (the only word).
-lock, A.S. *lák* (play): wed-*lock* (the only word).
-lock, **-lic**, A.S. *leác* (a plant): hem-*lock*, gar-*lic*.
-man, A.S. *mann* (person): wo-*man* (A.S. *wíf-man*).
-monger, A.S. *mang-ere* (dealer in mixed goods): fish-*monger*.
-red, A.S. *ræden* (counsel, condition): kin-d-*red*.
-red, A.S. *ræd* (rate): hund-*red* (the only word).
-ric, A.S. *rice* (dominion): bishop-*ric* (the only word).
-scape, Dutch *schap* (form, shape): land-*scape*.
-ship, A.S. *scipe* (form, shape): friend-*ship*.
-son, A.S. *sun-u* (son), a patronymic: Ander-*son*.
-stead, A.S. *stede* (place): bed-*stead*, Hamp-*stead*.
-tree, A.S. *tréow* (sawn timber): axle-*tree*.
-ward, A.S. *weard* (keeper): ste-*ward* (A.S. *stí-weard*).
-wife, A.S. *wíf* (female, not wife): fish-*wife*, mid-*wife*.
-wright, A.S. *wyrht-a* (workman): wheel-*wright*.

B. Inseparable :—

-d, **-de** (akin to p.p. Weak verbs): bloo-*d*, gle-*de* (a burning coal).

-el, **-le**, **-l**, A.S. *-el*, diminutive, or instrument: hov-*el* (dim. of A.S. *hof*, house), gir-*l* (dim. of *gör*, child), spin-d-*le* (a thing to spin with).

-en, **-n**, **-on**, A.S. *-en*: (1) dim. maid-*en*; (2) fem. vix-*en*, fem. of "fox"; (3) agent, wag-*on* (that which carries), rai-*n* (that which moistens); (4) akin to p.p. Strong verbs, bair-*n* (that which is born); (5) plural, ox-*en*.

-er, **-r**, A.S. *-or*, *-er*, instrument: lai-*r* (a thing to lie on), tim-b-*er* (a thing to build with).

-er, **-ier**, **-yer**, **-ar**, **-or**, A.S. *-ere* or *-iere*, agent: rid-*er*, cloth-*ier*, law-*yer*, li-*ar*, sail-*or*.

-ing, A.S. *-ing*, dim., part of a whole: farth-*ing* (the fourth of a penny), Rid-*ing* (division of Yorkshire).

-ing, A.S. *-ung*, *-ing*, abstract suffix: rid-*ing*.

-kin, chiefly Dutch, dimin.: lamb-*kin* or lamb-i-*kin*.

-ling, A.S. *-el* + *-ing*, double dim.: cod-*ling*, dar-*ling*.

-m, **-me**, **-om**, A.S. *-m*, *-ma*: hel-*m*, na-*me*, bes-*om*, doo-*m*.

-nd, **-and** (old suff. of pres. part., § 442): err-*and*, wi-*nd*.

-ness, A.S. *-nis*, *-nes*, *-ness*, abstract: dark-*ness*.

-ock, **-k**, A.S. *uc*, diminutive: bull-*ock*, stir-*k*.

-ow, **-w**, A.S. *-we*, Dative of *-u*: mead-*ow*, stra-*w*.

-st, **-t**, **-est**, A.S. *-st*, *-t*, *-est*: rus-*t*, twi-*st*, harv-*est*.

-ster, A.S. *es-tre*, originally fem.: spin-*ster*, song-*ster*.

-t, **-th**, A.S. *-ith*: leng-*th*, heigh-*t*.

-ter, **-ther**, **-der**, A.S. *-ther*, *-der*: laugh-*ter*, spi(n)-*der*, mo-*ther*.

-y, **-ey**, **-ie**, A.S. *-ig*, chiefly dim.: bod-*y*, hon-*ey*, bird-*ie*.

-y, A.S. *-e*, place of action: smith-*y* (smith's workshop).

475. Adjective-forming Suffixes.

A. Separable, or formerly Separable :—

-fast, A.S. *fæst*, firm, sure: stead-*fast*, shame-*faced* (for shame-*fast*, A.S. sceam-*fæst*).

-fold, A.S. *feald*: two-*fold*, mani-*fold* (for "many-fold").

-ful, A.S. *ful*, full: hope-*ful*, pocket-*ful* (noun).

-less, A.S. *léas*, loose, free from: fear-*less*, hap-*less*.

-like, A.S. *lic*, like: life-*like*, war-*like*.

-right, A.S. *riht*, direction: up-*right*.

-some, **-som**, A.S. *sum*: hand-*some*, bux-*om* (A.S. *bug-an*, to bend).

-teen (A.S. *tén*, ten), **-ty** (A.S. *tig*, ten): four-*teen*, for-*ty*.

-ward, A.S. *weard*, inclined to: fro-*ward* (A.S. *from-weard*).

-wart, A.S. *weorth*, worth: stal-*wart* (A.S. *stæl*, foundation).

-wise, A.S. *wis*, knowing: right-*eous* for "right-*wise*" (knowing the right).

B. Inseparable :—

-d, **-ed** (akin to p.p. Weak verbs): bal-*d*, gift-*ed*, ragg-*ed*.

-el, **-le**, **-l**, A.S. *-ol*, *-el*: scrann-*el*, fick-*le*, fou-*l*.

-en, **-n**, p.p. Strong verbs: drunk-*en*, op-*en* (that which is up).

-en, **-n**, A.S. *-en*, made of: wood-*en*, swi-*ne* (cf. Lat. su-*in*-us).

-er, **-r**, A.S. *-or*, *-er*: bitt-*er* (A.S. bit-*or*, biting), fai-*r*.

-ern (perhaps allied to A.S. *irn-an*, to run): north-*ern*.

-ish, **-sh**, **-ch**, A.S. *-isc:* mawk-*ish*, pal-*ish*.
-ly (inseparable form of A.S. *líc*, like): woman-*ly*.
-most, A.S. *mest*, double superl. *-ma* + *-est:* fore-*most*.
-ow, **-w**, A.S. *-we*, *-u:* call-*ow* (A.S. cal-*u*), slo-*w*.
-t, **-th** (akin to p.p. Weak verbs): swif-*t*, four-*th*, uncou-*th*.
-ther, A.S. *-ther*, Comparative suffix: o-*ther*, fur-*ther*.
-y, A.S. *ig:* might-*y*, an-*y* (A.S. ǽn-*ig*, from *án*, "one").

476. Adverb-forming Suffixes.

A. Separable, or formerly Separable:—

-meal, A.S. *mǽl-um*, Dative plur. of *mǽl*, a time: piece-*meal*.
-wards, A.S. *weard*, the *s* is possessive: back-*wards*.
-ways, A.S. *weg*, a way; the *s* is possessive: al-*ways*.
-wise, A.S. *wís-e*, manner: other-*wise*.

B. Inseparable:—

-er, **-re**, A.S. *-re* and *-r:* ev-*er*, he-*re*.
-ling, **-long**, A.S. *lung-a*, later *ling-a:* dark-*ling*, head-*long*.
-ly, A.S. *líc-e:* on-*ly*, happi-*ly*.
-n, A.S. *-nne:* whe-*n* (A.S. hwæ-*nne*), the-*n*.
-om, A.S. *-um*, Dative inflexion: seld-*om*, whil-*om*.
-s, **-ce**, **-se**, A.S. possessive *-es:* sometime-*s*, on-*ce* (A.S. *án-es*), el-*se* (A.S. *ell-es*).
-ther, A.S. *-der:* hi-*ther*, thi-*ther*, whi-*ther*.

477. Verb-forming Suffixes.

-en, **-n** (causal; akin to p.p. of Strong verbs): dark-*en*, ow-*n*.
-er (frequent. or continuat.): clamb-*er*, whimp-*er* (from *whine*)
-k (A.S. *-c*-ian, frequentative or intensive): har-*k*, hear-*k*-en.
-le, **-el**, **-l** (frequent. or continuat.): babb-*le*, sniv-*el*, knee-*l*.
-se, A-S. *-s*-ian: clean-*se*, glimp-*se*.
-sk (of Norse origin, "self"): ba-*sk* (bathe oneself).
-y (the *i* of A.S. *-ian*, Infin. suffix): ferr-*y*, tarr-*y*.

Section 2.—Noun Forms.

478. Feminine suffix "-ess."—Our old Feminine suffixes were *-estre* (cf. spin-*ster*, A.S. spinn-*estre*, a woman who spins), and *-en* (cf. vix-*en*, A.S. fyx-*en*, orig. the feminine of "fox"). These (with one more, of which no trace now remains) were eventually superseded by the Norman-French *-esse* (now spelt as *-ess*), late Latin *-issa*. Thus "songster" (which in A.S. *sang-estre* meant a female singer) became, after the meaning of the *-ster* had been forgotten, a noun of the common gender; so to form a Feminine the suffix *-ess* was added, making "song-stress."

479. Possessive inflexion.—The original ending was *-es*, which for some time continued to be a distinct syllable. It occurs as such, though very rarely, in Shakspeare:—

Larger than the moon-*es* sphere.—*Mid. N. Dream*, ii. 1.
To show his teeth as white as whal-*es* bone.—*Love's L. Lost*, v. 2.

When the -*es* became non-syllabic, the *e* was elided, and its loss was indicated by the apostrophe (§ 43).

480. Substitution of "his" for "s."—The Genitive or Possessive inflexion was sometimes spelt as -*is* instead of -*es*. When the noun was a foreign proper name, that had no real genitive of its own in our language, the *is* was often written apart from it. Owing to the uncertainty of initial *h*, the *is* became confounded with *his*:—

Decius Cæsar *his* tyme.—TREVISA, A.D. 1380.
For Jesus Christ *his* sake.—*English Prayer-Book*.

Note.—The old theory that our possessive inflexion *es* or 's came from *his* is, of course, ridiculous. We could never have said "Jane his bonnet."

481. Plural inflexions.—(*a*) Plurals in -*ies* (§ 35) are, in fact, formed quite regularly, because the original Singular ending was -*ie*, not -*y*; as *citie*, *cities*.

(*b*) Plurals in -*en* (§ 38) are from A.S. -*an* (as, steorr-*an*, stars). This ending long disputed the ground with -*es*. *Hosen*, plural of *hose*, occurs in Old Test., *Dan.* iii. 21; *shoon*, plural of *shoe*, in Shakspeare. Spenser has *eyen* for *eyes*, and *foen* for *foes*.

(*c*) Plurals in -*es* are from A.S. -*as* (as, "stán-as," stones). Originally this inflexion was not much more common than -*an*, though it has now become practically universal.

482. Mutation Plurals.—This is the name given to those plurals that are formed by a change of the root-vowel (see list in § 38). The *earliest* forms of these plurals were *mann-is* (men), *mús-is* (mice, cf. Lat. *mur-es*), *lús-is* (lice), *fót-is* (feet, cf. Lat. *ped-es*), *tóth-is* (teeth, cf. Lat. *dent-es*), and *gós-is* (geese). The Plural was formed simply by adding -*is* (= -*es*) to the Singular.

The effect of the vowel in -*is* was to change the vowel of the Singular noun into something more like itself; so that *mann*-is became *menn*-is, *mús*-is became *mýs*-is, *lús*-is became *lýs*-is, *fót*-is became *fét*-is, *tóth*-is became *téth*-is, and *gós*-is became *gés*-is. When the plural ending -*is* dropped off, as it did even in Anglo-Saxon times, nothing but the mutation of the root-vowel remained to indicate the plural. Hence in Anglo-Saxon we find *menn* = Eng. men, *mýs* = Eng. mice, *lýs* = Eng. lice, *fét* = Eng. feet, *téth* = Eng. teeth, *gés* = Eng. geese.

Many other nouns in our language were once formed by this

process of mutation.[1] The instances quoted are the remnants of what was once a larger class.

483. Same Form for Plural as Singular; see § 38 (*c*). In A.S. the plural forms of *deer*, *sheep*, *swine* were the same for the plural as for the singular, because the nouns were neuter. The A.S. plural of *yoke* was *geoc-u*, in which the final *u* became levelled (§ 435) to *e*, and the *e* became eventually silent. The word *score* was Plural, before it was ever used as a Singular. The foreign words *grouse*, *trout*, *cod*, *brace*, *dozen*, *gross*, and the native word *heathen*, all of which have the same form in the Plural as in the Singular, have followed the same model.

Section 3.—Adjective Forms.

484. Origin of the Articles.—The origin of the Indefinite article *a* or *an* from the A.S. numeral *án*, "one," is well in keeping with the fact that the Indefinite article is never used with any but Singular nouns, and that it still sometimes has the sense of "one":—

A bird (=*one* bird) in the hand is worth *two* in the bush.

The form "a" is short for "an," the latter being retained only before vowels or silent *h*; and *an* is merely an unaccented form of A.S. *án*.

In A.S. the form *the* was used as an Indeclinable relative, and not, as it now is, as a Demonstrative adjective. For all cases and genders of nouns, singular and plural (excepting the Nom. Sing. Masc. and the Nom. Sing. Fem., which had *sé* and *seó* respectively for their Definite articles), the Definite article was expressed by a declinable adjective containing the base *tha*, out of which we get our present forms *this*, *that*, *these*, *those*. Eventually the simple form "the" superseded every other for all cases and both numbers, and became, what it now is, the Definite article.

Note 1.—It is therefore opposed to history as well as to reason to consider the Articles a distinct part of speech. It is opposed to reason, because, wherever they are used, they discharge, as their origin would imply, the function of adjectives in limiting or defining the application of a noun. The universality of their use gives them, it is true, an exceptional character, which distinguishes them from ordinary adjectives; but this does not make them distinct parts of speech.

Note 2.—In such a phrase as "a many tears" (used by Tennyson, and commonly used in colloquial speech), there is no confusion of

[1] In German this process of mutation is called *Umlaut*. The English name, however, is quite as suitable, besides being more generally understood by English readers.

construction. *Many* is here not an adjective, but a noun from A.S. *menigu*, a multitude; and the preposition "of" is understood: thus "a many tears" = a multitude of tears.

This many summers on a sea of glory.—*Henry VIII.* iii. 2.

Compare "a thousand (of) pounds" (see § 38 (*e*) *Note*). The phrase *a few* has been formed in imitation of the phrase "a many"; that is, the numeral "few" is regarded as a Collective noun.

In the phrase "many a," *many* is a real adjective used in a Multiplicative sense (§ 51); thus "*many a* man" = many times one man.

Note 3.—On the origin of the adverb *the* used with Comparatives, see § 153.

485. Comparative forms.—In A.S. degrees of comparison were expressed by three flexional or synthetic methods, and by one analytical.

(1) Flexional: the A.S. *-ra*, answering to our *-er*, and the A.S. *-ast*, *-ost*, or *-est*, answering to our *-est*. The *r* of the Comparative was *s* at a still earlier stage, of which we retain a trace in our Comparative "wor-*se*."

(2) Flexional: *-ter*, *-ther* (Comparative suffix), of which we still have traces in our words "fur-*ther*," "o-*ther*," etc. Cf. Lat. "al-*ter*," "u-*ter*."

(3) Flexional (Superlative suffix): *-ma*, cf. Lat. "pri-*mus*." Of this we have traces in some double Superlative forms, such as "hind-*most*" (A.S. "hinde-*m-est*"). The suffix "most" is a misspelling of A.S. *mest*, through a confusion with the word named under (4).

(4) Analytical method: A.S. *mára* (more), *mǽst* (most). This came into use at a much later period (fourteenth century) than the flexional methods.

Section 4.—Pronoun Forms.

The following are among the most salient points:—

My, thy.—These are simply abbreviations of A.S. *mín*, *thín*. Thus the forms "mine," "thine" are much nearer the original, but a separate use has been assigned to them (§ 68) by modern idiom.

Ours, yours.—These are merely double Possessives. The inflexion *-s* (A.S. *-es*) has been added to another inflexion *-r* (A.S. *-re*, Genitive plural); as in A.S. *úre* (our), *úres* (ours). The secondary form "hers" is due to analogy.

It, that, what.—The final *t* is a neuter suffix; cf. Lat. "i-*d*," "illu-*d*," "quo-*d*."

Its.—This has taken the place of the old Neuter possessive *his*, which lasted till the Tudor period:—

No comfortable star did lend *his* light.—Shakspeare.

Along with the use of *his* we find *it* used as a possessive by Shakspeare:—

The hedge-sparrow fed the cuckoo so long,
That it had *it* head bit off by *it* young.—*King Lear*, i. 4.

Its (written without an apostrophe, since there never was a form *it-es*) was not well established till Dryden's time. Dryden uses nothing else (see § 454).

She.—Wrongly ascribed to the fem. Definite article *seó* (of which mention is made in § 484). It has come from the Mercian *scǽ* found in the Peterborough chapters of the *Old English Chronicle.* The spelling *she* is regularly formed out of *scǽ*.

Own.—From A.S. *ágen*, Past part. "possessed."

486. Myself, himself, etc.—The explanation of these forms is a very simple matter, if we attend to their history and avoid conjecture. The words occur in A.S. in such forms as *mín self-es* (of me the same), *mé self-um* (to me the same), *mec self-ne* (me the same, Acc.).

The first thing to be noted, as in fact the above forms show, is that *self* was originally not a noun, but an adjective which signified "same," as it still does in the following line; cf. *self-same* (adj.):—

At that *self* moment enters Palamon.—DRYDEN.

"Self" is still an adjective in the phrase *himself* (him the same). But, like many other adjectives, it came in modern times to be used as a noun, and acquired a plural *selves* formed on the analogy of "shelf, shelves." We must regard it as a noun in the phrase *my-self* (lit. my identity), *our-selves* (our identities). In the Tudor period *his-self* (his identity) was as common as *himself*:—

Who *his* own *self* bare our sins.—1 *Peter* ii. 24.

In low life we still hear the phrase, "He hurt *hisself.*"

The phrase *themselves* is due to a confusion of construction. Here *selves*, which should be the adjective "self" qualifying *them* (as in "himself" the "self" qualifies "him"), has received the form of a plural noun by attraction to the plural "them."

Note.—We can now see why it is wrong (as pointed out at the top of p. 158) to use *myself, himself*, etc., as subject to a verb. Such phrases presuppose that the corresponding personal pronoun has been mentioned already. "I *myself* (the identity of me, the very same person as the speaker) saw it." "He did it *himself*" (*i.e.* by himself, or for himself, or to himself). *Him* is here the Dative case, which in Old English required no preposition.

SECTION 5.—VERB FORMS.

487. Past tense.—The theory that the *d* or *t* of the Past tense in Weak verbs has come from *did* (as "love-did" = "loved") has been entirely exploded. The flexional method of thus forming the Past tense is from A.S. *-de* or *-te*, which again is traced further back to the Gothic inflexion *-da* or *-ta*.

Gothic.	*A.S.*	*English.*
brah-ta	broh-te	brough-t

In some Weak verbs we also find a difference of root-vowel, as *sell*, *sold*. In such verbs it is the Present tense that has changed, not the Past. Thus *sal-de* (sold) is regularly formed from the root *sal*; but this *sal* became *sel* by mutation (§ 482), through the influence of the *i* in the Infinitive suffix *-ian*; A.S. *sal-ian*, *sell-an*, Middle English *sell-en*, and finally (by the loss of final *-en*) *sell*.

488. Present Participle.—Of the three old forms of the Present Participle, *-and* was peculiar to the Northern dialect, *-ende* to the Midland, and *-inde* to the Southern (§ 442). The last spread into the Midland also, and fixed itself there. The *ind*, however, became changed to *ing*, owing apparently to the greater facility of pronouncing the latter syllable at the end of a word. The change was unfortunate in one respect: it reduced the Pres. part. to the same form as that of Verbal nouns ending in *-ing*, such as "binding," with which the Pres. part. is very apt to be confounded.

489. Past or Passive participle.—In Strong verbs the inflexion *-en* (though now in many cases lost) was so spelt in Anglo-Saxon; as "ge-cum-*en*" (come).

In Weak verbs the suffix *-d* or *-t* was likewise so spelt in Anglo-Saxon. From the very first it was quite distinct from the ending of the Past tense *-de* or *-te*, though by loss of the final *e* in *-de* or *-te* they became indistinguishable. The Past part. suffix *-t* or *-d* is the same as the *t* in Latin; cf. "ama-*t*-us," "moni-*t*-us," "rec-*t*-us," "audi-*t*-us." But the Past inflexion *-de* or *-te* is peculiar to Teutonic languages.

490. Infinitive.—In A.S. the Simple Infinitive (indeclinable) had the suffix *-an* or *-ian*, which after being levelled to *-en* (§ 435) was eventually lost. Thus we have "bind-*an*," "bind-*en*," "bind." In A.S. this Infinitive was never preceded by *to*, as it usually is in Modern English.

What we now call the Qualifying or Gerundial Infinitive was a phrase formed in A.S. by the preposition *tó* and by the inflexion *-anne*, which after being changed first to *enne* and then to *en* was eventually lost. Thus we have "tó bind-*anne*," "tó bind-*enne*," "tó bind-*en*," "to bind."

When the preposition *to* came to be added to the Simple Infinitive also (a process of which the earliest traces are seen about the end of the twelfth century), no difference *in form* between the two Infinitives was left. The *functions*, however, that is, the syntactical uses, of the two Infinitives are still as distinct as ever,—the Simple Infinitive having the force of a noun, the Gerundial that of an adjective or adverb (§ 127).

491. Gerund or Verbal noun in -ing.—The suffix *-ing* is from A.S. *-ing* or (as it was more commonly spelt) *-ung*. A word formed by adding *-ing* to a verb-stem, as "binding," was a noun pure and simple. The *-ung* or *-ing* was purely a noun-forming suffix, like *-th* in steal-*th*, or *-r* in stai-*r*, or *-l* in aw-*l*, or *-m* in doo-*m*. Though we now call such a word a gerund, it is properly speaking a noun in Modern English also. In this respect there is no breach of continuity from the time of Alfred the Great up to the present day.

As we approach the modern period, the habit grew up of omitting the preposition *of* after such nouns; cf. a similar omission in "on board (of) ship," "a thousand (of) pounds," "a many (of) tears," "despite (of) those riches" (Scott). Thus men began to say "showing compassion" for "showing (of) compassion." The omission of the preposition "of" made the noun "showing" look like a verb with the noun "compassion" as its object. "Showing" as a Pres. part. was known to be a verb already, and so "showing," the abstract noun, looked like a verb also.

It was thus the identity in form between the Pres. part. "show-*ing*" and the abstract noun "show-*ing*" which gave rise to the notion that the latter must be a verb like the former; and it was the omission of the preposition "of" which completed the illusion.

When the abstract noun "showing" was thus made out to be a part of the verb "show," it was very easy to coin a Past form "having shown" corresponding to the form of the Past participle:—

He was praised for *having shown* compassion.

For words thus used, such as "showing" and "having shown," "grammarians in despair have invented the term *gerund*" (Skeat); and we must now accept these forms as "developments of modern English" (Sweet).

But it should be clearly understood that there is no connection whatever between this modern Gerund and the old Gerundial Infinitive. The latter invariably ended in *-anne*, or *-enne*, or *-en* (§ 490), until (by about A.D. 1500) the inflexion died out altogether. The final *-enne* never took the form of *-inge* or *-ing*, and in fact it has no connection with it whatever.

PART VI.—SOUNDS, SYMBOLS, AND SPELLINGS.

CHAPTER XXXIV.—LETTERS, ACCENTS, SYLLABLES.

492. A letter (Latin *litera*, Fr. *lettre*) is a mark or symbol that stands for a certain sound. Without letters men can talk as fast as they like, but they cannot either read or write. A word, until it is written, is merely a sound, perceptible to the ear, but not to the eye.

Letters are subdivided into two great classes, vowels and consonants.

493. Vowel is from Lat. *vocalis*, Fr. *voyelle*,—L. *vox*, *vocis*, the voice. A vowel, as its etymology implies, stands for a *voice*-sound, *i.e.* a sound or tone produced by the unimpeded passage of the breath, without the help of a consonant. Thus it is quite as easy to say *e* as *be*.

494. Consonant (L. *con*, together with, *sonant-em*, sounding). This, as its name implies, stands for a sound that cannot be easily, if at all, produced except in company with a vowel. Thus it is not easy to pronounce the letter *b*, until we connect it with some vowel, as *be*. In fact, we find it so difficult to sound *b* by itself, that we have called the consonant *be*, not *b*.

495. The English Alphabet.—Our alphabet consists of 26 letters, of which 5 are vowels, 19 are consonants, and 2 are semivowels, *i.e.* dubious letters.

Vowels.—A, a; E, e; I, i; O, o; U, u.

Consonants.—B, b; C, c; D, d; F, f; G, g; H, h; J, j; K, k; L, l; M, m; N, n; P, p; Q, q; R, r; S, s: T, t; V, v; X, x; Z, z.

Semivowels.—Y, y; W, w.

The letter *y* is superfluous as a vowel; for it expresses precisely the same sound as *i*. Thus there is no difference of sound between the first syllables of *sin*-ner and *syn*-tax. As a consonant, however, the *y* is indispensable; for we could not express such words as *yoke*, *yet* without it.

The letter *w* as a vowel is even less useful (if this were possible) than *y;* for it cannot stand alone as *y* can, but is seen only in such combinations as *aw*, *ew*, *ow*, all of which can be quite as easily spelt *au*, *eu*, *ou*. As a consonant, however, the letter *w* is indispensable; for it enables us to express such words as *will*, *wax*, *wet*.

Note.—The vowels *i* and *u* (care being taken that *u* here stands for the *u* in *full*, and *not* for the *u* in *tune*) acquire the consonantal sounds of *y* and *w* respectively, when they are followed by other vowels. Thus *opinion* is sounded as if it were spelt *o-pin-yon* (three syllables). Similarly if we attempt to sound *uilliam* we get *William*. The letter *w* is merely a double *v*, though it is called a "double *u*." The symbol *v* is merely another form of *u*, and in Latin during the classical period *u* was the only symbol used.

496. **Digraph, diphthong.**—It is necessary to understand clearly what is meant by these two words.

A *digraph* is a compound **letter**; a *diphthong* is a compound **sound**. "Digraph" is from Greek *di*, two or twice, and *graph*, to write: it therefore means "a double letter." "Diphthong" is from Greek *di*, two or twice, and *phthong*-os, a sound: it therefore means "a double sound."

Owing to the fewness of our vowel-*symbols* and the multiplicity of our vowel-*sounds* we are sometimes forced to use a digraph for expressing a vowel-sound that is simple or uncompounded, as *au*. On the other hand, it sometimes happens (such is the perversity of our spelling) that we use a single letter to express a vowel-sound that is compound; as *u* in *tu-bu-lar*, sounded as *tyōō-byŏŏ-lar*.

Similarly we sometimes use a digraph to express a single consonantal sound, as *ph* in *Philip;* and a single consonant to express a double sound, as *x* in *tax*, sounded as *taks*.

497. **Voiceless and Voiced Consonants.**[1]—Consonants are subdivided into two great classes, the Voiceless and the Voiced. Voiced is the name given to those consonants which can be sounded to a slight extent *without the help of a vowel;* the Voiceless are those to which no sound whatever can be given without this help. The Voiced therefore have something of a

[1] *Voiceless* and *Voiced* are the names adopted by Professor Skeat. **Surd** (silent) and **Sonant** (sounding) are equally suitable. The names Hard and Soft, Sharp and Flat, are also used; but they are not suitable. An apple may be hard or soft, but not a consonant.

vocalic character, and are a connecting link between Voiceless consonants and Vowels.

Consonants as thus distinguished go for the most part in pairs. All consonants not included amongst these pairs are Voiced, with the exception of *h*, which is Voiceless.

Voiceless.	*Voiced.*	*Voiceless.*	*Voiced.*	*Voiceless.*	*Voiced.*
k	g	s	z	p	b
ch	j	t	d	f	v
sh	zh	th(in)	th(is)	wh	w

The distinction between Voiceless and Voiced can be easily verified by any one who will make the experiment on his own organs. We can sound *ka*, for instance, so long as the *k* is followed by a vowel. But if we cut off the *a* and try to sound the *k* alone, we cannot produce any sound whatever, though we are conscious of a feeling of muscular tension in the tongue. There is no *voice* in it ; and hence the consonant *k* is classed as Voiceless.

On the other hand, if we take the combination *ga*, and cut off the *a*, we find that without the assistance of this or any other vowel it is possible to make an audible guggle. This consonant is therefore classed among the Voiced.

The following facts are of very wide application :—

I.—When two consonants come together, voiceless consonants are assimilated in sound to voiced ones, or voiced to voiceless.

(*a*) In monosyllables the first letter usually holds its ground, and the second has to give way to it. Compare the *s* in *cats* with that in *lads*. In the first the *s* remains voiceless, because it is preceded by the voiceless *t*. In the second the *s* becomes a voiced letter, *i.e.* receives the sound of *z*, because it is preceded by a voiced *d*. Similarly compare the *d* in *looked* with that in *loved*, the *s* in *caps* with that in *cabs*.

(*b*) In dissyllables and compound words the first letter usually gives way to the second one ; as in *five*-teen, sounded and spelt as *fif*-teen ; *cup-board*, sounded, though not spelt, as *cub-board ; black-guard*, sounded, though not spelt, as *blag-guard*.

This process is very commonly at work in prefixes. Thus we have a*c*cent for a*d*cent, a*ff*lict for a*df*lict, a*p*pear for a*dp*ear, a*s*sent for a*ds*ent, a*t*tain for a*dt*ain, a*g*grieve for a*dg*rieve, a*l*lot for a*dl*ot, a*n*nul for a*dn*ul, a*r*rive for a*dr*ive, inte*l*lect for inte*rl*ect, o*c*cur for o*bc*ur, o*f*fer for o*bf*er, o*p*pose for o*bp*ose, pe*l*lucid for pe*rl*ucid, po*l*lute for po*rl*ute, su*c*ceed for su*bc*eed, su*p*port for su*bp*ort, etc.

II.—A voiceless consonant often receives the sound of a voiced one, when it is placed between two vowels. Thus in *breath* the *th* is voiceless; but in *breathe*, where it stands between two vowels, it is voiced. Again *rise* is sounded as *rize*, not as *rice*. *Lathe* is sounded, not as *lath*, but with the sound *th* as in *th*(is).

III.—When one consonant is substituted for another, as sometimes happens, a voiceless consonant is displaced by a voiceless one, and a voiced by a voiced. This is especially seen in doublets,—that is, pairs of words derived from the same original elements, but differently spelt:—

Croo*k*, cro*s*s (*k* substituted for *s*, both voiceless). A*p*titude, a*t*titude (*p* and *t*, both voiceless). Aprico*ck* (older spelling) and aprico*t* (*k* and *t*, both voiceless). Bar*b*, bear*d* (*b* and *d*, both voiced). *W*rap, *l*ap (*r* and *l*, both voiced). P*r*u*n*e, p*l*u*m* (*r* and *l*, *n* and *m*, both pairs voiced). *W*ard, *g*uard (*w* and *g*, both voiced).

In *sh*oe (A.S. *scó*) we find *sh* substituted for *sk* (both voiceless). So too in *sh*e (Midland *scǽ*). In "see*th*e," "sod*d*en," voiced *th* is interchanged with voiced *d*; so too in mur*th*er (older spelling), mur*d*er. In the 3rd Sing. "cast-*s*" (older form, cast-*es*, cast-*eth*) we find the voiceless *s* substituted for the voiceless *th*.

In A.S. final or medial *h* was sounded almost like *k*, as in "Lo*ch* Lomond." A survival of this occurs in the word *next* (=*nekst*), which in A.S. was spelt *nehst*. In modern English this *h* has been usually respelt as *gh*. In the words "lou*gh*" and "hou*gh*" (sounded as *lok*, *hok*), the original sound of the *k* has been retained. But in certain other words, as *enough*, *laugh*, *rough*, *trough*, *tough*, *cough*, the sound of *f* has been substituted for the sound of *k*, both letters being voiceless.

498. Accent, Emphasis, Quantity.—Roughly speaking, both accent and emphasis are the effect of *loudness* (which helps to produce distinctness), while quantity depends on the *time* that it takes to pronounce a syllable.

When we lay stress upon a *single syllable*, *i.e.* pronounce it more loudly and distinctly than the other syllable or syllables of the same word, this is called **Accent** (Latin *ad*, to, *cantus*, a song).

Sup-ply′, sim′-ply. Re-bel′ (verb), reb′-el (noun).

When we lay stress upon *an entire word*, *i.e.* pronounce it more loudly and distinctly than any other word of the same sentence or phrase, this is called **Emphasis** (Greek *en*, in or on, *phasis*, speech).

I appeal from Philip *drunk* to Philip *sober*.

Quantity means "the amount of *time* occupied in uttering a vowel or syllable." If the time so occupied is short, the vowel or syllable is said to be short; otherwise, it is said to be long.

A vowel can be long either by nature or by position. (1) Vowels long by nature are exemplified in *fate*, *fraud*, *smote*, *bite*, etc.; vowels short by nature are seen in *fat*, *pod*, *hit*, *wet*, etc. (2) Vowels long by position, but short by nature, are seen in *west*, *land*, *flint*, *stump*, *bond*. The vowels themselves in such words or syllables are not long, but they are said to be made long by position, because they are followed by a strong combination of consonants, which prevents the syllable from being sounded rapidly.

499. Importance of Accent in English.—In English as now spoken quantity counts for very little: accent is all-important. Thus the word *guard* is certainly a long syllable when it stands alone; but in the combination "blackguard" (sounded as *blag'-guard*) the accent thrown upon the first syllable compels us to make the second syllable as short as we can pronounce it. Again, the diphthong *u* (i.e. *u* sounded as *yoo*) is long by nature, as in *tube*. But in the adjective *tu'-bu-lar* the second *u*, though long by nature like the first one, is, owing to the want of accent, made as short as we can pronounce it.

Such is the effect of accent in our language that an unaccented syllable sometimes disappears altogether. Thus *ap-pren'-tice* has been reduced to *pren'-tice*; *dam'-o-sel* (older spelling) to *dam'-sel*; *co-roné* (Lat. "corona") to *crown*; *la-ven'-der-ess* to *laun'-dress*; *with-draw'-ing-room* to *draw'-ing-room*; *pun'-ish* to *punch*; *sa'-cris-tan* to *sex'-ton*; *pa-ral'-y-sie* (Gr. "paralysis") to *pal'-e-sy*, *pal'-sy*; *en-sam'-ple* to *sam'-ple*; *dis-port'* to *sport*; *hy-drop'-sy* to *drop'-sy*; *af-fray'* to *fray*; *es-quire'* to *squire*; *a-mend'* to *mend*; *ap-peal'* to *peal*; *de-spite'* to *spite*.

The part of speech to which a word belongs often depends upon the accent. If the choice lies between a verb and a noun, both spelt alike, the verb has the accent on the last syllable, the noun on the first. Of this we have at least sixty examples.

Com-pound' (verb), com'-pound (noun). Con-duct' (verb), con'-duct (noun). Con-fine' (verb), con'-fine (noun). Con-vert' (verb), con'-vert (noun). Con-vict' (verb), con'-vict (noun), etc.

If the choice lies between a verb and an adjective, the verb has the accent on the last syllable, as before:—

Ab-sent' (verb), ab'-sent (adj.). Fre-quent' (verb), fre'-quent (adj.).

If the choice lies between a noun and an adjective, the noun has the accent on the first syllable, as before, and the adjective on the second :—

Com′-pact (noun), com-pact′ (adj.). Min′-ute (noun), mi-nute′ (adj.). In′-va-lid (noun), in-val′-id (adj.).

Note.—Sometimes, however, there is no difference of accent; as *con-tent′* (adj. and verb), *con-tents′* (noun); *con-sent′*, *re-spect′*, *her′-ald*, *sup-port′* (all nouns and verbs); *con′-crete*, *pa′-tient* (both nouns and adjectives). Such examples are not common.

500. Syllabic division.—In dividing a word into syllables we must be guided by the pronunciation (which of course is very much affected by the accent), not by the etymology. "Word-division," says Professor Skeat, "has nothing to do with etymology. From a practical point of view *im′-pu-dence* is right, being based on the spoken language. It is only when we take the word to pieces, that we discover that it is formed from *im-* (for *in-*), the base *pud*, and the suffix *-ence*. Yet we divide the word as *im′-pu-dence*, not as *im-pud′-ence*. The spoken language has *pe-ruse′* at one moment, and *pe-ru′-sal* at another. It rightly regards ease of utterance, and nothing else."

We divide "banquet" into *ban′-quet;* we are compelled to do so by the accent. But if we followed the etymology we should have to divide it into *banqu-et*, and ignore the accent altogether; for the stem of the word is *banque*, Fr.

CHAPTER XXXV.—VOWEL-SOUNDS AND HOW THEY ARE SPELT.

501. Twenty vowel-sounds.[1]—If our alphabet were more perfect than it is, we should have one separate symbol to express each separate sound. Unfortunately it is very imperfect; for we have only five vowel-signs (*y* having been excluded as superfluous) to express four times as many sounds. Of these twenty vowel-sounds, sixteen are simple, and four are diphthongs. (The phrase "phonetic symbol" used below means the symbol used to

[1] The list of twenty sounds here given, though not the same as that given in some school-books, will, I trust, be accepted as correct; for it is the one on which all the best authorities are agreed,—Professor Skeat, Mr. Sweet, Miss Laura Soames, and Dr. Murray (in the introduction to the Oxford Dictionary). Dr. Murray's system is much more elaborate, but the basis is the same. As to the phonetic symbol most suitable for each sound, authorities are not equally unanimous. I have myself adopted those symbols which seemed likely to cause the least difficulty to a beginner, and which come nearest to those used in the current Dictionaries.

express or denote the *one particular sound* assigned to it. The reason why some are bracketed as pairs is explained in § 502.)

A. Four sounds[1] frequently denoted by the symbol *a*; one short, and three long; all simple, none diphthongal.

{ 1. Short: the sound of *a* in *marry*. Phonetic symbol **ă**.
{ 2. Long: the sound of *a* in *Mary*. Phonetic symbol **â**.
3. Long: the sound of *a* in *mason*. Phonetic symbol **ā**.

Note.—Observe that (3) is quite a distinct sound from (2). In sounding (2) you have to open the mouth a great deal wider than in sounding (3). In (2) the *a* is always followed by an *r*; in (3) it never is. No. (2) is merely No. (1) drawled or lengthened.

4. Long: the sound of *a* in *path*. Phonetic symbol **ȧ**.

E. Two sounds commonly denoted by the symbol *e*; one short, and one long; both simple, neither diphthongal.

5. Short: the sound of *e* in *fed*. Phonetic symbol **ĕ**.
6. Long: the sound of *ee* in *feed*. Phonetic symbol **ē**.

I. Two sounds commonly denoted by the symbol *i*; one short, and one long: the short is simple, the long diphthongal.

7. Short: the sound of *i* in *bit*. Phonetic symbol **ĭ**.
8. Long: the sound of *i* in *bite*. Phonetic symbol **ī**.

O. Three sounds commonly denoted, and a fourth occasionally denoted, by the symbol *o*; two short and two long; all simple, none diphthongal.

{ 9. Short: the sound of *o* in *lot*. Phonetic symbol **ŏ**.
{ 10. Long: the sound of *o* in *lost*. Phonetic symbol **au**.

Note.—Since the usual spelling is *au*, as in "fraud," this has been made the phonetic symbol in preference to *o*. But the use of the digraph *au* does not make the sound less simple than it is. In fact (10) is nothing more than (9) drawled or lengthened. If *dog* is drawled, it has the sound of *daug*. If the first syllable of *laurel* is shortened (as in practice it always is), it has the sound of *lŏrel*, rhyming with "moral." *Not* is merely the short of *naught*.

{ 11. Short: the sound of *o* in *o*-mit. Phonetic symbol **o'**.
{ 12. Long: the sound of *o* in *tone*. Phonetic symbol **ō**.

---

[1] To the four *a* sounds given above, some writers add two more, viz. the *a* in *fall* and the *a* in *want*. The latter is evidently a mistake. It creates a redundancy and leads to confusion; for the *a* in *want* is identical in sound with the *o* in *not*, and it never has the sound of *o* except when it is preceded by *w*. In fact, it is an *o* sound, and its connection with *a* is both accidental and exceptional. The former is not an *a* sound either, and is not expressed by *a* except when the *a* is followed by *l*. Professor Skeat associates only four sounds with the symbol *a* (see his Note printed in page 459 of my *English Grammar Past and Present*).

Note.—There is a great difference between (11) and (9). In sounding (9) you have to open your mouth rather wide, whereas in sounding (11) you almost close it. No. (12) is merely No. (11) drawled or lengthened.

OO. Two sounds commonly denoted by the digraph *oo;* one short, the other long; both simple, neither diphthongal.

{ 13. Short: the sound of *oo* in *stood.* Phonetic symbol **ŏŏ**.
{ 14. Long: the sound of *oo* in *stool.* Phonetic symbol **o͞o**.

U. Two sounds commonly denoted by the symbol *u;* one short, the other long; the short simple, the long diphthongal.

15. Short: the sound of *u* in *duck.* Phonetic symbol **ŭ**.
16. Long: the sound of *u* in *duke.* Phonetic symbol **ū**.

Oi. One sound commonly denoted by the digraph *oi;* diphthongal.

17. Long: the sound of *oi* in *toil.* Phonetic symbol **oi**.

Ou. One sound commonly denoted by the digraph *ou;* diphthongal.

18. Long: the sound of *ou* in *mouse.* Phonetic symbol **ou**.

Lastly, we come to two sounds, one short, the other long, and both simple or non-diphthongal. These have been called the Obscure, Neutral, or Indefinite sounds. For the expression of these sounds we have no vowel in our alphabet. So the expedient which the best authorities have agreed upon is to use ə (inverted *e*) for the phonetic symbol.

{ 19. Short: the sound of *er*[1] in gath′-*er.* Phonetic symbol **ə**.
{ 20. Long: the sound of *er*[1] in con-*fer′*. Phonetic symbol **əə**.

502. General results.—We have thus twenty vowel-sounds, of which sixteen are pure or simple, and four are mixed or diphthongal. The sixteen simple sounds are subdivided into (*a*) eight short, viz. **ă, ĕ, ĭ, ŏ, o′, ŏŏ, ŭ,** and **ə**; and (*b*) eight long, viz. **â, ā, ȧ, ē, au, ō, o͞o,** and **əə**. The four diphthongs are **ī, ū, oi,** and **ou**.

Sounds which in the above description are bracketed together as short and long are real pairs. Thus, the *a* of *Mary* is the

---

[1] In Scotland, however, and in some of the northern counties of England, the *r* is trilled, that is, distinctly sounded as *r*. Owing to this peculiarity of the Northern dialect, I have been reluctantly compelled to adopt from Mr. Skeat, Mr. Sweet, Miss Soames, and Dr. Murray the awkward-looking symbol ə. This sound is so natural to human speech that hesitating speakers use it to fill up the pauses in their sentences. In books such pauses are printed thus:—"I—*er*—am aware—*er*—that," etc.

drawled or lengthened sound of the *a* in *marry;* the *o* of *lost* is the lengthened sound of the *o* in *lot;* the *o* of *tone* is the lengthened sound of the *o* in *o*-mit; the *oo* of *stool* is the lengthened sound of the *oo* in *stood;* the *er* in con-*fer′* is the lengthened and accented sound of the *er* in gath′-*er*.

On the other hand, the sounds which are not bracketed together as short and long are not pairs. Thus the *ee* in *feed* is not the long sound of *e* in *fed;* the *i* of *bite* is not the long sound of *i* in *bit;* the *u* in duke is not the long sound of *u* in *duck.* Though the same vowel is used in each case, the sounds are entirely distinct. For instance, the sound of *ee* in *feed* pairs not with *ĕ*, but with *ĭ*. The sound of *ĭ* is actually expressed by *ee* in the word "breeches" (sounded short as if it were spelt *brĭches*). Again, the sound of *ā* pairs not with *ă*, but with *ĕ;* thus *waist′*-coat is sounded short as if it were spelt *wĕst′*-coat.

503. How the four diphthongs are produced.—Let us take each diphthong in turn.[1]

ī. The first vowel-sound that helps to make this diphthong is obsolete in modern English, though still heard in the north-country dialects, where the *a* of *man* has retained a sound intermediate between **ă** and **ȧ** (Nos. 1 and 4). This intermediate sound rapidly followed by the *i* of *bit* produces a third sound distinct from either. The spelling, *ai*, is seen in the word *aisle* (sounded as *īl*).

Note.—The sound of *ȧ*, when added to *i*, would produce a diphthong, like the sound of *ai* in *Isaiah, naive, Kaiser.*

ū. Made up of *ĭ* + *ōō*. These, when sounded rapidly in succession, give *yōō*, like the *u* in *duke* (sounded as "dyōōk").

oi. Made up of *au* (see No. 10 in § 501) + *ĭ*. The utterance of these two simple sounds in rapid succession produces a mixed sound distinct from both.

ou. Made up of *ȧ* (see No. 4 in § 501) + *ŏŏ*. The utterance of these two simple sounds in rapid succession produces a mixed sound distinct from both.

Note.—We now see very clearly what was stated above in § 496, that the use of a digraph or two letters to express a sound is no proof

[1] It has been pointed out by phoneticians (Skeat, Sweet, Soames, Dr. Murray) that the long vowels which I have written as **ā** and **ō** are usually sounded with the glides *i* and *u* respectively, as a^i, o^u, and that hence these vowels are in a certain sense diphthongal. They are not diphthongal, however, to the same extent that **ī**, **ū**, **oi**, and **ou** are. For the sake of simplicity I have followed Miss Laura Soames in treating them as simple vowels, not as diphthongs.

that the sound is diphthongal or mixed. Thus ī and ū, though expressed by single vowels, are both diphthongs; while **au, ŏŏ, ōō, əə**, though expressed by digraphs, are all simple sounds.

504. Spellings of the twenty vowel-sounds.—We shall follow the order of vowels, simple and diphthongal, given in § 501.

1. **ă**: m*a*d, pl*ai*d, h*a*v*e*, s*al*mon, thr*e*sh.
2. **â**: M*a*ry, *ai*ry, b*ea*rer, h*ei*ress, m*ayo*ralty, th*e*r*e*in.
3. **ā**: f*a*tal, f*a*t*e*, t*ai*l, pl*ay*, camp*aig*n, str*aigh*t, v*ei*n, th*ey*, r*eig*n, w*eigh*, st*ea*k, g*ao*l, g*au*ge, *eh*, d*ah*lia, h*alf*penny. French words: f*ê*te, cong*é*, ball*et*, champ*ag*ne, dem*es*ne.
4. **ȧ**: p*a*th, *a*rt, h*ea*rt, cl*e*rk, *au*nt, baz*aa*r, p*al*m, hurr*ah*, pl*ai*ster. Fr. words: v*as*e, écl*at*.
5. **ĕ**: b*e*d, h*ea*d, *a*ny, s*ai*d, s*ay*s, l*eo*pard, l*ei*sure, r*ey*nard, *a*t*e*, fr*ie*nd, b*u*ry.
6. **ē**: m*e*, th*e*m*e*, s*ee*n, *ea*ch, f*ie*ld, s*ei*ze,[1] k*ey*, C*æ*sar, pol*i*c*e*, inval*i*d, qu*ay*, p*eo*ple, rec*ei*pt, B*eau*champ.
7. **ĭ**: b*i*t, n*y*mph, pr*e*tty, g*i*v*e*, surf*ei*t, marr*ie*d, happ*y*, guin*ea*, donk*ey*, w*o*men, b*u*sy, br*ee*ches, s*ie*v*e*.
8. **ī**: *i*dol, tr*y*, m*i*n*e*, l*y*r*e*, s*ig*n, h*igh*, h*eigh*t, d*ie*, r*ye*, *is*land, *ai*sle, ch*oi*r, ind*i*ct, *eye*.
9. **ŏ**: fr*o*m, w*a*nt, sh*o*n*e*, l*au*rel, kn*ow*ledge, y*ach*t, h*ou*gh.
10. **au**: h*au*l, l*aw*, l*o*st, t*all*, t*al*k, p*ou*r, *ough*t, br*oa*d, s*o*r*e*, l*o*rd, w*a*r, w*a*ter, *augh*t, V*augh*an, g*o*n*e*.
11. **o'**: her*o*, foll*ow*, her*oe*s, foll*ow*ed, furl*ough*. Fr. dép*ôt*.
12. **ō**: n*o*, n*o*t*e*, b*o*th, t*oa*d, t*oe*, d*ough*, m*ow*, br*oo*ch, *oh*, y*eo*man, s*ew*, C*ock*burn. Fr. m*au*v*e*, b*eau*.
13. **ŏŏ**: st*oo*d, f*u*ll, c*oul*d, w*o*lf.
14. **ōō**: f*oo*l, t*o*mb, sh*oe*, m*o*v*e*, s*ou*p, thr*ough*, tr*u*th, bl*ue*, j*ui*ce, sl*eu*th-hound, sl*ew*, r*u*d*e*, man*œu*vre.
15. **ŭ**: sh*u*t, bl*oo*d, s*o*n, c*o*m*e*, t*ou*ch.
16. **ū** (=yōō): d*u*-ty, t*u*n*e*, d*ue*, s*ui*t, f*ew*, f*eu*d, l*ieu*, v*iew*, im-p*ug*n.
17. **oi**: c*oi*l, b*oy*.
18. **ou**: l*ou*d, d*ow*n.
19. **ə**: Chi'-n*a*, Sa'-r*ah*, suf'-f*e*r, squir'-r*e*l, but'-t*o*n, Eu'-r*o*pe, thor'-*ough*, tor'-t*oi*s*e*, fa'-m*ou*s, meer'-sch*au*m, waist-c*oa*t, cup'-b*oa*rd, pleas'-*u*r*e*, col'-l*a*r, mar'-t*y*r, bun'-k*u*m, an'-ch*o*r, ran'-c*ou*r, mur'-m*u*r (all in unaccented syllables. This sound is never accented).
20. **əə**: h*e*rd, *e*rr*e*d, h*ea*rd, b*i*rd, st*i*rr*e*d, t*u*rn, bl*u*rr*e*d, w*o*rd, *colo*-nel (sounded as k*er*'-nel). (All in accented syllables.)

One hundred and ninety spellings (not counting the French words) for twenty vowel-sounds.

505. Same spelling with different sounds.—We may now invert the process, and show how the same symbol (*i.e.* the same spelling) may be used to denote different sounds:—

[1] The following is a list of all the words in which *ei* has the sound of *ē*:—conceive, deceive, perceive, receive (and their derivatives), ceiling, seize, either, neither, plebeian, weir, weird, seignory, inveigle, counterfeit.

a : r*a*t, t*a*ll, p*a*th, m*a*ny, m*a*de, c*a*re, w*a*nt. stew*a*rd
a—e : r*a*v*e*, h*a*v*e*, *a*r*e*, *a*t*e*.
ai : m*ai*d, s*ai*d, pl*ai*d, *ai*sle.
au : *au*nt, h*au*nt, g*au*ge, m*au*ve, meer-sch*au*m.
e : h*e*, h*e*r, cl*e*rk, b*e*d, pr*e*tty.
e—e : th*e*r*e*, h*e*r*e*.
ea : h*ea*t, st*ea*k, h*ea*rt, h*ea*d.
ei : v*ei*n, l*ei*sure, s*ei*ze, sur-f*ei*t, h*ei*ght.
ey : th*ey*, k*ey*, *ey*e.
ew : n*ew*, s*ew*.
i—e : b*i*t*e*, n*i*ch*e*, pol*i*c*e*.
ie : f*ie*ld, d*ie*, s*ie*ve.
o : h*o*t, c*o*ld, w*o*lf, w*o*men, wh*o*m, s*o*n, butt*o*n, l*o*st, her*o*.
o—e : c*o*v*e*, pr*o*v*e*, l*o*v*e*, m*o*v*e*, sh*o*v*e*.
oa : l*oa*d, br*oa*d, cup-b*oa*rd.
oe : sh*oe*, t*oe*.
oo : h*oo*k, f*oo*l, br*oo*ch, fl*oo*d, d*oo*r.
ou : p*ou*r, y*ou*ng, th*ou*, s*ou*p, s*ou*l.
ough : r*ough*, hicc*ough*, c*ough*, h*ough*, tr*ough*, b*ough*, th*ough*, thr*ough*.
al : f*al*l, p*al*m, sh*al*l, hospit*al*.
ol : c*ol*d, w*ol*f, g*ol*f, sym′-b*ol*.
ar : *ar*′-row, *ar*t, col-l*ar*.

Note.—The reasons why our vowels came to express so many different sounds are—(1) because the Norman scribes, when they addressed themselves to the study of English, discarded the marks or accents denoting vowel-length in Anglo-Saxon words, and their example has been followed ever since; (2) because our vocalic symbols, though sufficient for the simple and pure language for which they were originally intended, are not sufficient for the very composite language that English has since become; (3) because one of the vocalic symbols (æ) used in A.S. has disappeared in modern English, though the sounds that it expressed have remained; (4) because in the sixteenth and seventeenth centuries a general shifting of the vowel-sounds took place, which was very seldom accompanied by a change of spelling; (5) because the sounds of certain vowels are affected by the proximity of certain consonants, the presence or absence of an accent, and by syllabic division; in short, the sound of a vowel varies with its surroundings.

For example, the vowel *a*, as shown above, is now used to express at least eight different sounds, viz. those exemplified in *rat, tall, path, many, made, care, was, steward.* (1) The sound of *a* in *rat* was represented in A.S. by the symbol *æ;* as this has become obsolete, *a* is made to do duty for it. (2) The sound of *a* in *tall* is produced by the liquid *l*, which has had the effect of prolonging the vowel and deepening its tone. (3) The sound of *a* in *path* was represented in A.S. by *á;* but as the accent has gone out of use, there is nothing but the simple *a* left to express this sound. (4) The sound of *a* in *many* (A.S. *manig*) may be ascribed to the frequent interchange of *a* and *e* in English; cf. A.S. *thenc-an, thank:* the sound of the *a* in *manig* has changed, but the spelling has remained. (5) The sound of *a* in *made* was represented in A.S. by *é* (very nearly); but as the sound of A.S. *é* has since shifted to that of *ee* in *seem*, the vowel *a* has been made to do duty for it. (6) The sound of *a* in *care* was represented in A.S. by *ǽ* (very nearly); but as this symbol has become obsolete, the vowel *a* followed by *re* has had to take its place. (7) The sound of *a* in *was* (=*wos*) is produced by the rounding of the lips in sounding the *w* that goes before; and in sounding the vowel *o*, the lips are somewhat rounded also. (8) The indefinite or neutral sound of *a* in *steward* arises from the want of accent on the syllable in which it stands.

CHAPTER XXXVI.—CONSONANTAL SOUNDS AND HOW THEY ARE SPELT.

506. Twenty-five Consonantal sounds.—In English as now spoken there are altogether *twenty-five* consonantal sounds. The symbols used to denote these sounds, if we place them as nearly as we can in the order of the alphabet, run as follows:—

1. b	4. g	7. k	10. n	13. s	16. w	19. ch	22. th(in)
2. d	5. h	8. l	11. p	14. t	17. y	20. ng	23. sh
3. f	6. j	9. m	12. r	15. v	18. z	21. th(is)	24. zh
							25. wh

507. Simple and Compound.—Out of the twenty-five sounds enumerated above all are simple or uncompounded except two, viz. *j* and *ch*. These are called by Dr. Murray (in the Oxford Dictionary) "consonantal diphthongs," because he, with other phoneticians, has analysed *ch* into *t* + *sh*, and *j* into *d* + *zh*. Thus the sound of *ritshes* cannot be distinguished from that of *riches;* nor the sound of *ridzhid* from that of *rigid* = *rijid*.

Though we have to accept this analysis on the word of the best authorities, and on the evidence of our own experience, it would be very inconvenient to write *tsh* for *ch*, and *dzh* for *j*. Moreover, the two sounds in question are of such frequent occurrence in our language, that *j* and *ch*, even if the sounds are diphthongal, deserve a place in the list of our consonantal symbols.

508. Redundant consonants.—It has been said that "our alphabet contains four redundant consonants—*c*, *j*, *q*, *x*." The statement may be admitted for the following reasons:—

C is superfluous, because (1) when it precedes *a*, *o*, or *u*, it expresses the sound of *k;* (2) when it precedes *e* or *i*, it expresses the sound of *s;* (3) when it is combined with *h*, as in *church*, the digraph *ch* has been analysed into *tsh*.

J is superfluous, because it has been analysed into *dzh*.

Q is superfluous, because it is never used except in combination with *u*, and the combination can be expressed equally well by *kw*, as in *awkward*. In A.S. the letters used were *cw*, as in *cwén*, a woman.

X is superfluous, because in such words as *extra* it is equivalent to *ks*, and in *example* to *gz*.

509. **Main divisions of consonants.**—The consonantal sounds can be classified according to the organ chiefly used in uttering them. Any part of our bodily structure that helps us to utter articulate sounds may be called an organ of speech. The chief organs are the tongue, the throat, the palate, the teeth, and the lips. By means of these organs the breath is modified as it passes through the larynx.

The most important of all these organs is the tongue; for the loss of this organ involves the loss of articulate speech. Since the tongue is the necessary helpmate to the other four organs, there is no separate class of Lingual (Lat. *lingua*, tongue).

The main divisions of consonants are as follows:—

I. **Gutturals** (Lat. *guttur*, throat): *k*, *g*, *ng*.
II. **Palatals** (Lat. *palatum*, palate): *ch*, *j* | *sh*, *zh* | *y*, *r*.
III. **Dentals** (Lat. *dent-em*, tooth): *t*, *d* | *s*, *z* | *n*, *l* | *th*(in), *th*(is).
IV. **Labials** (Lat. *labium*, lip): *p*, *b*, *m* | *f*, *v* | *wh*, *w*.

I. **Gutturals**: these three sounds are produced by raising the *back* of the tongue against the *soft* palate, viz. that part of the palate that lies farther back in the throat (Lat. *guttur*):—*k*, as in *k*een; *g*, as in *g*ood; *ng*, as in thi*ng* or fi*n*-ger. The last, though expressed by a digraph, is as simple a sound as the other two. It occurs only when it is followed by another guttural, *k* or *g*, as in bla*n*-ket, fi*n*-ger, or when it comes at the end of a word, as in thi*ng*, ridi*ng*. There is a great difference of sound between the *n* of fi*n*-(ger) and the *n* of fi*n*. The former is a guttural, which you cannot utter without opening your jaws; the latter a dental, which you can utter only with closed teeth.

II. **Palatals**: all these sounds are produced by raising the *front* of the tongue towards the *hard* palate, or palate proper (viz. that part of the palate that lies farther forward than the soft palate):—*ch*, as in *ch*air; *j*, as in *j*oke; *sh*, as in *sh*ip; *zh*, as in sei*z*ure; *y*, as in *y*ield; *r*, as in *r*ob. All of these are simple sounds with the exception of the first two (§ 507).

III. **Dentals**: all these sounds are produced by bringing the point of the tongue towards the teeth or upper gums:—*t*, as in *t*ail; *d*, as in *d*og; | *s*, as in *s*eal; *z*, as in *z*eal; | *n*, as in *n*ame; *l*, as in *l*ine; | *th*(in), as in brea*th*; *th*(is), as in brea*the*. In sounding the first pair, *t* and *d*, the point of the tongue touches the upper teeth. In sounding the second pair, *s* and *z*, it comes very near the roots of the upper teeth, but does not quite touch them. In sounding the third pair, *n* and *l*, it touches the upper gums. In sounding the fourth pair, *th*(in) and *th*(is), it is placed between the upper and the lower teeth.

IV. **Labials**: all these sounds are produced by closing the lips: *p*, as in *p*oor; *b*, as in *b*oon; *m*, as in *m*oon; | *f*, as in *f*ox; *v*, as in *v*ixen; | *wh*, as in *wh*ine; *w*, as in *w*ine. In sounding *p*, *b*, and *m* the lips are closed against each other, while the tongue is left to rest on the lower jaw. In sounding *f* and *v* the edges of the upper teeth are pressed against the lower lip, while the tongue rests on the lower jaw. In sounding *wh* and *w* the lips are rounded with the corners drawn together, while the tongue is almost in the same position as in sounding *g*. Hence *w* and *g* are liable to be interchanged, as in *w*ard (A.S. *w*eard), *g*uard (French spelling).

510. The Glottal "h" (Greek, *glottis*, mouth of the wind-pipe). "Glottal" is the name given to the open throat-sound expressed by the letter *h*. In sounding *h* we make no use of the palate, tongue, teeth, or lips. It is a mere breath-sound or aspirate, and stands alone in our alphabet.

The uncertainty about sounding or not sounding this unfortunate letter appears to have arisen in some way from the collision between English and French, which resulted from the Norman Conquest. In Anglo-Saxon the *h* was very distinctly sounded; in French very indistinctly. Hence the confusion.

511. Minor subdivisions of Consonants.—There are a few subdivisions of consonants, which cross with the four main divisions described above, and sometimes with one another.

Sibilants (Lat. *sibilantes*, hissing). On account of the hissing sound which they express, the name "sibilant" has been given to the letters *s*, *z*, *sh*, and *zh*.

Liquids (Lat. *liquidus*, flowing). This is the name given to the letters *l*, *m*, *n*, *r*, *ng*.

Nasals (Lat. *nasus*, nose); the name given to the three letters *n*, *m*, *ng*. These are called nasals, because in forming the sounds which they express the breath passes up the nose-passage and escapes through the nostril. If the nose-passage is blocked by a cold, *ng* (a guttural) is sounded almost as *g* (another guttural), *n* (a dental) almost as *d* (another dental), and *m* (a labial) almost as *b* (another labial).

Note.—When an *intrusive* consonant, *i.e.* one not belonging to the root, is inserted into a word, the intruder is usually of the same class as the consonant going before :—

Num-*b*-er (Lat. *nu-mer-us*) ; hum-*b*-le (Lat. *hum-il-is*) ; ten-*d*-er (Lat. *ten-er*) ; gen-*d*-er (Lat. *gen-er-is*). Observe the *m* and *b* are both labials, while the *n* and *d* are both dentals.

512. Spellings of the Consonantal sounds.—We shall take each of the twenty-five sounds in the order in which their respective symbols are given in § 506 :—

1. **b** : *b*ond (initial), e*bb* (final), *bu*oy, cu*p*-board.
2. **d** : bon*d*, la*dd*er, call*ed*, hor*de*, wou*ld*.
3. **f** : *f*elt, whi*ff*, *ph*legm, lau*gh*, ha*lf*, o*ft*en, sa*pph*ire, li*eu*-tenant (where *ieu*=*ef*).
4. **g** : *g*ame, e*gg*, *gh*ost, *gu*ard.
5. **h** : *h*ot, *wh*o.
6. **j** : *j*ob, *g*ist, *G*eor*ge*, ju*dge*, ju*dg*ment, sol*di*er, Greenwi*ch*, *g*aol.
7. **k** : *k*ill, *c*all, a*cc*ount, ba*ck*, bis*cu*it, *q*uell, li*qu*or, grotes*que*, a*ch*e, lou*gh*.
8. **l** : *l*ake, ki*ll*, is*l*and, ais*le*, gaze*lle*, sera*gl*io, Woo*lw*ich.
9. **m** : *m*end, ha*mm*er, hy*mn*, la*mb*, progra*mme*, phle*gm*, Ha*mp*den, dra*chm*.
10. **n** : pi*n*, i*nn*, dei*gn*, *kn*ee, *gn*aw, Jo*hn*, Linco*ln*, We*dne*sday, rib*and*, bor*ne*, A*nne*, coi*gne*.
11. **p** : *p*lace, ha*pp*y, ste*ppe*, Cla*ph*am, hiccou*gh*.
12. **r** : *r*ain, bo*rr*ow, *rh*ythm, *wr*ite, Nor*w*ich.
13. **s** : *s*elf, ki*ss*, den*se*, *c*ell, dan*ce*, *sc*ene, coale*sce*, *sch*ism, quar*tz*, *sw*ord, ha*st*en, i*sth*mus, *ps*alm, creva*sse*.
14. **t** : we*t*, ke*tt*le, gaze*tte*, *Th*ames, look*ed*, *tw*o, de*bt*, indi*ct*, recei*pt*, ya*cht*, cas*te*.
15. **v** : *v*est, ha*ve*, na*vv*y, o*f*, ne*ph*ew, ha*lve*.
16. **w** : *w*ine, *wh*en, s*u*ave, ch*o*ir.
17. **y** : *y*ield, un*i*on, hallelu*j*ah. French vi*gn*ette (*gn*=ny) cotil*l*on.
18. **z** : *z*eal, fi*zz*, hi*s*, clean*se*, sci*ss*ors, *X*erxes, fur*ze*, Wedn*es*day, Chis*w*ick, Win*ds*or, ven*is*on, *cz*ar, bu*s*iness.
19. **ch** : *ch*ur*ch*, ni*che*, la*tch*, na*tu*re, ques*ti*on, righ*te*ous, violon*c*ello.
20. **ng** : thi*ng*, fi*n*ger, to*ngue*, ha*nd*kerchief, Birmi*ngh*am.
21. **th**(is) : *th*en, soo*the*.
22. **th**(in) : brea*th*, Ma*tth*ew.
23. **sh** : *sh*all, A*s*ia, ti*ss*ue, pen*si*on, mousta*che*, fu*chs*ia, mi*ssi*on, fa*sh*ion, offi*c*iate, so*ci*al, o*ce*an, con*sci*ence, *sch*edule, vi*ti*ate, por*ti*on, lun*che*on, *ch*aise.
24. **zh** : sei*z*ure, lei*s*ure, occa*si*on, transi*ti*on. Fr. rou*ge*, ré*g*ime, *j*u*j*ube (sometimes sounded as *jujube*).
25. **wh** : *wh*ile (often sounded merely as *w*, except in North Britain).

One hundred and sixty-six spellings (not counting the French words) for twenty-five different sounds.

513. Same spelling with different sounds:—

c: violoncello, *c*at, *c*ity.
ch: a*ch*e, *ch*aise, su*ch*, dra*ch*m (silent).
j: *J*ew, *j*u*j*ube, hallelu*j*ah.
ge: rou*ge*, villa*ge*, *ge*t.
gi: *gi*ve, *gi*nger.
ti: no*ti*on, ques*ti*on, transi*ti*on.
s: ha*s*, ga*s*.
sc: *sc*ene, *sc*arce.
sch: *sch*eme, *sch*edule.
si: occa*si*on, disper*si*on.
th: *th*in, *th*is, *Th*ames.
x: e*x*tra, e*x*ample, *X*erxes. Fr. beau*x*.
ph: nym*ph*, ne*ph*ew.
gh: *gh*ost, lau*gh*, hou*gh*.
qu: li*qu*or, *qu*een.

514. Silent Consonants.

(1) **b** (after *m*): lam*b*, lim*b*, dum*b*, num*b*, plum*b*, clim*b*, clom*b*, tom*b*, wom*b*, crum*b*, thum*b*, com*b*, bom*b*: (the *b* is excrescent in *crumb*, *limb*, *numb*, and *thumb*; in the rest it is part of the root).

b (before *t*): dou*b*t, de*b*t, de*b*tor.

(2) **ch**: ya*ch*t, dra*ch*m, s*ch*ism.

(3) **g** (before *n* and *m*): *g*nat, *g*naw, *g*nash, *g*narled, *g*neiss, dei*g*n, fei*g*n, rei*g*n, champa*g*ne, campai*g*n, coi*g*ne, impu*g*n, phle*g*m.

(4) **gh** (final): hi*gh*, nei*gh*, wei*gh*, dou*gh*, slou*gh* (mire), plou*gh*, thou*gh*, throu*gh*, bou*gh*.

gh (before *t*): cau*gh*t, hau*gh*ty, frau*gh*t, fou*gh*t, nau*gh*t, thou*gh*t, sou*gh*t, bou*gh*t, tau*gh*t, mi*gh*t, ri*gh*t, etc.

(5) **h**: *h*eir, *h*our, *h*onour, *h*umour (where u = yoo), *h*onest, Jo*h*n.

Note.—*h* is sometimes silent in the middle of a word, as "ex*h*ibitor."

(6) **k** (before *n*): *k*now, *k*nack, *k*nave, *k*nead, *k*nee, *k*nell, *k*night, *k*nit, *k*nob, *k*nock, *k*not, *k*nuckle, *k*nack, *k*nout, *k*noll, *k*nacker, *k*napsack, *k*nife.

(7) **l**: cou*l*d, shou*l*d, wou*l*d; yo*l*k, fo*l*k; wa*l*k, ta*l*k; psa*l*m, pa*l*m; ha*l*f, ca*l*f; Linco*l*n.

(8) **n** (after *m*): autum*n*, hym*n*, condem*n*, dam*n*, colum*n*, lim*n*.

(9) **s**: vi*s*count, pui*s*ne (= puny), i*s*le, i*s*land, ai*s*le.

(10) **t** (after *s* and *f* and before *l* and *n*): has*t*en, lis*t*en, glis*t*en, mois*t*en, this*t*le, whis*t*le, wres*t*le, jos*t*le, of*t*en, sof*t*en.

(11) **w** (before *r*): *w*rap, *w*retch, *w*raith, *w*rath, *w*roth, *w*reath, *w*reck, *w*rite, *w*right, *w*rench, *w*rest, *w*rinkle, *w*riggle, *w*rist, *w*rithe *w*rong, *w*rought, a*w*ry.

w: s*w*ord, ans*w*er, t*w*o, *w*ho, Kes*w*ick, Chis*w*ick.

515. The letter "r."—In the Midland and Southern dialects the letter *r* in such words as *hair*, *deer*, *moor*, *pour*, is not sounded as a consonant (unless the next word or the next syllable begins with a vowel), but has the sound of the Indefinite vowel ə (described in § 501), so that here it helps to make a diphthong; as *hâə*, *dēə*, *mōōə*, *pauə*. It is not sounded as a *consonant* except before a word or syllable beginning with a vowel. Compare "*hair*," "the *hair'* of a man"; "*boor*," "a *boor*-ish man."

In the same dialects the letter *r* helps to form a triphthong or treble vowel-sound, in such words as *fire*, *pure*, *destroyer*, *power*, unless the next word or the next syllable begins with a vowel, in which case the *r*, as before, is sounded as a consonant.

In the Northern dialect, however, *i.e.* the dialect commonly spoken in Scotland and some of the northern counties of England, where the *r* is trilled, the letter *r* retains in full its consonantal character, and no such diphthongs or triphthongs are formed.

Exercise

(*a*) 1. Distinguish between *emphasis, accent, quantity*. 2. Give two instances in which words, identical in spelling, are distinguished one from another by accent. 3. "A perfect alphabet would contain a separate letter to represent every simple or elementary sound." Show that the letter *a* in English represents several simple or elementary sounds. 4. What single letters in our alphabet represent compound sounds? 5. "Our alphabet contains four redundant letters—*c, j, q, x*." Discuss this statement. 6. Write two words of one syllable, in the first of which the letter *i* represents a pure vowel sound, and in the second a diphthongal sound. 7. How do you account for the fact that the spelling of English words is often at variance with their pronunciation? 8. Give one example under each of the following to show that in some words—

(i.) The letter *i* represents a diphthongal sound.
(ii.) The letter *s* is written where *z* is sounded.
(iii.) A letter is not sounded at all.

9. State and illustrate the different sounds of the letter *s*. (*Oxford and Cambridge Locals.*)

(*b*) 1. What consonants are redundant in the English alphabet, and in what respects is our alphabet defective in consonants? 2. The sound of *a* in *hate* is expressed in several different ways in written English (as in *bait, may, whey, weight, gaol, gauge*, etc.). Show that there are also several ways in which the sound of *e* in *me* is represented in writing. 3. Give four true Diphthongs, four Liquids, four Sibilants, and four Labials. 4. Explain the terms *letter, diphthong, Labial, Palatal*. How many sounds has the combination *ough?* 5. Quote examples of English words containing *ei* or *ie* (four of each), and of verbs ending in *ceed* or *cede* (two of each). 6. What is a *diphthong?* Give six examples, all different, of so-called diphthongs which are not really diphthongs. 7. How many *true* diphthongs have we in the English language? Quote three words as examples of each of them. (*College of Preceptors.*)

APPENDIX ON DERIVATIONS.

In reading the following lists (which have been mainly compiled from Skeat's Etymological Dictionary), *the student is advised to note down on a separate piece of paper any words, as they occur, whose derivation he thinks he may forget. A few days afterwards he can go over these words privately without at first consulting the book, and see how many or how few of them he has mastered. He can of course refer to the book for verification.*

I.—WORDS DERIVED FROM PROPER NAMES.

Academy, from *Academia*, name of the grove where Plato taught. This grove was called after the hero Academus.

Amazon, a pugnacious masculine woman; called after a race of warlike women, the *Amazons* of Gr. mythology.

Arabesque, fantastic, of Arabian or Moorish design.

Argosy, a large merchant-ship, formerly spelt *aragousy* or *ragusy*. Originally "a ship of Ragusa," a port in Dalmatia. The name, however, became confused with that of the ship *Argo*.

Arras, a rich figured fabric used for a screen, curtain, etc. From the place *Arras*, a town of Artois.

Artesian, from *Artois*, where such wells were early in use.

Assassin, a secret murderer; from *hashishin*, "drinkers of hashish," an extract from Indian hemp, with which the Old Man of the Mountain in the 13th century stimulated his accomplices.

Atlas, a book of maps; from the Greek demigod *Atlas*, who was supposed to bear the world on his shoulders.

Attic, a room under the roof of a house; named after the *Attic* (Athenian) custom of building houses with a low upper story.

August, the month named after *Augustus* Cæsar.

Bantam, the fowl named after *Bantam*, a town in Java.

Bayonet, Fr. *bayonette*, named from *Bayonne*, in France.

Bedlam, Mid. Eng. *bedlem*, a corruption of *Bethlehem*, in Palestine; now applied to the lunatic hospital of St. Mary of Bethlehem.

Bluchers, a kind of half boot; named after General *Blucher*.

Bowdlerise, to expurgate; from a man named *Bowdler*, who published a Shakespeare cleared of all indelicate passages.

Boycott, to excommunicate; from Captain *Boycott*, who in A.D. 1880 was so treated by the Land League in Ireland.

Brougham, a four-wheeled vehicle; named after Lord *Brougham*.

Bunkum, tall talk ; from *Buncombe*, a county of North Carolina, the representative of which persisted in making "a speech from Buncombe," when the House was impatient to have the question put to the vote.

Calico, cotton-cloth, from *Calicut*, on the Malabar Coast, India.

Cambric, a kind of linen cloth ; from *Cambray*, in Flanders (France).

Canary, a kind of bird ; from the *Canary* Islands.

Canter, an easy gallop, at which the *Canter*-bury pilgrims rode.

Chaos, confusion ; the name given by the Greeks to the primeval state of the universe.

Chauvinism, reckless bragging about one's country ; from *Chauvin*, a character in a French play, who had a blind idolatry for Napoleon.

Cherry, Mid. Eng. *cheris;* named from *Ceras*-os, situated in Pontus, on the Black Sea.

Chimera, a wild creation of the fancy ; from Gr. *Chimæra*, a fabulous monster, with the head of a lion, the body of a goat, and the tail of a dragon.

Cicerone, Ital. *cicerone*, a guide ; from Latin *Ciceron*-em.

Copper, Mid. Eng. *coper ;* named after the island *Kupros* or *Cyprus*.

Cravat, a kind of neckcloth, such as was worn by the Croatians of Austria, whose name was often spelt as *Cravates*.

Currant, named after *Corinth*, whence the fruit first came.

Cynosure, centre of attraction ; Gr. *kunos oura*, "the dog's tail," the name given to the stars in the tail of the Lesser Bear.

Dahlia, from *Dahl*, a Swede, who introduced the flower into Europe.

Damask, Mid. Eng. *damaske*, cloth of Damascus (Syria).

Damson, Fr. *damaisine ;* a plum from Damascus.

Delf, earthenware, first made at *Delft*, in Holland.

Dollar, Ger. *thaler ;* first coined from the silver mines of Joachims-*thal*, in Bohemia.

Dunce, applied in ridicule by the disciples of Thomas Aquinas to the disciples of *Duns* Scotus, a Schoolman, who died A.D. 1308.

Epicure, one who is fond of good living ; from *Epicurus*, the Greek, who taught that happiness should be the great aim of life.

Ermine, the fur taken from the *Armenian* weasel.

Euphuism, an affected style ; from a book called *Euphues*, "the well-born," written by Lyly, A.D. 1579.

Fauna, collective name for the animals of a given area or epoch ; from *Faunus*, a rural demigod.

Filbert, the fruit of the hazel-nut ; from *Philibert*, a saint of Burgundy, whose anniversary falls in the beginning of the nutting season.

Flora, collective name for the vegetable products of a given area or epoch ; from *Flora*, the goddess of flowers.

Florin, a coin of *Florence*, the lily borne on it being the symbol of that town.

Fuchsia, named after *Fuchs*, the German botanist.

Fustian, a kind of coarse cloth ; Low Latin *fustaneum*, called after *Fustát*, another name of Cairo, in Egypt.

Galloway, a nag ; from *Galloway* (Scotland).

Galvanism, that branch of science which treats of electrical currents; from *Galvani*, the Italian scientist.

Gamboge, a gum brought from Cambodia (or *Cambogia*).

Gasconade, bragging; formed by adding *ade* to *Gascon;* the men of Gascony (France) were accounted great braggarts.

Gingham, a kind of cotton cloth; from *Guingamp*, in Brittany.

Gladstone, a travelling-bag called after the statesman of that name.

Gorgonise (Tennyson), to petrify; from the *Gorgon* named Medusa, a fabulous monster, whose look turned any one to stone.

Grimalkin, a cat; a corruption of **Grey Malkin**, the latter being the name of a cat *Mald-kin*, diminutive of *Mald* or *Maud*. Such etymologies have arisen from the habit of giving to favourite animals the names of men or women; for other examples see below under **Magpie, Jackdaw, Jackass, Martin, Parrot, Poll-parrot.**

Grog; after Admiral Vernon, who wore *grogram* (O. Fr. gros-grain) breeches, and was familiarly called "Old Grog." He made his sailors mix their rum with water.

Guillotine, an instrument for decapitation; named after the inventor.

Guinea, a coin named after gold from the *Guinea* coast.

Gypsy; named after *Egypt*, supposed to have been the original home of such men.

Hansom, a two-wheeled carriage; named after the inventor.

Hector, to treat with insolence; from the Trojan hero, *Hector*, who was so treated by Achilles.

Herculean, very strong and muscular; from *Hercules*, of Gr. mythology.

Hermetic, as in "hermetically sealed"; made perfectly air-tight; from *Hermes* Trismegistus, the reputed founder of the secrets of alchemy.

Hock; from the first syllable of "*Hoch*-heim" (lit. high home), a town in Germany where this wine was first made.

Holland, a kind of linen cloth first made in *Holland*.

Hollyhock, from the *hock* or mallow imported from the *Holy* Land.

Indigo, a blue dye, from *Indicum*, grown in India.

Italics, letters printed in sloping type; from Aldo, an *Italian*, who lived about A.D. 1500. Such letters were originally called Aldines.

Jackass; formed by adding *Jack* to the noun "ass."

Jackdaw; formed by adding *Jack* to the noun "daw." See above, **Grimalkin.**

Jacobin, a member of a political club in the French Revolution which first met in the hall of the *Jacobin* Friars, the Rue St. Jacques (*Jacobus*, James), in Paris.

Jacobite, an adherent of James II. (*Jacobus*), of the Stuart dynasty.

Jalap, the tuber of the plant called *Jalapa* in Mexico.

January, Lat. *Januarius*, named after Janus, the two-faced god, who saw the old year die and the new come in its place.

Jeremiad, a lamentation; from the book of Lamentations, ascribed to *Jeremiah* the Prophet.

Jersey, a fine woollen jacket, named after the Channel Island.

Jet, a black mineral, Old Fr. *jet, jaet*, from *Gagas, gagat*-em, a river in the south of Asia Minor.

Jovial, jolly, born under the lucky planet, *Jove* or Jupiter.

July, the month named after *Julius* Cæsar.

June, the month named after *Junius*, a Roman clan.

Laconic, brief, like the speech of the *Laconians* (Spartans).

Landau, a kind of coach, named from *Landau* in Germany.

Lazaretto, lazar-house, a house for the reception of diseased persons ; called after *Lazarus* in Luke's Gospel.

Lumber, named after the *Lombard*-room, where the Lombard broker of Italy stowed away his wares.

Lynch, to execute a supposed criminal by mob-law ; from John *Lynch*, an American of Virginia.

Macadamise, to pave a road with small broken stones, as was done by a Mr. *Macadam*, A.D. 1819.

Mackintosh, a waterproof overcoat, named from the inventor.

Magenta, a colour between pink and red ; discovered in 1859, the date of the battle of *Magenta*, in N. Italy.

Magnet, the lode-stone, Lat. *magnet*-em, first quarried from Magnesia in Thessaly.

Magpie, for *Margery-pie*. See **Grimalkin**. A pie is a kind of bird.

Malapropism, a grotesque misuse of words ; from Mrs. *Malaprop*, a character in Sheridan's comedy, "The Rivals."

Malmsey, a sweet wine ; from *Malvasia*, in Greece.

March, the month named after *Mars*, the god of war.

Martial, warlike, of the same origin as the above.

Martin, Martlet, a kind of swallow, the proper name *Martin* being given to the bird as a pet-name or nick-name. **Martlet** is from the dim. form *martinet*, in which the *n* has been changed to *l*. See **Grimalkin**.

Martinet, a rigorous disciplinarian ; from a French officer of that name in the army of Louis XIV.

Maudlin, sobbing, morbidly sentimental ; Mid. Eng. *Maudelein*, from Mary *Magdalene*, *i.e.* Mary of Magdala, who has been depicted as shedding tears of penitence.

Mausoleum, a magnificent tomb, orig. the tomb of *Mausolus*, king of Caria, in Asia Minor.

Meander, from *Mæander*, a winding river of Asia Minor.

Mentor, from *Mentor*, the fabled counsellor of Telemachus.

Mercurial, volatile ; inspired by the god *Mercurius*.

Mesmerise, to operate on the nervous system of a patient by means of the eyes or hands ; from *Mesmer*, a German physician, A.D. 1766.

Milliner, orig. one who deals in wares from *Milan*.

Mint, from Lat. *Moneta*, a surname of Juno, in whose temple at Rome money was coined.

Morocco, leather prepared in a certain way ; from *Morocco*, in Northern Africa.

Muslin, a very thin cotton cloth ; Fr. *mousse-line*, from *Mosul*, a city of Kurdistan.

Nankeen, a cotton cloth from *Nankin*, in China.

Negus, from Col. *Negus*, who first mixed the beverage.

Nicotine, tobacco-juice; from *Nicot*, the Frenchman, who first introduced the plant into France.

Pæan, a song of victory; orig. a song of healing; from *Pæan*, the physician of the gods.

Palace, from *Palatium*, the residence of Roman Emperors on one of the seven hills of Rome, which thus acquired the name of "Palatine."

Paladin, a knight-errant of the Middle Ages; another spelling of *Palatinus*, an officer of the Palace.

Palladium, a safeguard of liberty: a statue of the goddess Pallas, on which the safety of Troy was believed to depend, was called in Gr. *Palladion*, in Lat. *Palladium*.

Panic, sudden and extreme fright, ascribed to the influence of *Pan*, the god of shepherds and husbandmen.

Parchment, from *Pergamus*, in Asia Minor.

Paroquet, Fr. *perroquet*, borrowed from Sp. *periquito*, "little Perico, little Peter." See **Grimalkin**.

Parrot; from Fr. *perrot*, *pierrot*, "little Pierre, little Peter." See **Grimalkin**.

Pasquin, pasquinade, a lampoon: from a cobbler named *Pasquin*, distinguished for his powers of sarcasm.

Peach, Mid. Eng. *peche*, from Lat. *Persic*-um, a peach, so called because the tree was indigenous to Persia.

Peeler, a policeman; from Sir R. Peel, founder of the force.

Petrel, formerly *peterel*, "a little Peter," so called because the bird seems to walk on the surface of the water, as St. Peter did.

Phaeton, a kind of horse-carriage; in Gr. mythology *Phaeton* once drove the chariot of the sun.

Pheasant, Lat. *Phasian*-a avis; "the bird of the river Phasis," in Colchis. The final *t* is excrescent.

Philippic, a discourse or speech full of invective; the speeches delivered by Demosthenes against *Philip*, king of Macedon, were called "the Philippics."

Pinchbeck, a metal; from the inventor, 18th century.

Port, "the wine of Oporto."

Protean, said of anything that changes very often; from *Proteus*, a sea-god in Gr. mythology, who could change himself into an infinite number of forms.

Punch (1), a beverage made up of five ingredients, spirit, water, lemon-juice, sugar, spice; introduced from India: from *pancha*, the Indian word for "five."

Punch (2), a short humpbacked figure in a puppet-show; from *Punchinello*, Ital. *Pulcinello*, a droll clown in Neapolitan comedy.

Quince, a kind of apple; from *Cydon*, in Crete.

Quixotic, grotesque; from Don *Quixote*, the hero of the celebrated mock-romance called by that name.

Rhubarb; from *Rheum barb*-arum, "Rheum from the barbarian country." *Rheum* is from *Rha*, an old name of the river Volga.

Rodomontade, high-flown language: in allusion to the boastful character of *Rodomonte*, in the "Orlando Furioso" of Ariosto.

Sardonic, sneering; from a plant that grows in Sardinia (Gr. *Sardo*), which is said to screw up the face of any one who eats it.

Saturnine, melancholic, gloomy ; named after the planet *Saturn*.

Savoy, a crumpled kind of cabbage, brought from *Savoy*.

Shalloon, a light woollen stuff ; from *Chalons*, in France.

Shallot, shalot, a kind of onion ; from *Ascalon*, in Palestine.

Sherry, formerly spelt *sherris ;* from *Xeres*, in Spain.

Silhouette, a meagre form of portrait cut out in black paper, named (in derision) after a French minister of finance, Etienne de *Silhouette*.

Simony, traffic in ecclesiastical preferment ; from *Simon* Magus (Acts viii. 18).

Solecism, inaccuracy in speaking or writing ; from a town called *Soloi* in Cilicia, where a very corrupt kind of Greek was spoken.

Spaniel, a Spanish dog ; from *Espanol*, "Spanish."

Spencer, a short over-jacket, named after Earl *Spencer*.

Stentorian, very loud ; from *Stentor*, whose voice is said by Homer to have been as loud as that of fifty men all shouting together.

Stoic, stoical, indifferent to pleasure or pain, worthy of a Stoic, a school of philosophers founded by Zeno, who taught his pupils in a colonnade or *Stoa* in Athens.

Swede, a Swedish turnip of yellowish colour.

Tantalise, to excite a craving without satisfying it ; from the fabulous person called *Tantalus*, who in Gr. mythology stands up to his chin in water, which flies from his thirsty lips whenever he attempts to drink it.

Tawdry, flimsy, but showy ; formerly used only in the phrase "tawdry lace," which meant lace bought at *St. Awdry's* fair held on St. Awdry's day in the island of Ely.

Turkey, a large domestic fowl ; from *Turkey*.

Utopian, belonging to no man's land, too good ever to exist ; from *Utopia* (Gr. *Outopia*), "no man's land," the title of a book written by Sir Thomas More describing an ideal republic.

Volt, the standard unit of electro-motive force ; from *Volta*, an Italian electrician.

Volcano, from *Vulcanus*, the divine blacksmith.

Vulcanite, a hard, black substance, of which combs, buttons, etc. are made ; from *Vulcanus*, as shown above.

Worsted, twisted woollen yarn ; from *Worsted*, in Norfolk.

II.—WORDS FORMED BY COMPOSITION OR BY THE ADDING OF PREFIXES.

In this and the remaining sections of the Appendix A.S. *stands for Anglo-Saxon*, O. Du. *for Old Dutch*, O. Fr. *for Old French*, Scand. *for Icelandic*, O.H.G. *for Old High German*, Sp. *for Spanish*.

(*a*) Disguised Compounds.

Agnail : A.S. *ang-nægl*, a nail or hard knob that gives pain (*ang-*) ; the modern corrupted form is "hang-nail." See p. 371.

Apricot, formerly *apricock ;* Port. al + bri + coque, "the (*al*) early (*bri* = Lat. *præ*) ripe (*coque*)."

As : short for *al-so ;* A.S. *eál-swá* (quite so).

Atone : *at-one,* to reconcile or make *at one.*

Auger : corruption of *nauger ;* A.S. *nafu-gár,* from *nafu,* a nave, and *gár,* a piercer. "A nauger" was changed to "an auger."

Aught : A.S. *á-wiht,* one whit, anything whatever.

Back-gammon : a back-game ; A.S. *bæc* (back), *gamen* (game).

Bandog : Mid. Eng. *band-dogge,* a dog tied by a band, a watch-dog or ferocious dog.

Barley : A.S. *bær-lic,* that which is like *bear* or *bere* (barley). The last syllable has no connection with A.S. *léac,* a plant.

Barn : A.S. *bere,* barley ; A.S. *ern,* a place for storing.

Bay-window : a window having a "bay" or recess ; not the same word as "bow-window."

Bedridden : corruption of A.S. *bed-rída,* a bed-rider.

Beldam : a hag. Ironical : Fr. *belle,* beautiful, and *dame,* lady.

Bilberry : Scand. *böllr* (a ball), and *bær* (a berry).

Biscuit : *bis* (twice, Lat.), and Fr. *cuit,* Lat. *coctus,* cooked.

Brannew : for *brand-new,* new from the brand or fire.

Bridal : put for *bride-ale,* that is, a bride-feast. A.S. *brýd, calo.*

Bride-groom : for *bride-goom ;* A.S. *guma,* a man. In Mid. Eng. the Fr. *grome* was substituted for A.S. *guma.*

Brimstone : Mid. Eng. *bren-stoon,* burning stone.

Buck-wheat : from *beech-wheat,* because the grain resembles the mast of a beech-tree.

Bulwark : properly bole-work, from Scand. *bolr,* the stem or trunk of a tree ; cf. Fr. *boulevard.*

Bylaw : a town-law or municipal law ; from Scand. *by,* town. Not compounded with the adverb *by.*

Cenobite : one of a brotherhood of monks ; Gr. *koinos,* together ; *bios,* life.

Chaffer : for *cheap-fare ;* A.S. *ceáp,* bargain ; *far-u,* business.

Cobweb : A.S. *coppa,* a head (only known in the compound *átor-coppa,* a thing with poison in its head, a spider) ; A.S. *webb,* a web.

Colporteur : hawker ; Lat. *coll-um* (neck), *port-ator* (carrier).

Constable : Old Fr. *conestable,* Lat. *comes stabuli,* count of the stable.

Coverlet : Old Fr. *covre,* to cover ; and *lit,* Lat. *lectum,* a bed.

Curfew : Old Fr. *covre-feu,* a fire-cover.

Daisy = day's-eye, A.S. *dæges eáge.*

> That well by reason it men callen may
> The *dayesie,* or else the eye of day.—CHAUCER.

Dismal : gloomy : Old Fr. *dis mal,* Lat. *dies mali,* evil days.

Distaff : A.S. *distæf* for *dise-* (a bunch of flax) *stæf* (a staff).

Earwig : ear-creeper ; *wig,* from A.S. *wic-ga,* one that runs.

Eaves-dropper, one who stands under *droppings* from the *eaves* of a house, to listen to what is said inside the room.

Elbow : A.S. *el-boga* or *eln-boga,* lit. arm (*eln*), bending (*boga*).

Ember-days : A.S. *ymb-ryne ; ymb,* a circle ; *ryne,* a course : it means then periodic recurrence.

Emerod : more correctly *hemorrhoid ;* Gr. *haima* (blood), *rho*-e (a flowing) + *eid*-os (appearance).

Fellow: Scand. *fé-lag-i*, a partner in a *fé-lag*, from *fé*, property (Eng. *fee*), and *lag*, an association or laying together.

Filibuster, Span.: a corruption of Eng. *free-booter;* from Dutch *vrij* (free), and *buit*, booty, plunder.

Filigree: formerly spelt as *filigrane;* Span. *filigrana;* Lat. *filum*, a thread, and *granum*, grain, texture.

Freebooter: see **Filibuster** above.

Friday: A.S. *Frige-dæg*, day of *Frigu* (Love, Venus).

Fur-long = furrow-long, the length of a furrow.

Futtocks, for *foot-hooks*.

Gaffer, gammer: Eng. *grand-father* (hybrid); Fr. *grand-mère*.

Garlic: A.S. *gár-léac*, spear-leek; *gár*, spear.

Gantlet, gauntlet (in the phrase "to run the gauntlet"). Confused with *gauntlet*, a glove. The older form was *gantlope*, from Swedish *gat-lopp*, lit. "a gate-leap," where *gate* means street or way. To run the gauntlet is to run down a lane formed by two files of soldiers, who strike the offender as he passes.

Gospel: A.S. *god-spell*, "God story": story of life of Christ.

Gossamer: lit. *goose-summer*. The provincial English name is *summer-goose;* so called from the downy appearance of the film.

Gossip, lit. a sponsor in baptism; *god* and *sib* (related in God).

Grampus: Lat. *grandis piscis*, "great fish."

Grunsel, groundsill, threshold; from *ground* and *sill*.

Haberdasher: a seller of small wares; said to be from Old Fr. *hapertas*, with Eng. suffix *-er* (a hybrid word). But Dr. Murray says "origin unknown."

Handicap: hand i' (th') cap; a mode of drawing lots.

Handiwork: here the *i* answers to A.S. *ge;* as in A.S. *hand-ge-weorc*. In *handicraft* the *i* has been inserted by analogy.

Handsel, hansel: the first instalment of a bargain (Scand.). Lit. *hand-sale*, the conclusion of a bargain by shaking hands.

Harbinger: Old Fr. *herberge-our;* lit. one who goes before to secure a *herberge* (lodging for an army). (See next word.)

Harbour (Scand.): *her-bergi*, army-shelter. Old Fr. *herberge*.

Hawthorn: A.S. *haga*, a hedge, and *thorn*.

Heifer: A.S. *héah-fore*, from *héah* (high, full-grown), and *fore*, cognate with Greek *poris*, a heifer; A.S. *fearr*, a bull.

Henchman: Mid. Eng. *hensman, henchman*, a page; probably from A.S. *hengst*, a horse, and *man;* hence lit. "a groom."

Heyday: high-day; Mid. Eng. *hey*, high.

Hobby-horse: a horse-shaped toy; Scand. *hoppe*, a mare.

Hobnob: A.S. *hæbban*, to have, and *næbban*, not to have.

Humbug: from *hum*, to cajole, and *bug*, a terror.

Husband: lit. house-dweller; Scand. *hús-bóndi*.

Hussy, short for "house-wife"; A.S. *hús-wíf* (the house-woman).

Hustings, properly *husting;* from A.S. *husting*, borrowed from Scand. *hús-þing*, "house-thing"; a meeting of the house.

Icicle: A.S. *ís-gicel*, from *ís*, ice, and *gicel*, a small piece of ice.

Jeopardy: O. Fr. *jeu parti*, a divided game.

Kerchief: Old Fr. *covre-chef*, cover-to-the-head (*chef*).

Lady: A.S. *hláf-dige*, loaf-kneader.

Lammas: A.S. *hláf-mæsse*, loaf-mass; observed on 1st August.

Leman: A.S. *léof-mann*, dear one, from *léof*, lief, dear.

Lichgate: corpse-gate, from A.S. *líc*, a corpse.

Limpet: another form of *lamprey*. See **Lamprey**, in p. 373.

Livelihood: Mid. Eng. *livelode*, A.S. *líf* (life), and *lád*, a way.

Lord: A.S. *hláf-ord*, probably for *hláf-weard*, a loaf-keeper.

Lukewarm: lit. warm-warm; Mid. Eng. *leuk*, *luke*, tepid.

Malady, sickness: Lat. *malus*, bad; *habitus*, condition.

Malaria: Lat. *mala*, bad; *aria*, air.

Malinger, to feign illness: Lat. *male* (badly), *æger* (sick).

Maugre, in spite of: O. Fr. *mal-gré*; Lat. *male* (badly), *grat*-us (pleasing).

Mermaid: lake-maid, water-nymph; from A.S. *mere*, a lake.

Midriff: A.S. *mid-rif*; from *mid* (middle), and *hrif* (belly).

Midwife: from A.S. *mid*, with, and *wíf*, woman; female helper.

Mildew: A.S. *mele-deáw*, honey-dew; A.S. *mele*, *mil*, honey.

Mistletoe: lit. bird-lime twig; A.S. *mistel* (that which has *mist* or bird-lime), and *tán*, a twig.

Monday: A.S. *Mónan-dæg*, day of the moon.

Mortgage, lit. a dead pledge: Lat. *mort*-uus, and *gage*, a pledge.

Mulled-ale: corrupt. of *mould-ale*, a funeral feast; cf. **Bridal**, a marriage-feast.

Narwhal: the sea-unicorn; lit. corpse-whale, from Scand. *nár* (a corpse), and *hvalr*, a whale; so called from its pallid colour.

Naught, not: for *ne aught*; hence "naught-y." See **Aught.**

Neighbour: A.S. *neáh* (nigh), and *búr*, a husbandman.

Nickname: lit. an additional name. The *n* has been wrongly attached from *an*; hence "an eke-name" became "a nickname."

Nightingale: A.S. *nihte-gale*, a singer by night.

Nostril: A.S. *nos-þyrl*, nose-thirl, or nose-hole.

Osprey: the fish-hawk, lit. "the bone-breaker," doublet of "ossifrage"; Lat. *os*, *ossis*, a bone, and *frag-*, the root of *frang*-ere, to break.

Parboil: orig. to boil thoroughly; Lat. *per*, and *bullire*. But now "to boil partially," through confusion with *part*.

Parish: Mid. Eng. *par-ische*, Fr. *par-oisse*, Lat. *par-œcia*, Gr. *par-oikia*, "dwelling near."

Porpoise: O. Fr. *porpeis*; Lat. *porcus*, pig, and *piscis*, fish.

Prose: Lat. *pro* (forward), and *versa* (turned); shortened to *prorsa* and then to *prosa*, a forward or unembellished speech.

Puttock: *put*, a contraction of *poult* or *pullet*, and *hawk*; hence lit. a hawk that seizes pullets.

Quagmire: formerly *quake-mire*, a quaking mire.

Quinsy: formerly spelt *squinancy* or *quinancy*; Gr. *kunankh*-e, from *kun*-os (of a dog), *ankh*-e (pain).

Ransack: Icel. *rann*, a house, and *sæk*-ja, to search.

Rearmouse, a bat; A.S. *hrére-mús*, a fluttering or flying mouse.

Saturday: A.S. *Sætern-dæg* or *Sæter-dæg*, day of Saturn.

Scotfree, free from paying *scot* or *shot*, contribution.

Sennight, seven nights, a week.

Shelter: A.S. *scild-truma*, a shield-troop, a squadron or guard.

Sheriff: A.S. *scír-réfa*, a shire-reeve, officer of the shire.

Sirloin: from Old Fr. *sur* (over, upon), and *longe* (loin).

Sledge-hammer: lit. a hammer-hammer; A.S. *slecge*, hammer.

Somersault: Old Fr. *soubre-soult; soubre*=Lat. *super*, over; *sault*=Lat. *saltus*, a leap.

Squirrel: Lat. *skiur-ellus*, dim. of Gr. *ski-our-us* (shadow-tailed).

Stalwart: A.S. *stǽl-wyrðe*; *stǽl*, foundation, and *wyrðe*, worthy.

Starboard: A.S. *stéorbord*, steerboard; the steersman's deck.

Stark-naked: Mid. Eng. *start-naked*, lit. "tail-naked."

Step-child: A.S. *stéop-cild*, an orphaned child.

Steward: A.S. *stí-weard*, keeper of sties and cattlepens.

Stickleback, the little fish with *stickles* (prickles) on its *back*.

Stirrup: A.S. *stig-ráp*, a rope to climb up by.

Sunday: A.S. *Sunnan-dæg*, day of the sun.

Tadpole, a *toad* nearly all head or *poll*.

Tantamount: Lat. *tantus*; Fr. *à mont*, towards the mountain.

Thursday: A.S. *Thunres-dæg*, day of Thor or Thunder.

Topsy-turvy: orig. *topsy-tervy*. *Top-so-turvy* afterwards altered to *top-side-turvy*, as *up-so-down* was changed to *up-side-down*. *Turvy* means overturned, from A.S. *torfian* (to throw), Mid. Eng. *terven*.

Trade-wind: wind of a certain *trade*, tread, or trend (path).

Tramway, a railroad on *trams* (sleepers).

Tuesday: A.S. *Tiwes-dæg*, day of Tíw or Mars.

Twilight: lit. double (*i.e.* doubtful) light: from A.S. *twi-*, double.

Valhalla: Scand. *val-r*, the slain; *hall*, a hall.

Vinegar: Fr. *vin* (Lat. *vin-um*), and *egre* (Lat. *acre*, sour).

Walrus: Dutch *walrus*; Danish *hval-ros*, a whale-horse.

Wanton, undisciplined; A.S. *wan*, lacking; *togen*, disciplined.

Wassail: from A.S. *wes hál*, be thou whole or hale.

Wednesday: A.S. *Wódnes-dæg*, the day of Woden.

Wellaway: an exclamation of sorrow; sometimes corrupted to *welladay*; A.S. *wá lá wá*, woe! lo! woe!

Whitlow: a corruption of *quick-flaw*; a flaw in the *quick*.

Wilderness: A.S. *wild* (wild), *déor* (deer, animal).

Window: lit. "wind-eye"; Scand. *vindr* (wind), and *auga* (an eye).

Woman: A.S. *wif-man*; *wif*, a female, and *mann*, person.

Woof: A.S. *ó-wef*, for *on-wef*, lit. web on or across the weft.

World: lit. age of man; A.S. *wer*, man; *yldu*, old age.

Yesterday, from A.S. *geostra* (yester) and *dæg* (day).

Zoo-phyte, animal-plant: Gr. *zoön* (animal), *phuton*, plant.

(*b*) Mistaken or Apparent Compounds.

Acorn: not compounded of A.S. *ác* (oak) and *corn*. A.S. *æcern*, fruit of the field; from *æcer*, a field; cognate with Lat. *ager*.

Battle-ment: not from *battle*, but from Fr. *bastile*, a fortress.

Belfry: not compounded with *bell*. Old Fr. *ber-freit*, of Teutonic origin; *ber* or *berg*, to protect, and *freit*, a place of safety.

Blindfold: no connection with *fold*. A.S. *blind-fellen*, struck blind. The second word is p.p. of *fell*-an (to strike down) with intrusive *d*. The word was sometimes written *blind-felden*.

Bondage: not from "bond," but from A.S. *bonda*, a serf.

Caterpillar: not compounded with *pillar*. Fr. *chate*, a she-cat, and *peleuse* (Lat. *pilosa*), hairy. Old Fr. *chatepeleuse*, a weevil.

Chincough: not from *chin*, but *chink* = kink, a catch in the breath.

Counterpane: Old Fr. *contre-poinct*, Lat. *culcita puncta*, a quilt punctured or stitched. In older English counterpoint was used :—

Embroidered coverlets or *counterpoints* of purple silk.—NORTH.

Country-dance. This word has been wrongly included among compounds of mistaken origin. It is an English word signifying "rustic dance"; but it was borrowed by the French and misexplained as *contre-danse*, a dance in which the partners stand opposite (*contra*) each other.

Crayfish: Old Fr. *crevisse*; Old High Germ. *crebis*, a crab.

Curtail: Old Fr. *curt-ault*, Lat. *curt-us*, with suffix *-ault*.

Forgetful: A.S. *forgit-el*, the suffix *-el* having been confounded with *-ful*.

Frontispiece: Old Fr. *frontispice*, Late Lat. *fronti-spicium*, a front view. No connection with "piece."

Grey-hound: Scand. *grey* (dog), and *hundr* (hound).

Gridiron: Mid. Eng. *gridire*, Lat. *craticula*. In Mid. Eng. the word for "iron" was *iren* or *ire*. *Gridire* was changed to *gridiron*, because the *ire* was supposed to signify "iron."

Hand-cuff: apparently for *hand-cops*; *cops* means "manacle."

Hang-nail: not compounded with *hang*. See **Agnail**, p. 366.

Hiccough: a misspelling for *hiccock*, dim. of *hic* or *hick*, a catch in the voice imitative of the sound. Cf. "hacking cough."

Hogshead: more correctly *ox-head*. Dutch *oxhoofd*, ox-head.

Humble-pie: not compounded with *humble*, but *umble*, the entrails of a deer, given as a perquisite to the men who helped in the chase.

Humble-bee, the humming-bee; *humble* is here put *hummle*, freq. of *hum*.

In-voice: misspelling of *en-vois*, pl. of Fr. *en-voi*, a sending.

Iron-mould: not compounded with *mould*, but with *mole*, spot.

Isinglass: Dutch *huyzen-blas*, sturgeon-bladder, from which isinglass is made. The *g* after the *n* is intrusive; the *b* before the *l* has been lost.

Island: no connection with Fr. *isle*, Lat. *insula*. A.S. *ig-land*, in which *ig* alone means "island."

Lanthorn: Lat. *lanterna*; misspelt, because *horn* was once used for making the sides of lanterns.

Lapwing: A.S. *hleáp-wince*, "one who turns about (*wince*) in running (*hleáp*)."

Lime-house, a proper name of a place; for *lime-oast*, lime-kiln.

Loadstone, a stone that *leads*; A.S. *lád*, a way or course.

Lute-string: not compounded either with *lute* or *string*; for *lustring*, Fr. *lustrine*, a sort of lustrous silk. Lat. *lustr-are*, to shine.

Mongoose, an ichneumon: Indian word *mangús*.

Mushroom: Old Fr. *mouscheron*, an extension of *mousse*, moss.

Night-mare, an incubus; A.S. *niht* (night), and *mara* (a crusher).

Peacock. The word *pea* is borrowed from Lat. *pa-vo*, Gr. *ta-os*.

Pea-jacket: Dutch *pij*, a coat of coarse woollen stuff.

Penthouse: corrupt. of Fr. *a-pentis*, Lat. *appendicium*, appendage.

Periwig: not compounded with *wig*; *wig* is itself the short of *periwig*. Fr. *perruque*, Sp. *peluca*, from Lat. *pil-*um, hair.

Pick-axe: Mid. Eng. *pikois, pikeis;* no connection with "axe."

Policies (insurance paper): no connection with *policy*. Gr. *poly* (many), *ptukon* (a fold), a writing in many folds. Late Lat. *polecticum*.

Posthumous: not compounded with Lat. *humus*, the ground. A misspelling for *postumus*, "the last," superlative of *post*.

Primrose: not compounded with *rose*. Mid. Eng. *primerole*, dim. of Late Lat. *prim-ula*, which is itself a dim. of Lat. *prim*-a.

Rakehell: for Mid. Eng. *rakel*, Scand. *reikall*, a vagabond.

Rein-deer: not compounded with *rein*. Scand. *hreinn*, a deer.

Rosemary: Lat. *ros* (dew), *maris* (of sea): sea dew, sea spray.

Runagate: a corruption of *renegade;* Lat. *re*, again, and *negatus*, denied; one who has denied his faith.

Sandblind: lit. "half-blind"; A.S. *sám*, half, Lat. *semi*.

Sangreal: wrongly traced to *sang* (blood), *real* (royal, not real); the word is *san* (holy), *greal* or *grail* (dish). "The Holy Grail."

Service-tree, a kind of wild pear. Corruption of Mid. Eng. *serv-es*, plural, A.S. *syrf*, borrowed from Lat. *sorb*-us. Cf. *sorb*-apple.

Shamefaced: for *shame-fast;* cf. "sted-fast": A.S. *sceam-fæst*.

Slow-worm: A.S. *slá-wyrm*, a worm or snake that slays.

Sovereign: Late Lat. *super-aneus;* cf. *foreign*, Lat. *for-aneus*.

Surcease: Fr. *sursis*, p.p. of the verb *surseoir;* Lat. *super-sedere*.

Surround: for *sur-ound;* Lat. *super*, over, and *und-are*, to flow.

Titmouse: Scand. *tittr*, little; A.S. *máse*, small bird.

Touchy: corruption of *tetchy*, from Mid. Eng. *tetch*, a whim.

Turmoil: from Fr. *tremouille*, the hopper of a mill, so called because it is constantly in motion; Lat. *trem-ere*, tremble.

Uproar: not compounded of *up* and *roar*. Dutch *op-roer*, where *op* means "up," and *roer* means "commotion"; allied to A.S. *hrer-an*, to flutter; cf. **Rearmouse**, p. 369. "Roar" is from A.S. *rár-ian*.

Wall-eyed, "with a beam in the eye." Scand. *vagl*, a beam.

Walnut: not compounded with *wall*, but with A.S. *wealh*, foreign.

Wiseacre: Dutch *wijs-segger*, a wise-sayer.

Witchelm: A.S. *wice*, bending; cf. *wicker*, made of twigs.

Yeoman: Old Fris. *ga-man*, a villager, from *ga*, a village.

(*c*) Hybrid Compounds.

(*Compounds made up of words taken from different languages.*)

Arch-fiend: Gr. *arkh* (chief); A.S. *féond* (enemy, hence fiend).

Bandy-legged: Fr. *bandé* (bound); Scand. *leggr* (leg).

Bank-rupt: Du. *banck* (bench, table); Lat. *rupt*-us (broken).

Beef-eater: Fr. *boef, bœuf* (beef); Eng. *eater*, one who eats his master's beef; a servant. (The theory which made it a corruption of Fr. *buffetier*, a waiter at a side-board, has been disproved in Skeat's *Student's Pastime*, pp. 157, 158.)

Bigamy: Lat. *bis* (twice); Gr. *gam*-os (marriage).

Black-guard: Eng. *black* (A.S. *blæc*); Fr. *guard*.

Cause-way: Old Fr. *caucie* (Lat. *calciata*), paved; *way* (A.S. *wæg*).

Foumart: a polecat; A.S. *fúl* (foul); Fr. *marte* (a marten).

Grandfather, grandmother: Fr. *grand* (great); Eng. *father, mother*.

Haut-boy: Fr. *haut*, high; Dutch, *bosch*, wood.

Heir-loom: Fr. *heir* (Lat. *her-es*); Eng. *loom* (A.S. *ge-lóma*, tool).

Holly-hock: A.S. *hálig* (holy); Celt. *hoc*-ys (mallow). The flower was indigenous to the Holy Land.

Inter-loper: Lat. *inter* (between), and Du. *looper* (runner).

Kerb-stone: Lat. *curv*-us (curved), and A.S. *stán* (stone).

Knight-errant: Eng. *knight*; Fr. *errant* (wandering).

Lamprey, "licker of rocks"; Lat. *lamb*-ere (to lick), Gr. *petra* (a rock). Another form of the word is **Limpet.**

Macadamised: Gael. *mac* (son); Heb. *Adam*; Greek *-ise* or *-ize*, and Eng. suffix *-d*. (Four languages.)

Mari-gold: Heb. *Mary*; Eng. *gold*: so called from its colour.

Mil-dew: Lat. *mel*, honey; A.S. *deáw*, dew.

Nuncheon: Mid. Eng. *none-schenche*, "noon-drink": Lat. *nona*, ninth hour, noon; and A.S. *scenc*-an, to pour out drink.

Nut-meg: A.S. *hnut-a* (a nut); Mid. Eng. *muge*, Lat. *musc*-us.

Orchard: A.S. *ort-geard*; from Lat. (*h*)*ort*-us, garden; A.S. *geard*, enclosure. (The theory which identifies the first syllable with A.S. *wort* is now exploded.)

Os-trich: Lat. *avis* (bird); Gr. *strouth*-ion (a kind of bird).

Par-take, for *part-take*: Lat. *part*-em, Eng. *take* (from Scand. *tac*-a).

Pas-time: Fr. *pass*-er, to move onward; A.S. *tím*-a (time).

Ped-e-stal: Lat. *pes*, *ped-is*; A.S. *stæl*, a standing-place.

Pent-roof: sloping roof. Fr. *pente*, a slope; A.S. *hróf*, a cabin.

Piece-meal: Fr. *piece* (part); A.S. *mǽl* (a portion or time).

Pur-blind: orig. *pure-blind*; Lat. *pur*-us, A.S. *blind*.

Rigmarole: Scand. *ragmenni* (coward); Lat. *rotula* (a little wheel, hence *roll*). A coward's roll; a long stupid story.

Salt-cellar: first syllable, A.S. *sealt* (salt); the remainder of the word has nothing to do with "cellar," but is from Fr. *salière*, L. *salarium*, saltholder.

Sorb-apple: Lat. *sorb*-us (a wild tree); A.S. *æppel* (apple).

Spike-nard: Lat. *spic*-atus (spiked); Sanskrit *nalad-a* (nard).

Tar-pauling: A.S. *teoru* (tar); Lat. *pall*-ium (a coverlet).

(*d*) Disguised Prefixes.

Ab-: *av*-aunt (Lat. *ab ante*), *v*-an-guard (Fr. *av*-ant-garde), *adv*-ance, *adv*-ant-age (the last two derived, with the help of added suffixes, from Fr. av-ant, with an intrusive *d* between the *a* and the *v*).

Ad-: *ex*-cise (Dutch *aksiis*, corruption of Old Fr. *assise*, a tax; Lat. *ac* or *ad sess*-us, from *sedere*, to sit).

Ante-: *an*-cestor (Old Fr. *an*-cessour, Lat. *ante*-cessor, one who goes before).

Bi-: *ba*-lance (Fr. *ba*-lance, Lat. *bi*-lancem, having two scales).

Con-, co-: *cu*-stom (Lat. *con*-suetumen), *cur*-ry (verb, Old Fr. *con*-roi), *co*-ver (Old Fr. *co*-vrir; Lat. *co*-operire), *co*-venant (Old Fr. *con*-venant), *co*-unt (verb, Fr. *con*-ter, Lat. *com*-putare), *co*-unt (noun, Lat. *com*-item), *co*-uch (Old Fr. *cou*-cher; Lat. *col*-locare), *co*-st (Lat. *con*-stare), *co*-il and *cu*-ll (Old Fr. *coi*-ller, Lat. *col*-ligere), *co*-stive (Lat. *con*-stipatus), *cou*-sin (Lat. *con*-sobrinus), *cu*-rfew (O. Fr. *co*-vre-feu, covering of fires), *ke*-rchief (O. Fr. *co*-vre-chef, covering to the head).

De-: *di*-stil (Lat. *de*-stillare).

Dis-, di- : *des*-cant, *des*-habille (state of undress), *des*-sert (the last course at dinner), *de*-feat, *de*-fy, *de*-luge (Lat. *di*-luvium), *s*-pend (Lat. *dis*-pendere), *s*-tain (for *dis*-tain), *de*-bark (Fr. *des*-barquer, to land from a ship).

Ex-, e- : *a*-mend (but *e*-mendation), *a*-skance (*ex*-cansare, to go aslope), *a*-bash (Old Fr. *es-bahiss*, imitative), *af*-fray (Low Lat. *ex*-frediare), *a*-fraid (pp. of *affray*), *a*-ward (Old Fr. *es*- (Lat. *ex*-) ward-er), *as*-tonish (Old Fr. *es*-tonner, Late Lat. *ex*-tonare), *es*-cape (Old Fr. *es*-caper; Lat. *ex* cappâ, out of one's cape), *es*-planade (Lat. *ex*-planata), *es*-cort (Lat. *ex*-correctus, corrigere), *es*-cheat (Old Fr. *es*-chet, p.p. of *es*-cheoir, Lat. *ex*-cadere), *es*-say (Old Fr. *es*-sai, a trial; Low Lat. *ex*-agium, a trial of weight), *é*-carté (game at cards, lit. discarded), *is*-sue (Old Fr. *is*-sué, Lat. *ex*-ire), *s*-ample (Mid. Eng. *s*-ample, Old Fr. *es*-semple, Lat. *ex*-emplum), *s*-carce (Late Lat. *scarpsus*, short for *ex*-cerptus), *s*-corch (Old Fr. *es*-corcher, Lat. *ex*-cortic-are, take off bark or rind), *s*-courge (Old Fr. *es*-corgie, Lat. *ex*-coriata, flayed off), *s*-ombre (*ex* umbrâ, from the shade), *s*-camp (Old Fr. *es*-camper), *s*-camper (run away), *s*-luice (Lat. *ex*-clusa), *s*-cour (*ex*-curare), *s*-ewer (*ex*-aquaria), *s*-prain (Old Fr. *es*-praindre, Lat. *ex*-primere), *s*-quare (Lat. *ex*-quadrare; so also *s*-quadron).

Extra- : *stra*-nge (Lat. *extr*(*a*)-neous, external).

In- (*in*) : *an*-oint (Lat. *in*-unctus), *am*-bush (Low Lat. *im*-boscare, to set in a bush).

In- (*not*) : *en*-emy (Lat. *in*-imicus, hence *in*-imical).

Intra- : *entr*-ails (Old Fr. *entr*-ailles, Late Lat. *intr*(*a*)-alia).

Juxta- : *joust* (Late Lat. *juxt*-are), *jost*-le (freq. of Mid. Eng. *joust*-en).

Male- : *mau*-gre (in spite of, Fr. *mau*=Lat. male, *gré*=gratum, pleasing; hence the word means "ill-pleasing," "unpleasant").

Non- : *um*-pire (older form *num*-pire, Old Fr. *non*-per, peerless; *a numpire* was changed to *an umpire*).

Per- : *pil*-grim (Ital. *pellegrino*, Lat. *per*-egrinus), *par*-don (Lat. *per*-don-are), *par*-son (Lat. *per*-sona, lit. a mask, because an actor's voice *sounded through* it).

Post- : *pu*-ny or *puis*-ne (Old Fr. *puis*-né, Lat. *post*-natus, younger, born after; hence inferior in rank).

Pre- : *pre*-ach (Old Fr. *pre*-cher, Lat. *præ*-dicare), *pro*-vost (Old Fr. *pro*-vost or *pre*-vost, Lat. *præ*-positus, one placed in authority), *pr*-ize, *pr*-ison (Lat. *pre*-hensum, *pre*-hendere).

Pro- : *pr*-udent (short for Lat. *pro*-vident-em, one who looks before him).

Re- : *re*(*n*)-der (Fr. *ren*-dre, Lat. *red*-dere), *r*-ally (Fr. *r*-allier, Lat. *re*+alligare, to bind together), *r*-ansom (Old Fr. *ra*-enson, Lat. *red*-emptionem), *ru*-nagate (corrupt form of *re*-negade, Lat. *re*-negatus, p.p. of *re*-negare, to deny one's faith).

Retro- : *rear*-guard (older spelling *rere*-ward), *rere*-dos.

Se- : *s*-ober (Lat. *se*, apart; *ebrius*, intoxicated), *s*-ure, a short form of *se*-cure (Lat. *se*-curus).

Semi- : *sin*-ciput (lit. half the head, the fore part of the head).

Sub- : *su*-dden (Lat. *sub*-itaneus, Old Fr. *so*-dain), *so*-journ (Lat. *sub*+diurn-are, to stay, Old Fr. *so*-journ-er), *s*-ombre (traced by some to *sub*-umbrâ, under the shade; but see above, under **Ex**).

Super-: *sopr*-ano, *sover*-eign (older and more correct spelling *sovr*-an; no connection with *reign*, nor with Lat. *supre-mus;* derived from Late Lat. super-*aneus*), *su*-zer-ain (Late Lat. *sur*-ser-anus, Lat. *su*-rsum for *sub*-versum, upwards).

Trans-: *tres*-pass, *tre*-ason, *tres*-tle (Late Lat. *trans*-tellum, dim. of *trans*-trum), *tranc*-e (Fr. *trans*-e, Lat. *trans*-itum (a passing away).

Tri-: *tra*-mmel (Fr. *tra*-mail, Lat. *tri*+macula, a net).

Ultra-: *outr*(*a*)-age (Old Fr. *oltr*-age, excessive violence).

III.—DERIVATIVES FROM TEUTONIC (MAINLY A.S.) ROOTS.

Late Lat. *means post-classical Latin.* **Low Lat.** *means Latin coined from a Teutonic or other root which is not Latin at all.*

Ǣfen (*the latter part of the day*): eve, even, evening (A.S. ǽfnung, Mid. Eng. evening), eventide (A.S. ǽfentíd).

Æfre (*ever*): ever, every (the *y* is from A.S. ælc, each: so "every" means "ever each"), when-ever, who-ever, etc.

Ær (*before*): ere, early (A.S. ǽrlíc), erst (superl. degr. A.S. ǽrest, soonest), or (in the phrase "or ever," the "or" is a corruption of ǽr, and the "ever" is also a corr. of ǽr; so the phrase is tautological as well as doubly corrupt).

Ág-an (*to possess*): owe, own (adj., lit. possessed, A.S. ág-en, p.p. of ág-an), own (verb, A.S. ágn-ian), ought (A.S. áhte, pt. t. of ág-an, Mid. Eng. aughte or oughte).

Án (*one*): a or an (indef. art.), one, al-one or lone, on-ly (A.S. án-líc), lone-ly, lone-li-ness, any (A.S. ǽn-ig), at-one (to set at one), aught (A.S. á-wiht=a thing), ought (doublet of preceding, one-wiht), once (A.S. án-es, of one), nonce (as in the phrase "for the nonce," Mid. Eng. "for then anes"), an-on (A.S. on án, in one).

Bac-an (*to bake*): bake, batch (as much as is baked at once), baker, baxter (once a female baker, now a proper name).

Bælig, bælg (*a wine-skin*): bag (for balg, Mid. Eng. bagge), bag-at-elle (a hybrid dim.), baggage (a hybrid, with suffix -age), belly (A.S. bylig), bellows, bilge (the belly of a ship or cask), billow (lit. a swell or surge).

Ber-an (*to carry*): bairn, bear, barm (A.S. bearm, lap), barrow, wheel-barrow (Mid. Eng. barowe), berth, bier, birth, burden or burthen (A.S. byrthen, a load), forbear, overbearing.

Bed (*couch*): bed, bedstead (A.S. stede, station), bedridden (corr. from A.S. bed-rída, one who rides a bed, but cannot ride a horse; said orig. in derision).

Beód-an (*to command*): bid, beadle (A.S. býd-el, one who orders), bode (to foreshow, A.S. **bod**-ian, to announce).

Beorg-an (*to protect*): borough (A.S. burg, a fort, Mid. Eng. borwe), barrow (A.S. beorg, a grave-mound), borrow (A S. **borg**-ian, to give a pledge), burgess (Low Lat. burg-ensis), burgher, burgo-master, burrow (doublet of "borough"), bury (in the sense of town, as "Canter-bury," "Bury St. Edmunds," A.S. byrig, a protected place), bury (in the sense of interment, A.S. byrig-an or byrg-an).

Bet or **bat** (*good*): better (A.S. bet-era), best (A.S. betst, for bet-est), batten (lit. to make better), boot (A.S. bót, profit, improvement), boot-less, to boot.

Bidd-an (*to pray*): bead (orig. a prayer, now a bead for counting prayers), a bidding-prayer, beg (Mid. Eng. begg-en, A.S. bed-ec-ian, freq. of bidd-an).

Bind-an (*to fasten*): bind, band, band-age, band-box, bandog (a dog that is tied up), bend (A.S. bend-an, orig. to string a bow, hence to bend it), bandy-legged (bow-legged), banner (O. Fr. banière, Low Lat. banderia, a band or strip of cloth), bond, bondsman, body (A.S. bod-ig, "the little bond" that confines the soul), bod-ice (a corruption of "bodies," the orig. spelling), bundle (A.S. bund, from bunden, p.p. of bind-an, to bind).

Bít-an (*to hold between the teeth*): bite, bait (to cause to bite), bet (to wager, from Scand. beit-a, to cause to bite), a-bet, bit (a mouthful, small piece), bit (curb for a horse), bitter (A.S. bít-or, lit. biting), beetle (A.S. bít-el, a biting one), beetle (to project over, as in phrase "beetle-browed," *i.e.* with brows projecting like an upper jaw).

Bláw-an (*to puff*): blow, bladder (A.S. blædr, a blowing out), blast (A.S. blǽst, a blowing), blaze (A.S. blæse, a flame), blazon (extended form of preceding), blare (an older form of "blaze"), blister (O. Du. bluyster, a swelling), bluster (freq. to blow noisily).

Blend-an, **bland**-an (*to mix* or *confuse*): blend, blind (A.S. blind), blindfold (corr. of blind-felden, struck blind), blunder (Mid. Eng. blondr-en, freq. from Scand. blund-a, to doze, to be in a state of mental confusion).

Blíc-an (A.S.), **blink**-en (Du.) *to shine*: blank, blanch, blanket, bleach (A.S. blǽc, shining), blink, blench (to cause to blink), blight.

Blów-an (*to bloom as a flower*): blow (in the sense of blossom), bloom, blossom (A.S. blóst-ma), blood (A.S. blód, that which causes the bloom or flourishing of life), bleed (deriv. of blood, A.S. bléd-an), bless (A.S. blets-ian, to consecrate by blood).

Brec-an (*to break*): break, broke, breach, brick (Fr. brique, orig. a fragment, a bit), break-fast (A.S. fæst), break-water, brack-en (a fern growing on rough or broken ground).

Breów-an (*to boil, ferment*): brew, bread (A.S. bréad, *i.e.* flour that has been fermented), broth (A.S. bróth), brewis or brose (pottage, doublets formed from breów-an, O. Fr. brou-es).

Brún (*copper-coloured*): brown, bruin (the brown bear), brun-ette (brownish, fem.), burnish (to polish, lit. to enbrown), bronze (Fr. bronze).

Bú-an (*to cultivate*): boor (A.S. búr, ge-búr, a cultivator), neighbour (A.S. neáh-búr or neáh-gebur, a nigh or near cultivator), bond-age (A.S. bond-a, a servant of the soil), husband (Scand. hús, house, bóndi or búandi, occupier), bower (A.S. búr, Mid. Eng. bour, a chamber).

Búg-an (*to bend*): bow (noun and verb), bow-window (a semicircular window, not the same as bay-window), buxom (lit. bendsome, A.S. búg-sum, yielding, obedient), bight (A.S. bight, a bight or bay of water), bout (a turn), el-bow (A.S. el-boga; eln, arm = Lat. ulna).

Bulg-ja (Scand. *to swell out*): bulge, boil, bole (stem of a tree), bolster (A.S. bolster), bolt (a round strong pin, A.S. bolt), bowl (a round vessel, A.S. boll-a), bulk, bul-wark (lit. bole-work or log-work, whence Fr. boulevard).

Busc (*a thicket*): bush, am-bush, am-busc-ade (Low Lat. im-bosc-are, to place men in bushes), bosc-age (grazing, fodder), bouquet (O. Fr. bosquet, dim. of O. Fr. bos, Fr. bois).

Byrn-an, beorn-an, brinn-an (*to be in flames*, or *put into the flame*): burn, brand (sword, or burning piece of wood, A.S. brand, pt. t. of beorn-an), fire-brand, brand-new (that is, new from the fire), brand-ish (through Fr. brandiss-ant, pres. pt. of brand-ir, to wield a brand or sword), brand-y (formerly brand-wine or brand-y-wine, which, when the second word was dropped, became "brand-y," lit. "burnt or hot wine"), brim-stone (sulphur, Mid. Eng. brem-stoon or bren-stoon; Mid. Eng. brenn-en, to burn), brunt (an onset like a flash of fire), brindled or brinded (in the sense of streaked, as "a brindled cow").

Ceáp (*barter, price*): cheap, chaffer (A.S. ceáp, price, and A.S. faru, business), chap-man (A.S. ceáp-mann, a merchant), chop (to barter or exchange, Dutch koop-en, A.S. ceáp-ian), cope (to vie with, doublet of the preceding), keep (A.S. cép-an or cýp-an, a derivative of A.S. ceáp, price), Cheap-side (a street in the City of London, "the trade quarter").

Cocc (*a male bird*): cock, cockade (Fr. coquarde, fem. of coquard, saucy), cockloft (lit. a loft where cocks roost), coquette (fem. of Fr. coquet, a little cock), cocky (strutting as a cock), coxcomb (a fool named from his cock's comb or fool's cap), chick-en (A.S. cic-en, probably dim. of cocc), chick-en-pox, chick-en-hearted.

Cricc, crok (*a staff, a crook*): crick-et (dim. of cricc), crook, crutch, crochet (Fr. crochet, a little hook), crotchet, en-croach (to catch in a hook), crosier (O. Fr. croce, Low Lat. crocia).

Cropp (*the top of a plant*): crop, croup (the hinder part of a horse), crupper (Fr. croupière), group (Fr. groupe, a heap, a cluster).

Cunn-an (*to know*), **can** (used as pres. tense): can, con (A.S. cunn-ian, desiderative form of cunn-an), cunn-ing, uncouth (lit. unknown, A.S. cúth, known), cuddle (put for couth-le, to be familiar, to embrace), ken (A.S. cenn-an, causal form cunn-an), kith (A.S. cýth-the, native land, kindred).

Cwel-an, pt. t. **cwæl** (*to die*): quail, qualm (A.S. cwealm, lit. pestilence), quell (A.S. cwell-an, to cause to quail).

Cynn (*genus, race*): kin, kind (A.S. cynd, ge-cynd, nature), kind (adj. A.S. cynde, natural), kindle (to bring forth young), kindred (the first *d* is intrusive, A.S. cyn, and the suffix "red"), king (A.S. cyn-ing, a man of royal kin, A.S. cyne, royal), kingdom (A.S. cyne-dom).

Dǽl (*a share*): deal, dole, ordeal (lit. a dealing out, A.S. or= out).

Dó-n (*to perform, cause*): a-do (for "at do" = to-do, in the Northern dialect "at" was = to), deed (A.S. dǽd, a thing done), doff (do off), don (do on), doom (A.S. dóm, a thing decided on), deem (A.S. dém-an, lit. to express a doom or judgment), doomsday.

Drag-an (*to draw*): drag, draw, draggle, drawl, draught or draft (as in the phrase "a draught of fishes"), dredge, dregs, dray.

Dreós-an (*to drip*): drear or dreary (A.S. dreor-ig, gory, from A.S. dreór, gore), drizzle (freq. of dreós-an), dross (A.S. dros, that which settles down), drowse (A.S. drús-ian, deriv. from dreós-an), drowsy.

Drinc-an (*to drink*): drink, drench (to cause to drink), drunk-ard (A.S. drunc-, base of p.p. of drinc-an), drown (A.S. druncn-ian, to sink).

Dreóp-an (*to drop*): drop, drip (Scand. dryp), dribble (freq. of drip), driblet, droop.

Dryge (*dry*): dry, drought (from A.S. drug-ian, to dry), drug (O. Fr. drogue, Du. droog, dried roots being used medicinally), drugget (dim. of "drug," so called from coarseness of material).

Dún (*a hill*): dune, down, a-down (A.S. of dúne, off the hill), Snow-don, Hunting-don, Swin-don.

Dýf-an, dúf-an (*to plunge*): dive, diver, dove, didapper (a kind of bird, for dive-dapper, lit. "a dive-diver," a reduplicated word), dove-tail.

Eác (*also*): eke (adverb and verb), nick-name (for "an eke name," an additional name; the *n* of the article has been wrongly tacked on to "eke").

Eáge (*eye*): eye, daisy (A.S. dæges eáge, day's eye), window (Scand. vind-auga, "a wind-eye," the second word being another form of "eáge").

Eást (*east*): east, Easter (A.S. Eastre, the goddess whose festival was held in April), sterling (from "Easterling," man of the east, the name given to Hanse merchants, who frequented London in the spring).

Efeta (*kind of lizard*): eft, newt (Mid. Eng. newte, for "an ewte," ewte being a contraction of Mid. Eng. evete from A.S. efeta. For an explanation of the *n* in "newt" see above under **Eác**).

Eft or **æft** (*behind*): after, afterwards, ab-aft (A.S. a + bi + aft = on by aft).

Et-an (*to eat*): eat, eatable, fret (A.S. fret-an = for-et-an, to devour entirely), or-ts (from A.S. or = out, what is left, that which is uneaten, hence, the leavings: cf. ordeal under **Dǽl**, above), etch (to engrave with acids, Du. ets-en, to etch, to corrode).

Fang (*a seizing*): fang, fing-er (the *er* denotes agent), new-fangled (the *d* is excrescent, Mid. Eng. newe-fangel: the latter word signifies "ready to catch").

Far-an (*to travel, to go*): fare, farewell, thorough-fare, wel-fare, ferry (A.S. fer-ian, to cause to go, to convey across), ford (A.S. ford, a passage), frith or firth, war-fare (going to war), chaffer (A.S. ceáp faru; see above, p. 367).

Feó, feoh (*cattle*, hence *property*): fee, fellow (Scand. félagi, from fé, property, and lag, a laying together: hence "fellow" lit. means a sharer in property; Mid. Eng. felawe).

Feówer (*four*): four, fourth (A.S. feórtha), fourteen (A.S. feówer-tyne), forty (A.S. feówer-tig), farthing (A.S. feorthing, fourth part of a penny), fortnight (fourteen nights, A.S. feówertyne niht), firkin (fourth part of a barrel, O. Du. vier = A.S. feówer, four).

Fersc (*moving, on the move*, allied to **Far**-an): fresh, re-fresh, frisk, frisky, a-fresh, fresco (a painting in fresh plaster), fresh-et, fresh-man.

Fleóg-an (*to float in air*): flea (A.S. fleó), flee, flight (A.S. flyht), fledge (to furnish with feathers, Scand. fleyg-ja), fledge-ling.

Fleót-an (*to float on water*): float, afloat, fleet (A.S. fleót, a ship), fleet (swift, A.S. fleót-ig), flit (Mid. Eng. flitt-en), flutter (A.S. flotor-ian, to float about), flot-sam (Late Lat. fluct-at-ion-em, cognate with A.S. flot, the sea, and A.S. flot-a, a ship).

Fod-a (*what one eats*) : food, fodder (A.S. fód-or), feed (to give or take food, A.S. féd-an), forage (O. Fr. four-age, from Low Lat. fodrum), foster (A.S. fóstr-ian, to foster ; A.S. fóstor, nourishment).

Fore (*in advance*) : fore, a-fore, be-fore, first (A.S. fyrst, for-est), former (A.S. for-ma, first), fore-most, forward.

Fót (*foot*), pl. **fét** : foot, fet-lock (where "lock" means tuft of hair), fetter (shackle for the feet).

Freós-an (*to freeze*), p.p. **fror-en** : freeze, frozen, frost, frore.

Fúl (*foul*) : foul, filth (A.S. fylth), fou-mart (a polecat, Mid. Eng. ful mart, a foul marten).

Ful (*complete*): full, fill (A.S. fyll-an), ful-fil, fulsome (cf. winsome, buxom = bug-some).

Gá-n (a contracted form of **gang-an**, *to go*) : go, begone (A.S. bigán, or begán), gang (a crew of persons), gingerly (Scand. ging-la, freq. form, which seems to have been confounded with "ginger"), gangway.

Gár (*spear*) : gore (in the sense of spearing or stabbing), gar-lic (A.S. gár-leác, spear-leek), gar-fish.

Gást (*a spirit*) : ghost (the *h* is intrusive), ghast-ly. N.B.—"Aghast" is from A.S. a-gæst-an, to terrify, and has no connection with *gást* (spirit).

Geát (*an opening*) : gate (in the sense of door or opening), gate (in the sense of street or way), gait, gantlet (misspelt as "gauntlet"), gantlope (earlier form of the preceding, see above, p. 368).

Geót-an (*to pour*), p.p. **got-en** : in-got (that which is poured in), nugget (prob. doublet of the preceding ; formerly spelt "niggot" = an ingot : cf. *newt* under **Efeta**, and *nick* under **Eác**).

Gield-an, **gild-an** (*to pay up*) : guilt (fine for a trespass), yield, guild (a club, lit. the payment for entrance).

Git-an (*to obtain*) : get, be-get, for-get.

Gód (*good*) : good, goodwife, goody.

God (*the deity*) : goddess, godfather, godhead, good-bye (God be with you), gospel (A.S. spell, story, "the God story," the life of Christ), gossip (related in God ; in North. dial. "sib" means "relative").

Graf-an (*to engrave, cut*) : grave (in the sense of cut), en-grave, groove (a channel cut out), grove (properly a glade, A.S. gráf).

Gráp-ian (*to handle*), **gríp-an** (*to seize*) : grab, grapple, grapnel, grappling-iron, grip, gripe, grope (to handle, to feel one's way).

Grund (*ground*) : ground, grunsel or groundsill (threshold, A.S. syl, the base of a door), groundsel or groundswell (lit. "ground swallower," A.S. swelg-an, to swallow).

Habb-an (*to have*) : have, behave, behaviour, haft (A.S. hæft), haven (hæfene).

Hál (*whole, sound*) : hale, hail (in the sense of greet), hallow (A.S. hálg-ian, to make holy), holy (A.S. hál-ig), hallow-mass (the feast of All Hallows, All Saints), heal (A.S. hǽl-an, to make sound), health, holiday (for holy day), holly-hock (the hock or mallow from the Holy Land), wassail (A.S. wes hál, be thou hale), whole (Mid. Eng. hole, A.S. hál), whole-some, hali-but (Mid. Eng. hali-butte, the plaice used on holy days).

Hǽth (*untilled land*): heath, heath-en (lit. dweller on a heath), heath-er, hoid-en or hoyd-en (a romping girl, formerly a rustic, doublet of the preceding, from O. Du. heyd-en).

Hag-a (*enclosure, yard*): haw, hawthorn, hedge (A.S. hecg, a secondary form of A.S. hag-a), hagg-ard (O. Fr. hag-ard, wild, used of a hedge-falcon).

Hang-ian (*to suspend*): hang, hanker (freq. form, we still say "to hang about after a thing"), hinge (from Mid. Eng. heng-en).

Heald-an (*to keep*): hold, be-hold, up-hold, up-hol-ster-er (one who holds up things to sale; orig. spelling, up-hold-ster-er).

Hebb-an (*to lift up*): heave, up-heave, heft (formed from "heave" as haft is from "have"), heavy, heaven (A.S. heofon, or hefon; its connection with "hebb-an," however, has not yet been proved).

Herr or **here** (*army*): harbour (Mid. Eng. herberre, Scand. herbergi, lit. army-shelter), harbinger (Mid. Eng. herberge-our O. Fr. herberg-er, to harbour, to provide shelter for any one), herring (the fish being so named, because it came in shoals, like an army), harry (A.S. herg-ian, to devastate, as is done by an army), heriot (lit. military apparel, A.S. her-geatu).

Hlad-an (*to load*), pt. t. **hlód**: load, laden (p.p.), last (ship's cargo, A.S. hlæst), bal-last (lit. bad cargo).

Hleáp-an (*to jump* or *run*), pt. t. **hleóp**: e-lope, inter-loper, lap-wing (A.S. hleápe-wince, one who turns about in running), or-lop (Du. the deck of a ship, that which runs over the upper part of a ship). For "gauntlet" see above, **Geát**.

Hopp-ian (*to leap* or *dance*): hop, hopp-er (of a mill), hopple (a fetter for horses), hobble (doublet of the preceding), hobby, hobby-horse (a toy shaped like a horse).

Hreós-an (*to start up*): rouse, a-rouse, rush (Scand. ruske), rustle.

Hun-ig (*honey*): honey, honey-comb (A.S. hunig-comb), honey-suckle (A.S. hunig-súge, from A.S. súg-an, to suck).

Hwít (*white*): white, wheat (so called from the colour of the flour), whittle (a blanket named from its colour), Whit-Sunday (A.S. hwíta Sunnan-dæg, the Sunday when children were christened in white).

Lád (*a way* or *course*): lode, lead (A.S. lǽd-an), lode-star (the polar star, lit. the way-star, the star that leads), lode-stone (sometimes misspelt as load-stone).

Læssa (comp. of *little*): less (A.S. læssa), least (A.S. læst, contracted from læs-ast), lest (A.S. thý læs the, "for the reason less that").

Læt (*late, slow*): late, later or latter, latest or last, be-lated, let (in the sense of hinder, A.S. lett-an, to make late).

Lang, long (*extended*): long, along (A.S. and-lang), long (in the sense of wish, A.S. lang-ian), be-long (A.S. lang-ian), ling-er (A.S. leng-an, to put off), length (A.S. length), length-en.

Leáf (*foliage*): leaf, lobby (laube, a leaf-bower, Low Lat. lob-ia), lodge (O. Fr. loge, Low Lat. lobia).

Leás (*loose, false*); **los-ian** (*to set free, to part with*): loose, loos-en, leasing, (falsehood, A.S. leás-ung), -less (the suffix, as in "fear-less"), lose, lost, for-lorn (A.S. loren with intensive prefix), loss (A.S. los, destruction), louse (A.S. lús, destroyer).

Lecg-an, or **licg-an** (*to rest, abide*): lie, al-lay (A.S. á-lecg-an), lair (A.S. leger), law (A.S. læg, that which lies or is fixed), lay (to cause to lie down), out-lay, layer (doublet of lair), leaguer (a camp, see "All's Well," iii. 6. 27), be-leaguer, ledge (Scand. ligg-ja, to lie), ledger, low (Scand. lágr), re-ly (Lat. prefix re-, a hybrid).

Leóf (*dear*): lief, be-lieve (A.S. ge-lýf-an, to esteem dearly), leave (permission, A.S. leáf).

Leóht (*not heavy*): light, a-light (to descend from, A.S. of liht, the *a* being = A.S. *of*), a-light (to light upon; here the *a* = A.S. *on*), light-en (to alleviate).

Lif-ian (*to exist, to remain*): life (A.S. líf), a-live (A.S. on life, in life), live-long or life-long, live-ly (life-like), life-guard, livelihood (corr. of Mid. Eng. live-lode, "life-leading," A.S. líf lád), leave (A.S. lǽf-an, to leave a heritage, A.S. láf, that which remains).

Lust (*pleasure*): lust, list (A.S. lyst-an, to desire), list-less (put for lust-less).

Mæg (*I am able*), **mæg**-en (*strength*): may, dis-may (hybrid prefix), maiden (A.S. mægden, short for A.S. mæg-eth-en, dim. "one growing in strength"), main (A.S. mæg-en), might (A.S. mæht or miht).

Mearc (*bound, mark, border*): mark (a root kindred to Lat. marg-o, a border), de-marc-at-ion (an A.S. stem with Romanic affixes, and therefore a hybrid), march (in the sense of border), marque (as in the phrase "letters of marque," O. Fr. marque), marquee (a large tent, a bad spelling of Fr. marquise, orig. a tent for a marchioness or lady of rank), marquis (Low Lat. march-ensis, a prefect of the marches), marchioness (formed, with suffix -issa, from Low Lat. marchion-em, a prefect of the marches), margrave (prefect of the marches; Du. mark, a boundary, and graaf, a count), margravine (fem. of preceding), re-mark (Fr. re-marqu-er, to take note of).

Meng-an (*to mix*), **mang** (*a mixture*): mingle (freq. form of Mid. Eng. ming-en, A.S. meng-an), a-mong (A.S. on-mang, in a mixture), a-mongst (Mid. Eng. amonge, amonges, to which *t* was added), monger (dealer, trader, A.S. mangere, from A.S. mang-ian, to traffic in mixed goods), mongrel (for mong-er-el, an animal of mixed breed).

Mét-an (*to fall in with, to assemble*): meet, moot (as in the phrase "moot point," a point to be discussed in an assembly, A.S. mót), Witena-gemot (the Assembly of the Wise, that used to meet in Saxon times), moot-hall (hall of assembly), moot (verb, to moot a subject, bring it up for discussion).

Mid (*the central part*): mid, a-mid or amidst or midst (A.S. on middan, Mid. Eng. a-midd-e or a-midd-es, to which a final *t* was added), middle (A.S. midd-el), middl-ing (for midd-el-ing), mid-riff (A.S. hrif, the stomach), mid-ship (for a-mid-ship), mid-ship-man, mid-summer, mid-day, mid-wife (a woman who is with another, A.S. mid, with; no connection with "meed," a reward).

Mold-e (*dust, soil, earth*): mould, moldwarp (the animal that casts up mould, "Henry IV." iii. 1. 149), mole (shortened form of the preceding), mulled ale (corr. of muld-ale or mould-ale, a funeral ale or feast, from A.S. molde, the earth of the grave, and A.S. ealo, ale or feast; see above, p. 369), mould-er, mould-y.

Món-a (*the moon*): moon (lit. the measure of time), month (A.S. món-ath), Monday (A.S. Mónan-dæg, day of the moon-god).

Mów-an (*to cut grass*): mow, mead (A.S. *mǽd*, a field fit to be mowed), mead-ow (A.S. mǽd-u).

Næddre (*a snake*): adder (the initial *n* was confounded with *an*, the indef. article; cf. apron from napron (see **Mappa**, p. 398), umpire from numpire, *vide* **Par**, p. 401).

Neáh or **néh** (*adjacent*): nigh, near (A.S. neár, comp. of A.S. neáh), next (A.S. néhst, superlative of A.S. néhor, neáh), neighbour (A.S. neáh-gebúr or neáh-búr, lit. a nigh-husbandman).

Nós-u (*the nasal organ*): nose, nostril (=nose-thrill or nose-thirl, A.S. nósthyrl, the nose perforation; A.S. thyrl-ian, to bore a hole), nozzle (dim. of "nose").

Nú (*at the present time*): now, new (A.S. niwé, Mid. Eng. newe), new-fangled (A.S. fang-el, ready to catch), news (pl. new-es, new things, a transl. of Fr. nouvelles), re-new (a hybrid word, with Lat. prefix and Teut. stem).

Plætt-an (*to strike lightly*): pat (by loss of *l*), paddle (freq. of "pat," for pattle), patter (freq. of "pat").

Ræd-an (*to discern, advise*): read, rede (counsel), riddle (properly riddles, A.S. rǽd-else, a riddle, plur. rǽd-els-an, riddles), Ethelred the Unready (without rede or counsel, injudicious).

Reáf-ian (*to rob*): reave or be-reave, rover (a pirate).

Ríd-an, pt. t. **rád** (*to go on horseback*): ride, raid, road (A.S. rád), ready (A.S. ræde, equipped for riding), ar-ray (with Lat. prefix ad-), rai-ment (short for ar-rai-ment), bed-ridden (see above, p. 367).

Rów-an (*to propel with oars*): row, rudder (A.S. róther, a paddle).

Rúm (*space, a chamber*): room, roomy, rum-mage (for roomage, stowage; the verb "rummage" signifies to find room for close packing in a ship).

Sǽl (*time, season*): silly (A.S. sǽl-ig, lit. seasonable, then lucky, then simple or foolish).

Sár (*painful*): sore, sorry (A.S. sár-ig). No connection with "sorrow," from A.S. sorge.

Scád-an, or **sceád-an** (*to part* or *pour*): shed (as in "water-shed," that which sheds or parts the waters of a river), sheath (A.S. scǽth, lit. that which separates, hence a husk, shell, or pod), shoddy (that which is shed or thrown off in spinning wool).

Scæd, **scead**-u (*a shade* or *shelter*): shade, shadow, shed (a slight shelter).

Sceac-an (*to shake*, also *to run*): pt. t. **scóc**: shake, shock, shackle (A.S. sceac-ul, a loose bond), shank (A.S. sceanc-a, bone of the leg, named from its motion in running).

Sceap-an, or **scap**-an (*to form* or *fashion*): shape, ship (A.S. scip), skiff (doublet of preceding), skipper, land-scape, friend-ship.

Scearp (*cutting*): sharp, scarp, escarpment (Fr. escarpe, with suffix -ment), counter-scarp (Fr. contre scarpe), scrap, scrape (A.S. scearp-ian, to scarify), scramble (with intrusive *m*, freq. of "scrape").

Sceaw-ian (*to point out*): shew or show, sheen (A.S. scéne, Mid. Eng. schene), scavenger (for "scavager"; cf. messenger for "messager"; the *n* is in both words intrusive; scav-age=shew-age, a hybrid word formed with Teut. stem scav- and Romanic suffix -age).

Scer-an (*to cut*): shear, scar (a rock, Scand. sker, an isolated rock cut off from the mainland), scare, scarify, score (A.S. scoren, the number twenty denoted by a long cut in a stick), shard or sherd (A.S. sceard, a fragment, a thing cut), pot-sherd, share (A.S. scear-u, a portion, also a thing that cuts), plough-share, shore (A.S. score; cf. A.S. scor-en clif, a shorn cliff), short (A.S. sceort, cut off), skirt or shirt (Scand. skyrt, a short kind of kirtle).

Scild, sceld (*shield*): shield, shelter (a corr. of Mid. Eng. sheld-trume, "a shield-troop," which was frequently spelt as "sheltron" or "sheltrun"; A.S. scild, a shield, and A.S. truma, a troop).

Scóf-ian, scúf-an (*to push*): shove, shovel (A.S. scof-el), shuffle or scuffle (freq. of Scand. skuff-a, to push), sheaf (A.S. sceáf, a pile of corn shoved together).

Scót-ian or **sceót-an** (*to dart*), p.p. **scot-en**: shoot, shot, scot-free (A.S. scot, payment, a contribution to a common fund into which it is shot), scud, scuttle (freq. of preceding), shuttle (so called from being shot across the threads in weaving), shuttle-cock, skittish (Lowland Scotch, to *skit*, to caper about), skittles or skittle-pins (so called because *shot* at by a *skittle* or projectile).

Screáw-a (*a shrew-mouse fabled to have a venomous bite*): screw (a vicious horse), shrew (a scold of either sex), beshrew, shrewd (old sense, malicious), shrew-mouse.

Scún-ian (*to avoid*): shun, shunt, schooner (a misspelling for "scooner," a ship that glides along swiftly; A.S. scún-ian, orig. to speed or scud along).

Sing-an (*to resound*): sing, song (A.S. sang, from sang, pt. t. of sing-an), songster (A.S. sang-ystre or sang-es-tre, double suffix, -es and -tre), songstress (with a third suffix -ess, of Fr. origin), singe (A.S. seng-an, to cause to sing or resound).

Skerm-an (Old High Germ.), also **scirm-an** (*to fight*): scrimmage, skirm-ish (O. Fr. escarm-ouche), scara-mouch (a buffoon, derived from the preceding).

Slah-an, or **sleá-n** (*to kill*): slay, slaughter (of which the base is A.S. sleáht=Mid. Eng. slaught), sledge-hammer (A.S. slecge, a smiter, and A.S. hamor, hammer; a tautological compound).

Smít-an (*to deal blows*): smite, smooth (A.S. sméthe, orig. "flattened with a hammer"), smith (A.S. smith, one who works with the hammer).

Sníc-an (*to creep*): sneak, snake (A.S. snac-a, a crawler), snail (A.S. snægl, dim. of snac-a or snag-a).

Spinn-an (*to draw out threads*): spin, spindle (A.S. spinl), spider (Mid. Eng. spi-ther, which in A.S. would be spin-ther, one who spins), spin-ster (A.S. spinn-es-tre, a woman who spins).

Sprec-an (*to use the voice in talking*): speak (late A.S. spec-an), be-speak, speech (A.S. spǽc), spokesman (from Mid. Eng. spoke, pt. t. of speak; the *s* is intrusive, but after the analogy of words like "huntsman," "oarsman," etc.).

Stac-a (*a post*), **stic-ian** (*to set*): stick, stake, stickle-back, stock (A.S. stocc, a thing stuck down or fixed), stock-ade, etiquette (O. Fr. etiquet for estiquet, a small note stuck up on the gate of a court), ticket (doublet of the preceding), tick (credit, short for "ticket"), stitch (A.S. stice, a pricking sensation in the side).

Stæl (*standing-place for cattle*): stall, stale (kept too long standing), stalk (dim. from A.S. stæl), stallion (a horse not worked, but kept in a stall), stalwart (a misspelling for "stal-worth," A.S. stæl-wyrthe ; see above, p. 370).

Steóp (*orphaned*): step-child (A.S. steóp-cild), step-father (A.S. steóp-fæder), step-mother (A.S. steóp-móder).

Steór-an (*to guide a ship*): steer, steer-age (a hybrid word), star-board (the right side of a ship, on which the steersman stood), stern (the hind part of a vessel, the steerage place).

Stíg-an (*to climb* or *mount*): stag (the male, the mounter), stile (A.S. stig-el), stair (A.S. stǽgr), stirrup (A.S. stí-ráp, a rope to mount by), sty (A.S. stíg-o, a pen for cattle), steward (A.S. stí-weard, a keeper of enclosures).

Styb (*stump*): stub, stubble, stump (a nasalised form of "stub"), stubborn (stock-like, not easily moved, A.S. styb-or, with excrescent *n*).

Swer-ian (*to declare*): swear, an-swer (A.S. and-swer-ian, and= against), for-swear (A.S. for, depreciatory prefix).

Swil-ian (*to wash, to drink greedily*): swill, swill-tub, sculler-y ("sculler" is a variant of swiller, due to Scand. influence ; for the suffix *y* cf. pantr-y, smith-y, butter-y).

Swím-a (*dizziness*): swim, squeam-ish (a corr. of Mid. Eng. sweym-ous, a hybrid word), swindler (A.S. swind-an, a form of swim, to be dizzy, to act thoughtlessly).

Tádige, tádie (*a toad*): toad, tad-pole (a toad which is all "poll" or head), toad-eater (now contracted to "toady," a sycophant or mountebank who pretended to be ready to eat toads).

Tǽs-an, older form **tás**-ian (to pull about, tear): tease, touse, teas-el (A.S. tæsel, a plant), tussle (freq. of touse).

Takke (Mid. Eng. fastening, probably allied to Scand. **tak**-a, *take*): tack, tache (a blemish), at-tach, at-tack, de-tach, tetchy (now corrupted to "touchy").

Teár, tǽr (*fluid from the eye*): tear, train-oil (formerly spelt trane-oyle, O. Du. traen, tear : the drops that came out from whale's blubber).

Teóh-an, or **teón** (*to tug along*): tow, tow-line (A.S. toh-line, from tag-en, pp. of teóh-an ; A.S. line is from Lat. lin-ea), tug (from pt. t. plur. of A.S. teóh-an), tuck (to gather in a dress, from the same root as "tug"), wan-ton (A.S. wan-towen, untrained, from A.S. wan, deficient, and towen=togen, p.p. of teóh-an), tie (A.S. tyge, teág, or teáh, a rope for pulling).

Thersc-an (*to beat*): thresh or thrash, thresh-old (=thresh-wold, A.S. thersc-wald, later Sax. thersc-old; A.S. wald or weald; threshold is the piece of wood constantly beaten by the tread of feet).

Threó, thrí (*three*): third (A.S. thridda), thrice (Mid. Eng. thri-es, of three), thir-teen (A.S. threó-tyne), thirty (A.S. thri-tig), riding (for thrid-ing, one of the three divisions of Yorkshire).

Tíd (*time*) ; **tíd**-an (*to happen*) : tide, be-tide, Whitsun-tide, tidings (Mid. Eng. tid-inde, afterwards spelt as tidings, things that happen).

Tred-an (*to put the foot on anything*) : tread, trade, trade-wind (a wind that follows a certain course), treadle (what we tread on in a lathe or in a cycle).

Treówe, or **trúwe** (*firm, certain, believed*): true (Mid. Eng. trewe), trow (A.S. treów-ian, to believe), troth or truth (A.S. treówthu), be-troth, truce (Mid. Eng. trewes, the plural of "trew," a pledge, from A.S. "trúwa, a contract), trust (Scand. traust, of the same base as "true").

Twá (*two*): be-tween (A.S. be-tweónan), betwix-t (the *t* is excrescent, Mid. Eng. be-twix-e, A.S. be-twih), twelve (A.S. twelf, twelfe, Goth. twá-lif, which means "two over ten"; "lif" means remaining; ten and two over; see **Lif**-ian, above), twenty (A.S. twén, twegen, twain, and A.S. tig, ten), twice (A.S. twíg-es), twig (shoot of a tree, the part of a branch, which is necessarily double), twill, twin (A.S. ge-twinne), twine (A.S. twín, a twisted or doubled thread), twist (A.S. twist-; from A.S. twí-), with suffix *-st*, as in bla-st, from blow).

Wác-an, **wac**-ian (*to arise, cease from sleep*): wake, a-wak-en, watch (A.S. wæcce), a-wait (O. Fr. a-wait-ier; from O. High Ger. wahta, a watchman; hence the phrase "lie in wait"), waits (musical watchmen), bivouac (Fr. bivouac, orig. bivac; Ger. beiwache, a keeping watch, from bei, near, and wach-en, to watch).

Wæpen (*an implement of war*): weapon, wapentake (A.S. wæpen-ge-tǽc-e, lit. weapon-touching, hence a district governed by a man whose authority was conferred by the touching of weapons).

Wær (*cautious*): wary, a-ware, be-ware, ware (merchandise, A.S. war-u, heed, care), warn (A.S. wearn-ian), weir (A.S. wer, a dam, a protection), warr-ant, guarantee (O. Fr. garantie).

Wæter (*water*): water, otter (A.S. otor, dweller in water).

Warre (*fighting*): war, war-fare (A.S. far-u, a setting out or going), guerilla (irregular warfare, lit. "a little war," dim. of Fr. guerre, war).

Weard (*keeper*): ward, a-ward, ward-en, guard (Fr. garde, the French spelling of "ward"), guardian (doublet of "warden"), re-ward, re-gard, ward-robe (a place for keeping robes), van-guard (see **Ab**-, p. 373).

Wed (*a pledge*): wed (verb, A.S. wedd-ian, lit. to pledge in marriage), wed-lock (A.S. wed-lác, A.S. lác, sport), wage (a gage or pledge, stipulated payment), wager (a bet).

Weder (*the state of the air*): weather, weather-beaten, weather-bitten ("Winter's Tale," v. 2. 60), wither (lit. to expose to the weather).

Wef-an (*to weave*): weave, web (A.S. webb), weft, woof (a corr. of Mid. Eng. oof, and this is a contraction of A.S. ó-wef, lit. on the wef or warp).

Weg-an (*to carry, bear, lift*): weigh, wain (A.S. wægn or wǽn), wag-on or wagg-on (A.S. wægn), wag, wagg-le.

Wíf (*a woman*): wife, woman (a corr. of A.S. wíf-man, the word "man" being formerly applied to both sexes; in the 12th century it became "wumman").

Wiht (*a person* or *thing*): whit (a particle), wight (a person), aught (A.S. á-wiht, one whit), naught (aught with negative prefix), not (contr. of preceding).

Will-an (*to desire*): will, wild (A.S. wild, untamed), wilderness (A.S. wildern-nesse, Mid. Eng. wilderne, formed with suffix *n* from

A.S. wilder, a wild animal; "wilder" is from A.S. wild and deór, a wild animal), be-wilder (to lead astray), weal (A.S. wela, prosperity), wealth, well (according to wish), wel-fare, wel-come.

Wind (*the air in motion*): wind, wind-fall, wind-mill, wind-ow (Scand. vindr-auga, lit. wind-eye), winn-ow (A.S. windw-ian, to expose to wind).

Wind-an (*to turn round*): wind, wend, wand-er (freq. of preceding), windlass (Scand. vind-áss, from áss, a pole or rounded beam; the *l* is intrusive), wonder (A.S. wund-or, a thing from which one turns aside in awe), wondrous (a corr. of Mid. Eng. wonders, poss. case of "wonder," and therefore adverbial, not an adjective; in A.S. the adj. was wundor-lic, "wonder-like").

Wit-an (*to know*): wit (noun and verb), wise (in the sense of discreet, A.S. wís, orig. form wit-sa, possessed of wit), wis-dom (A.S. wís-dóm), wise (in the sense of manner, A.S. wíse, way), like-wise, other-wise, guise (doublet of "wise"), dis-guise (a hybrid formation), twit (A.S. æt-wít-an, to reproach), wise-acre (O. High Ger. wízagó, a prophet, which in A.S. became wítega), witch (A.S. wicca, mas., or wicce, fem.), wicked (the stem of this word is A.S. wicc-, as in the preceding), wit-ness (A.S. wit-nes, testimony), wiz-ard (=witt-ish-ard), I wis (supposed to be=I know, but really from Mid. Eng. ywis or iwis, certainly, this being from A.S. ge-wis), witena-gemot (assembly of the wise; see above under **Met**-an).

Wring-an (*to twist*): wring, wrick (Mid. Eng. wrikk-en, as in the phrase "to wrick one's ankle"), rickets (derived from the preceding), wrig (to move about, A.S. wrig-ian), rig (a frolic, or prank, for "wrig"), wriggle (freq. of "wrig"), wrangle (freq. of "wring"), wrench (A.S. wrenc or wrence, a twist), wrinkle (a little twist), wrong (A.S. wrang; orig. pt. t. of verb "wring-an"), wry (A.S. wrig-ian, to incline towards), a-wry.

Wríth-an (*to twist about*): writhe, wrath (A.S. wráth, pt. t. of the verb writh-an), wreath (A.S. wrǽth, a twisted band), wrest (A.S. wræst-an, to twist forcibly, to distort), wrestle (freq. of preceding), wrist (A.S. wrist, that which turns the hand about), wroth (A.S. wráth).

Wyrc-an (*to make anything*): work (verb, A.S. wyrc-an; noun, A.S. weorc or werc), wright (workman, A.S. wyrhta), cart-wright, wheel-wright, ship-wright.

IV.—DERIVATIVES FROM LATIN ROOTS.

N.B.—Observe distinction between **Late Lat.** *and* **Low Lat.** (*p.* 375).

Ac-er, acr-em (*sharp*): acer-b-ity, acr-id, acri-mon-y, eager (Fr. aigre), vin-egar (Fr. vin-aigre, sour wine).

Ac-u-ere, **ac-ut**-um (*sharpen*): acute, ague (shivering fit, Fr. aigu).

Æd-es (*a house*): ed-i-fice, ed-i-fy, ed-i-fic-at-ion.

Æqu-us, **æqu-al**-is (*just, equal*): ad-equ-ate, equ-at-ion, equ-i-ty, in-iqu-i-ty, equ-al, equ-al-i-ty, equ-anim-i-ty.

Æstim-are, **æstim-at**-um (*to value*): aim (O. Fr. aesm-er, Lat. ad æstim-are), esteem, estim-at-ion.

Æv-um (*age*): co-ev-al, medi-ev-al, prim-ev-al.

Ag-er, **agr**-i (*field*): agr-ar-ian, agri-culture, per-egr-in-at-ion, pilgrim (O. Fr. pelegrin or pelerin, Lat. per-egr-inus).

Ag-ere, **act**-um (*to do*): act, ag-ent, ag-en-cy, ag-ile, amb-ig-u-ous, cog-ent (from co-ig-entem), en-act, ex-ig-ent, prod-ig-al (Late Lat. prod-ig-al-is).

Ali-us (*other*): ali-as, ali-bi, ali-en, ali-quot.

Al-**ter** (*second of two*): alter (v.), alter-cation, altern-ate, altr-u-ism, sub-altern.

Alt-us (*high*): alt-ar, alt-i-tude, alt-o, ex-alt, haught-y (O. Fr. haut, high), haut-boy (Fr. bois, wood; Ital. o-boé).

Am-are, **amat**-um (*to love*): amat-ory, am-i-able, am-ic-able (Lat. amic-us), am-or-ous (Lat. am-or, noun), en-amour, en-em-y (in-im-ic-us), in-im-ic-al, en-m-i-ty.

Anim-a (*life, breath*); **anim**-us (*mind*): anim-al, anim-ad-vert, anim-ate, anim-os-i-ty, equ-anim-i-ty, magn-anim-ous, pusill-anim-ous, un-anim-i-ty.

Ann-us, **ann**-i (*year*): ann-als, anni-vers-ary, ann-u-al, bi-enn-i-al, per-enn-i-al, sept-enn-i-al, cent-enn-i-al.

Ante- (prefix, *before*): ancient (Late Lat. anti-an-us, with excrescent *t*), anterior, antique (Fr.), antic (a doublet of the preceding), van (Fr. av-ant, Lat. ab ante).

Aper-ire, **apert**-um (*to open*): aper-i-ent, Apr-il (because the earth then opens to yield new fruits), apert-ure, overt (Fr. ouvert, open, unconcealed), overt-ure.

Ap-**pell**-are, **ap**-**pell**-**at**-um (*to call*): ap-peal, ap-pell-at-ive, inter-pell-at-ion (here *inter* displaces *ad*), peal (short for ap-peal).

Apt-us (*fit*): apt, ad-apt, ad-ept, apt-i-tude, att-i-tude (doublet of the preceding by the substitution of *t* for *p*), in-ept.

Aqu-a (*water*): aqu-at-ic, aqu-e-duct (aquæ ductus, Lat.), aqu-e-ous, ewer (O. Fr. ewer, from L. aqu-arium, a vessel for holding water).

Arc-us (*bow*): arc, arc-ade, arch, arch-er (Fr. archier, Late Lat. arc-ar-ius).

Ard-eo, **ars**-um (*to burn*): ard-ent, ard-our, ars-on.

Arm-a (*arms*); **arm**-are, **arm**-**at**-um (*to arm*): al-arm (Ital. all' arme, to arms!), al-arum (doublet of *alarm*), ambry (stone closet, Fr. armoire, Lat. arm-arium), arm-ad-a (Lat. arm-at-a classis, an armed fleet), arm-a-ment, arm-i-stice, arm-our (Lat. arm-at-ura), arm-y (O. Fr. armée, an armed body of men).

Ars, **art**-is (*art*): art, artful, art-i-fice, art-illery, art-ist, art-i-san (as if from Late Lat. art-it-i-anus), in-ert.

Art-us (*joint*): art-i-cle, art-ic-ul-ate.

Aud-io, **aud**-**it**-um (*to hear*): aud-i-ble, aud-i-ence, aud-it (he hears), ob-ed-i-ent, ob-ed-i-ence, obeisance (doublet of preceding), ob-ey, Oyez (hear ye, which a crier pronounces as O yes).

Aug-eo, **auct**-um (*to make larger*): auct-ion, aug-ment, Aug-ust, auth-or (Lat. auct-or), aut-umn (auct-umn-us, the season of increase or harvest).

Aur-um (*gold*): aur-e-ole, auri-ferous, or (*gold*, in heraldry), or-i-el (O. Fr. or-i-ol, Late Lat. or-i-ol-um, Lat. aur-e-ol-um, lit. a recess ornamented with gold), ori-flamme (auri flamma, the old standard of France).

Av-is (*bird*): avi-ary, au-spice or au-spices (Lat. avis spicium, the watching of birds for purposes of augury), au-gury, bus-tard (formerly bis-tard, Lat. avis tarda, a slow-flying bird), os-trich (O. Fr. os-truce, Lat. avis + Gr. strouth-ion).

Barb-a (*beard*): barb, barb-el (bearded fish), barb-er, barbed (as a horse), beard.

Bell-us (*fair, fine*): belle, beau, beau-ty, bel-dam, bella donna (Lat. bella domina), em-bell-ish.

Bib-ere (*to drink*): bib, bev-erage (O. Fr. bovraige), bev-y (Fr. bev-ée, a company), im-bibe, im-bue, wine-bibber.

Bis (*twice*); **bin-i** (*two at a time*): bin-ary, bin-ocular, com-bine, ba-lance (Fr. ba-lance, Lat. bi-lanc-em), bi-furcate (furca, fork).

Brev-is (*short*): breve, brev-et, brev-i-ary, brev-i-ty, brief, ab-brev-i-ate, a-bridge.

Caball-us (*horse*): caval-ier, caval-cade, caval-ry, cheval-ier, chival-ry (Fr. cheval).

Cad-ere, cas-um (*to fall*): case, cas-cade, cas-u-al, cad-ence, chance (doublet of preceding), co-in-cide, de-cad-ence, de-cay, de-cid-u-ous, es-cheat (O. Fr. eschet, rent, Lat. ex cad-ere), ac-cid-ent, in-cid-ent, oc-cas-ion, oc-cid-ent.

Cæd-ere, cæs-um (*to cut* or *kill*): cæs-ura, circum-cise, con-cise, de-cide, ex-cis-ion, in-cis-ive, ce-ment (Lat. cæmentum, cæd-i-mentum), chisel (Late Lat. cis-ellus, for cæs-ellus), homi-cide, sui-cide, infanti-cide.

Calx, calc-em (*stone, lime*): chalk, calc-areous (for calc-arious), calc-ulus, calc-ul-ate, causeway (Lat. calc-i-ata, paved, to which Eng. "way" has been added; a hybrid compound: see p. 372).

Camer-a (*apartment*): cham-b-er, chamber-lain (for chamber-ling, O. Fr. chambrelenc), comrade (Sp. camarada, a company, an associate).

Camp-us (*plain*): camp, camp-aign, camp-estral, champ-agne, champ-aign, champ-ion (Late Lat. camp-ion-em, a combatant), de-camp, en-camp, scamp (O. Fr. es-camp-er, *to flee*, Lat. ex campus), shamble.

Cancell-us (*grating*): cancel, chancel, chancell-or, chancery (for chancel-ry).

Cand-ere (*to be white*), **candid-us** (*white*): cand-id, cand-id-ate, cand-le (Lat. cand-el-a), kindle, cannel-coal, cand-our, chandel-ier, chandl-er, in-cand-escent.

Can-ere, cant-um; **cant-are, cant-at-um** (*to sing*): cant, ac-cent, cant-icle, cant-o, chant, chanticleer, chant-ry, des-cant, en-chant, in-cant-at-ion, in-cent-ive, pre-cent-or, re-cant.

Can-is (*dog*): can-ine, kenn-el (O. Fr. chen-il).

Cap-er, capr-i (*a goat*): caper, cabriolet, cab (short form of preceding), capri-corn, cap-rice (Ital. capriccio, a whim, a frisk like a goat's).

Cap-ere, capt-um (*to take* or *hold*): ac-cept, anti-cip-ate, cab-le, (Late Lat. cap-ul-um, a holding rope), capt-ive, cait-iff (doublet of the preceding), cap-able, catch (Late Lat. capt-i-are), chase (O. Fr. chac-ier), con-ceit, con-ceive, ex-cept, in-cipi-ent, inter-cept, pre-cept, pur-chase (O. Fr. pur-chacer), re-cipe (*take it*), sus-cept-ible.

Caps-a (*a vessel*), allied to **cap-ere**: case, capsule, case-ment, cash (orig. the box in which cash was kept), en-case, sash (corruption of Fr. châsse, Lat. capsa).

Caput, capit-is (*head*): a-chieve (O. Fr. a-chef, Lat. ad caput, to a head), a-chieve-ment, cabbage (from Ital. capuccio, a little head), cape, capit-al, capit-at-ion, capit-ol, capit-ul-ate, capt-ain (Late Lat. capit-an-eus), cattle (Late Lat. capit-al-e), chapt-er, chatt-els, chief (O. Fr. chef, chief), de-capit-ate, hatchment (corruption of ach'-ment, shortened form of achieve-ment), oc-ciput, pre-cip-ice, sin-ciput (lit. half head, semi caput).

Car-o, **carn**-is (*flesh*): carn-al, carn-age, carn-at-ion, carn-i-val, carr-ion, charn-el, in-carn-a-dine, in-carn-at-ion, carn-i-vor-ous (Lat. vor-are, to devour).

Car-us (*dear*): car-ess, char-i-ty, cher-ish.

Cast-us (*pure, chaste*): caste (lit. a pure breed), chaste, chast-en, chast-ise, in-cest, cast-i-gate.

Caus-a (*cause*): ac-cuse, be-cause, caus-at-ive, ex-cuse, re-cus-ant, ruse (a trick, Fr. ruse, O. Fr. reüser, Lat. re-cus-are).

Cav-us (*hollow*): cage, cave, cajole (O. Fr. cageol-er, to chatter like a bird in a cage), con-cave, ex-cav-at-ion, gabion (Ital. gabbione, augm. of Late Lat. gabia, a cage), gaol or jail (O. Fr. gaole, Late Lat. gabiola).

Ced-ere, **cess**-um (*to make way* or *yield*): cede, abs-cess, ac-cede, ancestor (O. Fr. an-cess-our, Lat. ante-cess-or), ante-ced-ent, ac-cess, ac-cess-ory, de-cease (Lat. de-cess-us), ex-ceed, excess, ex-cess-ive, inter-cede, pre-de-cess-or, re-cede, re-cess, se-cede, se-cess-ion, suc-ceed, suc-cess, suc-cess-ive.

Cent-um (*a hundred*): cent (as in "per cent"), cent-en-ary, cent-enn-i-al, cent-i-grade, cent-i-pede, cent-u-ple, cent-ur-ion, cent-ur-y.

Cern-o, **cret**-um (*to distinguish*): con-cern, de-cree (Lat. de-cret-um), de-cret-al, dis-cern, dis-creet, se-cret, se-cret-ary.

Chart-a (*paper*): card, chart, carte (as in "carte blanche"), cart-el, cart-oon, cart-ouche, cart-r-idge (doublet of "cart-ouche," the *r* is intrusive, the -idge is a corr. of -ouche), charter.

Cing-ere, **cinct**-um (*to surround*): cinct-ure, en-ceinte (Lat. in-cinct-a, lit. girt in), pre-cincts, shingles (Lat. cing-u-lum), suc-cinct.

Civ-is (*a citizen*): **civ-il**-is (adj.): civil, city (short for civ-i-ty, Lat. civ-i-tatem), cit-i-zen, cit-a-del (Fr. citadella, dim. form).

Clar-us (*clear, bright*): clear, clar-et, clar-i-fy, clar-i-on, de-clare, glaire (O. Fr. white of egg).

Claud-ere, **claus**-um (*to shut*): clause, cloist-er, close, clos-et, con-clude, con-clus-ion, re-cluse, se-clus-ion, sluice (O. Fr. es-cluse, Lat. ex-clusa aqua, shut-off water).

Cliv-us (*a slope*): ac-cliv-i-ty (sloping up), de-cliv-i-ty (sloping down), pro-cliv-i-ty (sloping forward).

Cognosc-ere, **cognit**-um (*to know*, compounded of *con* and *gnosc*-ere): cognit-ion, cognis-ant, connoisseur (a knowing one), in-cognit-o, re-cognise, re-cognis-ance, re-cognit-ion, reconnaissance, re-connoitre (O. Fr. recognoistre).

Col-ere, **cult**-um (*to till*); col-on-y, cult-ure, cult-i-vate, agri-cult-ure.

Com-es, **comit**-is (*companion*): count (from stem *comit*), count-y (Lat. comit-at-us), con-stable (Lat. comes stabuli, count of the stable), con-comit-ant.

Co-oper-ire (*conceal*): cover (O. Fr. covr-ir), cover-let (O. Fr.

covre-lit, a bed-cover), covert, cur-few (O. Fr. covre-feu, a fire-cover), dis-cover, ker-chief (O. Fr. covre chef, head-cover). N. B.—Re-cover is from Lat. *re-cuper*-are, an entirely distinct root.

Coqu-ere, **coct**-um (*to cook*): bis-cuit (Fr. bis-cuit, twice cooked), cake (?), cook, con-coct, de-coct-ion, kitchen (A.S. cicen, Lat. coqu-ina, cook-house), pre-coc-i-ous (Lat. præcox, -coc-is, early ripe), apri-cot (formerly spelt as apricock, Port. al bricoque, the early ripe. The *al* was merely the Arabic article; the *bri* was from Lat. *præ*).

Cor, cord-is (*heart*): core, ac-cord, ac-cord-ing-ly, con-cord, con-cord-at, cour-age, dis-cord, re-cord, re-cord-er.

Cor-i-um (*hide*): cuir-ass (Fr. cuir, leather), ex-cori-ate, scourge, (O. Fr. es-corgie, Lat. ex-coriata, a leather whip).

Corn-u (*a horn*): corn, corn-el, corn-el-ian, corn-er (Late Lat. corn-er-ia), corn-et, uni-corn.

Coron-a (*a crown*, n.), **coron**-are, **coron-at**-um (v.): corn-ice (Late Lat. coron- or corn-ic-em, a border), coroll-ary (Lat. coroll-a, dim. of coron-a), coron-al, coron-er (Late Lat. coron-at-or, a crown officer), coron-et (dim. of Fr. corone), coron-at-ion.

Corp-us, **corpor**-is (*body*): corps, corpse, corse, corp-u-lent, cor-pus-cle, cors-et, cors-let, corpor-al, corpor-at-ion, in-corpor-ate.

Cre-are, **cre-at**-um (*to make*): create, creat-ure, creole (Sp. criollo, a negro, corruption of cre-ad-illo, dim. of cre-ad-o, one educated, well brought up), pro-create, re-cre-at-ion. (No connection with *recreant:* see next word.)

Cred-ere, **credit**-um (*to believe*): cred-ence, cred-ible, cred-it, cred-ul-ous, grant (from Late Lat. form of *credent-*), re-creant (pres. part. of Fr. re-croire, Lat. re-cred-ere), mis-creant (one who misbelieves).

Cresc-ere, **cret**-um (*to grow*): ac-cret-ion, ac-crue (O. Fr. ac-creu), cresc-ent, con-crete, de-crease, de-cre-ment, ex-cresc-ence, re-cruit (ill formed from Fr. recruter, to levy troops), in-cre-ment, crew (formerly spelt as crue, short for O. Fr. accrue, reinforcement).

Crux, **cruc**-is (*cross*): cross (O. Fr. crois), cruc-i-al, cruc-i-fy (Lat. cruci-fig-ere, to fix on the cross), crus-ade, ex-cruc-i-ate, cruise (to cross the sea, through Dutch kruis-en, to cruise).

Cub-are, **cubit**- or **cubat**-um (*to lie down*): cov-ey (O. Fr. covce, brood of partridges), con-cub-ine, cub-it, in-cub-ate, in-cub-us, in-cumb-ent (Lat. cumb-ere, another form of cub-are), re-cumb-ent.

Culp-are, **culp-at**-um (*to blame*): culp-able, culp-r-it (the *r* is intrusive, as in part-r-idge, cart-r-idge), ex-culp-ate, in-culp-ate.

Cur-a (n.), **cur**-are, **cur-at**-um (*to take care of*): cure (verb and noun), ac-cur-ate, cur-ate, cur-i-ous, proctor (short form of pro-cur-at-or), pro-cure, prox-y (Lat. pro-cur-at-io), scour (O. Fr. es-cur-er, Lat. ex-cur-are), sine-cure (Lat. sine curâ, without any trouble), se-cure, sure (short form of secure), as-sure, en-sure. (No connection with *care*, A.S. car-u, cear-u.)

Curr-ere, **curs**-um (*to run*): course, con-course, con-cur, corridor (Ital. corridore, a passage or gallery running along), cors-air, cours-er, cour-ier, curr-ent, curr-en-cy, curr-i-cle, curs-ory, dis-course, ex-curs-ion, in-cur, oc-cur, re-cur, pre-curs-or, re-course, suc-cour (Lat. suc-curr-ere, to help).

Curv-us (*bent*), **curv**-are, **curv-at**-um (*to bend*): curve, curb, curv-at-ure, curv-et, kerb-stone (a misspelling for curbstone).

Damn-are, **damn-at**-um (*to condemn*): damn, con-demn, damage (Late Lat. damn-at-icum), damn-at-ion, in-demn-i-fy, in-demn-i-ty. (No connection with *doom*, A.S. dóm.)

D-are, **dat**-um (*to give*): ad-d, data (things granted), date, dat-ive, die (Fr. dé, O. Fr. det), e-dit-ion, per-dit-ion, render (Fr. rendre, Lat. red-dere), rendezvous (Fr. render yourselves, Lat. reddite vos), rent (Fr. rente, Lat. red-dita), sur-render (Lat. super rendere), tra-dit-ion, treason (O. Fr. traïson, doublet of the preceding).

Deb-ere, **debit**-um (*to owe*): deb-ent-ure (Lat. deb-ent-ur, they are owed, they are due, 3rd pers. plur. passive), deb-it, debt, debt-or, due (O. Fr. deu, deue, p.p. of Fr. devoir, to owe), du-ty, en-deavour (Fr. devoir), in-debt-ed, debit-able.

Dec-**em** (*ten*), **decim**-us (*tenth*), **den**-i (*ten at a time*): dean (Lat. decan-us, one set over ten men), decan-al (belonging to a dean), dec-enn-i-al (Lat. ann-us, a year), decim-al, decim-ate, den-ary.

Dens, dent-is (*a tooth*): dent-al, dent-ist, dandelion (Fr. dent de lion, tooth of a lion), dent-i-frice (Lat. fric-are, to rub), dent-it-ion, in-dent, in-dent-ure.

Dic-are, **dic-at**-um (*to say*): ab-dic-ate, con-dit-ion (for con-dic-ion), de-dic-ate, in-dex, in-dic-ate, pre-dic-ate, preach (Fr. prêcher), pre-dic-a-ment.

Dic-ere, **dict**-um (*to say*); **dict**-are, **dict-at**-um (freq. of **dic**-ere): ad-dict, contra-dict, dict-ate, dict-at-ion, dict-at-or, dict-ion-ary, ditto (Ital. ditto, that which has been said), ditt-y, e-dict, in-dict, in-dite, inter-dict, pre-dict, bene-dict-ion, benison (doublet of preceding), male-dict-ion, malison (doublet of preceding), ver-dict (Lat. vere dictum), juris-dict-ion.

Di-es (*day*); **diurn**-us (*daily*): ad-journ (Late Lat. diurn-are), di-al, di-ary, diurn-al, journ-al, journ-ey (Late Lat. diurn-ata), so-journ (so = Lat. sub), meri-di-an (Lat. medius dies, *r* having been substituted for *d*).

Dign-us (*worthy*); **dign**-ari, **dign-at**-us (*to think worthy*): deign, con-dign, dign-i-ty, dain-ty (doublet of "dignity"), dign-i-fy, dis-dain, in-dignat-ion.

Doc-ere, **doct**-um (*to teach*): doc-ile, doct-or, doct-r-ine, doc-u-ment, in-doct-r-in-ate.

Dol-or (*pain*), **dol**-ere (*to be in pain*): dole-ful (a hybrid word), dol-our, dol-or-ous, condole, in-dol-ence (lit. freedom from pain, hence ease, idle-ness).

Domin-us (*lord*); **domin**-ari, **domin-at**-us (*to act the lord*): dam, dame (O. Fr. dame, Lat. domin-a), dam-sel (O. Fr. dam-ois-ele), danger (O. Fr. dangier, as if from a Late Lat. domin-i-arium, power to harm), domain or demesne, domin-ate, domin-eer, domin-ion, don (Spanish title), donna, duenna, dungeon or donjon (Late Lat. domn-ion-em, a dungeon-tower), pre-domin-ant, mademoiselle (Fr. lit. my girl, miss).

Don-are, **don-at**-um (*to give*): con-done, donat-ion, par-don (Fr. par-donn-er, Lat. per-don-are).

Dos, dot-is (*dowry*): dower (Lat. dot-arium), dowr-y, dow-a-ger (coined from dow-age, endowment), en-dow, en-dow-ment.

Duc-ere, **duct**-um (*to lead*); **duc**-are, **duc-at**-um (*to lead*); **dux, duc**-is (*a leader*): ab-duct-ion, ad-duce, con-duce, con-duct, con-duit (doublet of "conduct"), de-duct, doge (Ital. from duc-is), douche

(Ital. doccia, docc-i-are, Late Lat. duct-i-are), duc-al, ducat, duke, duch-ess, duch-y (Late Lat. ducat-us, a dukedom), duct, duct-ile, e-duce, e-du-cate, in-duct, pro-duce, re-doubt (an intrenched place of retreat, from Lat. re-ductus), sub-due (O. Fr. souduire, Lat. sub-ducere), tra-duce (Lat. trans-ducere).

Du-o (*two*); **dubit**-are, **dubit-at**-um (*to be of two minds*): du-al, deuce, double (Lat. du-plus), doublet, doubt, dozen (O. Fr. dosaine, from doze (twelve), Lat. duo-decim, with suffix -aine), dubious, du-et, du-el, du-plex, in-dubit-able, re-doubt-able.

Dur-us (*hard*); **dur**-are, **dur-at**-um (*to last*): dur-ing, dur-able, dur-ance, dur-at-ion, dur-ess (Lat. dur-it-ia, O. Fr. dur-esce), en-dure, ob-dūr-ate.

Ed-ere, **es**-um (*to eat*), **esc**-a (*food*): ed-ible, esc-ulent, ob-ese (one who has eaten largely).

Em-ere, **empt**-um (*to buy*): ex-empt, per-empt-ory, prem-ium (præ em-ere or im-ere, to take beforehand), prompt (pro empt-us), im-prompt-u, red-eem, red-empt-ion, ransom (doublet of the preceding).

E-o, **i**-re, **it**-um (*to go*); **iter**, **itiner**-is (*journey*): amb-i-ent, amb-it-ion, circu-it, commence (Lat. com = "cum," initiare, to begin), ex-it, eyre (O. Fr. eire, journey, Lat. itiner-is), errant (as in the phrase "knight-errant," a travelling or wandering knight, from O. Fr. err-er, or eir-er, pres. part. err-ant, from Lat. itiner-are, not from Lat. err-are), in-it-i-al, issue (O. Fr. issuë, fem. of issu, p.p. of issir, to go out, Lat. ex-ire), it-in-er-ary, ob-it, per-ish (from Fr. periss-, Lat. per-ire), prætor or pretor (præ itor, one who goes before), preter-ite, sed-it-ion, sudden (O. Fr. sudain, Late Lat. sub-it-an-us), trans-it, trance, trans-i-ent, trans-it-ory.

Exempl-um (*example*): en-sample, example, exempl-ary, sample, sampler.

Extra (*outside*): extr-an-eous (Lat. extr-an-eus), estrange (Fr. estranger, from Lat. extr-an-eus), strange (short for estrange), strang-er, extra (as "an extra," "extras"), exterior, extreme, extrinsic, external.

Fabric-are, **fabric**-atum (*to fashion*); **fabric**-a (n.): fabric, forge (O. Fr. forge), fabric-ate, fabric-at-ion.

Fac-ere, **fact**-um (*to make*): af-fect, bene-fit, bene-fact-or, com-fit, counter-feit, de-feat (O. Fr. de-fait, p.p. of de-faire), de-fect, deficit (it fails or falls short), ef-fect, ef-fic-ac-y, fac-simile (short for "factum simile," made like), fact-ion, fact-it-i-ous, fac-totum (Lat. fac-ere totum), fashion (doublet of "faction"), feas-ible (from O. Fr. fais-ant, pres. part. of faire), fet-ish or fet-ich (Fr. fét-iche, from Lat. factiti-us), feat (O. Fr. fait, doublet of "fact"), feat-ure, honori-fic, in-fect, magni-fy, per-fect, pre-fect, pro-fici-ent, pro-fit, re-fect-ory, suf-fice, sur-feit, terri-fy, stupe-fy.

Faci-es (*face*): face, faci-al, de-face, ef-face, faç-ade (face of a building), super-ficies, sur-face.

Fac-il-is (*easy*): dif-ficul-ty, facile, facul-ty, facil-i-tate.

Fall-ere, **fals**-um (*to deceive, disappoint*): fail, fall-acy, false, falter (O. Fr. falt-er), fall-ible, fault (Ital. falt-a, a defect), de-fault-er.

Falx, **falc**-is (*a sickle*): falch-ion (a bent sword), de-falc-ate, falc-on (so named from its hooked beak).

F-ari, **fat**-um (*to speak*): af-fable (Lat. ad fabilis), fable (Lat. fabula), fay (O. Fr. fae, Late Lat. fata, a goddess of destiny), fairy (O. Fr. faerie, enchantment), in-ef-fable, in-fant (Lat. in- (not), fant-em, speaking), in-fant-ry ("in-fant" once signified servant, and foot-soldiers were at first the servants of knights), ne-far-i-ous, pre-face (Late Lat. præ-fat-ium).

Fer-re, **lat**-um (*to bring* or *carry*): circum-fer-ence, con-fer, de-fer, de-fer-ence, dif-fer, dif-fer-ence, in-fer, of-fer, pre-fer, re-fer, suf-fer, trans-fer, fer-tile; di-late, de-lay (O. Fr. delai, Ital. dilata, that which is put off or deferred), di-lat-at-ion, pre-late, pre-lacy, re-late, trans-late, il-lat-ive, super-lat-ive, cor-re-lat-ive.

Ferr-um (*iron*): farr-ier, ferr-ous, ferr-ug-in-ous (Lat. ferr-ug-in-em, iron rust).

Fid-es (*faith*); **fidel**-is (*faithful*); **fid**-ere (*to trust*): af-fy, af-fi-ance, af-fidavit (he has pledged, from Late Lat. fid-are), con-fide, de-fy, de-fi-ance, dif-fid-ent, faith (O. Fr. feid, Mid. Eng. feith), fidel-i-ty, feal-ty, in-fidel, per-fid-i-ous, per-fid-y.

Fil-um (*thread*): de-file (to march in a file), en-fil-ade, file (of soldiers, as in the phrase "rank and file"), fil-a-ment, fil-i-gree (Lat. gran-um), fill-et (dim. of O. Fr. fil, a thread or string), pro-file.

Fing-ere, **fict**-um (*to fashion*): ef-fig-y, faint, feint, feign, fict-ion, fig-ment, fig-ure, con-fig-ur-at-ion, trans-figure.

Fin-is (*end*): af-fin-i-ty, con-fine, de-fine, fin-ance (Late Lat. fin-antia, settlement by paying), fine (Lat. fin-it-us, well finished off), fin-ic-al, fine (a tax, Law Lat. fin-is), fin-ish, fin-ite, re-fine, super-fine. The phrase "in fine" means "lastly, in short, to sum up."

Firm-us (*strong*); **firm**-are, **firm-at**-um (v.): firm, af-firm, af-firm-at-ive, con-firm-at-ion, farm (Late Lat. firm-a, O. Fr. ferme, a fixed rent, hence an establishment that pays rent), firm-a-ment, in-firm-i-ty.

Flagr-are, **flagr-at**-um (*to burn*); **flam**-ma for **flag**-ma (*a flame*): flagr-ant, flame, con-flagr-at-ion, flam-beau, flam-ingo, in-flamm-able.

Fl-are, **flat**-um (*to blow*): in-flate, flat-u-lent, flute (O. Fr. flaute, fleute), flout, flue (short of "flute").

Flos, **flor**-is (*a flower*); **flor**-ere (v., *to flourish*): flower, flour, flor-al, ef-flor-esce, flor-id, flos-cule, flour-ish.

Flu-ere, **flux**-um (*to flow* or *swell*); **fluct**-us (*a wave*): af-flu-ence, con-flu-ent, fluct-u-ate, flu-id, flux, floss (doublet of "flux"), flush (another doublet), in-flu-ence, in-flu-enza (doublet of "influence"), in-flux, super-flu-ous.

Foli-um (*leaf*): foli-age, ex-foli-ate, foil, foli-o, tre-foil, port-foli o.

Fort-is (*strong*): force, fort, forte, com-fort, ef-fort, fort-i-tude, fort-i-fy, fort-alice (Late Lat. fort-alitia), fortress (O. Fr. forteresce, fortelesce, doublet of "fortalice"), en-force, re-in-force.

Frang-ere (for **frag**-ere), **fract**-um (*to break*): de-fray (O. Fr. de-fray-er, to pay expenses), fract-ion, fract-ure, frag-ment, frag-ile, frail (doublet of "fragile"), in-fract-ion, in-fringe, ir-re-frag-able, re-fract-ory, re-frain (the burden of a song, O. Fr. re-freindre, to break back).

Frat-er, **fratr**-is (*brother*): frat-ern-al, friar (O. Fr. freire, a brother), frat-ern-ise, fratr-i-cide.

Frons, **front**-is (*front*, *brow*): af-front, con-front, ef-front-ery, front-al, front-ier, front-is-piece (a misspelling of "frontispice," Late Lat. front-i-spicium, a front aspect), front-let.

Fru-i, **fruct**-us and **fruit**-us (*to enjoy*); **frux, frug**-is (*produce*): fruit, fruct-i-fy, fru-it-ion, fruit-er-er, fruit-age, frug-al, frug-al-i-ty.

Fug-ere, **fugit**-um (*to flee*): fugit-ive, fugue, re-fuge, re-fug-ee, centri-fug-al, febri-fuge, subter-fuge.

Fund-ere, **fus**-um (*to pour out, to melt*): found (to cast metal), found-ry, fuse, fus-il, fus-ible, con-found, con-fuse, dif-fuse, ef-fuse, fois-on (O. Fr. fois-on, Lat. fus-ion-em), fu-tile (that which is easily poured forth, for Lat. fud-tilis), in-fuse, pro-fuse, re-fund, re-fuse, suf-fus-ion, trans-fuse.

Fund-us (*bottom*); **fund**-are, **fund-at**-um (*to found, to establish*): fund, found, found-er (to go to the bottom), found-at-ion, fund-a-ment-al, pro-found.

Gaud-ere, **gavis**-um (*to enjoy*); **gaud**-ium (*gladness*): gaud (show, ornament), gaud-y, joy (O. Fr. goye, joye), en-joy, jewel (O. Fr. joy-el, dim. of "joye"; no connection with "jocale," as has been asserted), re-joice.

Gel-u (*frost*); **gel**-are, **gel-at**-um (*to freeze*): gel-id, con-geal, gelat-ine, jelly (formerly "gelly," Fr. gelée, Lat. gelat-um).

Gens, gent-is (*clan, stock*): gent-ile, gent-eel, gent-le, gent-ry.

Gen-us, **gener**-is (*kind*, allied to **gens**, as above): con-gen-ial, con-gen-it-al, de-gener-ate, gen-d-er (the *d* is excrescent), en-gend-er, en-gine (Lat. in-gen-ium), gin (short form of preceding), gener-al, gener-ate, gener-ic, gener-ous, gen-i-al, gen-ius (Lat. word, inborn faculty), gen-u-ine, indi-gen-ous, in-gen-i-ous, in-gen-u-ous, pro-gen-it-or, pro-gen-y, re-gener-ate.

Ger-ere, **gest**-um (*to carry on*): jest (O. Fr. geste), con-ger-i-es, con-gest-ion, di-gest, ex-ag-ger-ate, gest-at-ion, gest-ic-ul-ate, gest-ure, re-gist-er, sug-gest-ion.

Gradu-s (*a step* or *degree*); **grad**-i, **gress**-us (v.): grade, ag-gress-ion, con-gress, de-grade, di-gress, e-gress, gradi-ent, gradu-al, gradu-ate, in-gredi-ent, in-gress, pro-gress, retro-grade, retro-gress-ion, trans-gress-or.

Grand-is (*grand, great*): ag-grand-ise, gaffer (for grand-father), gammer (for grand-mother), gramercy (in Chaucer, graund mercy, Fr. grand merci), gram-pus (Lat. grandis piscis), grand-ee, grand-eur, grandi-loquent.

Gran-um (*a grain, corn*): grain, en- or in-grain, gran-ary, garner (doublet of "granary"), garn-et (Late Lat. gran-at-us), grange (Late Lat. gran-ea, a barn), granite (Ital. granito, lit. speckled stone), gran-ule, gren-ade (Ital. gran-ad-o, Lat. gran-at-um, full of seeds), gren-ad-ier, pome-gran-ate (O. Fr. pome grenate), gran-ul-ar, gran-ul-at-ion, fili-gree (Lat. filum + granum).

Grat-us (*pleasing*); **grat**-ia (*grace, thanks*): grace, a-gree (Fr. à gré, to one's pleasure), con-grat-ul-ate, grate-ful, grat-i-fy, grat-is, grat-i-tude, grat-u-it-ous, grat-u-ity, in-grat-i-ate, in-grate, maugre (malgré).

Grav-is (*heavy*); **grav**-ari, **grav-at**-um (v.): grave, ag-grav-ate, grief, ag-grieve, gravit-ate, gravit-at-ion.

Grex, greg-is (*flock*); **greg**-ari, **greg-at**-um (v.): ag-greg-ate, con-greg-ate, e-greg-i-ous, se-greg-ate, greg-arious.

Gurg-es (*whirlpool*) ; Late Lat. **gorg**-ia (*throat*): gorge, garg-le, garg-oyle, gorg-e-ous (the throat swelling with pride), gorg-et, gurg-le (Ital. gorgoglia).

Hab-ere, **habit**-um (*to have*) ; **habit**-are, **habit-at**-um (freq. of hab-ere) : able (O. Fr. habile, abile, able), aver-age (Late Lat. averagium, O. Fr. aver, property in cattle, horses, etc.), co-habit, de-bil-i-ty (de hibilis or habilis, not able, not up to the mark), des-habille (un-dress), ex-hibit, habil-i-ment, habit-u-al, habit-able, habitat (it dwells there), in-habit, in-hibit, prebend (Lat. præ habenda), pre-bend-ary, pro-hibit, provender (Late Lat. præbenda, food allowance).

Hær-ere, **hæsit**-um (*to stick*) ; **hæsit**-are, **hæsit-at**-um (freq. of preceding) : ad-here, ad-her-ent, ad-hes-ive, co-here, hesit-ate, in-her-ent.

Hær-es, **hæred**-is (*one who inherits*) : heir, hered-it-ary, her-it-age, in-herit, heir-loom (a hybrid, A.S. lóma, a tool).

Hom-o, **homin**-is (*man*) ; **human**-us (adj. of homo) : hom-age (Late Lat. hom-aticum, the service of a man or vassal), hom-i-cide, hum-an, hum-ane.

Hosp-es, **hospit**-is (*host* or *guest*) : host (hospit-em), hospice (hospiti-um), hospit-able, hospit-al, hostel, hostler or ostler, hotel, spittle.

Hum-us (*ground*) ; **humil**-is (*lowly*) : ex-hume, hum-b-le (the *b* is intrusive), humil-i-ty, humil-i-ate. N.B.—"Post-humous" is not from "humus," but is a misspelling of Lat. *postumus* or *postimus*, the last.

Imbecill-us (*weak*) : imbecile, embezzle (obs. Fr. verb *imbécill*, to diminish, subtract from).

Insul-a (*island*) : isle, insul-ar, insul-ate, isol-ate. No connection with "island" (see p. 371).

Jac-ēre (*to lie down*) : ad-jac-ent, gist (O. Fr. gist, Lat. jacet, "it lies," the point wherein the matter lies), joist (a timber on which the boards of a room lie).

Jac-ĕre, **jact**-um (*to throw*) ; **jact**-are, **jact-at**-um (freq. of jac-ere) : jet (O. Fr. jett-er, Lat. jact-are), ab-ject, ad-ject-ive, amice (O. Fr. amicte, Lat. amictus, from am- (for ambi-)+jactus, "a garment thrown round one"), con-ject-ure, de-ject-ion, e-jacul-ate (Lat. jac-ul-um, a dart), e-ject, in-ject, jet-sam (jact-at-ion-em), jetty (O. Fr. jettée), jut (doublet of "jet"), ob-ject, pro-ject, sub-ject, pro-ject-ile, tra-ject-ory.

Joc-us (*a jest*) : joke, jeopardy (O. Fr. jeu parti, a divided game), joc-ose, joc-ul-ar, juggler (Lat. joc-ul-at-or, a jester).

Ju-dex, ju-dic-is (*judge*) ; **judic**-are, **judic-at**-um (v.) : ad-judge, ad-judic-ate, judic-at-ure, judic-i-al, judic-i-ous, pre-judge, pre-judice.

Jug-um (*a yoke, a joining*) : con-jug-al, con-jug-at-ion, jug-ul-ar (from Lat. jug-ul-um, collar-bone, which joins the neck and shoulder), sub-jug-ate.

Jung-ere, **junct**-um (*to join*) : join (O. Fr. joindre), joint, ad-join, en-join, in-junct-ion, junct-ion, junct-ure, joint-ure (doublet of preceding), junt-o (Sp. junto), junt-a (Sp. junta, fem. of junto), re-join, sub-join, sub-junct-ive.

Jus, jur-is (*law*) ; **jur**-are, **jur-at**-um (*to take an oath*) ; ab-jure, ad-jure, ad-just (Lat. just-us), con-jure, in-jure, juri-dic-al, juris-dict-ion, jur-ist, jur-or, jur-y (Fr. jurée, Lat. jur-at-a, a body of sworn men), just (Lat. just-us), just-ice, just-i-fy, per-jure.

Juv-are, **jut**-um (*to help*) : ad-jut-ant, co-ad-jut-or, aid (O. Fr. aid-er, Late Lat. ad-jut-are, freq. of ad-juv-are).

Juven-is (*young*) : juven-ile, jun-ior (short for juven-ior), juni-per (lit. youth-producing), gin (short for geneva, a corruption of Fr. genevre, a juniper tree).

Lac, lact-is (*milk*) : lacteal, lettuce (from Lat. lact-uca, the milky herb).

Lacert-us (*an arm*) : lizard (Fr. lesard, Lat. lacerta), al-ligator (Sp. el-lagarto, *the* lizard, *i.e.* the great lizard).

Lac-us (*a pool*) : lake, lac-ustrine, lag-oon (Lat. lac-una).

Læd-ere, **læs**-um (*to do harm to*) : col-lide, col-lis-ion, e-lide, les-ion.

Lamb-ere (*to lick*) ; lamb-ent, lamp-rey (a fish so called from Late Lat. lam-petra, licker of rocks).

Laus, laud-is (*praise*) ; **laud**-are, **laud-at**-um (v.) : laudable, laud-at-ory, allow (to admit or approve of, Fr. al-lou-er, Lat. ad laud-are. Ye *allow* the deeds of your fathers.—Luke xi. 48).

Lav-are, **lav-at**-um or **laut**-um (*to wash*) : lave, lav-at-ory, laundr-ess (lavender-ess), laundry (Late Lat. lavanderia), lava (molten rock), lavender, lot-ion.

Leg-are, **leg-at**-um (*to depute*) : al-lege, al-leg-at-ion, col-league, col-lege, de-leg-ate, leg-acy, leg-ate, leg-at-ee, re-leg-ate.

Leg-ere, **lect**-um (*to read, to gather*) : coil (O. Fr. coill-er, Lat. col-lig-ere, to gather together), cull (doublet of preceding), col-lect, di-lig-ent, e-lect, e-lite (Fr.), e-leg-ant, e-lig-ible, intel-lect, intel-lig-ence, lect-ion, lesson (doublet of "lection"), lect-ure, leg-end, leg-end-ary, leg-ible, leg-ion, leg-ume (a pod), neg-lect (the *g* is intrusive), neg-lig-ence, pre-di-lect-ion, re-col-lect, se-lect, re-lig-ion (referred by some to **Lig**-are, *q.v.*).

Lev-is (*light*) ; **lev-are, lev-at-um** (*to make light*) : al-lev-i-ate, e-lev-ate, leaven (Lat. levamen, that which raises the flour), leger-de-main (O. Fr. legier (from Late Lat. lev-i-arius) de main, light of hand), Levant (Ital. levante, the east, where the sun rises), levée, lev-er (Lat. lev-at-or, the lifter), lev-ity, lev-y, re-lev-ant, re-lieve.

Lex, leg-is (*law*) : leg-al, loy-al (doublet of "legal"), leal (a second doublet of "legal"), legis-lator, leg-ist, leg-it-im-ate, al-leg-i-ance, privi-lege (private right).

Liber (*free*) ; **liber**-are, **liber-at**-um (*to make free*) : de-liver (O. Fr. de-livre, Lat. de-liber-are), liber-ate, liber-tine, liber-ty, liv-ery.

Lib-er, libr-i (*a book*) : libr-ary, lib-el, libr-etto.

Libr-a (*a pound, a balance*) : de-liber-ate (to weigh in the balance), livre (Fr.), level (O. Fr. livel, Lat. lib-ella, dim. of "libra"), equi-libr-ium.

Lic-et (*it is lawful*), **licit**-um : lic-ence, il-licit, leis-ure (O. Fr. leis-ir, to be allowed ; the suffix *-ure* is from the Fr. infin. ending *-ir*), lic-ent-i-ate, lic-ent-i-ous.

Lig-are, **lig-at**-um (*to bind*) : al-lig-at-ion, al-ly (O. Fr. a-li-er, Lat. ad-lig-are), al-li-ance, league, li-able (formed with suffix -able from

Fr. li-er), lien (Fr. lien, Lat. lig-amen, a thing that binds), lig-a-ment, lig-at-ture, ob-lige, ob-lig-at-ion, rally (re + allier, to re-ally, or re-assemble), re-lig-ion (doubtful, see **Leg**-ere).

Lim-es, **lim-it**-is (*a boundary*); **lim**-en, **limin**-is (*a threshold*): lim-it, de-lim-it-at-ion, lint-el (Late Lat. lintell-us, for lim-it-ellus, dim. of limit-is), e-limin-ate, pre-limin-ary.

Linqu-ere, **lict**-um (*to leave*): de-linqu-ent, de-re-lict, re-lic (Lat. re-liqu-i-æ), re-lict, re-linqu-ish, re-liqu-ary.

Lin-um (*flax*); **lin**-e-a (*a string*): line, de-lin-e-ate, lin-e-age, lin-e-al, lin-e-a-ment, lin-e-ar, lin-en (orig. an adj., "made of flax"; cf. flax-en), lin-ing, linn-et (the bird that feeds on flax seed), lin-seed, lint (Lat. lint-e-um).

Liqu-ere (to melt): liqu-id, lique-fy, liqu-id-ate, liqu-or. N.B.—"Liquorice" has no connection with "liquor"; see Liquorice under Greek Roots, V.

Lit-er-a (*letter*): letter (Fr. lettre, Lat. lit-era), lit-er-al, lit-er-at-ure, il-lit-er-ate, ob-lit-er-ate.

Loc-us (*a place*); **loc**-are, **loc-at**-um (v.): al-loc-ate, al-low (Fr. al-lou-er, to assign, grant), col-loc-ate, couch (O. Fr. couch-er, Lat. col-loc-are), dis-loc-ate, lieu (Fr. lieu), lieu-ten-ant (Lat. locum tenens), loc-al, loc-ate, loc-o-motion.

Locust-a (*a locust*): locust, lobster (A.S. loppestre, lopust, corr. of Lat. locusta).

Loqu-i, **loc-ut**-us (*to speak*): loqu-ac-ious, al-loc-ut-ion, circum-loc-ut-ion, col-loqu-y, e-loc-ut-ion, e-loqu-ent, ob-loqu-y, soli-loqu-y, ventri-loqu-ist.

Luc-is (gen. of **lux**, *light*); **luc**-ere (*to shine*): luc-id, e-luc-id-ate, luc-u-brat-ion (worked out by lamp-light, from Lat. luc-u-brum, a light), pel-luc-id, trans-luc-ent.

Lud-ere, **lus**-um (*to play*): al-lude, al-lus-ion, col-lude, col-lus-ion, de-lude, e-lude, lud-i-crous, pre-lude.

Lu-men, lumin is (*light*, formed from **luc**-men; see **Luc**-is above): il-lumin-ate, limn (shortened form of "lumin-en," Mid. Eng. limn-en), lumin-ary, lumin-ous.

Lun-a (*moon*, from **luc**-na, light-giver): lun-ar, lun-at-ic, lun-a-cy, sub-lun-ary.

Lustr-are, **lustr-at**-um (*to throw light*, from the root **luc**; see above): lustre, il-lustr-ate, lustr-ous, lutestring (corr. of lustr-ing, a sort of shining silk).

Mag-n-us (*great*); **mag**-is-ter (a great man, a master): mag-is-trate, magn-animity, magn-ate, magn-i-fic-ent, magn-i-fy, magn-i-loqu-ence, main (O. Fr. magne, maine), maj-esty, maj-or, mayor (doublet of major), master (O. Fr. maistre, Lat. magister), max-im (from superl. max-im-us), max-im-um, miss (contraction of "mis-tress"), mister, mistress.

Mal-us (*bad*): mal-ady (Lat. mal-, and habitus, condition), mal-apert (Lat. male, badly, and apert-us, open), mal-aria (Ital. aria, air), male-diction, malison (doublet of the preceding), mal-ign, mal-inger (Lat. æger, sick), mal-treat, mal-vers-at-ion, maugre (O. Fr. mal-gré).

Mand-are, **mand-at**-um (*to give an order*): com-mand, com-mend, com-modore (Sp. from Lat. com-mend-at-or), counter-mand, de-mand, mandate, re-com-mend, re-mand, Maundy Thursday (Mid. Eng.

mandee, from Lat. mandatum novum, "a new command," John xiii. 34).

Man-ere, **mans**-um (*to abide, remain*): man-or (O. Fr. man-oir, a mansion), manse (Late Lat. mans-a, a dwelling), mans-ion, mas-tiff (prob. from Late Lat. mansatinus canis, a house-dog), menagerie (orig. a place for keeping household animals, Fr. ménage, O. Fr. mesnage), menial (one of a household, O. Fr. mesnee, with added suffix), messuage (Late Lat. messuagium), per-man-ent, re-main, remnant (for re-man-ent).

Man-us (*the hand*): a-man-u-ensis, main-tain (Lat. manu tenere), man-acle (Lat. man-icula), man-age (O. Fr. man-ege), mani-fest, mani-ple (Lat. manipulus, a handful), mani-pul-ate, manner (O. Fr. man-iere), manœuvre (Lat. manu opera), manu-al, manu-facture, manu-mission, manure (doublet of "manœuvre"), manu-script.

Mapp-a (*a cloth* or *napkin*): map, apron (formerly napron, O. Fr. naperon, augm. form of O. Fr. nape, a cloth, Late Lat. nap-a, a corruption of Lat. mappa. The initial *n* of "napron" was confounded with *an*, the indef. article. Thus "napron" became "apron," just as "numpire" became "umpire"; see below under **Par**).

Mar-e (*sea*); **mar-in**-us (adj.): mar-ine, mar-in-er, mar-itime, sub-mar-ine, rose-mar-y (Lat. ros mar-is, dew of the sea: not from Lat. *rosa*, a rose).

Mat-er, matr-is (*a mother*): mat-ern-al, matri-cide, matr-ic-ul-ate, matr-i-mony, matr-ix, matr-on.

Med-i-us (*middle*): demi- (from Lat. di, apart, and medius, separated in the middle), im-med-i-ate, mean (in the sense of "middle," O. Fr. meien, Late Lat. medi-an-us), med-i-ate, medi-ev-al, medi-ocre, Medi-terr-an-ean, meri-di-an (corr. of Lat. medi-di-an-us), mezzo-tinto (Ital. half tinted), mizen or mizzen (O. Fr. misaine), moiety (Fr. moitié, Lat. medi-e-tat-em).

Mel, mell-is (*honey*): mar-mal-ade (O. Fr. marmelade, Lat. mĕli-malum, honey apple or quince), melli-flu-ous, mil-dew (a hybrid, Lat. mel, and A.S. deáw, dew), mol-asses (Sp. mel-aza).

Me-min-i (*I remember*, from a base **min**); **memor**-is (*mindful*): memory, com-memor-ate, memoir, memor-and-um, memor-i-al, re-mem-b-er (the *b* is intrusive), re-min-isc-ence, memento (remember thou).

Mens, ment-is (*mind*, akin to the base **min** in "me-*min*-i," as above): com-ment (Lat. com-ment-ari), de-ment-ed, ment-al, ment-ion.

Merg-ere, **mers**-um (*to dip*): e-merge, e-merg-en-cy, im-mers-ion, sub-merge.

Merx, merc-is (*merchandise, traffic*): a-merce (O. Fr. a = Lat. ad, and merc-ier, to pay off), com-merce, mark-et (Lat. merc-at-us), mart (doublet of market, mark't), merc-ant-ile, merc-en-ary, merc-er, merch-ant, merch-and-ise, Merc-ur-y (the god of traffic).

Met-iri, **mens**-um (*to measure*; akin to A.S. *met*-an, to mete): meas-ure (O. Fr. mes-ure, Lat. mens-ura), com-mens-ur-ate, di-mens-ion, im-mense, mens-ur-at-ion.

Mill-e (*a thousand*): mile (a thousand paces, a Roman mile), mill-ion, b-ill-ion, mil-foil (thousand leaf), mill-enn-ium.

Min-æ (*threats*); **min**-ari, **min-at**-us (v.): men-ace (Lat. min-ac-em), a-men-able (easy to lead, Fr. a-men-er, to lead, Late Lat.

min-are, to lead), com-min-at-ion, min-at-ory, de-mean (to conduct, O. Fr. de-mener, to conduct: distinct from de-mean, to lower, to debase), de-mean-our, mien (the general bearing of a man), mine (to excavate, Late Lat. min-are, to follow up a lode), min-er-al, pro-men-ade (from O. Fr. pro-men-er, to walk, with added suffix).

Min-or (*less*) ; **minu**-ere, **min-ut**-um (*to make less*) : ad-min-is-ter, di-min-ish, di-min-ut-ion, min-im (from Lat. superl. min-im-us), min-is-ter, min-strel (Late Lat. min-is-tr-al-is), min-or, min-or-i-ty, min-u-et, min-ute, mystery (a trade or craft, misspelling for "mis-tery," Lat. min-is-ter-i-um. The "mystery plays" were so called because they were acted by craftsmen or trained men).

Mir-ari, **mir-at**-us (*to wonder at*) : ad-mire, mir-a-cle, marvel (Fr. merveil, a wonder, Lat. mir-abile), mir-age, mir-ror (Late Lat. mir-at-or-ium).

Misc-ere, **mixt**-um (*to mingle*) : misc-ell-an-eous (Lat. misc-ell-us, mixed), mixt-ure, pro-misc-u-ous, meddle (O. Fr. medl-er or mesl-er, Late Lat. misc-ul-are, to mix), medley (O. Fr. medl-ee, Fr. mêlée ; spelt by Tennyson as "mellay").

Mitt-ere, **miss**-um (*to send*) : ad-mit, ad-miss-ion, com-miss-ary, com-mit, com-miss-ion, com-pro-mise, de-mise, dis-miss, e-mit, inter-miss-ion, miss-al (a mass-book, "mass" being formed from Lat. miss-a, through A.S. mæsse), mess, mess-age, miss-ion, miss-ile, miss-ive, o-mit, o-miss-ion, per-mit, pre-mise, pre-miss, pro-mise, pro-miss-ory, sub-mit, sur-mise (O. Fr. sur-mise, orig. an accusa-tion), trans-mit.

Mod-us (*measure, manner*) : mode, mood (doublet of "mode"), ac-com-mod-ate, com-mod-i-ous, in-com-mode, mod-el, mod-er-ate, mod-ern, mod-est, mod-i-fy, mod-ul-ate, mould.

Mon-ere, **monit**-um (*to advise*) : ad-mon-ish, mon-u-ment, pre-mon-ish, sum-mon, sum-mons, monster (Lat. monstrum, for mon-es-trum, a warning), mon-et-ary, mon-ey, mint (all three from Mon-eta, the warning one, a surname of Juno, in whose temple at Rome money was coined ; see **Mint**, p. 364).

Mors, **mort**-is (*death*) ; **mor**-i, **mortu**-us (v.) : mort-al, mor-bid (Lat. mor-bus, disease), mort-gage, mort-i-fy, mort-main (dead hand), mortu-ary, murrain (O. Fr. moreine, morine, carcase of a beast).

Mos, **mor**-is (*manners, custom*) : mor-al, mor-al-ist, de-mor-al-ise, de-mure (O. Fr. de murs, of good manners), mor-ose (of surly manners).

Mov-ere, **mot**-um (*to move*) : com-mot-ion, e-mot-ion, mob (Lat. mob-ile vulgus, the fickle crowd), mob-ile, mo-ment (short for Lat. mov-i-mentum), mot-ive, mot-or, mut-iny (O. Fr. meute, a sedition ; cf. Fr. é-meute), pro-mote, re-mote, re-move.

Mun-us, **muner**-is (*a gift, service*) : com-mune (Lat. munis, ready to be of service), com-mon, muni-cipal, im-mune, muni-fic-ence, re-muner-ate.

Mut-are, **mut-at**-um (*to change*) : com-mute, moult (the *l* is intru-sive), mew (orig. a cage for moulting hawks, O. Fr. mue, a moult-ing), mut-ual, per-mut-at-ion, mut-able, im-mut-able.

Nasc-i, **nat**-us (*to be born*) : nat-al, in-nate, co-gnate, nasc-ent, nat-ion, nat-ive, naive (doublet of "native"), nat-ure, pre-gnant, preter-nat-ur-al.

Nav-is (*a ship*); **naut**-a (*a sailor*): nave (a church being likened to a ship), naus-eous, naut-ic-al, naut-ilus, nav-al, nav-ig-able, nav-y, nav-vy (a labourer employed in digging a canal for navigation).

Neg-o, **negat**-um (*to say no*): ab-neg-ate, deny (O. Fr. de-nei-er, Lat. de-neg-are), neg-at-ion, neg-at-ive, re-neg-ate or runagate (Lat. re-neg-atus, one who has denied his faith).

Noc-ere (*to hurt*): in-noc-ent, in-noc-u-ous, nox-i-ous, ob-nox-i-ous, nuisance (Fr.).

Norm-a (*rule*): norm-al, ab-norm-al, e-norm-ous, e-norm-ity.

Nosc-ere (for **gnosc**-ere), **not**-um (*to know*): bi-nom-ial (Lat. nom-en, nomin-is, a name), de-nomin-ate, i-gno-ble, i-gnomin-y, i-gnore (Lat. in + gnor-are), no-ble, no-bili-ty, nomen-clat-ure, nomin-al, not-ice, not-i-fy, not-orious, noun, pro-noun, quaint (O. Fr. coint, Lat. cognit-us, well known), ac-quaint (O. Fr. a-coint-er), re-nown.

Not-are, **not-at**-um (*to mark*); **not**-a (n.): note, an-not-ate, de-note, con-note, not-able, not-ary.

Nov-us (*new*); **nov**-are, **nov-at**-um (*to make new*): in-nov-ate, novel, nov-it-i-ate, novice (doublet of the preceding), re-nov-ate, re-new (doublet of re-nov-ate).

Nunti-us (*messenger*); **nunti**-are, **nunti-at**-um (*to bring tidings*): nunci-o (Ital. papal messenger), an-nounce, an-nunci-at-ion, e-nunci-at-ion, pro-nounce, re-nounce.

Nutri-re, **nutrit**-um (*to nourish*): nutri-ment, nurse, nour-ish, nurt-ure (Lat. nutrit-ura), nutrit-i-ous, nutrit-ive.

Odi-um (*hatred*): an-noy (Lat. in odio), an-noy-ance, en-nui (Fr.), noi-some (for an-noi-some), odi-ous.

Od-or (*smell*); **ol**-ere (for **od**-ere, *to smell*): od-our, ol-fact-ory, red-ol-ent.

Ol-esc-ere, **ult**-us (*to grow*): ad-ol-esc-ent, ad-ult, co-al-esce, co-al-it-ion.

Op-us, **oper**-is (*work*); **oper**-ari, **oper-at**-um (v.): co-oper-ate, in-ure (O. Fr. eure, uevre, Lat. in opera), manœuvre (Lat. manus, the hand), man-ure (doublet of preceding), oper-a, oper-ate.

Orb-is (*circle*): orb, orb-it, ex-orb-it-ant.

Ord-o, **ordin**-is (*order, rank*): ord-er, dis-ord-er, ord-er-ly, co-ordin-ate, extra-ordin-ary, in-ordin-ate, ord-ain, ordin-al, ordin-ance, ord-nance (doublet of preceding), ordin-at-ion, prim-ord-i-al, sub-ordin-ate.

Os, **or**-is (*the mouth*); **or**-are, **or-at**-um (*to speak*): ad-ore, in-ex-or-able, or-a-cle, or-at-ion, orison (doublet of preceding), or-at-or, ori-fice, or-al, os-cul-ate, per-or-at-ion.

Os, **oss**-is (*a bone*): oss-e-ous, os-prey (Lat. ossi-frag-us, lit. a bone-breaker), ossi-frage (Lev. xi. 13; doublet of the preceding), ossi-fy.

Ost-i-um (*door*): usher (Lat. ost-i-arius, doorkeeper).

Pag-us (*a village*): pagan, paynim (contr. of pagan-ism), peas-ant (O. Fr. pais-an, Lat. pag-ensis; the *t* is excrescent).

Pal-us, **pal**-i (*a stake*): pale, pal-ette, pal-is-ade, pall-et, pole.

Pand-ere, **pass**-um (*to open*): com-pass, ex-pand, pace (Lat. pass-us), pass, passage, pass-port (Lat. port-a, a gate), pas-time, sur-pass, tres-pass (Lat. trans, beyond).

Pang-ere, **pact**-um (*to fasten*): com-pact (adj.), impact, im-pinge, page (Lat. pag-ina, "pag-" being the earlier form of "pang-"), pag-e-ant.

Pan-is (*bread*): ap-pan-age, com-pan-ion, pann-ier, pantry (Late Lat. pan-et-aria).

Pann-us (*a piece of cloth*): pane (patch of cloth or of glass), counter-pane, pann-el, pan-icle, pawn.

Par, **par**-is (*equal*): pair, par, par-i-ty, dis-par-i-ty, ap-par-el, com-peer, dis-par-age, um-pire (O. Fr. nom-pair, Lat. non-par, the odd man who decides between two others. "Num-pire" became "um-pire" just as "napron" became "apron," under the mistaken notion that *n* belonged to the article *an*).

Par-are, **par-at**-um (*to shave off, to get ready*): pare, ap-par-at-us, com-pare, com-par-i-son, em-per-or (Lat. im-per-at-or), em-pire, im-per-at-ive, im-per-i-al, par-ade (Fr.), parry (Fr. par-er, to guard), para-pet (Ital. pett-o, the breast, "that which guards the breast"), para-sol ("that which keeps off the sun"), prepare, rampart (O. Fr. rem-part, from re + im (= in) + parat-us), re-pair, se-par-ate, sever (O. Fr. sevr-er), sev-er-al, ap-par-at-us.

Par-ĕre, **part**-um (*to bring forth*): par-ent, part-ur-i-ent, part-ur-it-ion, re-pert-ory, ovi-par-ous, vivi-par-ous, viper (contr. of preceding), puer-per-al.

Pars, **part**-is (*a portion*): part, parse (to say to what part of speech a word belongs), a-part (Fr. à part, Lat. ad partem), a-part-ment, com-part-ment, de-part, im-part, parcel (contr. from Lat. part-ic-ella), par-take, part-i-al, part-i-cip-ate, part-ic-le, partisan (Late Lat. part-it-i-anus), part-it-ion, part-ner (Late Lat. part-it-ion-arius), part-y (Lat. part-it-a), re-part-ee.

Pasc-ere, **past**-um (*to feed*): pabulum, past-or, past-el (Lat. past-illum, a little loaf), past-ille, past-ern, past-ure, pest-er (O. Fr. em-pestr-er, to hobble a horse at pasture), re-past.

Pat-ere (*to lie open*): pat-ent, pat-en (Lat. pat-ena, pat-ina), pan (contr. of preceding), pail (Lat. pat-ella, dim. of Lat. pat-ina).

Pat-i, **pass**-us (*to suffer*): com-pass-ion, com-pat-ible, pass-ion, pass-ive, pati-ent.

Pauper (Fr. **pauvre**, *poor*): pauper, poor, poverty, im-pover-ish-ment.

Pax, **pac**-is (*peace*); **pac-isc**-i, **pact**-us (*to make an agreement*): pact, com-pact (n.), ap-pease (O. Fr. a-pais, Lat. ad pacem), pac-i-fy, peace, pay (Lat. pac-are, to discharge a debt), re-pay.

Pell-ere, **puls**-um (*to drive*): com-pel, com-puls-ion, im-pel, im-pulse, pelt (Lat. pult-are for puls-are), pro-pel, pulse, puls-at-ion, push (O. Fr. pouss-er, Lat. puls-are), purs-y (short-winded, O. Fr. pouss-er or pouls-er, to gasp for breath), re-pel, re-puls-ive.

Pend-ĕre (*to hang*); **pend**-ĕre (*to weigh*), **pens**-um: pend-ant, ap-pend, ap-pend-ix, com-pend-i-ous, com-pens-ate, counter-poise (O. Fr. pois-er, to weigh, Lat. pens-are), de-pend, dis-pense, im-pend, pans-y (Fr. pensée, thought, the pansy being considered the flower of thought), pend-ul-um, pens-ion, pens-ive (thoughtful), pent-house (O. Fr. apentis, Lat. ap-pend-ic-i-um), per-pend-ic-ul-ar, pre-pense, pro-pens-ity, re-com-pense, spend (Lat. dis-pend-ere), sus-pend.

Penn-a (*a feather*): pen, penn-ant, penn-on, pin, pin-ion, pinn-acle.

Per-iri, **per-it**-us (*to try*): ex-peri-ence, ex-pert, per-il (Lat. per-ic-ulum), peril-ous, par-lous (doublet of preceding).

Pes, ped-is (*foot*): bi-ped, ex-ped-ite, despatch (O. Fr. despecher, lit. "to unfetter," Late Lat. dis-pedic-are, from Lat. ped-ica, a fetter), im-peach (Late Lat. im-pedic-are), im-pede, im-pedi-ment, pawn (O. Fr. paon, Late Lat. pedon-em, a foot-soldier), ped-e-stal (A.S. stæl; "pedestal" is therefore a hybrid), ped-estr-ian, pion-eer (O. Fr. peon or paon, a foot-soldier), quadru-ped, centi-pede.

Pet-ere, **pet-it**-um (*to seek*): ap-pet-ite, com-pet-ent, com-pet-it-or, im-pet-us, pet-ul-ant, re-peat, re-pet-it-ion.

Pil-us (*a hair*): cater-pillar (Lat. cat-us, cat, and pilosus, "hairy cat"; O. Fr. chate-peleuse; Mid. Eng. catyrpel), de-pil-at-ory, perruque (Fr.), periwig (doublet of the preceding), plush (Fr. pil-uche, Late Lat. pil-ucius), wig (short for periwig).

Ping-ere, **pict**-um (*to paint*): pict-ure, depict, paint, pig-ment pi-ment-o (Port.), pint (Fr. pinte, Sp. pinta, a spot or mark).

Pi-us (*devout, holy*): pi-ous, im-pi-ous, ex-pi-ate, pi-ac-ular, pi-ety, pity (a doublet of the preceding).

Plac-ere, **placit**-um (*to please*): com-plac-ent, com-plais-ant (doublet of preceding), plac-id, plea, plead (Lat. placit-um), pleasure (Fr. plais-ir, infin. of the Fr. verb).

Plang-ere, **planct**-um (*to beat the breast in token of grief*); **plag**-a (*a blow*): com-plain, plague, plaint, plaint-ive, plaint-iff (doublet of preceding).

Plan-us (*level*): plain, plane, plan, es-plan-ade (from O. Fr., Lat. ex-plan-at-a), explain, piano-forte (Ital. piano, soft, Lat. planus).

Plaud-ere, **plaus**-um (*to clap the hands*): ap-plaud, ex-plode, plaud-it (from Lat. plaudite, clap your hands), plausible.

Plect-ere, **plex**-um (*to plait*): com-plex-ion, com-plex, per-plex, sim-ple, du-plex, du-plic-i-ty.

Pl-ere, **pl-et**-um (*to fill*); **plen**-us (*full*): ac-com-pl-ish, com-ple-ment, com-plete, com-pli-ment (Ital. complire, to fill up), com-ply, com-pli-ant (Ital. com-plire), de-plet-ion, ex-plet-ive, im-ple-ment, plen-i-tude, plen-ty (for plen-i-ty, Lat. plen-i-tat-em), re-plen-ish, re-plete, sup-ple-ment, sup-ply.

Plic-o, **plic-at**-um or **plic-it**-um (*to fold* or *bend*): ply, ac-com-plice, ap-ply, com-plic-ate, com-plic-i-ty, de-ploy (Fr. dé-ploy-er), dis-play (Lat. dis-plic-are, to unfold), em-ploy, ex-plic-ate, ex-plicit, ex-ploit, im-plic-ate, im-ply, plait, pleat (doublet of preceding, Lat. plic-at-um), pli-ant, plight (Lat. plic-it-a), plot (short for "com-plot," Lat. com-plicit-um), re-ply, sup-ple, sup-pli-cant, sup-pli-ant, sup-pli-cate.

Pœn-a (*punishment*); **pun**-ire, **pun-it**-um (v.): pain, im-pun-i-ty, pen-al, pen-ance, pen-it-ence, pun-ish, punch (doublet of the preceding), re-pent.

Pon-ere, **posit**-um (*to place*): post, ap-posite, com-pon-ent, com-post, com-pound (the *d* is excrescent), de-pon-ent, de-posit, de-posit-ion, de-pôt, dis-posit-ion, ex-pon-ent, ex-pound (with excrescent *d*), im-post, inter-posit-ion, op-posite, posit-ive, post-illion (Ital. postig-lione), post-ure, pre-posit-ion, pro-pound, pro-vost (Lat. præ-posit-us), pur-pose (Lat. pro-posit-um), re-posit-ory, sup-posit-ion.

Porc-us (*a pig*): pork, porcu-pine (Lat. spina, a thorn; O. Fr. porc espin), porpoise (O. Fr. por-peis, Lat. porcus piscis, a pig-fish), porcelain (Fr. porcelaine or pourcelaine, Ital. porcellana, the Venus-shell, so named from the curved back, resembling a pig's back, of its upper surface. The same name was applied to earthenware, because its polished surface resembled the surface of the Venus-shell).

Port-a (*a gate*): port, port-al, port-cullis (porte coulisse, lit. a "sliding door"), Porte (the Sublime Porte, "the high gate," the Turkish Government), port-er (Lat. port-arius, gate-keeper).

Port-are, **port-at-um** (*to carry*): port (demeanour), de-port, dis-port, ex-port, im-port, in-sup-port-able, port-er (Lat. port-at-or, carrier), pur-port, re-port, sport (short for "dis-port"), trans-port-at-ion.

Posse (*to be able*); **pot-ens** (*able*): poss-ible, potent, posse (used as noun, meaning power), power (M.E. pöer, the *w* is intrusive; O. Fr. po-er, to be able), puissant (Fr. puis-sant, mighty; from Lat. possent-em, though no such participle is found).

Prehend-ere, **prehens**-um (*to take hold of*): prehens-ile, ap-prehend, ap-prent-ice (Late Lat. ap-prent-ic-i-us), prentice (short form of preceding), ap-prise (O. Fr.), com-prehend, com-prise, enter-prise, im-pregn-able (the *g* is intrusive, O. Fr. im-pren-able, "untakeable"), prise (a lever), pris-on (Lat. prens-ion-em), prize (Fr. prise, a thing captured, a seizure), re-prehend, re-pris-al, sur-prise.

Prem-ere, **press**-um (*to press* or *squeeze*): com-press, de-press, ex-press, im-print (O. Fr. em-preinte), print, re-print, re-prim-and (Fr. re-prim-ande, a thing that ought to be repressed), sprain (O. Fr. es-preindre, Lat. ex-prim-ere).

Pret-i-um (*price, value*): ap-preci-ate, de-preci-ate, praise, ap-praise, dis-praise, preci-ous, price, prize (O. Fr. pris, a price or value).

Prim-us (*first*): prim, prime, prim-ary, prim-ate, prem-ier (doublet of "primary"), prim-eval, prim-it-ive, primo-genit-ure, prim-rose (not from "rose," but a corruption of Mid. Eng. primerole), prince (Lat. prin-ceps, "taking the first place," primus capere), prin-ciple, prior.

Prob-are, **prob-at**-um (*to probe* or *test*): probe, proof, prob-able, ap-prob-at-ion, ap-prove, im-prove, re-prieve (Mid. Eng. re-prev-en, to reject), re-prob-ate, re-prove.

Prope, **pro-pi**-or, **proxim**-us (*near, nearer, nearest*): ap-proach (O. Fr. a-prochi-er, Lat. ap-propi-are), ap-proxim-ate, prop-inquity, proxim-i-ty, re-proach (Fr. re-proch-er).

Pung-ere, **punct**-um (*to prick*): pung-ent, punct-ure, ap-point, com-punct-ion, ex-punge, poign-ant, point, pounce, punch (to perforate), punch-eon, punct-ilio, punct-u-al, punct-u-at-ion.

Put-are, **put-at**-um (*to think*): am-put-ate, com-pute, count (doublet of the preceding), ac-count, dis-count, dis-pute, re-pute, re-put-at-ion.

Quær-ere, **quæsit**-um (*to seek*): ac-quire, con-quer, dis-quisit-ion, en-quire, ex-quisite, in-quest, in-quisit-ion, per-quisite, quest, quest-ion, re-quest, re-quire.

Quat-ere, **quass**-um (*to shake*): quash, con-cuss-ion, dis-cuss, per-cuss-ion, rescue (for re-ex-cutere).

Quatu-or (*four*); **quadr**-us (*square*): quadr-angle, quad-rant, quadr-enni-al, quadri-later-al, quadr-ille, quadr-oon (one who is a fourth part black), quadru-ped, quadru-ple, quarantine, quarry (Late

Lat. quadr-aria, a place for digging out stones to be squared), quart, quart-an, quart-er, quart-ern, quart-ette, quatr-ain (a stanza of four lines), quire (O. Fr. quaier), squad (O. Fr. esquadre, from Late Lat. ex-quadrare), squadron, square.

Quer-i, **quest**-us (*to complain*): quer-ul-ous, quarrel (Lat. querel-a), queri-moni-ous, cry (Lat. quirit-are, freq. of quer-i), de-cry (to cry down, to condemn).

Qui-es, **qui-et**-is (*rest*); **qui-esc**-ere (v.): quiet, ac-qui-esce, ac-quit (Late Lat. ac-quiet-are), coy (O. Fr. coit, Lat. quiet-us), de-coy, quit, quite, re-qui-em, re-quite.

Rad-ere, **ras**-um (*to scrape*): rase, raze, raz-or, e-rase, rail (Fr. raill-er, Late Lat. radul-are), raill-ery, rash (O. Fr. rasche, Late Lat. ras-ic-are, to scratch).

Radi-us (*a streak of light*); **radi**-are, **radi-at**-um (v.): ray, radi-ant, radi-at-ion, ir-radi-ate.

Rap-ere, **rapt**-um (*to snatch away*): rap-id, rap-ac-i-ous, rap-ine, rapt-ure, rav-age, rav-ine, rav-ish.

Reg-ere, **rect**-um (*to rule*); **reg-ul**-a (n.): a-droit (Fr. à droit, Lat. ad di-rect-um), cor-rect, di-rect, dirge (short for Lat. di-rige, direct thou), dress (O. Fr. dress-er, Late Lat. di-recti-are), e-rect, escort (O. Fr. escorte, Lat. ex cor-rect-us, put right), in-sur-gent (Lat. in-sub-reg-ere), in-sur-rect-ion, rect-angle, rect-ify, rect-i-linear, reg-i-men, regi-ment, reg-ion, surge (Lat. surg-ere, for sub-reg-ere), source (Lat. sur-rect-um), re-source, re-sur-rect-ion, rule (Lat. regul-a), reg-ul-at-ion, sortie (Late Lat. sur-rect-ire).

Regn-um (*reign*); **regn**-are (v.); **rex**, **reg**-is (*king*): reign, inter-regn-um, realm (Late Lat. reg-al-i-men), reg-al, royal (doublet of the preceding), regi-cide.

Rip-a (*a bank* or *shore*): ar-rive (ad ripam), ar-rival, riv-er (Late Lat. rip-arius, O. Fr. riv-iere; not derived from Lat. rivus).

Riv-us (*a stream of water*): riv-ul-et (Lat. riv-ul-us, dim. of rivus), de-rive, de-riv-at-ion, riv-al (one who uses the same brook as another).

Robur, **robor**-is (*strength*): robust, cor-robor-ate.

Rog-are, **rog-at**-um (*to ask*): ab-rog-ate, ar-rog-ant, de-rog-ate, inter-rog-at-ive, pre-rog-at-ive, pro-rogue, super-e-rog-at-ion, sur-rog-ate.

Rot-a (*a wheel*); **rot-und**-us (adj.); **rot**-are, **rot-at**-um (v.): rot-at-ory, rot-ate, rot-at-ion, control (O. Fr. contre role, Lat. contra rotul-us, dim. of rot-a), comptroll-er or controll-er, roll (Lat. rot-ul-are), rot-und, round (doublet of rotund), roul-eau (a roll of paper), roul-ette, round-el, round-el-ay, row-el (Late Lat. rot-ella, dim. of rot-a), sur-round.

Rump-ere, **rupt**-um (*to break*): rupt-ure, ab-rupt, cor-rupt, dis-rupt-ion, ir-rupt-ion, rote (O. Fr. rote, Mid. Eng. bi rote, in a beaten track), route (Fr. a beaten track, a rutt), rout, rout-ine, rut (a wheel-track). (No connection with *rota*, a wheel.)

Sac-er (*sacred*); **sacr**-are, **sacrat**-um, or **sanc**-ire, **sanct**-um (*to make sacred*, with intrusive *n*): con-secr-ate, ex-ecr-ate (for ex-secr-ate), sacer-dot-al, sacr-a-ment, sacri-fice, sacri-lege, sacrist-an (Late Lat. sacrista), sexton (doublet of the preceding), saint (Lat. sanct-us), sanct-i-fy, sanct-i-moni-ous, sanct-ion, sanct-u-ary.

Sal, **sal**-is (*salt*); **sals**-us (adj.): sal-ad (Fr. sal-ade), sal-ary (Lat.

sal-arium, salt-money), sal-ine, salt-cellar (put for salt-selar, of which the first syllable (A.S. sealt) is superfluous: O. Fr. saliere, a salt-holder, Lat. sal-arium), salt-petre (Lat. sal petræ, salt of the rock), sauce (Lat. sals-a), saus-age (Fr. saucisse, Lat. sals-ic-ium).

Sal-ire, **salt**-um (*to leap*): sali-ent, as-sail, as-sault, de-sult-ory, ex-ult, in-sult, re-sult, sally (Fr. saillie), sal-mon (the leaping fish), ex-ile (for ex-sile; but derived by some from ex solo, one banished from his native soil).

Sal-us, **sal**-ut-is (*health*); **salv**-us (*safe, sound*); **salv**-are, **salv**-at-um (*to save*): safe (Mid. Eng. sauf, Fr. sauf, Lat. salv-us), sage (a plant, Mid. Eng. sauge, Fr. sauge, Lat. salv-ia), salu-bri-ous, salut-ary, salute, salv-age (O. Fr. salv-age, Late Lat. salv-aticum), salv-er (Sp. salv-ar, a plate on which viands are tasted, to make sure that they contain no poison).

Sap-ere (*to taste, to be wise*): sapi-ent, in-sip-id, sage (in the sense of wise, Late Lat. sabi-us, for sapi-us), sav-our (Lat. sap-or).

Scand-ere, **scans**-um (*to climb*): scan (short for scand), a-scend (a for Lat. ad), con-de-scend, scale (Lat. sca-la for scad-la), escalade (Sp. escalado, a scaling), scans-ion, tran-scend.

Sci-re (*to know*): sci-ence, con-sci-ence, con-sci-ous, sci-ol-ist (a smatterer).

Scrib-a (*writer*); **scrib**-ere, **script**-um (*to write*): script, scrip (doublet of the preceding), scribe, a-scribe (Lat. a=ad), circum-scribe, con-script, de-scribe, de-scry (doublet of the preceding, O. Fr. de-scrire, short form of de-scrivre), post-script, pre-scribe, scribble, script-ure, scriv-en-er (Late Lat. scrib-an-us, a notary).

Sec-are, **sect**-um (*to cut*): bi-sect, dis-sect, in-sect, inter-sect, scion (O. F. cion, a cutting), sect-ion, seg-ment, sick-le (A.S. sic-ol, Lat. sec-ul-a), tri-sect. For "sect," see **Sequ**-i, below.

Sed-ere, **sess**-um (*to sit*): as-sess, as-size (doublet of "assess"), as-sid-u-ous, ex-cise (a misspelling of O. F. assise, Du. aksiis, a tax), hostage (Late Lat. ob-sid-i-at-icus, a hostage), in-sid-i-ous, pos-sess, pre-side, re-side, re-sid-ue, sed-i-ment, see (of a bishop, Lat. sed-es), sess-ion, sizar (for as-siz-er, one who receives an allowance), sub-side, sub-sid-y, super-sede, sur-cease (not from "cease," but a corr. of O. Fr. sur-sis, sur-sise, intermitted), siege (ob-sid-ium).

Sen-ex, **sen**-is (*old*): sen-ate, seign-i-or (Fr., from Lat. sen-i-or), sen-ile, sen-i-or, sir, sire, sirrah, surly (sir-like, *i.e.* domineering).

Sent-ire, **sens**-um (*to feel*): scent (with intrusive c), sense, as-sent, con-sent, pre-sent-i-ment, re-sent, sens-u-al, sent-ence, sent-i-ment.

Sequ-i, **sec**-**ut**-us (*to follow*): con-sec-ut-ive, con-sequ-ent, en-sue, ex-ec-ute (for ex-sec-ute), in-trin-sic (O. Fr. intrin-seque, Lat. intra + in + sequ-i), ob-sequies, per-sec-ute, pro-sec-ute, pur-sue (doublet of pro-sec-ute), sec-ond (Lat. sec-und-us, O. Fr. sec-ond), sect (Late Lat. sect-a; no connection with sec-are, to cut), sept (doublet of the preceding), sequ-el, sequ-ester, sue, suit, suite (doublet of the preceding).

Ser-ere, **sert**-um (*to put in a row*): ser-i-es, as-sert, con-cert (for con-sert), de-sert (in the sense of wilderness), dis-sert-at-ion, ex-ert (for ex-sert), in-sert, serr-ied.

Serv-us (*servant*); **serv**-ire, **serv**-**it**-um (*to serve*); **serv**-are, **serv**-at-um (*to keep*): serve, serf, con-serve, de-serve (Lat. de-serv-ire), de-sert (in the sense of merit), des-sert (from O. Fr. des-serv-ir, to take away the courses at dinner), ob-serve, ob-serv-at-ion, re-serv-oir (Lat. re-serv-at-orium), sergeant or serjeant (Lat. serv-i-ent-em).

Sign-are, **sing-at-um** (*to make a mark*); **sign**-um (n.): sign, as-sign, con-sign-ment, counter-sign, de-sign, en-sign, seal (Lat. sig-illum, dim. of sig-n), sign-et, sign-al.

Simil-is (*like*); **simul**-are, **simul-at**-um (*to pretend*): simil-ar, as-semble, as-simil-ate, dis-semble, dis-simil-ar, sembl-ance, re-semble, simil-i-tude, simult-an-eous (with intrusive *t*).

Sol-us (*alone*): de-sol-ate, sol-emn (Lat. solus and annus, year), sol-i-tary, sol-i-tude, sol-o (Ital.), sullen (O. Fr. sol-ain, Late Lat. sol-an-us).

Solv-ere, **sol-ut**-um (*to loosen*, or *to pay*): solve, ab-sol-ute, dis-solve, dis-sol-ute, re-solve, sol-u-ble, sol-ut-ion.

Spec-ere, **spect**-um (*to behold*): speci-es, a-spect, circum-spect, con-spic-u-ous, de-spise (Lat. de-spic-ere, to look down on), de-spite (Lat. de-spect-us), especi-al (O. Fr. especial, Lat. speci-al-is), espy (O. Fr. espi-er), ex-pect (for ex-spect, Lat. spect-are, freq. of spec-ere), per-spect-ive, per-spic-ac-ity, respite (Lat. re-spect-us), speci-e (money in gold or silver), speci-men, speci-ous, spect-a-cle, spect-re, spec-ul-ar, spec-ul-ate, spice (speci-es, which in Late Lat. meant a drug), spite (short for "despite"), spy (short for "espy"), suspicion.

Spir-are, **spir-at**-um (*to breathe*): spirit (Lat. spir-it-us), sprite (doublet of preceding, Fr. esprit), sprightly (a misspelling for sprite-ly), spir-acle (Lat. spir-ac-ulum, a breathing-hole), a-spire, con-spire, ex-pire, in-spire, per-spire, re-spire, tran-spire. For "Spi-ral," see Greek Roots, V., *in loco*.

Spond-ere, **spons**-um (*to pledge*): spons-or, cor-re-spond, de-spond, espouse (O. Fr. espous-er, the *e* not being part of the root), re-spons-ible, spouse (Lat. sponsa).

St-are, **stat**-um (*to stand*): ar-rest (Lat. ad + re + stare, O. Fr. ar-rest-er), circum-stance, con-stant, contra-st (Fr. contrast-er, Lat. contra-st-are), cost (O. Fr. cost-er, Lat. con-st-are), dis-(s)tant, sta-ble, con-stable (Lat. comes stabuli, "count of the stable"), con-stabul-ary (a collection of constables), e-stabl-ish, state, e-state (doublet of the preceding), ex-tant, in-stance, inter-stice (Lat. inter-stit-ium), ob-stacle, rest (Lat. re-stare, Fr. rest-er), rest-ive (Fr. rest-if, drawing backwards), stage (Late Lat. stat-ic-um), sta-men, stanza (Late Lat. stant-ia), stat-ion-ary, stat-ion-ery, stat-ue, stat-ure, sub-stance, super-stit-ion.

Statu-ere, **statut**-um (*to establish*): stat-ute, in-stit-ute, de-stit-ute, con-stit-ut-ion.

Stern-ere, **strat**-um (*to spread flat*): stray, street, con-stern-at-ion, pro-strate. (No connection with "strew.")

String-ere, **strict**-um (*to draw tight*): string-ent, strict, a-string-ent, strain, strait, stress (Late Lat. strict-i-are), con-strain, dis-(s)tress, dis-(s)trict, re-strain. N.B.—*Straight* has no connection with *strait*, but is derived from A.S. *streht*, p.p. of *strecc*-an, to stretch.

Stru-ere, **struct**-um (*to build*): struct-ure, con-struct, con-strue, de-stroy, in-struct, in-stru-ment, super-struct-ure.

Super, **supra** (*above*); **suprem**-us, **summ**-us (*highest*): sum, summ-it, con-summ-ate, soprano (Ital., from Late Lat. super-an-us), sover-eign (a misspelling of Mid. Eng. soverain, Late Lat. super-an-us), super-ior, supern-al, supra-mund-ane, supreme, suzerain (Late Lat. surser-an-us, from Lat. sursum, turned up, sub (up) versum (turned)).

Tal-ea (*a slip of wood*): tail-or (a cutter out, Fr. taill-er, to cut), de-tail, en-tail, in-tagl-io (Ital. a wood-carving), re-tail (to sell by cuttings or small amounts at a time), tall-y (Fr. taille, a notch).

Tang-ere (with intrusive *n*), **tact**-um (*to touch*): tact, tang-ent, at-tain (Lat. ad + ting-ere), at-taind-er, at-taint (not allied to "taint," Lat. tinct-us), con-tact, con-tag-ion, con-ta-min-ate (Lat. con-ta-men for con-tag-men), con-tig-u-ous, en-tire (Lat. in-teg-er), red-in-teg-rat-ion, tang-ible, tax (O. Fr. tasque, Late Lat. taxa, tax).

Teg-ere, **tect**-um (*to cover*): teg-u-ment, detect, in-teg-u-ment, pro-tect, tile (A.S. tig-ele, Lat. teg-ul-a).

Temp-us, **temp-or**-is (*time*): temp-or-al, con-temp-or-aneous, extempore ("from the time," impromptu), temp-est-as, tense (Fr. temps).

Tend-ere, **tens**-um (*to stretch, to bend to*): tend, at-tend, con-tend, dis-tend, dis-tent-ion, ex-tent, in-tent-ion, in-tense, in-tens-ive, os-tens-ible, os-tent-at-ion, por-tend, pre-tend, pre-tens-ion, super-in-tend-ent, tend-er (in the sense of "offer"), tend-on (Late Lat. tend-on-em), tens-ion, tent (a pavilion), tent-er (as in the phrase "tenterhooks").

Ten-ere, **tent**-um (*to hold*); **tent**-are, **tent-at**-um (freq. form, *to try* or *test*): abs-tain, ap-per-tain, ap-pur-ten-ance, con-tain, con-tent, con-tin-ent, con-tin-ue, con-tin-u-ous, coun-ten-ance (Lat. con-tin-entia), de-tain, enter-tain, im-per-tin-ent, per-tin-ac-ity, rein (O. Fr. reine, Ital. redina, Late Lat. re-tin-a), re-tain, re-tin-ue, sus-tain, taunt, tempt, at-tempt, ten-ac-i-ous, ten-ant, ten-e-ment, tenet (he holds), ten-on, ten-or, tent-acle, tent-at-ive, ten-ure.

Ter-ere, **trit**-um (*to wear* or *rub*): trite, con-trite, at-trit-ion, de-tri-ment, trit-ur-ate, tri-bul-at-ion, try (Fr. tri-er, Late Lat. trit-are).

Terr-a (*the earth*): terr-ace, in-ter, dis-in-ter, in-ter-ment, par-terre (Fr. par terre, along the ground), sub-terr-an-ean, tur-een (a bad spelling of Fr. terrine, an earthen pan), terr-ene, terr-ier (lit. a dog that burrows), terri-tory.

Tex-o, **text**-um (*to weave*): text, con-text, pre-text, toil (in the sense of net, Fr. toile, Lat. tel-a for tex-la, a thing woven), toil-ette (dim. of preceding), sub-tle (Lat. sub-til-is, lit. "finely woven"), text-ile, text-ure, tissue (Fr. tiss-er, to weave, Lat. tex-ere).

Torqu-ere, **tort**-um (*to twist*): tort-ure, con-tort, dis-tort, ex-tort, tart (O. Fr. tarte, Lat. tort-a), torch (Late Lat. tort-ia), tor-ment, tort-oise (Mid. Eng. tortuce, South Fr. tortesa, so named from its crooked feet), truss (Fr. trousse, O. Fr. truss-er, Late Lat. tort-i-are, to twist), trouss-eau (dim. of Fr. trousse), trowsers (Fr. trousses, breeches).

Trah-ere, **tract**-um (*to draw* or *drag*): tract, trait, trace (Fr.

trac-er, Late Lat. tract-i-are), abs-tract, at-tract, con-tract, de-traction, en-treat, por-trait, por-tray, pro-tract, re-treat, tract-able, trail (O. Fr. traail, Late Lat. trah-ale), train (Late Lat. trah-in-are), treat, treat-ise, treat-y.

Turb-a (*a crowd, confused mass*); **turb-ul**-a (dim.): turb-id, dis-turb, per-turb, turb-ul-ent, trouble (Fr. troubl-er, Late Lat. turb-ul-are).

Umbr-a (*shade*): umbr-age (Fr. ombr-age, Lat. umbr-aticum), ad-umbr-ate (to foreshadow), umbr-ella (Ital. umbrella, dim. of umbr-a), umber (Fr. ombre, short for terre d'ombre, earth of shadow, a brown earth used for shadowing by painters).

Ungu-ere, **unct**-um (*to smear*): ungu-ent, oint-ment (doublet of the preceding), an-oint, unct-ion.

Un-us (*one*); **null**-us (*none*, from *ne ullus*, *ullus* being the short for *unulus*, dim. of *unus*): un-ity, an-nul, null, un-ion (in the sense of oneness), un-ion (in the sense of pearl), on-ion (doublet of the preceding), un-animous, un-i-corn, un-ique (Lat. un-ic-us), un-i-son (Lat. son-us, a sound), un-ite, un-i-voc-al.

Ut-i, **us**-us (*to use*): use, us-age, ab-use, per-use, us-ury, us-urp (Lat. usum + rumpere, or perhaps Lat. usu + rapere), ut-ensil, ut-il-ise, ut-il-ity.

Vag-us (*wandering*); **vag**-ari, **vag-at**-us (v.): vague, vagr-ant (with intrusive *r*), extra-vag-ant, vag-ary, vag-a-bond.

Val-ere (*to be strong*): val-id, a-vail, con-val-esc-ent, counter-vail, pre-val-ent, vale-dict-ion, val-i-ant, val-our, val-ue, val-e-tud-in-ar-ian.

Veh-ere, **vect**-um (*to carry*): veh-icle, con-vex, in-veigh, veil (Lat. vel-um, a sail, so called because it carries or propels a ship), vein (conveyer of blood), re-veal, veh-e-ment, ven-ous, vex (Lat. vex-are, intens. form of veh-ere).

Ven-ire, **vent**-um (*to come*): vent-ure, ad-vent, a-ven-ue (Fr. a-ven-ir, Lat. ad-ven-ire), contra-vene, con-vene, con-ven-i-ent, con-vent, co-ven-ant (O. Fr. con-ven-ant), inter-vene, in-vent, par-ven-u (part. of Fr. par-ven-ir, to thrive), pre-vent, re-ven-ue, sou-ven-ir, ven-ue.

Vert-ere, **vers**-um (*to turn* or *change*): verse, ad-verse, ad-vert, ad-vert-ise, contro-vers-y, con-vers-at-ion, di-verse, di-vers (doublet of the preceding), di-vert, di-vorce, in-verse, prose (Lat. prosa, for prorsa, pro-versa, turned forward), re-verse, sub-vert, tra-verse, vers-ion, a-vers-ion, vert-ebra, vert-ex, vert-igo, vort-ex.

Ver-us (*true*): ver-y, a-ver, ver-ac-ious, ver-dict (Lat. vere dict-um), ver-i-fy, veri-simil-i-tude, ver-ity.

Vi-a (*road*): con-vey, con-voy (Late Lat. con-vi-are), de-vi-ate, de-vi-ous, en-voy, im-per-vi-ous, in-voice (corr. of en-vois, Eng. plural of Fr. en-voi, a sending).

Vid-ere, **vis**-um (*to see*): vis-ion, ad-vice (O. Fr. a vis, Lat. ad vis-um), ad-vise, en-vy (Lat. in-vid-ia), in-vid-i-ous, e-vid-ent, im-pro-vise, pro-vid-ent, prud-ent (doublet of the preceding), pur-vey, view, re-view, re-vise, sur-vey, vis-age, vis-or or viz-or, vista (Ital.), vis-it, vis-ible, vit-re-ous (Lat. vitrum, for vid-trum).

Vinc-ere, **vict**-um (*to conquer*): vict-ory, con-vince, e-vict, e-vince, in-vinc-ible, vanquish (O. Fr. veinquiss, of verb veinquir).

Vind-ex, **vind-ic**-is (*avenger*): a-venge, re-venge, venge-ance, vind-ic-ate, vindic-tive (short for vindic-at-ive).

Viv-ere, **vict**-um (*to live*); **viv**-us (*alive*); **vit**-a (*life*): con-viv-i-al, re-vive, sur-vive, vi-ands (Lat. viv-enda), vi-per (Lat. vivi-para, producing living young), vi-tal, viv-ac-i-ty, viv-id, vivi-section, vict-u-als.

Voc-are, **voc-at**-um (*to call*); **vox**, **voc**-is (n.): voice, vouch, ad-voc-ate, ad-vows-on (Lat. ad-voc-at-i-on-em), a-voc-at-ion, a-vouch, con-voke, pro-voke, voc-i-fer-at-ion, vouch-safe, voc-al, vowel (doublet of the preceding).

Volv-ere, **vol-ut**-um (*to roll*): vol-u-ble, con-vol-ut-ion, con-volv-ul-us, de-vol-ut-ion, e-volve, re-volt (Fr. re-volte), vault (O. Fr. volte, from Lat. vol-ut-us), vol-ume.

Vov-ere, **vot**-um (*to vow*): vote, vot-ive, de-vote, de-vout (a doublet of the preceding), vow (O. Fr. vou, Lat. vot-um).

Vulg-us (*the common people*): vulg-ar, di-vulge.

V.—DERIVATIVES FROM GREEK ROOTS.

Ag-ein (*to lead*): dem-ag-ogue (Gr. dem-os, people), ped-ag-ogue (Gr. paid-os, a boy), syn-ag-ogue (Gr. sun, together, "house of assembly").

Ag-on (*struggle*): ag-on-y, ant-ag-on-ist (Gr. anti, against).

Akolouth-os (*one who follows*): acolyte (Late Lat. acolythus).

Akr-os (*at the top*): acro-bat (Gr. bat-es, walker), acro-polis (Gr. polis, city), acro-stic (Gr. stikh-os, a line).

Alg-os (*pain*): neur-alg-ia (Gr. neur-on, nerve), nost-alg-ia (home-sickness, Gr. nost-os, return).

Allēl-on (*of each other*): par-allel (Gr. para, by the side of), par-allel-o-gram (Gr. gramma, something written).

All-os (*other*): all-egory (Gr. egoria, speech), all-o-pathy (Gr. path-e, suffering).

Ana-khor-ein (*to retire; "ana" is merely a prefix*): an-chor-ite (one who has retired from the world).

Anem-os (*wind*): anem-o-meter (Gr. metron, a measure), anemone (wind-flower).

Angel-os (*messenger*): angel, arch-angel (Gr. arkh-e, leadership), ev-angel-ist (Gr. eu, well).

Anth-os (*a flower*): antho-logy, poly-anthus (Gr. pol-us, many).

Anthrop-os (*man*): anthrop-o-logy, mis-anthrope (Gr. misos, hatred), phil-anthrop-y (Gr. phil-os, a lover).

Arkh-e (*beginning, headship*); **arkhai**-os (*ancient*): archa-ic, archæ-o-logy, archa-ism, arch-ives, arch-i-pelago, arch-i-tect, mon-arch (Gr. mon-os, alone), hept-arch-y (Gr. hepta, seven), hier-arch-y (Gr. hier-os, sacred), olig-arch-y (Gr. olig-oi, few), patri-arch (Gr. pater, a father), an-arch-y (Gr. an, not).

Arist-os (*best*): arist-o-crat (Gr. krat-ein, to rule), arist-o-crac-y.

Arithm-os (*a number*): arithm-et-ic (Gr. arithm-et-ik-e, science of numbers), log-arithm (ratio-number).

Arkt-os (*a bear*): arct-ic, ant-arct-ic, arct-urus (Gr. ouros, watcher or guard).

Ast-er (*a star*): astr-o-logy, astr-o-nom-y (Gr. nom-os, law), ast-er-isk (isk is Gr. dim. suffix), aster-oid (a minor planet, Gr. eidos, appearance). N.B.—"Dis-aster" is not of Greek origin, but from Lat. dis- (in the sense of ill) and astr-um, a star.

Athl-on (*a struggle*): athl-ete, athl-et-ic.

Atm-os (*vapour*): atmo-sphere (Gr. sphair-a, a globe).

Aut-os (*self*): auto-bio-graphy (Gr. bios, life, and Gr. graph-ein, to write), auto-crat (Gr. krat-ein, to rule), auto-graph, auto-maton (Gr. stem, mat-, moving), auto-nomy (self-government, Gr. nom-os, law), aut-opsy (Gr. opsis, sight), auto-type (Gr. tup-os, a model).

Ball-ein (*to throw*); **bol**-e (*act of throwing*); **blem**-a (*a throw*): hyper-bol-e, sym-bol, para-bol-a, para-ble (lit. a comparison), em-blem.

Bapt-ein (*to dip*): bapt-ise, bapt-ism, bapt-ist.

Bar-os (*weight*): baro-meter, bar-i-tone.

Bas-is (*going*); **bet**-es (*goer*): base, bas-is, bas-ic, dia-bet-es, acro-bat.

Bibli-on (*a scroll*); **bibl**-os (*a book*): Bible (the book), bibli-o-graphy, bibli-o-mania, bibli-o-pole (Gr. pol-ein, to sell).

Bi-os (*life*): bio-logy, bio-graphy, amphi-bious (Gr. amphi, on two sides, dubious).

Blapt-ein, (fut.) **blaps**-o (*to damage*): blas-pheme (Gr. phem-e, speech), blame (doublet of the preceding, O. Fr. blasm-er), blas-phem-y (Gr. phem-e, saying, word).

Bom-bux (*silk, cotton*): bom-bast (lit. cotton-wadding, hence padding, affected language), bom-bas-ine.

Bronkh-os (*wind pipe*): bronch-ia, bronch-itis.

Butis, **boutis** (*a flank*): bottle (Late Lat. buticula, dim. of butica, Mid. Eng. botel, Fr. bouteille), butler (for bottler, Mid. Eng. boteler), butlery (for bottlery, Mid. Eng. botelerie, confused with "butter").

Daim-ōn (*a supernatural being, a divinity*): demon, demon-î-ac, demon-o-logy.

Dek-a (*ten*): dec-ade, deca-gon (Gr. gon-ia, a corner), deca-logue, deca-hedron (Gr. hedra, a seat or base), deca-syllable.

Dem-os (*people*): dem-o-crat (Gr. krat-ein, to rule), dem-o-crac-y, dem-ag-ogue (Gr. ag-ein, to lead), en-dem-ic, epi-dem-ic, demo-graphy (the study of races with reference to mortality, sickness, etc.).

Di-ait-a (*mode of life*): di-et, di-et-et-ic, di-et-ary.

Di-dask-ein (*to teach*): di-dact-ic (having instruction for its aim).

Dok-ein (*to think* or *seem*); **dox**-a (*opinion*): dog-ma, dog-ma-tic, dog-mat-ise, ortho-dox (Gr. orth-os, straight, right), hetero-dox (Gr. heter-os, other, different).

Dra-ein (*to do, to act*): dra-ma, dras-tic.

Drom-as, **dromad**-os (*running*, adj.); **drom**-os (*course*): hippo-drome (Gr. hipp-os, a horse), dromed-ary.

Dunam-is (*power*): dynam-ics, dynam-ite, dynam-o-meter (power-measure).

Dus (*ill*, used only as a prefix): dys-entery (Gr. enter-on, intestine), dys-pept-ic (Gr. peptik-os, fit for digesting).

Ekh-o (*a sound*): echo, cat-ech-ise, cat-ech-ist, cat-ech-umen (from Gr. part. -oumenos).

Eid-os (*appearance, form*): metall-oid (and all other compounds ending in oid), eido-graph (Gr. graph-ein, to write), kal-eido-scope (Gr. kal-os, beautiful, and scop-ein, to see), id-ol (Gr. eid-ōl-on) id-o(l)-latry (Gr. latr-eia, worship), id-ol-ise, id-yll ("a little picture," Gr. eid-ull-ion).

Eik-on (*figure, image*): ic-on (image or picture), ic-on-o-clast (Gr. klast-es, a breaker).

Eir-on (*a dissembler*): ir-on-y, ir-on-ic-al.

Ele-ein (*to pity*); **ele-em**-on (*pitiful*): alms (A.S. ælmesse, formed from Gr. el-e-em-os-un-e, pity), ele-em-os-yn-ary (adj. of "alms," formed by adding Lat. suffix -ary).

Elektr-on (*amber*): electr-ic, electr-ic-i-ty, electr-o-type, electr-o-meter, electr-o-cute (to put to death by electricity, a recent coinage, formed apparently on the analogy of the word "execute").

Enter-on (*intestine*): enter-ic, enter-itis, dys-entery (Gr. dus, ill).

Erem-os (*desert*): erem-ite, herm-it (doublet of the preceding).

Erg-on (*a work*): en-erg-y, en-erg-et-ic, metall-urg-y, lit-urg-y (Gr. lei-tos, public), surg-eon (from Gr. kheir-urg-eon; kheir, the hand).

Ethn-os (*nation*): ethn-ic, ethn-o-logy, ethn-o-graphy, ethn-arch.

Eu (*well*, used only as a prefix in English): eu-char-ist (Gr. khar-is, thanks), eu-log-ise (Gr. log-os, speech), eu-log-y, eu-phem-ism (Gr. phēm-ē, saying), eu-phon-y (Gr. phon-e, the voice), eu-phras-y (the plant called eye-bright, Gr. phrain-ein, to delight), eu-phu-ism (pp. 362, 416, Gr. phu-ein, to produce), eu-thanas-ia (easy death, Gr. than-at-os, death), ev-angel-ist (Gr. angel-os, a messenger).

Gal-a, **gal-akt**-os (*milk*): galax-y.

Gam-os (*marriage*): mono-gam-y (Gr. mon-os, single), bi-gam-y (Lat. bis, twice: hence this word is a hybrid), poly-gam-y (Gr. pol-us, many), mis-o-gam-ist (Gr. mis-os, hatred).

Gast-er, **gastr**-os (*belly*): gastr-ic, gastr-it-is, gastr-o-nom-y.

Gē (*the earth*): ge-o-log-y, ge-o-graph-y, ge-o-centr-ic, ge-o-metr-y, apo-gee (Gr. apo, from), peri-gee (Gr. peri, around).

Gen-os (*kind*); **genes**-is (*origin*): genes-is, genea-log-y (Gr. genea, birth), hydro-gen (Gr. hudr-os, water), nitro-gen (Gr. nitr-on, potash), ox-y-gen (Gr. ox-us, sharp).

Gi-**gnosk**-ein (*to know*): gnom-on, gnost-ic, physi-o-gnom-y (Gr. phus-is, natural appearance), dia-gnos-is (Gr. dia, through), pro-gnos-is (Gr. pro, beforehand), pro-gnost-ic-ate.

Gloss-a (*tongue*): gloss-ary, di-glot (Gr. dis, twice), glott-is (mouth of the windpipe), epi-glottis (Gr. epi, at or upon).

Gluk-us (*sweet*): gluc-ose (a variety of sugar), glyc-er-ine, liquorice (a misspelling of Gr. glycyrrhiza, glukus (sweet) and rhiza (a root); the correct spelling is found in Pliny's *Nat. Hist.* (Latin); but this was afterwards corrupted to "liquiritia"; hence the misspelling in English).

Gon-ia (*an angle* or *corner*): penta-gon, hexa-gon, dia-gon-al.

Graph-ein (*to write*); **gram**-ma (*what is written*): graph-ic, di-graph, dia-gram, epi-gram, graph-ite, mono-gram, mono-graph, bio-graph-y, epi-graph-y (the art of deciphering inscriptions), geo-graph-y, para-graph, tele-graph (Gr. tel-e, distant), physio-graph-y, biblio-graph-y (Gr. biblion, a book), gramm-ar, pro-gramme (Fr. programme).

Gumn-os (*naked*): gymn-ast, gymn-astic, gymn-asium, gymnosophist.

Hagi-os (*holy*): hagi-o-logy, hagi-o-scope.

Haim-a, **haimat**-os (*blood*): hæm-or-rhage, Gr. rhag-e, a rent), hæmat-ite (red iron ore), emerod (corr. of "hemorrhoid," Gr. haimorrhoïd-es, Gr. rho-os, flux).

Hair-ein (*to take*); **haires**-is (*the act of taking, choice*): heres-y, heret-ic, heresi-arch, di-æresis (a mark of separation), syn-æres-is (the fusion of two vowels into a diphthong), aph-æres-is (the removal of a letter or syllable from the beginning of a word).

Heli-os (*the sun*): helio-centric, helio-scope (Gr. skop-os, seeing), helio-trope (Gr. trop-os, turning).

Hemer-a (*day*): ep-hemer-al (lasting for a day).

Hier-os (*sacred*): hiero-glyph-ics (Gr. gluph-ein, to engrave): hiero-phant (Gr. phant-es, one who shows or explains), hier-arch (one who presides over sacred rites, Gr. arkh-ein, to be at the head).

Hipp-os (*horse*): hippo-drome (Gr. drom-os, a course), hippo-griff (Gr. grups, a griffin), hippo-potamus (Gr. potam-os, a river).

Histor-ia (*research, narrative*): history, story, histori-o-graph-er.

Hod-os (*a way, a road*): ex-od-us, peri-od, meth-od, episode (lit. a side entrance or additional entrance; Gr. epi (besides) + eis (into) + hodos).

Hol-os (*whole, entire*): cat-hol-ic (Gr. kata, according to), holocaust (Gr. kai-ein, to burn).

Hom-os (*the same*); **homoi**-os (*similar*): homo-geneous (Gr. gen-os, kind, race), homo-log-ous, an-omal-ous (Gr. omal-os, even, related to "homos," the same), homœo-path-y (Gr. path-e, suffering).

Hud-or (*water*): hydr-a, otter (allied to A.S. otor, p. 385), hydr-ant, hydr-ate, hydr-angea (a flower whose seed-vessel is cup-formed, Gr. angei-on, a cup), hydr-aul-ic (Gr. aul-os, a pipe), hydro-dynam-ics (dunam-is, power), hydro-gen (generator of water, Gr. gen-, producer), hydro-pathy (the water-cure, Gr. path-e, suffering), hydro-phob-ia (Gr. phob-ein, to fear), dropsy (short for Gr. hydro-pisis, water-thirst), hydro-statics.

Ide-a (*notion*, or *picture in the mind*): idea, ideal, ideal-ise.

Idi-os (*peculiar to oneself*): idi-om, idi-ot (orig. a private person), idio-syn-crasy (Gr. sun (with) -kras-is (mixture), hence composition, temperament).

Is-os (*equal*): iso-bar (Gr. bar-os, weight), iso-therm (Gr. therm-os, hot), iso-sceles (Gr. skel-os, a leg).

Kai-ein, (fut.) **kaus**-o (*to burn*): caust-ic, cauter-ise, encaust-ic.

Kal-ein (*to call*); **kles**-is (*a calling*): ec-cles-i-ast-ic (Gr. ecclesia, the calling out, the church).

Kal-os (*beautiful*): cali-graphy, calo-type, cali-sthen-ics (Gr. sthen-os, strength), kal-eido-scope (Gr. eid-os, form, and scop-ein, to see).

Kan-on (*rule*): canon, canon-ise, canon-ic-al.

Ken-os (*empty*): ceno-taph (Gr. taph-os, a tomb).

Kentr-on (*a goad, a point*): centre, con-centr-al, ec-centr-ic.

Khol-e (*bile*): chol-er, chol-er-a, melan-chol-y.

Khor-os (*a band of dancers and singers*): choir, chor-us, chor-al, chor-ist-er.

Khri-ein (*to anoint*); **khris**-is (*anointing*): Christ (khrist-os, the anointed), chrism, Christ-mas (Lat. miss-a, A.S. mæsse).

Khrom-a (*colour*): chrom-at-ic, a-chrom-at-ic, chrome or chromium (a metal that exhibits beautiful colours).

Khron-os (*time*): chron-icle, chron-icl-er, chrono-log-y, chrono-graph, syn-chron-ous (=con-temp-or-ary, of Latin origin).

Khrus-os (*gold*): chrys-al-is, chrys-al-ite (a kind of stone), chrys-anth-em-um (a kind of flower, Gr. an-thos, a flower).

Kist-e (*a box*): cist (hence A.S. cyste), chest (doublet of the preceding), cist-ern (found only in Lat. cist-ern-a).

Kler-os (*lot*): cler-ic, clerk (short form of cleric), clerg-y, cler-ic-al.

Klin-e (*a bed*); **klin**-ein (*to lie down*): clin-ic-al, clin-ique (nursing home), en-clit-ic, clime, climate, ac-clim-at-ise, clim-ax, anti-clim-ax, clim-ac-ter-ic.

Koima-ein (*to sleep*); **kom**-a (*sleep*): coma, com-at-ose, cem-et-ery (Gr. koim-et-er-ion, a sleeping-place).

Konkh-e (*shell*): conch, conch-o-log-y.

Kosm-os (*order*): cosmos, cosm-ic-al, cosm-o-gon-y (Gr. gon-e, coming into existence), cosm-o-graphy, cosm-o-polite (Gr. polit-es, a citizen), cosm-et-ic (Gr. kosm-et-es, an adorner).

Kran-ion (*a skull*): cran-ium, cran-i-o-logy.

Krat-os (*power*): demo-crat, dem-o-crac-y, arist-o-crac-y, pluto-crat (Gr. plout-os, wealth).

Kris-is (*judgment*); **krit**-es (*a judge*): cris-is, crit-ic-al, crit-er-ion hyper-crit-ic-al, hypo-crite, hypo-cris-y.

Krupt-ein (*to hide*): crypt, crypto-graphy (secret writing), apo-cryph-a, apo-cryph-al, grotto (Ital. grotta), grot-esque (Fr. grot-esque, Ital. grot-esca).

Kub-os (*a solid square*): cube, cub-ic-al. N.B.—No connection with "cubicle," from Lat. *cub*-are, to lie down.

Kukl-os (*circle*): cycle, en-cycl-ic-al, cycl-one (augm. form), cycl-oid (Gr. eid-os, form), en-cyclo-pædia (Gr. paid-ei-a, instruction), cycl-ops (Gr. ops, the eye).

Ku-on, poss. **kun**-os (*a dog*): cyn-ic, cyn-ic-al, cyn-os-ure (Gr. kun-os our-a, the dog's tail: north pole star), quinsy (formerly spelt "squinancy," the *s* being a contraction of *es*=Lat. ex: from Gr. kun-ankh-e, a dog-throttling, a bad kind of sore throat).

Kuri-os (*lord*): kirk (Gr. kuriak-e, the Lord's house), church.

Lab- (*take*); **lēps**-is (*taking*); **lem**-ma (*a thing taken*): syl-lable (the last *l* is intrusive), di-lem-ma, epi-leps-y, cata-leps-y.

La-os (*people*): lay, lay-man, la-ity.

Leg-ein (*to say* or *choose*); **lex**-is (n.); **log**-os (n.): ana-log-y, apo-logue, apo-log-y, cata-logue, deca-logue (Gr. deka, ten), dia-lect, dia-logue, ec-lect-ic, ec-logue, epi-logue, eu-log-y (Gr. eu, well), mono-logue (Gr. mon-os, single), pro-logue, syl-log-ism (Gr. sun, with), log-ic, log-arithm (Gr. arithm-os, a number, "ratio-number"), lex-ic-on, lex-ic-o-grapher. N.B.—The reference of "elegy" to the root *leg*- is unsupported by evidence. It comes from Gr. eleg-os, a lament.

Leip-ein (*to leave*); **leips**-is (n.): ec-lipse, el-lipse, ec-lipt-ic, el-lipt-ic-al.

Lith-os (*stone*): litho-graph, litho-tom-y (Gr. tom-e, cutting), aerolite, mono-lith, neo-lith-ic (Gr. neos, new or recent), palæo-lithic (Gr. palai-os, ancient).

Lu-ein (*to loosen*); **lus**-is (n.): ana-lyse, ana-lys-is, ana-lyt-ic, dia-lys-is, para-lys-is, palsy (doublet of the preceding).

Mart-ur (*a witness*): martyr, martyr-dom (a hybrid, since the suffix is A.S.), martyr-o-log-y, proto-martyr (Gr. prōt-os, first).

Math-em-a (*learning*): math-em-at-ics.

Mekhan-e (*contrivance*; Lat. **machin**-a): mach-ine, mechan-ic, mechan-ics, mechan-ist.

Mel-as (*black*): melan-choly, Mela-nes-ia (Gr. nes-os, an island).

Metall-on (*metal*; Lat. **metall**-um): metal, mettle (doublet of the preceding), mettle-some, high-mettled, metall-urg-y (Gr. erg-on, work).

Met-er, **metr**-os (*mother*): metro-polis (Gr. polis, city).

Metr-on (*measure*): met-er, metre, metr-ic, hyper-metric-al, hexameter (Gr. hexa, six), penta-meter (Gr. pente, five), baro-meter (Gr. baros, weight), thermo-meter (Gr. therm-os, hot), hydro-meter (Gr. hudr-os, water).

Mikr-os (*small*): micro-cosm (Gr. kosm-os, order or universe), micro-scope (Gr. skop-ein, to see).

Mim-os (*imitator*): mim-ic, panto-mime (Gr. pant-os, poss. of pas, all).

Mis-os (*hatred*): mis-anthrope (Gr. anthrop-os, man), miso-gam-ist (Gr. gam-os, marriage), miso-gyn-ist (Gr. gun-e, a woman).

Mon-os (*alone, single*): monk (Gr. mon-akh-os, solitary), mon-ach-ism, mon-ad (a unit), mon-ast-ery (Gr. mon-ast-es, one who lives alone), minster (doublet of the preceding, through A.S. mynster), mon-arch, mon-ody (Gr. od-e, a song), mono-chord (Gr. khord-e, a musical string), mono-gamy (Gr. gam-os, marriage), mono-gram (Gr. gram-ma, something written), mono-graph (a treatise on a single topic), mono-lith (Gr. lith-os, a stone), mono-logue, mono-mania (madness on a single subject), mono-poly (Gr. pol-ein, to sell, "sole right of selling"), mono-theism (Gr. the-os, god), mono-syllable, mono-ton-ous (Gr. ton-os, a tone).

Morph-e (*shape, form*): a-morph-ous (shapeless), Morpheus (the "shaper," the Gr. god of dreams), morph-ia, meta-morph-os-is (Gr. meta-, a suffix denoting change), morpho-log-y (the science of comparative forms).

Mu-ein (*to be closed*); **must**-es (*one who is initiated into a secret order*): myst-ic, myst-ery, myst-er-i-ous.

Naus (*a ship*): nausea (Gr. nausia, sea-sickness), naut-ic-al, naut-il-us.

Nekr-os (*dead body*): necro-polis, necro-mancy (Gr. mantis, a prophet).

Ne-os (*new*): neo-phyte (a new convert, Gr. phut-on, a plant), neo-log-y, neo-lith-ic (Gr. lith-os, a stone, "the more recent Stone Age").

Nom-os (*law*): astro-nomy (Gr. astron, star), gastro-nomy (Gr. gaster, belly), Deutero-nomy (Gr. deuter-os, second), eco-nomy (Gr. oik-os, house).

Oik-ein (*to dwell*); **oik**-es-is (n.): eco-nomy, di-oc-ese, di-oc-es-an, par-ish (Gr. par-oik-ia, Fr. par-oisse), par-och-i-al (adj. of "parish"), ec-u-men-ic-al (Gr. oik-ou-men-e, the inhabited world, applied by the Jews to the Roman empire).

Okto (*eight*): octa-gon (Gr. gon-ia, angle), octo-pus (Gr. pous, foot), octo-syllabic.

Onom-a, **onom-at**-os (*a name*): onomato-pœia (the literary device by which the sound is made to echo the sense, Gr. poi-ein, to make), syn-onym, syn-onym-ous, an-onym-ous, patr-onym-ic, hom-onym (Gr. hom-os, the same).

Opt-esthai (*to see*); **ops**-is (*sight*): opt-ics, opt-ic-al, opt-ic-ian, syn-ops-is (a collective or summary view, Gr. sun, with), syn-opt-ic, pan-optic-on.

Organ-on (*an instrument*): organ, organ-ic, organ-ise, dis-organ-ise, re-organ-ise.

Oste-on (*bone*): osteo-logy (the science of bones).

Ox-us (*sharp*): oxy-mor-on (Gr. mor-os, foolish), par-oxysm, oxy-tone.

Path-os, **path**-e (*suffering*): path-et-ic, path-os, sym-path-y, anti-path-y, allo-path-y (Gr. all-os, other, different), homœo-path-y (Gr. homoi-os, similar, like), patho-logy.

Pais, paid-os (*boy*): ped-ag-ogue (Gr. ag-ein, to lead or direct), ped-ant, pedo-baptism (infant baptism), en-cyclo-pæd-ia (Gr. kukl-os, a circle).

Palai-os (*ancient*): palæo-lith-ic (belonging to the Old Stone Age), palæo-graphy, palæo-zoic (Gr. zo-on, animal), palæ-ont-o-logy (science of ancient existences; Gr. ont-a, existences).

Pas, pan-tos (*all*): pan-ac-ea (Gr. ak-os, cure), pan-dect (Gr. dekt-os, received), Pan-dora (Gr. dor-on, a gift), pan-egyr-ic (fit for a full assembly, Gr. agor-a, assembly), pan-orama (Gr. horama, a sight), pan-the-ist, pan-oply (a full suit of armour, Gr. hopl-on, a weapon), panto-mime (Gr. mim-os, an actor).

Pau-ein, (fut.) **paus**-o (*to cease*): pause (through Late Lat. paus-are, to cause to rest; confused with *pose*, from Lat. pon-ere, pos-it-um).

Pente (*five*): Pente-cost (fiftieth), Penta-teuch (teukh-os, a book, in later Greek), penta-gon (Gr. gon-ia, a corner), penta-meter (a line in five feet).

Petra (*a rock*): petri-fy, petr-el (dim. of Peter), lam-prey (licker of rocks, Lat. lamb-ere, to lick, compounded with *petra*, a rock; a hybrid word).

Phag-ein (*to eat*): sarco-phagus (Gr. sarx, sark-os, flesh).

Phain-esthai (*to appear*); **phant**-os (*displayed*): phant-as-y, fancy (doublet of the preceding), phant-asm, phant-om (doublet of the preceding), phen-omenon (a thing that appears), phase.

Phem-i (*to speak*): pro-phet, pro-phes-y, blas-pheme (Gr. blapt- or blas-, to injure), blame (doublet of the preceding), eu-phem-ism.

Pher-ein (*to carry*): peri-phery (Gr. peri, around), phos-phor-us (Gr. phos, light).

Phil-os (*loving*): phil-anthropy (Gr. anthrop-os, man), phil-harmon-ic, Phil-ip (Gr. hipp-os, horse), phil-o-log-y (the study of words; Gr. log-os, word), philo-mel (nightingale, Gr. mel-os, melody), philo-soph-y (Gr. sophia, wisdom), philtre (a love potion). N.B.—The last word has no connection with *filter*, to strain through *felt*.

Phon-e (*voice*): phon-et-ics, phono-graph, sym-phon-y, eu-phon-y, caco-phon-ous (Gr. kak-os, bad).

Phos, **phot**-os (*light*): phos-phorus (Gr. pher-ein, to bear), photo-graph.

Phraz-ein (*to tell*): phrase, peri-phras-is, para-phrase (Gr. para, alongside of), phrase-o-logy.

Phren, **phren**-os (*mind*): phren-zy, phren-et-ic, frantic (doublet of the preceding), phren-o-logy.

Phu-ein (*to produce*); **phus**-is (*nature*); **phut**-on (*the thing born*): phys-ic, phys-ics, physi-o-logy, physi-o-gnomy (Gr. gnomonia, means of knowing), physi-o-graphy, zo-o-phyte (Gr. zo-on, animal), neo-phyte (Gr. ne-os, new).

Plass-ein (*to mould*): plast-ic, plast-er, plasm, proto-plasm.

Plat-us (*broad*): plate, pate (the crown of the head; the *l* has been lost), place (Lat. plate-a, Gr. plat-eia, fem. of plat-us), plaice (a kind of fish, so called from its flatness), piastre (Fr. piastre, Ital. piastra, a plate of metal), piazza (a chief street, Lat. platea), plane (kind of tree, Gr. plat-an-os), plan-tain (named from its spreading leaf), plant (A.S. plante, Lat. plant-a, Gr. plat-us), plat-eau, plat-i-tude, platt-er, plat-in-a (a metal), platform (Fr. plate-forme).

Pneum-a (*breath*): pneum-at-ics, pneum-on-ia.

Poi-ein (*to make*): po-et, po-em, po-esy, po-et-ry, onomatopœia (see above, under **Onom**-a), pharmaco-pœia (Gr. pharmak-on, a drug).

Pol-ein (*to sell*): mono-pol-y (Gr. monos, sole), biblio-pole (book-seller).

Pol-is (*city, state*): pol-ice, pol-it-y, pol-i-cy, pol-it-ics, cosmo-pol-ite (Gr. kosmos, the world), metro-polis. N.B.—"Polite" is from Lat. *polit*-us, polished, not from Gr. *polit*-es, citizen.

Pol-us (*many*): poly-anthus (Gr. anth-os, flower), poly-archy (Gr. arkh-e, rule), poly-chrome (Gr. khroma, colour), poly-gam-y (Gr. gam-os, marriage), poly-glot (Gr. glossa or glotta, tongue), poly-gon (Gr. gon-ia, angle), Poly-nes-ia (Gr. nes-os, island), poly-pus (Gr. pous, foot), poly-techn-ic (Gr. tekn-e, art), poly-theist.

Pous, **pod**-os (*foot*): tri-pod.

Prass-ein (*to do*); **prag**-ma (*thing done*): pract-ice, pract-ise, prag-mat-ic-al.

Presb-us (*old*), **presb-uter**-os (*older*): presbyter, priest (doublet of the preceding, A.S. preóst), Prester (John, of Abyssinia).

Prot-os (*first*): proto-plasm (see above under **Plass**-ein), proto-col (Gr. kolla, glue, "a first leaf glued on to a manuscript"), proto-type, proto-martyr.

Pseud-os (*a falsehood*): pseud-onym, pseudo-martyr, pseudo-prophet.

Psukh-e (*life, mind*): psych-ic, psych-o-logy, met-em-psych-os-is (transmigration of souls).

Pur, **pur**-os (*fire*): pyre, pyr-it-es (a fire-stone), pyro-techn-ics (Gr. tekhn-e, art or contrivance), pyr-acanthus (Gr. akantha, a prickly shrub that forms a red berry).

Rhe-ein (*to flow*); **rheum**-a (n.): rheum, rheum-at-ism, rhythm (measured motion), hemo-rrh-oid (see **Haim**-a, above), emerod (doublet of the preceding), diar-rhœa, catarrh (flowing down, Gr. kata, down).

Sarx, **sark**-os (*flesh*): sarc-asm (tearing the flesh), sarco-phagus (Gr. phag-ein, to eat).

Sit-os (*bread*): para-site (Gr. para, by the side of; one who has his food at another's expense).

Skandal-on (*that which trips up*): scandal, slander (doublet of the preceding), scandal-ise.

Skhiz-ein (*to split*); **skhism**-os (n.): schism, schism-at-ic.

Skhol-e (*leisure*): school, shoal (of fishes, doublet of preceding), schol-ar, schol-ium, schol-i-ast, schol-ast-ic.

Skop-ein (*to see*); **skop**-os (n.): scope, micro-scope (Gr. mikr-os, little), epi-scop-al (Gr. epi, over), bishop (A.S. bisceop, Lat. episcopus, Gr. episkopos, overseer), stetho-scope (Gr. steth-os, the breast), tele-scope (Gr. tel-e, at a distance), spectro-scope (Lat. spectr-um, an image).

Soph-os (*wise*): soph-ism, soph-ist, soph-ist-ry, philo-soph-er.

Speir-a (*a coil*): spir-al. N.B.—No connection with "spire," a tapering body, A. S. spír.

Sphair-a (*a ball*): sphere, hemi-sphere (Gr. hemi, half), spher-ic-al.

Stas-is, **stem**-a (*standing*): apo-stas-y, ec-stas-y, sys-(s)tem.

Stell-ein (*to send*); **stol**-e (*equipment*): stole, apo-stle, epi-stle, epi-stol-ary, apo-stol-ic.

Stere-os (*solid*): stereo-scope, stereo-type.

Stikh-os (*a line*): dis-(s)tich, hemi-stich, acrostic (see above, **Akr-os**).

Strat-os (*army*): strat-ag-em (for strat-eg-em), strat-eg-y, strat-eg-ist. (In these words the *eg* is from Gr. *hēg*-, which signifies "to lead.")

Stroph-e (*a turn*): stroph-e (the turning in a Gr. choral dance or song), apo-stroph-e, anti-stroph-e.

Suk-on (*a fig*): syca-more (Gr. mor-os, a mulberry), syco-phant, (lit. fig-shower, Gr. phant-es, one who shows).

Suringx, **suring**-os (*a squirt*): syringe, syrinx (a wind instrument made of reeds), syring-a (a plant whose stems were used for musical pipes).

Takt-os (*arranged*); **tax**-is (*arrangement*): tact-ics, syntax. N.B.—*Tact* is from Lat. tact-us, tang-ere, to touch.

Tekhn-e (*art*): techn-ical, poly-techn-ic.

Tel-e (*afar*): tele-scope, tele-graph, tele-phone, tele-path-y.

The-a-esthai (*to behold*); **the-or**-ia (*a seeing*): the-a-tre, the-or-y, the-or-em, amphi-theatre.

The-os (*God*): the-ism, a-the-ism, apo-the-os-is (deification), theo-crac-y, theo-log-y, theo-gon-y (Gr. gon-ia, birth), the-urg-y (Gr. erg-on, work, "supernatural agency"), theo-soph-ist, en-thus-i-asm (Gr. en + theo + ousia, the state of being in God, inspiration), poly-the-ism, pan-the-ism (God identified with the universe).

Theri-on (*wild beast*): treacle (Gr. theri-ake, viper's flesh, under the notion that such flesh was an antidote against a viper's bite).

Therm-os (*hot*): therm-al, iso-therm (Gr. is-os, equal), therm-o-met-er.

Thes-is, **thek**-e, **them**-a (*a placing*): theme, thesis, apo-thec-ary, hypo-thec-ate, hypo-thes-is, syn-thes-is, ana-them-a, treas-ure (Gr. thes-aur-os; the meaning of aur-os is unknown).

Tom-e, **tom**-os (*a cutting*): ana-tom-y, tome, a-tom (Gr. "a" signifying *not*; the uncut or indivisible), en-tom-o-logy, epi-tom-e.

Ton-os (*stretching*): tone, tune, at-tune, mono-ton-y, ton-ic, in-tone.

Top-os (*place*) : top-ic, top-o-graphy, U-top-ia.

Tox-on (*bow*) ; **tox-ik**-on (*poison*) : in-tox-ic-ate.

Trag-os (*a he-goat*) : trag-ed-y (Fr. tragédie, Lat. trag-œdia, Gr. trag-odia, from ōd-e, a song : the buskins covering the actors' feet were made of goat-leather), trag-ic, trag-ic-al.

Trakh-us (*rough*) : trach-ea (windpipe), trache-o-tom-y (see **Tom**-os, above).

Treis (*three*) : tri-pod (Gr. pod-os, a foot), tri-gon-o-metry (Gr. gon-ia, angle), tri-chord (Gr. khord-e, a string), Tri-nit-y (Lat. un-us, one, "three in one, and one in three"), tri-log-y (a triad of plays or volumes), tress (Gr. trikha, three times), tri-ad (a set of three).

Trogl-ē (*a cave*) : troglo-dyte (cave-dweller, Gr. dut-es, one who enters).

Trop-e (*a turn*) : tropics, helio-trope (Gr. heli-os, the sun ; "the plant that turns toward the sun").

Tup-os (*impression*) : type, anti-type, typ-ic-al, stere-o-type (Gr. stere-os, solid), typ-o-graphy.

Zel-os (*emulation*) : zeal, zeal-ot, zeal-ous (a hybrid, because the suffix is Latin), jeal-ous (doublet of the preceding).

Zo-on (*animal*) ; **zodi**-on (dim.) : zodi-ac (Gr. zodi-ak-e), zo-o-phyte (Gr. phut-on, a plant), zo-o-log-y.

INDEX OF SUBJECTS AND SELECTED WORDS.

The references are to pages.